Enclosing the Neolithic

Recent studies in Britain and Europe

Edited by

Alex Gibson

BAR International Series 2440
2012

BAR

Since 1974

British Archaeological Reports

First published in 2012
BAR International Series 2440

Enclosing the Neolithic: Recent studies in Britain and Europe

ISBN: 978 1 4073 1039 8

Printed in England

All BAR titles are available from:

British Archaeological Reports Ltd
Oxford
United Kingdom
Phone +44 (0)1865 310431
Fax +44 (0)1865 316916
Email: info@barpublishing.com
www.barpublishing.com

Originally published by Archaeopress in conjunction with British Archaeological Reports (Oxford) Ltd/Hadrian Books Ltd the Series principal publisher, in 2012

Table of Contents

List of Contributors

BRADLEY, Richard (Prof)
Department of Archaeology
University of Reading
Whiteknights,
Reading RG6 6UR
UK

BROPHY, Kenneth (Dr)
Archaeology
Schoolof Humanities
Gregory Building
University of Glasgow
Glasgow G12 8QQ
UK

CONVERTINI, Fabien (Dr)
Institut National de Recherches Archéologiques
Préventives et LAMPEA – UMR 7269
Km delta
561 rue Etienne Lenoir
30900 Nîmes
FRANCE

DAVIS, Steve (Dr)
UCD School of Archaeology
Newman Building
University College Dublin
Belfield,
Dublin 4
IRELAND

FIELD, David (Mr)
2 West Nolands Farm Cottages
Yatesbury, SN11 8YD
UK

GIBSON, Alex (Dr)
Archaeological Sciences
University of Bradford
Bradford, BD7 1DP
UK

HARDING, Jan (Dr)
School of History, Classics and Archaeology
Newcastle University
Newcastle upon Tyne, NE1 7RU
UK

LARSSON, Lars (Professor)
Department of Archaeology and Ancient History
University of Lund
SE-221 00 LUND
SWEDEN

LEARY, Jim (Mr)
Archaeologist (prehistory)
English Heritage
Fort Cumberland
Portsmouth, PO4 9LD
UK

NEEDHAM, Stuart (Dr),
Langton Fold,
North Lane,
South Harting,
West Sussex GU31 5NW
UK

NAUBAUER, Wolfgang (Prof)
LBI for Archaeological Prospection and Virtual
Archaeology
University of Vienna
1-1190 Vienna
Austria

NOBLE, Gordon (Dr)
Department of Archaeology
University of Aberdeen
St Mary's Building
Elphinstone Road
Aberdeen AB24 3UF
UK

O'SULLIVAN, Muiris (Professor)
UCD School of Archaeology
Newman Building
University College Dublin
Belfield
Dublin 4
IRELAND

PARFITT, Keith (Mr)
Field Officer
Canterbury Archaeological Trust
92A Broad Street
Canterbury
Kent CT1 2LU
UK

POLLARD, Joshua (Dr)
Archaeology
University of Southampton
Avenue Campus
Highfield
Southampton, SO17 1BF
UK

STOUT, Geraldine (Dr)
Archaeological Survey of Ireland
Department of Arts, Heritage and the Gaeltacht
Custom House
Dublin 1
IRELAND

TUREK, Jan (Dr)
Department of Archaeology
University of Hradec Králové
Rokitanského
62 500 03 Hradec Králové
CZECH REPUBLIC

VALERA, António Carlos (Dr)
Direcção do Núcleo de Investigação Arqueológica
- NIA
ERA Arqueologia SA.
Cç. de Santa Catarina, 9C
1495-705 Cruz Quebrada – Dafundo
PORTUGAL

Enclosure

Alex Gibson

Enclose – surround with a wall, fence etc. Shut in on all sides. Fence in so as to make it private property. Seclude from the outside world. (Concise Oxford Dictionary).

The need to enclose is a basic one. Children build dens, to hide away, to give them secrecy and security. The bones of saints are enclosed in golden caskets encrusted with precious stones not just to preserve the relics but to make a statement as to their specialness and the piety of those charged with their keeping. Various walls, fences and hedges define our gardens over which territorial disputes can occasionally arise. The walled gardens of country estates do not just define the lands around the great house but make a statement as to the wealth of its owners and the manpower that they could once command. Enclosures can contain or exclude. The example of the estate wall is a case in point, providing security for those who live within and making a prohibitive statement to would be poachers and trespassers. Such a statement was made on a grand scale by the attempt to enclose the Roman Empire by walls and fences across the *limes*. No frontier of such a length could ever be successfully defended across its entirety but this is irrelevant, it was the statement that was important: Roman within and Barbarian beyond.

We enclose areas and things for a variety of reasons. The famous Neolithic rock art panel called the Swastika Stone on Ilkley Moor, a stone's throw from where I write, is enclosed by railings to keep erosive feet off the stone; to help preserve the motif from unwitting damage caused by the curious. Fields are enclosed not just as a sign of ownership but also to contain stock or to keep stock off growing cereals. Iron Age houses may be enclosed by a drip gully to facilitate drainage, by a bank and ditch or various hedges or stockades, to protect stock and inhabitants against predators, human or otherwise. Indeed the present writer has, at various times, asked different student groups (school children, undergraduates and extramural students) to list what they see as essential components of a 'Prehistoric Settlement'. Houses (invariably round), stock pens and various 'activity areas' are common features but, in nearly every case, the ideal settlement is enclosed by a fence, hedge or bank and ditch. Enclosing one's property might seem to be a fundamental human need.

Enclosures need not comprise solid barriers. On a sports field the ball must be kept within due bounds though the playing space is demarcated simply by a painted line. A car park may be defined by bollards spaced widely enough to allow pedestrian access but close enough to exclude cars except by the proper routes. Access to our university campus is restricted by road barriers – access permitted only to those on university business or to staff who have paid the requisite dues. A bandstand may be enclosed only by the upright roof supports but the space is nevertheless delineated. In prehistory, stone circles are permeable boundaries but the areas that they enclose are nevertheless well defined.

All of these examples, and clearly there are many more, have one thing in common: they enclose space. But in so doing they perform two main functions that need not be mutually exclusive – they contain and exclude. Furthermore, they define and display.

From early in the Neolithic, this need to enclose is obvious amongst our field monuments. Human remains are enclosed within a variety of chambered cairns and mortuary structures: they are places of containment. These small monuments may themselves be enclosed in mounds. Sometimes these mounds continue to be accessible such as in the case of the Cotswold-Severn tombs and later passage graves or the mounding may be a final act closing one particular episode of a monument's life. Causewayed enclosures, more widespread in their British and European distribution than initially envisaged, represent complex enclosures in part permeable (the ditch causeways) and in other parts impenetrable with unbroken banks and occasional palisades.

The enigmatic cursus monuments of the middle Neolithic exhibit planning and survey on a dramatic scale. Often over 100m wide and several kilometres long, their banks and ditches are slight in comparison to the scale of the monument yet they scythe their way across landscapes with some long lost intent. Opposed entrances are located in their longer sides. Entrance to these enclosures is proscribed, controlled, regulated not from end to end as favoured by the 'processionists' but rather across and through these elaborate barriers.

In the century or so before 3000 BC there is a fundamental change in British monumental architecture. The causewayed enclosures cease to be built though they may still be visited. The rectangular and elongated cursus monuments are a short-lived phenomenon. Instead, circles form the enclosures of choice.

These circles take many forms. Circles of stones, circles of posts, circles of earth. Stone circles vary in their monumentality from the colossal stones of Avebury (Wiltshire) to stones barely visible above the ground at Rhos-y-Beddau (Powys). Timber uprights vary from stakes to full-sized tree trunks. Earth circles vary from the small enclosed cremation cemeteries at Dorchester on Thames (Oxfordshire) to Durrington Walls (Wiltshire) some 400m across. Some earth circles may be defined by causewayed ditches, others by continuous ones. Yet more may have one or two formal entrances. Ditches may be accompanied by banks, sometimes slight, sometimes truly monumental, sometimes external to the ditch, sometimes not, sometimes central to two ditches. Stone banks in upland areas define a variety of cairn forms – kerbed cairns, ring cairns. Some circular sites are defined by mounds and not by spaces.

We can take this variety further. Not all (indeed few) circles are circular. The pedant might say that stone circles are in fact polygons the uprights marking spots on a circle connected by straight lines. Certainly ring ditches frequently show an irregularity to their construction as if points have been laid out then connected by lines that do not quite follow the desired arc. Stone and timber circles have oval forms and flattened and egg-shaped stone circles are well known. Whilst some variations from the circle may be attributed to uneven topography, others are clearly intentional and by design.

Astronomical alignments have been identified, assumed and invented at many of these sites. Being circular, the number of orientations is presumably almost limitless. But rigorous appraisal at an increasing number of sites makes it now unarguable that during the third and second millennia BC, the movements of the sun and moon were being observed and that solsticial and equinoctial events were being celebrated. As these events involve the setting and rising of the sun, they cannot be divorced from landscape for it is the rising and setting of the sun at particular times and at particular places on the horizon that are being observed: where earth and heavens come together. We do not need to imply a calendrical function in the modern sense, despite some claims, no monument can be demonstrated to have been laid out so specifically, but midwinter and midsummer, spring and autumn are important times of the agricultural year and as such needed marking. Leap years were doubtless an unknown concept: midwinter always happened at midwinter when the days were shortest and the sun stood still. And, just as surely, spring would follow.

What was happening inside these enclosures is also varied. Burials are nearly always encountered but not necessarily in large numbers. There is also the problem of stratigraphy for it is not always possible to determine whether the burials and enclosures were contemporary: were burials added to enclosures or were old but remembered burial events later enclosed. Certainly many of the more recently excavated sites are demonstrating that they had a long history, detailed biographies, of which the enclosure is only a part, and often a secondary one. Where stone and timber circles coincide with banked and ditched enclosures, the latter element can nearly always be demonstrated to be secondary. Sites had been chosen as special, marked by burials or monuments and unmarked by long-gone ritual practices before there was the need to define them with earth, either encircling or covering. Indeed enclosure of these sites was far from universal and some, indeed most, stone and timber circles had no need of further enclosure.

These earthen enclosures, like the natural horizon, are bounded by a perimeter of 360°. They represent the world in microcosm. Land beyond the boundary, beyond the horizon, is not unknown but it is different. There may be different people there, different landscapes, different dangers real or perceived. Living space may well be limited to the horizon, especially in a wooded environment, thus for ritual purposes, the sacred space is even smaller, even more restricted and more private with access limited to the few, rituals controlled and proscribed. Participants would be active or passive depending on their status. Some might perform, some others partake while yet more might simply watch. The increasing evidence for feasting, however, suggests that what was happening at these sites was truly important to each community and probably also to neighbouring groups. Cattle were imported, pigs slaughtered, goods exchanged and matches made.

Circular monuments are ubiquitous in the British and Irish Neolithic. The uniformity of their design must point towards a shared ideology, even cosmology. The benefits of a circle hardly need repeating – easily laid out from a centre peg, maximum area enclosed for perimeter dug therefore a truly economical shape. But such are belief systems that forms often pay little heed to economy of effort and difficulty of design and elaboration of design may be important. Thus cursus monuments albeit simple in shape involved elaborate laying out to ensure Pythagorean proportions.

The papers in this volume address some of these issues and strands of research. Originating in a weekend conference in Oxford in Spring 2012 – *Henges: a Late Neolithic Conundrum* - this volume, in its first part, presents thought provoking papers by well known British and Irish archaeologists, each involved in the study of circular earthen monuments at both a national and regional level. Scotland, Ireland, Wessex and Kent form regional syntheses against a historical perspective set in chapter 1. That the earth circle is not a purely insular phenomenon is then demonstrated by various regional European syntheses, two of which (Neubauer and Valera) were presented at Oxford whilst the others were commissioned for this volume.

Enclosure is the common theme, but there are also other threads running through the tapestry. The need for enclosure, the place of enclosures within the biographies of given locales, the function(s) of the enclosures, their date, their origins, their variation over time, their roles in society. Everywhere their emergence and demise seems to represent ideological changes, perhaps related to sun worship or at least celestial observation and the emergence of new pan-European warrior elite in the mature Bronze Age. There is scope for another volume on this theme alone but swansongs fit the British evidence as well as the Iberian. Dates may vary across Europe, but responses seem to be similar.

It is hoped that these overviews will gather together a great body of data from across Europe into a single volume. It is also hoped that this volume will act as a springboard for further research by younger scholars. The editor would like to extend his thanks to all who supported the Oxford conference, to all who contributed to the lively discussions, to the speakers for the relaxed but authoritative way in which they delivered their lectures and especially to all the contributors to this volume for their cooperation in the speedy delivery of their papers.

An Introduction to the Study of Henges: Time for a Change?

Alex Gibson

Abstract

This paper summarises 80 years of 'henge' studies. It considers the range of monuments originally considered henges and how more diverse sites became added to the original list. It examines the diversity of monuments considered to be henges, their origins, their associated monument types and their dates. Since the introduction of the term, archaeologists have often been uncomfortable with it. It was introduced in inverted commas and those commas continued to be used for over 30 years. With the introduction of the term 'hengiform' the strictures of definition that characterised the monument class collapsed and an increased variety of circular and oval monuments were included under the henge aegis. It is suggested here that the term 'henge' has outlived its usefulness as we no longer know what we mean by it. Instead we should adopt an objective viewpoint and recognise these earth circles as just one manifestation of the tradition of circularity that pervades the third and second millennia BC.

Keywords: Henge, Earth Circle, Stone Circle, Timber Circle, Neolithic, Bronze Age, Ritual.

Introduction

The problem with henges is that archaeologists no longer know what they mean by the term. The term has become increasingly applied to a variety of sites that now go far beyond the strictures that were originally defined. It is an understandable problem because, since the time of Kendrick and Hawkes, a considerable variety of circular sites have been discovered through aerial survey and geophysical prospection. Many of these circular sites date from the middle or later Neolithic and we can now generalise that in the last quarter of the fourth millennium BC, the inhabitants of Britain became fixated with circular and oval enclosures of earth, wood and stone. The ubiquity of the circle from such a fairly precise chronological horizon clearly points to shared (or at least related) cosmologies throughout Britain and Ireland which persisted, though perhaps with modification, for almost two millennia. Henges, timber circles, stone circles, ring-ditches, kerb cairns, disc barrows, ring cairns, penannular enclosures, causewayed ring ditches, palisade enclosures, enclosed cremation cemeteries, stake circles, round barrows and round cairns encapsulate this focus on circularity and there are clear relationships, similarities and shared grammatical constructs within these monuments but what now constitutes a henge?

Origins of the term – previous work

When Kendrick (Kendrick and Hawkes 1932) defined the term 'henge monuments', he used inverted commas around the word 'henge' throughout the chapter devoted to the phenomenon. He stated at the outset (Chapter VII) that 'under this rather curious heading I am going to group a number of prehistoric 'sacred places' which I cannot, or dare not, sort out into period chapters' (Kendrick and Hawkes 1932, 83). He admits that the name is derived from Stonehenge and Woodhenge (Figure 1) the two sites that head the list but it must be remembered that even the name 'Woodhenge' was derived from its better-known lithic neighbour and was an appellation that grew as the excavations progressed and the complexity of the site was gradually revealed. During this process, the overall similarity to the layout of the stones at Stonehenge was recognised and prior to the excavations the low-mounded site had been known as 'the Dough Cover' (Cunnington 1929). This derivative labelling continues to be used, so in the popular press, Sarn-y-bryn-caled (Powys) was named the Welsh Woodhenge, a palisade barrow around a buried tree stump at Holme-next-the-sea in Norfolk was christened Seahenge as befitted its present (but not

FIGURE 1: STONEHENGE AND WOODHENGE. THE TWO SITES THAT HEADED KENDRICK'S LIST.

original) environment and another 'Wooden henge' has been discovered by the recent geophysical survey of the Stonehenge environs. This latter misuse of the term betrays the apparent complexity of the site comprising as it does one ring (possibly 2) of pits, a causewayed ring ditch and a barrow.

Kendrick was at once apologetic for 'coining the phrase'. He admitted that 'some readers may not approve of my including as members of the same family certain apparently empty 'rings' and 'stone circles'. He goes on to say that the interpretation of these sites as meeting places or temples is not unequivocal and nor are they necessarily of one date, but rather they are unified in being round, not primarily for burial, and 'belong, as far as it is possible to tell, either to the late Neolithic period or the first half of the Bronze Age' (Kendrick and Hawkes, 1932, 83). Included in the subsequent description are Stonehenge and Woodhenge, The Sanctuary (notably with no ditch), Avebury, Durrington Walls, Dorchester (Oxon), Eyam Moor stone circle (Derbys), Porlock stone circle (Somerset), two ditched enclosures at Hengwm (Gwynedd), the Ysceifiog barrow (Flintshire) and he further refers to Elgee's description of 'ceremonial' and 'burial' circles in east Yorkshire – which is confusing given that he has already stated that henges were not primarily associated with burial. The chapter is not comprehensive, however, concentrating as it does on documenting recent interventions rather than offering a corpus of sites.

From the outset, therefore, even to the originators of the term, ' henge' was an unhappy monumental category. It was not confined to earthwork enclosures (The Sanctuary was included) but rather it was loosely defined and consequently applicable to a large number of diverse monuments from ditched enclosures, timber circles, stone circles and elements of round barrows. But despite the instability of this foundation, it has formed the basis for numerous theoretical archaeological pyramids.

Four years later, in his report on the excavations at Arminghall (Norfolk), Grahame Clark, in looking for 'the affinities of the monument' published a list and distribution map of monuments that he considered comparable (Clark 1936). Clark was the first to define the monument class properly as

> '*a well-known class*, possessing certain easily defined features. At the centre of all of them is a more or less circular area on which stand stone or timber uprights..... The central area is defined by a bank, and, where the material for this can more easily be quarried from the ground, by a ditch; as a general rule the ditch is placed within the bank, and where there are two ditches the inner one is normally the larger. Access to the central area is given by a single or often by two opposite entrances; where there is a ditch, the entrance is represented by an unexcavated causeway. (ibid 23, my emphasis).

Clarke regarded the internal ditch and external bank arrangement as a crucially defining feature and furthermore the presence of internal settings of stones or posts was also one of the fundamental characteristics of a henge. This said, however, the main sites listed in Clark's text are supplemented by an additional appendix of sites of similar shape where no internal features have been recognised including sites such as Durrington Walls (before discovery of the timber circles), Thornborough Rings in N Yorkshire and King Arthur's Round Table in Cumbria. On his distribution map, Clark records 20 probable 'henge' monuments (he too continues to use the term in inverted commas) amongst which are the Stripple Stones in Cornwall and Brodgar and Stennes in Orkney. Clark also acknowledges that 'within this class of monuments....there is scope for many variations in detail' (ibid, 23). He describes, for example, the variations in ditch form – internal at Arbor Low (Derbyshire), none at Mayburgh (Cumbria), external at Stonehenge (Figure 2). At once the loose definition is loosening further.

When discussing function, Clark is at pains to point out the considerable amount of labour that must have been invested in some of these sites: the quarrying of the large ditch at Avebury, the transportation of the stone to Stonehenge and the felling of the massive oak posts at Arminghall and Woodhenge would have involved a great deal of effort. They were therefore sites of importance to those who constructed them. He concludes that internal ditches were not overtly defensive and the sites were therefore used for ritual or ceremonial and he concurs with St George Gray's amphitheatre hypothesis that the banks may have served as viewing platforms with the spectators denied physical access to the interior by the ditch (Gray, 1935). He did not want to speculate further regarding prehistoric religion but felt that the sepulchral evidence had been exaggerated and that some burials, such as that of the infant with split skull at Woodhenge, may have been dedicatory. Regarding date, Clark considers the Peterborough Ware from below the bank at Avebury to act as a *Terminus Post Quem* for the bank and refers to Peterborough Ware and Beaker in the ditch. Rusticated Beaker was, of course, found on the floor of the inner ditch in his own excavations at Arminghall. A barbed and tanged arrowhead from the base of the Arbor Low ditch was similarly invoked to suggest a Beaker date. Gorsey Bigbury (Somerset) produced Beaker pottery from the ditch and he also commented that 'there is a suspicion that Durrington Walls belongs to the same period' (Clark 1936, 30). This 'suspicion' is doubtless attributable to Farrer's 1917 excavations through the bank at Durrington Walls where, beneath the bank and in a layer of charcoal, a fragment of pottery identified as Beaker was found. The sherd has since been lost but Farrer's description of the sherd's fabric and combed cross-hatching certainly seems to support the Beaker identification made for him by Cunnington and Blackmore (Farrer 1918, 100).

In 1938, Piggott considered the dating of these sites, albeit not in great detail. He linked the stone circles and henges with his 'Groove Ware' (sic.) and Beaker groups

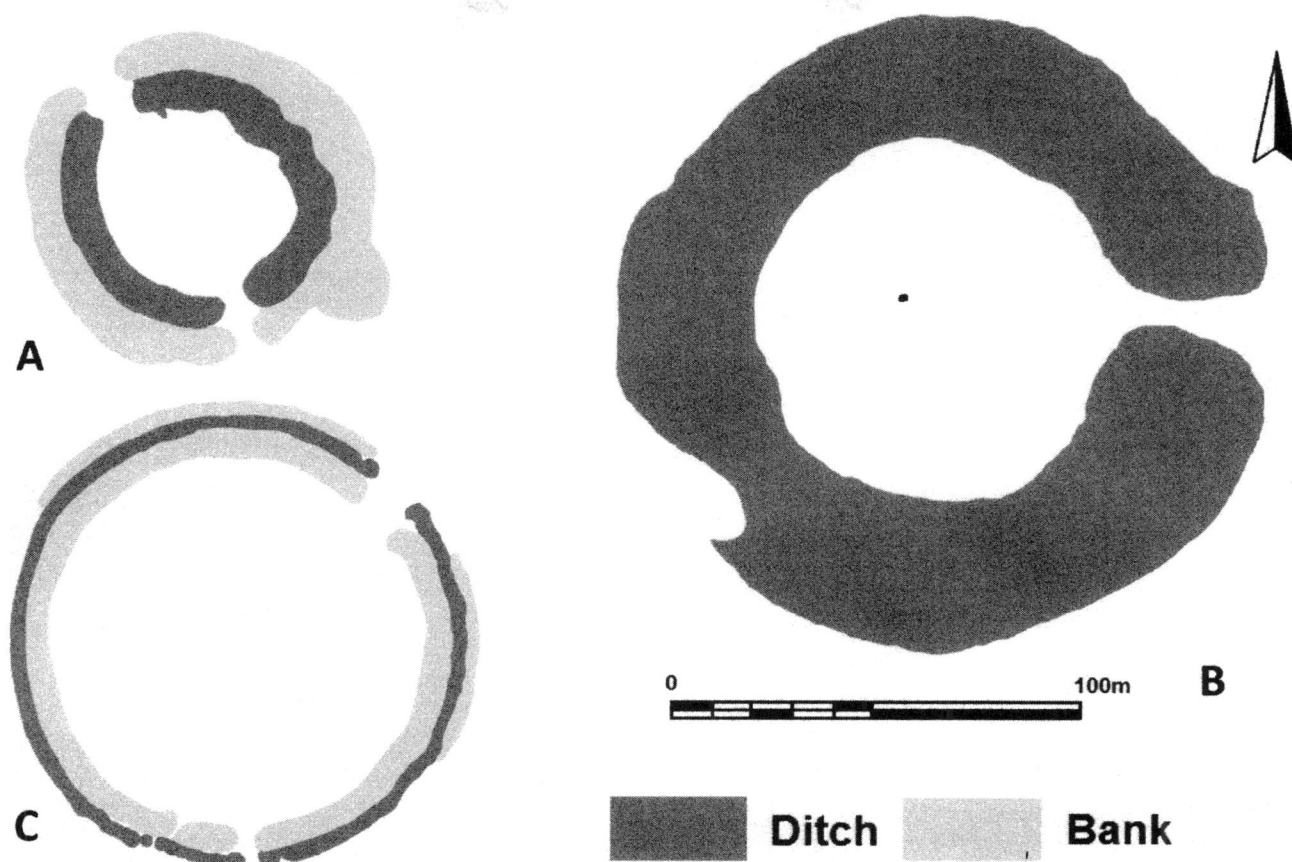

FIGURE 2: DIFFERENCES IN DITCH POSITION. A – ARBOR LOW, DERBYSHIRE. B – MAYBURGH, CUMBRIA. C – STONEHENGE, WILTSHIRE.

and he sees the monuments as 'essentially the product of a lowland culture with a relatively soft subsoil enabling encircling ditches to be dug with ease' (Piggott 1938, 57). Consequently stone circles, were upland phenomena where ditch-digging was more difficult but where orthostats were abundant. Arbor Low and Avebury were seen as a fusion of the two traditions. This observation was later taken up by Burl (1969; 1976).

A year later, Stuart and Peggy Piggott described the stone and earth circles in Dorset (Piggott and Piggott 1939). In this work they distinguish two sub-groups of henges on entrance alone and in particular whether they have one or two. Once again ' henge' is in inverted commas as if no-one has yet come to terms with the label. We are also informed that the first sub-group, with one entrance, tend to have their entrances to the NE while the two-entranced henges are orientated NW-SE (ibid, 140). They reiterate that henges are a lowland phenomenon, perhaps related to 'the A Beaker people from Holland and the Rhineland' while the stone circles represent a highland phenomenon perhaps allied to the Breton origin of the 'BI Beaker folk' (ibid 141).

Piggott's two sub-types were adopted by Atkinson in his co-authored report on the excavations at the Dorchester

on Thames (Oxon) cursus complex (Atkinson et al. 1951). Here the excavation of a variety of circular enclosures provided the opportunity for Atkinson to deliver an up to date synthesis and overview of the type. Atkinson actually suggested that 'the term "henge monument" is redundant' (Atkinson et al. 1951, 81) as only Stonehenge could be proved unequivocally to have had a 'hanging' (i.e.lintelled) structure. He nevertheless decided to retain the name as a convenient way of avoiding 'cumbrous definition' or 'insufficiently specific' words such as 'Sanctuary'. An external bank, internal ditch and 1 or 2 entrances were Atkinson's defining features of henges: he rejected continuous ring banks and free-standing stone and timber circles.

According to his definition, Atkinson listed 36 sites that could reasonably claim to be henges, 13 belonged to Class I, 17 to Class II and 6 to the new Class IIa (Atkinson et al. 1951, 94-5). Atkinson added the Class IIa sub-division to describe henges with double entrances and double ditches flanking a central bank. There was no similar sub-division of the Class I type despite the well documented double ditches of Arminghall. Atkinson also identified 5 dubious examples amongst which were Marden and Durrington Walls. Furthermore, he noted that whilst Class II and IIa henges were found across the size range (ibid, 85, Fig 27),

Class I tended to be under 400ft (122m) in diameter. By virtue of the artefacts found in the few excavated examples, Atkinson concluded that the Class I henges were earlier than Class II. Excavations at Class I henges had produced middle Neolithic pottery as well as Grooved Ware and artefacts traditionally held to be later Neolithic such as skewer pins and transverse arrowheads. Beaker, of course, had been found in comparatively large quantities at Gorsey Bigbury but to date no mature Bronze Age finds had come from Class I henges. Class II monuments, however, had a tendency to Beaker and Bronze Age associations (Food Vessel at the diminutive Fargo Plantation, Wiltshire). Avebury, despite having 4 entrances, was included in Class II and tentatively associated with 'A-Beaker'.

The orientation of the entrances of henge monuments was also analysed as part of Atkinson's study and he concluded that Class II and IIA monuments had no common orientation but only a tendency towards a NW-SE axis whilst the entrances of Class I monuments avoided the SW-SE arc.

In his review of the Dorchester excavation report, Clark (1954) was unhappy with Atkinson's use of the word 'henge'. Clark still used the name in inverted commas and explained that 'the term "henge", first applied generically to a class or family of analogous monuments, has stuck because it seems to characterise in a word a well-defined category of monument. The fact that on strictly etymological grounds the term 'henge' can only be applied to Stonehenge itself is irrelevant so long as we are all agreed what we mean to apply by it....The leading formal elements of 'henge' monuments have been generally understood to comprise: (a) a central, more or less circular area supporting stone or timber uprights; (b) a bank, and, where material for this was obtained by excavation, a ditch, which was normally, though not invariably, inside the bank; and (c) one or two entrances giving access to the central area through bank and, where present, ditch' (Clark 1954, 91).

Given this reiteration of his original definition, Clark suggests that none of the Dorchester sites are henges as first and foremost they lack uprights. 'Scale is not a criterion on which one would necessarily care to lay much stress in making formal comparisons, but it is surely significant that, if we exclude the site in Fargo Plantation which equally lacks the feature of an interior structure, the Dorchester sites are all substantially smaller than the smallest recognised 'henge' monument' (ibid 92). He goes on to say that Atkinson's report's great achievement was in bringing to light a *new* monument type to British Neolithic studies and he issued the 'plea' that 'this should not be obscured by referring the new monuments to a well-defined category, a leading feature of which they so conspicuously lack' (ibid 92). Interestingly, Clark then noted the similarity of some of the Dorchester sites with Stonehenge I and in consequence suggests that the Dorchester circles may therefore be the progenitors of the henge *sensu stricto*. In other words, Atkinson had

extended the original definition to include many of the middle and later Neolithic circular forms with which we began. Clark's observation fell largely on deaf ears and the loosening term was soon to be completely unravelled.

In 1967, following his work at Priddy Circles, Somerset, Tratman added a further 15 henge sites to Atkinson's corpus. Two years later Burl could list 78 henges as defined by Atkinson 'a roughly circular bank with one or more entrances' and he regards Clark's insistence that these should enclose internal structures as 'an attractive but misleading hypothesis' (Burl 1969, 3). Burl nevertheless is uncertain about including Fargo Plantation and some of Atkinson's Dorchester sites in his corpus. Fargo Plantation is a burial site, possibly borrowing from henge architecture whilst the Dorchester circles may better be seen as 'cremation cemeteries quite possibly ancestral to the Wessex henge-tradition'. This can be taken further and given the presence of internal ground-surface cremation deposits surviving in this heavily ploughed environment, it may be suggested that the interiors had been protected for a considerable time, perhaps by an internal mound. Burl was the first to look at henges in detail, describing associations, distribution, size, outlying stones, internal portal stones or posts, internal timber structures, internal pit circles, internal stone circles, burials and orientations. He recognised eleven regional groups and he also defined the term 'circle-henges' for those that combined the respective earthwork and megalithic elements of henges and stone circles.

Also in 1969, following his excavations at Durrington Walls, Wainwright undertook a review of henges. Benefiting from the increase in the use of aerial photography in archaeology, but ignoring Clark's criticisms that have already been described, he was able to add 31 sites to Atkinson's 1951 corpus but he also introduced a new word to the archaeological literature: 'hengi-form' - a word that has been widely used, mis-used and even abused since. He refers to some 'hengi-form' sites recently photographed from the air in Scotland (Wainwright 1969, 116) and describes some of the Dorchester sites as 'not true henges but rather of hengi-form type' which is a tacit admission that the typology advocated by Kendrick, Clark, Piggott and, to a lesser degree, Atkinson has now broken down. It is a compromise between Atkinson's descriptions of the Dorchester sites and Clark's critical review. Wainwright defines 'hengi-form' sites as those which have henge characteristics but are less than 100ft (*c*.30m) in diameter. He includes in this group the small Class I enclosure at City Farm, Hanborough (Oxon) (Case *et al.* 1965) and the diminutive Class II enclosure at Fargo Plantation (Figure 3). He further proceeds to include other upland variants such as the enclosed cremation cemeteries of southern Scotland and northern England and here the picture starts to become really confused.

Wainwright identifies some of the small enclosed cremation cemeteries being excavated in northern England and Southern Scotland as 'hengi-forms'. At Whitestanes

Moor in Dumfriess Scott-Elliot and Rae had excavated a turf-covered stone bank with an internal diameter of 30ft (9.1m) (48ft (14.6m) overall) which enclosed 8 cremations, 1 with a Bronze Age cup (Scott-Elliot and Rae 1965). The excavators labelled their site as an enclosed cremation cemetery and never mentioned the 'henge' (or even hengi-form) word preferring to find parallels for their site elsewhere in Scotland and in the Northumberland excavations of Jobey (see below). Meanwhile Radley was excavating similar sites in the Pennines and in particular a site at Brown Edge on Totley Moor another 'hengi-form' according to Wainwright. The Brown Edge site comprised an earthen bank surrounding a flat area with a central cairn covering cremations associated with Collared Urns. 'The ring-work is related in general form, function and age to other earth circles, cairn circles and stone circles found in the Pennines and elsewhere' (Radley 1966, 1). Radley went on to consider that 'the ring bank with a central cairn is comparable to the true Wessex disc barrow, lacking only the ditch' (Radley 1966, 22). Radley goes on to suggest that comparable Pennine sites but having entrances 'produce a form reminiscent of a henge or …pond barrows which have entrances' (ibid).

Jobey was also resisting temptation to link some of his Northumberland sites to henges. In his excavations at Alnham, Jobey (1966) described a small double-entranced enclosure (Cairnfield A, burial 3) with internal ditch and external bank (Figure 3). The ditch was no more than 3ft (0.9m) wide and 1ft (0.3m) deep and had probably enclosed a low, robbed central mound. From the 18ft (5.5m) diameter central area, a flint scraper and a fragment of jet, possibly from a cup, was recovered hinting at its Bronze Age date. Jobey compared this site to the Class II "henge" (sic) form but he did this only tentatively

preferring instead to use comparisons with the Roxburgh Saucer Barrows.

There is no doubt that some of these sites bear *superficial* similarities to classic henge ditch and bank morphology but in extending his definition to hengi-form, away from the intention of the original term, Wainwright has opened up the label 'henge' to encompass any circular or oval earthwork of putatively Neolithic or Bronze Age date and, like Burl and Atkinson before him, he has dispensed with the need for internal structures, one of the defining characteristics of the original definition.

In 1971, Catherall proposed a new classification for henges and offered an insight as to their origins acknowledging that the complexity of the class appears to increase with excavation. Catherall classified the sites by their internal arrangements recognising that this limited the classification to excavated examples however he felt it unlikely that further excavation would increase the range of internal features. He proposed a six-fold classification based on internal elements: A – circles of pits, B – timber structures, C – stone circles, D – central structures, E – central burials and F – portal stones and posts. There were hybrid forms therefore Balfarg, with its portal stones, stone and timber circles and its central burial might be a B/C/E/F hybrid. Atkinson had already suggested that single entranced henges (Class I) were, in the main, earlier than the double entranced types (Class II) and Catherall's scheme broadly supported this hypothesis although his Class F monuments were exclusively single entranced. Associated ceramics also broadly supported a type A – F progression with Mildenhall and Impressed wares associated with types A-C and Bronze Age ceramics associated with types C-F. Catherall followed Clark (1954)

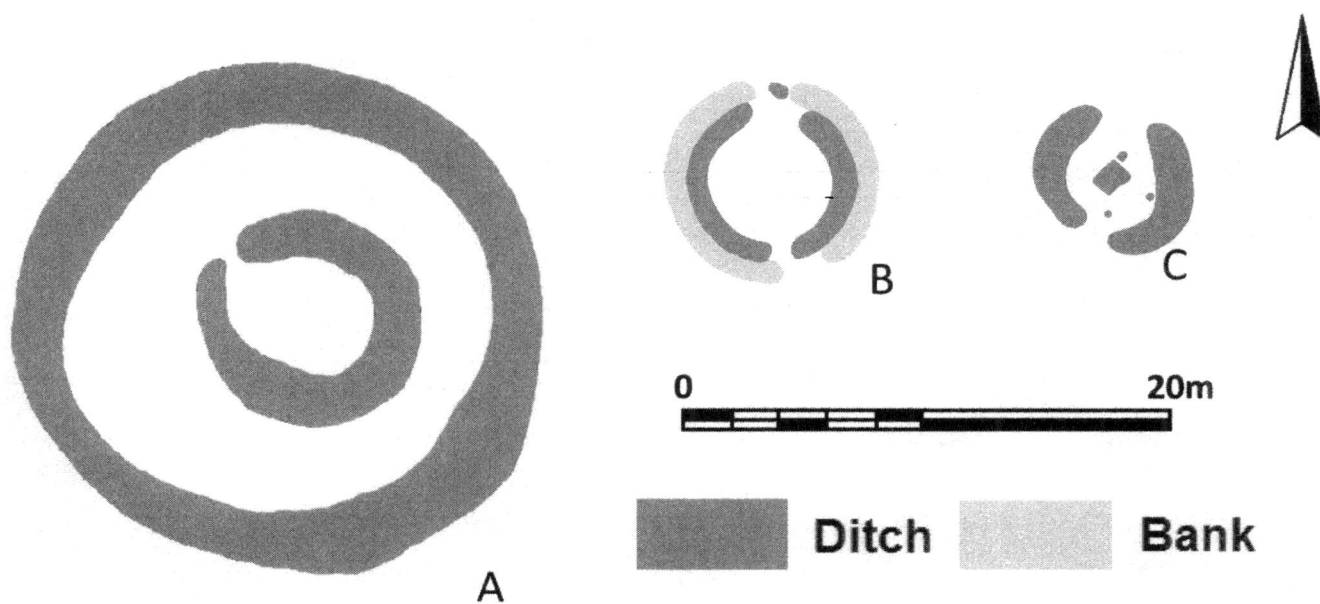

FIGURE 3: 'HENGIFORMS'. A – CITY FARM, HANBOROUGH, SITE 4, OXFORDSHIRE. B – ALNHAM, NORTHUMBERLAND. C – FARGO PLANTATION, WILTSHIRE.

by suggesting that the circular cremation cemeteries at sites such as Dorchester, Stonehenge I and possibly also Cairnpapple Hill may be contenders for the origins of henges, the broad contemporaneity of these earlier sites reinforced by the bone skewer pins found with the cremations. He further disagrees with Atkinson (Atkinson *et al.* 1951) who regarded the ditches of henges as purely quarry ditches providing material for the all important bank and instead proposes that the ditches may have had a non-utilitarian function and, again based on Dorchester, that the causewayed ditches may well be an early feature ultimately derived from Causewayed Enclosures.

In 1986, following on from his 1973 thesis, Clare attempted to straighten the tangle that henge and hengiform terminology had become. Clare proposed to dispense with the idea that internal uprights should form a distinguishing characteristic of these sites but rather 'it is…the perimeter to which the features belong which forms the primary characteristic of these sites previously called henges' (1986, 282). He outlines the confusion between henges and ring-ditches and concludes that 'we are not dealing with a clear-cut monument type but a permutation of practices and features….' (ibid). Using a system of matrix analysis in his comprehensive review, Clare concluded that 'there is no clear distinction between those sites previously called "henges" and those described as "hengiform" (*op. cit.* 283). This conclusion is reiterated in his concluding section (*ibid* 307) where he also makes the observant remark that while the perimeters are important they 'may have been added to an existing site': a conclusion that is becoming increasingly apparent in recent excavations (see below).

Clare's follow-up article in the following year examined the possible origins of his henge and hengiform classes. Clare points out that not only do henges share some features with causewayed enclosures, but that they also share features with earlier Neolithic 'mortuary enclosures' (another

unsatisfactory label) and that henges and hengiforms often occur in proximity to (sometimes actually enclosing) these earlier sites (Figure 4). He sees henges and hengiforms developing out of a 'milieu or nexus' of sites and traditions (1987, 468).

Clare considered a large number of morphologically similar sites and an impressive range of variables in order to attempt to bring order out of classification chaos. It was a brave and useful attempt to disentangle and re-order the henge problem but it did not meet with universal acceptance (Barclay 1989). Barclay felt that a stricter definition of the term henge was needed. He felt that Piggott's first separation of the monument type into class I and II depending on the number of entrances was 'still the most useful' (1989, 260). Other monument types (stone circles, ring-ditches, ring-cairns etc) doubtless had 'complex relationships' with henges proper enjoying similarities of architecture, sepulchro-ritual deposition and even site histories of modification, but these acknowledged similarities still did not make a ring-ditch a henge.

Meanwhile, in 1987, Harding and Lee had published their assessment of henges based largely on excavation and aerial photographic data (Harding with Lee 1987). Their pictorial and descriptive catalogue is still invaluable to anyone interested in henge monuments and its critical approach to the aerial photographic evidence did much to put henge studies back on track. Harding and Lee reinforced Atkinson's definition as a circular or near circular monument defined by a ditch within a bank and with one or two entrances and attribute many of the then (and now) current problems of classification to the fact that 'many current writers broaden the classification…to include sites that would formerly have been excluded' (*op. cit.* 12). They go on to discuss the problems of interpretation based purely on morphology, especially regarding class I henges and point out that many single-entranced internally ditched enclosures may have an agricultural function and

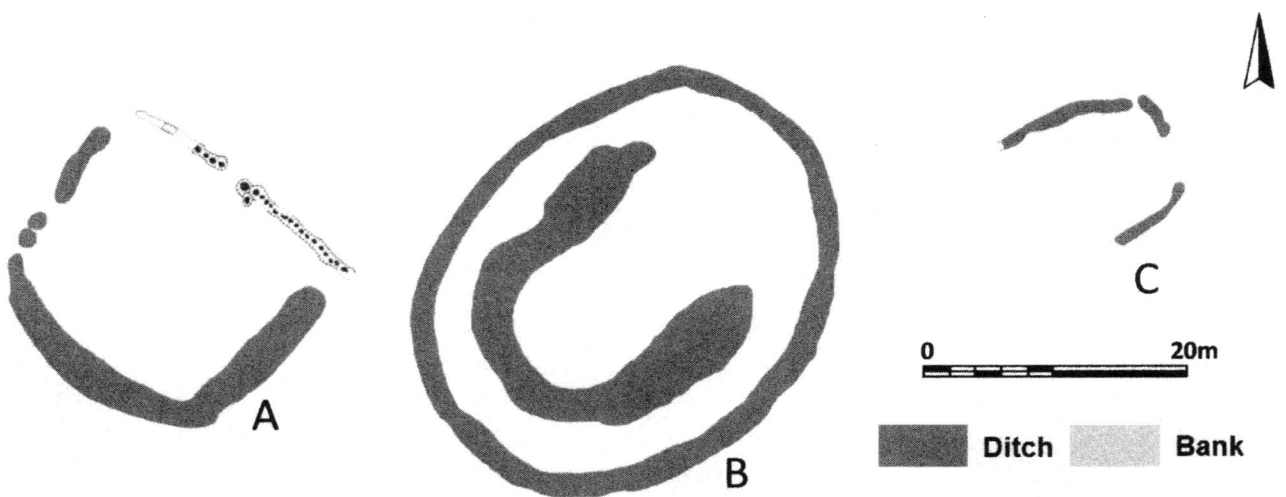

FIGURE 4: NEOLITHIC 'MORTUARY ENCLOSURES'. THE ORIGINS OF HENGES? A – GRENDON, NORTHAMPTONSHIRE. B – HORTON, MIDDLESEX. C – ALDWINCLE, NORTHAMPTONSHIRE.

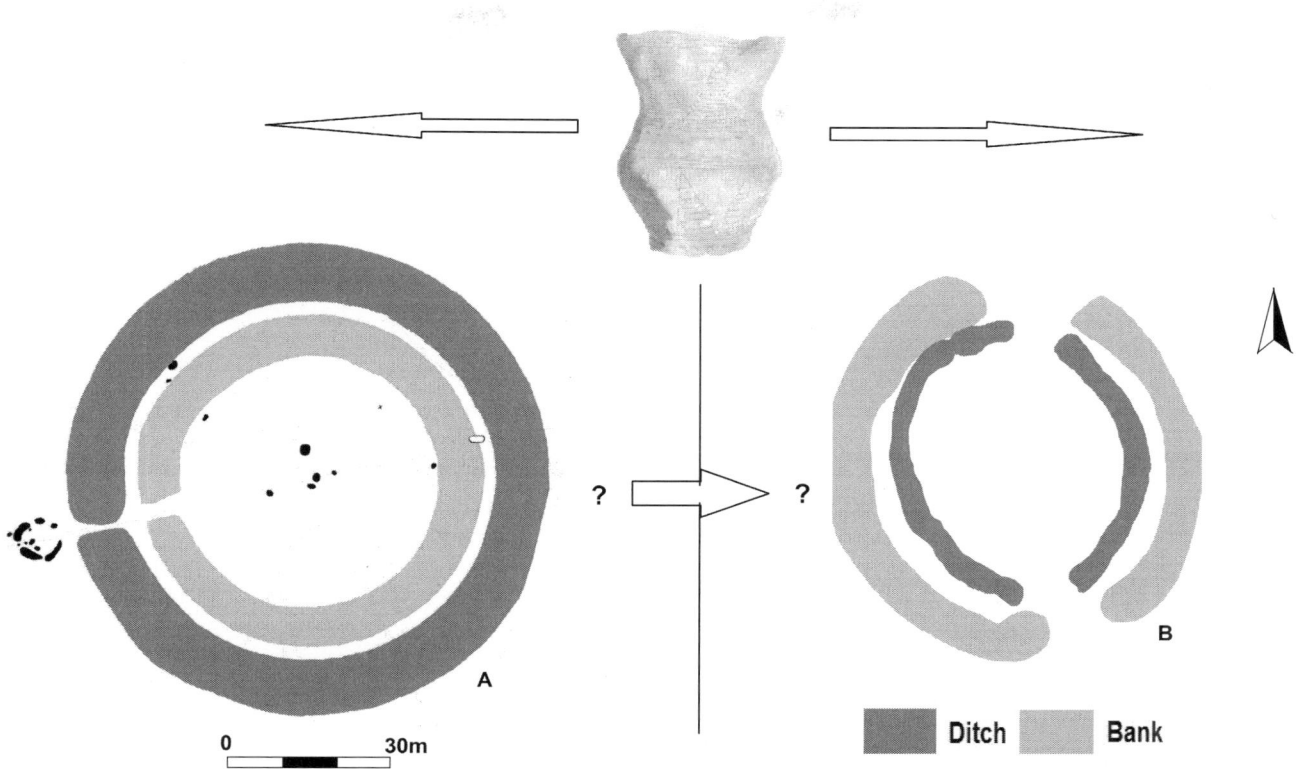

FIGURE 5: ATKINSON'S HYPOTHETICAL SCHEME FOR HENGE DEVELOPMENT AND CHRONOLOGY. CLASS I PRE-DATE BEAKER, CLASS II ARE BEAKER OR LATER. CLASS I MAY HAVE INFLUENCED CLASS II. A – LLANDEGAI A, GWYNEDD. B – CAIRNPAPPLE HILL, WEST LOTHIAN.

be very much later than the Neolithic or Bronze Age (for example Roman signal stations, hut circles and post mills).

By such strict adherence to Atkinson's original definition, Harding and Lee reduced the corpus to 22 'classic' excavated sites and 20 slightly excavated or unexcavated 'classic' sites. The large Wessex henges they termed 'henge-enclosures' while the smaller sites with henge-like characteristics they termed 'mini-henges'. They also recognised other related circular forms such as segmented ring-ditches and ring-cairns but avoided the use of the term 'hengiform' (though it does creep into the gazetteer). When discussing scale, and using the internal diameter as the most frequently available measurement (as opposed to crest to crest of ploughed-out banks) they suggest that 14m is the cut off point between classic and mini-henges and that single entrance henges tend to be slightly smaller than the double entranced ones as originally noted by both Atkinson (*et. al* 1951) and Burl (1969). Similarly ditch width should be over 2.5m in classic henges. The next major synthesis was that of Jan Harding in 2003 who very much followed Harding with Lee's typology of mini-, classic and super-henges.

The origin of henges

Such was the concern as to what a henge actually was or which features defined a henge of whatever type, few archaeologists attempted to look at the origins of the class. Clark (1936, 31-2) suggested that the wooden elements

of henges might come, with the Beaker Folk, from the palisade and post-circle barrows of the Low Countries but he also pointed out that the chief Dutch investigator of such phenomena, Albert van Giffen, was of the opinion that the Dutch barrows were themselves influenced by British henges. A discussion of British and Dutch timber circles below barrows suggested to Clarke that the jury was out as to which influenced which. Clark went on to examine Callendar's (1927) hypothesis that stone circles were derived from cairn peristaliths and suggested that it may be that the 'stone "henges" (may be) ancestral to the wooden ones' (1936, 36). Without an absolute chronology at his disposal, however, Clark was forced to admit that 'we are left with two hypotheses (Dutch palisade barrows and the British Megalithic tradition) and in the present state of knowledge it is difficult to choose between them. Fortunately this is not necessary; we are not writing one of these synthetic works wherein all difficulties must be resolved....' (1936, 39, my brackets).

Atkinson (1951, 93) was not convinced by either theory. He started with the generally accepted theory that class II henges were Beaker in date and if so, they must be a native manifestation of the Beaker culture as they lacked direct parallels in Europe. However Class I henges had either produced pre-Beaker artefacts or had produced Beaker from secondary contexts. Class I henges might therefore be the influence for the Class II monuments (Figure 5). As for the origins of the Class I sites, that was 'no less obscure than the origins of the communities to which they belong' (1951, 96). As mentioned above, Clark (1954) saw the Dorchester sites not as henges *sensu stricto* but, given their Neolithic associations, perhaps as the progenitors of the henge tradition.

Wainwright favoured the roughly circular forms of Causewayed Enclosures as the progenitors of henges (1969). Neither Causewayed Enclosures nor henges were permanently settled but rather appeared to have been visited seasonally when rituals involving feasting, burial and deposition took place though the evidence for feasting and ritual was scant at henges. Burl (1976, 25) followed Wainwright to a degree. He noted the connection of Causewayed Enclosures and henges with stone axes suggesting that one may have replaced the other as meeting places for exchange and social discourse. The earliness of Llandegai A (see below) and the perfect Group VI axe from beneath the bank might argue for an origin in areas close to axe production.

Harding and Lee consider the potential contribution of the growing number of central European enclosures of the post-LBK Lengyel and Rössen cultures (now known as *Kreisgrabenanlagen*) as possible influences however their dating now suggests that they are earlier than henges by as much as a millennium and that they appear to have been comparatively short-lived phenomena associated, in central Europe with the appearance of the Lengyel culture *c.* 4900-4500 cal BC (Daim and Neubauer 2005: Melichar and Neubauer 2010). It remains a possibility that some of these *Kreisgrabenanlagen* may still have been visible as earthworks or functioned as important locales for a considerable time after their construction and it may be that the shared circularity and, to a lesser extent, astronomical alignments between these sites and British henges may be common responses to shared or similar beliefs however the difference in time and space between the central European and British phenomena make any direct relationship unlikely.

Harding and Lee, like Wainwright and Burl, regard Causewayed Enclosures as more likely precursors of henge monuments citing the discontinuous ditches, the treatment of these ditches and the placed deposits within them and in the interiors. There are differences, of course, and the 'domestic' material at Causewayed Enclosures is certainly more abundant than it is at henges. Some henges lie close to Causewayed Enclosures and may have taken over their roles as meeting places however the similarities in both form, site-history and distribution are general rather than specific and they conclude that there is 'little ... that suggests a background specifically in Causewayed Enclosures' (Harding with Lee 1987, 59). They further look to Neolithic round barrows and cite Duggleby Howe, North Yorkshire, with its encircling causewayed ditch. They also see a formative phase for circular monuments perhaps evolving from Mortuary Enclosures and interrupted ring ditches of the Neolithic though rarely do these possess the scale of construction found amongst henges. Instead Harding and Lee look to a variety of circular monuments

such as pit circles and post circles below barrows as equally influencing henges. They conclude that 'no one source can provide an adequate background for all the features represented on them (i.e. henges)' (*op. cit.*, 61, my brackets). Clare (1987) largely supported this view also drawing attention to Neolithic mortuary enclosures as mentioned above.

Indeed Causewayed Enclosures, and in particular those with internal fences or palisades may well have influenced the emerging class of middle and late Neolithic Palisaded Enclosures. These represent a considerable increase in scale from the Causewayed Enclosure stockades and involve the felling of considerable numbers of mature oak trees. Starting in the last few centuries of the fourth millennium cal BC they continue through the later Neolithic, the early examples pre-date henges and they are often found in association with them (Gibson 2002; Brophy and Noble, this volume). The largest so far discovered, at Hindwell, Powys, encloses a staggering 34ha, is three times the area of Durrington Walls and probably involved the felling of a minimum of 1400 mature oak trees.

Jan Harding (2003) did not look so much towards the Continent or indeed the Earlier Neolithic for the origins of henges but preferred to see the emergence of a series of circular enclosures which he termed formative henges. He benefitted from an increased radiocarbon chronology and saw sites with early dates such as Stonehenge I, Llandegai A and Stennes (all Class I henges) as being formative. Stonehenge and Llandegai A were also unusual in having external ditches. The ditches around megalithic tombs and Neolithic round barrows such as Maes Howe, The Giant's Ring at Ballynahatty, Co. Antrim and Duggleby Howe are also cited as possible atypical and therefore formative henges. Flagstones in Dorset with its late fourth millennium radiocarbon dates, its interrupted ditch, its circular form and incorporation of human burials may, with Stonehenge, link formative henges to Causewayed Enclosures and suggest 'a continuity between the late fourth and early third millennium BC' (2003, 13). To these may be added the Thames Valley sites such as the Neolithic penannular ring ditches at Shepperton (Jones 2008), Horton (Preston 2003) and Imperial College Sports Ground (Barclay *et al.* 2009) with their irregular ditch profiles, human burials and association with Impressed Ware. With radiocarbon dates spanning c.3600-3300 cal BC these sites are earlier than Stonehenge 1 and may be related to the early monuments at Dorchester. Harding goes on to suggest that the emergence of the circular tradition may represent a fundamental change in religion away from ancestor cults represented by multiple burials and long mounds to more individual burial and different monument forms. This seems to have taken place at the end of the fourth millennium.

Burrow also favoured the idea of formative henges in his review of the Welsh and western English material (2010) and once again noted a sepulchral connection in the earlier monuments. Like all other commentators, Burrow suffers from the paucity of secure radiocarbon dates and had to rely largely on educated speculation in his identification of these early sites which, by his own admission, made his conclusions the more tentative. Indeed, subsequent excavation of one of his possible formative henges (Walton Court, Powys) has returned a mid third millennium date (Jones 2010).

Variety in henges

The variety of monuments that became increasingly added to the henge corpus was excellently outlined by Clare over a quarter of a century ago and needs little reiteration here (Clare 1986). One of the problems is that sites are being recognised from aerial photography or other prospection techniques without the benefit of excavation and classifying a site by morphology alone can be dangerous leading to the possible confusion of monuments from different periods as admirably demonstrated by Harding and Lee (1987). Indeed a recent review of Welsh henges by the present writer has identified a number of later prehistoric enclosures that had originally been erroneously (perhaps hopefully) identified as henges (Gibson forthcoming (a)).

With Wainwright's introduction of the word 'hengiform' free reign was given to include monuments of all sizes and indeed of different forms. Amongst the better known henges, for example Stonehenge and Llandegai

A (Gwynedd) have internal banks, but Llandegai A has a single entrance while Stonhenge has 2, possibly 3 (Figure 6). Woodhenge has a single entrance but an external bank and possibly an internal mound. The original name for Woodhenge prior to its excavation was the 'Dough Cover' so named after its low domed interior (Cunnington 1929). Cunnington attributed the mounded interior to agricultural processes suggesting that the chalk had been eroded near the ditch by circular ploughing around the ditch edge. It may be however, that the chalk in the central area had been protected from the plough by a low mound which, in its turn had been ploughed away. If the mound hypothesis is accepted, then Woodhenge resembles Dyffryn Lane, Powys, which also had a single entrance and an internal mound but Dyffryn Lane enclosed a stone circle while Woodhenge enclosed the site of a timber one. At the double-entranced site at LLandegai B the ditch is 4m wide and encloses a circular area roughly 70m in diameter (Figure 7) whilst at Vaynor, Ceredigion, the ditch is twice as wide yet encloses a comparatively small oval internal area averaging only 16m in diameter (Barber and Pannet 2006): compare this with the ditch at Duggleby Howe which averages 6.5m across yet encloses a massive area some 370m in diameter. In terms of diameter Duggleby compares well with Durrington Walls, but at this latter site the ditch was over twice as wide and twice as deep. Durrington Walls also had an external bank, Duggleby had

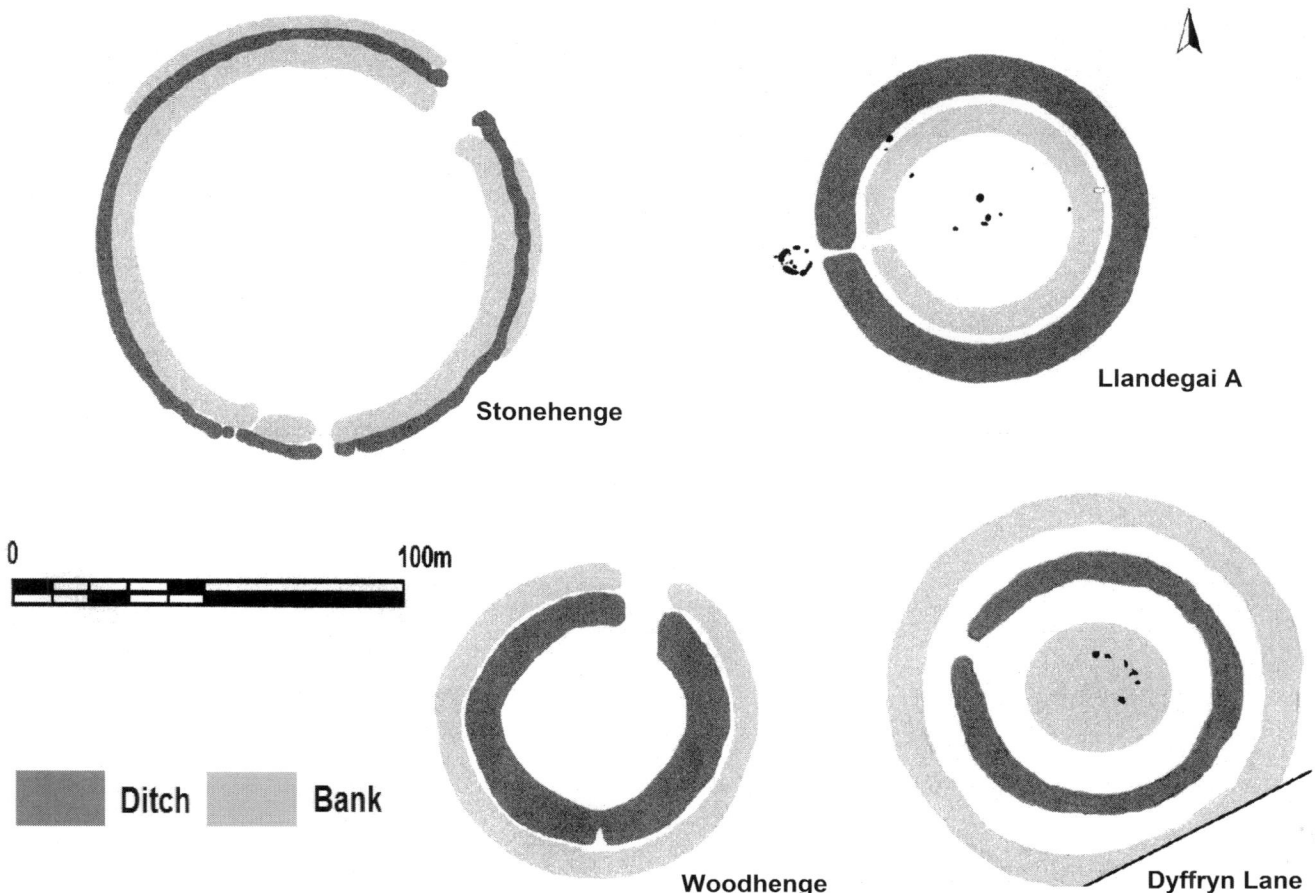

FIGURE 6: VARIATION IN HENGE BANK LAYOUT.

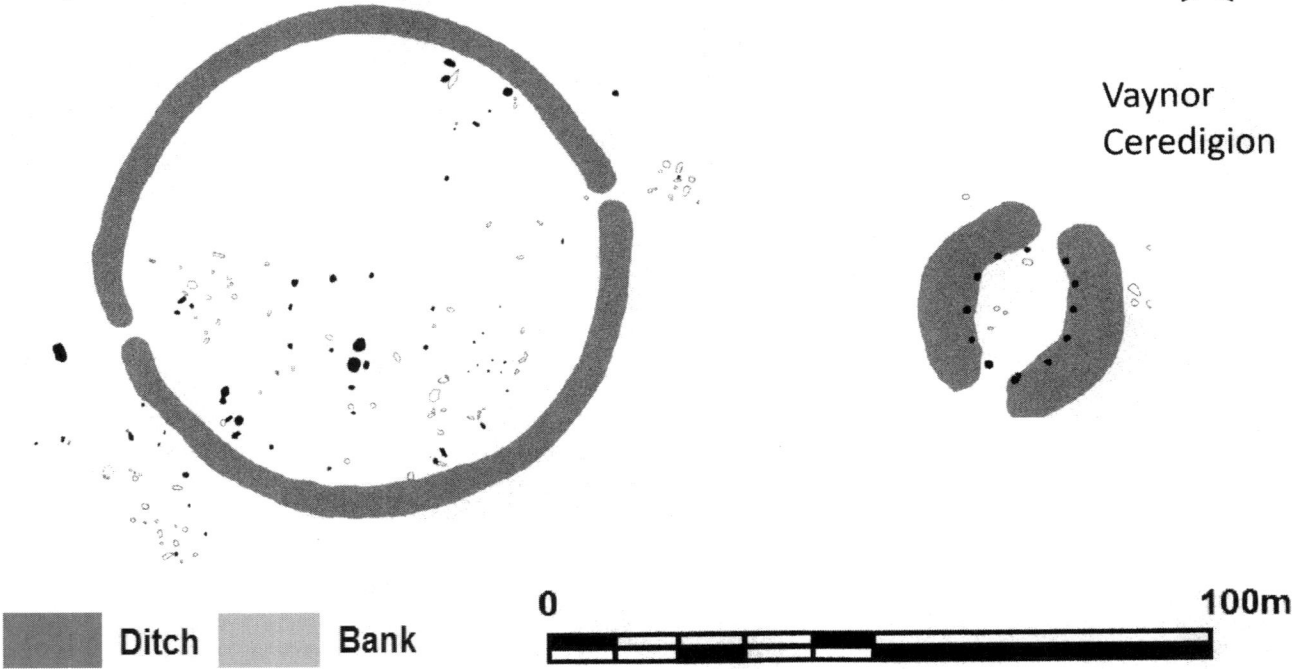

Llandegai B
Gwynedd

Vaynor
Ceredigion

Ditch   Bank

0   100m

FIGURE 7: COMPARISON IN DITCH DIMENSIONS BETWEEN THE LARGE LLANDEGAI B, GWYNEDD AND THE SMALL VAYNOR, CEREDIGION. NEITHER SITE APPEARS TO HAVE HAD BANKS.

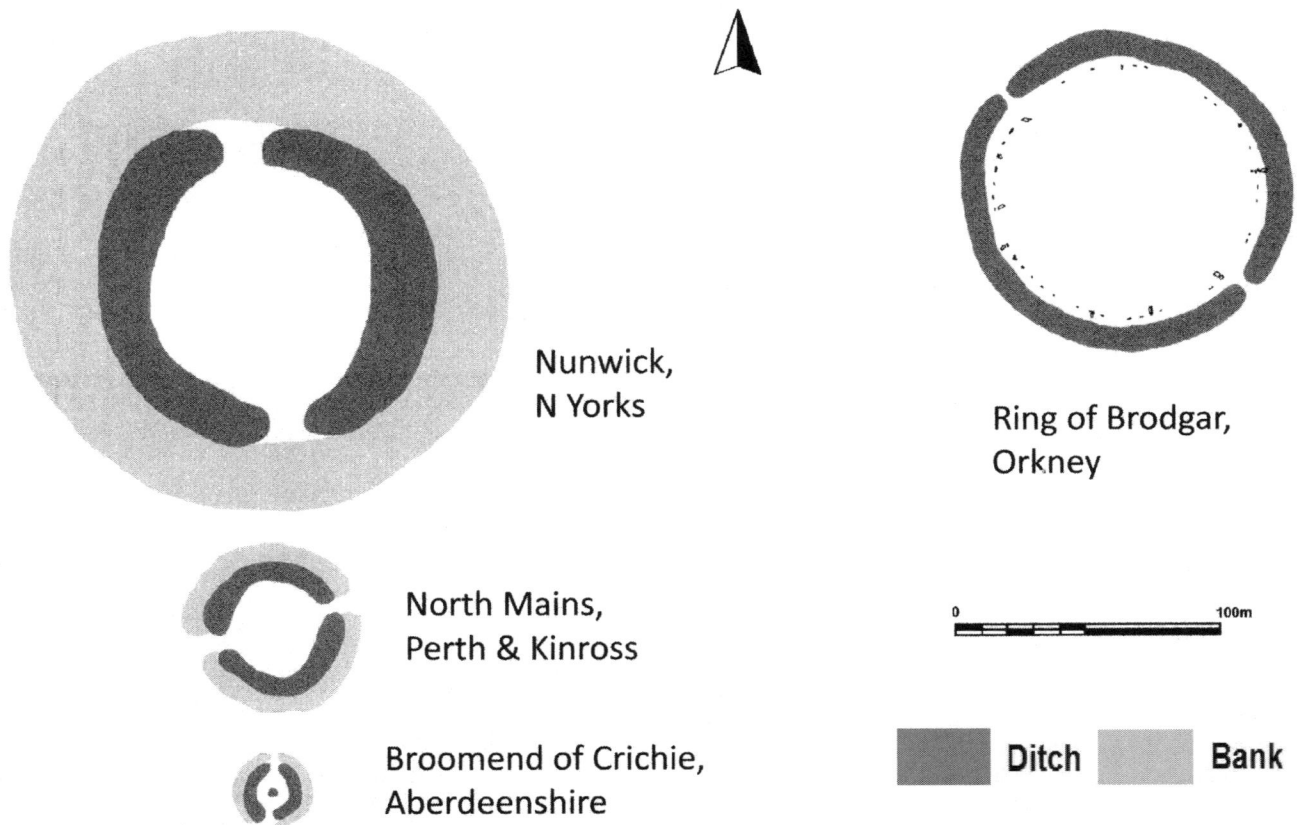

Nunwick,
N Yorks

Ring of Brodgar,
Orkney

North Mains,
Perth & Kinross

Broomend of Crichie,
Aberdeenshire

0   100m

Ditch   Bank

FIGURE 8: DIFFERENCES IN INTERNAL DIAMETER IN RELATION TO DITCH AND BANK DIMENSIONS.

Stennes, Orkney

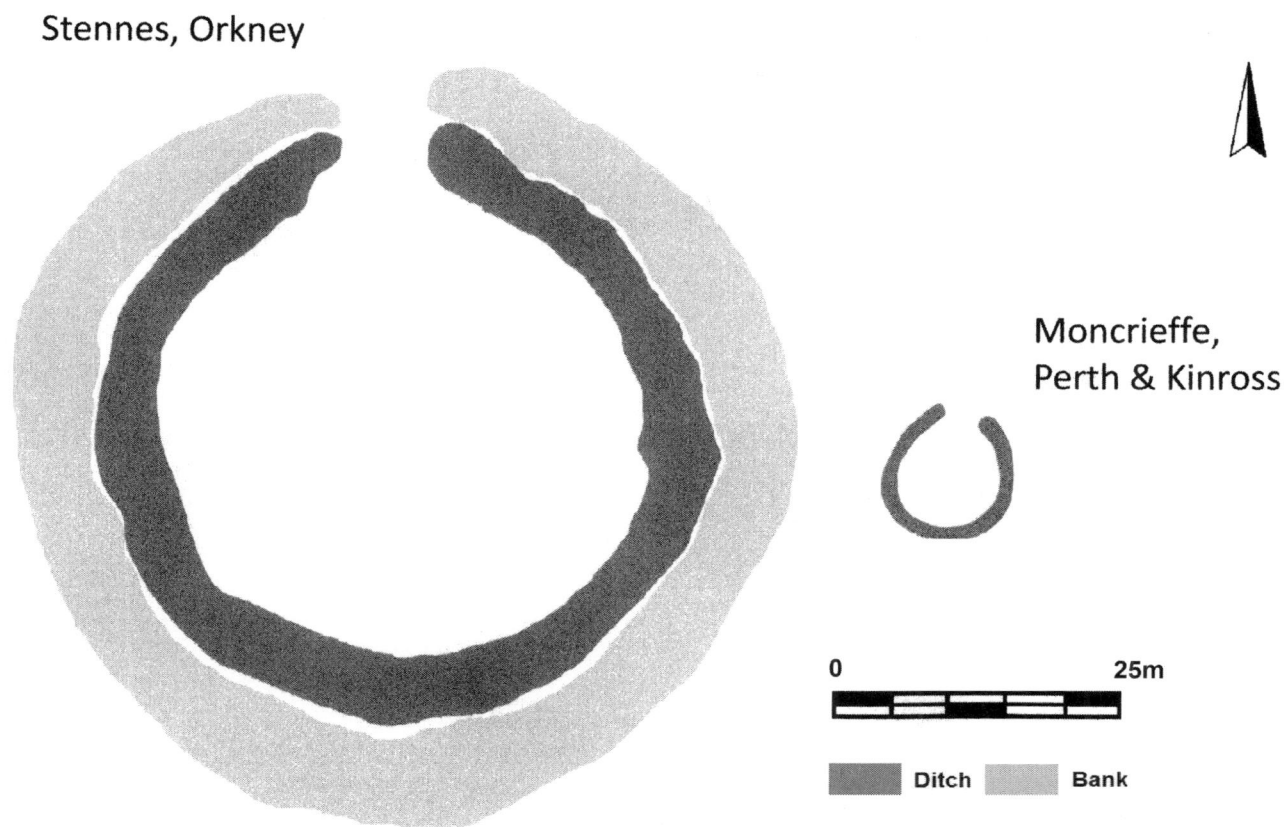

Moncrieffe, Perth & Kinross

FIGURE 9: TWO CLASS I SITES GREATLY DIFFERING IN SIZE AND SEQUENCE.

none. The class II henge at Nunwick, North Yorkshire has an internal area averaging some 85m in diameter (Dymond 1963) enclosed by a ditch some 13m wide but less than 2m deep (Figure 8). The similarly shaped monument at North Mains, Perth and Kinross, measured only some 33m across with a ditch 6-11m wide and up to 3m deep. In contrast the still smaller class II Broomend of Crichie, Aberdeenshire, (c.15m internal diameter) had a 6m wide ditch of similar depth. At the other extreme, Brodgar, Orkney, has an internal diameter of c.110m but with a rock cut ditch little deeper or wider than North Mains (3m deep and 10m wide as weathered – Renfrew 1979 fig 15). Loanhead of Daviot, · Aberdeenshire, and Fargo Plantation share the Class II form. The former averages 11m in internal area with a ditch under 1m wide and 0.25m deep whilst the latter averages half the diameter of Loanhead yet has ditches 1.5m wide. Neither have banks. If Bradley's suggestion that the Loanhead ditch was a palisade slot is accepted, then the form takes on a greater significance (Bradley 2011).

At the classic single-entranced site at Stennes, Orkney, the internal area averaged 45m in diameter and the ditch averaged 3.5-4m across and over 2m deep (Figure 9). The henge enclosed the well known stone circle and other internal features and Ritchie (1976) regarded the stone circle as primary. At 10m in internal diameter, the morphologically similar single-entranced enclosure at

Moncrieffe, Perth and Kinross, is less than a quarter of the size of Stennes and with a much smaller ditch only 1.4m wide and up to 0.75m deep (Stewart 1985). This enclosed a circle of pits but, according to the excavator, the ditch was backfilled before a stone circle was added. In contrast, at Broomend of Crichie, Dyffryn Lane, and Balfarg, Fife, the stone circles appear to have been earlier than the enclosures and this sequence has also been inferred at other sites such as Arbor Low, Cairnpapple Hill (West Lothian), and possibly even at Avebury.

Indeed there is now a considerable body of data to suggest that enclosing ditches were late in many site sequences. Grooved Ware at Woodhenge comes from under the bank so was clearly at the site before the earthwork was constructed. The enclosure is also most likely to be secondary to the timber circles and possibly even the later stone setting (Pollard and Robinson 2007). It may be that the Woodhenge earthwork is associated with a possible low internal mound and perhaps also the off-centre burial though, given the degree of excavation at the site, this must remain hypothetical and is unlikely to be resolved. Despite this, the layout of the timber circles and by analogy with other sites such as North Mains, Broomend of Crichie and Dyffryn Lane a long sequence at Woodhenge can be suggested (Figure 10).

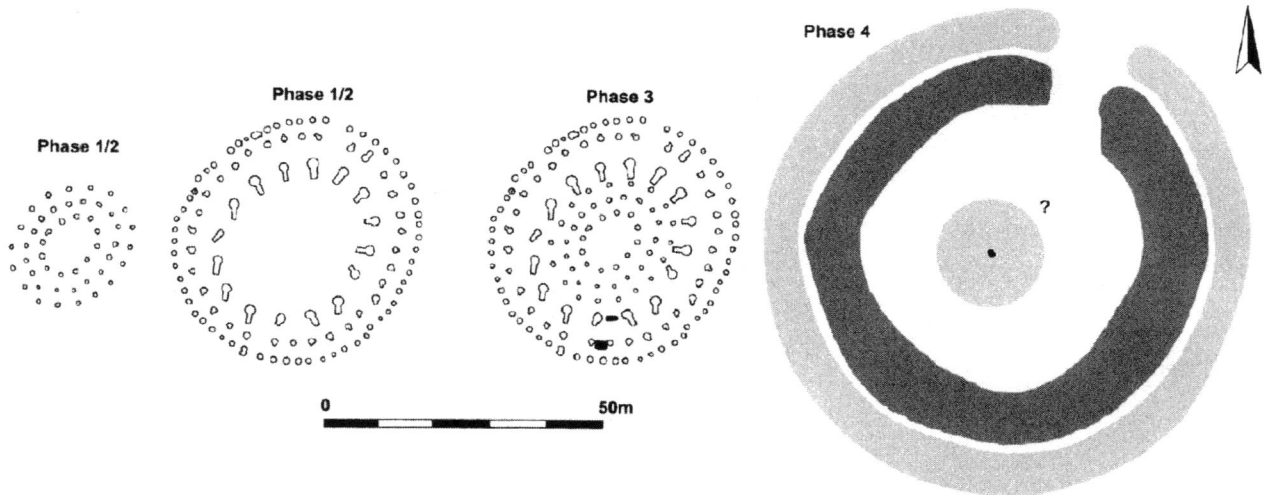

FIGURE 10: POSSIBLE PHASING AT WOODHENGE, WILTSHIRE

It is clear from the south-facing ramps in the northern arc of ring C that these posts could not have been erected whilst rings D, E, and F were extant. Their lack of orientation on the enclosure entrance also suggests that their arrival at the site was not hindered by the earthwork. Similarly the construction of rings D, E and F would have been difficult if the posts of ring C were in place. The ramps of ring B face outwards and once again logic suggests that they are most likely to pre-date the enclosure and to post-date ring C. The stone setting post-dates rings C and B as does the enclosure bank and ditch. The place of the crouched infant sacrifice at the centre of the monument remains unresolved. The mode of burial may suggest that it is Beaker or later however crouched infant burials are known from the beginning of the third millennium at, for example, Duggleby Howe (Gibson and Bayliss 2010). The position of the grave across the axis of the timber circles might draw comparison to the altar stone at Stonehenge, however it may equally draw analogy with the central burials at Broomend, Balfarg, North Mains, Cairnpapple Hill and possibly also Arbor Low and Dyffryn Lane. A low internal mound possibly existed at Woodhenge and certainly existed at Dyffryn Lane and Cairnpapple Hill and can be inferred at Balfarg (Gibson 2010a) so it may be with this mound that the enclosure ditch and child burial are associated in the closing centuries of the third millennium. That the monument continued to be a focus of attention can be demonstrated by the burial dug into the floor of the eastern section of the ditch and dated to the second quarter of the second millennium.

Thus a protracted relative sequence can be proposed. Phase 1 comprises rings D, E and F. These went out of use and were replaced by rings B, C, and A. These rings were replaced by a stone setting. The enclosure ditch was excavated on a slightly different alignment and provided material for an external bank and possibly a low mound covering the child inhumation. This act effectively closed the interior of the site and brought to an end the rituals that must have been practiced in this arena. Finally a burial was placed in the ditch in the Early Bronze Age c.1800 – 1600 cal BC.

The outward facing post ramps at North Mains and the unidirectional south-facing ramps at Arminghall similarly argue for the primacy of the timber phases: an hypothesis finally proven by the radiocarbon dating of a cremation sealed by the bank at North Mains (Barclay 2005). The primacy of the timber circle at Milfield North, Northumberland, is not in doubt as the postholes were sealed by the outer bank (Harding 1981). In 2010 it was suggested that the proximity of stones to the inner edge of the ditch argued for the primacy of stone circles at 'circle-henges' (Gibson 2010b). The ramps at the Devil's Quoits, Oxon, support this hypothesis and resemble the post ramps at North Mains. Bradley (2011) has taken this further by highlighting not just the proximity of the stones to the ditch edge, but also the change in orientation between the pre-enclosure ovals and the enclosure entrances at Broomend of Crichie, Cairnpapple Hill and Arbor Low.

The secondary nature of the enclosing earthwork, therefore, may well explain the peculiar configuration of henge monuments, namely the internal ditch and external bank. Were the earthworks to enclose an area that was already ritually important, then the external bank would not compromise the internal space. The ditch could be excavated close to the perimeter of that space and the bank spread away from it, outside the special area. The external bank may therefore be purely practical. Irregular banks (Avebury, Arbor Low) and sites without banks (Vaynor, Llandegai B) might suggest the relative importance of the ditch as the main delineating feature (Gibson 2010b).

There are therefore considerable differences in detail, sequences, site form and size amongst monuments usually labelled henges. The only real uniting factor is the presence of a ditch and the lack of 'domestic' detritus (but see Gorsey Bigbury – Jones 1938).

Links with other monuments

The direct links with other monuments, of which the enclosing ditch plays a component part have already been illustrated above. But these earthwork enclosures are frequently associated with other earlier and later monuments in what have been called ritual complexes. This is not the place to detail such complexes and Harding and Lee (1987) have already examined this phenomenon but a few examples from diverse regions will serve to illustrate the point.

Dyffryn Lane, for example is only 500m SE of the Lower Luggy long barrow and Neolithic enclosure (Gibson 2010b) and is itself surrounded by a complex of cropmark barrows and ring-ditches, some of which appear to be penannular. A cursus monument has recently been located to the west (Jones 2009). Links with cursus monuments are well known at Dorchester (Atkinson *et al.* 1951), Barnack and Maxey, Cambridgeshire, (Harding with Lee 1987, 77 and 89) where again ring-ditches and penannular enclosures are also present. North Mains is part of a cluster of round barrows and ring ditches in the Earn Valley (Barclay 1983) Whilst in the Tay Valley, penannular and double entranced enclosures are in close association with the palisaded site at Forteviot, Perth and Kinross, datable to the first half of the third millennium (Brophy and Noble 2011).

Interesting at these sites is the juxtaposition of other circular ditched enclosures, usually termed ring-ditches, yet it is not always clear what features single out the henge. In some cases the henge has a wider and more prominent ditch however as we have seen above, the ditches at other henges can be slight indeed.

Current dating

In 1939, Piggott had suggested that henges were linked to 'Beaker Folk' however the tendency of late has been to regard henges as later Neolithic phenomena extending into the Beaker period and beyond. The reason for this earlier start is clearly the dates of c.3000 cal BC for Stonehenge I (Cleal *et al.* 1995), the later Neolithic (now mid-late Neolithic) 'Dorchester Culture' artefacts such as maceheads and bone skewer pins from Atkinson's excavations at the type-site and elsewhere and the high-profile Grooved Ware-producing excavations at the Wessex henges, particularly Durrington Walls and Woodhenge as well as further north at Balfarg, North Mains and even Stennes. The idea of formative henges in terms of circular ditched sites linking the fourth and mid third millennia has already been discussed.

The problem with dating henges, however, is what to date. Firstly, and as outlined above, the whole issue of 'what is a henge' has become hopelessly confused since the monument class was first defined. How can we be sure in such an environment that the site we are dating is in fact a henge?

Leaving aside the well-known contaminant possibilities such as old oak and curated human and animal remains, unless there are helpfully placed deliberate and fresh deposits such as articulated bone on the ditch floor (not silts), then we cannot be certain that what we are dating is the construction of the henge. Even then the ditch may have been kept clean for a considerable period before the articulated bone was deposited. Dates and/or finds from beneath the bank can only provide *Termini Post Quos* (*TPQ*) dates while deposits in the ditch, no matter how low down (with the exception of deliberately placed deposits mentioned above) can at best provide *Termini Ante Quos (TAQ)* determinations. Material from features within or outside the henge can at best only date the activity at the site unless there is a stratrigraphic relationship between the dated feature and henge perimeter in which case once again *TPQ and TAQ* dates are the best that can be expected. However these can still be informative as can site layout and associations.

Increased radiocarbon dating is also starting to suggest that 'things we call henges' are quite long-lived phenomena, lasting from just before 3000 BC until the first half of the second millennium (Harding 2003, Figure 6). It would appear that some 'types' of hengiform may actually be long-lived. Thus the small single-entranced 'hengiform' at Sarn-y-bryn-caled Site 2 (Gibson 1994) seen as a formative henge by Burrow (2010) is virtually identical in shape to the enclosed Bronze Age cremation cemetery at Balneaves, Angus (Russell-White *et al.* 1992). The former dates to the beginning of the third millennium (Gibson 2010c), the latter to the middle of the second millennium and the evidence for a bank at both sites is by no means certain. The ditch surrounding Maes Howe suggests it was dug in the early third millennium (Renfrew 1979), the ditch around Duggleby Howe in the mid third millennium (Gibson forthcoming (b)) though it must be remembered that Duggleby is over twice the size of the Maes Howe enclosure.

Indeed many of the dates for henges are of poor integrity. Many come from unidentified and/or bulked samples from the ditch silts and given the mobility of charcoal in the soil must be treated with extreme caution. For example it has been recently pointed out that the dates for the Milfield henge complex in Northumberland derive from samples that 'consist of bulked unidentified charcoal' (Waddington 2011, 287-8.). Waddington claims that the age at death offset may affect these dates and whilst this is true, the real situation is much worse. Such charcoal may have washed in from earlier features cut by the henge ditch and destroyed by its weathering. Just such a scenario is used to explain the early dates for the Milfield 'droveway' that passes through the henge complex (Waddington 2011, 290).

The site that is consistently identified as a formative henge, largely from its internal bank and therefore its similarity with Stonehenge, is Llandegai A. Dates for this monument at the end of the fourth millennium are often cited, but analysis of the contexts for these dates suggest that the dating of the henge is far from secure. An axial alignment is formed through the entrance of the henge from the central Pit A1 to a causewayed ring-ditch outside the entrance. The cremation burial in pit 370 just to the south of the eastern end of this alignment was dated to the 32nd-31st C cal BC (Lynch and Musson 2004). The three dates from the causewayed ring ditch outside the western entrance span the 37th to 29th C cal BC at 2 sigma (34th-29th C at 1 sigma) but the dates are largely derived from oak charcoal so may well suffer from the old wood effect and are at best TPQs for the ring-ditch. Nevertheless, the common axis of this ring-ditch the central axis of the henge and the broadly contemporary central Pit A1 (also dated from oak charcoal) attest a broad association. The position of pit 370 appears to extend this alignment to the western edge of the enclosure but this was sealed by the bank and produced a Mesolithic date.

The date from layer 4 in the ditch of Llandegai A is from above the primary silts in the ditch. At first sight this suggests that the ditch was silting in the 34th-27th C cal BC but again we must question the integrity of this sample which comprised bulked charcoal including oak. Given the middle Neolithic activity inside and outside the henge, this material (and the fragmentary middle Neolithic pottery) may easily be derived from earlier eroded contexts and have been incorporated into the silts as a result of natural weathering as was claimed for the Milfield droveway. It is argued here that none of the dates from Llandegai A date the construction of the henge and that they provide at best a TPQ. The cremation burial from F13 in the north-east quadrant, however dates to the 18th – 20th centuries cal BC over 1 millennium later than the axial features. It is argued here that the henge may date to any time within that millennium.

Two sets of C14 dates from Dyffryn Lane ostensibly act as TPQ dates for the henge construction. The first, associated with Impressed Ware pits below the bank and derived from short-lived charcoal, ranges from approximately the 30th to 29th Centuries cal BC. The second, also derived from short-lived charcoal from a hearth below the bank dates to 26th-25th Centuries cal BC (Gibson 2010b). The difference in context however is important. The pits were sealed by a thin buried soil beneath the bank whilst the hearth lay on top of this and directly below the bank material. We can safely accept the hearth dates as the more accurate and the Impressed Ware dates as considerably pre-dating henge construction. Might we have been so well informed had the site formed part of a machine-stripped landscape excavation?

If the radiocarbon dates are taken at face value, Class I henges span the period 3500cal BC –cal AD 700 (Figure 11). There are clearly outliers that can be seriously questioned such as the late date from Lairg, Maxey and Stennes which may show that the henge was still receiving attention but are more likely to derive from natural processes. The early dates from Shepperton confirm this

penannular enclosure as belonging to the middle Neolithic ring-ditch series. That from Whitton Hill is on old and unidentified charcoal and the Llandegai dates have already been discussed, and hopefully dismissed. The date from Arminghall with its large margin of error compounds with the plateau in the radiocarbon curve and dates the timber circle rather than the henge.

If we look at only the dates that provide construction dates or TPQ dates for the construction of the Class I henges (such as samples from ditch floors and buried soils) the corpus reduces considerably but the basic date range is still maintained. Once again Sarn-y-bryn-caled may be considered a Middle Neolithic penannular enclosure but even if this is dismissed, we still have the early date for Stennes. The dates for Woodhenge are interesting. The latest comes from the burial cut into the base of the eastern ditch section. The Cunningtons did not notice a cut through the silts. We are left with two scenarios. Either the original British Museum dates date the enclosure to the early Beaker period or they are derived from old weathered material and the burial in the base of the ditch dates the construction of the monument. The problem is not easily resolvable. One involves the dismissing of two similar dates from the same general context, while the other perhaps puts an over-reliance on the Cunningtons' excavation methodology.

This approach may be considered parsimonious however if we include features from within the henge interiors and ditches which certainly date the use of the monuments the date range is much the same. Our three general, parsimonious and selected datasets agree that single entranced henges span the period 3000 cal BC to about 1200 cal BC.

As has been mentioned above, Class II henges with opposed or near-opposed entrances are generally considered to be later with Beaker or mature Early Bronze Age associations. A view of all radiocarbon dates from Class II henges suggests that this is not the case however the early Broomend of Crichie dates date pre-henge activity as is almost certainly true for Balfarg compounded by the old wood factor (Figure 12). The Yeavering date is also undoubtedly from derived material and the Ferrybridge henge is dated from possibly residual material on top of the phase 1 bank (Roberts 2005). Once again the parsimonious approach considerably reduces the corpus and this does indeed suggest that class II henges are a chalcolithic phenomenon. The dates for the construction and use of these sites following the selection criteria adopted for the class I sites however shows a much more limited date range starting with the introduction of Beakers in the 25th C cal BC and continuing into the Early Bronze Age but not really lasting beyond the currency of late Beakers (Needham 2005).

The date ranges for the Class I and Class II henges are very different. The former spans 2 millennia, the latter less than one. The longevity of the class I sites can also

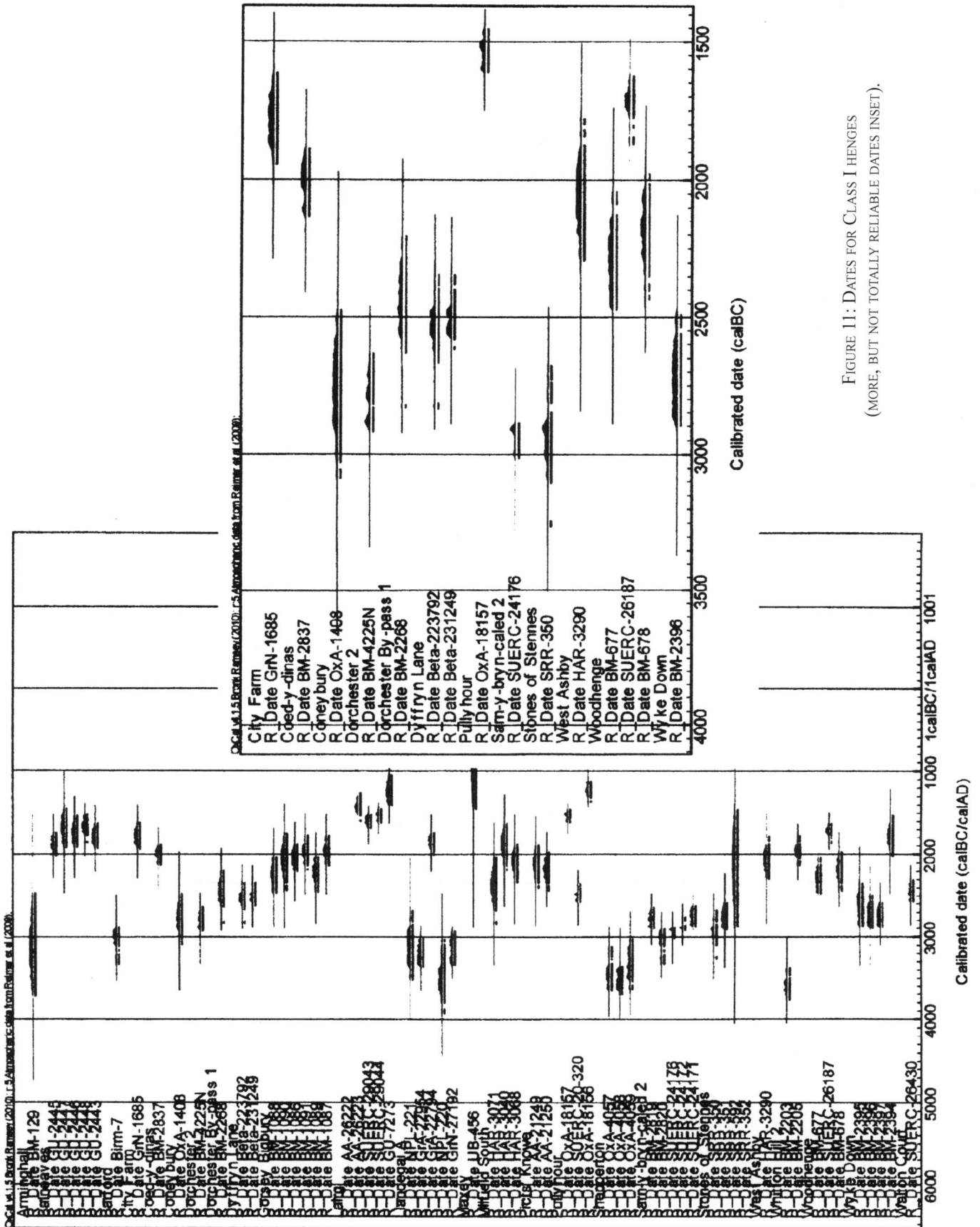

FIGURE 11: DATES FOR CLASS I HENGES
(MORE, BUT NOT TOTALLY RELIABLE DATES INSET).

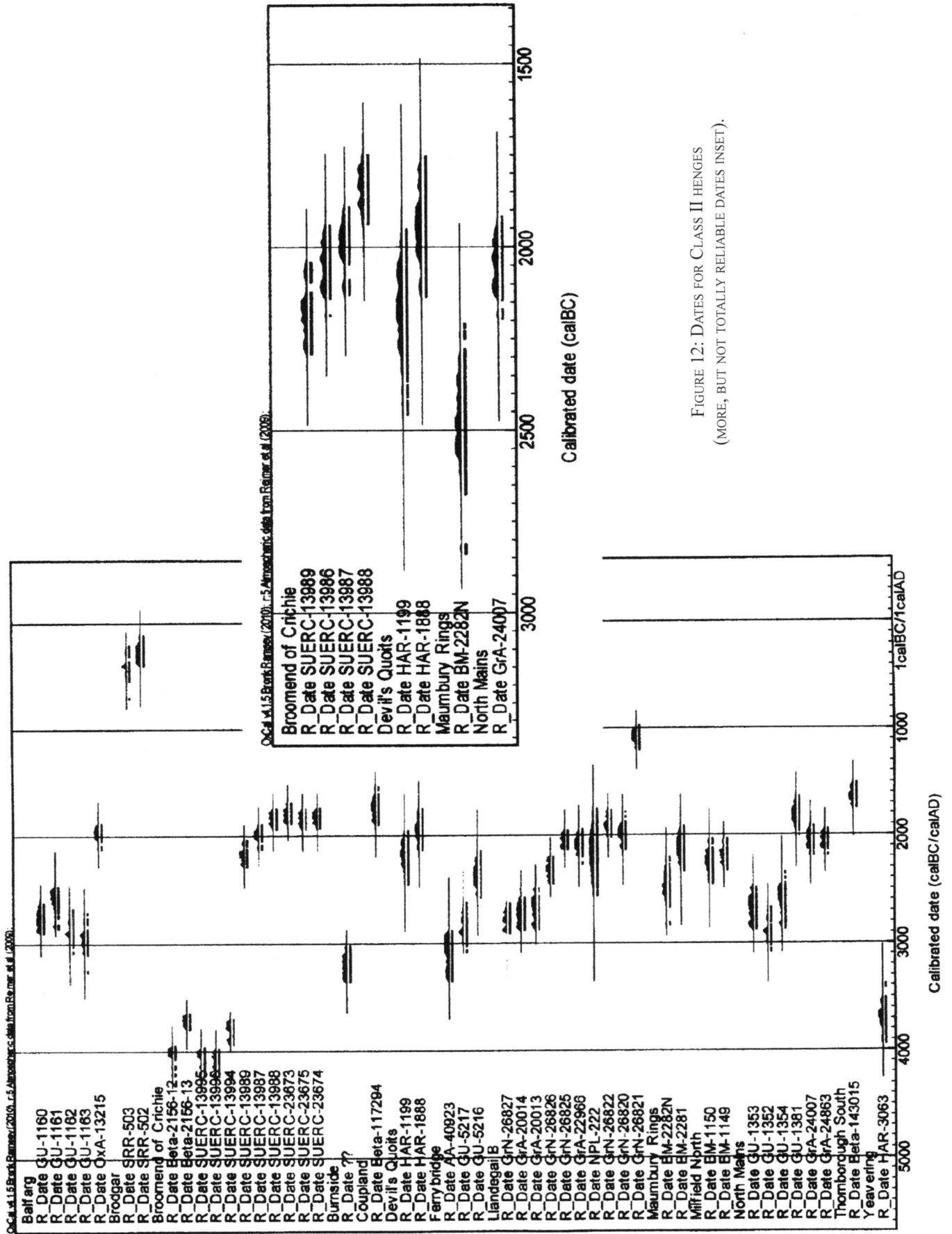

FIGURE 12: DATES FOR CLASS II HENGES
(MORE, BUT NOT TOTALLY RELIABLE DATES INSET).

be compared with their great diversity and form. Small sites are both early (Sarn-y-bryn-caled 2, Dorchester 2) and late (Balneaves, City farm, Lairg, Pullyhour) with larger sites adopting the middle of the range. This similar chronological rise and fall has been suggested for timber circles (Gibson 1994; 1998) and there is a growing amount of evidence to suggest that it may also be true for stone circles that are notoriously difficult to date but that similarly span this long period.

It now seems that there is a distinct dichotomy within the henge classes. A long-lived and varied tradition of single-entranced enclosures with a much more chronologically defined and morphologically homogenous group of double-entranced enclosures.

Time for a change

The problem with henges is of our own making. We have seen that from the introduction of the name until the 1960's the term was usually cited in inverted commas intimating a general unease with the label for almost 30 years. We have seen that there are (at least) three types and according to this typology, Stonehenge is not a henge, nor for that matter is Llandegai A. Nevertheless the classifications were stretched to allow these unusual sites to be included. Not only are there henges with internal and external banks, but there are 'henges' with no banks at all such as the class II site at Vaynor (Barber and Pannet 2006), Brodgar (Renfrew 1979), Llandegai B (Lynch and Musson 2004), and the causewayed ditch at Duggleby Howe (Gibson forthcoming b). The only consistent features then seem to be a ditch and a tendency towards circularity. Indeed non-existent banks as mentioned above or irregular banks (Arbor Low) suggest to the present writer that it is the ditch that is the important feature. Often dug wide and deep in relation to their diameters they form considerable trenches around their foci perhaps symbolically to contain what lies within their perimeter as suggested by Warner (2000). The idea is attractive but its impact is lessened to a degree in the cases of those sites without banks and the pure practicality of internal ditches and external banks (or indeed ditches with no banks) has already been discussed above. Harding and Lee examined henge ditch width in relation to site diameters but no real patterning was visible but they nevertheless suggested that henge ditches should be over 2.5m wide and that anything 'less substantial than this are simply not accepted into the canon of henge sites' (1987, 40). But this seems a somewhat arbitrary boundary.

The idea of formative henges might also be seriously questioned. It is difficult to see how these largely circular sites developed into the more geometrically uniform oval monument (Class II) with two entrances, especially when the single entranced form continues in currency throughout and beyond the Class II timespan. These Class II sites do tend to make a better homogenous grouping than do the Class I monuments. They range considerably in size but do appear to be Beaker or later in date and are united in their opposed entrances and often slightly asymmetric

outline. As already pointed out by Bradley (2011) there is a fundamental difference between the single and double entranced henges beyond simple morphology: the former prescribe entrance and exit by the same pathway, the latter allow passage through the monument. This must have an important bearing on the ways in which these sites were used and suggests a fundamental difference between the 2 classes. Indeed this can be taken further and class II would not only allow passage through but also entry from two directions. This may be important given Loveday's suggestion that Class II henges may have been constructed on or near to ancient routeways as later fossilised by Roman roads (Loveday 1998).

When the term 'henge' was coined to refer to a specific number of sites it was already inadequate as the sites were diverse. With increased aerial prospection, increased dating and the growth of developer-funded archaeology, so the diversity of circular Neolithic and Bronze Age ditched enclosures has similarly expanded. Surely it is time to stop shoe-horning diverse sites into an out-dated and now inadequate class of monument. The henge has served us well but it may be time to put it to rest: we are reminded of Atkinson's claim that the term henge was redundant as early as 1951. But 'henge' is emotive and to the lay person the mystery of the name conjures up the mystery of the distant past. 'Henge' invokes ideas of Neolithic rituals and ceremonies, of temples and sanctuaries to the extent that it has been applied to some monuments which cannot be termed henges in the archaeological sense: Seahenge (a palisade barrow at Holme-next the-Sea) and the Welsh Woodhenge (as the press referred to the timber circle at Sarn-y-bryn-caled). As archaeologists, however, we are trained to be objective. Thus some archaeologists will excavate Neolithic timber houses, whilst the more cautious will acknowledge them only to be 'timber structures'. With this objectivity in mind, the present writer advocates the abandonment of 'henge'.

There can be no denying that shortly before 3000 BC there was a dramatic change in monument construction. Causewayed Enclosures and Long Barrows ceased to be built and the laying out of elongated Cursus monuments occupied but a brief episode. Monuments constructed after 3000 BC are almost exclusively circular or oval be they of stone, timber or earth.

Stone circles range in date from 3000 to approximately 1200 BC. Timber circles are broadly contemporary though both monument types have problems with their dating relying on conveniently placed material in the stoneholes and charring of the outer rings of the timber uprights. Both are later Neolithic in their origins, sharing their initial horizons with the advent of Grooved Ware. They both continue through the Beaker or Chalcolithic period. Both cease to be built in the Bronze Age their demise coinciding with that of the Food Vessel and Urn traditions. There are distinct groupings and types within both the stone and timber circle classes. In the case of stone circles there are the large open circles of Cumbria, the smaller rings of Dartmoor, four posters, flattened circles, oval circles, embanked circles, the low simple circles of Wales to the complexity of Callanish and Stonehenge. In timber circles there are single, double and multiple forms of both circular and oval rings. Both monument types connect with Bronze Age burial monuments with timber circles found below and around barrows and stone circles merging with the kerb and ring-cairn traditions.

Circles defined by ditches are no different. Their variety of form has been the subject of much of this paper. The earliest examples are exactly contemporary with the earliest circles of stone or wood and they too suffer from an imprecise chronology. Like stone and timber circles, they are varied in their size and architecture but they are clearly part of the same tradition of circularity as stone and timber circles and indeed the three monument types may overlap physically for example at Balfarg and Stanton Drew. Their construction ceases at the same time in the Bronze Age. They also merge with contemporary burial monuments, particularly in the lowland zone as outlined by Clare over 25 years ago (1986).

Back in 1939, in an article in Antiquity, the Piggotts described the earth circles of Dorset. They used 'henge' in inverted commas and acknowledged the variety in the class. If we have circles of stone and wood, then why not also earth. The term is not loaded with prejudice, interpretation or emotive baggage but rather treats these sites with the same objectivity as their stone and timber counterparts. The term can be sub-divided. Thus we might have penannular earth circles, oval earth circles, embanked earth circles, concentric earth circles and so on. Neither does size matter because the objective name is equally applicable to both small sites such as Sarn-y-bryn-caled 2 and the larger sites such as Brodgar in the same way as the stone circle class spans the range from four posters to Avebury. By using such a simple and descriptive name we also acknowledge the links with other contemporary circles noting only the differences in the media of their construction. 'Henge' has done us well but should now be put to rest.

Double-entranced earth circles, however, share a very similar form and grammar regardless of their size. They usually comprise an oval area formed by two unequal segments of curved ditch and again a bank is not obligatory. The form is also found in timber and in stone and as Bradley has shown, they almost certainly operated in a way different to the single-entranced enclosures. These may be a class apart and certainly seem to be much more restricted in date. They may well have had a specialised role within the general milieu of earthen circles. If henge is to be retained then it may be to these distinctive monuments that the label may be applied.

Bibliography

Atkinson, R.J.C, Piggott, C.M. and Sandars, N.K. 1951. *Excavations at Dorchester, Oxon. First Report*. Oxford: Ashmolean Museum.

Barber, A. and Pannet, A. 2006. Archaeological Excavations along the Milford Haven to Aberdulais Natural Gas Pipeline 2006: A Preliminary report. *Archaeology in Wales*, 46, 87-99.

Barclay, A. Beavan, N., Bradley, P., Chaffey, G., Challinor, D., McKinley, J., Powell, A. and Marshall, P. 2009. New Evidence for Mid-Late Neolithic Burial from the Colne Valley, West London. *PAST, The newsletter of the Prehistoric Society*, 63, 4-6.

Barclay, G. 1983. Sites of the third millennium bc to the first millennium ad at North mains, Strathallan, Perthshire. *Proceedings of the Prehistoric Society*, 113, 122-281.

Barclay, G. 1989. Henge Monuments: Reappraisal or Reductionism? *Proceedings of the Prehistoric Society*, 55, 260 – 62.

Barclay, G. 2005. The 'henge' and 'hengiform' in Scotland. In Cummings, V. and Pannett, M. (eds), *Set in Stone. New Approaches to Neolithic Monuments in Scotland*, 81-94. Oxford: Oxbow Books.

Bradley, R. 2011. *Stages and Screens. An Investigation of Four Henge Monuments in Northern and North-eastern Scotland*. Edinburgh: Society of Antiquaries of Scotland.

Brophy, K. and Noble, G. 2011. Big Enclosures: The Later Neolithic Palisade Enclosures of Scotland in their Northwestern European Context. *European Journal of Archaeology*, 14 (1-2), 60-87.

Burl, H.A.W. 1969. Henges: Internal Features and Regional Groups. *Archaeological Journal*, 126, 1-28.

Burl, H.A.W. 1976. *Stone Circles of the British Isles*. New Haven and London: Yale University Press.

Burrow, S. 2010. The formative henge: speculations drawn from the circular traditions of Wales and adjacent counties. In Leary, J., Darvill, T. and Field, D. (eds) *Round Mounds and Monumentality in the British Neolithic and Beyond*, 182-196. Neolithic Studies Group Seminar Papers 10. Oxford: Oxbow Books.

Callendar, J.G. 1927. Recent Archaeological Research in Scotland. *Archaeologia*, 77, 87-110.

Case, H., Bayne, N., Steele, S., Avery, G. and Sutermeister, H. 1965. Excavations at City Farm, Hanborough, Oxon. *Oxoniensia*, 29/30, 1-98.

Catherall, P.D. 1971. Henges in Perspective. *Archaeological Journal*, 128, 147-153.

Clare, T. 1986. Towards a Reappraisal of Henge Monuments. *Proceedings of the Prehistoric Society*, 52, 281-316.

Clare, T. 1987. Towards a Reappraisal of Henge Monuments: Origins, Evolution and Heirarchies. *Proceedings of the Prehistoric Society*, 53, 457 – 478.

Clark, G. 1936. The Timber Monument at Arminghall and it's Affinities. *Proceedings of the Prehistoric Society*, 2, 1 – 51.

Clark, J. G. D. 1954. Review of Atkinson *et al.* 1951. *Antiquaries Journal,* 34, 91 – 2.

Cleal, R. M. J., Walker, K. E. and Montague, R. 1995. *Stonehenge in its Landscape: Twentieth Century Excavations.* London: English Heritage.

Cunnington, M. 1929. *Woodhenge.* Devizes: Wiltshire Archaeological and natural History Society.

Daim, F. and Neubauer, W. (eds) 2005. *Zeitreise Heldenberg Geheimnisvolle Kreisgräben Niederösterreichische Landaustellung 2005.* Wien: Verlag Berger - Horn.

Dymond, D.P. 1963. The 'Henge' monument at Nunwick, near Ripon, 1961 Excavation. *Yorkshire Archaeological Journal,* 41, 98-107.

Farrer, P. 1918, Durrington Walls or Long Walls. *Wiltshire Archaeological and Natural History Magazine,* 40, 95-103.

Gibson, A.M. 1994. Excavation at the Sarn-y-bryn-caled Cursus Complex, Welshpool, Powys, and the Timber Circles of Britain and Ireland. *Proceedings of the Prehistoric Society,* 60, 143-223.

Gibson, A.M. 1998. *Stonehenge and Timber Circles.* Stroud: Tempus.

Gibson, A.M. 2002. The Palisaded Enclosures of Britain. In A. Gibson (ed) *Behind Wooden Walls.,* 5-23. BAR International Series 1013. Oxford: Archaeopress.

Gibson, A.M. 2010a. Dating Balbirnie: recent radiocarbon dates from the stone circle and cairn at Balbirnie, Fife, and a review of its place in the overall Balfarg/ Balbirnie site sequence. *Proceedings of the Society of Antiquaries of Scotland,* 140, 51-77.

Gibson, A.M. 2010b. Excavation and survey at the Dyffryn Lane henge complex, Powys, and a reconsideration of the dating of henges. *Proceedings of the Prehistoric Society,* 76, 213 – 248.

Gibson, A. M. 2010c. New dates for Sarn-y-bryn-caled, Powys, Wales. *Proceedings of the Prehistoric Society,* 76, 351-6.

Gibson, A.M. Forthcoming (a). What's in a Name? A Critical Review of Welsh 'Henges'

Gibson, A. M. Forthcoming (b). Report on the excavation at the Duggleby Howe causewayed enclosure, North Yorkshire, May - July 2009. *Archaeological Journal,* 168.

Gibson, A.M. and Bayliss, A. 2010, Recent Research at Duggleby Howe, North Yorkshire. *Archaeological Journal,* 166 (2009), 39-78.

Gray, H. St G. 1935. The Avebury Excavations 1908-22. *Archaeologia,* 84, 99-162.

Harding, A. 1981. Excavations in the Prehistoric Ritual Complex near Milfield, Northumberland. *Proceedings of the Prehistoric Society,* 47, 87-135.

Harding, A. with Lee, G. 1987. *Henge Monuments and Related Sites of Great Britain.* BAR British Series 175. Oxford: British Archaeological Reports.

Harding, J. 2003. *Henge Monuments of the British Isles.* Stroud: Tempus.

Jobey, G. 1966. Excavations on Palisaded Settlements and Cairnfields at Alnham, Northumberland. *Archaeologia Aeliana,* fourth ser, 44, 5 – 48.

Jones, N.W. 2009. Dyffryn Lane Cursus, Berriew, SJ19810147. *Archaeology in Wales,* 49, 101-104.

Jones, N.W. 2010. *Walton Court Farm Ring Ditch: Trial Excavation and Survey 2009-10.* Clwyd-Powys Archaeological Trust Report No 1025.

Jones, P. 2008. *A Neolithic Ring Ditch and Later Prehistoric Features at Staines Road Farm, Shepperton.* Monograph 1. Woking, Spoilheap Publications.

Jones, S.J. 1938. The Excavation of Gorsey Bigbury. *Proceedings of the University of Bristol Spelaeological Society,* 5 (1), 3-56.

Kendrick, T.D. and Hawkes, C.F.C. 1932. *Archaeology in England and Wales, 1914-1931.* London: Methuen and Co.

Loveday, R. 1998. Double Entranced Henges – Routes to the Past?. In A. Gibson and D. Simpson (eds) *Prehistoric Ritual and Religion. Essays in Honour of Aubrey Burl,* 14-31. Stroud: Alan Sutton.

Lynch, F. and Musson, C. 2004. A Prehistoric and Early Medieval Complex at Llandegai, near Bangor, North Wales. *Archaeologia Cambrensis,* 150 (2001), 17 – 142.

McInnes, I.J. 1964. A Class 2 Henge in the East Riding of Yorkshire. *Antiquity,* 38, 218 – 9.

Melichar, P. and Neubauer, W. (eds) 2010. *Mittelneolithische Kreisgrabenanlagen in Niederösterreich.* Wien: Verlag der Österreichischen Akademie der Wissenschaften.

Mercer, R.J. 1981. The Excavation of a Late Neolithic Henge-type Enclosure at Balfarg, Markinch, Fife, Scotland. *Proceedings of the Society of Antiquaries of Scotland,* 111, 63-171.

Needham, S. 2005. Transforming Beaker Culture in North-West Europe; Processes of Fusion and Fission. *Proceedings of the Prehistoric Society,* 71, 171-218.

Piggott, S. 1938. The Early Bronze Age in Wessex. *Proceedings of the Prehistoric Society,* 4, 52 – 106.

Piggott, S. and C.M. 1939. Stone and earth Circles in Dorset. *Antiquity,* 13, 138 – 158.

Pollard, J. and Robinson, D. 2007. A Return to Woodhenge: the Results and Implications of the 2006 Excavations. In Larsson, M. and Parker Pearson, M., *From Stonehenge to the Baltic. Living with Cultural Diversity in the Third Millennium BC,* 159-168. BAR International Series 1692. Oxford: Archaeopress.

Preston, S. 2003. *Prehistoric, Roman and Saxon Sites in Eastern Berkshire. Excavations 1989-1997.* Monograph 2. Reading: Thames Valley Archaeological Services.

Radley, J. 1966. A Bronze Age Ring-work on Totley Moor and other Bronze Age Ring-works in the Pennines. *Archaeological Journal,* 123, 1 – 26.

Renfrew, A.C. 1979. *Investigations in Orkney.* London: Society of Antiquaries of London.

Ritchie, J.N.G. 1976. The Stones of Stenness, Orkney. *Proceedings of the Society of Antiquaries of Scotland,* 107, 1975-6, 1 – 60.

Roberts, I. (ed) 2005. *Ferrybridge Henge: The Ritual Landscape. Archaeological Investigations at the Site* of the Holmfield Interchange of the A1 Motorway. Wakefield: West Yorkshire Archaeological Services.

Russell-White, C.J., Lowe, C.E. and McCullagh, R.P.J. 1992. Excavations at three Early Bronze Age Burial Monuments in Scotland. *Proceedings of the Prehistoric Society*, 58, 285-323.

Scott-Elliot, J. and Rae, I. 1965. Whitestanes Moor Sites 1 and 80. An Enclosed Cremation Cemetery. *Transactions of the Dumfriesshire and Galloway Natural History and Antiquarian Society*, 42, 51 – 60.

Stewart, M. 1985. The Excavation of a Henge, Stone Circles and Metal-working Area at Moncrieffe, Perthshire. *Proceedings of the Society of Antiquaries of Scotland*, 115, 125-50.

Tratman, E.K. 1967. The Priddy Circles, Mendip, Somerset. Henge Monuments. *Proceedings of the University of Bristol Spelaeological Society*, 11 (2), 97-125.

Waddington, C. 2011. Towards Synthesis: Research and Discovery in Neolithic North-East England. *Proceedings of the Prehistoric Society*, 77, 279-320.

Wainwright, G.J. 1969. A Review of Henge Monuments in the Light of Recent Research. *Proceedings of the Prehistoric Society*, 35, 112-33.

Warner, R. 2000. Keeping out the Otherworld: The Internal Ditch at Navan and other Iron Age "hengiform" Enclosures. *Emania*, 18, 39-44.

Henging, Mounding and Blocking: The Forteviot Henge Group

Kenneth Brophy and Gordon Noble

Abstract

Our understanding of henge monuments in Scotland has radically changed over the past few decades, not just the dating and variation of these monuments, but also in terms of what the term 'henge monument' actually means. In this paper a brief summary of recent key developments in the study of henge monuments in Scotland will be presented. These developments will be considered in light of recent excavations at the Forteviot cropmark complex, Perth and Kinross, Scotland. These cropmarks were first recorded in the 1970s, and although the complex is dominated by a huge later Neolithic palisaded enclosure, the cropmarks of a range of henge-like, circular and pennanular features were also recorded. In 2008-2010, excavations were carried out at four of these circular monuments. This paper will focus on the results of work at three of these sites, all conforming to the henge ground plan. The larger monuments – Forteviot 1 and 2 – were both shown to have lengthy and complex sequences of activity stretching across much of the 3rd millennium BC. The implications of these results will be discussed in relation to the wider ongoing rethink of henge monuments in Scotland. In particular there seems to be a concern with containing and closing down these spaces, utilising three techniques: henging, mounding and blocking.

Keywords: Scotland, Neolithic, Bronze Age, henge monument, barrow

Preamble

The henge monuments of Scotland are being deconstructed. The chronology, typology, context, role and purpose of these earthwork enclosures have undergone a radical re-assessment over the past decade. In part this has been due to a series of significant excavations of henges in mainland Scotland, some of which date back over 30 years. Within this context, a range of new dating evidence has emerged; this has been accompanied by reflection on the source of these dates and how closely they can be associated with the henge earthworks. The number of possible henge monuments has also increased greatly, bolstered by widespread cropmark evidence. With this has come a closer focus on variability (in terms of size and internal features) and less emphasis on the reductive processes of typology. The work of two individuals in particular – Gordon Barclay and Richard Bradley, who between them have excavated a range of henges in eastern and northern Scotland – has been extremely influential in terms of teasing apart henge earthworks from the features that they enclose, and has pushed henge chronology into the Bronze Age. The impact of their work on henges has been felt elsewhere in the British Isles (to which this volume attests), and we are now in a position to reverse the situation where the Scottish henges once 'played a limited role in general accounts of these monuments' (Bradley 2011, xvi). It is within this new chronological and temporal context that recent excavations of a group of henge-like monuments in central Scotland, at Forteviot, Perth and Kinross should be contextualised. The results of these excavations will be briefly summarised in this paper, and some thoughts on the chronology and the nature of henge monuments derived from these excavations will be considered.

Scotland's henges: form

There are over 80 henge monuments in Scotland (Figure 1), the bulk of them known only as cropmarks (for the most recent overviews of these sites, see Barclay 2005). This number has increased rapidly in recent decades, largely due to the advent of concentrated aerial reconnaissance

in Scotland in 1976. These monuments are found across Scotland, including in the northern isles of Orkney, but more are known in the east than the west. Regional variations are apparent, with the Orkney monuments, and those of the north and north-east, for instance, forming distinct regional traditions (Barclay 2005, 85-6). The location within the landscape of these monuments is typical of elsewhere in Britain: most sites are located in lowland river valleys, often close to rivers, although there are rare upland exceptions (Harding 2003).

The henge monuments in Scotland typically fulfil the 'classic' morphological definition of a henge monument, that is, with an external bank, internal ditch, and one or two (opposed) entrances, all defining a circular to oval space (hence their inclusion within the class). Within this group of monuments, however, there are some notable exceptions to these 'norms', such as the apparently bankless Ring of Brodgar, Orkney, or the non-opposed entrances at Balfarg, Fife. There is a good deal of size variation within this group as well, with two sites over 100m in diameter at the upper end of the scale (although nothing on the scale of the 'super-henges' of southern England). The majority of the monuments classified as henges lie at the lower end of the scale, typically known by the rather awkward term 'hengiform', or more recently 'mini-henges'. Mini-henges were defined by Harding and Lee (1987, 37) as monuments with an *internal* diameter of less than 14m. This term was coined to respond to the increasing range of small henge-like forms being recorded as cropmarks. Barclay (2005) used the term 'hengiform' (and also 'henge') with care, preferring to highlight a continuum of variation within henge diameter (Figure 1). More recently, Bradley's (2011) programme of investigations at henges in the northern half of Scotland has explicitly explored a regional tradition of mini-henges, sites Barclay has termed 'pocket sized' henges (2005, 81). This work has teased out some key characteristics shared within and beyond this group of monuments, to which we will later return.

The coining of the terms 'hengiform' (Wainwright 1969) and 'mini-henge' has had several interesting implications.

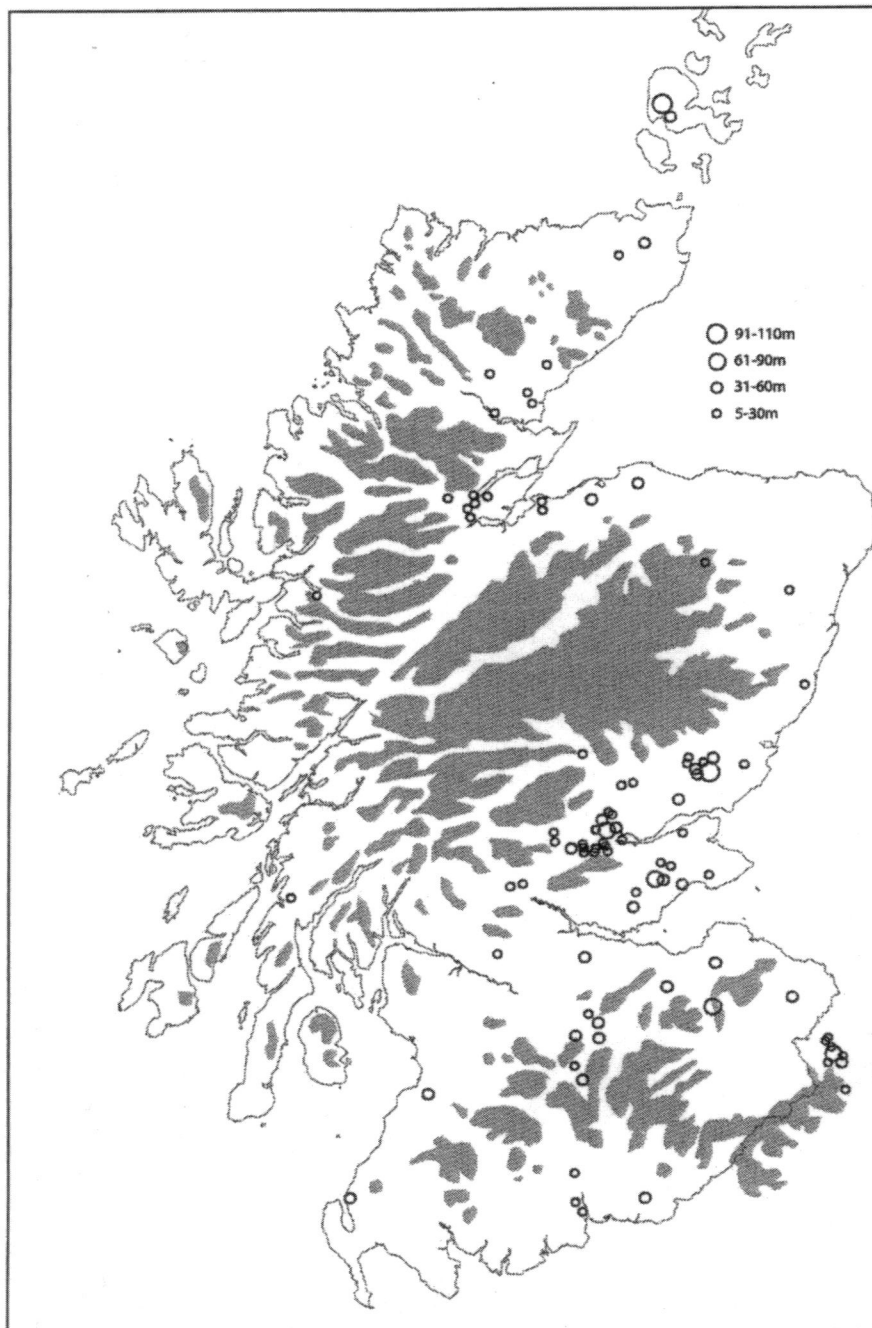

FIGURE 1. MAP SHOWING THE LOCATION OF THE HENGE MONUMENTS OF SCOTLAND, WITH DIFFERENTIAL DIAMETER INDICATED (FROM BARCLAY 2005)

that of Bronze Age funerary traditions (particularly interesting given what we now know about henge chronology (see below)). This temporal and interpretive shift reflects a growing understanding that henge monuments were far more than just a ditch and bank, and that in fact these earthworks are located in places that had very long sequences of use. This includes pre-henge activity, from pit-digging and cremation burials, to the erection of timber posts and standing stones, but also re-use (often with major modification) from the early Bronze Age onwards, for deposition, burial and metal-working. If we are to regard henges as being related in some way to other, small, pennanular enclosures, and also that the earthworks are but one phase of activity at these sites, then an understanding of henge chronology is imperative.

Scotland's henges: chronology

Our current understanding of the chronology of these monuments suggests that the idea of 'henging' (enclosing a circular space within earthworks including an *internal* ditch) had a remarkable temporal currency. Indeed the first and last henge earthworks in Britain may well be found in Scotland, potentially spanning a period of over 1500 years. The notion that henges originated in the north has been prompted by the very early dates associated with animal bones found on the base of the ditch at the Stones of Stenness, Orkney (Ritchie 1976). Dated to the late fourth millennium / early third millennium cal BC, Stenness is an atypically early 'classic henge' (Harding 2003, 12). The Orcadian origins of henges and Grooved Ware have become increasingly emphasized and entangled in recent years (cf. Thomas 2010). However, the nearby Ring of Brodgar, also on Mainland Orkney, appears to be later based on recent OSL dating of the rock-cut ditch base (Colin Richards pers comm). Other early henge dates are surprisingly rare in Scotland, and convincing Grooved Ware / henge associations are equally rare. The 'Grooved Ware henge' of Balfarg Riding School (BRS), Fife, provided a date range of 3340-2880 cal BC (Barclay

It vastly widened the number of monuments that could be classified in the henge monument continuum, and so muddied the clarity of the henge label (Gibson, this volume). This has inevitably increased the blurring of the class with a series of other pennanular sites, often of the early Bronze Age, including barrows, cremation cemeteries, pit-enclosures, segmented ditched enclosures and so on (cf. Harding and Lee 1987; Barclay 2005). On one hand this could be viewed as problematic when making sense of the cropmark record, but on the other hand it has placed at least some henges into a different interpretive framework, and Russell-White 1993), dates derived from charcoal found in the ditch in 'near primary' contexts, and found in association with Grooved Ware (Barclay 2005, 91). The only dates associated with the nearby, and much larger, Balfarg henge, are derived from postholes within the henge itself (Mercer 1981). Recently Gibson (2010a, 72) has tentatively assigned the construction of the Balfarg henge earthworks to the 'end of the 2nd half of the third millennium', post-dating the Grooved Ware phase of use of these locations; despite the dates and pottery from the BRS ditch, Gibson has suggested this too was an early Bronze Age enclosure in a location which had been used extensively in the Neolithic.

Therefore 'early henges' (aka Late Neolithic henges) are apparently exceptions, outnumbered by the remarkable sequence of early (and even later) Bronze Age dates for most other recently excavated henges in Scotland. Bradley's recent excavations of henges at Broomend of Crichie, Aberdeenshire, and Pullyhour, Caithness, Highland, have shown both to be almost wholly Bronze Age monuments. The circular earthwork at Pullyhour was in fact probably created in the middle centuries of the 2nd millennium BC (Bradley 2011, 122). As we shall see, the dating sequences derived from Forteviot suggest that both henges 1 and 2 had earthworks that appear to have emerged in the second half of the 3rd millennium BC. Likewise, a date from a cremation below the North Mains henge bank provides a *terminus post quem* for bank construction of 2140-1960 cal BC suggesting Bronze Age construction (Barclay 2005, 86). Although the date of construction of a henge at Pict's Knowe is not entirely clear (and for a fuller discussion on this, see Thomas 2007, 145ff) peat beneath the henge bank was dated to 2400-1850 cal BC, meaning this earthwork was also certainly a Bronze Age rather than Neolithic monument.

The implications of these results are startling for anyone brought up safe in the knowledge that henge monuments were a Late Neolithic phenomenon. Yet some words of caution are required before going any further. Firstly, the range of dates we have seem to reflect variations within the henge class itself and so cannot be applied uniformly across all undated monuments, never mind cropmark sites. For instance, as already noted, mini-henges could be viewed as a distinctive group morphologically, and perhaps also chronologically. Bronze Age dates are largely derived from monuments which could be characterised as 'small or otherwise unusual' (Barclay 2005, 85). Secondly, how we date henges and earthworks (and indeed what is being dated) is very much open to debate and as such perhaps emphasis needs to move beyond single radiocarbon dates of questionable provenance. Given the obvious problems with trying to date earthwork enclosures solely from ditch contents, radiocarbon dates should be treated with caution, and it may be that more use will need to be made of *terminus post quem* and *terminus ante quem* dates, while the exploration of sub-bank deposits and the continued development of OSL dating should be research priorities. Thirdly, the very idea of dating a henge is a creation of

archaeological discourse. It reflects our tendency to compress all aspects of 'henge monuments' into a single phase, and also the undue primacy given to the earthwork elements of these sites. We know from many excavated examples that the ditches and banks were but one 'phase' of the use-life of these locations (cf. Harding 2003; Barclay 2005; Bradley 2011; Gibson 2010b and this volume).

The implications of this dating evidence, even with these caveats in mind, are startling. At least some henge earthworks need to be situated within entirely different frameworks, perhaps the most noticeable being a change from the traditional Grooved Ware-ritual narratives, and consider for instance the increasing association of henge earthworks with Beaker pottery and Bronze Age mortuary activity. It seems likely that in some instances the act of 'henging' may have had more of a funerary role than was previously imagined. For instance, the North Mains ditch and bank seem to have been created at the same time as burials were being inserted into this space, and the nearby conical barrow was being constructed (Barclay 2005; Bradley 2011). At a more prosaic level, how henges are dealt with in research framework contexts also needs to be reviewed, and what role they played in the Chalcolithic of Scotland (if indeed there was one) also needs to be considered. It is within this dynamic intellectual backdrop that our excavations at the Forteviot henge group took place, and it is to these henge monuments that we now turn.

The Forteviot henge group

Over multiple seasons of reconnaissance (in 1973-1975 and 1977) St Joseph documented a remarkable complex of cropmarks in a large field immediately to the south of the small Perthshire village of Forteviot, Perth and Kinross. He noted that these cropmarks were 'of a nature so remarkable as to justify a second note' (1978, 48), and it is easy to see why: the complex is dominated by a large sub-circular palisaded enclosure with circumference of almost three-quarters of a kilometre, and bounded on one side by an escarpment (Figures 2-3). A number of much smaller circular cropmark enclosures were also identified within and around this 'stockade' as St Joseph called it; the most northerly three interpreted as 'bronze age ritual structures', with two southerly outliers thought to enclose burials. The word henge did not appear in St Joseph's initial report on these monuments, even to describe an obviously henge-like enclosure that he recorded within the palisaded enclosure. Forteviot was subsequently characterised as one of only seven henge 'clusters' in Britain by Harding and Lee (1987, 43-4, 409-12), consisting of five henge variants. In part these interpretations were derived from repeat reconnaissance since the mid 1970s by the Royal Commission on the Ancient and Historical Monuments of Scotland (RCAHMS) which fleshed out the detail of this complex as well as identifying much later activity here. These henge-like monuments, consisting of a disparate group of small pennanular enclosures, have generally been interpreted as 'enclosures', 'ring-ditches' or henge

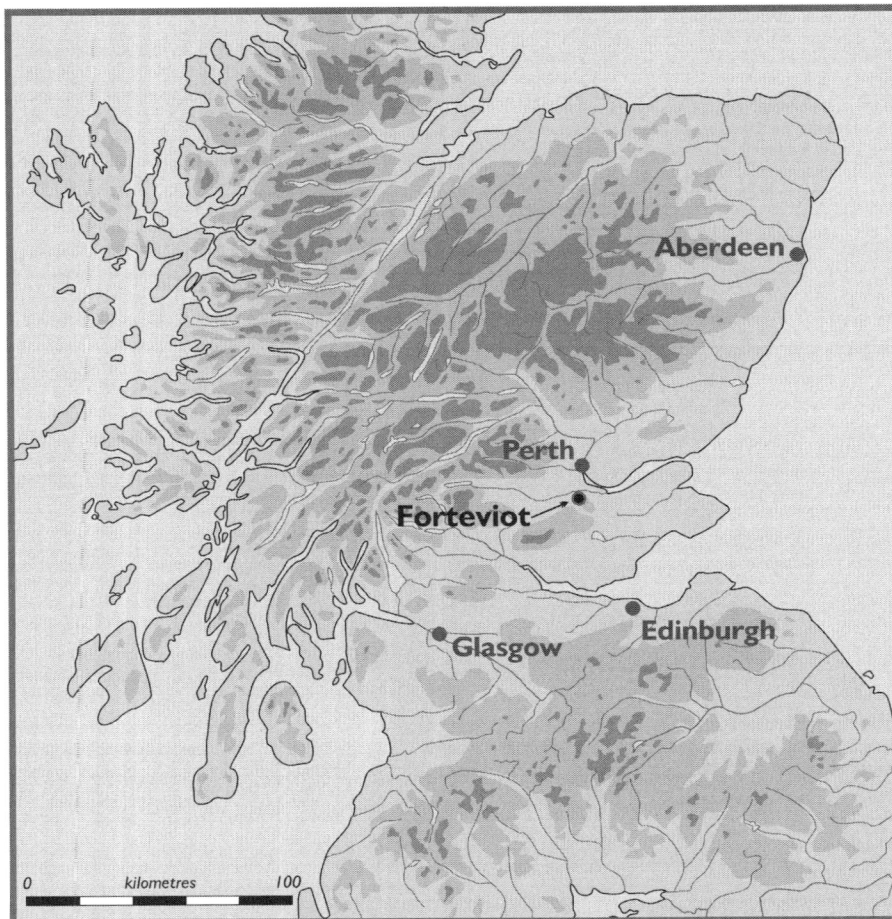

FIGURE 2. LOCATION MAP FOR FORTEVIOT

TABLE 1: THE FORTEVIOT HENGE GROUP

SERF site name (see Figure 3)	St Joseph (number and comment)	Harding & Lee 1987 (cat. no. and comment)	NMRS number and classification
Henge 1	4: No interpretation given	312: Probable henge	NO01NE 33: Henge (possible)
Henge 2	1: 'Bronze Age ritual structure'	Not listed	NO01NE 30: Enclosure or henge
Henge 3	2: 'Bronze Age ritual structure'	310: Probable henge	NO01NE 31: Henge (possible)
Triple-cist structure	3: 'Bronze Age ritual structure'	311: Causewayed barrow	NO01NE 32/238: Enclosure or henge (possible)
Mini-henge	Not listed	313: Possible mini-henge	NO01NE 33: Henge (possible)
Un-named ring-ditch	5: No interpretation given	314: Causewayed barrow	NO01NE 34: Ring ditch

monuments within the National Monuments Record of Scotland (NMRS) since their discovery; the assumption is that these were either contemporary with, or slightly later than, the palisaded enclosure, which since its discovery has been assumed to be later Neolithic. (See Table 1 for a summary of the classifications used at Forteviot to date.)

Since 2006, the Strathearn Environs and Royal Forteviot project (SERF) has been investigating the cropmarks south of Forteviot (for a project overview see Driscoll st al. 2010). The main objective of this project has been to investigate two significant periods when this location was a centre of power and ceremony: once in prehistory, as evidenced by the aforementioned cropmarks, and once again in the early medieval period when historical references show that Forteviot was, in the 9th century AD, a Pictish royal centre, and location of the *palacium* of Kenneth Mac Alpin, an early king of what was to become Scotland (Aitchison 2006; Alcock and Alcock 1992). A rich collection of early medieval carved stones from the area, and cropmarks indicating an extensive early medieval cemetery on the south-east edge of the modern village, add weight to the historical records. The SERF project has sought to explore the long-term development of Forteviot, and to investigate the relationship between Neolithic / Bronze Age monuments and early medieval activity. Within this context excavations between 2007 and 2010 focused on a number of elements of the prehistoric complex (and the results of this work to date have been summarised elsewhere (Noble and Brophy 2011a)).

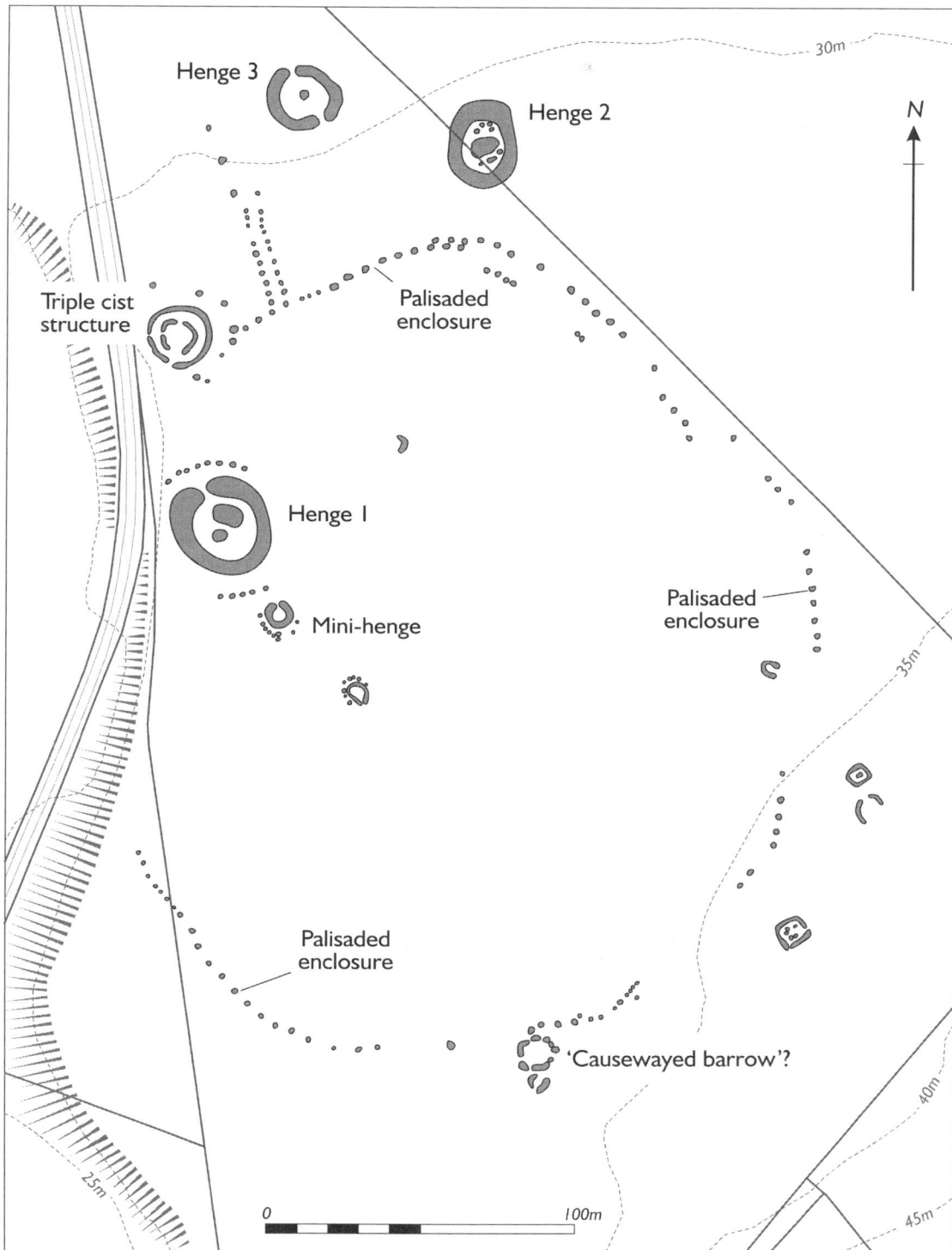

Figure 3. The Forteviot cropmark complex, with sites mentioned in the text annotated
(© SERF Project)

Although the focus of this account is the nature of the 'henge monuments' at Forteviot, these are framed by the palisaded enclosure, around and within which these monuments appear to have congregated (Figure 3). Investigated over two seasons (2007 and 2009), this monument was shown to have been defined by an irregular boundary of differentially spaced large oak posts, set into ramped postholes, forming an enclosure some 260m in diameter with a narrow entrance avenue on the north side. No smaller posts, stakes or palisades were found between these posts, although severe plough truncation may have removed such traces; however there is circumstantial evidence for an earthwork component to this boundary and living trees could well have been incorporated into the monument. The posts were erected in the period 2900-2500 cal BC, and given the scale of the endeavour required

25

this may well have been a 'construction site' for quite some time. As the monument declined, posts were in some cases removed, in others burnt, and still others left to rot *in situ*, but it seems likely that the boundary of this monument had an enduring presence in the landscape, even when ruinous (and again the results of these excavations are summarised elsewhere (Noble and Brophy 2011b)).

Between 2007 and 2010, four of the henge-like monuments identified as cropmarks in and around the palisaded enclosure were investigated. Three are discussed here: henge 1 and 2, and a 'mini-henge'. The fourth was not henge-like in character, but may have been a prominent part of the post-henge barrow cemetery that appears to have developed here, and will be returned to briefly later.

Henge 1

The largest henge within the Forteviot complex is located within the northern half of the palisaded enclosure, close to the western escarpment. Identified by Harding and Lee as a 'probable henge' (1987, 412), this has been the prevailing interpretation since, and cropmarks also indicated a timber or pit circle surrounding this monument. Henge 1 was excavated over two seasons in 2008 and 2009, during which time the vast majority of the monument was exposed. A series of internal and external features were investigated (only some of which had shown as cropmarks) as well as the henge ditch (Figure 4). The monument was shown to have a relatively small enclosed interior, some 22m in diameter, a space defined by a large ditch which was in places up to 10m wide, and between 2.1 and 3m deep. No trace of a bank was found beyond some amorphous silt spreads on the exterior edge of the ditch. Assuming a bank of similar width to the ditch, the monument probably had an overall diameter of some 55-65m. There was a single entrance on the NNE side of the monument; excavations in the eastern ditch terminal recovered a few sherds of comb impressed Beaker in the lower fills (Wilkin 2011). No other diagnostic artefacts were found within secure contexts related to henge ditch (although a few sherds of abraded 'prehistoric pottery' were recovered from a secondary fill). Little evidence was found for activities within the henge associated with the earthwork element of the monument, and the interior of the henge was heavily disturbed by later activity including the digging of a massive elongated pit in the early medieval period. Ditch fills suggested that, for the most part, the ditch silted naturally, being waterlogged for some time on at least one occasion early in the life of the earthworks. Occasional acts of burning within the henge were suggested by infrequent burnt deposits thrown into the interior side of the ditch; these deposits included burnt soil and turves. Dates were recovered from various fills and levels within the ditch indicating use between 2468–1938 cal BC (Figure 5), suggesting the earthworks, and associated activities, were likely confined to the early Bronze Age. However, these dates do only offer a *terminus ante quem* for ditch digging albeit some were derived from early fills.

Extensive evidence was found for activity in this location before the earthworks were constructed. The earliest dated evidence for activity here was a late Neolithic cremation cemetery, found within the undisturbed western half of the henge interior area. In use for an unknown duration within the period 3090-2638 cal BC this consisted of the discrete deposits of the cremated remains of some 18 individuals, associated with 16 bone 'skewer pins' (Leach 2012). Some of these cremations may have been contained in organic bags, or wooden vessels. A cremation found at Cairnpapple Hill has recently been found to be broadly contemporary with the Forteviot cemetery (Sheridan et al 2010) and numerous cremation burials from Stonehenge have also been found to have a similar date (Parker Pearson st al. 2009). The Forteviot cemetery seems to have had an enduring significance; its location would be used for ceremony and burial for a millennium after its establishment. This memorialisation may have been maintained by the sealing of the cremation cemetery beneath a mound; this would explain why this area, later to become the henge interior, remained largely undisturbed by later activity or the plough. Still earlier activity in this location was hinted at by the discovery of an apparently broken standing stone, over which several cremations had been deposited. This area was subsequently enclosed by a timber circle with a diameter of around 45m in the period c.2850-2500 cal BC. It is likely that this timber circle defined the footprint for the subsequent henge bank which would have overlain whatever remained of this timber setting (again offering a *terminus post quem* for henging at this site). Timber circles are commonly found in association with henges, but they are almost always *inside* henges (Gibson 2004; Millican 2007); a notable parallel is the slightly smaller Milfield North henge in Northumberland, although this monument also had an internal timber circle (Harding 1981). Despite this apparent inversion of the norm, the typical sequence for such monuments was maintained: timber circle first, henge second.

Several centuries after the henge earthworks were dug, the henge played host to an elaborate high status burial (Noble and Brophy 2011a). This consisted of a monumental sandstone-lined cist within a large oval pit dug into the southern extreme of the henge interior. This cist, rather like the succession of burials inserted into Cairnpapple Hill, straddled the henge ditch; by the time of this burial (2150-1900 cal BC) the ditch was almost two-thirds full. No bones survived within this cist, but evidence for a body has been suggested through phosphate analysis and sampling. However, an elaborate series of grave goods accompanied this burial including two daggers, a fire-making kit, several wooden objects, and all of this was accompanied by a large bunch of meadowsweet flowers. The cist was sealed by a four-tonne sandstone slab with an enigmatic carving on the interior side. The insertion of this cist into the deepest zone of the henge enclosure furthest away from its entrance was accompanied by the conversion of this open space into a mounded place, as well as what could be viewed as a slighting of the henge boundary. A cairn of quarried basalt and waterworn stones overlay the cist, sourced from

FN09 Pre-excavation plan

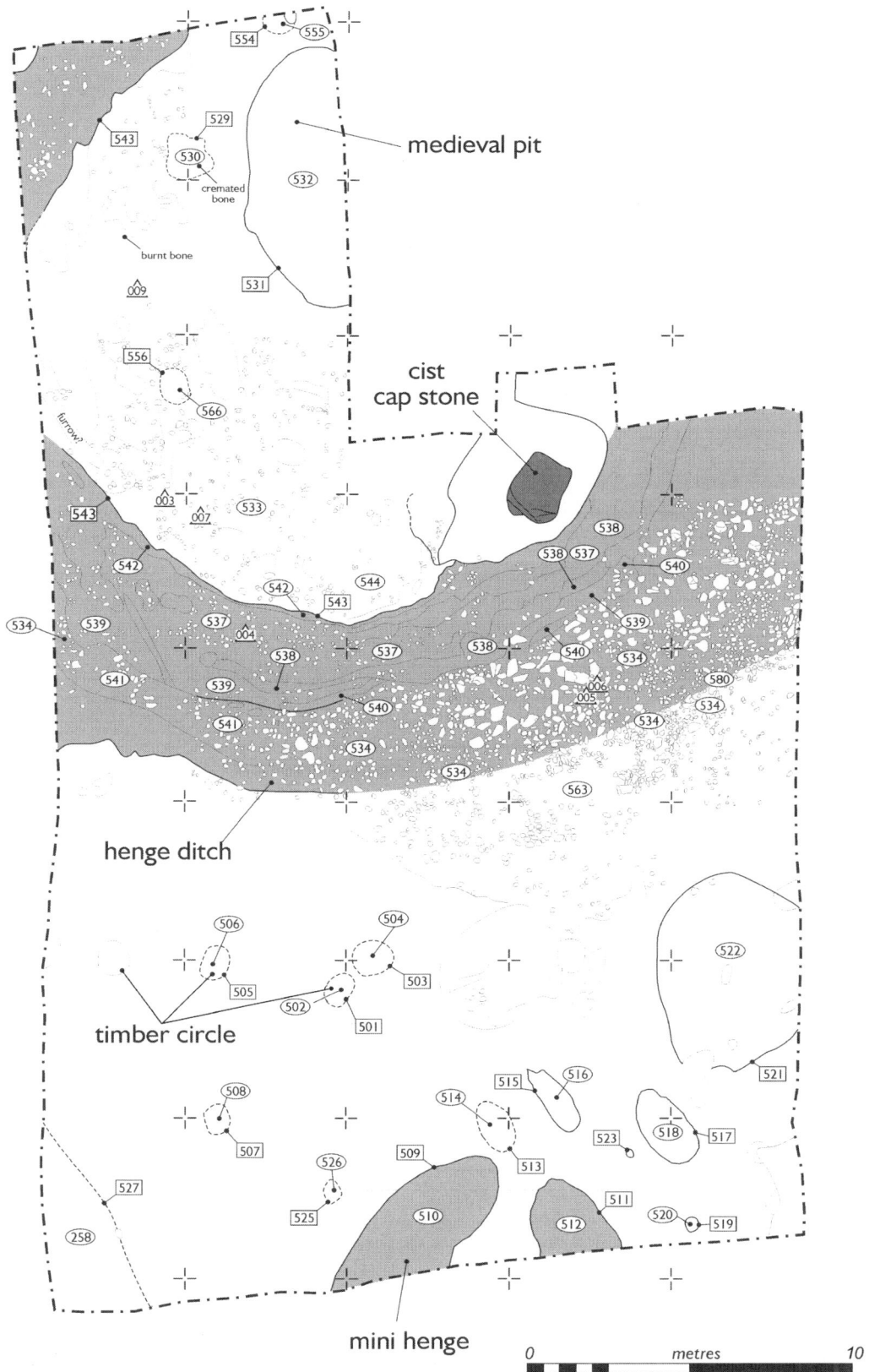

FIGURE 4. Plan of the trench opened over henge 1 in 2009, showing the henge ditch, dagger cist capstone, timber circle, mini-henge and cremation cemetery (© SERF Project)

various points in the landscape; the quantity of stonework across the southern and eastern areas of the henge suggests this structure may have been substantially larger than was needed just to cover one cist, although its full extent is unknown and it probably did not cover the entire interior area of the henge. Subsequent early medieval incursions into the henge caused a good deal of disturbance, which included the digging of a large pit in the northern half of the henge, and it is likely this activity, as well as post-medieval ploughing of the field, reduced the cairn and henge earthworks to their current condition.

Henge 2

This enigmatic monument is situated outside the palisaded enclosure, about 20m to the north of the northern palisade line, and 150m to the north-east of henge 1 (Figure 3). As a cropmark, this monument is not obviously a henge, with a possible single entrance on the eastern side hinted at only by a less dense cropmarking in that location (notably it is not included in the Harding and Lee 1987 catalogue). Geophysical survey in early 2010 confirmed this stretch of the boundary ditch to be 'anomalous'. Upon excavation, and investigation of this anomalous area in particular, it was concluded that this had been a henge-like enclosure in an earlier incarnation, which was subsequently 'converted' to a completely bounded space (perhaps even a barrow) with the digging away of the entrance causeway. As with henge 1, there was also clear evidence for the use of this location before, and after, the henge earthworks were dug. Henge 2 is smaller than henge 1, and more oval in plan, but with an

equally disproportionate boundary to enclosed space ratio (Figure 6). The internal area of the monument measures about 13m east–west by 18m, enclosed by a substantial ditch with width of up to 6m and depth of at least 1.7m. As with henge 1, the only material culture associated with the lower fills of this ditch were Beaker potsherds, although in more substantial quantities. Sherds of two, perhaps three, all-over-corded (AOC) Beakers were recovered from very low in the henge ditch fill sequence in the area we identified as initially being a henge ditch terminal (Wilkin 2011). Some sherds were accompanied by chunks of shattered stone and some charcoal, perhaps part of a single act of deposition. No trace of a bank was found. As with henge 1, little evidence was found for activity within the henge that could have been contemporary with the henge earthwork / Beaker phase of this monument, although further Beaker sherds were found scattered across several features within the henge (see below). A series of dates from the henge ditch suggested activities with dates ranging from c.2400 cal BC through to the first half of the 2nd millennium BC (Figure 5).

Before the henge earthworks were constructed, a rectangular setting of substantial timber posts stood in this location, roughly contemporary with the pre-henge 1 timber circle, and post-dating palisaded enclosure construction. This monument was defined by perhaps seven posts, three on either side of the structure, and one 'gable end' post equidistant between the most northerly 'corner' posts. The structure measured about 8.5m by 4m and lay on the same axis as the later henge (albeit the exact

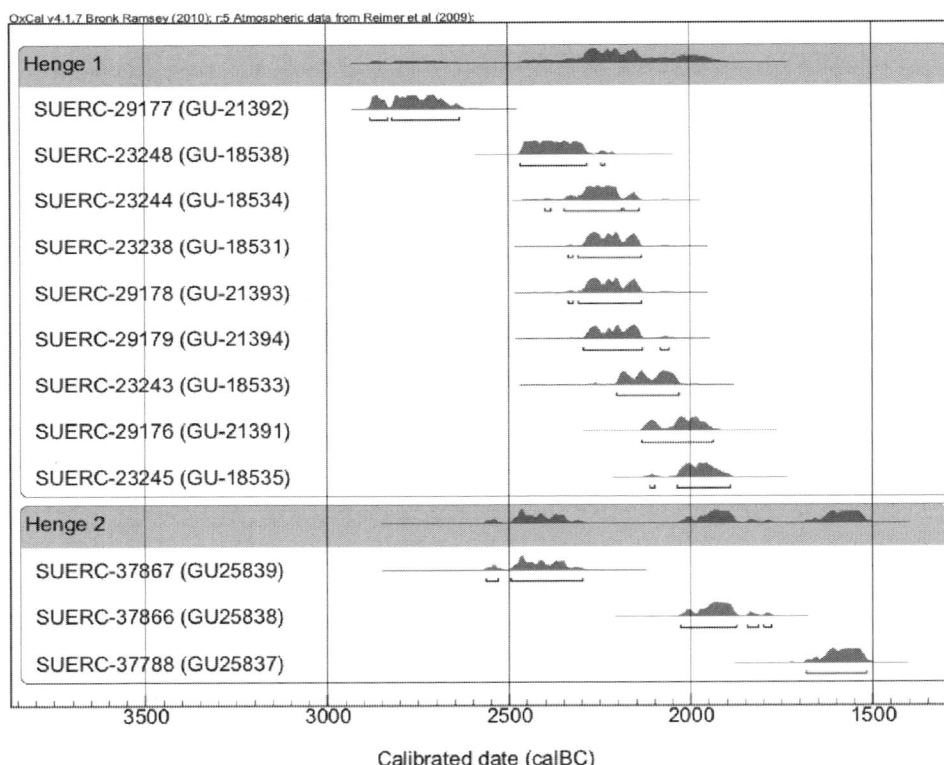

FIGURE 5. RADIOCARBON DATES FROM HENGE 1 AND HENGE 2 DITCH DEPOSITS

FIGURE 6. VERTICAL AERIAL VIEW OF FORTEVIOT HENGE 2 DURING EXCAVATION IN 2010. THE BLOCKED ENTRANCE AREA IS UNDER INVESTIGATION TOWARDS THE TOP OF THE IMAGE (©FLYING SCOTSCAM AND SERF PROJECT)

form and composition of this structure is unclear due to later disturbances within the monument). This structure may have been a setting of free-standing posts rather than a roofed structure, but a centrally placed stone-filled pit was located where one would expect to find a hearth within a building. The postholes were notable for their lengthy (perhaps even disproportionately large) ramps, akin in scale to those found at the Holywood North timber cursus monument, Dumfries and Galloway (Thomas 2007), and in the upper fills of two of these postholes were scattered sherds of three more AOC Beakers (Wilkin 2011). These may have been 'planted' across the site in a depositional act contemporary with, or following, henge construction and occurred when posts no longer stood or were highly decayed. The posthole ramps were in some instances cut by the henge ditch, offering a *terminus post quem* for ditch digging.

At some point after the enclosure of this location, and after some natural silting of the ditch had occurred, the causeway seems to have been dug away, effectively blocking off the interior of the henge from easy access, and creating a continuous ditch that by that stage may have been less than 1m in depth. The 'blocking ditch' was 4.5m wide and

up to 0.85m deep; the size of the causeway gap is unclear but was probably initially no more than 3m to 5m across. The 'blocking' of the henge in this way may relate to the conversion of this monument from an enclosed space to a blocked and perhaps mounded place. Although they cannot be connected chronologically, the transformation of this monument may have been associated with a near centrally placed burial. Within the henge a crude squarish 'cist' had been constructed and within the cremated remains of a female or young male (Leach 2012) had been placed in association with a complete tripartite Food Vessel and a single (abraded) AOC Beaker sherd. A date for this burial is awaited, but we do know that this type of vessel generally dates to the period 2150-1800 cal BC (Wilkin 2011). Other burials may also have been present within this monument (or indeed inserted into the putative barrow or mound) but as with henge 1, there is evidence for later alteration and serious disturbance within the interior of this monument. Various episodes of Iron Age and early medieval activity were recorded within the enclosed area, including a massive pit which filled almost a third of the interior area of the monument. A lack of rubble within and around the henge suggests any mound here would have had a different composition from the cairn / mound at henge 1.

Figure 7. The northern half of the Forteviot mini-henge pre-excavation, 2009. Note the very narrow entrance causeway, and possible tree throw just outside the entrance (© SERF Project)

Mini-henge

A third henge was investigated in 2009, albeit a site of such a small size that even the term mini-henge is applied with some caution. This monument was initially recorded by St Joseph as a cropmark, and Harding and Lee characterised it as a 'possible mini-henge' (1987, 412). It is situated just 12m to the south of the outer ditch edge of henge 1, and was partially exposed within our 2009 trench (Figures 3 and 7). This small enclosure measured perhaps no more than 4m to 5m internally, bounded by a ditch which was up to 2.5m wide and at least 0.9m deep. As a whole, this structure was no more than 9m or 10m across (assuming the presence of a bank) with a single, very narrow 'entrance' causeway on its northern side. (This was less than 1m wide.) Despite this being on the small side even for a mini-henge, there are strong reasons for considering it in relation to this class. In plan, it appears to have been a more or less exact copy of henge 1 albeit one-sixth of the size of its neighbour: both share the same plan and axis, both have a single entrance on the NNE side, both have disproportionate boundaries, and both are surrounded by a timber circle. The mini-henge's timber circle was defined by relatively large postholes (with postpipes of up to 0.7m) and would have had a diameter of 12-14m (the complete circuit has not been recorded as cropmarks). A single radiocarbon date derived from willow charcoal found in the lower ditch fill was early Mesolithic, almost certainly

indicative of activity within this complex millennia prior to the construction of any monuments rather than relating to the construction or use of this monument. Indeed it is not unreasonable to assume, given the close proximity, and similar form in plan, that the mini-henge and henge 1 were closely contemporary and may have mirrored one another's development but we also cannot rule out a later act of mimicry. If we assume the presence of banks, then these monuments may have more or less touched one another, perhaps even merged, and clearly shared a close association. No internal features have been recorded, nor any material culture recovered, and there was no evidence for a mound here (although this is not to say there was not one).

Henge 3, the triple-cist structure and other pennanular cropmarks

Two further circular enclosures have been identified from cropmarks to the northern side of the palisaded enclosure (Figure 3). The enclosure closest to the palisaded enclosure, and near the edge of the escarpment, was excavated in 2009 and shown to be a remarkable double ditched or palisaded enclosure with a stone-lined triple-cist and pit with a whole Beaker within its interior space. As yet we have no dates for this monument, although it may well be some-kind of timber-framed barrow structure or cult building, and offers yet another example of the variable funerary rites carried out at this complex (Noble and Brophy 2011a). The other circular enclosure – henge 3 – looks quite convincingly henge-like as a cropmark, but as yet has not been excavated (Figure 3). It is located about 50m to the north of the palisaded enclosure, and 40m to the west of henge 2. This 'henge' is sub-circular in plan, with a diameter to the outer edges of the ditch of about 25m. The boundaries take the form of two more or less symmetrical 'sausage-shaped' ditches, leaving two entrance gaps directly opposite one another, on the NNW and SSE sides of the monument. This alignment accords well with other monuments in this complex, with the palisaded enclosure avenue, and henge 1 axis sharing this orientation. Cropmarks indicate a single circular pit-feature within this henge, nothing on the scale of the much larger (and much later) 'blobs' within henges 1 and 2. Harding and Lee's site 314 (1987, 412) is situated right on the southern edge of the palisaded enclosure and again has not been excavated. As a cropmark it measures 10m across, and may have had a main entrance on the east side; their interpretation of a 'causewayed barrow' seems a good as any. Cropmarks hint at further circular enclosures of various shapes and sizes at Forteviot, although these are fragmentary and their overall form and nature remains unclear; some may be later prehistoric or early medieval barrows.

Other Strathearn henges

The henge group at Forteviot sits within a river valley, Strathearn, with a selection of unusual, and often small, henges in the vicinity. Most are located on the south side of the river. A second henge group has been identified at Leadketty, 4km to the west of Forteviot. There are clear parallels to Forteviot here, down to the inclusion of these monuments in association with a huge palisaded enclosure, albeit all of these sites are known only as cropmarks and have not yet been excavated. There are at least three possible mini-henges here, one of which encloses an internal area of only about 2m within a ditch also about 2m wide and only a hint of an entrance causeway; this might best be described as a mini-mini-henge. A second slightly larger hengiform is located 10m away, and looks rather more henge-like with a horseshoe plan and single entrance, albeit with an overall diameter (including ditches) of only about 12-15m. The third mini-henge here lies just to the south, perhaps no more than 3-4m across internally and with a single entrance. Other cropmarks here may also be henge-variants, including a large circular ditched enclosure in the field to the north, with diameter of about 35-40m and a single entrance on the northeast side. This site has not previously been classified as a henge, perhaps because of the relatively narrow ditch, and it sits near a putative causewayed enclosure (Barclay 2001, 151). A number of other circular pennanular cropmark enclosures have been identified at Inverdunning House just to the east; again these may, or may not, be henges.

A number of henges in the valley have been excavated. The site of Belhie lies about 8km west of Forteviot, and was highlighted by Harding and Lee (1987, 44) as a possible henge cluster, although few sites here are truly convincing as henges and again all are cropmarks. Two adjacent pennanular monuments (amongst several in a location also marked by a standing stone) were excavated in 1988 in advance of pan-busting. The smaller of the two monuments here, about 5m across internally, was interpreted as a mini-henge with Beaker sherds recovered from the ditch whereas the other, slightly larger, enclosure was a cremation cemetery (Ralston 1988, 27). The unusual multi-phase mini-henge at Moncrieffe is situated about 9km to the east of Forteviot on the north side of the Earn. It was excavated in 1974 (and indeed completely dismantled and moved to a garden location nearby) in advance of motorway construction (Stewart 1987). This complex monument had an internal diameter of only 9m; the ditch enclosed an area with a small timber circle, and various cairns and stone settings were subsequently inserted into this monument (for a succinct summary, see Bradley 2011). The much larger (up to 35m internal diameter) 'classic' double entrance henge at North Mains (upriver from Forteviot) was excavated in advance of airfield expansion in 1979 (Barclay 1983). A complex sequence of activities here included two timber circles, massive henge earthworks, and a series of inhumation and cremation burials associated with Beakers, Food Vessels, and Urns. As noted above, at least one cremation pre-dated the bank (Barclay 2005, 88). A large barrow was located 300m to the west, with an elaborate internal timber frame.

Exclusion or inclusion?

The henge *earthworks* of Strathearn have a few things in common: they largely belong in one form or another to the Chalcolithic / Early Bronze Age, most have some kind of Beaker and / or funerary association; there is also evidence for lengthy histories of activity pre-henge enclosure, as well as later re-use. But why were these earthworks constructed (in some cases drawing on substantial physical effort) and why do the boundaries seem so out of proportion with the space enclosed? There has been much debate about the nature of henge boundaries, and whether the ditch, or the bank, is more important, but recent discussion has focused on the impact these earthwork would have on those experiencing the monuments (e.g. Bradley 1998, 2007; Thomas 1999; Harding 2003). The establishment of these substantial boundaries with limited entrance points would have impacted on the ability of people to get inside, or even to see and hear what was happening within the enclosed space. Over the past decade, a compelling narrative has emerged to explain henging: henge earthworks were constructed to separate the internal space off from the rest of the world. This was not to keep people and prying eyes out – but *to trap something inside, to seal something in*. The idea initially emerged from an attempt to explain the internal ditch / external bank arrangement at late Iron Age enclosures in Ireland. Warner (2000) suggested that this was because the boundary was defending the outside world from something *inside* the enclosure, something dangerous. This could be some trace of past activities, spirits, the dead or even some kind of practice or activity that was taboo or dangerous. Barclay (2005, 92) developed this idea with relation to Scotland's henges, suggesting that the act of creating earthworks around certain historical location may have derived from a strategy of containment, and that what lay within the henge was something society had to be 'defended' from. More recently, Bradley (2011, xviii) has considered the creation of seclusion and proscribed entry and exit points as elements of henge earthwork architecture that suggested that whatever happened within henges was transformative and liminal. Such dangerous and chaotic activities may well have created forces that needed to be contained, perhaps even kept secret from external eyes.

These are compelling ideas, and at Forteviot, there does seem to have been a huge amount of effort that went into making it difficult to get in *and* out of the henges (Figure 8). Henging was employed to good effect, restricting access to the interiors of henges 1 and 2 to a single entrance with super-wide earthworks that would be overkill if the logic was simply to restrict access to the interior space. Yet perhaps even this was not enough. The various traces within these monuments, of timber structures and the ancestors, were not simply sealed off with henge earthworks. At Forteviot 2, the henge was subsequently 'blocked' off altogether for external access by the removal of the causeway, while at least some of the internal area of henge 2 was mounded over, sealing in what lay beneath for ever. We would argue, then, that the processes of blocking and mounding were other (perhaps more extreme) strategies employed to seal in and contain. There is no shortage of evidence for materials, activities and structures in certain locations that seem to have become closed off in these ways. At henge 1, as with Cairnpapple, an ancient burial ground was enclosed within the henge earthworks. For henge 2 (as well as many other henges) timber posts, perhaps partially rotted, collapsed or burnt stumps, were enclosed. At other henges this might have been burning events, deposition in pits or old stone settings; memories and traces of activities from the past. Henging may not simply have been a process of memorialisation, but rather a response to a sudden transformation or redundancy in the status of the places enclosed. Henging transformed these places and how they could have been experienced, acts of remembering, but also of forgetting.

Transcending these boundaries, and access to the internal spaces, perhaps became still more difficult through time. The digging away of the causeway at Forteviot henge 2 is a stark example of a rather dramatic attempt to seal off the henge interior, perhaps associated with a specific burial in that interior. Other hints at attempts to control or impede the entrance areas of henges 1 and 2 are suggested by undated cut features (pits and / or postholes) found at the edge of henge ditch terminals at both sites. A tree throw sat immediately in front of the entrance of the mini-henge, a location which may or may not be a coincidence, but this (if contemporary) would have at the very least have made entering and leaving this tiny space awkward. The phenomenon of blocking henge entrances has recently been identified by Bradley at several henges in northern

Scotland. A range of strategies were identified which 'impeded access to the interior' at Pullyhour, Migdale and Lairg including the erection of timbers or standing stones, the digging of pits, and the establishment of small cairns (Bradley 2011, 158); in some cases this may even have been part of the 'decommissioning' of the monument, something we should be aware of for the Forteviot henges. A quick glance at other henges in Scotland suggests blocking is much more common than has previously been acknowledged. A number of upstanding mini-henges in the Highlands, including Cononbridge and Achilty, have internal banks with a single entrance, and a continuous bank on the exterior; this peculiar arrangement could be explained if the bank had been extended to block the causeway. The cropmark henge at Logieside, also Highland (see Wainwright 1969, 129), is an internally ditched single-entrance enclosure; parchmarks suggest a continuous bank (Harding & Lee 1987, 374) blocking access to the causeway. The cropmark record may well repay a closer inspection to identify blocking features such as postholes, pits and screens within the entrance area to henges. For instance, the potential cropmark henge / barrow at Langleypark, Angus consists of an apparently continuous ditch with an internal 'barrow-like' structure; one side of the monument has a strange large pit obscuring the ditch (see Harding and Lee 1987, 417) which looks rather similar to the blocked entrance on the northeast side of Forteviot 2. And this phenomenon may not be restricted to Scotland: Bradley has noted external complete banks and internal ditches with a single entrance at some Irish Bronze Age 'ring barrows' such as Reanascreena, County Cork (2011, 177 ff) while a large pit was found in the entranceway of Ringlemere henge, Kent (Parfitt, this volume).

By modern times, the henge at Pullyhour had taken on the appearance of a 'mound' (Bradley 2011, 165) and mounding may have been the final and most extreme way that henge interior locations were sealed in, literally buried. That some henges became mounds is not in doubt: Gibson (2010, 72) has recently argued for instance that a mound was constructed within Balfarg henge. But some locations were mounded without ever being henges. The act of constructing a round(ish) mound (often with similar diameter to mini-henges) offered a tangible and effective means to cover something up. Barrows of the late Neolithic and early Bronze Age often mark locations which, like henges, had long histories of activities. These activities were brought to a close by mound construction. Within Strathearn, the early Bronze Age North Mains barrow offers an obvious example, built on a location marked by much earlier farming activity, and constructed over time utilising a complex timber skeleton defining the barrow form. For a time the thick mound enclosed a small internal circular space, accessible to the outside world for a time but only via a narrow passage. The whole mound sat within a complete ditch circuit, a henge with no entrance or bank, and the diameter of this mound was almost exactly the same size as the interior area of Forteviot henge 1. Further afield, the barrow at Pitnacree, Strathtay, Perth and Kinross, is also a location that was used for a range of different activities in the earlier Neolithic but by the end of that period (perhaps even in the early Bronze Age) the site had been completely sealed in by an earthen and stone mound. The activities pre-mound included the construction of a series of structures including split-post uprights, a horseshoe-shaped stone bank and a stone rectangular structure. This was also a location that had once been cultivated, saw the deposition of early Neolithic potsherds, played host to dramatic burning events and was used for the deposition of cremations (Coles and Simpson 1965; Noble 2006). Dynamism, interactivity and bodily interaction with this place were put to a stop by the construction of a mound of earth, stone and turf with a diameter of 28m, perhaps toward the end of the 3rd millennium BC (Sheridan 2010, 46-7).The finality of this action also involved 'blocking' the entrance to one of the earlier, but soon-to-be buried, structures (Coles and Simpson 1965; Sheridan 2010). And this act of mounding forced an entirely new set of engagements upon this location that were raised up from the ground, played out through for instance the erection of a standing stone atop the mound associated with charcoal dated to 2130-1770 cal BC (Sheridan 2010, 47) as well as the insertion of some 'secondary' burials into the mound. (Indeed one facet of henge blocking may well have been

to stop people digging directly into the ground in certain locations.)

The sequence at Pitnacree is remarkably similar to some of the henges in Perth and Kinross, with a long sequence of pre-earthwork activities including the erection of timber posts and the deposition of cremated remains, and very different post-earthwork activities largely centred on burials. Furthermore, the processes of henging and mounding seem to have played themselves out in the same sites and locations. The North Mains barrow has a henge element (ditch) while Forteviot henge 1 (and perhaps 2) has mound or cairn elements in a later incarnation. At Forteviot, the pennanular cropmark record offers tantalising glimpses of still more variations on these forms. Several other mounds are identifiable for instance. One of these is still upstanding, the Mijas Cairn, located in a rough patch of woodland adjacent to the field the main cropmark complex is found in, about 175m to the southwest of the palisaded enclosure southern boundary. This monument consists of a stony round mound, measuring 22m in diameter, and with a maximum height of 1.4m; recent topographic survey work as part of the SERF project here found no indication of a ditch surrounding this mound. The width: height ratio of 15:1 suggests that this may be a late Neolithic barrow (Barclay 1999; Brophy 2010). Excavations at the triple-

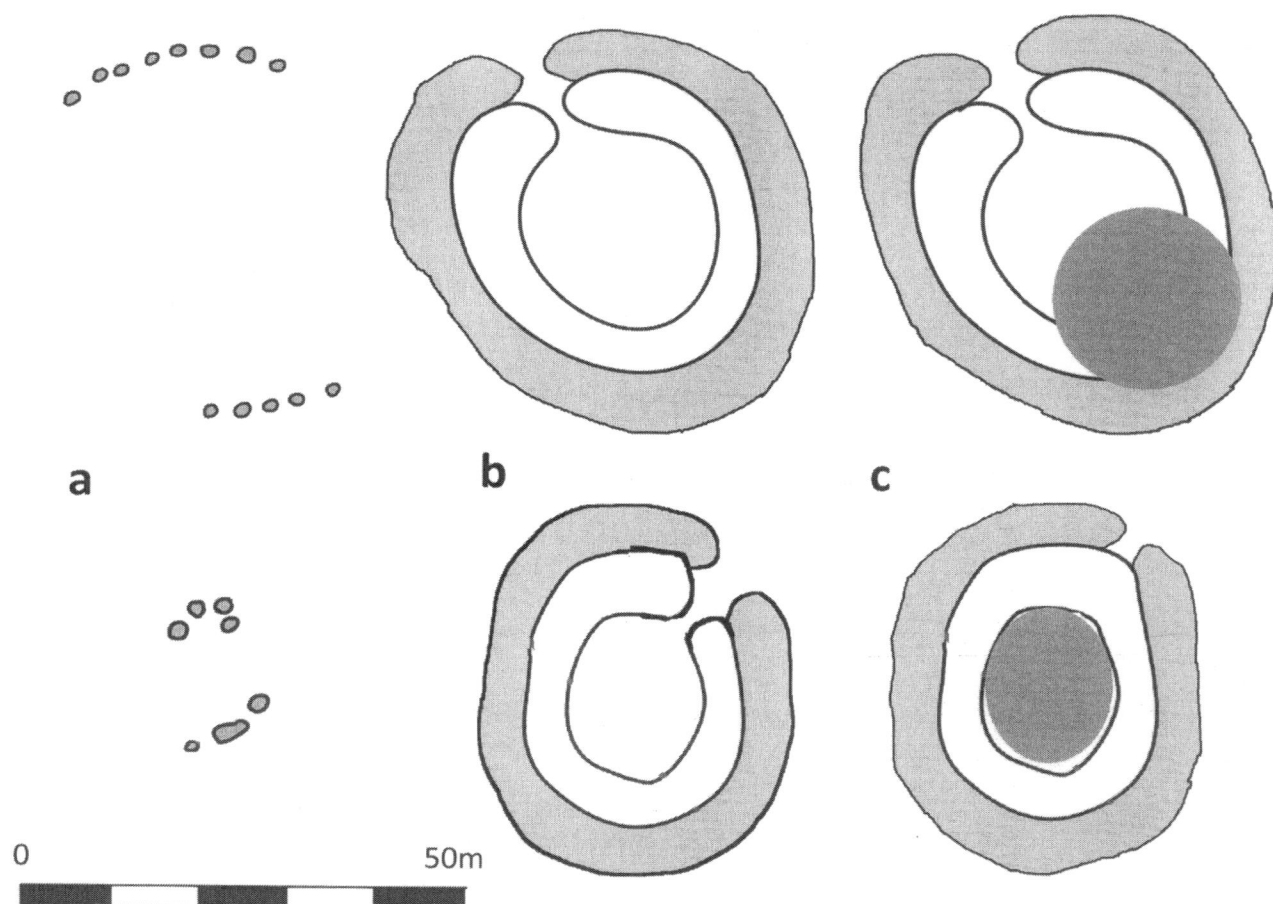

FIGURE 8. SCHEMATIC DIAGRAM OF HENGING, MOUNDING AND BLOCKING AT FORTEVIOT

cist structure at Forteviot have revealed what may be the frame of another mounded barrow. Therefore, at Forteviot the group of monuments characterised as a henge cluster by Harding and Lee (1987) include a range of significant places in the 3rd millennium BC that were subject to henging, blocking and mounding, until all that was left was a group of impenetrable, solid mounds.

Conclusion

In this paper, in outlining the results of our excavations at Forteviot, we have contributed to a discourse where the term henge hangs a little more loosely than it used to. The act of henging seems to have had an incredible spatial and temporal currency, and unite a wide range of types of places and areas of land. Places that were henged had diverse histories, temporalities and social contexts. Yet when considered as an act, a verb, rather than a thing, a noun, the word henge begins to make a little more sense as a *common response to something*, rather than as a cultural or temporal identifier. The earthwork element of these monuments inevitably altered the experience of these places, regardless of the scale of the earthworks, changing these places for ever, clearly defining an inside and an outside more explicitly than had been possible (or even desirable) before at places that had already had long life-histories. Henging was an emphatic act, and was made more explicit still in some cases by the blocking of henge entrances by extending the ditch, or the bank (not apparently both though), or even the construction of a mound within the henge, or overlapping its boundaries. These actions – henging, blocking, mounding – seem to be associated with putting places beyond use, moments of no return. In some instances such acts decommissioned monuments altogether, while in others activity was still attracted to the fringes or raised areas of these places (upper ditch fills, secondary burials high in mounds). These sealing activities were often, although by no means in all cases, accompanied by burial, apt as traces of earlier activities were also being buried away inside the closed henge or beneath a mound.

Our excavations at Forteviot have revealed a fascinating complex of circular monuments, some henges, some barrows / cairns, and some a combination of both. Something about these places seems to have had a fascination for people in the 3rd millennium BC, perhaps even at some points in times a horrid fascination. The establishment of a cremation cemetery (perhaps itself a mound) after 3000 cal BC, and the erection of hundreds of oak posts in a range of different settings in the following centuries, transformed the dynamic of this place forever. And within and around this massive but increasingly ruinous enclosure, the ghosts of posts, and the ancient burial mound may have become places that were less about veneration and ceremony, and more about control, concealment and eventually containment. The newly dead were introduced to these places, and new rules were developed which seem to have required acts of henging,

blocking and mounding. Once again, these places were changed forever and there was no going back.

Acknowledgements

We would like to thank Alex Gibson for inviting one of us (KB) to participate in the weekend event from which this book is in part derived. This created the opportunity to explore some of the issues covered in this paper with Alex, and Richard Bradley, which was very helpful in preparing the final version of this paper. Comments were gratefully received on an earlier version of this paper from Gordon Barclay and Rebecca Younger, both of whose insight into henges in general has helped inform this paper. We would like to acknowledge the generous support the SERF Project has received from Historic Scotland, the British Academy and the Society of Antiquaries of Scotland. Thanks to our co-directors of SERF, Steve Driscoll and Ewan Campbell, and the project manager, Tessa Poller for their support. We would like to thank Gordon Barclay for permission to reproduce figure 1. Figures 2, 3 and 4 were prepared by Lorraine McEwan. Figure 6 is reproduced courtesy of Flying Scotscam. Figure 5 was compiled by Adrian Maldonado. And of course none of our observations on the Forteviot henges and mounds would have been possible without the hard work of dozens of team members who have worked in Forteviot since 2006. For summaries of the SERF excavations to date and interim reports, visit out project website:

www.gla.ac.uk/schools/humanities/research/archaeologyresearch/projects/serf/

References

Aitchison, N. 2006. *Forteviot: a Pictish and Scottish Royal Centre*. Stroud: Tempus.

Alcock, L. and Alcock, E. A. 1992. Reconnaissance excavations on Early Historic fortifications and other royal sites in Scotland, 1974-84; 5: A) Excavations & other fieldwork at Forteviot, Perthshire, 1981; B) Excavations at Urquhart Castle, Inverness-shire, 1983; C) Excavations at Dunnottar, Kincardineshire, 1984. *Proceedings of the Society of Antiquaries of Scotland*, 122, 215–87.

Barclay, G. J. 1983. Sites from the third millennium bc to the first millennium ad at North Mains, Strathallan, Perthshire. *Proceedings of the Society of Antiquaries of Scotland*, 113, 122–281.

Barclay, G. J. 1999. A hidden landscape: the Neolithic of Tayside, in A. F. Harding (ed.), *Experiment and design: Archaeological studies in honour of John Coles*, 20–29. Oxford: Oxbow.

Barclay, G. J. 2001. Neolithic enclosures in Scotland, in T. Darvill and J. Thomas (eds.), *Neolithic enclosures in Atlantic Northwest Europe*. Oxford: Oxbow.

Barclay, G. J. 2005. 'The 'henge' and 'hengiform' in Scotland', in V. Cummings and A. Pannett (eds.), *Set in stone: new approaches to Neolithic monuments in Scotland*, 81-95. Oxford: Oxbow.

Barclay, G. J. and Russell-White, C. J. 1993. Excavations in the ceremonial complex of the fourth to second millennium BC at Balfarg / Balbirnie, Glenrothes, Fife. *Proceedings of the Society of Antiquaries of Scotland*, 123, 43–210.

Bradley, R. 1998. *The Significance of Monuments*. London: Routledge.

Bradley, R. 2007. *The Prehistory of Britain and Ireland*. Cambridge: Cambridge University Press.

Bradley, R. 2011. *Stages and Screens: an investigation into henge monuments in northern and north-eastern Scotland*. Edinburgh: Society of Antiquaries of Scotland.

Brophy, K. 2010. '...a place where they tried their criminals': Neolithic round mounds in Perth and Kinross, in J. Leary, T. Darvill and D. Field (eds.), *Round mounds and monumentality in the British Neolithic and beyond*, 10 – 27. Oxford: Oxbow.

Driscoll, S. T., Brophy, K. and Noble, G. 2010 The Strathearn Environs and Royal Forteviot Project (SERF), *Antiquity 84 Project Gallery*, www.antiquity. ac.uk/projgall/driscoll323/

Gibson, A. 2004. Round in circles. Timber circles, henges and stone circles: some possible relationships and transformation. In R. Cleal and J. Pollard (eds.), *Monuments and material culture*, 70–82. Salisbury: Hobnob Press.

Gibson, A. 2010a. Dating Balbirnie: recent radiocarbon dates from the stone circle and cairn at Balbirnie, Fife, and a review of its place in the overall Balfarg / Balbirnie site sequence. *Proceedings of the Society of Antiquaries of Scotland*, 140, 51–77.

Gibson, A.M. 2010b. Excavation and survey at the Dyffryn Lane henge complex, Powys, and a reconsideration of the dating of henges. *Proceedings of the Prehistoric Society*, 76, 213 – 248.

Harding, A. F. 1981. Excavations in the prehistoric ritual complex near Milfield, Northumberland. *Proceedings of the Prehistoric Society*, 47, 87–135.

Harding, A.F. and Lee, G. E. 1987. *Henge monuments and related sites of Great Britain*, BAR British Series 175. Oxford: British Archaeological Reports.

Harding, J. 2003. *Henge Monuments of the British Isles*. Stroud: Tempus.

Leach, S. 2012. *Report on the human skeletal remains excavated from the prehistoric ceremonial complex site at Forteviot, Perthshire (2008-2010)*. Unpublished Report.

Millican, K. 2007. Turning in circles: a new assessment of the Neolithic timber circles of Scotland. *Proceedings of the Society of Antiquaries of Scotland*, 137, 5–34.

Noble, G. 2006. *Neolithic Scotland: timber, stone, earth and fire*. Edinburgh: Edinburgh University Press.

Noble, G. and Brophy, K. 2011a. Ritual to remembrance at a prehistoric ceremonial complex in central Scotland: excavations at Forteviot, Perth and Kinross. *Antiquity*, 85, 787–804.

Noble, G. and Brophy, K. 2011b. Big enclosures: the later Neolithic palisaded enclosures of Scotland in their Northwestern European context. *European Journal of Archaeology*, 14.1-2, 60–87.

Mercer, R. 1981. The excavation of a late Neolithic henge-type enclosure at Balfarg, Markinch, Fife, Scotland. *Proceedings of the Society of Antiquaries of Scotland*, 111, 63–171.

Parker Pearson, M., Chamberlain, A., Jay, M., Marshall, P., Pollard, J., Richards, C., Thomas, J., Tilley, C. and Welham, K. 2009 'Who was buried at Stonehenge?' *Antiquity*, 83, 23–39.

Ralston, I. 1988. Belhie (Auchterarder Parish): enclosed cremation cemetery, minihenge and other cropmarked features. *Discovery and Excavation in Scotland*, 1988, 27.

Ritchie, J. N. G. 1976. The Stones of Stenness, Orkney. *Proceedings of the Society of Antiquaries of Scotland*, 107, 1–60.

St Joseph, J. K. 1978. Air reconnaissance: recent results 44. *Antiquity*, 52, 47–50.

Sheridan, A. 2010. Scotland's Neolithic non-megalithic round mounds: new dates, problems and potential, in J. Leary, T. Darvill and D. Field (eds). *Round mounds and monumentality in the British Neolithic and beyond*, 28–52. Oxford: Oxbow.

Sheridan, A., Bradley, R. and Schulting, A. 2010. Radiocarbon dates arranged through the National Museums of Scotland Archaeology Department during 2008/9. *Discovery and Excavation in Scotland New Series*, 10, 212–4.

Stewart, M. E. C. 1987. The excavation of a henge, stone circles and metal-working area at Moncrieffe, Perthshire. *Proceedings of the Society of Antiquaries of Scotland*, 115, 125–50.

Thomas, J. 2007. *Place and memory: excavations at the Pict's Knowe, Holywood and Holm Farm, Dumfries and Galloway, 1994–8*. Oxford: Oxbow.

Thomas, J. 1999. *Understanding the Neolithic*. London: Routledge.

Thomas, J. 2010. The Return of the Rinyo-Clacton Folk? The Cultural Significance of the Grooved Ware Complex in Later Neolithic Britain. *Cambridge Archaeological Journal*, 20(1), 1–15.

Wainwright, G. J. 1969. A review of henge monuments in light of recent research. *Proceedings of the Prehistoric Society*, 35, 112–133.

Warner, R. B. 2000. Keeping out the otherworld: the internal ditch at Navan and other 'Iron Age' hengiform enclosures. *Emania*, 18, 39–44.

Wilkin, N. 2011. *Forteviot prehistoric complex, Perth & Kinross. Beaker and Food Vessel pottery report*. Unpublished report.

Henges in Ireland: New Discoveries and Emerging Issues

Muiris O'Sullivan, Stephen Davis and Geraldine Stout

Abstract

For many years Irish archaeologists have acknowledged the circular form of Neolithic and Bronze Age ritual monuments in Ireland but have generally avoided using the term 'henge' to describe these sites in the acknowledgement that there were significant differences in form and date with the British material. Accordingly, the Irish sites were described as 'embanked enclosures'. Recent studies over the last 20 years has highlighted the range in types and dates of these enclosures and intensive survey of areas such as the Boyne Valley has shed new light on these enclosures as well as considerably augmenting the database. This paper examines the Irish evidence and illustrates how the use of new techniques such as LiDAR can shed new light on these sites, even in already well-surveyed areas.

Keywords: Henge, Embanked Enclosure, Boyne Valley, LiDAR.

Introduction

In Britain the term *henge* is well established in the archaeological literature following its initial definition some 80 years ago (Kendrick and Hawkes 1932, 83). By contrast the Irish literature tended to avoid the term until the 1990s. It was mentioned occasionally – as a monument type associated with Beaker in Britain (Herity and Eogan 1977) or having ambiguous links with the Irish embanked enclosure (O'Kelly 1989; Cooney and Grogan 1994) – but the henge as a distinctive monument type was not targeted comprehensively. In part this was because researchers in Ireland tended to regard the Irish form, known as an embanked enclosure, as something different from the henge as understood in Britain. More recently, however, the relationship between embanked enclosures in Ireland and henges in Britain has been explored with increasing confidence (Stout 1991; Cooney 2000; Bradley 2007), and there has been a greater interest in henges as a monument type in Ireland (e.g. Condit and Simpson 1998; Danaher 2005). This has become feasible as the concept of a *henge* has evolved in Britain with the inevitable blurring of the original definition, and as new types of discoveries challenge established classifications in Ireland. On both sides of the Irish Sea there appears to be some generalized agreement on monuments that might be termed *henges*, or at least discussed in that context, with an emerging mutual appreciation that henge sites generally represent something more complex than a circular enclosed space constructed and used within a defined timeframe in the prehistoric past (Map 1).

Modern overviews have tended to highlight clustered complexes of earthen, wooden and occasionally stone or pit-defined enclosures in special prehistoric landscapes in Ireland, such as the Boyne Valley, Tara and Ballynahatty (Stout 1997, 301-303; Cooney 2000, 165-173; Bradley 2007, 113-122). The chronological emphasis in these reviews has generally focused on the third millennium BC; increasingly relying on the dating of the timber and pit-defined enclosures at these places more so than the earthen ones, but Bradley also draws attention to the lengthening chronology of henge locations. Both Cooney (2000) and Bradley (2007) explore the links with comparable complexes in Britain, especially Orkney, and the merits of a modulated regional approach are reinforced here.

The current paper reviews the history and use of the henge concept in Ireland and uses the evidence from relevant excavated sites to indicate some interesting patterns of chronology and context. As shown below, it is probably too early to attempt a definition of Irish henges here, principally because our knowledge of these monuments beyond the Boyne Valley remains comparatively limited in spite of the advances made over the past twenty years in particular. The second half of the paper focuses on the Boyne Valley and neighbouring parts of county Meath, analysing the evidence from LiDAR data in respect of earthworks deemed to be henges, including some previously unidentified examples. The results of this analysis demonstrate that even a previously surveyed landscape can yield new enclosures and new information on established sites when scrutinized anew with improved technology. In turn this shows the incompleteness of our knowledge about the occurrence and variety of henges across Ireland. Data from the relatively small proportion of excavated sites demonstrates the chronological complexities of these locations. A list of two reasonably well established variants of henges in Ireland and a third, miscellaneous group is provided in tables 1-3, with some data on each site where available. Omitted from these lists are the timber- and pit-defined circles of the Boyne Valley and Ballynahatty, as well as ritual ponds, but these are discussed occasionally in the text.

From embanked enclosures to henges and beyond

The term *embanked enclosure*, embracing a broad range of circular enclosures in Ireland that 'began early and lasted to the end of prehistoric times', was coined to describe an enclosed ritual space constructed from earth as distinct from standing stones (Ó Ríordáin 1953, 93). A quarter of a century later, Ruaidhrí de Valera's revised edition of Ó Ríordáin's publication left the interpretation intact but highlighted examples with very large diameters in the Boyne Valley region and at Ballynahatty, Co. Down. It was

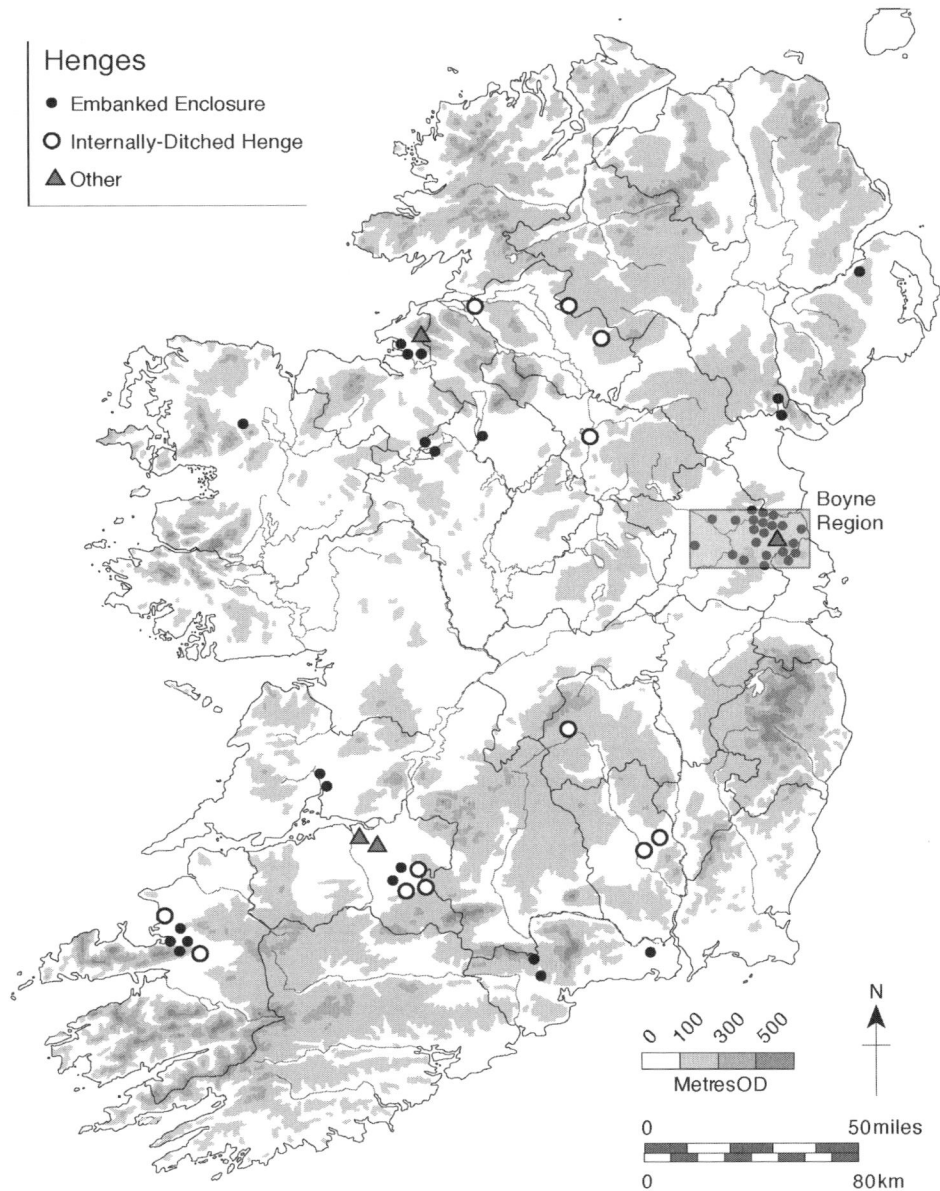

FIGURE 1: EMBANKED ENCLOSURES IN IRELAND.

now generally accepted that these embanked enclosures represented a late Neolithic or Early Bronze Age tradition and the sequential relationship with passage tombs seemed to be reinforced when the Monknewtown, Co. Meath enclosure (Figure 2) was excavated and produced both Carrowkeel and Beaker pottery (Sweetman 1976).

The classification *embanked enclosure* in Ireland was designed specifically to exclude stone circles and it was this distinction that helped to underpin a traditional Irish resistance to the term *henge*, deriving from the hanging lintel at Stonehenge. In this context a small number of embanked stone circles became a focus of interest. The examples at Grange near Lough Gur, Co. Limerick and Castleruddery, Co. Wicklow are the most frequently cited specimens of this group. The Grange enclosure in particular is important because a substantial portion of it was excavated by Ó Ríordáin (1951), and the results weighed

heavily on subsequent interpretations. The excavator regarded Grange as a hybrid stone/earth circle and dated it to the Beaker period at the beginning of the Bronze Age. In the 1990s, arising from discoveries at Knowth, there was a greater awareness of the widespread occurrence of Grooved Ware in Ireland including at the Grange Stone circle, which pushed the dating back into the final centuries of the Neolithic (Roche 1995; Eogan and Roche 1997). As such the Grange Stone Circle was deemed to be broadly contemporary with the post-passage tomb centuries in the Boyne Valley (Cooney 2000, 80) when open air circles were being defined by various means (soil banks, wooden posts, standing stones and pits) and a Grooved Ware horizon flourished before overlapping with a succeeding Beaker phase at the very end of the Neolithic (ibid.2000, 165-7). However, the interpretation of Grange was then markedly altered by Helen Roche who demonstrated that the enclosing bank was apparently constructed on top of a

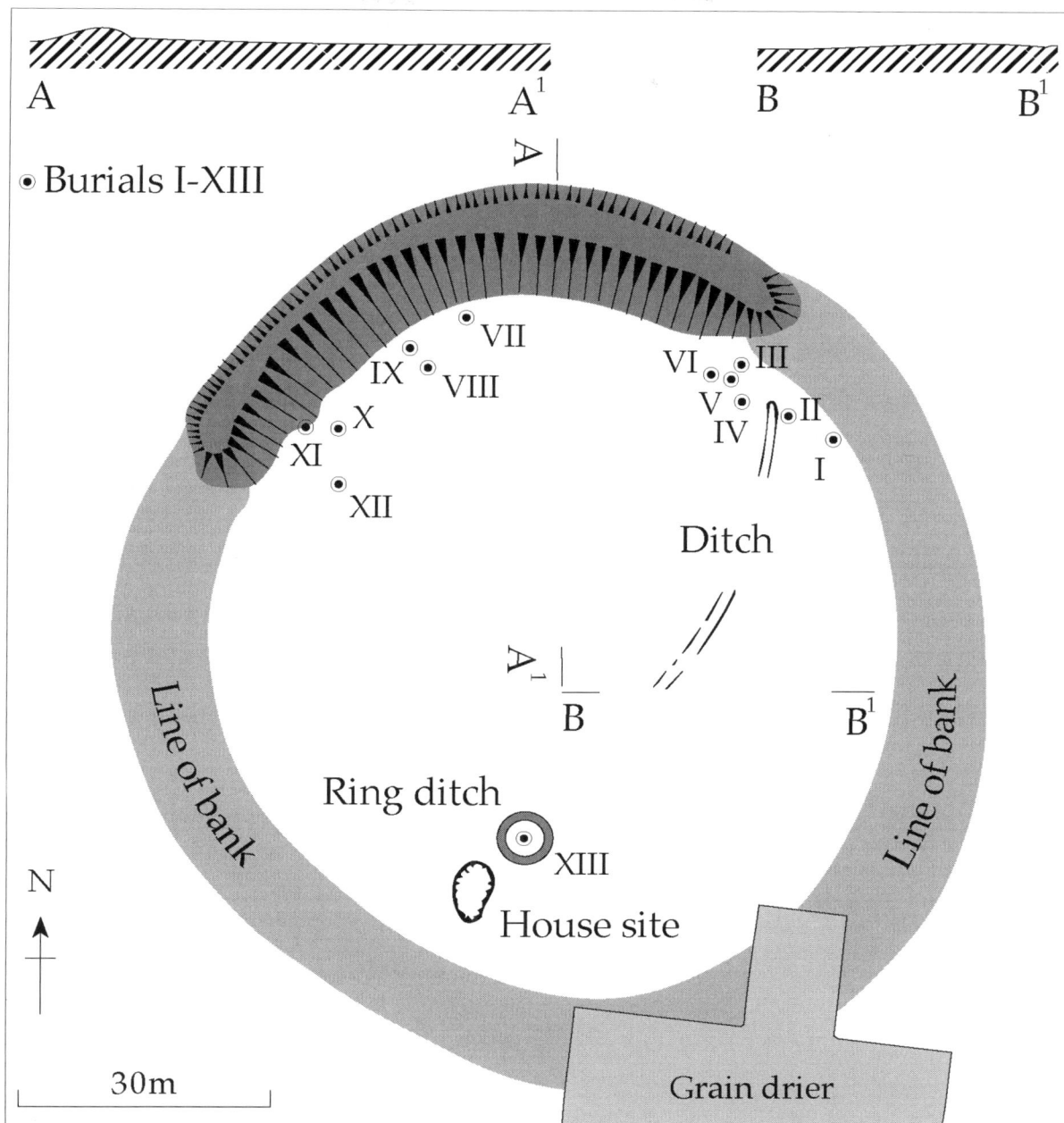

Figure 2: The henge at Monknewtown showing the partially destroyed bank and the internal features revealed by excavation (after Sweetman 1976).

Late Bronze Age horizon, with Grooved Ware also present not only under the bank and in the enclosed space (as was Beaker) but also in re-deposited turf layers within the bank (Roche 2005). As Roche herself acknowledged, however, the construction of the Late Bronze Age monument at a site already rich in Late Neolithic material may reflect an enduring sense in prehistory that this was a special place. The occurrence and nature of other monuments in the immediate neighbourhood - stone circles, an embanked enclosure, a megalithic tomb and a standing stone - suggests that here was a ritual focus located within 300m of the shore of Lough Gur and directly across the water from the broadly contemporary settlement on the Knockadoon peninsula less than 1km away.

The Giant's Ring at Ballynahatty, Co. Down, located on a ridge beside the River Lagan, is also known to be situated amongst a variety of other prehistoric features of a ceremonial nature (Hartwell 1998). This earthwork is nearly 200m across with a bank originally c.15-16m wide at the base and surviving to a height of some 4m. A megalithic chambered tomb occurs at the centre of the interior, and some distinctive cists containing Carrowkeel bowls and cremations (like miniature passage tombs) were found north-west of the enclosure. Timber enclosures were also found in this area, one of them remarkably like the one excavated at Knowth and Grooved Ware was present in both cases. There appears to be limited information on the flat cemetery and multiple cist cairn recorded in this

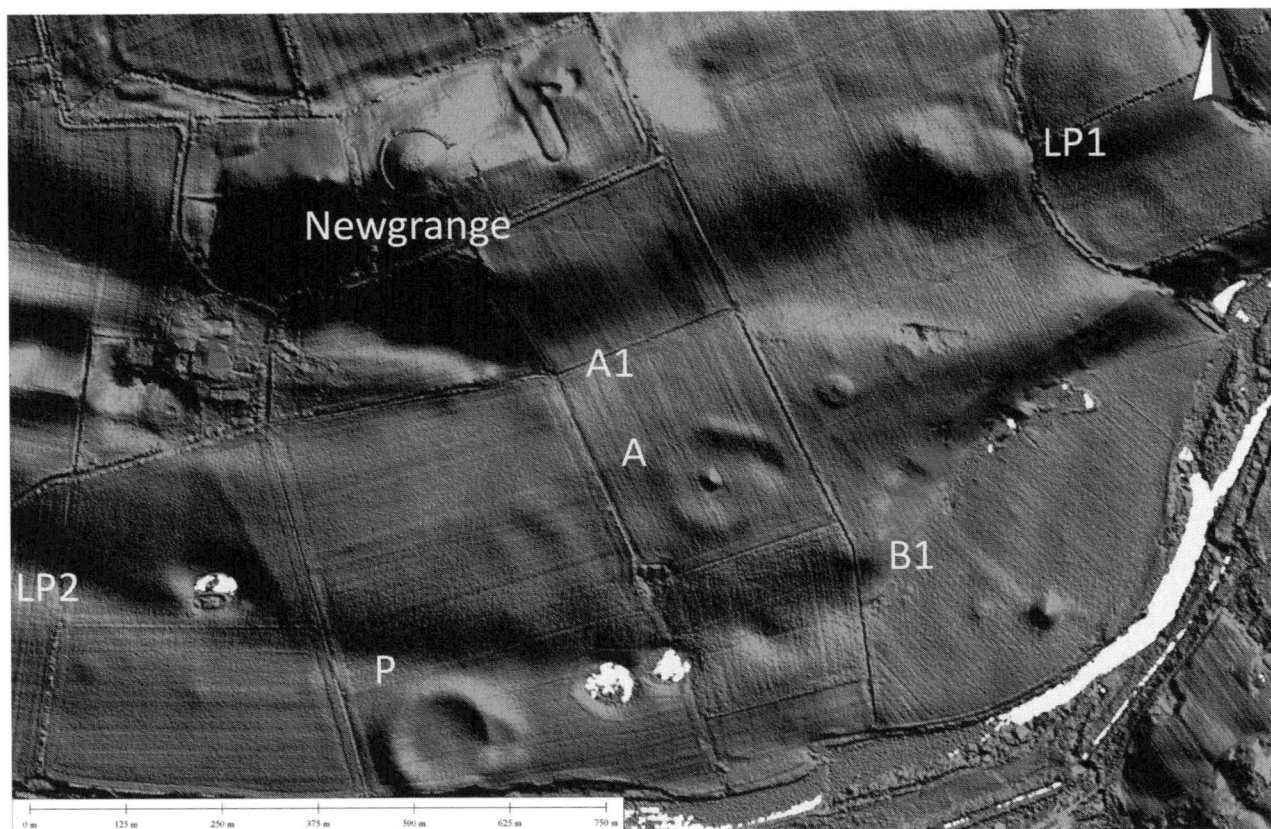

FIGURE 3: HENGES LOCATED BETWEEN NEWGRANGE AND THE RIVER BOYNE.

area but it has been assumed that these were Bronze Age features. Beyond that the subsequent story of the site is lost in the mists of prehistory. However, its later Neolithic and Early Bronze Age elements tend to influence and reinforce the interpretation of other sites, notably Monknewtown in Co. Meath.

The embanked enclosure at Monknewtown (Figure 2), often cited in the context of the Boyne Valley later Neolithic, was excavated by Sweetman (1971; 1976) who recorded both Carrowkeel pottery and Grooved Ware at this partially destroyed embanked enclosure. In a sense this was seized upon as confirmation of a Later Neolithic date for the monument but it overshadowed the fact that burials with Food Vessel and Late Bronze Age pottery were also recovered at the site (See Smyth 2008, 16-19). Radiocarbon dates from the site ranged between the mid-Neolithic and late medieval periods. One Late Bronze Age burial occurred at the centre of a ringditch that, as noted by Roche (2004), was similar to four examples revealed within the Grange enclosure during Ó Ríordáin's excavations. The evidence points to a succession of activity at Monknewtown, extending in this case over more than two millennia from around 3000 BC, a possibility already raised by Waddell (1998, 110). The Monknewtown circle was constructed fewer than 200m from a passage tomb in the same townland. A nearby circular pond, seemingly man-made, has sometimes been compared with the King's Stables in the Navan Fort

complex, Co. Armagh, an artificially constructed swamp from which Late Bronze Age material is known. Condit (1996, 23), however, wondered if the Monknewtown pond might be part of a widespread Late Neolithic horizon in the Boyne Valley and this seems to be confirmed by a Late Neolithic radiocarbon date (Beta-288747: 2840-2480 cal BC) from the basal fill of the ditch at a depth of $c.1.90m$ (Davis st al. 2010, 143). The Monknewtown pond consists of an inner area $c.30m$ in diameter surrounded by a bank measuring $c.15m$ wide and an outer ditch some 10m wide. The depth of the ditch is $c.1.5$-$2m$ below the surrounding ground level and the interior is 1m deeper again.

The embanked enclosures of the Boyne Valley (Figure 3) are most typically characterized by a flat-topped earthen bank breached by a single entrance and having an external diameter of more than 100m, enclosing a circular or oval space that is domed or hollowed in profile and frequently marked by interior features (Stout 1991, 246-7). Other elements regarded as diagnostic include the absence of a ditch and the presence of an enhanced entrance, although it should be noted that only two reasonably confirmed examples of enhanced entrances are known, at Newgrange Sites A and P. It was noted that a variety of equivalent or similar enclosures were to be found in other parts of the Irish countryside (Stout 1991, 282-284; Condit and Simpson 1998), including some previously undiscovered possibilities such as those in the Lee Valley, Co. Kerry (Table 1).

Table 1: Class 1 henges (embanked enclosures) in Ireland

County	Townland	Dims	Entrance	association	Reference	RMP NO.
Clare	Coogaun	x3m	SW		Stout 1991,2x1	CL034-143
Clare	Knopoge	29m	S	wedge tomb	Condit & Grogan 1994, x-12	CL042-091
Down	Ballynahhatty	225m		passage tombs	Stout 1991,2x2	Co. Down
Kerry	Ballyseedy	50m	?	passage tomb?	Connolly & Condit 1996, 8-12	KE038-093
Kerry	Dromavally					KE038-131
Kerry	Tonavane					KE038-113
Kerry	Flemby				Connolly & Condit 1996, 8-12	KE039-202001
Leitrim	Kilclaremore	20m	?	Cairn complex	Moore, M. 2003, 129	LE028-003
Limerick	Bulgadenhall	70m		ring ditch		LI040-230
Limerick	Grange	95m	?	stone circle	O' Nuallain , S. & Cody, E. 1996, 3-14	LI032-002
Louth	Balregan	57m		Stone circles	O'Donnchadha, B. 2006, 324	LH007-001008-
Louth	Carn Beg	?	E	Stone circle	Buckley 1988,53-54	LH007-012
Mayo	Richmond	34m	?			MA038-180
Meath	Balrath	160m	SE	embanked enclosure	Stout 1991, 255-257	ME032-011
Meath	Belpere/Odder	240m	W	ring ditches	Stout 1991, 257	ME037-008
Meath	Carranstown				Steve Davis per. comm..	ME027-078
Meath	Carranstown/ Caulstown	140m	SW		Davies, S et al 2010, H12-ii	ME027-078
Meath	Fourknocks	110m	NNW	passage tomb	Stout 1991, 259	ME033-025
Meath	Fourknocks				Steve Davis per. comm.	ME033-052
Meath	Irishtown	245m	E/W	Embanked enclosure	Stout 1991, 263, 264	ME038-011
Meath	Micknanstown	140m	E	passage tomb	Stout 1991,265-267	ME033-013
Meath	Monknewtown	107m	?	passage tomb and pond	Stout 1991,267	ME019-016001
Meath	Newgrange Site A	175m	E	Embanked enclosure	Stout 1991,26-269	ME019-049002
Meath	Newgrange Site A2				Steve Davis per. comm.	ME019-112
Meath	Newgrange Site P	175m	E	passage tomb	Stout 1991, 26-271	ME026-006
Meath	Newgrange Site LP2	164m	?	Mound or cairn	Steve Davis per. comm.	ME019-094
Meath	Newgrange Site B1	125m	?		Steve Davis per. comm.	ME019-058002
Meath	Oristown	60m	W	Teltown complex	Conor Newman pers comm.	ME017-050
Meath	Riverstown	150m	SE	ring ditches	Stout 1991, 271-272	ME031-032
Meath	Stackallen	110m	SW?	passage tomb	Stout 1991, 271-274	ME018-024
Meath	Dowth Site Q	165m	SW	passage tombs	Stout 1991, 259	ME020-010
Meath	Dowth Site Q1	?			Steve Davis per. comm.	ME020-075
Meath	Dowth Site Q2	?			Steve Davis per. comm.	ME019-53
Meath	Heathtown	200m	?	ring ditches	Stout 1991,259-263	ME033-011
Meath	Kilbrew	142m	W	embanked enclosure	Stout 1991, 263-265	ME038-010
Meath	Rathcarran				Steve Davis per. comm.	ME030-035
Meath	Corballis				Steve Davis per. comm.	ME028-070
Roscommon	Ballinphuill	54m	W/NE		Stout 1991,283	RO005-041
Roscommon	Knockadoobrosna	70m	NE	Emnbanked enclosure	Stout 1991,283	RO006-118001
Roscommon	Knockadoobrosna	96m	?	Mound	Stout 1991,283	RO006-118007
Sligo	Cumeen	111m	?	Tumulus	Timoney 1984, 284	SL014-047001
Sligo	Knockatober	65m	S	Portal tomb	Stout 1991,283	SL021-051
Sligo	Lisnalurg	150m	SW		Thornton [Stout] 1980, 168	SL014-012001
Waterford	Castletown	90m	?	passsage tombs	Stout 1991, 283-284	WA017-060
Waterford	Coumaraglin Mt	24m	SW	Cairn complex	Moore 1995, 210	WA023-066020

Table 2: Class 2 henges (internally ditched enclosures) in Ireland

County	Townland	Dims	Entrance	Association	Reference	RMP No.
Cavan	Banagher	42m	NNE	Passage tomb	Cody 2002, 77-98	CV026-004006
Fermanagh	Sheebeg	70m	SE	mound	Thornton 1980, 136-7	N. Ireland
Fermanagh	Knockbeg	50m	SE		Thornton 1980, 134-5	N. Ireland
Kilkenny	Annamult	35m	W/E/SE		Gibbons, 1990, 6	KK027-022
Kilkenny	Clashwilliam	50m	?		Gibbons 1990,6-7	KK024-024
Kerry	Carrigeenwood	60m	E		Castleisland Survey	KE024-006
Kerry	Garryard	77m	East		Toal 1995, 71	KE010-017
Laois	Newtown-Skirk	96m		Standing stone	Cunningham 1987, 63-4	LA021-021001
Limerick	Bohergeela	70m	N?	Lough Gur	O'Kelly, 1942,90	
Limerick	Mortgage	70m	SE	Lough Gur	O'Kelly, 1942,90	
Limerick	Rathmore N	42m	E	Lough Gur	O'Kelly, 1944,90	
Tipperary South	Lismortagh	140m	?	Ring barrow		TS062-010003-
Tyrone	Craghan	85m	E/W		Thornton 1980	N. Ireland

Table 3: Other henges in Ireland

County	Townland	Dims.	Entrance	Association	Reference	RMP No.
Limerick	Friarstown	112m	?	henge	Kelly & Condit, 1998, 18-22	LI013-089
Limerick	Friarstown	165m	?	henge	Kelly & Condit, 1998, 18-22	LI013-094002
Meath	Grange	80m	East	passage tomb	Steve Davis per. comm.	ME033-024
Sligo	Tonaforte	85m	East		Danaher, 2007	SL014-224

As in Britain the discovery of new sites led to a blurring of established characterizations. Some specimens correspond quite closely to Wainwright's definition of a henge as 'a circular area of variable size enclosed by a bank and ditch, the former normally sited outside the latter and broken by one or more entrances' (1989, 14). The Irish sites in question are low-lying, internally ditched, externally embanked enclosures located frequently near a river and varying in size from 26-85m in diameter. Generally there appears to be a single entrance but at Guillane East, Co. Kerry and Craghan, Co. Tyrone a double entrance is visible. Examples of these smaller enclosures are distributed widely across Ireland with small concentrations in North Kerry and Small County, Co. Limerick (Table 2). The pair of banks with intervening ditch recorded at the partially excavated enclosure at Tonafortes in Co. Sligo, to be reviewed further below, suggest that other variants of the henge phenomenon may exist beyond classes 1 and 2.

The possibility that at least some late prehistoric royal enclosures in Ireland may have originated as henge-type monuments was reviewed by Newman (1997,174-7). These large enclosures, represented most notably at Ráith na Ríg on the Hill of Tara in Co. Meath, Navan Fort in Co. Armagh and Knockaulin in Co. Kildare, are characterized by internal ditches and external banks. The evidence for a Neolithic origin at these sites is inconclusive but Newman notes that a site that he excavated at Raffin, Co. Meath featured an earthwork constructed in later prehistory near the end of a long sequence that began in the Neolithic period and continued into the first millennium AD. This enclosure had been levelled by bulldozing but Newman was able to identify a succession of human interventions

at the site, beginning around 3000 BC and involving the construction of a multi-ringed post circle in the Early Bronze Age, an oval plank-palisaded enclosure around the 11th century BC, a circular structure in the Late Bronze Age, interpreted as a double-walled round house (D: 13m), followed by the surrounding henge-like enclosure and a centrally placed ringditch with surrounding timber circle in the early centuries AD (Heritage Council undated).

To suggest that Ráith na Ríg at Tara originated as a Late Neolithic henge monument may seem optimistic in the face of evidence indicating an Iron Age date (Roche 2002, 64-6). However, a small stretch of palisade located between Duma na nGiall and Roche's Iron Age palisade/ditch combination yielded a radiocarbon date (GrA-17670) in the range 2469 – 2347 cal BC while another palisade located east of the mound yielded a similar date (O'Sullivan 2005, 49-50). Neither could be projected as part of a large curvilinear enclosure but their presence is in keeping with the repeated interventions at the adjacent passage tomb from around 3000 BC to the 17th century BC. Nearby activity in the Late Bronze Age and Iron Age (ibid., 221-235; Roche 2002), not to mention the many other prehistoric monuments on the Hill of Tara, add up to a general continuum not unlike Raffin, Monknewtown and Grange. On the other hand the monumental evidence for a henge is slim. Even the oft-quoted large enclosure located north of Ráith na Ríg and defined by a ditch with flanking pits as traced by geophysical survey is spatially most obviously associated with the Iron Age enclosure Ráith na Senad with which its centre coincides (Fenwick and Newman 2002). This enclosure incorporates the passage tomb Duma na nGiall at its southern end and also the undated but arguably Bronze Age barrow incorporated amongst the outer ditches of Ráith na Senad on the north-western side (Grogan 2008). Excavation may yet date this enclosure to the Late Neolithic, providing a parallel for the large Newgrange pit circle and the large timber enclosure at Ballynahatty. Until then Rath Maeve, located 1km south of the main Tara focus, is a considerably less contentious case (Stout 1991, 257-8; Newman 1997, 190), although not without complications.

The slightly ovoid enclosure at Rath Maeve measures approximately 275m in maximum diameter including the bank which varies from 7-15m wide (Stout 1991, 257-258). Ongoing fieldwork at the site under the direction of Finola O'Carroll promises to develop into an important contribution towards the study of large embanked enclosures in the region. Although presumed to be an embanked enclosure, Rath Maeve has yielded geophysical results that suggest a history extending into the Early Medieval period. The most extensive array of earthworks revealed in the interior resembles Early Medieval settlement enclosures of a type found at several locations along the nearby M3 but there is also a striking circular enclosure with a prominent and seemingly unbroken ditch, measuring some 40m in exterior diameter. This is presumably a prehistoric site, possibly equivalent to some of the smaller enclosures noted below as possible henge antecedents elsewhere. Another suggested prehistoric enclosure, located southwest of the first but still in the interior, may have been even larger. Only the eastern half of this second feature occurs within the area of the geophysical survey, but enough is visible to suggest that it was apparently overcut by the Early Medieval enclosure and might originally have been c.60m in diameter. Both of these internal enclosures occur in the western half of the interior. The examination of Rath Maeve is still in its infancy but the results will be awaited with enormous interest.

An embanked enclosure (Class 1) was partially excavated in advance of road schemes at Balregan 1, Co. Louth (O'Donnchadha, B 2006, 321). Balregan 1 is located on a promontory above the confluence of the Kilcurry and Castletown Rivers, c.3.5km to the southeast of the estuary at Dundalk Bay. An early illustration of the site (Wright 1758) shows a ritual complex which includes cairns, standing stones, a stone alignment and stone circles which have long since disappeared. Excavations revealed an encompassing bank created from material quarried either side of the bank and a foundation core of water-rolled stones, which represented part of a circular enclosure with an internal diameter of c.46m and external diameter of 57m (A stone core has also been identified at the embanked enclosures in Ballynahatty, Co. Down and Newgrange Site P in Co. Meath). An entrance in the south-southeast with a slightly expanded terminus on its northern side corresponded to a similar feature in the outer ditch. The southern side of the entrance was marked by an oval, stone edged, pit that may have supported a standing stone such as those illustrated by Wright (1758). Four pits were

found in the interior of the Balregan enclosure, within the internal quarry, and a shallow pit was recorded at the south end of the enclosure bank. The fill of one pit contained burnt human bone which represented part of an adult, with skull fragments indicating a young adult female. This appeared to be an intact burial composed of selected bone from a funerary pyre. Similar pit burials have been found at the henge at Monknewtown, Co. Meath (Sweetman 1976, 28–36). A small quantity of burnt cattle and sheep/goat bone came from the external quarry. Fragments identified as dog and horse came from the upper, possibly deliberate, fill. The dating for the site is largely dependent on the stratigraphic relationship between the enclosure and the Middle and Late Neolithic pottery assemblages found under the bank. Deposits containing Neolithic pottery were partly disturbed during the construction of the monument. Grooved Ware came from the upper layer of the external ditch and a deposit that overlay the ditch fill: If, as the excavator suggested, this ditch remained open for only a short period the pottery evidence indicates that the Balregan enclosure dates from the later Neolithic.

In preparation for the construction of the Sligo inner relief road a portion of an enclosure at Tonafortes, identified as a henge by Condit and Simpson (1998), was excavated by Danaher (2005). This concentrated specifically on the entrance area which happened to fall within the take of the roadway on the eastern side of the monument. The causeway between the ditch terminals was 8.20m wide and the terminal on the northern side was noticeably deeper than that on the south. Apart from the construction there was little evidence of human activity from the building phase, but a small number of prehistoric artefacts were encountered and charcoal from the stony basal fill of the ditch, interpreted as a rapid re-fill, produced a radiocarbon date of 2460-2140 cal BC. The interior space at Tonafortes, measuring 45m across, is enclosed by two banks with an intervening ditch. This is atypical in the Irish series but the site lies within 3-4km of the Carrowmore passage tomb complex and occurs in an area where a variety of monuments from a succession of prehistoric eras are known, including an earlier Neolithic causewayed enclosure at nearby Magheraboy (Danaher 2004). In classic henge mode the morphology of the Tonafortes enclosure creates an inward-looking situation, further emphasised by the location of the monument at the centre of a natural amphitheatre defined by the surrounding mountains: Knocknarea to the west, Ben Bulben to the north and the Ballygawley Hills to the north-east.

The assumption that the construction of all henges and related earthworks in Ireland can automatically be attributed to the Late Neolithic or Early Bronze Age is questionable. In Britain, as pointed out by Bradley (2011), henge monuments are generally defined in terms of their enclosing earthwork because this is the most obvious feature, especially in aerial photography, and it was assumed until relatively recently that this element was primary, with other features established in the enclosed space either at the same time or later. He questions this

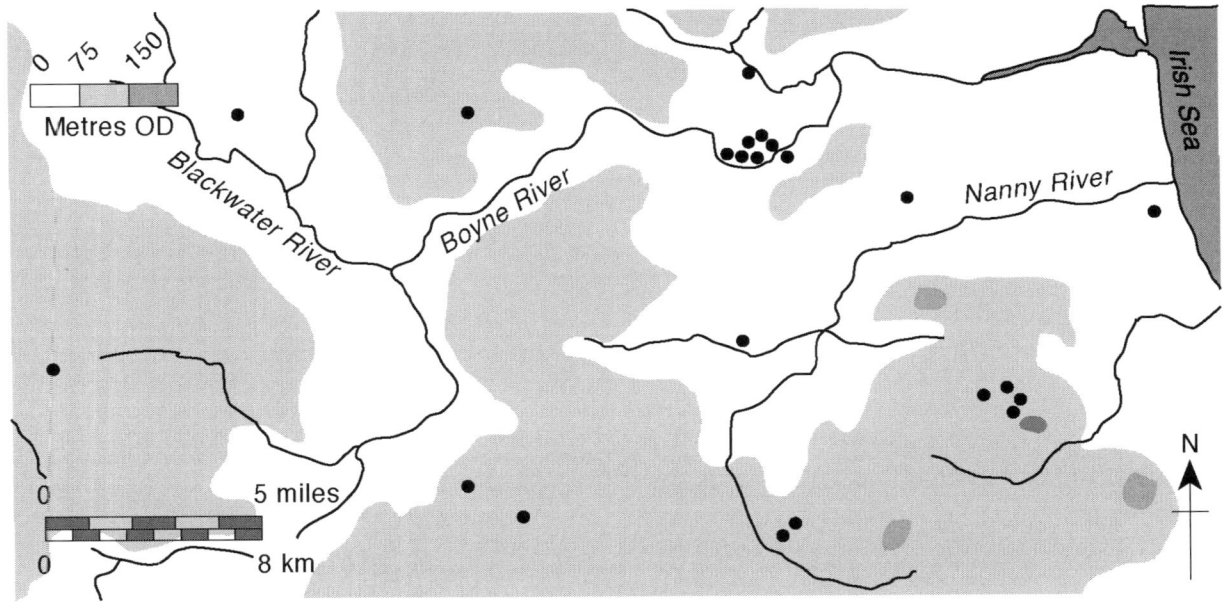

FIGURE 4: EMBANKED ENCLOSURES IN CO. MEATH.

generalization, noting contrary evidence cited by Gibson (2004), and presents evidence from a number of sites in Scotland to demonstrate that the earthwork is but one element of a complex history at these sites. At Broomend of Crichie, for example, excavations revealed an extensive array of features ranging from the later third millennium to the mid-second millennium BC and other sites appeared to extend into the Late Bronze Age (Bradley 2011, 181). O'Brien (2004, 334) makes a similar point in relation to sites in Ireland that had been claimed as circle henges (*i.e.* stone circles surrounded by a ditch with external bank). The evidence from the Grange site discussed above makes

effectively the same point for Irish henge monuments. At Grange the enclosure may have been the last major development at a site that had been a focus of activity for close to two thousand years. This mirrors the interpretation of the Raffin site (Newman 1997, 177).

Condit and Simpson (1998) reviewed the possible henges and related sites across the Irish countryside, sub-dividing them as follows: earthen embanked enclosures, internally ditched enclosures, embanked stone circles, circle henges, timber circles, 'royal' enclosures and ritual ponds. Although very useful in its time, this classification is already in need

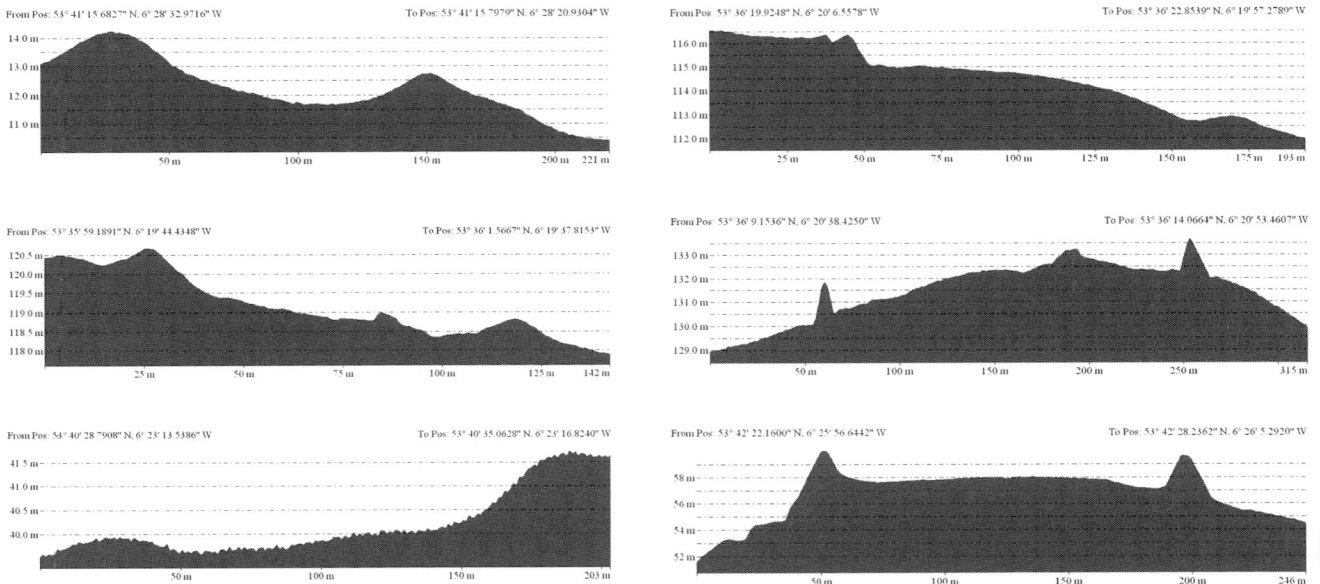

FIGURE 5: LIDAR-GENERATED CROSS SECTIONS OF IRISH EMBANKED ENCLOSURES, SHOWING FROM TOP: LEFT - SITE P AT BRÚ NA BÓINNE (W-E), FOURKNOCKS/MICKNANSTOWN (SW-NE), CARRANSTOWN (SE-NW). RIGHT - MICKNANSTOWN (SW-NE), HEATHTOWN (SE-NW), DOWTH HENGE AT BRÚ NA BÓINNE (SE-NW).

of revision. The reliance on overt morphological features with insufficient regard for associated structures is a weakness in itself, but not a fatal one. A more fundamental difficulty is the emerging evidence, some acknowledged by the authors at the time and some published since then, that the structures on which the classification is based are not from a neatly defined period in prehistory, specifically the Late Neolithic/Early Bronze Age continuum. To take an example, while timber circles from the period in question occur at Knowth and also near the great earthen embanked enclosure at Ballynahatty, as well as Raffin and along various motorway corridors, the timber circle at Lismullin near Tara is an Iron Age structure, albeit erected beside what seems to have been a focus of ritual digging throughout the Neolithic. Furthermore, O'Brien presented some new evidence and a rigorous critique of other evidence to question 'the very existence of circle henges as a separate sub-class in Ireland' (2004, 337). The embanked stone circle at Grange has been clarified by Roche (2004) but this clarification has shown that the structural basis of the classification dates no earlier than the Late Bronze Age. The royal enclosures remain unresolved, with teasing Neolithic (and sometimes Bronze Age) elements recurring at these Iron Age sites. Irrespective of these difficulties Condit and Simpson have helped to crystallize the debate on the types of site to be considered in discussions of henges in Ireland. Moreover their identification of ritual ponds as a type of henge is reinforced by the Late Neolithic radiocarbon date from the Monknewtown example, which focuses renewed attention on the King's Stables at Emain Macha and other relevant ponds, including the one located between sites A and P at Newgrange. The map accompanying their paper demonstrates the widespread occurrence of these sites, especially in the eastern part of the country and counties Sligo, Roscommon, Clare and Limerick, with further sites discussed in the text. For the purpose of the lists provided in Tables 1 and 2 here, a simple classification is adopted.

Definition and comparison

As indicated above, henges in Ireland are some distance from resolution. Too much depends on a small number of excavations, most of which were at unrepresentative sites or were not designed to address research questions associated specifically with henges. Nevertheless a few recurring themes can be recognized:

- Monuments claimed to be henges are circular or oval in plan and appear to be associated with spaces that attracted activity, usually of a ritual nature, over a period that extended from the Middle or Late Neolithic to the Late Bronze Age and sometimes the Iron Age.

- Leaving aside those enclosures constructed in other media (e.g. timber- and pit-defined or waterfilled circles), henges known or presumed to have been built in the Late Neolithic are generally constructed by scooping soil from the interior to create a bank or by digging a ditch immediately inside the bank.

- Banks are sometimes broad and are broken by one or two entrances, the exact number of which is difficult to establish without excavation.

- The most commonly occurring pottery at these sites is Grooved Ware, Beaker and Late Bronze Age coarse ware, sometimes all three.

- Internal features are common but are poorly understood due to a dearth of comprehensive excavation.

- Other ritual monuments tend to occur in the neighbourhood, and sometimes a group of embanked enclosure appear to cluster together (Stout 1991, 246; Condit and Simpson 1998, 47).

The most recognizable and acceptable class of Irish henge monuments is undoubtedly the embanked enclosure. Their profusion in the Boyne Valley and along other river valleys in Co. Meath (Figure 4) has prompted linkages with the passage tomb tradition. The spatial associations are obvious in the Boyne Valley and Fourknocks while the occurrence of Carrowkeel ware at Monknewtown and Ballynahatty strengthens the link, but the association between henges and passages tombs is not always so obvious elsewhere and it is possible that the spatial coincidence might in part be explained by the association of both monument types with rivers. In any case Monknewtown is slightly atypical, being at the smaller end of the scale by comparison with the spatial extent of other sites. The excavated sites beyond the Boyne Valley, including Tonafortes (two banks with intervening ditch), emphasise not so much the commonalities as the morphological variety of monuments discussed under the term *henge* (See tables 1-3 here).

Enclosures with banks and internal ditches or no ditches continued to be raised in Ireland until at least the end of prehistory. Ringbarrows present a difficulty because they vary considerably in size. Ráith Gráine at Tara for example comprises a circular mound surrounded by a ditch and external bank with a diameter of *c*.70m while discernible almost at the centre of this enclosure is a smaller barrow consisting of a low mound surrounded by a ditch with a diameter of *c*.13.5m. Whether or not these features represent a single construction, they highlight the range of sizes and forms to be found amongst Irish ringbarrows. One characteristic that helps to distinguish ringbarrows from henges in Ireland is the general absence of an entrance from the former, although the occurrence of an entrance in ringditch variants of the ringbarrow complicates the discussion around problematic sites like Dún Ruadh, Co. Tyrone (Simpson 1993; Condit and Simpson 1998, 56; O'Brien 2004, 324).

It must also be noted that the long history recorded at sites like Grange and Monknewtown brings other circular monuments into consideration that have not generally been discussed previously in the context of henges. The enclosure at Johnstown South near Arklow, Co. Wicklow is a case in point. Excavations by Martin Fitpatrick (Fitzpatrick 2008) revealed it to be a subcircular prehistoric enclosure defined by a low bank, *c.*0.5m high and 9-10m wide containing an interior measuring *c.*36m north-south and 33m east-southwest. No entrance was identified but the denuded condition of the bank on the western side cautions against drawing inferences from the absence. The bank was composed mainly of stone including both larger uprights and smaller stones scattered around. The majority of the artefacts appear to be from the Bronze Age and Roche (2004, 115) mentions the pottery at this site as a comparator for the Late Bronze Age coarse ware from Grange. Intriguingly, however, the excavator noted the presence of decorated pottery, including two pieces of cord-impressed ware, possibly an Early Bronze Age indicator. A preliminary sorting of the flints revealed that amongst the predominating flakes and cores there were hollow-based arrowheads, a barbed and tanged arrowhead, a leaf-shaped arrowhead and scrapers. In addition to these hints of Early Bronze Age and even earlier activity at the site, there was a strong medieval presence. Pending a fuller excavation report, we are left to wonder about reported cremation pits, one of them stone-lined, found within the enclosure and to a lesser extent the smelting and other industrial activity recorded at the site. Its multi-period history and the mixing of burial, industrial and possibly some domestic activity makes this a site worthy of consideration. A similar complexity of activity through time was recorded in the centre of the great hillfort at Rathgall, also in Co. Wicklow, at which Condit and Simpson (1998) have previously drawn attention to the large unbroken ringditch, some 35m in diameter with a circular structure at its centre. Banagher in Co. Cavan is another interesting complex with evidence of an internally ditched, externally embanked enclosure, two stone circles, two megalithic tombs (at least one a type of passage tomb with decorated stones) and two barrows (Cody 2002).

In comparing definitions of henges and embanked enclosures from Britain and Ireland, some points of commonality are clearly evident, as well as substantial differences. In Britain henges are considered to range in size from *c.*20m upwards, with structurally similar sites of less than 20m sometimes termed 'hengiform enclosures' and large, irregularly shaped monuments termed 'henge enclosures'. They are commonly agreed to be enclosed by a boundary earthwork although the form of this is somewhat contentious. In the UK this earthwork is generally possessed of an internal ditch with one, two or occasionally more entrances. In an Irish context while elements of this definition are maintained they do not necessarily stand up to criticism. For example, the presence of an inner ditch is not universal. Furthermore in an Irish context the number of entrances, where they are evident, is most commonly one. Two entrances are evident at Dowth but the NE entrance has been interpreted as a later feature; at Newgrange Site P the suggested western entrance is

visible only as a crop mark and may relate more to the bank composition than to a formal entrance.

The Irish definition of 'embanked enclosures' includes sites towards the smaller end of the UK henge category (in excess of 25m, at least until challenged by Bradley 2011) and specifically calls for a single entrance and a flat-topped bank with no mention of an internal ditch. A possible clustering pattern, still somewhat vague in detail, is also implied within this definition. One of the more distinctive recurring features of the embanked enclosure in Ireland is that 'the broad, ditchless bank which defines the enclosure is constructed from earth scooped out from the interior of the site', as articulated by Condit (1993) following Stout (1991) and reiterated by Condit and Simpson (1998). Although this is likely to be an over simplification, it diverges from the diagnostic bank with inner ditch that predominates amongst British henges and serves as a starting point for discussion.

The embanked enclosures of Co. Meath

Co. Meath is particularly well supplied with embanked enclosures (Figure 4). These are concentrated along the Boyne as well as the Nanny and Delvin amongst other rivers, their distribution apparently related to that of earlier prehistoric sites such as passage tombs, and to watercourses, a hitherto understudied aspect. Thirteen sites were surveyed by Stout (1991) within this area, of which Rath Maeve and Riverstown near Tara appeared to be western outliers. Recent analysis of LiDar data (see below) has identified a number of other possible sites, with a particular concentration in the Brú na Bóinne World Heritage Site (but with other potential sites distributed elsewhere, generally in proximity to watercourses, examples being Rathcarran and Corballis These recent surveys have also raised a number of questions regarding the sub-division of sites under the broad umbrella of 'embanked enclosure'.

Site form: The classic form of an Irish embanked enclosure is generally thought to comprise a large, circular enclosure, with a broad, flat-topped bank of indeterminate height, lacking any sharp internal ditch, but instead possessed of a broad, shallow scarping from which the bank itself was constructed (Stout 1991; Condit 1993). The best example of a site which meets all of these criteria is to be found at Micknanstown, Co. Meath, to the north of Fourknocks. However, many sites deviate substantially from this definition and even Micknanstown is not without its problems in this regard, with suggestions that the flat-topped bank has been significantly modified.

While domed interiors arising from scarping are evident at Dowth, Heathtown and Micknanstown, information from LiDar suggests that the most frequently encountered form resembles a shallow bowl with no obvious indication of scarping (Figures 5 and 6). The best preserved example of a typical 'Boyne'-type enclosure is Newgrange Site P, which lies adjacent to the Boyne to the south of Newgrange

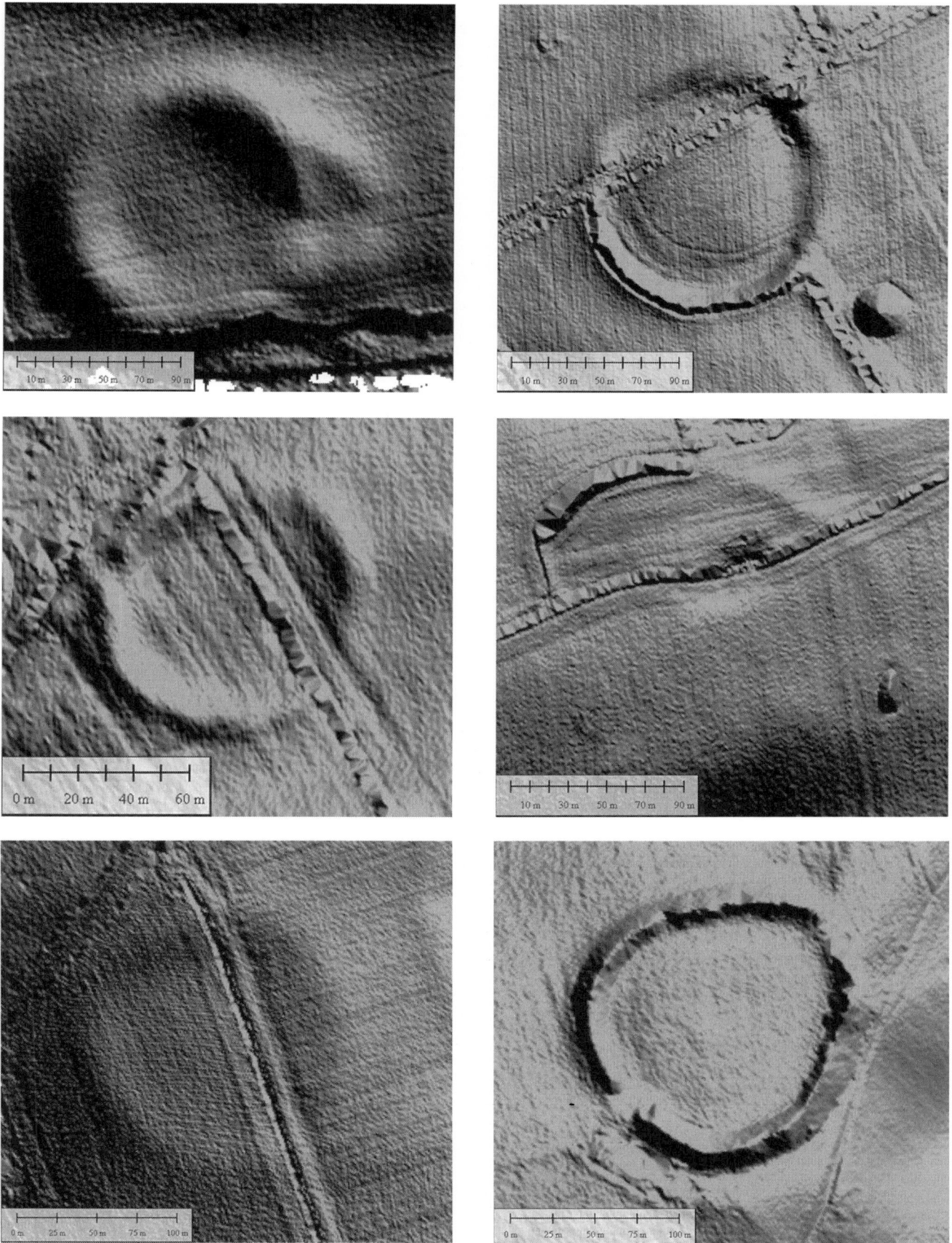

Figure 6: LIDAR-derived aerial images (standard analytical hillshade) representing the six enclosures illustrated in the previous image. Left - Site P, Fourknocks/Micknanstown, Carranstown. Right – Micknanstown, Heathtown, Dowth Henge.

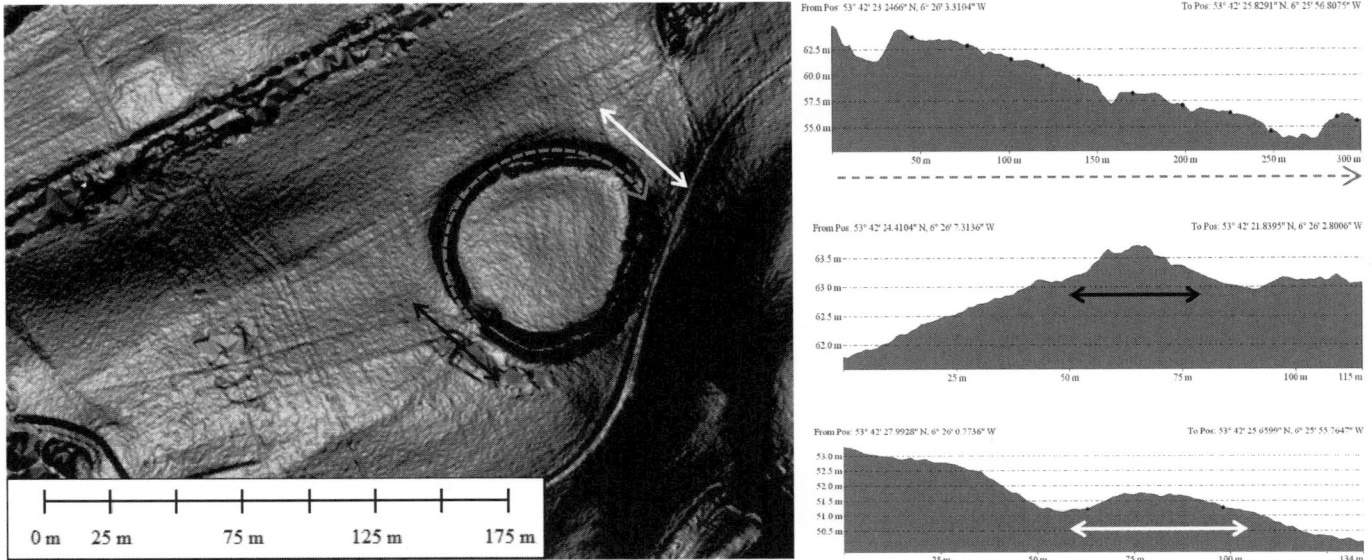

FIGURE 7: DOWTH HENGE (SITE Q AT BRÚ NA BÓINNE). LEFT - SLOPE-SHAPED DIGITAL ELEVATION MODEL (DEM) SHOWING SCARPING AROUND THE CONVEX INTERIOR AND THE FAINT OUTLINE OF AN INTERNAL ENCLOSURE BESIDE THE SOUTH-WEST ENTRANCE. RIGHT - CIRCUMFERENTIAL SECTION (ALONG DASHED LINE) SHOWING ENTRANCES WITH ASSOCIATED EXTERIOR RAISED AREAS (BLACK AND WHITE ARROWS).

passage tomb. It is a massive site, *c*.160m in external diameter with substantial remaining banks up to *c*.2m high in places and exceptionally broad (*c*.35m). Both Site P and its sister site in Newgrange townland, Site A, are unusual in that they have a second, associated enclosure which takes the form of an alcove abutting the main enclosure, to the east at Site P and the northeast at Site A. At Site P this alcove encloses the one clear entrance which faces due east. A second entrance to the site has been suggested to lie directly opposite in the western bank, where a clear break in the crop mark delimiting the bank is evident (1995 OSI AP). On the surface, however, there is no clear break in the bank coincident with this second entrance and it may represent a difference in bank construction, a possible repair or an earlier entrance feature. Both the interior and exterior of the Site P enclosure show some slight scarping but this is almost invisible without advanced visualisation techniques.

With the exception of the additional alcove, the interior form evident at Newgrange Site P is prevalent among the Boyne enclosures, with examples at Newgrange Site A, Rathcarran, Fourknocks/Micknanstown, Corballis and Carranstown. In the majority of cases the remaining bank section is considerably less imposing than at Site P, often less than 0.5m in height. As a broad definition, these are large sites, usually in excess of 100m in diameter (although Fourknocks/Micknanstown is an exception at *c*.65m). Typically they are located on very slightly sloping ground in lowland, floodplain situations, making one bank of the enclosure appear slightly elevated. Recent geophysical survey at the Carranstown example (Davis *st* al. 2011) revealed an archaeologically quiet space, with the

interior of the enclosure showing even less activity than the exterior. No ditching of any description was evident through magnetometric survey and the enclosing bank also yielded almost no magnetometric signal, suggesting that bank construction (i.e. presence or absence of stone revetment) may vary on a site by site basis.

Despite a similar external diameter to Newgrange Sites A and P, Dowth henge is in most other ways substantially different from the other large Boyne enclosures (Figure 7). In shape it is ovoid, narrowing to a point in the northeast and flattened to the southwest, as opposed to the subcircular plan of Sites A and P. It has high (in excess of 4m in places) banks which are not flattened; these are interrupted by two breaks (measuring c. 15 m), one towards the northeast, the other to the southwest. There has been some debate regarding the originality of both entrances. One of the authors (Stout 1991, 259) for example has previously suggested that the external form of the northeast entrance, considered in the context of mapping evidence, points to this being a later feature. Morphologically, however, there appears to be little difference between the internal and external form of the two gaps. Furthermore the presence of a raised 'routeway' feature, running from the banks of the Boyne east of Clogherlea stone circle and through Dowth henge, passing through both entrances, suggests that the northeast entrance is at least of some antiquity.

While the main group of Boyne enclosures have a saucer-like profile, with little to no obvious rise towards their centre, at Dowth this profile is inverted owing to the obvious internal scarping from which much of the bank material was presumably derived. Local Relief Modelling

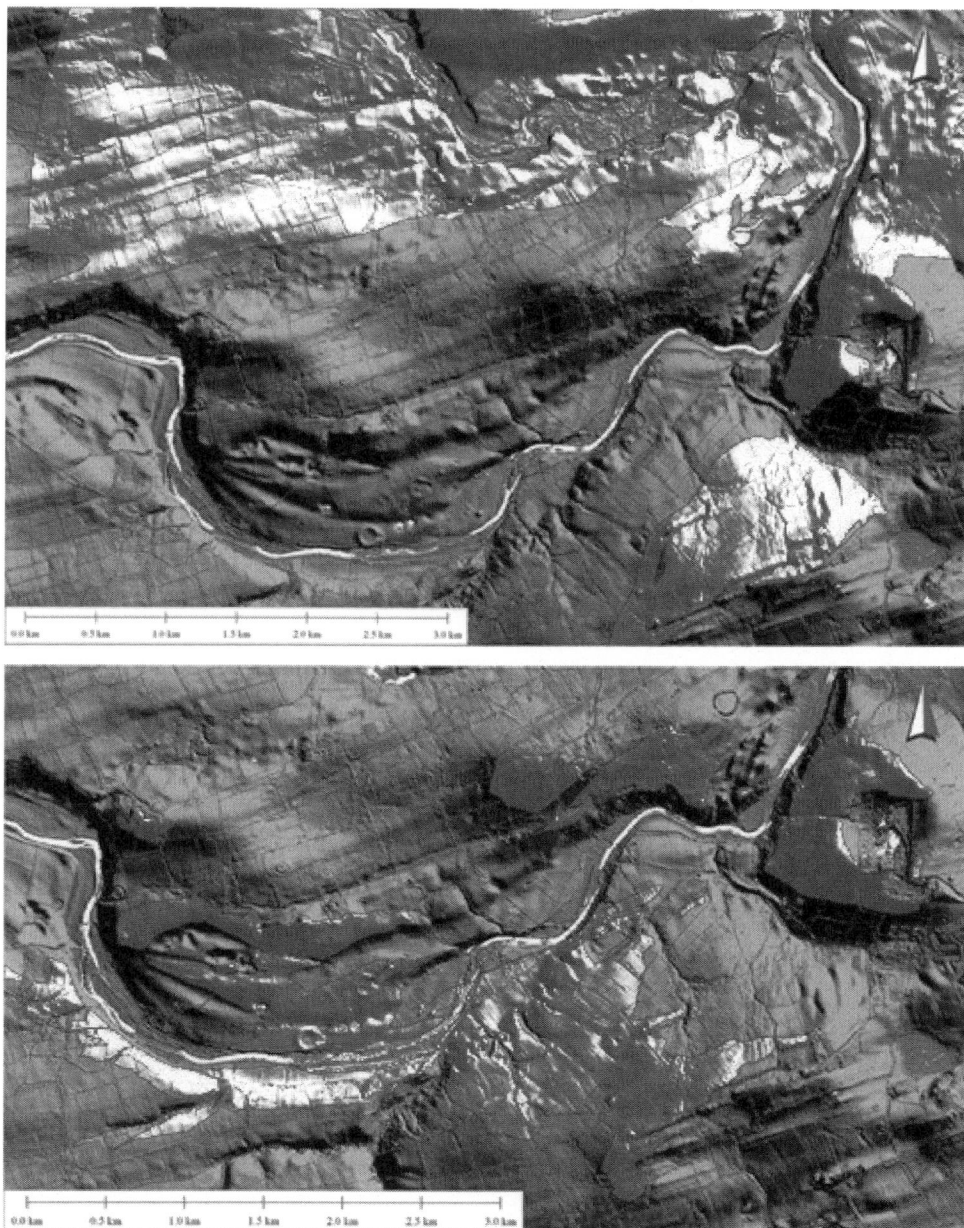

Figure 8: Viewshed analysis. Upper - Views to Dowth henge from Brú na Bóinne region. The transmitter and receiver heights were both set to 2m, the transmitter located on the highest point of the bank to provide maximum visibility (Note lack of visibility from within Brú na Bóinne itself). Lower - View to Site P. Again the transmitter and receiver heights were set to 2m but in this case the transmitter was placed centrally within the enclosure to demonstrate this site's contrasting lack of seclusion.

(Hesse 2010) also demonstrates that scarping has also occurred external to the bank. This echoes the mode of construction seen at Balregan, Co. Louth where internal and external ditches were excavated.

The aspect of Dowth henge also differs substantially from the other enclosures within the Brú na Bóinne Heritage Site (Figure 3). While Newgrange Sites A and P are unquestionably low lying, occupy relatively flat terrain, and are considerably overlooked both by the Newgrange ridge and the south bank of the Boyne, Dowth henge is in an elevated location and is notable for being one of the least visible monuments within the entire Brú na Bóinne landscape (Figure 8). Furthermore, Dowth henge is situated upon a significant slope, the lowest section facing downwards towards the river and away from the great passage tomb mounds. This suggests that while the presence of such a monumental ritual enclosure in proximity to the similarly monumental tumuli is hardly coincidental, its association is perhaps more with the Boyne itself than with earlier Neolithic monuments.

Within the Meath enclosures, the closest parallel for Dowth henge is the largely destroyed site at Heathtown (Stout 1991, 259-60). While only two short sections of upstanding bank remain, traces of approximately half of the circumference arc still visible through aerial photography and survey. These define a site that would have been strongly flattened on one face (the northeast), reminiscent of the southwest face of the Dowth henge. However, the absence of the southwestern portion of Heathtown means that its full form is unknown. Heathtown occupies a small rise in otherwise low-lying ground and domes noticeably towards the centre (again, like Dowth). Where they still remain, the banks are sharp and moderately high (2-2.5m); however, the scarping at Heathtown is less clear, with a relatively narrow inner ditch (c.3.5m across) and potentially traces of a slight outer ditch. A recent magnetometer survey at the site implies some relatively ephemeral features within the enclosure, in particular several small circular anomalies and a series of high-intensity ferrous signals grouped at the highest point of the site (Davis st al. 2011). Survey also highlights the presence of a *bona fide* internal ditch as opposed to merely a scarped area, suggesting a genuine parallel with British henge monuments (as well as similarities with potential Irish parallels such as Ráith na Ríg on the Hill of Tara, Co. Meath).

Of the other Meath sites with some resemblance to Dowth, consideration should also be extended to Stackallan and the sites at Irishtown/Kilbrew (Stout 1991, 263-4). Stackallan once again occupies a position just off the crest of a rise, in this case on the western bank of a low hill. It is slightly ovoid in form, though not as clearly as Dowth Henge, being slightly flattened to the southwest. Somewhat like Dowth, the site is visually isolated from the surrounding landscape. Indeed, viewshed analysis indicates that the interior of the site is almost totally hidden from external viewpoints. This is not the first time that henge enclosures have been characterized as screens (Bradley 2007, 128). The site again slopes considerably, with the lowest point being located in the southwest corner. The bank morphology is again sharp, and a slight outer ditch is evident in profile. However, the interior of the site shows no evidence for scarping and has a smooth, saucer-shaped profile akin to Newgrange Sites P and A at the Brú na Bóinne Heritage Site.

The two sites at Irishtown and Kilbrew again occupy moderately high ground and are not overlooked by other areas in the vicinity. The Irishtown enclosure is a particularly unusual example, effectively enclosing the base of a low hill within a monumental bank. While in its current form this is less than 0.5m in height, it is very broad (c.25m). This is a strikingly large enclosure, measuring c.230m in external diameter, and represents a significant construction effort. It is subcircular, with some sections (most notably to the north and west) straight-banked. Rather than being centred on a slight rise, in the case of Irishtown the central portion of the enclosure is c.6m higher than the surrounding bank. The adjacent enclosure at Kilbrew is placed similarly to those

at Stackallan and Dowth, just off a slight rise. While the exterior banks of Irishtown and Kilbrew are intervisible there is no visual connection between the interior of the two enclosures, even accounting for the elevated nature of the central portion of the Irishtown site. Once again, the best preserved bank sections at Kilbrew have a sharp profile, while, owing to its position spanning a slight ridge, the interior of the site rises to a slight dome when viewed from a NW-SE direction.

Possible precursors and adjuncts: Newgrange Site A and Dowth henge.

As previously described, Newgrange Sites A and P possess an unusual annex-like feature, clearly encompassing the entrance at Site P and probable entrance at Site A. The sequence of construction here is unclear. It is possible that the annex structures might represent earlier enclosures which have been partly overbuilt in the construction of the large enclosures, or they may delineate contemporary entrance features or even later additions. Aerial imagery implies that they are at least of different construction to the main enclosing bank. In older imagery a clear parch-mark is visible around the inner shoulder of the main bank, mirroring the stone revetment recorded by Collins (1957) at Ballynahatty. This is absent from the annex feature. The manner of construction is clarified somewhat by later imagery (1995 OSI) which shows a double parchmark for Newgrange Site P – the main internal bank ghosted by a narrow external parchmark which is contiguous with the eastern annex. The construction sequence at Ballynahatty is hypothesised to have incorporated an external gravel 'guide' enclosure as a possible precursor to the main monument. Given the contiguous nature of the external parchmark and the annex, coupled with the very similar intensity of the parchmark in both cases it seems likely that the manner of construction here is similar and that the annex is not immediately contemporary with the main enclosure. It is not beyond the bounds of possibility that the very low profile Newgrange Site LP1 which has a limited magnetometric signature represents such a guide enclosure where a more substantial enclosure was never constructed (Davis st al. 2010).

At Newgrange Site A the main central enclosure is surrounded by up to three smaller enclosures. One of these, most clearly visible using 'SkyView Factor' (Kokalj st al. 2011) is evident as an additional annex facing approximately northwest. Two further small enclosures are present at the northwest and northeast. These are extremely low profile with a total external vertical height of no more than 15cm and an approximate external diameter of c.75m. They have broad, flat-topped banks, in excess of 12m in diameter and could themselves be classified as embanked enclosures. At the Dowth henge, a low-profile enclosure with a diameter of c.60m is visible just inside the southwest entrance. This subsidiary enclosure appears 'D-shaped' in form, owing to its southwestern portion having apparently been removed by scarping in the construction of the bank section. Rather than directly opposite the entrance, the subsidiary enclosure is located slightly to the north of the entranceway. The apparent removal of a portion of this internal enclosure in the construction of the main bank suggests that it predates either the main phase of bank construction or a post-construction phase of bank remodelling. The presence of these smaller enclosures at Newgrange Site A and Dowth henge suggests that such smaller enclosures might have been complete circles preceding the large enclosures.

The immediate environment of Dowth henge is somewhat complicated by its historic past. Early ordnance survey mapping of the Dowth estate include both a race course and deer park, alongside numerous 'tree rings', clustered in the vicinity of the henge itself. Some of these are still visible as tree rings in the current landscape, while others remain as crop marks only. Without further testing it is impossible to determine whether these represent later demesne features or are potentially archaeological in origin. If related to the henge they would be reminiscent of the situation at Lisnalurg located southwest of Carrowmore in Co. Sligo, where a circular embankment forms a rim around a hollow in which a circular earthwork (internal diameter *c*.75m) is centrally located.

Landscape characteristics

In some areas of Ireland, clusters of embanked enclosures are evident (Table 1). Of these, the Brú na Bóinne World Heritage Site is most notable, with Fourknocks, the Lee Valley and the Boyle area of Roscommon also representing clusters of three or more sites, generally within *c*.2km of each other and sometimes (e.g. at Brú na Bóinne) much less. However, clustering does not appear to be a universal phenomenon, with many sites standing in apparent isolation.

Similarly, while some sites are apparently focussed on areas of significant earlier Neolithic activity (again the Boyne and Fourknocks are obvious examples, with the Tralee group in proximity to the supposed passage tomb at Ballycarty) this is not always especially clearcut (e.g. the Roscommon group). While a number of sites are located within perhaps 2km of passage tomb(s) it is debatable how important this proximity may have been in determining the location of the enclosure. Numerous significant clusters of passage tombs (in particular upland clusters) are, as yet, lacking any recognised embanked enclosure within their vicinity. While this may be a function of our inability to actually locate these sites within the landscape, it may suggest that the presence of a passage tomb was perhaps not the defining factor in locating such enclosures. It is plausible to suggest that the same criteria may have been important in choosing the location of both enclosure and tomb.

The range of physical locations for these enclosures is somewhat variable. While many (e.g. Dowth , Heathtown, Carranstown, Ballyseedy, Stackallan, Irishtown) occupy locally high ground or encompass a low rise, thereby restricting views to the interior of the site while maximising views from its exterior, this is by no means always the case, as is clear in the case of Newgrange Sites A and P. Here the chosen location appears to be at the base of a river terrace. Similar locations are evident at Site LP1, Balrath and Tonafortes (Co. Sligo), with the terrace edge perhaps emphasising the height of one slope of the enclosure.

As discussed earlier, while henge sites may have their roots in the late Neolithic – with suggestion of earlier origins such as the mid-Neolithic date and Carrowkeel bowl from Monknewtown and abundant broad-rimmed pottery at Balregan – their role as *foci* within the landscape persisted through time, in some cases to the early medieval period and beyond, as exemplified for example by the siting of a tower house within the enclosure at Kilbrew or the occurrence of a likely early-medieval settlement at Rath Maeve. While the lack of sound chronological framework is clearly an issue, in some cases these sites appear to be situated within and perhaps central to landscapes featuring contemporary or slightly earlier or later archaeological activity

Into the future

In spite of efforts by a small group of authors to draw attention to these monument types, supplemented by data from excavations old and new, and the appearance of invaluable reviews over the past twenty years, this overview reveals that our knowledge of the broad range of Irish henges beyond the Boyne Valley remains partial and haphazard. Even within the Boyne Valley and wider Co. Meath region where the embanked enclosure variant has received considerable attention over the years, recent analysis of LiDar data demonstrates how many potential sites have previously remained undiscovered and how much more there is to be revealed about basic issues like the topographical context of henges. In addition no relatively intact example in the core Boyne Valley region has yet been comprehensively excavated as a research project, although Finola Carroll's work at Rath Maeve near the Hill of Tara may go some way towards filling the void. As Bradley has noted, henges are only one form of several ritual enclosure types to be found in Ireland, ranging from the Neolithic to the Iron Age. Initially a regional approach may prove to be rewarding, involving localized surveys in which henge variants may be identified amongst the variety of other circular enclosures.

Assuming Tonafortes in Co. Sligo is a genuine henge, which in spite of the limited evidence is a reasonable assumption, it raises the possibility that the double bank with intervening ditch at this site may be a regional feature. As seen above, the enclosures in the wider Boyne/Delvin region of Co. Meath are not uniform in structure but most are based on a univallate template. Another interesting feature of the Tonafortes specimen is its relatively smaller diameter (85m including the outer bank) by comparison with the Boyne Valley embanked enclosures which range upwards from more than 100m. On the other hand most of the suggested examples in Limerick and Kerry have smaller diameters than Tonafortes. The implication of a regional variation from east to west supports the existence of regional groups defined on the basis of enclosure structure in Ireland and Britain (Wainwright 1969, 114-116). On the other hand, the chonological intricacies revealed at excavated sites and the difficulty of establishing a date for the earthwork itself at some of these shows that regional variation may not be the only factor at play. As in Britain, henges in Ireland are resistant to easy generalizations. This underlines the need for a coordinated study of henges across Britain and Ireland, generating comparative data and insights from well chosen regional surveys.

References

Bradley, R. 2007. *The Prehistory of Britain and Ireland*, Cambridge: Cambridge University Press.

Bradley, R. 2011. *Stages and Screens: An Investigation of Four Henge Monuments in Northern and Northeastern Scotland*. Edinburgh: Society of Antiquaries of Scotland.

Buckley, V.M. 1988. Ireland's Stonehenge - a lost antiquarian monument rediscovered, *Archaeology Ireland*, 2 (2), 53-4.

Cody, E. 2002. A complex of prehistoric monuments at Banagher, County Cavan, *Journal of the Royal Society of Antiquaries of Ireland*, 132, 77-98.

Collins, A.E.P. 1957. Excavations of the Giants Ring, Ballynahatty. *Ulster Journal of Archaeology*, 20, 44-50.

Condit, T. 1993. Ritual enclosures near Boyle, Co. Roscommon, *Archaeology Ireland*, 7 (1), 14-16.

Condit, T. 1996. Late Neolithic ritual – earthen ceremonial enclosures, *Archaeology Ireland*, 11(3), *Brú na Bóinne* supplement.

Condit, T. and Gibbons, M. 1988. A henge-type monument at Castletown, Co. Waterford, *Decies*, 37, 4-7.

Condit, T. and Grogan, E. 1994. The later prehistoric landscape of southeast Clare, *The Other Clare*, 18, 8-12.

Condit, T. and Simpson, D.D.A. 1998. Irish hengiform enclosures and related monuments: a review. In Gibson, A. and Simpson, D.D.A (eds), 45-61.

Connolly, M. and Condit, T. 1998. Ritual enclosures in the Lee valley, Co. Kerry, *Archaeology Ireland*, 12 (4), 8-12.

Cooney, G. 2000. *Landscapes of Neolithic Ireland*. London: Routledge.

Cunningham, G. 1987. *The Anglo-Norman Advance into the South-West Midlands of Ireland*, 1185-1221. Roscrea: Parkmore Press.

Danaher, E. 2004. Symbolic enclosure: A tantalising Neolithic space in the north-west, *Archaeology Ireland*, 19(4), 18-21.

Danaher, E. 2005. Tonafortes: A ceremonial enclosure in county Sligo, *Archaeology Ireland*, 20(3), 12-15.

Danaher, E. 2007. *Monumental beginnings: The archaeology of the N4 Sligo InnerRelief Road*, 43-59. Dublin: NRA.

Davis, S. Megarry, W., Brady, C., Lewis, H., Cummins, T., Guinan, L., Turnere, J., Gallagher, C., Brown, T. and Meehan, R. 2010. *Boyne Valley Landscapes Project: Phase III Final Report 2010*. Kilkenny: Heritage Council.

Eogan, G. & Roche, H. 1997. *Excavations at Knowth*, 2. Dublin: Royal Irish Academy.

Fenwick, J. and Newman, C. 2002. Geomagnetic Survey on the Hill of Tara, Co. Meath, 1998-9, *Discovery Programme Reports* 6, 1-17.

Fitzpatrick, M. 2008. http://www.excavations.ie/Pages/Details.php?Year=&County=Wicklow&id=4125

Gibbons, M. 1990. The archaeology of early settlement in Co. Kilkenny. In Nolan, W. and Whelan, K. (eds) *Kilkenny: History and Society*, 1-32. Dublin: Geography Publications.

Gibson, A. and Sheridan, A. 2004. *From Sickles to Circles: Britain and Ireland at the Time of Stonehenge*. Stroud: Tempus.

Gibson, A. and. Simpson, D.D.A (eds), 1998. *Prehistoric Ritual and Religion*. Stroud: Sutton Publishing.

Grogan, E. 2005. *The North Munster Project* (two volumes). Dublin: Wordwell.

Grogan, E. 2008. *The Rath of the Synods, Tara, Co. Meath: Excavations by Seán P. Ó Ríordáin*. Dublin: Wordwell.

Hartwell, B. 1998. The Ballynahatty complex. In A. Gibson and D.D.A. Simpson (eds), 1998, 32-44.

Heritage Council. undated. http://heritagecouncil.ie/unpublished_excavations/section10.html

Herity, M. and Eogan, G. 1977. *Ireland in Prehistory*, London: Routledge & Kegan Paul Ltd. Reprinted 1996.

Hesse, R. 2010. LiDar-derived Local Relief Models – a new tool for archaeological prospection. *Archaeological Prospection*, 17, 67-72.

Kelly, E. and Condit, T. 1998. Limerick's Tara, *Archaeology Ireland*, 12 (2), 18-22.

Kendrick, T. and Hawkes, C. 1932. *Archaeology in England and Wales 1914-1931*. London: Methuen.

Kokalj, Ž., Zakšek, K. and Oštir, K., 2011. Application of sky-view factor for the visualization of historic landscape features in LiDar-derived relief models. *Antiquity*, 85, 263-73.

Moore, L. 1918-21. Notes, *Journal of the Kildare Archaeological Society*, 11, 199-200.

Moore, M. 2003. *The Archaeological Inventory of County Leitrim*, Dublin: Stationery Office.

Newman, C. 1997. *Tara – An Archaeological Survey*. Discovery Programme Monographs, 2. Dublin: Royal Irish Academy.

O'Brien, W. 2004 (Con)fusion of tradition? The circle henge in Ireland. In Gibson and Sheridan (eds), 2004, 323-338.

O'Donnchadha, B. 2006. Balregan henge. In Bennett, I. (ed.) *Excavations 2003: Summary accounts of archaeological excavations in Ireland*, 324 (91221). Dublin: Wordwell.

O'Kelly, M. J. 1942. A survey of the antiquities in the barony of Small County, Co. Limerick, *North Munster Archaeological Journal*, 3 (2), 75-97.

O'Kelly, M. J. 1944. A survey of the antiquities in the barony of Small County, Co. Limerick, *North Munster Archaeological Journal,* 4 (1), 16-53.

O'Kelly, M.J. 1989. *Early Ireland: an introduction to Irish Prehistory*. Cambridge: Cambridge University Press.

Ó Nualláin, S. and Cody, E. 1996 A re-examination of four sites in Grange townland, Lough Gur, Co. Limerick, *North Munster Antiquarian Journal,* 37, 3-14.

Ó Ríordáin, S.P. 1951. Lough Gur Excavations: The Great Stone Circle (B) in Grange Townland, *Proceedings of the Royal Irish Academy,* 54C, 37-74.

Ó Ríordáin, S.P. 1953. *Antiquities of the Irish Countryside* (third edition). London: Methuen.

O'Sullivan, M. 2005. *Duma na nGiall: The Mound of the Hostages, Tara.* Dublin: Wordwell.

Roche, H. 2002. Excavations at Ráith na Ríg, Tara, Co. Meath, 1997. *Discovery Programme Reports,* 6, 19-82.

Roche, H. 2004. The dating of the embanked stone circle at Grange, Co. Limerick. In H. Roche, E. Grogan, J. Bradley, J. Coles and B. Raftery, *From Megaliths to Metals: Essays in Honour of George Eogan*, 109-116. Oxford: Oxbow.

Simpson, D.D.A. 1993. Dún Ruadh – a real Irish henge. *Archaeology Ireland,* 7(2), 14-15.

Smyth, J. 2008. *Brú na Bóinne World Heritage Site: Research Framework*, Consultation Draft. Kilkenny: Heritage Council.

Stout, G. 1991. Embanked enclosures of the Boyne region, *Proceedings of the Royal Irish Academy,* 91C, 245-284.

Stout, G. 1997. The Bend of the Boyne, County Meath. In F.H.A. Aalen, K. Whelan and M. Stout, *Atlas of the Irish Rural Landscape*, 299-315 Cork: Cork University Press.

Sweetman, P.D. 1971. An earthen enclosure at Monknewtown, Slane: Preliminary Report, *Journal of the Royal Society of Antiquaries of Ireland,* 101, 135-40.

Sweetman, P.D. 1976. An earthen enclosure at Monknewtown, Slane, Co. Meath. *Proceedings of the Royal Irish Academy,* 76C, 25-72.

Thornton, G. M. [Stout, G.] 1980. *A survey of the earthen enclosures of the Boyne Valley and related sites*, unpublished M.A. thesis, University College, Dublin.

Timoney, M. 1984. Earthen burial sites on the Carrowmore peninsula, Co. Sligo. In Burenhault, G., *The Archaeology of Carrowmore*, 319-25. Stockholm: University of Stockholm.

Toal, C. 1995. *North Kerry Archaeological Survey*. Tralee: FAS.

Topping, P. 1992. The Penrith Henges: A survey by the Royal Commission on the Historical Monuments of England, *Proceedings of the Prehistoric Society,* 58, 249-64.

Waddell, J. 1998. *The Prehistoric Archaeology of Ireland*. Galway: Galway University Press.

Wainwright, G. L. 1969. A review of henges in the light of recent research, *Proceedings of the Prehistoric Society,* 35, 112-33.

Journeys and Juxtapositions. Marden Henge and the View from the Vale

Jim Leary and David Field

Abstract

This short paper sets out a summary of a project to investigate the henge at Marden and its surroundings in the Vale of Pewsey, which includes an excavation carried out in 2010 across the footprint of the now demolished Neolithic mound known as the Hatfield Barrow and the discovery of a well-preserved Neolithic building surface and midden. It argues that whilst archaeologists have traditionally focussed on the Wessex chalk upland, the real action happened in the river valleys, with rivers and springs being of particular significance to communities during the Neolithic period.

Keywords: River, valley, Greensand, henge enclosure, mound, sweat lodge, feasting

Introduction

It is easy to presume that all the great Neolithic Wessex monuments are situated on chalk. The Wessex chalkland sites have been, and continue to be, well researched and extensively excavated (see Pollard this volume). Monuments on these upland areas have enjoyed a very different later history to the lowland vales, which in the case of the latter's has not generally favoured the preservation of prehistoric monuments. The higher chalk has been somewhat more insignificant in historic times, considered poor for cultivation and marginal for settlement. The porous nature of the chalk and low water retention makes it difficult, without dewponds or modern water stands, to even graze cattle throughout the year. In contrast, the lower lying areas, particularly the spring line of the Greensand bench, have rich fertile soils that are highly suitable for agriculture and settlement. This unfortunately also means that traces of earlier activity tend to be destroyed (Field 2008; Field 2011; Field et al. in press).

The Vale of Pewsey, for example, is a west to east oriented valley, some 5-7km wide that is situated between the escarpments of Salisbury Plain and Marlborough Downs. This low-lying area would appear on the face of it to be largely devoid of monumental activity. As a result, it is excluded from the Stonehenge and Avebury World Heritage Site, which covers only the chalk upland zones to the south and north respectively; the Vale separating the WHS into two areas. This is despite the fact that the Pewsey Vale contains the largest Neolithic henge in the British Isles: Marden henge (also dubbed the Hatfield Enclosure in English Heritage literature).

The monument is located immediately north of the village of Marden, close to one of the sources of the River Avon (Figure 1). The underlying geology for the most part of the Vale is Upper Greensand, which until recently has been unresponsive to cropmarks and magnetic signals making aerial photography and geophysical prospection unrewarding. Further, the rich and fertile nature of the land with well-drained loamy soils has led to repeated cultivation during the historic period and the subsequent destruction of all but the most intractable of earthworks.

It is not difficult to see how a certain belief that few prehistoric monuments ever existed there prevails, and why archaeologists are drawn away towards the bright lights of the chalk uplands.

The Hatfield Barrow is a good example of this wanton destruction. The Reverend John Mayo described this large conical mound that once stood in the centre of Marden henge as 'about 70 or 80 yards diameter and about 30 feet high' (64-73m diameter by 9m high) (Gough 1806, 159), and it was said to be the second largest in Wiltshire after Silbury Hill (letter to Salisbury Journal Monday December 2, 1776). It was evidently under the plough before 1789 (Withering 1822, 210–48: ref to Marden 236), and by 1806 its height had been reduced to 22.5 feet (7m) (Hoare 1821, 5–6) as a result of cultivation; indeed Cunnington was able to report that the wheat harvested from the mound produced 'six Sacks' [of grain] (Cunnington MSS, Devizes Museum).

Following the excavation of a shaft from the summit to the base in 1807 by Richard Hoare and William Cunnington, which recovered animal bone, pottery and 'two small parcels of burned human bones' (Hoare 1821, 6), the shaft collapsed. Hoare subsequently noted that 'On revisiting this ground in the autumn of 1818, I had the unexpected mortification to find that the great barrow had been completely levelled to the ground, and no signs remained of its previous existence' (Hoare 1821, 7). The drive for intensive cultivation in the area had evidently led directly to demolition of the Hatfield Barrow; albeit the farmer taking advantage of the damage caused by the antiquarians.

Despite this however, the henge bank that surrounds the site has survived the intervening millennia reasonably well in places, a testament to its size perhaps, whilst a circular enclosure of similar diameter to the Hatfield Barrow, located in the southern part of the henge, has endured extraordinarily well; although that did not always seem to have been its fate. Hoare recalled of the southern enclosure: 'In digging within the area, we found a few bits of old pottery and a little charred wood, but no marks of any interment. Its elegant form has been much defaced by tillage and soon will probably be entirely lost' (Hoare

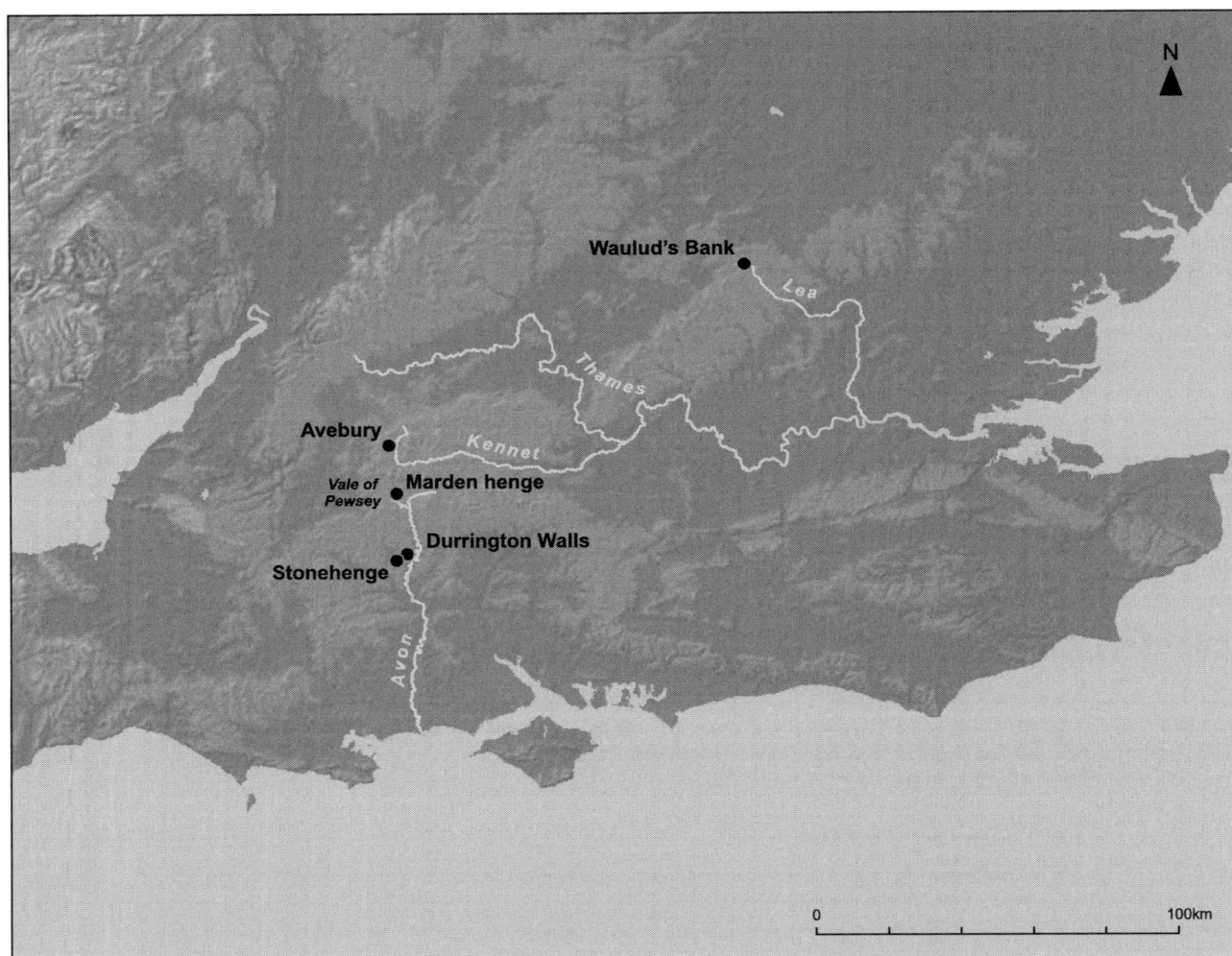

FIGURE 1: LOCATION MAP SHOWING MARDEN HENGE AT THE HEAD OF THE RIVER AVON, WITH DURRINGTON WALLS AND STONEHENGE. ALSO SHOWN ARE AVEBURY HENGE AT THE HEAD OF THE RIVER KENNET AND WAULUD'S BANK AT THE HEAD OF THE RIVER LEA (©EDDIE LYONS/ENGLISH HERITAGE).

1821, 7). Thankfully it was not and it remains today as a dramatic feature within Marden henge.

In more recent times, Marden henge has seen very little research, especially when compared to the henge enclosures on the chalk upland. Geoffrey Wainwright carried out some exploratory excavations there in 1969 in order to compare the site with the recently excavated Durrington Walls henge and to ascertain whether wooden structures similar to those at Durrington existed at Marden (Wainwright et al., 1971). He focused on the northern of two entrances and recovered material that confirmed the Neolithic nature of the site (Fig. 2). Trenches placed at the terminals revealed that the ditch was originally some 2m deep and 13.5m wide. A considerable amount of Grooved Ware pottery along with antler picks and lithic material was recovered from these trenches. Just within the northeast entrance lay a possible circular timber structure. A skeleton of a young female was also recovered from relatively high up in the enclosure ditch and is likely to be later in date.

It was the desire to understand the Neolithic use of the Vale of Pewsey in light of recent re-analysis of a number of the Neolithic monuments on the chalk that led to the development of an English Heritage project focussing on Marden henge and the area surrounding it. Initially a series of non-intrusive surveys were undertaken, including a topographic survey (Figure 2), geophysical survey and aerial survey (Field et al. 2011). The aerial survey had a wider remit and took in much of the Vale of Pewsey for the English Heritage National Mapping Programme. This discovered that the Vale is far from devoid of prehistoric monumental activity with evidence for what could be a long mortuary enclosure alongside another henge to the south of that reported here and not far away a ring-ditch cemetery as well as a possible long barrow (Carpenter and Winton 2011). As a result, questions raised by the surveys regarding Marden henge were targeted by excavation and three areas were excavated in four trenches from June to September 2010 (Figure 2). These areas were the location of the Hatfield Barrow, a newly identified southeastern entranceway and the inner enclosure to the south.

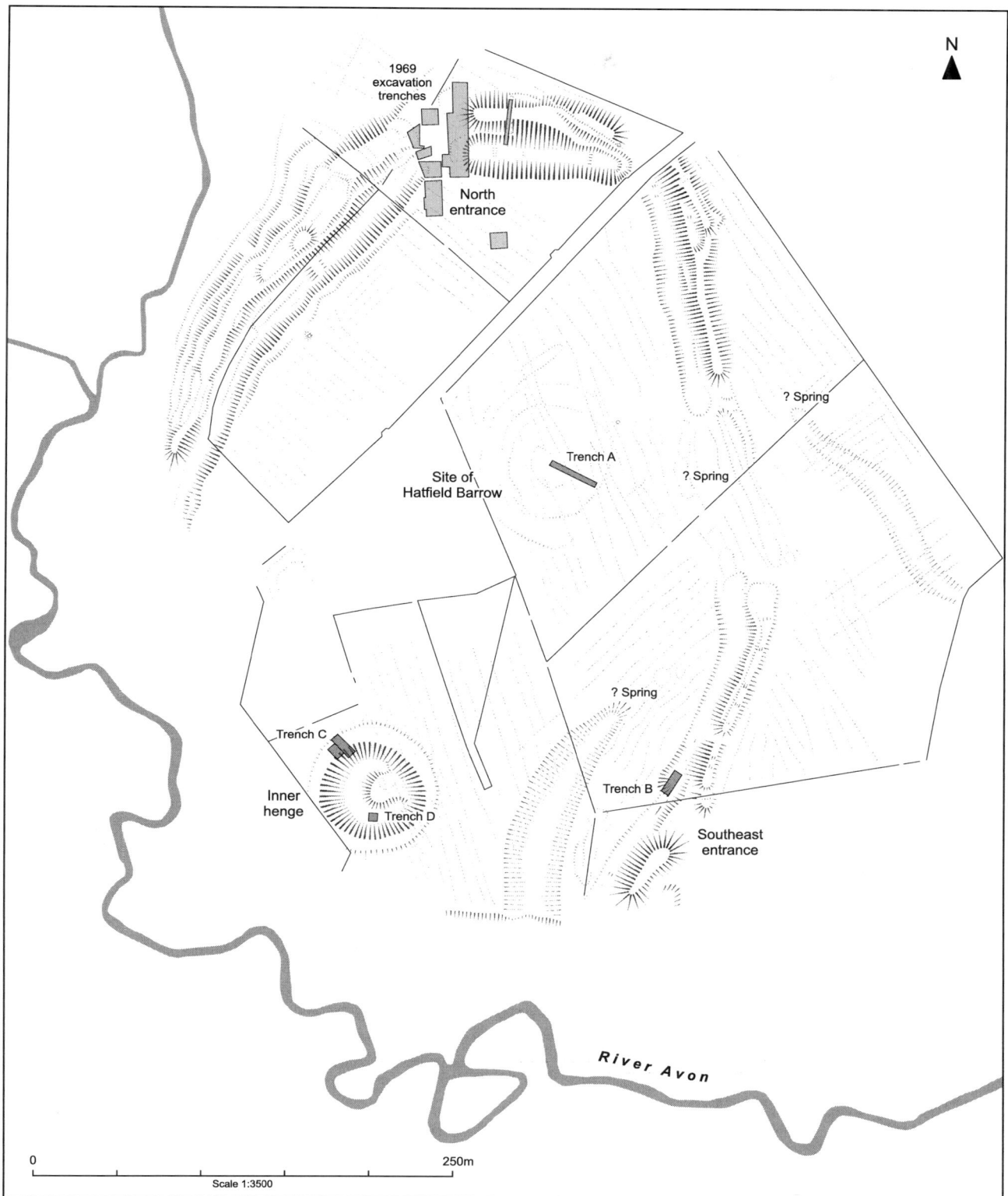

Figure 2: The topographic survey of Marden henge showing the entrances and internal features, such as the site of the Hatfield Barrow, the inner enclosure, and possible springs. Also shown are the trench locations (1969 and 2010). Note the proximity of the River Avon. (©Eddie Lyons/English Heritage).

The henge enclosure

The lowland setting of Marden and the brooks, streams and springs are of interest and perhaps key to understanding it. Marden henge itself is set hard against the floodplain (here less than 200m wide) of one branch of the River Avon, which rises nearby at Beechingstoke and is supplemented by a number of small rivulets fed by springs in the immediate locality. Island place names such as Patney and Pewsey emphasise that much of the area is low-lying and provide a reminder that the northern part of Beechingstoke Parish lay on the edge of Cannings Marsh (Field et al. 2011). Enclosing an area of 11ha within its ditch, the Marden henge enclosure is larger than its major Wessex counterparts, whilst its unusual irregular U-shaped plan form is dramatically different. The English Heritage surveys indicate that it comprises a series of four straight lengths of apparently uncoordinated earthwork bank with associated internal ditch sections, each of which is in excess of 100m long (Figure 2; Field et al. 2011). These lengths are separate but conjoined and clearly it is not a monument of formal plan, but one that has to a certain degree developed *ad hoc*. The river bluff completes the line of the perimeter to the south and emphasises that the relationship of river and enclosure was a close one (Figure 2). In both shape and topographic location Marden henge compares very favourably to the possible henge at Waulud's Bank in Luton, which actually encloses five springs and is located at the source of the River Lea (Fig. 1; Anon 1972; Dyer

1956, 9–16; 1961–3, 57–64; Kennett 1972, 3). However, despite this comparison, the huge Marden enclosure does not easily fit into any classification.

Springs appear to have been incorporated within and around the Marden enclosure and even today when the water companies have taken great quantities out of the aquifer the enclosure ditch still holds water for part of the year. On the east side a break in both bank and ditch coupled with a deviation in its course appears to be influenced by the location of a spring. A little beyond and outside the henge is a sinuous linear depression, which appears to mark the course of a former or seasonal water feature. While another similar linear feature inside the henge starts abruptly to the south of this gap in the earthworks and runs down the slope, discharging into the River Avon (Figure 2). Springs have also been previously noted as feeding into the Hatfield Barrow ditch (see below). The north entrance to the enclosure faces towards the source of the Avon, visible a kilometre away, while the southeast entrance (discovered as a result of the English Heritage survey, which also demonstrated that the previously noted putative eastern entrance was a product of more recent damage) faces towards the farther side of a river meander. It is as though the purpose of the ditch was to metaphysically capture the passage of the water in the north and ease it round the meander loop; certainly, the river appears to be an integral part of the enclosure perimeter, even if the permeable Greensand would not have held flowing

FIGURE 3: THE SOUTHEAST ENTRANCE UNDER EXCAVATION. THE DITCH TERMINAL CAN CLEARLY BE SEEN, AS CAN THE LINEAR ARRANGEMENT OF GRAVEL ALONG THE ENTRANCE, ALIGNED SOUTHEAST NORTHWEST, TO THE RIGHT OF THE PICTURE WITH AN EXCAVATION SLOT THROUGH THEM (ADAM STANFORD, ©AERIAL-CAM/ENGLISH HERITAGE).

water for long (see also Richards 1996). This provides a nuanced perspective in a developing acceptance of ditches as a barrier to malign spirits (Darling 1998; Field 2004; Gibson 2004; for the Bronze Age: Taylor 1951, 132–4; for the Iron Age: Field and Smith 2008; Warner 2000). Here one can also imagine that the entrances could act as foci for a journey or route along the River Avon; a routeway that may have existed long before the henge enclosure (*cf.* Harding this volume; Loveday 1998; for similar ideas regarding hillfort ditches see Field and Smith 2008).

A little over 9m of the henge enclosure ditch was investigated during the 2010 excavation in a trench measuring 15m by 5m, showing that in this area it measured 5m wide and was 2.5m deep, at which point the water table was reached (Figure 2, Trench B; Figure 3). The ditch terminated at this location – the side steeply and smoothly rising up from the base to a rounded, regular end, forming one side of the southeastern entrance to the henge. A series of silty sandy fills were recorded within the ditch cut, and whilst Grooved Ware pottery was recorded throughout this sequence, it was far from a notable assemblage, particularly when compared to that recovered in 1969 from the ditch fills around the northern entrance. In contrast, the struck flint assemblage was comparatively large and included a broken flint stem interpreted as belonging to an arrowhead similar to two others found in the inner henge to the south (below).

Within the southeastern entranceway was a series of compact flint gravel layers clearly forming a deliberately laid surface and sitting within a shallow, linear cut (Figure 3). The gravel deposits were made up of three distinct re-metalling episodes and may well form a routeway into and out of the henge; if so, the projected line would lead southeast down to the River Avon and this may be comparable to the gravel routeway identified leading from the southeastern entranceway to the river at Durrington Walls (see Pollard this volume). Assuming this to be the case, it again highlights the physical connection between the monument and the river, and if the enclosure was placed on a routeway along the River Avon, travellers could continue down to the river and on to Durrington Walls where another gravel routeway would lead them into that henge, and then continuing on to Stonehenge via its routeway and link to the river: the Avenue. Such a journey may have been experienced as a narrative as people moved between monuments.

The Hatfield Barrow

Water may well have also been present around the Hatfield Barrow. The mound was visited by James Norris, a local naturalist, in 1798, who described the huge ditch that surrounded the mound as forming 'a sort of moat, which does not become dry even in the midst of summer' and was fed by springs (Withering 1822), while Richard Hoare in 1812 also noted that the ditch retained water (Hoare 1821). The ditch was cored in 2010 showing it to be around 5m deep (with an organic waterlogged medieval horizon

further up the sequence). The ditch of the Hatfield Barrow was located by all the English Heritage survey techniques which provided accurate locational information, and allowed a trench measuring 13m by 3m to be excavated over the footprint of the mound (Figure 2, Trench A). This uncovered a series of earlier features, the earliest of which were two irregular tree hollows, presumably reflecting an episode of tree clearance, or perhaps storm damage, sometime prior to the construction of the mound. This was overlain by a spread of burnt material containing frequent fragments of hazelnut shell, occasional calcined animal bone fragments, struck flint and twelve fresh sherds of Grooved Ware pottery (representing a minimum of five vessels). A narrow semi-circular gully and two postholes cut this burnt layer, clearly indicating a continuation of activity focused on that area.

The remnants of the Hatfield Barrow mound (only surviving to a height of 0.15m) was recorded over this, and animal bone fragments and struck flint were recovered from it. Cutting this material in what would have been the centre of the mound was a posthole measuring 0.75m in diameter and 0.35m deep with clear traces of a post pipe (with a diameter of 0.12m). This posthole cut the surviving mound material, and given that the posthole was itself likely to have been sealed by further mound material (based on the various suggested heights of the mound), we can propose at least three phases to the mound (mound material, posthole, further mound material). This is based on the limited evidence available, and we may imagine that, like Silbury Hill, it comprised many more phases than this. Like other Neolithic monuments, the mound clearly developed from earlier activity and the area had a demonstrable history.

The ditch surrounding the Hatfield Barrow should have been evident in the southeastern end of the trench; however, an edge was never clearly identified during the excavations and not, in the event, recorded on site. It is likely that significant damage to the edge of the ditch occurred during the process of nineteenth century ground levelling and subsequent ploughing which has made the area where a ditch cut should be evident very ambiguous.

The southern inner enclosure and building surface

Against the southern boundary of the henge, hard against the scarp for the River Avon floodplain lies the enigmatic southern inner enclosure, which was clearly recorded by all the English Heritage surveys (Figure 2). With an internal ditch and external bank nearly 1m high, it could be classified as a henge, although the dramatic profile of the feature provides an impression of an amphitheatre, with a small and slightly domed central area that is lower than the surrounding ground surface and offset to the north, and other interpretations, such as the location of a ritual shaft, can not be ruled out. No entrance is clearly visible, although this may be concealed by a modern hedge line and the effects of ploughing. The overall dimensions, 90m in diameter, are similar to those of the Hatfield

Barrow and it is interesting to note that the north-south paired arrangement is reflected in the north and south circle/barrow features at Avebury, Durrington Walls and Stonehenge.

Excavation in 2010 of part of this inner enclosure proved to be some of the most spectacular on site. A trench was excavated on the northwest side of the bank, whilst a second trench measuring 5m by 5m was opened up over the ditch to the southwest (although this trench was closed after reaching a depth of 1.1m) (Figure 2, Trenches C and D respectively).

The bank was formed of Greensand and contained a rich assemblage of cultural debris such as fragments of animal bone, a broken bone awl, and struck flint, including an extremely well made ripple-flaked oblique arrowhead. Layers of flint gavel were used on the inner scarp of the bank, presumably to stabilise the slope, preventing the sandy bank deposits from being eroded into the ditch below, but possibly also to mark it out in a different colour and surface material. No similar deposit was recorded on the outer edge of the bank. The circular ditch evident on the inside of this bank was presumably also cut at the time the bank was erected, although the cut and primary fills of this ditch were not excavated. An auger was drilled through the fills, showing that the ditch was at least 3.7m deep from the top of ditch fills. Just metres from the floodplain the ditch is likely to have held water and should it have done so, its raised internal area may have stood clear and be connected to some water-related ceremony.

Embedded within this bank sequence was a well-preserved rectangular chalk building surface, which had a large sunken area containing evidence for a hearth in its centre (Figure 4). Whilst analogous to those discovered at Durrington Walls (Pollard this volume), it also shows differences, with a sunken central area and hearth rather than a raised hearth platform. The chalk used to form this surface had been crushed and packed down to create a compact and flat surface. The nearest exposure of this chalk lies some 2km distant, and may well be a deliberate reference or symbolic link to the chalk upland sites. The surface measured 7.4m long (northwest to southeast) and five metres wide (northeast to southwest), and where visible was around 0.1m thick. The southeastern edge of the surface had been damaged slightly, possibly the result of small-scale later ploughing.

The sunken area within the surface was roughly square (3.8m by 3.3m) and sunken by 0.18m below the rest of the surface. Although only the southern quadrant was exposed during this excavation, the chalk used for the sunken area could be seen to continue seamlessly up the inner face to

FIGURE 4: THE MARDEN BUILDING SURFACE. PART OF THE SUNKEN AREA AND HEARTH ARE REVEALED WITHIN THE EXCAVATED QUADRANT. NOTE THE CIRCULAR FEATURE AROUND THE HEARTH. PHOTOGRAPH FACING SOUTHEAST TOWARDS THE CENTRE OF THE INNER ENCLOSURE. THE SCALES ARE BOTH 2M. (©ENGLISH HERITAGE).

join the rest of the surface on the higher level (Figure 4). Along the inner face of the sunken area the chalk appeared to have been re-applied, with a slightly brighter white chalk used for the final skim.

The central part of the sunken area within the building contained evidence for a circular hearth surrounded by a gully or circular feature, and dominated the sunken space (Figure 4). Intense burning had modified the colour of the chalk within the hearth, turning it a pinky-orange colour. Only one quarter of the hearth was exposed during the excavation, but assuming that it is regular, we can interpolate its diameter, including the surrounding feature, as 2m. The building surface, with its white colour, clean, straight lines and circular hearth, to the modern eye at least, has an aesthetic quality.

A discrete deposit of over one hundred sherds of exceptionally decorated Grooved Ware pottery from a minimum of seven vessels was recorded on the southeastern side of the floor surface and clearly indicates a placed deposit, possibly in the entrance of the building. If this was the entrance, it faced southeast towards the centre of the inner enclosure. The sherds were well preserved with a number re-joining. The range of vessels is exceptional, including six jars and a bowl with interior decoration in

the form of lozenges (Russell 2012), whilst sherds from another pot had a very thin coating of bone ash applied to the exterior surface before firing, giving the pot a distinctive cream to light grey colour (White 2012), and one wonders (and technology is not yet able to determine this) whether the ash was formed of animal or human bone.

Outside the building and on the northeastern side was another hearth, this time filled and surrounded by a thick layer of charcoal (Figure 5). The presence of two hearths, one internal and the other external is interesting. One interpretation is that the structure formed a sweat lodge-like building, whereby stones heated in the external fire (which clearly had an open flame) were brought into the structure and placed in the central hearth; water, perhaps obtained from the henge ditch or the Avon, could then be poured on these stones to produce a steam bath or sauna effect, likely as part of a purification ritual (Figure 6). This may explain the considerable quantities of charcoal outside the building but not inside. Large quantities of small but highly burnt sarsen fragments (as one might expect when heating stones to a high temperature) recovered from the charcoal spread around the external hearth certainly seem to support such an interpretation. However the building is interpreted, the internal hearth takes up so much of the sunken floor space that it indicates a focus upon the hearth

FIGURE 5: THE BUILDING SURFACE UNDER EXCAVATION. THIS SHOWS THE TOPOGRAPHIC POSITION OF THE BUILDING ON THE TOP OF THE BANK, WHICH SLOPES DOWN ON THE SOUTHEAST SIDE TOWARDS THE CENTRE OF THE INNER ENCLOSURE. THE EXTERNAL HEARTH AND BURNT SPREAD ARE ON THE FAR SIDE OF THE SURFACE, AND THE MIDDEN IS TO THE BOTTOM RIGHT OF THE PICTURE. THE SUNKEN AREA AND HEARTH ARE YET TO BE EXCAVATED.
(ADAM STANFORD, ©AERIAL-CAM/ENGLISH HERITAGE).

FIGURE 6: A RECENTLY USED SWEAT LODGE (MISSING ITS SKIN COVERING) IN CALIFORNIA, USA IN 2011. IT SHOWS BOTH THE EXTERNAL WOOD FIRE WHERE STONES HAVE BEEN HEATED UP AND THE INTERNAL HEARTH WHERE THE HOT STONES ARE PLACED AND WATER POURED OVER THEM. NOTE THE CHARCOAL SPREAD AROUND THE EXTERNAL FIRE. JUST OUT OF THE FRAME TO THE LEFT IS A PILE OF HEAVILY BURNT STONE. SWEAT LODGES REQUIRE A REGULAR SOURCE OF WATER AND ALTHOUGH NONE IS SEEN IN THIS PHOTOGRAPH, A STREAM RUNS IMMEDIATELY BEHIND THE SWEAT LODGE. PETER TOPPING IS IN THE FOREGROUND WITH DAVID FIELD BEHIND. (©JIM LEARY).

FIGURE 7: PART OF THE MIDDEN TO THE SOUTHWEST OF THE BUILDING. ARTICULATED ANIMAL BONE CAN CLEARLY BE SEEN. (©ENGLISH HERITAGE).

and a function other than a structure in which to live and sleep.

On the opposite side of the building, and again immediately outside, was a midden deposit (Figures 5 and 7). The deposit was dominated by animal bones, mostly pig and representing joints of meat (Figure 7). A number of the bones, particularly the longbones, were scorched, charred and calcined, and fine butchery marks were evident on some of these. The presence of a number of refitting epiphyses together with the lack of gnawing in the bone assemblage indicate that the bones were fresh when deposited and had not been subsequently disturbed (Worley 2012). The pottery from this midden represents the largest assemblage of Grooved Ware from the 2010 excavations, comprising 135 sherds from a minimum of thirteen vessels (Russell 2012). The sherds were large and well preserved and many re-join and are exceptional in terms of their decoration. Three bowls are represented, all with neatly executed internal decoration, as are several decorated jars. Two lug handles are also present, one of which may be anthropomorphic (Russell 2012). A complete bone awl was also recovered.

This midden clearly originated from a single event that involved the preparation of a large amount of food, and it is tempting to see it as the result of a feast, presumably associated with the use of the building or part of a closing ceremony when the structure was demolished; either way the surface, midden and external hearth and associated charcoal spread were buried together. Certainly rather than being evidence for the everyday, the remains appear to be special and whatever went on must have had a significant performative quality – one that involved many people. The sequence has the whiff of the morning after the night before about it; and these activities may well have been accompanied by music, dancing and story telling, temporarily transforming the space and soundscape; a sensuous experience with the smell of roast pork combined with vibrant sights and sounds, aided by the unusual and highly decorated pottery. Such place-temporality gives us a small but vivid and significant insight into one of the transformative activities that went on within the henge enclosure.

The inner enclosure bank was evidently then remodelled as further sandy material was piled over it, sealing the midden, charcoal spread and remains of the chalk surface. It is uncertain how soon after the activity described above this would have been, however, good preservation of the chalk surface and artefacts and ecofacts within the midden suggest that this may have been relatively rapidly completed. This later bank also contained a quantity of cultural material, including animal bones, worked flint (including a small barb possibly from another ripple-flaked arrowhead), Grooved Ware pottery sherds, and a number of fragments of bone pins and awls. The bank was also enhanced at this point with a revetment of Greensand stone blocks – two revetments were recorded on the outer edge and one on the inner. Further bank material overlay this, giving it its final form. These later contexts contained further fresh sherds of Grooved Ware pottery and a small assemblage of struck flint, including another superbly made ripple-flaked oblique arrowhead, which should be considered alongside the other arrowhead mentioned above, as well as the stem from the enclosure ditch (Fig.8). Although these arrowheads and stem were recovered from different phases they are near identical and likely to have

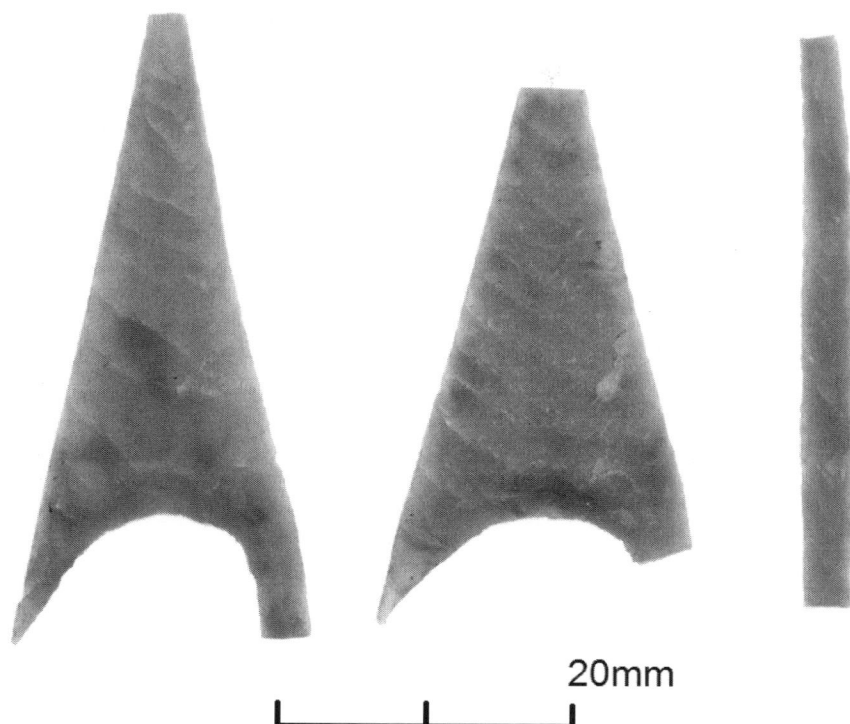

20mm

Figure 8: The Marden ripple-flaked oblique arrowheads and stem.
(Ian Leonard, ©English Heritage).

been made by the same hand (Bishop et al. 2011; Bishop 2012), which perhaps has some bearing on the timing of the phases. They are of outstanding quality and one wonders whether they were items deliberately brought to the site and deposited therein.

The inclusion of this 'event' within the make-up of the bank is of interest, for we should not think of henge banks as simply upcast earth from the ditch. Where excavated, henge banks often show evidence for greater complexity, for example the bank at Woodhenge contains significant quantities of cultural debris (see Pollard this volume), whilst the bank at Avebury, which also had an earlier phase, contained clusters of antlers. The banks therefore contain the power and the evidence of what went before; a material biography of the community. The artefacts and events were contained and wrapped by later bank material; a feature noted within the mound at Silbury Hill (Leary and Field 2010; Leary and Field in press). At Marden, the bank was in effect a linear mound. These events were written into the history of the bank, forming a narrative as they developed and grew. In this way, the materials that made up the banks may be of more importance than the form or shape of the enclosure, challenging our notion of a henge as an architectural blueprint. The question arises as to whether other similar buildings occur elsewhere on, and indeed within, the henge bank. It is perhaps time to revisit other henges and pose certain questions, for example, are the layers of burnt flints recorded in the bank at Woodhenge

(see Pollard this volume) proxy evidence for further sweat lodge type buildings?

Conclusion

The preliminary excavations at Marden henge have provided a glimpse of some of the activities that went on inside the enclosure. Clearly, it was a place with a long history: Mesolithic flints were recovered from the site, both from the 1969 excavations and from 2010, and elsewhere the Greensand incorporates large numbers of Mesolithic flint scatters, and the Vale of Pewsey may too; whilst the features under the Hatfield Barrow evidence prior activity. We can envision this juxtaposition of the past and the present as an interweaving of oral history, stories and the legitimisation and use of space. By modifying the old in favour of the modern, continuities and discontinuities are created in a continual process of imagining and re-imagining.

Clearly multiple activities occurred within the enclosure, which included the possible use of a sweat lodge as well as feasting activity, with its implied large, although perhaps occasional, aggregations of people. Activities included artefacts that can hardly be described as 'everyday', and include at least three exceptional flint arrowheads, as well as an unusually large number of Grooved Ware bowls, all decorated internally with complex motifs, and jars with rare decorative schemes. The fact that a large section of the perimeter incorporates the river as part of the enclosure suggests that a focus upon the river, or access from or to the river, were critical parts of the functionality of the henge. The southeast entrance with its possible southeast aligned routeway, as well as the placed deposit in the southeast of a similarly aligned building all point to the importance of axes, perhaps related to the solstice, or sunrise more generally. If the former, this may imply a calendrical rhythm to some proceedings, alongside other occasional rhythms that may relate to, for example, particular stages of life cycles.

We can also see from this brief discussion that river valleys in the Wessex area offer fertile ground for the study of Neolithic archaeology. The lack of intensive agricultural activity on the chalk downs has led to the good preservation of monuments and attracted ever more archaeological investigation, privileging and indeed fetishizing sites like Stonehenge at the expense of others. This is not to deny the importance of the chalk, or indeed the monuments located on it, but developments in remote sensing and the National Mapping Programme have already demonstrated that a plethora of monuments and ceremonial sites are distributed along river valleys. Perhaps we should now re-focus research excavations away from the Wessex chalk and concentrate efforts on other parts of the drainage basin, particularly where monuments may be threatened by continued agricultural activity.

Indeed, it is perhaps the juxtaposition of the monuments near rivers that is of greatest significance, and it has been suggested that polities are likely to have been based on the drainage pattern (Field 2008). We have argued elsewhere that the enormous Silbury Hill (and Avebury henge) is located at the source of a large and important river system (the Kennet/Thames) flowing west to east (Field et al. in press; Leary 2010; Leary and Field 2010; Leary and Field in press); perhaps Marden, which developed into the largest henge in the country, is equally placed at the head of the River Avon, a north south flowing river system (Figure 1). Their position at the very source of these rivers emphasises ownership, belonging, ancestry, and a right of tenure along the valley, in both metaphysical and practical senses, and it may be no coincidence that the monuments decrease in size the further downstream one travelled. The use of these huge monuments as backstops to different river systems implies that the valleys themselves may well be caught up in different and perhaps competing networks. The river valleys channel movement and create routes, both terrestrial and riverine, and emphasise, metaphorically and literally, the notion of a journey. Marden henge, with its north and southeastern entrances, directed, focused and controlled this movement.

Acknowledgements

We wish to thank all colleagues involved in the successful completion of the Marden henge project, and thank the specialists, particularly Barry Bishop, Mike Russell and Fay Worley, for use of unpublished material, and for their continued analysis. With thanks to Eddie Lyons for producing the figures. We are very grateful to the landowners James Hues and Philip Warner, and tenants Mark and Phillippa Carpenter for all their help; also to Sue Shepherd-Cross for her support. The text has benefitted greatly from discussion with various colleagues, particularly Josh Pollard, Mike Parker Pearson, Dave McOmish and Peter Topping. Jim Leary wrote his contribution to this paper during sabbatical leave from English Heritage as the 'Field Archaeologist in Residence' at the McDonald Institute for Archaeological Research, Cambridge University. Both English Heritage and the McDonald Institute are warmly thanked. All due regard is owed to Alex Gibson who co-organised the original conference with Jim Leary.

References

Anon 1972. Waulud's Bank. *Current Archaeology,* 30, 173–7.

Bishop, B. 2012. Assessment of the flint, in J. Leary *Marden henge excavations: archaeological assessment report.* Unpublished report, English Heritage.

Bishop, B., Leary, J. and Robins, P. 2011. Introducing the 'Long-tailed oblique' arrowhead: examples from Marden henge, Wiltshire, and Santon Warren, Norfolk. *PAST,* 68, 1–2.

Carpenter E. and Winton H. 2011. *Marden Henge and Environs, Vale of Pewsey, Wiltshire. A report for the National Mapping Programme.* Research Department Report Series 76 - 2011. Swindon: English Heritage.

Darling, P. 1998. Aerial archaeology in Africa: the challenge of a continent. *AARG News, Newsletter of the Aerial Archaeology Research Group,* 17, 9–18.

Dyer, J. F. 1956. A secondary Neolithic camp at Waulud's Bank, Leagrave, Bedfordshire. *Bedfordshire Archaeological Journal,* (1995), 9–16.

Dyer, J. F. 1961–3. Waulud's Bank, Leagrave. *Bedfordshire Magazine,* 8, 57–64.

Field, D. 2011. Neolithic ground axe-heads and monuments in Wessex. In V. Davis, V and M. Edmonds (eds.) *Stone Axe Studies III,* 325–32. Oxford: Oxbow.

Field, D. 2008. *Use of land in central southern England during the Neolithic and Early Bronze Age.* BAR British Series 458. Oxford: British Archaeological Reports.

Field, D. 2004. Engraved sequences and the perception of prehistoric country in south east England. In J. Cotton, G. Crocker and A. Graham(eds.) *Aspects of archaeology and history in Surrey: trends towards a research framework for the county,* 39–49. Guildford: Surrey Archaeological Society.

Field, D., Leary, J. and Marshall, P. In press. Neolithic Silbury in Context. In J. Leary, D. Field and G. Campbell *Silbury Hill: The largest prehistoric mound in Europe.* Swindon: English Heritage.

Field, D., Martin, L. and Winton, H. 2011. *The Hatfield earthworks, Marden, Wiltshire. Survey and investigation.* Research Department Report Series 96 - 2011. Swindon: English Heritage.

Field, D. and Smith, N. 2008. *Croft Ambrey, Aymestry, Herefordshire: analysis of earthworks at Croft Ambrey.*

Research Department Report Series 36-2008. Swindon: English Heritage.

Gibson, A. 2004. Round in circles. Timber circles, henges and stone circles: some possible relationships and transformations, in R. Cleal and J. Pollard (eds.) *Monuments and material culture. Papers in honour of an Avebury archaeologist: Isobel Smith*, 70–82. Salisbury: Hobnob Press.

Gough, W. and R. 1806. (Trans) (originally published 1610) *William Camden's Britannia*. London: John Stockdale.

Hoare, R. C. 1821. *A history of Ancient Wiltshire 2*. London: Lackington, Hughes, Harding, Maver and Lepard.

Kennett, D. H. 1972. Bedfordshire Archaeology, 1971–72. *Bedfordshire Archaeological Journal*, 7, 89–98.

Leary, J. 2010. Silbury Hill: A monument in motion, in J. Leary, T. Darvill and D. Field (eds.), *Round mounds and monumentality in the British Neolithic and beyond*, 139–52. Oxford: Oxbow.

Leary, J. and Field, D. In press. Ways of understanding prehistoric Silbury. In J. Leary, D. Field and G. Campbell *Silbury Hill: The largest prehistoric mound in Europe*. Swindon: English Heritage.

Leary J. and Field D. 2010. *The story of Silbury Hill*. Swindon: English Heritage.

Leary, J., Field, D. and Russell, M. 2010. Marvels at Marden henge. *PAST*, 66, 14–6.

Loveday, R. 1998. Double entrance henges – routes to the past, in Gibson, A. and Simpson, D.D.A. (eds.) *Prehistoric Ritual and Religion*, 14–31. Stroud: Sutton.

Richards, C. 1996. Henges and water: towards an elemental understanding of monumentality and landscape in Late Neolithic Britain. *Journal of Material Culture*, 1(3), 313–36.

Russell, M. 2012. Assessment of pottery. In J. Leary *Marden henge excavations: archaeological assessment report*. Unpublished report, English Heritage.

Taylor, H. 1951. The Tynings Farm barrow group. Third report. *Proceedings of the University of Bristol Speleological Society*, 6, 111–73.

Wainwright, G. W., Evans, J. G. and Longworth, I. H. 1971. The excavation of a late Neolithic enclosure at Marden, Wiltshire. *Antiquaries Journal*, 51 (2), 177–239.

Warner, R. 2000. Keeping out the Otherworld: the internal ditch at Navan and other Iron Age 'hengiform' enclosures. *Emania*, 18, 39–44.

White, H. 2012. SEM-EDS and XRD analysis of 'slipped' sherd from [93034]. In J. Leary *Marden henge excavations: archaeological assessment report*. Unpublished report, English Heritage.

Withering, W. 1822. *From the miscellaneous tracts of the late William Withering M.D. F.R.S. etc to which is prefixed a memoir of his Character and Writings in two volumes*. London: Longman.

Worley, F. 2012. Assessment of the animal bones. In J. Leary *Marden henge excavations: archaeological assessment report*. Unpublished report, English Heritage.

Conformity, Routeways and Religious Experience –
the Henges of Central Yorkshire

Jan Harding

Abstract

A remarkable cluster of eight giant henges in central Yorkshire are testament to an extraordinary dynamic of building and worship. Built across an area which does not appear to have been permanently occupied, their distinctive and almost identical design — characterised by a pair of opposed entrances, outer ditches, and a uniform size — reflected their role as socially-neutral meeting-places in a system of trans-Pennine exchange and religious worship. The monuments appear to have been built intermittently, and as 'projects' they reproduced, celebrated and partly brought into being new types of social reality and identity. There were also important spiritual reasons for building enclosures here, especially across the Ure-Swale Interfluve where six of the eight henges are located. It will be argued this was a place of religious renown and that the monuments, along with their connecting routeways, were part of a sophisticated system of worship with parallels to historic pilgrimage.

Keywords: henges, exchange, landscape, pilgrimage, religion, rivers, routeways, Yorkshire

Introduction

Since the earliest recognition of henges as a distinctive class of Neolithic monument there have been attempts to typologically sub-divide them. Their varying size led to the identification of 'hengiforms', 'henge-enclosures' and 'mini-henges', whilst interruption by either single or double entrances resulted in a major distinction between 'Class I' and 'Class II' enclosures, and further sub-division on account of the number of ditches dug (Piggott and Piggott 1939; Atkinson et al. 1951, 82, 91; Burl 1969; Wainwright 1969; Harding and Lee 1987, 31). Other schemes of classification were based on what the earthworks enclosed (most notably Catherall 1971). These studies neatly emphasise the physical diversity of henges, yet it has proved far trickier to consider what variations in design tell us about the role, meaning and significance of these monuments. Their contrasting forms are often seen to reflect the scale of cultural interaction with which they are related, with the larger henges acting as regional centres serving the many, the smaller henges as local meeting-places for lesser groups of people (most notably, Renfrew 1973; Barnatt 1989, chapter 5; Earle 1991). They are assumed, in other words, to be part of a continuum of religious activity, yet the alternative — that variations in their location, design, and structural or depositional histories indicate a range of very distinctive intentions and motivations on the part of their builders and users during the late Neolithic — is also clearly relevant and may suggest the henge phenomenon is far less coherent (see, for example, Bradley 1993, 100-11; Gillings *et al* 2008, chapter 6).

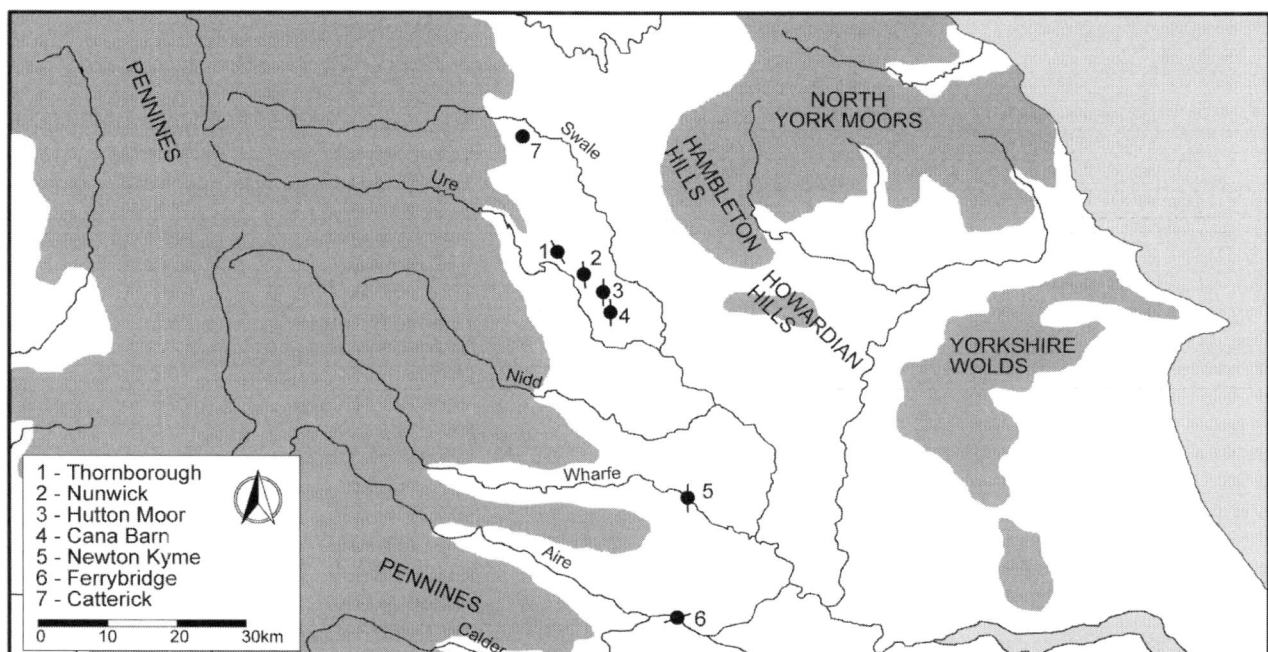

FIGURE 1: THE HENGES OF CENTRAL YORKSHIRE WITH AXIAL LINES SHOWING THEIR ALIGNMENT

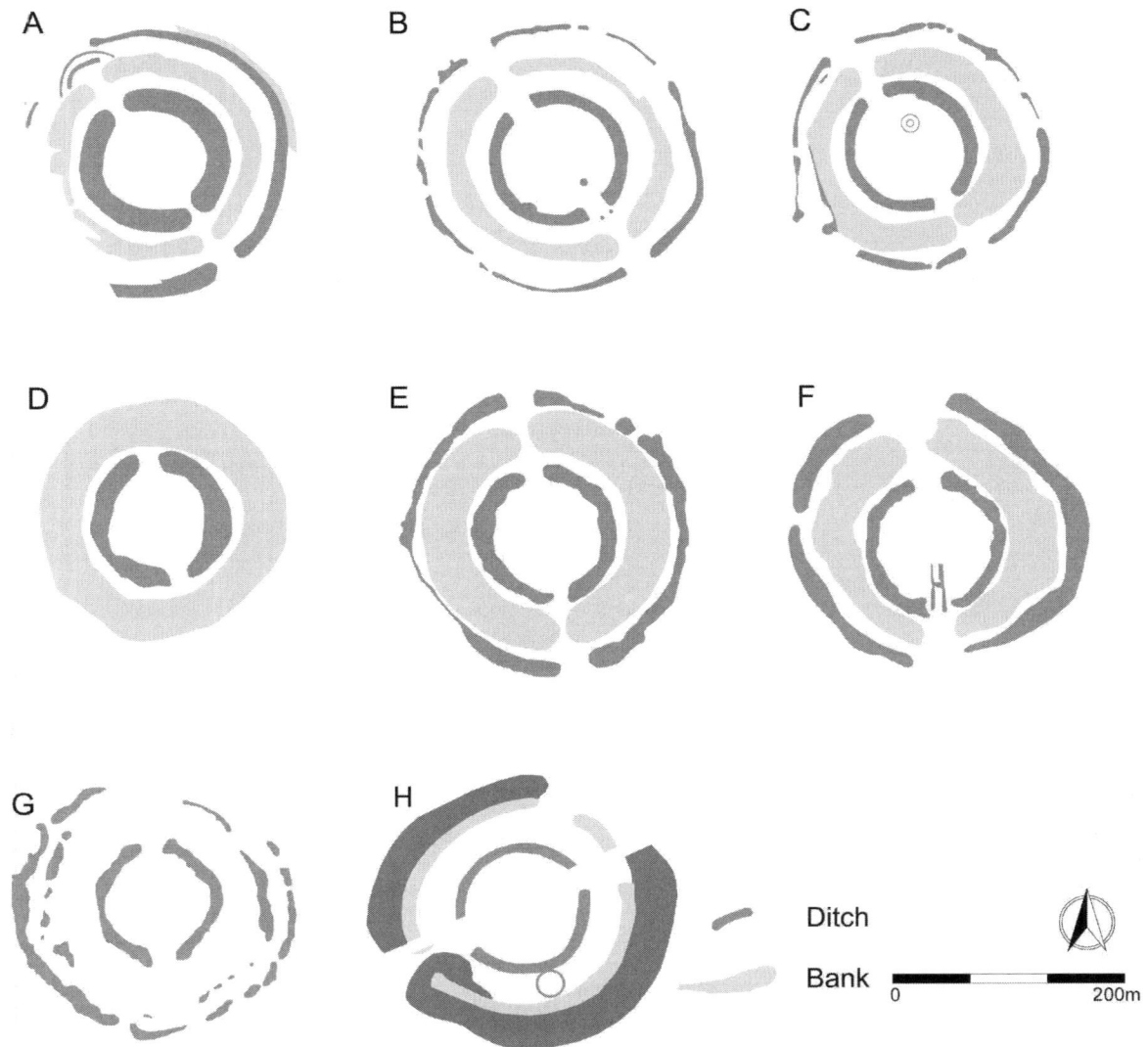

FIGURE 2: PLAN OF YORKSHIRE'S DOUBLE-ENTRANCED HENGES: A. NORTHERN THORNBOROUGH; B. CENTRAL THORNBOROUGH; C. SOUTHERN THORNBOROUGH; D. NUNWICK; E. HUTTON MOOR; F. CANA BARN; G. NEWTON KYME; H. FERRYBRIDGE (A-F ARE ORIGINAL TRANSCRIPTIONS FROM AERIAL PHOTOGRAPHS, G. AFTER HARDING AND LEE 1987, 311, H. AFTER ROBERTS ET AL. 2005, FIG 135)

Some of the differences in henge layout, and also, therefore, in their use and meaning, may have played out regionally since 'certain henges with architectural similarities happened to be close to one another' (Burl 1969, 10). Undoubtedly the most distinctive of all the geographically defined groups of henges are the eight enclosures clustered together in central Yorkshire — Ferrybridge, Newton Kyme, Cana Barn, Hutton Moor, Nunwick, and the three at Thornborough (Figures 1 and 2) — representing all but one of the known Class IIA enclosures. Each possesses a pair of wide adjacent entrances, and, with the single exception of Nunwick (Figure 2 D), an outer ditch, or in the case of Newton Kyme, two outer ditches (Figure 2 G). They are also very similar in size with inner areas and outer enclosures of 80-102m and 202-254m across respectively (from Harding and Lee 1987). Their conspicuously linear distribution on or close to a broad north-south shelf of magnesium limestone and marl, flanked by the Pennines to

the west and low-lying vales to the east, certainly contrasts with the small number of henges found elsewhere in Yorkshire (Harding 2003, 100-103), and along with their almost identical appearance, suggests they were the product of similar intentions and motivations. Their distinctiveness is emphasised by the lack of parallels nationally. Only the Big Rings henge, far to the south at Dorchester-on-Thames in Oxfordshire, shares their architectural features — and indeed, is similarly sized with an outer earthwork some 193m across (Whittle et al 1992, 184) — although a double-ditched, but single-entranced, enclosure at Condicote in Gloucestershire is comparable (Saville 1983).

To have eight giant henges clustered together in an area only 58km from north to south attests to an extraordinary dynamic of building and worshipping in this part of Yorkshire. But what exactly was this dynamic and how can we explain the enclosures' distinctive design? I wish to explore these issues by considering the henges' apparent association with routeways and exchange. The possibility they were strategically positioned meeting-places along well-used pathways for people and objects could certainly explain the little we know about their structural sequence of building, including the digging of outer ditches. Yet this does not account for why it was necessary to build six of the enclosures in the Ure-Swale Interfluve and less than 12km apart. Adopting the idea they were placed in an otherworldly or liminal landscape, it will be contested that each henge was carefully sited along a highly structured pathway or pilgrimage route in order to articulate narratives about people's creation myths, their landscapes, and their relationships with each other. This interpretation requires further research, and especially fieldwork, but has clear implications for our understanding of late Neolithic Britain by implying a level of planning, coordination and religiosity only rarely considered appropriate to third millennium BC communities.

Exchange, interaction and henge design

If large henges were the religious capitals of surrounding socio-political territories we would expect this part of Yorkshire to be densely populated in the late Neolithic. Yet the little we know about settlement patterns suggest otherwise. Recorded multi-period lithic assemblages from Thornborough, Marton-le-Moor, and further north at Catterick and Scorton — all from the low-lying reaches of the Ure-Swale Interfluve (Figure 1) — are of modest size, and with traits, like the almost total absence of complete flakes with cortex, or their small number of cores, which are generally indicative of periodic short-term occupation (see Brooks 2003, 35; Dickson 2011; Harding in press, chapters 5; Rowe 1998; Speed 2003a; 2003b; 2004; 2008a; 2008b; 2010; in prep; Tavener 1996). The tiny number of lithics collected further south around the Ferrybridge henge tells a similar picture (Brooks 2005). There is certainly nothing to indicate dense habitation near to any of these monuments and the available palaeoenvironmental evidence suggests that extensive deforestation and clearance did not start across the interfluve until the Bronze Age (Bridgland et al. 2011, 258-64). Given this, it is noteworthy that the bulk of this flint — representing as much as 80% of the material collected by fieldwalking and excavation at Thornborough (Harding in press, chapter 5) — most likely originated from coastal tills some 80km to the east. It is nearer this source, across the chalklands of the Wolds, that one finds larger quantities of lithics (Manby 1974; 1975), suggesting that eastern Yorkshire was actually the focus of settlement during the Neolithic. It therefore seems the river-strewn lowlands flanking the Pennines were only temporarily occupied, with many of the people worshipping at the henges travelling long-distances from the east to do so.

The possible importance of movement to those who built and used the henges may actually be implicit to their design. That all eight possess a pair of opposed entrances (Figure 2), creating a central axis through each site, highlights the

significance of this characteristic to the meaning and use of the enclosures. Their presence suggests 'that the concept of the thoroughfare was as important as that of boundedness' (Harding and Lee 1987, 34), and indeed, Roy Loveday (1998), whilst noting the general correlation between the alignments of double-entranced sites nationally and the course of nearby Roman roads, concluded that henges of this design were quite literally strung out along routeways. This would explain their linear distribution in central Yorkshire, an observation taken further by Blaise Vyner (2007), who used their clustering along part of the narrow shelf of magnesium limestone and marl between Nottingham to the river Tees — a natural routeway which historically connected the English Midlands with northern England (Brennand et al. 2007, 390; Vyner 2000, 103) — to suggest a 'Great North Route'. This configuration is certainly indicative of a key channel of movement, as is their very deliberate association with the rivers Ure, Wharfe and Aire (Figure 1), with at least some of these monuments located 'close to the lowest readily fordable points on each of the rivers' (Vyner 2007, 75), and also, therefore, near to key Roman centres and the headports of the Middle Ages (Moorhouse 2003, fig. 53). These rivers offered connections across the low-lying vales, but also westward to the Pennine uplands and North West England beyond, and eastward to the hills of eastern Yorkshire, the coast, and the Humber Estuary. The henges may have therefore been 'strategically placed for access' (Manby 1979, 76), with movement either following the rivers, or using them as navigable arteries as in later periods (Moorhouse 2003, fig. 53).

But why would people be travelling along this routeway in the first place — and be building henges or worshipping within them as they did so? Their motivations were surely diverse, but at least one reason may have been trans-Pennine exchange. Large numbers of polished Cumbrian stone axes, originating from the mountains of the central Lake District, are known to have moved eastward to the Yorkshire and Lincolnshire Wolds, and down the river Trent into the north Midlands (Bradley and Edmonds 1993, 162, fig. 9.8; Clough and Cummins 1988, map 6; Manby et al. 2003, 47, 49). Similarly, the till flint from Yorkshire's coast is found in abundance across eastern Cumbria, and was clearly moving in the opposite direction (Cherry and Cherry 1987; 2002; Lynch 2005). Hence, the henges could have been strategically sited meeting-places or 'staging posts' where people congregated to trade information, resources and objects (Manby 1979, 76-77); and given that Cumbrian axes and Yorkshire flint have a wider if less dense distribution (Clough and Cummins 1988, map 6; Waddington 1999, 155), they may have even acted as hubs in a system of exchange connecting communities further afield. The six enclosures clustered in the interfluve are all close to the river Ure — which flows through Wensleydale, dissecting much of the Pennines west to east — along what was probably the quickest natural route between the Great Langdale 'axe factory' in the Lake District and the lowlands of central Yorkshire. Its role as a routeway is emphasised by the orientation of the henges themselves, which are broadly parallel with the river's course (Figure 1; see also Richards 1996, 330), perhaps indicating people's approximate direction of travel. To the south of the interfluve is Newton Kyme, whose north-south orientation across the nearby river Wharfe suggests an association with a crossing-point, and Ferrybridge, aligned north-east to south-west as if directing travellers either eastward along the river Aire, and then to the Humber Estuary, or westward across the Pennines following the course of the Aire and the Calder (Figure 1).

It would not be surprising for exchange and worship to be closely interwoven, for the largest religious centres around the world have often fulfilled a range of roles, their sacredness used to sanctify other tasks. It implies the henges were meeting-places where spiritual and economic transactions could freely occur, but this would only happen if they were seen to 'belong' to no one group, or put another way, were regarded as socially-neutral religious centres which served the many. Their clustering outside of people's 'homeworlds', in a geographically liminal landscape flanking the Pennines, would help in this regard — as it would if the 'many' were involved in their construction. Certainly the scale of these sites suggest a large labour force, and the possibility that building was completed periodically by those gathering together to exchange and complete other related activities is perhaps indicated by the little we know about the history of construction. Excavations at Ferrybridge have demonstrated a complex sequence whereby the initial bank was built around 3000 BC during at least three discrete construction events with spoil from a deepening inner ditch, with additional upcast material, from a shallower outer ditch, being added during two further episodes some time in the third millennium BC (Roberts et al. 2005). Through intermittent construction the earthwork got progressively more monumental, as would be expected if building was integral to the periodic meetings or festivals occurring there. Other sites have not benefited from a comparable scale of excavation, but 'a similar staged construction might have occurred for Thornborough's central henge' given the heaps of earth recorded in its bank section by Nicolas Thomas in 1952 (Roberts et al. 2005, 235; see also Thomas 1955, 433) — although the outer ditches of all three monuments here could have conceivably been built first (Harding in press, chapter 4) — and the same can be said for the 'traces of tip-lines and the interleaving of loads' discovered at nearby Nunwick during the excavation of its henge bank (Dymond 1963, 100, fig. 3.). Hence, it is very possible that each of the henges was the outcome of periodic construction, their massive earthwork perimeters, and unusual double ditch circuits, reflecting a need to constantly reinstate or regenerate relationships resulting from the coming-and-going of people along the closely associated routeways.

Intermittent construction has been suggested for other British henges, and in late Neolithic Orkney 'disjointed and staggered labour' reflected their building becoming 'a dramatic arena for strategies of ritualized competition

and social dominance' (Richards 2004, 108, 111; see also Barrett 1994, 26). There may be merit in this connection to concepts of power, but the essential religiosity of monument building should not be overlooked. The creation of sacred architecture is itself an offertory or propitiatory ritual (Jones 2000b, 243), and as such, its completion on the scale evident in central Yorkshire demonstrates the willingness of people to toil for one another and for the spirits and gods associated with these enclosures, thereby creating a narrative around which communities could unite irrespective of their differences. The henges are therefore best considered as 'projects' whose development was testament to the commitment and sincerity of their builders to specific beliefs and to trans-Pennine interaction. Their wide double-entrances may have divided sites into two halves, with each perhaps constructed by different groups from different areas, so that their eastern and western halves were built by people from eastern Yorkshire and Cumbria respectively. Yet if their layout was testament to the relationships they embedded, these were two parts of a whole, and as a monument 'grew' — both spatially and temporally — then so did the density and standing of the connections between generations of builders. The very layout of the henges could have therefore represented, celebrated and partly brought into being new types of social reality and new types of identity across a landscape which was geographically liminal to its many users. As with all offertory or propitiatory ritual, the acts required repeating, so building was the means by which beliefs and relations were reproduced (see Jones 2000b, 245-51). Successive generations were tied-in to a system of interaction and contact which was materially important to their existence, and presumably, spiritually essential to their futures.

These projects were probably highly orchestrated from the outset. A deeper understanding of their building must await further fieldwork, but it is striking how periodic construction nonetheless resulted in remarkably similar sites. Inner ditches enclose an area of uniform size (Figure 2), and the possibility a standard layout was being followed is most clearly demonstrated by Nunwick, Hutton Moor, Cana Barn, and the northern and southern Thornborough enclosures, all with external diameters of between 92m and 100m (after Harding and Lee 1987, 307-17). The similarity is too striking to ignore, especially if we consider that Big Rings and Condicote, the two other double-ditched henges, had inner enclosures with estimated diameters of 108-111m and 103m respectively (Harding and Lee 1987, 159, 228), whilst the single bank and ditch circuit at King Arthur's Round Table, the nearest henge monument to the west of the Pennines in Cumbria, covered an area between 96m and 111m across (after Harding and Lee 1987, 102). If this suggests the popularity and use of an idealised design — which may reveal nothing more than the use of a standard unit of measurement equating to a hundred paces — then the same can be concluded for the rest of their layout. Despite the greatly varying condition of these earthworks — the best preserved sites being the northern and central henges at Thornborough (Fig 2 A and B) — their banks and ditches would have been comparably impressive in size once complete (Dymond 1963; Harding in press, chapter 4; Roberts et al. 2005), and their outer ditches, which in some instances were almost certainly left causewayed, dug to a similar layout. Whether these outer circuits were added later, or built first, their overall size indicates they too were predetermined, as do less obvious features like their straightened arc around the south-east course of Cana Barn, Newton Kyme and central Thornborough. There is, therefore, little doubt that with the possible exception of Nunwick (see below), these monuments 'emerged' into a 'finished' state.

The intermittent reproduction of an idealised design raises many intriguing questions. One can only speculate as to the builders' intentions, yet it was surely linked to their attempts to orientate themselves in the world, both literally and metaphorically, and to their emphasis on the connectivity of past and present. Reproduction may have been achieved by copying an earlier archetypal 'origin' site,

and across the Ure-Swale Interfluve we could be seeing successive building as new sites replaced existing religious centres, reflecting the expected ebb-and-flow of alliances, affiliations and relationships over the lengthy period when axes and flint were exchanged. If so, the differences which do exist in the layout of these monuments — such as the digging of a second outer ditch at Newton Kyme, the apparent building of an outer bank along part of the eastern side of the northern henge at Thornborough, or the wide berm between the inner ditch and bank at Ferrybridge (Figure 2) — could reflect the changing motivations of builders as time passed. Individual sites could have been built at different times and to different agendas, the henges closely respecting, and perhaps partly creating, wider socio-political development. Some building projects may have even placed less importance on the dutiful copying of the archetype. However, there is an alternative, and perhaps more interpretively challenging scenario, whereby the henges were broadly contemporary, part of a single

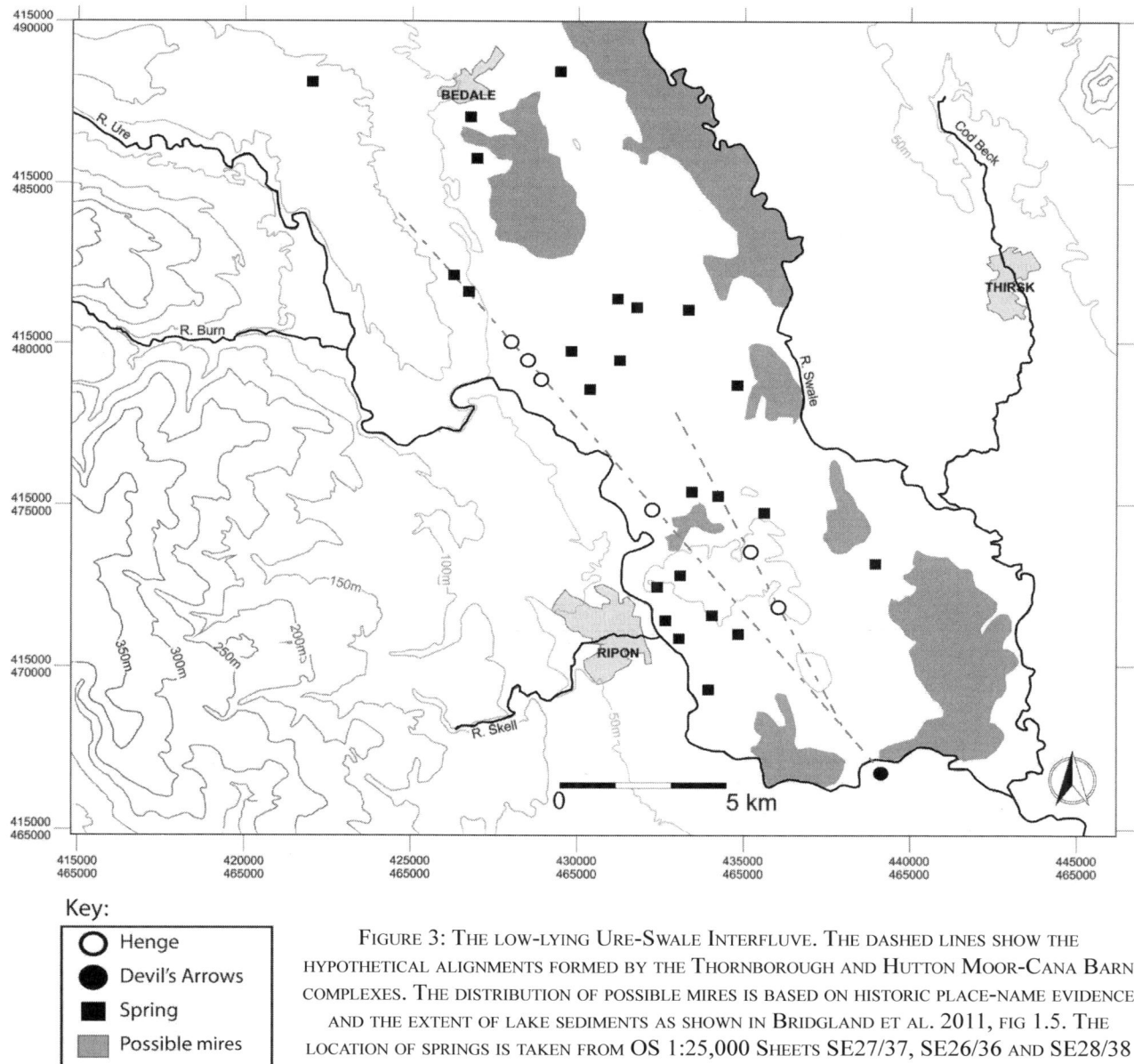

FIGURE 3: THE LOW-LYING URE-SWALE INTERFLUVE. THE DASHED LINES SHOW THE HYPOTHETICAL ALIGNMENTS FORMED BY THE THORNBOROUGH AND HUTTON MOOR-CANA BARN COMPLEXES. THE DISTRIBUTION OF POSSIBLE MIRES IS BASED ON HISTORIC PLACE-NAME EVIDENCE AND THE EXTENT OF LAKE SEDIMENTS AS SHOWN IN BRIDGLAND ET AL. 2011, FIG 1.5. THE LOCATION OF SPRINGS IS TAKEN FROM OS 1:25,000 SHEETS SE27/37, SE26/36 AND SE28/38

Key:

○ Henge
● Devil's Arrows
■ Spring
▨ Possible mires

FIGURE 4: LOOKING WEST FROM CANA BARN (TOP) AND NORTH-WEST FROM HUTTON MOOR (BOTTOM)

plan which saw a massive commitment to henge building. If this was the case, then a religious imperative — such as the development of an increasingly popular cult with its own beliefs, practices and spiritual associations — must have surely been responsible for driving people on both sides of the Pennines to unite in the replication of an idealised design on such a massive scale. This widespread and labour-intensive use of homologised architecture would ultimately have engendered connectivity, trust and assurance which 'sets the stage and calls the assembly to attention' (Jones 2000b, 45).

Religion, pathways and pilgrimage

It can certainly be argued these impressive henges were built across this part of central Yorkshire for reasons other than their siting affording good communication, contact and exchange. People may have congregated here in the first place because parts of this landscape, and especially the Ure-Swale Interfluve where most of the henges are found, were places of religious renown. Popular religious centres with the largest temples are often in landscapes which possess important symbolic resources or in some way appear atypical or unique, each being regarded as what Mircea Eliade, the well-known historian of religion, described as 'hierophanies', or instances of the sacred world breaking into the lived world and revealing itself to believers (for an overview, and references therein, see Jones 2000b, 33-35). The interfluve is characterised by broad rivers, numerous springs and extensive mires (Figure 3; see also Bridgland et al 2011; Moorhouse 2004, 30-31), and given the spiritual value Neolithic communities evidently placed on watery features like rivers and bogs (see, for example, Bradley 1990, 57ff; Fowler and Cummings 2003), these associations perhaps indicate the area was favoured for religious supplication and ritual appeasement. The interfluves' distinctiveness is even more pronounced when one considers the natural deposits of gypsum here, or more specifically, the subsistence hollows or sinkholes created since prehistory by its underground dissolution (Cooper 1986; 2000; Powell et al 1992, 15-18, 94-95; see also Dickson and Hopkinson 2011, 36-37, 199). The sudden and violent appearance of what are often very large steep-sided shafts, which then quickly filled with water, must have been both striking and deeply unsettling, even if the event itself went unwitnessed; and it was surely understood in religious terms, perhaps, like springs, as an opening or point of access with an underworld. Hardly surprising, then, that gypsum was deliberately incorporated into the monuments of the interfluve, including, most spectacularly, their use to coat the henge banks at Thornborough (Cornwall 1953; Thomas 1955; Harding in press, chapter 6). It seems likely that the very physicality of this landscape gave it an otherworldly appearance which matched its geographical liminality, thereby providing spiritual motivation aplenty for visiting.

If the building of six giant enclosures across the interfluve reflects the landscapes' fundamental religiosity, then the latter may also explain the exact location of the henges (Figure 3). Given the probable expanses of wetland it seems likely that people moved along the more elevated ridge of land immediately to the north-west of the likely crossing-point across the Ure, on the southern banks of which is found the impressive standing stones of the Devil's Arrows (Burl 1991). It was upon this ridge that Hutton Moor and Cana Barn were built, 1.7km apart, and surrounded by a cluster of springs, including at Hallikeld 2.4km to the north-west on the alignment created by both henges. These enclosures are actually located across the highest part of the southern interfluve and currently overlook surrounding areas (Figure 4). Cana Barn is unusually sited on a slope, so that even within the more forested Neolithic landscape it is likely to have enjoyed extensive westerly views of a hilly area with a large number of springs, the Ure valley beyond, and the flanking hills of the Pennines. There are no views northwards and eastwards except from along the top of the ridge beyond the henge's northern entrance. By contrast, visibility from Hutton Moor is most extensive to the north-west, north and east, although woodland could have conceivably prevented all of these. A ridge immediately to the south and west blocks the view here, and ensures the two henges are not intervisible. Clear differences are therefore apparent in the setting of Cana Barn and Hutton Moor, yet the views they afford are complementary. The location of both henges contrasts markedly with the more low-lying Thornborough complex sited 8km to the north-west. Here three clearly intervisible henges, aligned north-west to south-east across the only large plateau found in the southern part of the interfluve, enjoy very limited views of the surrounding landscape, although the limestone ridge immediately to the west, along with the much more distant Hambleton Hills, could have been evident. Thornborough is also associated with a cluster of springs, including a notable concentration around the modern village of Well, whose location 2.4km to the north-west and on the same alignment as the monuments, exactly matches the relationship between the other two henges and the Hallikeld springs.

Both complexes appear carefully sited in topographically distinct landscapes which may have provided contrasting experiences to worshippers. As such, they suggest the deliberate positioning of henges as part of a unified vision. Their relationship to Nunwick, the other interfluve henge, is not at all clear, yet it seems anything but coincidental that it was placed on the alignment created by the orientation of the Thornborough complex, which, if continued even further southwards, is also replicated by the location and course of the Devil's Arrows (Figure 3). One possibility is that a remarkable 'symbolic geometry' stretched across this landscape during the late Neolithic, of which Nunwick was part. Yet its setting is clearly different to the other henges. It lies on a terrace close to the Ure — rather than on the more distant and higher drier ground preferred by the other enclosures — possibly with a stream immediately to the east. It most likely enjoyed no views of the surrounding landscape. Nunwick's association with waterways could certainly demonstrate the religious appeasement or celebration of water's spirituality, but it may also help explain why of all the henges this is the only one without an outer ditch: perhaps it was abandoned during the inundation of the surrounding landscape, explaining why it wasn't favoured for later round barrow building like the other henges. The soils excavated under and in the lower portion of its bank, along with the primary silting of its ditch, had certainly been greatly affected by hydrological action (Proudfoot 1963). It may even be possible that Nunwick was earlier than the other enclosures, as was believed by its excavator (Dymond 1963, 100) — an original act of supplication, dedicated to the spirits and deities of water, which was subsequently respected by building the three Thornborough henges, and the Devil's Arrows, on the same alignment.

The landscape may have also orchestrated the short journey between enclosures. Whilst it is impossible to ascertain exact routeways, or indeed, people's direction of travel, there are hints of the intimate relationship between topography and movement. Those coming from Cumbria, heading eastward along Wensleydale and then perhaps visiting the springs at Well, would have moved across the latter's hilly terrain before being presented with extensive views as they travelled south along the ridge

(Figure 5). This was the first opportunity to see what lay to the east of the Pennines, and the view, which extends across the lowlands to the Hambleton Hills, would have added greatly to their sense of entering a different world. It was also the first occasion to see the giant enclosures, and the fact all three henge banks were probably covered in gypsum made them stand-out from the extensive woodland of the surrounding landscape. These travellers would have then descended to the monuments, their approach to the northern henge emphasised by what appears to be an alignment of impressive upright posts leading directly to the monument (Harding in press, chapter 5). By contrast, those moving in the opposite direction, coming perhaps from eastern Yorkshire, are most likely to have crossed the Ure in the general vicinity of where the Devil's Arrows is located — in itself perhaps a memorable act — before immediately starting the gentle ascent of the undulating ridge on which Cana Barn is sited (Figure 6). The most direct route would have taken them directly to the southern entrance of the former monument. Hence, in each instance the landscapes' topography, reinforced by its border of hills to the north-west and the river to its south, could have emphasised the act of 'crossing over' into a new spatial domain.

FIGURE 5: LOOKING SOUTH-EAST FROM THE RIDGE BETWEEN WELL AND NOSTERFIELD (COPYRIGHT COURTESY OF DICK LONSDALE)

FIGURE 6: VIEW OF THE RIDGE ON WHICH CANA BARN AND HUTTON MOOR ARE LOCATED LOOKING NORTH-EAST FROM LINGHILLS

There may be other examples of topography physically orchestrating experience by creating thresholds or boundaries for people to cross. The most direct route between the Thornborough complex and the henges of Hutton Moor and Cana Barn, irrespective of whether you were heading south or north, took the traveller across a landscape less elevated than the plateau and ridge on which the monuments are sited; a landscape presumably dominated by woodland and dissected by frequent streams. Its character generated a very different experience to travelling than elsewhere in the interfluve, and in contrast to the experience of visiting the henges, presumably offered limited visibility. Indeed, it could have been a difficult landscape to traverse — especially if parts of it were seasonally waterlogged, as already suggested for the area close to Nunwick — which in itself would have helped differentiate between the two complexes. Accordingly, to move out of this area on to the drier monumental landscapes involved ascent, albeit up gentle slopes, and irrespective of the full extent of tree cover, it seems highly likely the henges themselves would not have been visible until the last moment, a pattern apparently repeated between Hutton Moor and Cana Barn, their exact siting either side of an intervening ridge suggesting highly structured patterns of movement and visibility across this complex. That both henges were deliberately kept 'hidden' until the last moment, most likely in an attempt to maximise their impact on worshippers, is borne out by neither being sited on the highest parts of this ridge, including the hill immediately to the west of the complex. It is even possible that Hutton Moor was approached via a narrow and steep valley which runs to its west and north-west, and from the bottom of which the earthwork was unlikely to have been visible.

Movement across this landscape may have therefore been divided into short stages or legs, with each of these, and the henges with which they are associated, drawing directly on natural features like springs, contrasting views of the world, and if the fieldwork around Thornborough is typical (see Harding in press, chapter 5), a series of highly structured 'sacred landscapes', to create texture and meaning. These routes were admittedly short, for the henges are today no more than an hour's walk apart — they nevertheless fulfilled an important role. Religious centres are at their most effective if those who are about to worship within them are ready to break free of their normal worldly limits and accept, or surrender to, the spiritual nourishment offered by their sacred architecture (Jones 2000a, 60ff). However, this 'sense of ritual' (Bell

1992, 50ff) is rarely in the minds of worshippers prior to their visit; rather, it has to be orchestrated or invoked. One can only speculate as to how this may have been achieved, but it is easy to imagine these routeways as possessing their own spirituality, akin perhaps to the 'ancestral tracks' recognised by anthropologists (see, for example, Munn 1992, 113; Morphy 1995). They were likely symbolically charged, and in the same way that Australian Aboriginal society believed their ancestors had quite literally left their mark on the landscape, creating a series of special or sacred places, then Neolithic travellers could have similarly ascribed meaning. The subtle changes in topography, the more pronounced ridges of drier ground, the mires and springs, and the gypsum collapses which characterise the Ure-Swale Interfluve, all created a rich mosaic of places which quite literally livened peoples' beliefs about the world, and by moving amongst them, and thereby stepping back temporally to get 'inside' the founding values of spiritual existence, they were creating an understanding essential to an appropriate 'sense of ritual'. If so, it seems likely that some of these natural places witnessed their own rituals, acts which may have looked forward to the ceremony of being inside the henges, and indeed, the social relationships embedded during these occasions.

Journeying along these routes would have therefore helped 'prepare' worshippers, alluring them into the right frame of mind for the transformative experience of approaching, entering, and indeed, building the henges. Irrespective of what exactly happened within these enclosures, and how it was organised, their earthworks — which in their latter stages would have towered over the worshippers, denying them views of the surrounding landscape — confronted and challenged beholders, invoking the bewilderment and disorientation necessary if they were to achieve the total transcendence of worldly limits, and hence accept the strangeness, alterity and potential of the spirit world. Acts of frenzied building would certainly be possible given the correct 'sense of ritual'. The routeways were essential to making all this happen, and like the monuments, part of a sophisticated network of religiosity inscribed across the interfluve. If correct, this was a remarkable feat reminiscent of some of the pilgrimage routes of world religions, and indeed, the parallel has been drawn elsewhere for other parts of Neolithic Britain (notably Loveday 1998; in press; Renfrew 2000, 16-18). Each phase of this journey, and visit to a henge, could have formed part of a narrative which made distinct statements about the cosmos and the relationships embedded within its creation and meaning, thereby drawing worshippers into a dialogue about 'divinity, world creation, and human purpose' (Jones 2000a, 90). This was especially poignant given the monuments themselves were mnemonic devices which spoke, through their history of activity, of human relationships and patterns of affiliation. It is impossible to say if people travelled to and worshipped at all these henges, or visited just one, as is often the case with temples along pilgrimage routes (Jones 2000a, 34), but either way these travellers would be in little doubt as to the spiritual significance of the area. Likening what was

happening here to pilgrimage certainly helps explain the adherence of its built places to shared elements of design, for the replication of key shrines is a composite part of these routes (see Loveday 1998, 26, 30). Replication was the means of ensuring a shared material language and the dissemination of key religious messages about the cosmos; and given this, the building of no less than six henges across such a small area indicates the cogency of what was being created here.

This logic, or religious imperative, could have extended across an even larger area. The close similarities between the design of Newton Kyme and Ferrybridge and the henges of the interfluve suggest connections extending southwards. These two sites are spaced nearly 21km apart, comparable to the distance of 23km between Newton Kyme and the Devil's Arrows (Figure 1), suggesting a spatial pattern which may equate to what is no more than a day's walk. Their relationship to the sacred enclosures and routes of the interfluve poses some obvious questions, including if they were contemporary, or indeed, also sited in landscapes of religious renown. There is no doubt as to their strategic location — with both sited on the junction of upland and lowland, close to the openings of Wharfedale and Airedale — but little else can be said with any certainty. Superficially at least, nothing about their setting suggests they too were placed in landscapes which may have been considered atypical and therefore of special religious significance. This could accord with the plan of the two henges. Of all the sites in central Yorkshire, these are the most deviant, with Newton Kyme (Figure 2 G) possessing an additional outer ditch, and Ferrybridge an unusually wide berm between inner ditch and bank (Figure 2 H), perhaps demonstrating a weakening of the archetypal norm the further one is from the interfluve. It may even be this is why Ferrybridge is associated with 'eight possible hengiform monuments' (Roberts and Richardson 2005, 200), a type of site not yet recorded at any of the other henges. If their overall similarities of design suggest they too were part of a pilgrimage route, then they may have been paying homage to the sacredness of the area to the north, suggesting perhaps that not all the enclosures of central Yorkshire were perceived to be of equal religious value. That the henge at Ferrybridge marked the southern extent of the route is perhaps indicated by the river Aire being the last of the great rivers descending from the Pennines and flowing east-west across its flanking lowlands. Beyond here very different socio-political realities may have prevailed.

More problematic is whether these connections continued across the north of the interfluve. Whilst the sites at Thornborough are the northernmost double-ditched henges, it can not be ruled out that people were travelling further, to the late Neolithic monuments known to cluster around Catterick near the river Swale (Figure 1), including a large double palisade enclosure (Hale et al. 2009) and a 'ringwork' or possible single-circuit henge (Moloney et al. 2003, 9-13). That no double-ditched henge appears to have been constructed could be taken as indicating that the area was somehow used and perceived differently than was the southern interfluve, and the fact that the 'ringwork' closely replicates the architecture of Mayburgh in Cumbria, and indeed the enclosures of third millennium Ireland, by having no ditch (Bradley 2007, 134-35) suggests that a different set of social affinities may have operated here. Nevertheless, Blaise Vyner (2007) imagined his 'Great North Route' extended to the Swale — bending westward to Thornborough to avoid 'the carr lands of the Swale margin' (Bridgland et al. 2011, 218-19) — and even further northwards to the rivers Tees, Wear and Tyne. Alternatively, that the sites at Catterick are directly north of the course established by Hutton Moor and Cana Barn, could suggest a routeway running along a ridge between extensive mires both to the east and west, parallel with and alongside the current A1M road artery (Figure 3). If so, it implies an even more complex pattern of pathways and places of worship for travelling pilgrims, with Thornborough sited on a route connecting Wensleydale to Yorkshire's low-lying vales. Connectivity to the northern interfluve could suggest that different complexes attracted different audiences, and that henges lacked finite meaning, their symbolism and significance shifting according to the background, group affiliations and personal expectations of those worshipping there.

That the litany and symbolism of worship had to appeal to a range of peoples is perhaps borne out by one further characteristic of the henges. It has been observed how temples on historic pilgrimage routes are often kept both physically and metaphorically 'empty', a deliberate attempt, it seems, to create 'a religious void, a ritual space capable of accommodating diverse meanings and practices', and thereby ensuring that they become a 'vessel into which pilgrims devoutly pour their hopes, prayers and aspirations' (Earle and Sallnow 1991, 15). There are obvious problems with drawing too closely on historic pilgrimage as an analogy, yet this observation could explain one noticeable feature of all these monuments — the absence of structures within them. Their interiors have admittedly seen little investigation, the only excavation being a tiny evaluation at the central Thornborough henge (Thomas 1955, 433, fig. 2); and aerial photography and geophysical prospection indicates single features like the 'H' shaped feature at Cana Barn (Figure 2 F), or the circular anomaly at the central Thornborough henge (Figure 2 B; Harding in press, chapter 4), both associated with their entrances. Nevertheless, what they appear to lack are complex structures like the timber and stone circles associated with henges elsewhere, an absence matched by the monuments being kept remarkably clean, with little or no discarded artefacts (Harding in press, chapter 5). Many inner settings pre- or post-date surrounding earthworks, but their absence in Yorkshire indicates the henges were kept largely empty throughout their use. Their builders might have refrained from over-prescribing what occurred within them in an attempt to accommodate different traditions and backgrounds. Within such uncluttered arenas it was easier for disparate beliefs and practices to coalesce.

Conclusion

The above discussion suggests that the henges of central Yorkshire were connected to a distinctive and quite remarkable socio-religious dynamic. As such, it demonstrates that whilst henges can be regarded as the result of shared traditions of building and believing which stretched across the British Isles, they were also the product of more local processes and issues. What may have emerged in central Yorkshire was a distinctive set of traditions, practices and materials which were well suited, for at least a short time, to the coming-and-going of people from very different backgrounds, and which, in this instance, help us understand the distinctive architectural traits and locations of henges. The flourishing of the double-ditched henges, linked together by prescribed routes and associated narratives, served to articulate or regulate relationships in a landscape which may have been spiritually and strategically important to many dispersed communities. These empty henges, where people periodically gathered to build and worship, were well suited to a range of important socio-political roles, including no doubt the need 'to reassert social identity, exchange information concerning both local and more global matters, and expose and attempt to alleviate internal disputes' (Silverman 1994, 14). Without them, crucial social links would have withered and died. Hence, the henge phenomenon, which affected many third millennium communities across the British Isles, was in Yorkshire translated and understood within a regional context, giving rise to an inventive conformity in the design of sacred architecture. If we wish to understand henges more generally we must create biographies which acknowledge the distinctive trajectories of local areas.

Acknowledgements

I am grateful to Marie-Claire Ferguson for the illustrations and to Gary Speed, of Northern Archaeological Associates, for making available unpublished archaeological reports.

References

Atkinson, R. J. C., Piggott, C. M. and Sandars, N. K. 1951. *Excavations at Dorchester, Oxon: First Report*. Oxford: Department of Antiquities, Ashmolean Museum.

Barnatt, J. 1989. *Stone Circles of Britain: Taxonomic and Distributional Analyses and a Catalogue of Sites in England, Scotland and Wales*. BAR British Series 215 (i and ii). Oxford: British Archaeological Reports.

Barrett, J. C. 1994. *Fragments from Antiquity: an Archaeology of Social Life in Britain, 2900-1200 BC*. Oxford and Cambridge: Blackwell.

Bell, C. 1992. *Ritual Theory, Ritual Practice*. New York and Oxford: Oxford University Press.

Bridgland, D., Innes, J., Long, A. and Mitchell, W. 2011. *Late Quaternary Landscape Evolution of the Swale-Ure Washlands, North Yorkshire*. Oxford: Oxbow Books.

Bradley, R. 1990. *The Passage of Arms*. Cambridge: Cambridge University Press.

Bradley R. 1993. *Altering the Earth: the Origins of Monuments in Britain and Continental Europe* (The Rhind Lectures 1991-92). Monograph No.8. Edinburgh: Society of Antiquaries of Scotland.

Bradley, R. 2007. *The Prehistory of Britain and Ireland.* Cambridge: Cambridge University Press.

Bradley, R. J. and Edmonds, M. 1993. *Interpreting the Axe Trade. Production and Exchange in Neolithic Britain.* Cambridge: Cambridge University Press.

Brennand, M., Brown, F., Howard-Davis, C. and Lupton, A. 2007. Synthesis, in F. Brown, C. Howard-Davies, M. Brennand, A. Boyle, T. Evans, S. O'Connor, A. Spence, R. Heawood and A. Lupton, *The Archaeology of the A1(M) Darrington to Dishforth DBFO Road Scheme*, 379-410. Lancaster Imprints 12. Oxford: Oxford Archaeology North.

Brooks, I. P. 2003. Flint and chert, in C. Moloney, R. Holbrey, P. Wheelhouse and I. Roberts, *Catterick Racecourse, North Yorkshire: the Reuse and Adaptation of a Monument from Prehistoric to Anglian Times*, 35-36. Archaeology Service Publications 4. Wakefield, West Yorkshire Archaeology Service.

Brooks, I.P. 2005. Flint artefacts, in I. Roberts (eds.), *Ferrybridge Henge: the Ritual Landscape*, 143-49. Leeds: Archaeological Services WYAS.

Burl, H. A. W. 1969. Henges: internal features and regional groups. *Archaeological Journal,* 126, 1-28.

Burl, A. 1991. The Devil's Arrows, Boroughbridge, North Yorkshire: the archaeology of a stone row. *Yorkshire Archaeological Journal,* 63, 1-24.

Catherall, P.D. 1971. Henges in perspective. *Archaeological Journal,* 128, 147-53.

Cherry, J. and Cherry, P. J. 1987. *Prehistoric Habitation Sites on the Limestone Uplands of Eastern Cumbria.* Research Volume 2. Kendal: Cumberland and Westmorland Archaeological Society.

Cherry, J. and Cherry, P. J. 2002. Coastline and upland in Cumbrian prehistory. *Transactions of the Cumberland and Westmorland Antiquarian and Archaeological Society* II, 1-21.

Clough, T. H. McK. and Cummins, W. A. 1988. *Stone Axe Studies Volume 2: the Petrology of Prehistoric Stone Implements from the British Isles.* Research Report No 67. London: Council for British Archaeology.

Cooper, A. H. 1986. Subsidence and foundering of strata caused by the dissolution of Permian gypsum in the Ripon and Bedale areas, North Yorkshire, in G.M. Harwood and D.B. Smith (eds.), *The English Zechstein and Related Topics*, 127-39. Oxford, London, Edinburgh, Boston, Palo Alto, Melbourne, Geological Society Special Publications No 22.

Cornwall, I. W. 1953. Thornborough (middle) rings. *Proceedings of the Prehistoric Society,* 19 (2), 144-47.

Dickson, A. 2011. Appendix 2: lithics, in A. Dickson and G. Hopkinson, *Holes in the Landscape. Seventeen Years of Archaeological Investigations at Nosterfield Quarry, North Yorkshire*, 271-310. http://www.archaeologicalplanningconsultancy.co.uk/index.php

Dickson, A and Hopkinson, G. 2011. *Holes in the Landscape. Seventeen Years of Archaeological Investigations at Nosterfield Quarry, North Yorkshire.* http://www.archaeologicalplanningconsultancy.co.uk/index.php

Dymond, D. P. 1963. The 'henge' monument at Nunwick, near Ripon: 1961 excavation. *Yorkshire Archaeological Journal,* 161, 98-107.

Earle, T. 1991. Property rights and the evolution of chiefdoms, in T Earle (ed.), *Chiefdoms: Power, Economy and Ideology*, 71-99. Cambridge,: Cambridge University Press (School of American Research Advanced Seminar Series).

Earle, J. and Sallnow, M. J. 1991. Introduction, in J. Earle and M. J. Sallnow (eds.), *Contesting the Sacred: the Anthropology of Christian Pilgrimage*, 1-29. London: Routledge.

Fowler, C. and Cummings, V. 2003. Places of transformation: building monuments from water and stone in the Neolithic of the Irish Sea. *Journal of the Royal Anthropological Institute,* 9, 1-20.

Gillings, M., Pollard, J., Wheatley, D. and Peterson, R. 2008. *Landscape of the Megaliths. Excavation and Fieldwork on the Avebury Monuments, 1997-2003.* Oxford: Oxbow Books.

Hale, D., Platell, A. and Millard, A. 2009. A late Neolithic palisaded enclosure at Marne Barracks, Catterick, North Yorkshire. *Proceedings of the Prehistoric Society,* 75, 265-304.

Harding, A.F. and Lee, G.E. 1987. *Henge Monuments and Related Sites of Great Britain. Air Photographic Evidence and Catalogue.* BAR British Series 175. Oxford: British Archaeological Reports.

Harding, J. 2003. *Henge Monuments of the British Isles.* Stroud: Tempus.

Harding, J. In press. *Cult Centres, Religion and Pilgrimage: the Neolithic and Bronze Age Monument Complex of Thornborough, North Yorkshire.* York: Council for British Archaeology Research Report.

Loveday, R. 1998. Double entrance henges — routes to the past?, in A. Gibson and D. Simpson (eds.) *Prehistoric Ritual and Religion: Essays in Honour of Aubrey Burl*, 14-31. Stroud: Sutton Publishing.

Loveday, R. In press. Religious routine and pilgrimage in the British Isles, in C. Fowler, J. Harding and D. Hofmann (eds.), *The Oxford Handbook of Neolithic Europe.* Oxford: Oxford University Press.

Jones, L. 2000a. *The Hermeneutics of Sacred Architecture: Experience, Interpretation, Comparison. Volume One: Monumental Occasions. Reflections on the Eventfulness of Religious Architecture.* Cambridge, Massachusetts: Harvard University Press.

Jones, L. 2000b. *The Hermeneutics of Sacred Architecture: Experience, Interpretation, Comparison. Volume Two: Hermeneutical Calisthenics. A Morphology of Ritual-Architectural Priorities.* Cambridge, Massachusetts: Harvard University Press.

Lynch, H. 2005. *A Study of Cross Pennine Exchange during the Neolithic*. Unpublished PhD thesis, Newcastle University.

Manby, T. G. 1974. *Grooved Ware Sites in the North of England*. BAR British Series 9. Oxford: British Archaeological Reports.

Manby, T. G. 1975. Neolithic occupation sites on the Yorkshire Wolds. *Yorkshire Archaeological Journal* ,47, 23-59.

Manby, T. G., King, A. and Vyner, B. 2003. The Neolithic and Bronze Age: a time of early agriculture. In T. G. Manby, S. Moorhouse and P. Ottaway (eds.), *The Archaeology of Yorkshire: an Assessment at the Beginning of the 21st Century*, 35-113. Occasional Paper No. 3. Leeds: Yorkshire Archaeological Society.

Moloney, C., Holbrey, R., Wheelhouse, P. and Roberts, I. 2003. *Catterick Racecourse, North Yorkshire. The Reuse and Adaptation of a Monument from Prehistoric to Anglian Times*. WYAS Publications 4. Wakefield: Archaeological Services WYAS.

Moorhouse, S. 2003. Medieval Yorkshire: a rural landscape for the future. In T. G. Manby, S. Moorhouse and P. Ottaway (eds.), *The Archaeology of Yorkshire: an Assessment at the Beginning of the 21st Century*, 181-214. Occasional Paper No. 3. Leeds: Yorkshire Archaeological Society.

Moorhouse, S. 2004. Thornborough henges: a landscape through time. *Medieval Yorkshire, 33*, 19-33.

Morphy, H. 1995. Landscape and the reproduction of the ancestral past. In E. Hirsch and M. O'Hanlon (eds.), *The Anthropology of Landscape: Perspectives on Place and Space*, 184-209. Oxford: Clarendon Press.

Munn, N. D. 1992. The cultural anthropology of time: a critical essay. *Annual Review of Anthropology, 21*, 93-123.

Piggott, S. and Piggott, C. M. 1939. Stone and earth circles in Dorset. *Antiquity, 13*, 138-58.

Powell, J. H., Cooper, A. H. and Benfield, A. C. 1992. *Geology of the Country Around Thirsk*. London: HMSO Memoir for 1:50,000 Geological Sheet 52.

Proudfoot, B. 1963. Soil Report. In D. P. Dymond, The 'henge' monument at Nunwick, near Ripon: 1961 excavation. *Yorkshire Archaeological Journa,l 161*, 103-07.

Renfrew, C. 1973. Monuments, mobilization and social organization in neolithic Wessex. In C. Renfrew (ed.), *The Explanation of Cultural Change*, 539-58. London: Gerald Duckworth.

Renfrew, C. 2000. The auld hoose spaeks: society and life in Stone Age Orkney. In A. Ritchie (ed.), *Neolithic Orkney in its European Context*, 1-20. Cambridge: McDonald Institute Monographs.

Richards, C. 1996. Henges and water: towards an elemental understanding of monumentality and landscape in late Neolithic Britain. *Journal of Material Culture, 1*, 313-26.

Richards, C. 2004. A choreography of construction: monuments, mobilization and social organization in Neolithic Orkney. In J. Cherry, C. Scarre and S.

Shennan (eds.), *Explaining Social Change: Studies in Honour of Colin Renfrew*, 103-13. Cambridge: McDonald Institute Monographs.

Roberts, I. and Richardson, J. 2005. Discussion and synthesis. In I. Roberts (eds.), *Ferrybridge Henge: the Ritual Landscape*, 191-222. Leeds: Archaeological Services WYAS.

Roberts, I., Stead, I. M., Rush, P., Sitch, B. J., McHugh, M. and Milles, A. 2005. Appendix 1: excavation of the henge bank and ditches, 1991: a summary report. In I. Roberts (eds.), *Ferrybridge Henge: the Ritual Landscape*, 223-35. Leeds: Archaeological Services WYAS.

Rowe, P. 1998. *Flint Report — Nosterfield 1991, 1994-1996*. Unpublished report.

Saville, A. 1983. Excavations at Condicote henge monument, Gloucestershire, 1977. *Transactions of the Bristol and Gloucestershire Archaeological Society, 101*, 21-47.

Silverman, H. 1994. The archaeological identification of an ancient Peruvian pilgrimage center. *World Archaeology, 26*(1), 1-18.

Speed, G. 2003a. *Tancred Quarry, Scorton, North Yorkshire: Archaeological Watching Brief*. Unpublished Northern Archaeological Associates Report 03/137.

Speed, G. 2003b. *Bridge Road, Brompton on Swale, North Yorkshire: Archaeological Post-Excavation Assessment*. Unpublished Northern Archaeological Associates Report 03/141.

Speed, G. 2004. *Tancred Quarry Scorton, North Yorkshire: Phase 2 Archaeological Watching Brief*. Unpublished Northern Archaeological Associates Report 04/110.

Speed, G. 2008a. *Scorton Quarry, North Yorkshire, Area 1A: Archaeological Monitoring and Excavation Post-Excavation Assessment Report*. Unpublished Northern Archaeological Associates Report 08/39.

Speed, G. 2008b. *Scorton Quarry (Areas 2 and 4B), North Yorkshire: Programme of Archaeological Investigation Report*. Unpublished Northern Archaeological Associates Report 08/89.

Speed, G. 2010. *Scorton Quarry, North Yorkshire. Area 3(1) Archaeological Excavation and Watching Brief: Post-Excavation Assessment Report*. Unpublished Northern Archaeological Associates Report 10/29.

Speed, G. In preparation. *Excavations at Hollow Banks Quarry, Scorton, North Yorkshire. Volume 1*.

Tavener, N. 1996. Evidence of Neolithic activity near Marton-le-Moor, North Yorkshire. In P. Frodsham (ed.), *Neolithic Studies in No-Man's Land. Papers on the Neolithic of Northern England from the Trent to the Tweed*, 183-88. Newcastle: Northumberland Archaeology Group Northern Archaeology 13/14.

Thomas, N. 1955. The Thornborough Circles, near Ripon, North Riding. *Yorkshire Archaeological Journal, 38*, 425-46.

Vyner, B. 2000. Lost horizons: the location of activity in the later Neolithic and early Bronze Age in north-east England. In J. Harding and R. Johnston (eds.), *Northern Pasts. Interpretations of the Later Prehistory of Northern England and Southern Scotland*, 101-10. BAR British Series 302. Oxford: British Archaeological Reports.

Vyner, B. 2007. A Great North Route in Neolithic and Bronze Age Yorkshire: the evidence of landscape and monuments. *Landscapes,* 1, 69-84.

Waddington, C. 1999. *A Landscape Archaeological Study of the Mesolithic-Neolithic in the Milfield Basin, Northumberland.* BAR British Series 291. Oxford: British Archaeological Reports.

Wainwright, G. J. 1969. A review of henge monuments in the light of recent research. *Proceedings of the Prehistoric Society,* 35, 112-33.

Whittle, A., Atkinson, R. J. C, Chambers, R. and Thomas, N. 1992. Excavations in the Neolithic and the Bronze Age complex at Dorchester-on-Thames, Oxfordshire, 1947-1952 and 1981. *Proceedings of the Prehistoric Society,* 58, 143-202.

Ringlemere: A Pit/Post Horseshoe and Henge Monument in East Kent

Keith Parfitt and Stuart Needham

Abstract

The excavation of a ditch-enclosed mound at Ringlemere Farm, Woodnesborough, Kent, has revealed a rich body of evidence relating to a long and varied sequence of prehistoric activity. Following low-level Mesolithic and Early Neolithic activity in the area, the Late Neolithic period saw a great increase in activity apparently of both domestic and ceremonial nature, though not necessarily at the same time. Aside from the mound, still just visible in 2001, the most prominent archaeological feature was a substantial enclosure ditch with a north-facing entrance and indirect evidence for an external bank typical of the monuments that have come to be known as henges. The area enclosed was found to have more than 230 cut features of varied character and we present some preliminary interpretations of elements of multiple structural phases. Most relevant to the present discussion is a ring of pits or post holes, actually in the form of a horseshoe facing east-south-east and possibly pre-dating the enclosure. Associated with the pre-mound activity was a large assemblage of Grooved Ware, a much smaller quantity of Beaker pottery and large quantities of flintwork, but unburnt bone was absent due to adverse soil conditions.

Sometime around the turn of the third/second millennium BC, the addition of a central mound transformed the henge monument into a barrow of large diameter, though not necessarily of exceptional height. Full excavation of the part that had survived the plough gave little indication that this particular mound had served as a place for burial, but a large feature dug into its centre produced a spectacular Early Bronze Age cup of beaten gold and part of a rare amber pendant. The composite henge-cum-barrow monument appears to have served as a focal-point for the subsequent development of a group of at least eight other prehistoric ring-ditch/barrow monuments. It is argued that the re-shaping of the monument may conceal a more fundamental continuity in its socio-functional position; the deposition of the cup and amber objects were a celebration of that position.

Keywords:- Kent; Durlock Stream; Late Neolithic; Early Bronze Age; Grooved Ware; henge; post ring; domestic structures; round barrow

Introduction

The discovery of a henge monument at Ringlemere, near Sandwich in east Kent came about in a rather unorthodox way – in the course of chasing the context of a spectacular Early Bronze Age gold cup which had been found by metal-detectorist Mr Cliff Bradshaw in November 2001 (Parfitt 2003a; Parfitt 2003b). At the findspot, in the middle of a large field, there was a low, but quite distinct rise and Bradshaw himself immediately realised that this might be the ploughed down remains of a previously unknown round barrow; subsequent excavation confirmed this. The threat of continuing plough erosion made the full excavation of this prehistoric mound a priority, in order to seek a context for the cup, to investigate any other related contexts and to recover any further artefacts, whether *in situ* or disturbed. The project became a collaborative venture between the Canterbury Archaeological Trust and the British Museum, with annual fieldwork being undertaken between 2002 and 2006.   Financial assistance was provided by the British Museum, the British Academy, English Heritage and Kent Archaeological Society. The excavation team was drawn from Canterbury Archaeological Trust, Dover Archaeological Group, British Museum staff and students from several university archaeology departments.

Before work began it was naturally speculated that the gold cup might derive from a rich Early Bronze Age burial, in the 'Wessex' tradition, that had been struck and scattered by the plough as this cut through the last remnants of an important round barrow. Ultimately, however, the fieldwork provided little evidence to support the view that

either the cup or two contemporary amber objects derived from formal burials (Needham at al. 2006). Meanwhile, field-walking on and around the site brought to light a marked concentration of prehistoric flintwork, including a quantity of finely worked scrapers and other implements. The assemblage indicated significant activity during the Neolithic and Bronze Age periods. Geophysical survey and aerial photograph analysis further revealed that the visible barrow was not isolated but the largest monument in a group of circular ditched enclosures, and the only one with part of a mound surviving.

Excavation of the barrow began in March 2002. Within a few days, the quantity of Late Neolithic Grooved Ware pottery recovered had surpassed that of any other site in east Kent, strongly suggesting that the site had earlier roots and was not simply a Bronze Age round barrow. As excavation progressed, it emerged that the development of the site had been both long and complicated, with the gold cup apparently deposited relatively late in the main sequence of use of the monument. An outline of the site sequence has been published in Needham at al. 2006 (see also Parfitt and Needham 2007a; Parfitt and Needham 2007b), but the final detailed phasing of a complex set of structures will come in the full excavation report currently in preparation. The following summary must therefore be taken as an interim statement on work in progress.

Local topography and landscape

Ringlemere (NGR TR 2938 5698) is located in the eastern-most part of Kent, 14.5km east of Canterbury and 3.75km

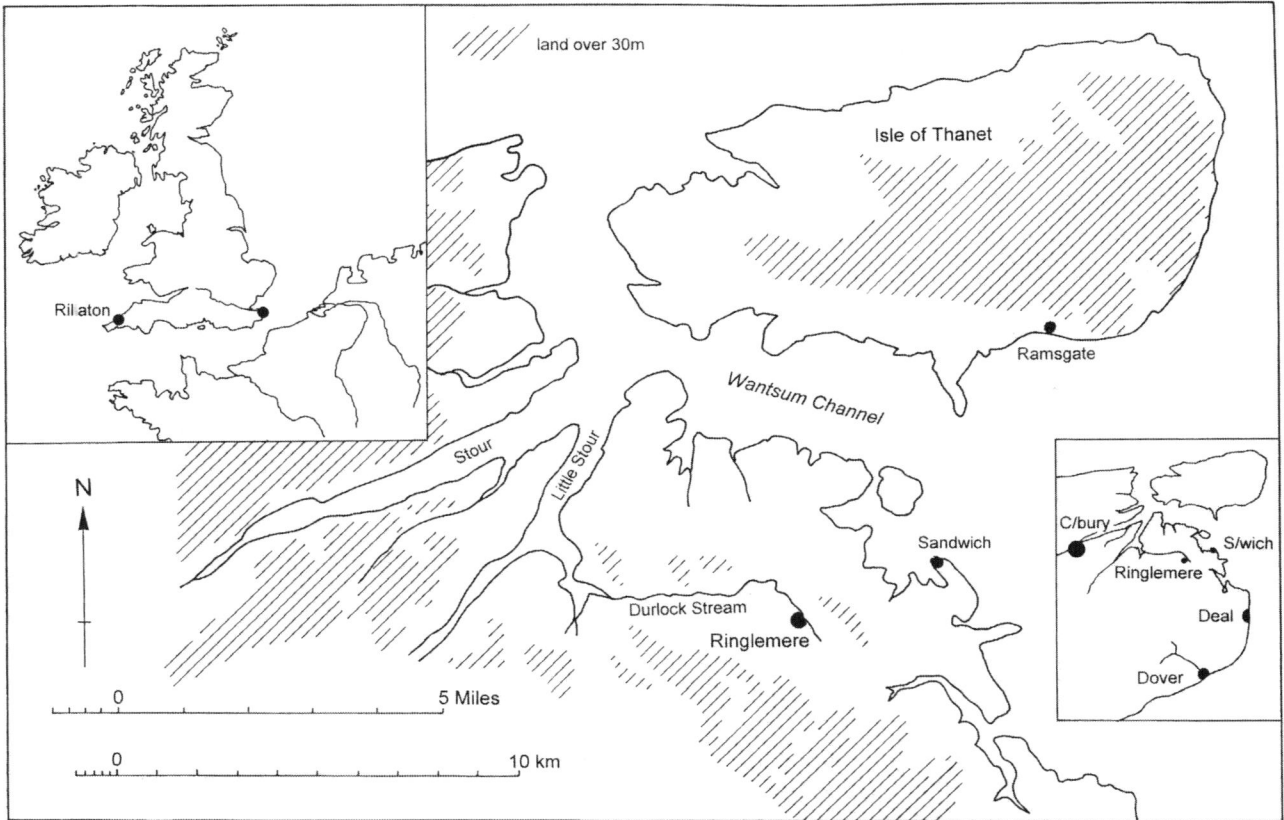

FIGURE 1: MAP OF NORTH-EAST KENT SHOWING THE LOCATION OF RINGLEMERE IN RELATION TO THE WANTSUM CHANNEL
(WITH INSET LOCATION MAPS).

west-south-west of Sandwich (Figure 1). The site lies at the foot of the North Downs dip-slope, in the parish of Woodnesborough, with Ringlemere Farm some 400m to the south-east (Figure 2). The surviving barrow mound is situated at an elevation of between 10 and 13m above mean sea level and is positioned towards the bottom of a long, north-east facing slope which constitutes the southern side of the valley of the Durlock Stream. The underlying geology here is head brickearth, with some gravel, over Thanet Beds clay.

Today, the Durlock Stream begins at a spring which rises just below the site (Figures 1 and 2) and flows along the foot of the Downs for about 6km westwards to join with the Wingham River which itself empties into the Little Stour near Ickham (Needham at al. 2006, fig. 2). In the past, the Durlock probably rose a little higher up the valley to the east. A network of modern field ditches in that direction often contain flowing water during periods of wet weather and could be vestiges of a more permanent fan of feeder streams at times of higher water table. The soils flanking the stream today comprise mostly fertile loams. Overall, the valley is relatively broad and shallow, offering little shelter from winds of any direction, but its northern slopes are a little steeper than the southern side where the Ringlemere monument complex is located.

The valley's northern slopes define one side of a ridge of Eocene sands that separates the Durlock valley from

the south-western edge of an extensive tract of low-lying marshland, now drained. This marsh represents the silted remains of the former Wantsum Channel. Throughout the prehistoric and Roman periods the Wantsum was open water, dividing the Isle of Thanet from the mainland of Kent (Figure 1). Archaeological evidence for activity around its shores suggests this was a much used water-way, providing sheltered landing places for local mariners and visiting traders, and a safer, shorter alternative to rounding the North Foreland for vessels travelling between the Thames estuary, the southern North Sea and the English Channel. Clark (in Bennett at al. 2008, xv) has recently high-lighted the importance of the Wantsum during the prehistoric period. Its sheltered waters could have provided an extensive natural harbour, which, significantly, lay at the very crossing point of two of Europe's greatest ancient waterway trading corridors; one running down the River Rhine, across the southern North Sea and up the River Thames; the other running through the English Channel from its Atlantic portals and then up the eastern coasts of Britain all the way to Orkney and Shetland. From the Early Bronze Age at least and until well into the historic period, these routes were regularly used by travellers, traders, colonists and invaders moving through north-west Europe, so that the lands around the Wantsum shore occupied a pivotal position.

Ringlemere probably lay between 3 and 4km inland from the prehistoric shoreline of the Wantsum and the site could not be seen from the water because of the intervening ridge.

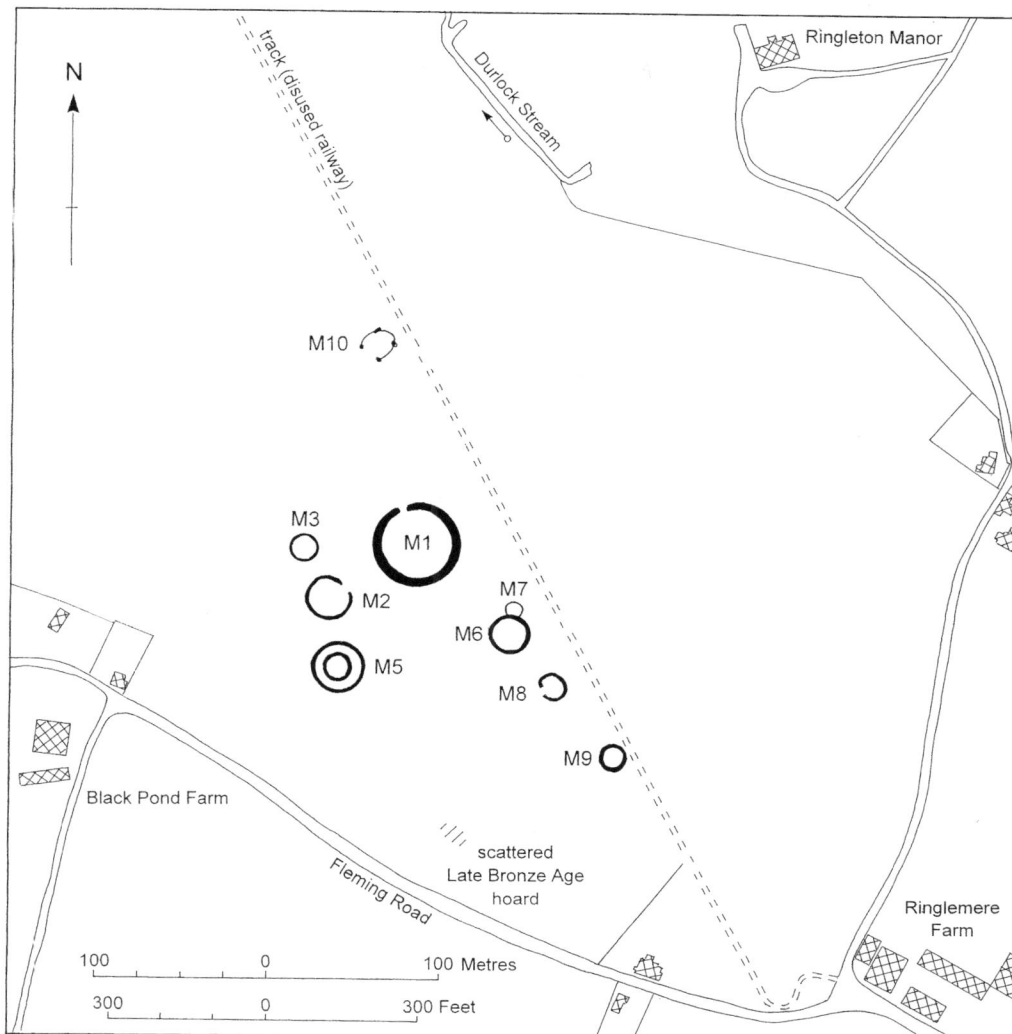

FIGURE 2: PLAN OF THE RINGLEMERE SITE SHOWING THE LOCATION OF THE EXCAVATED HENGE-BARROW (M1), ADJACENT RING-DITCHES (M2, 3, 5–9) AND OTHER DISCOVERIES.

Further west, the Little Stour and the Wingham River may once have formed a broad southern inlet opening off the main Wantsum Channel and capable of navigation by vessels with shallow draught (Figure 1). The existence of nearby landing places for water-borne traders and travellers could be significant for Ringlemere, not only in terms of the long-distance exchange connections implied by the Early Bronze Age exotica from the site itself and local finds of Neolithic axe fragments of non-local stone, but also more generally for the reception of changing cultural ideas and customs. Nevertheless, clear views to the Wantsum Channel, the Isle of Thanet and the open sea beyond were apparently not important in the actual siting of the Ringlemere complex, which lies in a more secluded position behind the coastal strip.

Neither does Ringlemere seem to have been located on any major land route. What is thought to represent a significant prehistoric trackway, leading inland southwards from the former shore of the Wantsum, passes through Wingham (present B2046), a few kilometres to the west of the site. Local east–west routes follow the higher ground on either

side of the Durlock valley, with the Roman road from Canterbury to Richborough taking advantage of the ridge to the north.

The lower reaches of the Durlock Stream and the Wingham River are today filled with a complex sequence of riverine clays and peat deposits. Study of peat samples recovered from a site near Wingham church during the 1960s, about 5km west of Ringlemere, generated an important pollen sequence. Dated by a single radiocarbon age determination of 3195±110 BP (1617–1049 cal BC; Q-110) analysis suggested that the region had been extensively deforested, presumably through agriculture, by sometime in the middle of the Bronze Age (Godwin 1962, 90). Subsequent work at Ringlemere has suggested that areas of long-term pasture already existed in the locality by Late Neolithic times (Heathcote 2003; Needham at al. 2006, 9).

It is becoming increasingly clear that east Kent – both the Isle of Thanet and the opposing part of the mainland – was once rich in prehistoric remains, especially round barrows, but the region has been intensively farmed and most ancient sites are now quite invisible on the surface (e.g. Parfitt 2006; Champion 2007, 87–92; Moody 2008, 94, fig. 45). Many had probably already been lost to the plough by the start of the eighteenth century so that early antiquaries could see little of interest here and, as a consequence, there is no long-garnered corpus of prehistoric excavation data and artefacts. Against this background of a heavily ploughed modern landscape, the survival of the basal part of a barrow mound at Ringlemere at once appeared to be of exceptional archaeological importance. The array of key information subsequently recovered from the site by excavation provides a clear object lesson in just what might have been lost at more heavily damaged sites.

The Ringlemere monument complex

Prior to the start of the Ringlemere project, the Durlock valley itself had seen little in the way of archaeological fieldwork, with few recorded sites or finds. Our intensive investigations have now established the presence at Ringlemere of a previously unknown complex of at least eight prehistoric ring-ditch/barrow monuments (designated M1–3, 5–8 and 10; Figure 2). Fieldwalking of some 13ha of land around this complex has shown that the entire area is covered by an unbroken, light to moderate, surface scatter of prehistoric flintwork, implying regular activity here during the Mesolithic, Neolithic and Bronze Age periods.

M1 is the substantial barrow associated with the Bronze Age cup, but excavation evidence suggests that this mound was a secondary feature, built on the site of an earlier henge (Needham at al. 2006, 16–30). This composite henge-cum-barrow monument appears to have served as a focal-point for the subsequent development of a group of smaller barrows and ring-ditches. Of these, Monuments 2, 3 and 5 consist of a line of ring-ditches running along the contour just above M1, following a localised outcrop of gravel on the valley side. Each of them could once have encircled a mound, but no traces survive today. In 2007 M3 was fully excavated and M2 sampled with a single trench (Parfitt and Corke 2009, 26). Unlike M1, these heavily plough-damaged sites have yielded relatively little information and few finds and features.

A little further downslope is a second linear arrangement of at least four ring-ditches (Figure 2; M6, M7, M8 and M9) extending in a south-easterly direction from M1 and again running along the contour of the valley-side. None of these sites has yet been excavated. Some 60m to the north of M1 lies M10, located by geophysical survey. Again unexcavated, it is difficult to interpret, although its most obvious characteristics seem to be four irregular anomalies that occur close to the cardinal points of the compass, at a distance of around 14m from each other. These could represent large irregular pits or post settings. They appear to be either incorporated into, or superimposed onto, a faint ring-ditch. Square four-post settings often form the core of Late Neolithic timber structures, as seen for example at Durrington Walls (Wainwright and Longworth 1971, 26 fig. 11, 42 fig 17), Durrington G68 (Pollard 1995b),

Stanton Drew (David at al. 2004, 349 fig. 7), Machrie Moor (Haggarty 1991, 61–2), Knowth (Eogan and Roche 1997, 101) and Ballynahatty (Hartwell 1998), but these are of much smaller dimensions with sides between 3.5 and 7.5m. Comparison can also be made with the four-stone settings known in upland areas. Such a setting at the heart of the Mayburgh henge (only a single stone surviving) appears to have been 15 x 15m (Topping 1992, 250–3). It is tempting to relate M10 to these structures, but soilmarks can be very fickle.

The henge-cum-barrow, M1

Working intermittently, as cropping of the field allowed, the surviving remains of the barrow mound (maximum height 0.50m), the complete interior of the underlying henge (diameter 42m, area 1350m^2), and about two-thirds of its enclosure ditch (of total circumference 145m) were fully excavated between 2002 and 2006. The remainder of the ditch fill is not imminently threatened by ploughing and has been left intact for future generations to investigate. No prehistoric burials were located and there are no conclusive grave-like features. However, the pre-barrow soil was found to be well preserved and over 230 cut features provide a wealth of detail concerning pre-mound activity on the site (Figure 3). These pre-mound contexts are associated with a sizable assemblage of Late Neolithic Grooved Ware, a little Beaker pottery and large quantities of flintwork. In fact, a good quantity of comparable cultural material was also recovered from the mound remnant, which transpired to be formed of decayed turves. The implication is that the turf had been collected from an artefact-rich topsoil outside the enclosure, presumably a continuation of the preserved topsoil under the mound.

At an early stage in the first season of excavation it was established that the monument incorporated a large ring-ditch. As investigation and understanding of the site progressed in successive seasons, it appeared increasingly likely that this enclosing ditch was not directly related to the barrow, but instead to a phase of pre-mound activity. The substantial proportions of the ditch and the size of the area it enclosed, subsequently reinforced by the discovery of an entrance causeway along with some slight evidence for the former presence of an outer bank, all pointed to it having been a henge monument (in the classic definition – see Gibson this volume) in an earlier phase. The associated Late Neolithic assemblage demonstrated significant pre-Bronze Age activity, but one of the key questions then became to what extent were the extensive artefact remains and numerous cut features directly associated with the assumed ceremonial enclosure. While henges were clearly a familiar feature of the Late Neolithic landscape, it is now established that similar monuments continued to be built in the Chalcolithic and into the earliest Bronze Age (e.g. Gibson 1998; Harding 2003; Needham 2012), so we could not even assume that the enclosure belonged to the Late Neolithic. Despite extensive excavation of the ditch fills, finds were few and the lower levels particularly sterile, so they provide little assistance with dating.

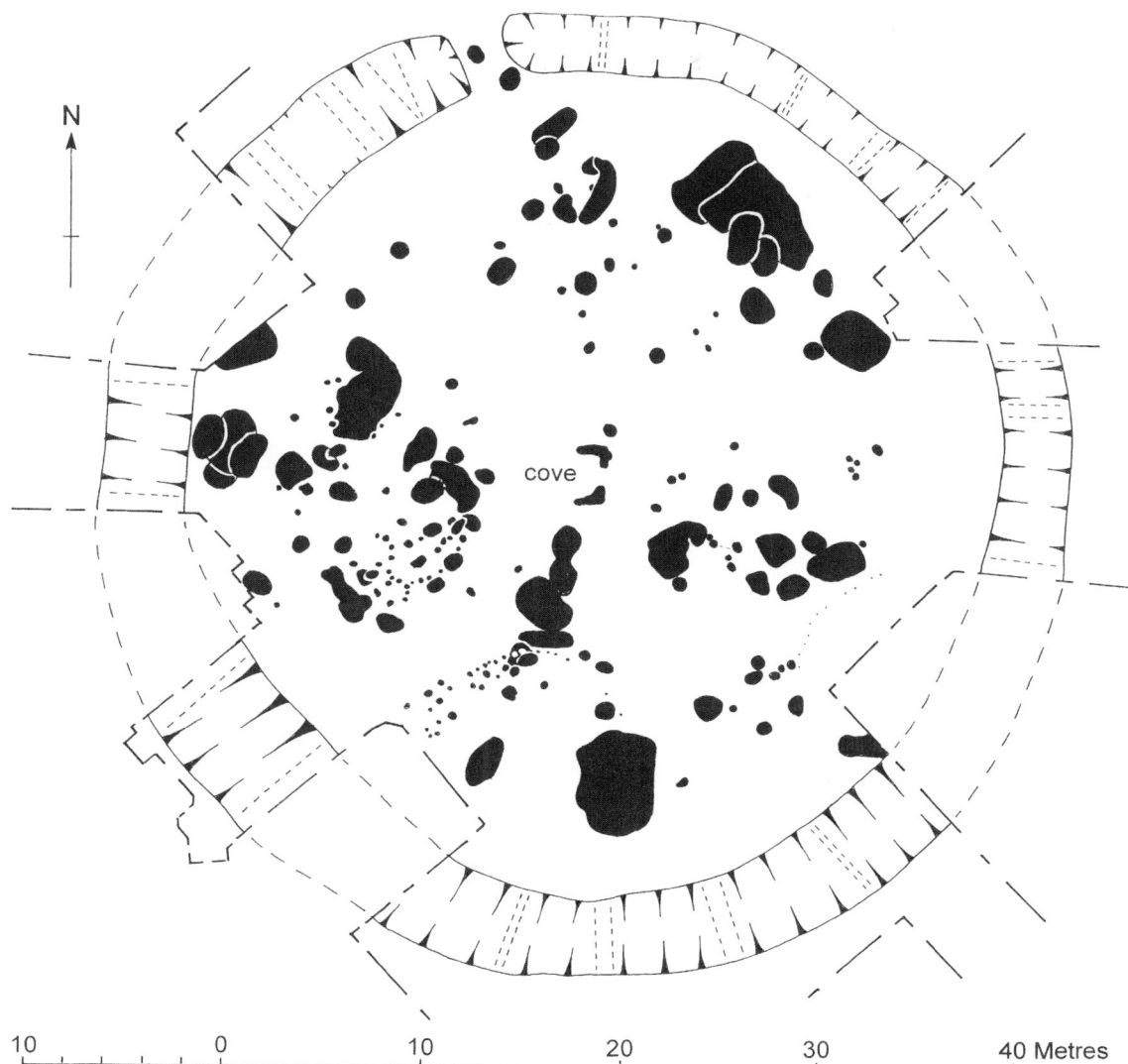

FIGURE 3: PLAN OF PRE-BARROW FEATURES ASSOCIATED WITH THE HENGE MONUMENT.

A further complication for the sequence arose as it became apparent that a ring of pits or post holes could be disentangled from the mass of features. Although forming an oval plan, open at one end, this ring was essentially concentric with the henge ditch; again the question of contemporaneity or succession came to the fore, especially since a succession from a timber circle to an enclosure has been shown to be the case at some other sites (e.g. Gibson 1998, 36; and this volume).

The enclosure

A defining feature of henge monuments generally is the presence of a bank *outside* the ditch (for history of definition and complications, see Gibson above). No bank survived at Ringlemere, but at a number of points around the circumference of the ditch, the character of the fill suggested that more material was slipping in from the outside than the inside. Particularly noticeable were deposits of gravel which occurred too high in the sequence of fills to have weathered directly from the natural

outcrop where this was exposed in the sides of the ditch. These layers appeared to be derived from some external source which has since been entirely removed. The simplest explanation is that this source was an encircling bank, partially formed of gravel, that had originally lain immediately outside the ditch but which has subsequently been deliberately levelled and/or erased by agricultural activity.

The henge ditch enclosed a near-circular area, though slightly longer in its N–S axis (Figure 3). Internally, it was between 41.50m (E–W) and 43.75m (N–S) across and externally, between 49.50m (E–W) and 51.50m (N–S). The ditch was of substantial proportions, but it has been truncated by a negative lynchet on all except the north-west side. What survives varies between 2.50 and 6.00m wide across the top and 0.90 to 1.50m deep. Up to 1m of its original depth could have been removed by ploughing in certain places. Although it was fairly constant in profile, with convexly sloping sides and a broad, flat base between 1 and 1.5m across, it is nevertheless clear that the ditch could not originally have been dug to standardised dimensions. Outside the area affected by the lynchet, just east of the north entrance, the ditch was 3m wide and 1.26m deep. By contrast, on the south-west side it survived 6m wide and still 1.45m deep after substantial plough erosion had occurred. There seems little doubt that the width of the original ditch would initially have been increased by natural erosion of its sides cut through gravel and clay-loam, but this increase would be variably counter-balanced by reduction as a consequence of the truncation. There was no convincing evidence for any re-cutting of the ditch. Its lowest fills were frequently laminar in composition and had clearly been water-laid. This implies that the ditch had held water, at least in wetter seasons, although probably due to the nature of the clayey subsoil rather than as any specific design feature.

On the northern side, a deliberate break occurred in the circuit of the ditch (Figure 3). This seems to have formed the only entrance into the enclosure; it is unlikely that another existed in the unexcavated ditch segments, but one should not forget the existence of henges or related enclosures with markedly non-opposed entrances, notably at Balfarg (Mercer 1981) and Stonehenge (Cleal *et al* 1995, 66 fig. 36). The entrance at Ringlemere survived to about 2.50m wide, although erosion of the ditch terminals may have reduced its original width a little. There appeared to have been no attempt to make the ditch on either side of this entrance any deeper or more impressive than in other parts of the circuit. The surface of the natural gravel across the entrance causeway and for several metres outside was carefully examined but there was evidence for neither wear of the subsoil surface, nor any other activity in front of the entrance. It seems likely that any significant deposits or shallow features here had been previously removed through centuries of plough erosion.

The only feature discovered in the entrance was a single large pit. This was cut 0.65m deep and was set in line with the middle of the ditch and slightly to the west of centre (Figure 3). It seems likely that it once held a large post, placed in the gap between the ditch terminals, either as a blocking structure or to constrict entry into the monument. Standing posts or stones are known in the entrances of other henge-type enclosures, such as Balfarg, Stones of Stenness, Stonehenge, Avebury and Mount Pleasant Site IV.

The internal feature complex

The fact that virtually all cut features occur inside the ditch, even though we excavated several sizable areas outside, may not be as significant as it appears. It has already been mentioned that the ground surface outside the monument came to be substantially reduced, by up to 1m, before being slowly restored by centuries of accretion under plough action. The initial reduction in level may itself have been partly due to erosion from agriculture before accretion took over as the dominant process. However, we now think it probable that a large part of the peripheral

ground-level reduction was caused by the excavation of, firstly, top soil and, secondly, underlying silt in order to construct the two-material barrow. Whatever the cause, all but the deepest of pre-existing cut features outside the ditch will have been totally carved away. The near exclusive distribution of features inside the henge is thus merely a matter of differential survival.

The ditch enclosed some 1350m^2 of gently sloping ground, in which about 235 separate archaeological features were recorded (excluding animal burrows, of which there were many). Virtually all apparently pre-dated the mound (Figure 3), that is to say, they were not visible during excavation until either the top of the buried soil or, in most cases, underlying subsoil was reached. This palimpsest of features included variously sized hollows, pits and post holes, a number of stake holes and three hearth-like features. Little in the way of obvious patterning or regular alignments is discernible at first glance. Clearly, several different phases of activity must be represented, although there are comparatively few instances where intercutting features allow fragments of a relative chronology to be constructed. The features could theoretically range in date from well before the construction of the henge monument up until a point in time immediately preceding the erection of the barrow. Indeed, on disentangling some elements of the palimpsest and taking account of chronological evidence available, we suspect strongly that the features represent a long sequence spread over two millennia, or a little longer. Identifying significant structures and groupings amongst such a palimpsest, with only minimal stratigraphic and close artefact dating evidence available, is always a challenge. After protracted study of the plans, however, a number of potentially significant groupings of features have been identified. We will only touch on some here in advance of the final report.

Most immediately obvious from the plan, and indeed obvious on site, are two L-shaped slots right at the centre of the enclosure. Originally, these probably contained timber uprights for a small rectangular structure aligned north–south and measuring *c*. 2.4 by 1.2m. This structure was apparently originally open to the west, with a more restricted opening to the east, and it has previously been described as a 'cove' (Figure 3; Needham at al. 2006, 12–13); similar rectilinear structures have been identified at or near the centre of an increasing number of henges and other ceremonial circles (but also in other locations, *ibid*, 17–28; see also Bradley 2011, 108–11) and on the strength of this recurrent association we suggest that the cove belongs with an active use-phase of the enclosure. This does not of course mean that the two were constructed at exactly the same time.

The long axis of the cove, lying N–S, does not line up exactly with the entrance, but there is a gently curving line of four features that seems to form a link between entrance and the centre of the site. We can also link in other feature sets, which, taken all together, result in a cardinally oriented layout of the henge interior. The various features concerned do not obviously make sense associated with other structural phases. They include an 'avenue' of four posts running west from the arms of the cove and a laid bed of flint cobbles on the floor of the ditch at its southernmost point. Within the corridor running eastwards from the cove are three pits, each of which contained a complete or near-complete Beaker pot; one had in addition the lower half of a second vessel. While one pit, that containing the second vessel portion, might have been just large enough to have contained a small, tightly crouched inhumation (subsequently decayed), the other two were rather small to be graves, although one could not entirely rule out crouched infants. We seem more likely to be witnessing a non-burial form of deposition involving (near-)complete pots, although presumably still of a ritual nature. Concern for marking cardinal positions is a recognized feature of henges (Gibson 1998, 77) and sometimes this extends to patterns that respected all four; for example, the corridors fanning out within the Mount Pleasant site IV multiple timber circles (Wainwright 1979, 22–8), or the foci for artefact deposition at Woodhenge (Pollard 1995a). If the Beaker-yielding pits are indeed associated with the henge and cove at Ringlemere, then they imply a later third millennium BC date. Dating this phase otherwise is problematic, since there is no useful evidence from the primary ditch silts, while two radiocarbon dates on charcoal flecks from the cove are very divergent and have to be discounted (Needham at al. 2006, 46).

The discovery on plan of a pit or post ring has already been mentioned. This could not be recognized in the field because of the limited area of the interior under excavation in any one season. Indeed, it was not readily apparent even on plan because of the fairly wide and not entirely regular spacing of the features. Nevertheless, the ring was suspected before the final season and it gains support from the facts that, firstly, it is more or less concentric with the enclosure ditch – as is the case at many other sites – and, secondly, the features involved cannot be better attributed to other structures. To be precise, the 'ring' is either an oval or a horseshoe open to the ESE and enclosing an area of 30 x 25.5m; the uncertainty derives from a choice between two pairs of features at the ESE end, but there may now be grounds for favouring the horseshoe interpretation (Figure 4; to be detailed in the final report).

Horseshoes, or open oval structures, can of course be paralleled elsewhere, most famously in the inner stone settings at Stonehenge (c. 14 x 13m), but not forgetting the similar sized one (c. 13 x 13m) made of eight substantial posts at Arminghall, Norfolk (Clark 1936). The post or stone ring at Cairnpapple is also, strictly speaking a horseshoe, albeit with a rather narrow opening at the SSE end (Piggott 1947–8, fig 3); its area of 32 x 26m is very similar to that at Ringlemere. Such horseshoe plans are of course echoed in the shape of single-entrance henges, some of which are elongated like the Ringlemere and Cairnpapple settings.

One of the features on the southern side of the Ringlemere pit/post ring was overlain by one of the three hearth-like features, all of which had quite heavily burnt clay within a shallow pit (0.12, 0.17 and 0.18m deep) sealed by the buried soil. Associated with this 'hearth' was a small amount of unidentifiable cremated bone, recently radiocarbon dated to 2885 – 2640 cal BC (4176 ± 28 BP; OxA-25853). This suggests that the digging of the horseshoe (and the erection and demolition of the posts, if such there were) dates to the early third millennium BC. The presence of cremated bone in pits or post holes is of course known at a few comparable sites of Late Neolithic date, such as Cairnpapple (Piggott 1947–8), Llandegai A (Lynch and Musson 2001, 48–54), Meusydd (Jones 2009), Stonehenge (Parker Pearson at al. 2009) and Dorchester-on-Thames site 3 (Whittle at al. 1992, 169–75). The latter was an egg-shaped circle of 12 posts, 21 x 18m across, with a NW-SE long axis. The context at Llandegai is often described as a 'cremation circle', but one of the present writers has suggested the cut features could have supported a cove-like structure around which the cremated bones came to be deposited (Needham at al. 2006, 26–7).

Little else can be securely associated with the horseshoe. However, a pair of post holes or pits is fairly symmetrically positioned at the centre of the ring, the line between them being transverse to the long axis (Figure 4). There is also another pair of post holes straddling the main axis just to the south-east, towards the horseshoe's entrance. Together these suggest either two 'portals' or a trapeziform structure. One of the more central features was cut by the southern L-slot of the cove, thus seemingly confirming the sequence from an early third millennium post/pit ring to a quite different, cardinally-oriented layout later in that millennium. Only the latter can be linked to the henge enclosure, given the spatial patterning observed, and it is possible that the post/pit horseshoe was unenclosed, as was the case at many other sites. However, it is worth noting in passing that the ring-preceding-enclosure sequence was not universal. Setting aside durable stone settings, the case of Balfarg (Mercer 1981) is instructive for here the various linear and circular alignments that can be extracted from the total and complicated feature palimpsest suggest strongly that some (though not necessarily all) timber structures coexisted with the enclosure (Needham at al. 2006, 25 fig. 20). Again, Richard Bradley has suggested that the inner pit/post ring at Milfield North was in contemporary use with the enclosing henge-style earthwork (2011, 106–7).

Having provisionally identified two structural sets of probable ceremonial character, it remains to consider the mass of other features. Some of these do present coherent sets; for example, a triple arc of post holes alongside Hearth I (but not necessarily contemporary with it) in the south of the enclosure, looks convincing as one side of an oval or sub-square structure. Reconstruction would suggest overall dimensions of about 11.5 x 9m and slightly offset post hole pairs on both the surviving NE and NW sides could suggest entrance porches. This compares well with, for example, the dimensions of the inner wall of the

Ringlemere pit/post horseshoe

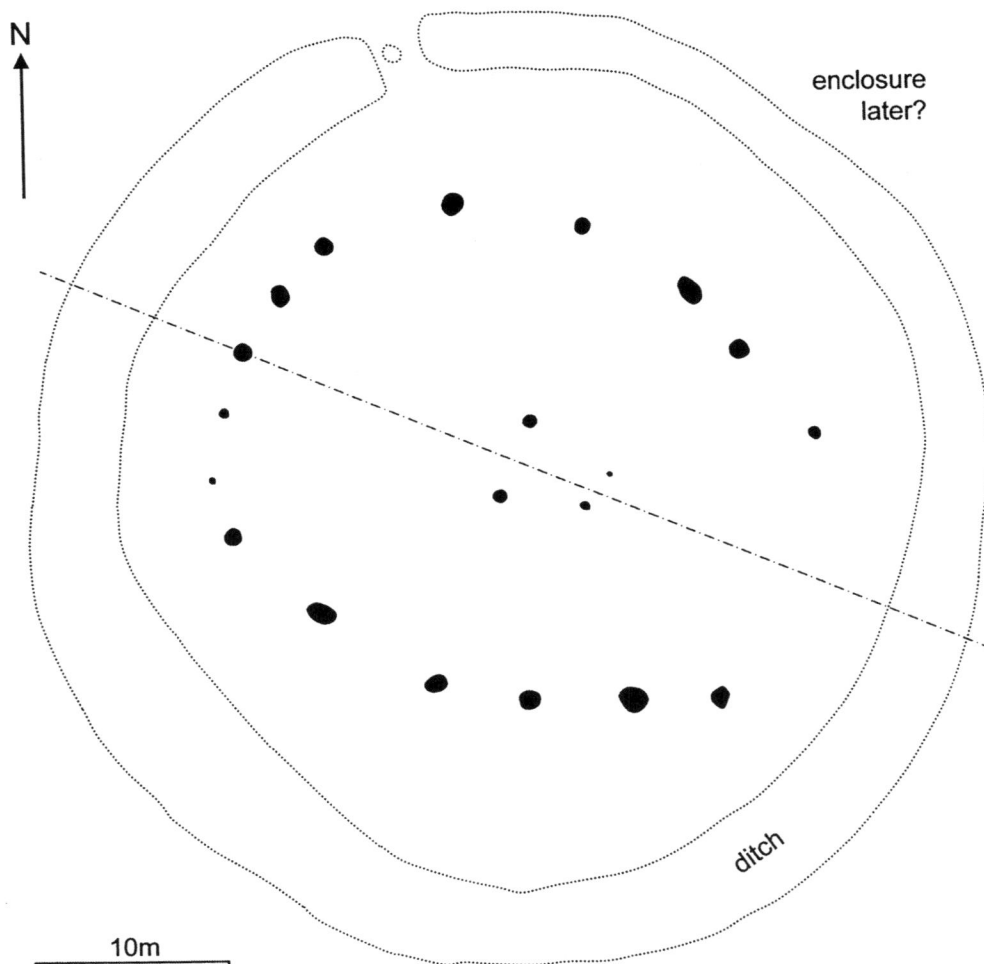

FIGURE 4: PROVISIONAL PLAN OF THE PIT/POST HORSESHOE.

large house (house 8) at Barnhouse, Orkney (Richards 2005), and is only a little smaller than the buildings at, for example, Machrie Moor site 1 (Haggarty 1991, 61 ill. 5), Durrington North Ring and Durrington G68, Wiltshire (Darvill 1996, 94 fig 6.8 nos 1 and 2; Pollard 1995b).

A compact mass of features around Hearth III in the western sector is more confusing; nevertheless, it is possible to reconstruct one complete oval post ring, albeit of tiny dimensions (2.8 x 1.9m), within which lies the hearth, and, outside, a series of further concentric arcs or lines, which must be more like screens than parts of entire buildings. This complex is more difficult to reconcile with a straightforward domestic use; the inner ring seems far too small for comfort, given the central hearth, and we may have to consider some non-residential function. It is, though, noteworthy that very small oval structures, only a little larger than this, are known on other Late Neolithic sites (Darvill 1996, 94 fig 6.8 no. 7, 96 fig. 6.10 nos 2, 3, 9 and 13). At Ringlemere there is also tentative evidence for a rectilinear post structure amongst a feature cluster

in the northern sector, but it appears to have survived incompletely.

In our working model we take most of these to be structural elements associated with the mass of Grooved Ware 'occupation' material and datable to the early half of the third millennium BC, although there is some ambiguity as to whether they preceded or followed the post/pit horseshoe. However, radiocarbon evidence now suggests a longer time depth to the 'occupation'; a curving line of stake holes inside the ditch in the south-east sector, possibly the last remains of a circular or oval building, has been dated to the Early Neolithic (3770 – 3645 cal BC; 4921 ± 30 BP, OxA-25857) on an *in situ* charred stake tip. Another line of larger features may date close to the turn of the fourth and third millennia. There is also evidence in the form of flintwork and perhaps occasional features for Mesolithic activity on the site.

Nothing has been said yet of a series of rather large pits. Most of these are difficult to relate to the provisional structural phases outlined, but they undoubtedly represent varied phases. One group just inside the ditch on the north-east side is almost certainly much later than the Late Neolithic to Early Bronze Age use of the monument. On the other hand, some are definitely early – for example, a medium-sized pit cut by the southern sub-square building just described. A few might have held substantial timbers but it has not been possible to suggest these belonged to anything more than isolated posts or limited settings of uprights.

One of the distinctive features of Ringlemere that will have become obvious is the co-occurrence of ceremonial type structures and a mass of 'occupation' refuse. At first sight, this will attract comparison with other refuse-rich henges, especially those in Wessex such as Durrington Walls, Mount Pleasant and Woodhenge; and we should not forget others with more limited material in association, such as Gorsey Bigbury, Balfarg Riding School or Coneybury. The occurrences of dense refuse have invited explanations

in terms of feasting by large seasonal gatherings of people, combined with reverential deposition around the ceremonial structures. However, one crucial difference at Ringlemere is that virtually no debris was entering the enclosure ditch as it filled up, contrasting with most other sites. So, this gives added poignancy to our on-going consideration of the interplay between occupation and ceremonial activity on this particular site.

The round barrow

At a later stage, probably around the turn of the third/second millennia BC, the 'open' enclosure, with any structures that were still standing inside, was transformed by the raising of a mound, probably covering the whole of the interior. The mound comprised two distinct components: a central core of soft, decayed turf, encircled by a ring of orange-brown clay-loam (Figure 5). By implication, the latter material would originally have spread right across the top, whence it has subsequently been removed by

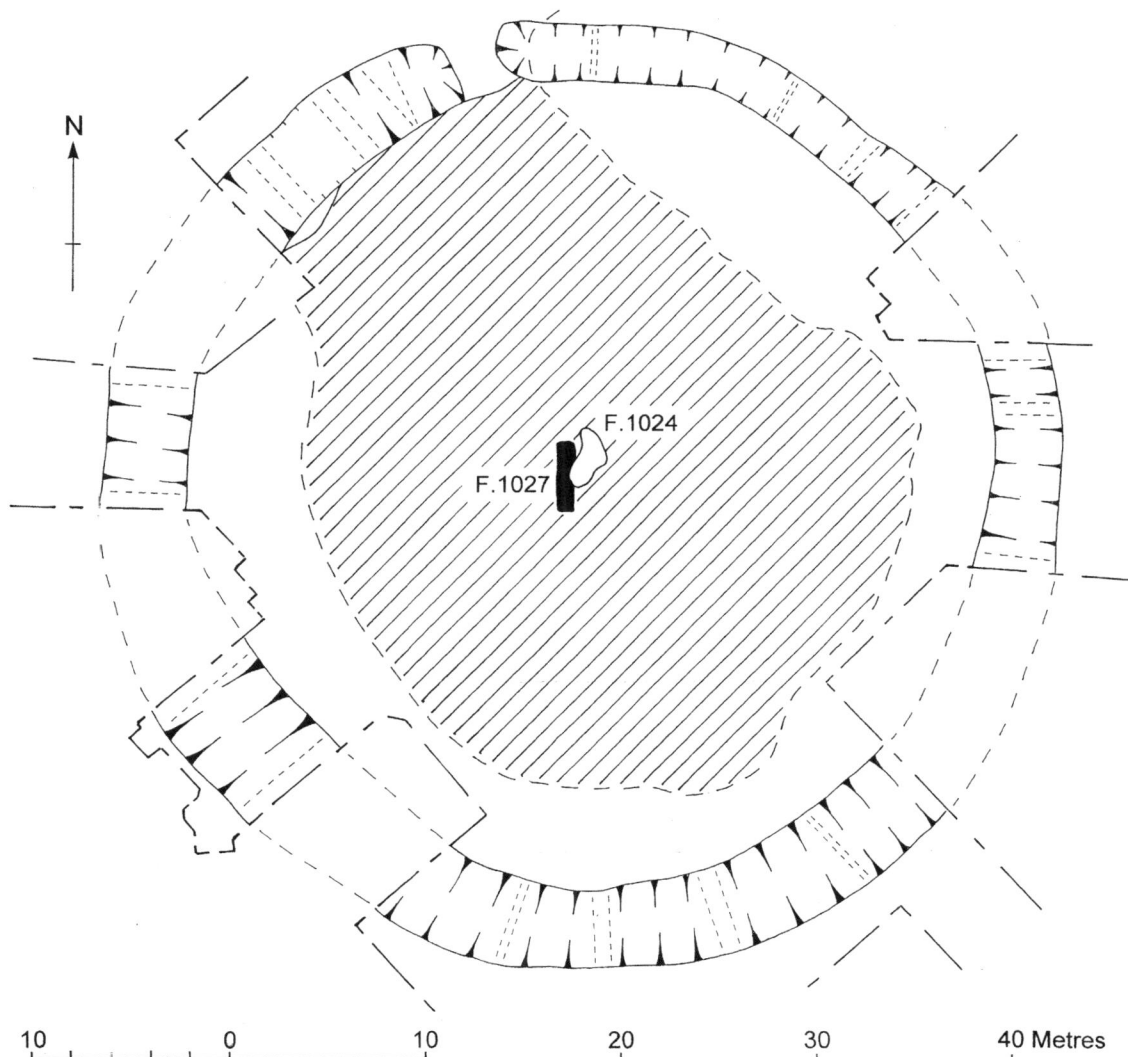

FIGURE 5: PLAN OF THE SURVIVING BARROW MOUND (SHADED) SHOWING THE ASSOCIATED FAÇADE TRENCH (F. 1027) AND THE LATER PIT (F. 1024) WHICH PROBABLY HELD THE GOLD CUP.

erosion and ploughing. As we have already noted, the turf core contained much residual midden material in the form of struck flint, calcined flint and broken pottery (again, mostly Grooved Ware with a much smaller quantity of Beaker), clearly derived from earlier activity at the site and evidently coming from somewhere outside the enclosure. At no point did we identify in the extant mound make-up the distinctive deposits of green clay and gravel through which the enclosure ditch had been cut; this implies that the material in the mound did not include up-cast from the ditch.

The quarrying of the material for the mound from outside the earlier enclosure has implications for morphology and scale. The two-material mound would have been impressive in its diameter, filling the whole of the old interior, some 42m across. Nevertheless, we have expressed reservations as to whether it was ever particularly high by comparison with other aggrandized barrows (Needham at al. 2006, 29). Certainly, it is unlikely that the centre of the mound would have been much more than 1m high when the central façade was dug through it (Figure 5, F. 1027), although it is possible that this was done at an intermediate stage in its raising (e.g. just the turf core). It is impossible now to know whether more was added and, if so, how much. Regardless of absolute height above ground level, however, one effect of quarrying the peripheral zone would have been to give a greater sense of height, the mound rising out of a broad basin.

The lack of any secure evidence for formal burials has been discussed before (Needham at al. 2006, 28–9) and was not overturned in the final stages of excavation. The feature cut into the centre of the turf core that contained one of the amber objects and probably the gold cup is not readily matched among Early Bronze Age graves (Figure 5, F. 1024). Only one of the underlying Beaker containing pits might possibly be a grave, but even if this was the case, it is not certainly connected to the erection of the mound. A pit cut into the old ground surface under the northern sector of the mound did yield a small amount of cremated bone, but this now appears to be considerably earlier than the Early Bronze Age. Rather than for the purposes of burial *per se*, we have previously given consideration to the mound serving as an elevated platform (*ibid*) for ceremonial activity associated with the developing Early Bronze Age monument complex around it. Attention was drawn to some parallel associations between henges and mounds, and since then there has been the publication of the additional example from Dyffryn Lane, Powys, where the evidence is again persuasive that the mound was added later to a pre-existing enclosure (Gibson 2010). Alex Gibson is also suggesting that Woodhenge may once have had a mound (this volume).

Whether the M1 mound pre-dated all the surrounding ring-ditches we cannot know. But in any case its reconfigured morphology may partly disguise a degree of continuity in the ritual centrality of M1 across the complex ideological transition from Late Neolithic to early metal age. An element of continuity is also seen in the erection of a new structure, the timber façade, bedded into the centre of the turf mound, but not dissimilar in length and orientation to the long axis of the underlying cove it replaced. The burial of the gold and amber finery in the mature Early Bronze Age could have been essentially a celebration of the continuing and long-held importance of M1 in the local social landscape.

Bibliography

Bennett, P., Clark, P., Hicks, A., Rady, J. and Riddler, I. 2008. *At the Great Crossroads Prehistoric, Roman and medieval discoveries on the Isle of Thanet 1994–95.* Occasional Paper No. 4. Canterbury: Canterbury Archaeological Trust.

Bradley, R. 2011. *Stages and Screens: an Investigation of Four Henge Monuments in Northern and North-eastern Scotland.* Edinburgh: Society of Antiquaries of Scotland

Champion, T. 2007. Prehistoric Kent. In J.H. Williams (ed) *The Archaeology of Kent to AD 800*, 67–132. Canterbury: Kent County Council.

Clark, G. 1936. The timber monument at Arminghall and its affinities. *Proceedings of the Prehistoric Society,* 2, 1–51.

Cleal, R.M.J., Walker, K.E. and Montague R. 1995. *Stonehenge in its Landscape: Twentieth Century Excavations.* Monograph 10. London: English Heritage.

Darvill, T. 1996. Neolithic buildings in England, Wales and the Isle of Man. In T. Darvill and J. Thomas (eds) *Neolithic Houses in Northwest Europe and Beyond,* 77–111. Neolithic Studies Group Seminar Papers 1 and Oxbow Monograph 57. Oxford: Oxbow Books.

David, A., Cole, M., Horsley, T., Linford, P. and Martin, L. 2004. A rival to Stonehenge? Geophysical survey at Stanton Drew, England. *Antiquity* 78, 341–58.

Eogan, G. and Roche, H. 1997. *Excavations at Knowth, 2: Settlement and Ritual Sites of the Fourth and Fifth Millennia bc.* Dublin: Royal Irish Academy.

Gibson, A. 1998. *Stonehenge and Timber Circles.* Stroud: Tempus.

Gibson, A. 2010. Excavation and survey at Dyffryn Lane henge complex, Powys, and a reconsideration of the dating of henges. *Proceedings of the Prehistoric Society* 76, 213–48.

Godwin, H. 1962. Vegetational History of the Kentish Chalk Downs as seen at Wingham and Frogholt. *Veröffentlichungen des Geobotanischen Instituts Zürich,* 37, 83–99.

Haggarty, A. 1991. Machrie Moor, Arran: recent excavations at two stone circles. *Proceedings of the Society of Antiquaries of Scotland* 121, 51–94.

Harding, J. 2003. *Henge Monuments of the British Isles.* Stroud: Tempus.

Hartwell, B. 1998. The Ballynahatty Complex. In A. Gibson and D. Simpson (eds) *Prehistoric Ritual and Religion: Essays in Honour of Aubrey Burl.* Stroud: Sutton, 32–44.

Heathcote, J. 2003. Geoarchaeological assessment of buried soil, mound material and ditch deposits. In K. Parfitt 2003a.

Jones, N.W. 2009. Meusydd timber circles and ring-ditch, Llanrhaeadr-ym-Mochnant, Powys: excavation and survey, 2007. *Archaeologia Cambrensis*, 158, 43-68.

Lynch, F. and Musson C. 2001. A prehistoric and early medieval complex at Llandegai, near Bangor, North Wales. *Archaeologia Cambrensis*, 150, 17–142.

Mercer, R. 1981. The excavation of a late Neolithic henge-type enclosure at Balfarg, Markinch, Fife, Scotland, 1977-78. *Proceedings of the Society of Antiquaries of Scotland* 111, 63–171.

Moody, G. 2008. *The Isle of Thanet, from Prehistory to the Norman Conquest*. Stroud: The History Press.

Needham, S. 2012. Case and place for the British Chalcolithic. In M.J. Allen, J. Gardiner and A. Sheridan (eds), *Is there a British Chalcolithic: People, Place and Polity in the Later Third Millennium*. Prehistoric Society Research Paper 4.

Needham, S., Parfitt, K. and Varndell, G. 2006. *The Ringlemere Cup: Precious Cups and the Beginning of the Channel Bronze Age*. British Museum Research Publication 163. London: British Museum.

Parfitt, K. 2003a. *Ringlemere Farm, Woodnesborough, Kent, Spring 2002: Assessment Report and Updated Project Design.* (unpublised C.A.T. archive report submitted to English Heritage, May 2003)

Parfitt, K. 2003b. Bronze Age Discoveries at Ringlemere Farm, Woodnesborough. *Archaeologia Cantiana,* 123, 390–391.

Parfitt, K. 2006. Ringlemere and ritual and burial landscapes of Kent. In Needham at al. 2006, 47–52.

Parfitt, K. and Needham, S. 2007a. Amber, gold and a Bronze Age Barrow. *Current Archaeology* 208, 41–46.

Parfitt, K. and Needham, S. 2007b. Excavations at Ringlemere Farm, Woodnesborough, 2002–2006. *Archaeologia Cantiana* 127, 39–55.

Parfitt, K. and Corke, B. 2009. Ringlemere, Woodnesborough. *Canterbury's Archaeology 2007–2008* (32nd Annual report of the Canterbury Archaeological Trust), 25–7.

Parker Pearson, M., Chamberlain, A., Jay, M., Marshall, P., Pollard, J., Richards, C., Thomas, J., Tilley, C. and Welham, K. 2009. Who was buried at Stonehenge? *Antiquity,* 83, 23–39.

Piggott, S. 1947–8. The excavations at Cairnpapple Hill, West Lothian, 1947–48. *Proceedings of the Society of Antiquaries of Scotland,* 82, 68–123.

Pollard, J. 1995a. Inscribing space: formal deposition at the Later Neolithic monument of Woodhenge, Wiltshire. *Proceedings of the Prehistoric Society,* 61, 137–56.

Pollard, J. 1995b. The Durrington 68 timber circle: a forgotten Late Neolithic monument. *Wiltshire Archaeological Magazine,* 89, 122–5.

Richards, C. 2005. *Dwelling among the Monuments: the Neolithic Village of Barnhouse, Maeshowe Passage Grave and surrounding Monuments at Stenness, Orkney.* Cambridge: McDonald Institute Monograph.

Topping, P. 1992. The Penrith henges: a survey by the Royal Commission on the Historical Monuments of England. *Proceedings of the Prehistoric Society,* 58, 249–64.

Wainwright, G.J. 1979. *Mount Pleasant, Dorset: Excavations 1970–1971*. London: Society of Antiquaries Research Report 37.

Wainwright, G.J. and Longworth, I.H. 1971. *Durrington Walls: Excavations 1966–1968*. Research Report 29. London: Society of Antiquaries of London.

Whittle, A., Atkinson, R.J.C., Chambers, R. and Thomas, N. 1992. Excavations in the Neolithic and Bronze Age complex at Dorchester-on-Thames, Oxfordshire, 1947–1952 and 1981. *Proceedings of the Prehistoric Society,* 58, 143–201.

Living with Sacred Spaces: The Henge Monuments of Wessex

Joshua Pollard

Abstract

By asking why henge monuments might be constructed in the first place, and in the locations where they were, we might better be able to understand their form and purpose. Here the matter is approached at two scales: first at a macro level by asking why the Wessex region should have become such a focus for monument construction during the first three quarters of the 3rd millennium BC. The second is more specific and seeks to understand the local conditions in which places might be transformed and become sufficiently sanctified to require monumentalisation. It is argued that places and their properties, powers and politics all played their part.

Keywords: Wessex, henge, settlement, monumentalisation, sacredness

The sheer concentration and often immense scale of the later Neolithic (*c*.3000-2400 BC) monuments of Wessex marks the prehistory of this region of southern Britain as something exceptional. On the chalklands of Wiltshire and Dorset are found the great monument complexes around Avebury, Stonehenge, Knowlton and Dorchester (Darvill 2006; Lawson 2007; Pollard and Reynolds 2002); while on the greensand of the Vale of Pewsey, between Avebury and Stonehenge is the Marden henge – possibly the largest monument of its kind (Wainwright 1971). Not far to the west, and surely related to the Wessex complexes, are the stone circles, henge enclosures and other constructions on deposits of Keuper Marl at Stanton Drew, Somerset (David et al. 2004); here including the second largest stone circle in the British Isles (Figures 1-4). Superlatives might abound – the world's largest prehistoric stone circle at Avebury; Europe's largest prehistoric mound at Silbury Hill; megalith transportation over the longest recorded distance in prehistoric Europe at Stonehenge; and so on (though note a Welsh victory when it comes to timber monuments, with the colossal palisade at Hindwell, Powys: Gibson 1999). It is hardly surprising then that the monuments of Neolithic Wessex have attracted a lengthy and sustained history of research; although it is also sobering to reflect that many basic questions relating to the period within this region remain to be addressed.

There has been a good body of work on the henge monuments of Wessex over the last decade, with renewed excavations at Stonehenge (Darvill and Wainwright 2009; Parker Pearson 2012), Avebury (Gillings et al. 2008), Durrington Walls and Woodhenge (Parker Pearson 2012; Parker Pearson et al. 2006), and Marden (Leary et al. 2010). A new henge has been discovered through excavation at Bluestonehenge (Parker Pearson et al. 2009), and further details of the structure of the Mount Pleasant henge has been revealed through aerial photography (Barber 2004). This period has also seen the publication of the excavations on the Wyke Down 2 henge on Cranborne Chase (French et al. 2007). The results provide a set of better chronologies and a much enhanced understanding of the role of these monuments. Their temporal span runs from the very beginning of the 3rd millennium BC (Stonehenge 1), with the larger 'henge enclosures' of Avebury (in its second phase), Mount Pleasant, Durrington Walls and probably

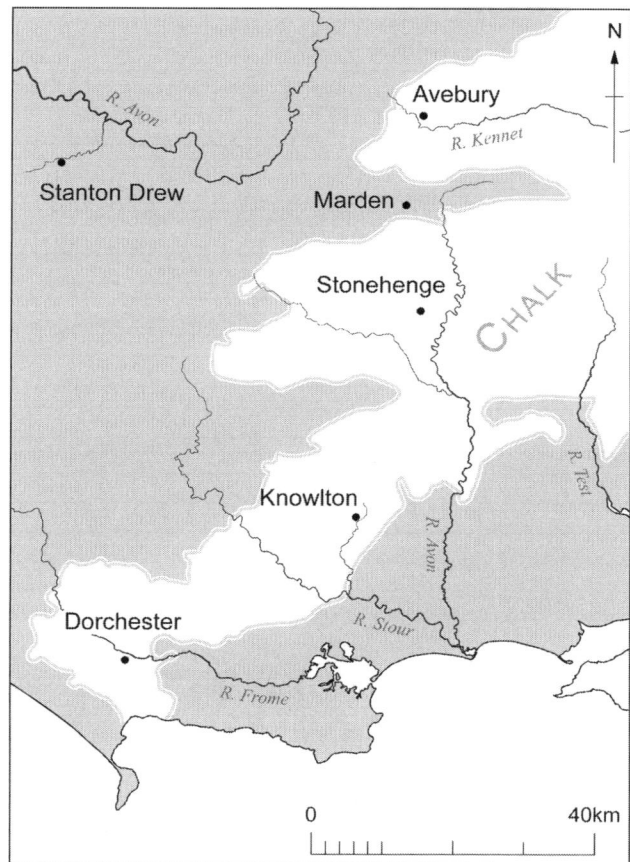

FIGURE 1. THE WESSEX REGION (DRAWING: ANNE LEAVER)

Marden falling within the period c.2800-2500BC (Parker Pearson 2012; Pitts 2001, Pollard and Cleal 2004). Of the smaller henge earthworks, Wyke Down 2 and Coneybury look to belong early in the 3rd millennium BC, while those enclosing Woodhenge and Bluestonehenge belong in the second half of that millennium (Barrett et al. 1991; Cleal and Pollard 2012; French et al. 2007; Pitts 2001; Richards 1990). Origins might be sought more distantly (even from Orkney given the early dates from sites such as Stenness: Richards 2005), or more locally among a range of circular earthwork constructions that include the Flagstones enclosure at Dorchester (Healy 1997) and the pit circle at

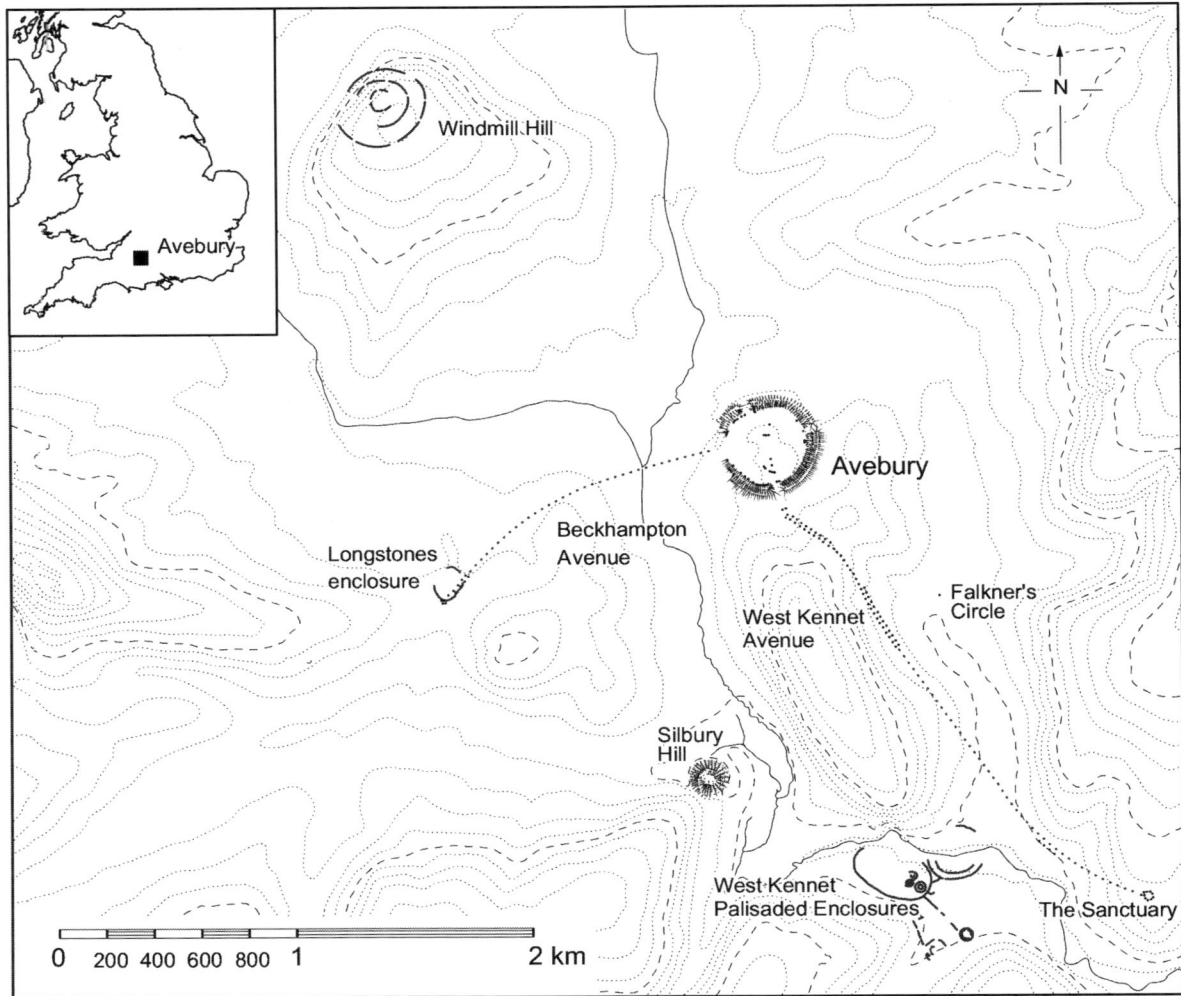

FIGURE 2. THE AVEBURY MONUMENT COMPLEX (DRAWING: RICK PETERSON)

Monkton up Wimborne on Cranborne Chase (French et al. 2007).

There is great variety in the format and structure of the region's henge monuments (cf. Harding 2003; Harding and Lee 1987). The henge earthworks themselves enclose settings of standing stones (Stonehenge, Avebury, Bluestonehenge, Stanton Drew, Site IV at Mount Pleasant), former timber settings (Woodhenge, Durrington Walls, Stanton Drew, Site IV, Coneybury), smaller henges (Durrington Walls, Mount Pleasant, Marden), large mounds (Marden), or nothing (visible) at all (Wyke Down). A number of related structures share 'henge-like' characteristics, including the Sanctuary near Avebury (Cunnington 1931), where an outer stone circle effectively substitutes for a henge earthwork, and the inner palisade enclosures at West Kennet, which 'wrap' smaller timber structures in much the same fashion (Whittle 1997). Such variety highlights both the inadequacy of our classificatory schemes (Gibson, this volume), and the possibilities for combination and appropriate deployment of a repertoire of architectural devices that presented themselves to Neolithic communities (Thomas 2004). At a general level, what might have mattered most were the properties of the substances – stone, earth, timber, and so forth – that were engaged to create these monuments. The idea, for instance, that stone was ontologically connected to ancestral realms, while timber held a closer connection to corporeal life, does hold remarkably well through various sets of material associations for complexes such as those around Stonehenge and Avebury during the middle of the 3rd millennium BC (Parker Pearson and Ramilisonina 1998; Parker Pearson et al. 2006). Perhaps because of perceived transformatory and life-giving properties, streams, rivers and other water features also hold a recurrent connection with many of these monuments, *regardless of their form* (cf. Leary and Field 2010).

The concern is not, then, to become embroiled in complex discussion over categorisation, because the answers to many of our questions relating to these constructions do not lie within typological refinement (Bradley 1998, 2000). By asking why monuments might be constructed in the first place, and in the locations where they were, we might be better able to understand their form and purpose. Here the matter is approached at two scales: first at a macro level by asking why Wessex should be so different, and why the region should have become such a focus for

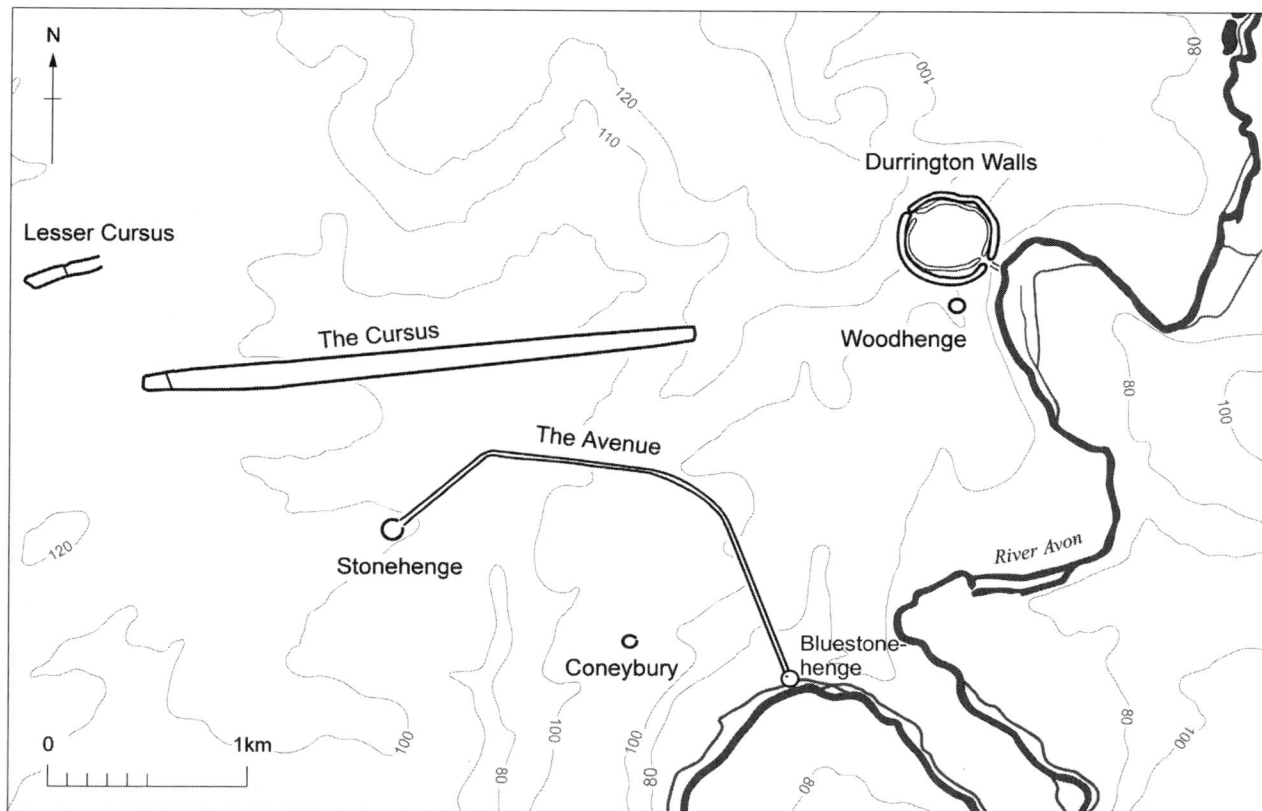

FIGURE 3. THE STONEHENGE MONUMENT COMPLEX (DRAWING: ANNE LEAVER)

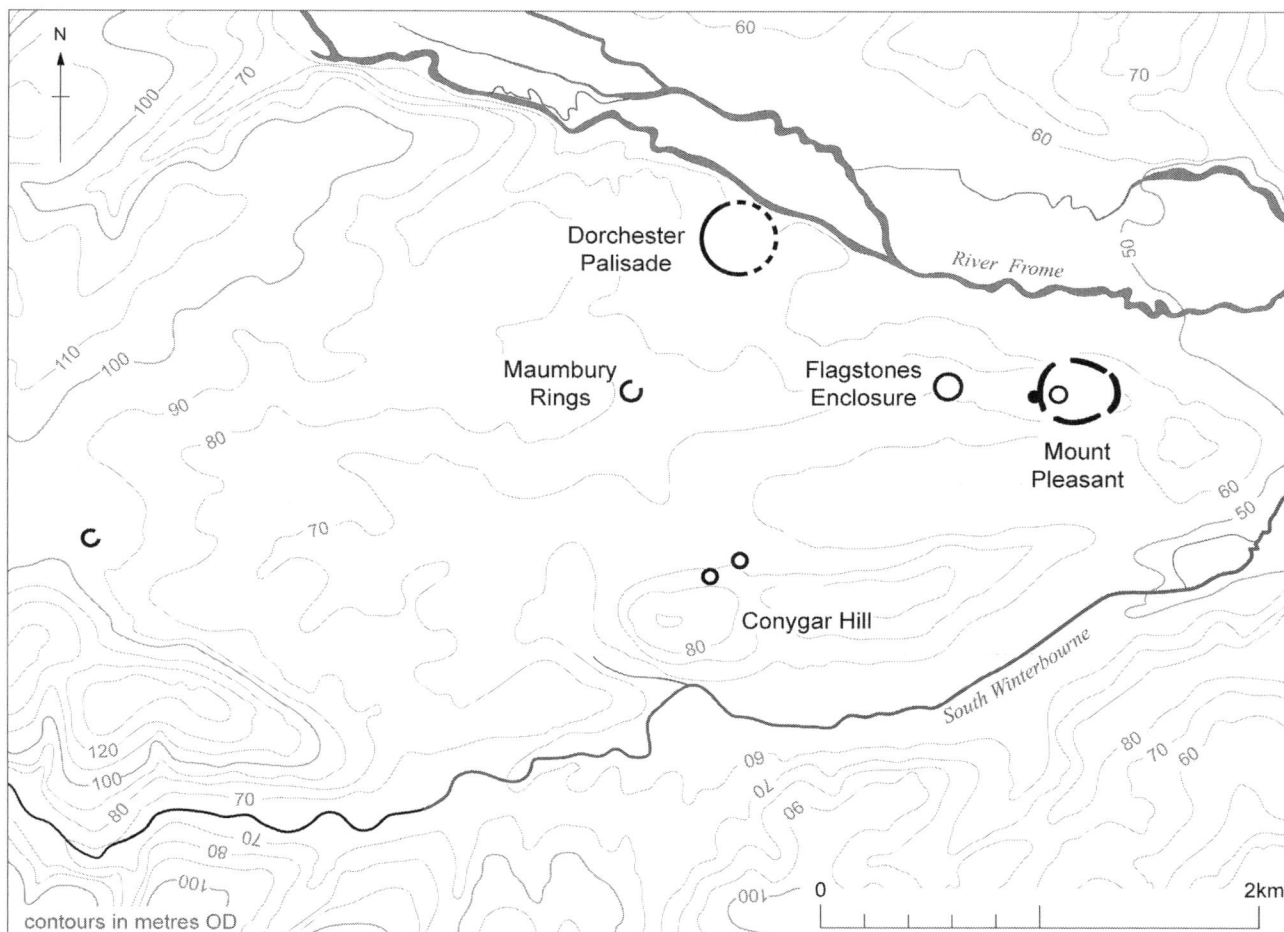

FIGURE 4. THE DORCHESTER MONUMENT COMPLEX (DRAWING: ANNE LEAVER)

monument construction during the first three quarters of the 3rd millennium BC. The second is more specific and seeks to understand the local conditions in which places might be transformed and become sufficiently sanctified to require monumentalisation. Places and their properties, powers and politics all played their part. In particular, there often exists a close link between settlements and settlement histories and the eventual creation of henges, highlighting processes by which the status of certain locations could shift over time, some becoming progressively more sacred (and others not). This process often involves a sanctification of structures and material traces.

Why Wessex?

It is stressed above that events displayed in Wessex during the later Neolithic are not typical of those of many other regions of Britain. They are somewhat remarkable, and we must account for this. Several features, both historic and inherent to the region make it distinctive.

Beginnings

First, there is the issue of longer, pre-Neolithic histories of activity within the wider region. It is striking that, with the exception of Cranborne Chase (Barrett et al. 1991, 29-30; French et al. 2007, 219-20), the higher areas of chalkland later occupied by Neolithic monuments seem not to have attracted a sustained late Mesolithic presence, perhaps because they were both too dry and largely devoid of concentrations of game. In the Stonehenge landscape what late Mesolithic activity has been identified is confined to the corridor of the Avon valley; while that in the wider environs of the Avebury landscape is largely focused further downstream along the Kennet or on the claylands to the west (Darvill 2006; Pollard and Reynolds 2004). For the Avebury region, Whittle (1990) proposed a process of infill early in the Neolithic, and this remains a viable model. The relative 'emptiness' of these landscapes could have afforded them a distinctive character – one that was more closely connected to the new worlds of Neolithic living than older frames of reference.

Identity and place

Second, the broader distribution of distinctive types of earlier Neolithic monuments and certain forms of material culture mark out this part of southern Britain as a zone of overlap between different traditions that might be generalised as 'eastern' and 'western'. Both (eastern) earthen and chambered (western) Cotswold-Severn style long mounds overlap here (Darvill 2004; Kinnes 1992). The principal concentration of causewayed enclosures occurs in a north-east–south-west band running from the Upper Thames Valley onto the Wessex chalk (Oswald et al. 2001, fig. 1.1). Two of the largest of these – Windmill Hill and Hambledon Hill – are located in similar topographic positions on the edge of the high chalk facing out to the north and west, reflecting connections seen in the material culture deposited on those sites (Mercer and

Healy 2008; Whittle et al. 1999). Undoubtedly, part of the role of these large enclosures was to facilitate and mediate contacts between different communities (Edmonds 1999), both sites potentially possessing very wide 'catchments' for periodic gatherings that could have brought together people from regions as distant as the South-Western Peninsular, Cotswolds, the south coast and Middle Thames Valley. Aspects of the early-mid-4th millennium BC artefact record also highlight the overlap of different cultural traditions along the Wessex chalk. The area lies at the junction of two different earlier Neolithic 'families' of pottery – Southern Decorated Wares and South-Western styles (Darvill 2010, fig. 33). Wessex is perhaps less a fault line, than a liminal zone in which communities with two or more distinct senses of origin met. That status was maintained into the 3rd millennium BC, when even larger scale gatherings are implied by massive public monuments such as Avebury, Stonehenge and Mount Pleasant. Their spheres of influence are hinted at by the long distances over which animals (and so people) were moved, into and across the region as illustrated by data coming from recent strontium and oxygen isotope work carried out by the Feeding Stonehenge Project (Viner et al. 2010). In its principal stone phase, Stonehenge might even have stood as a monument that represented the uniting of previously fractious communities from across southern Britain (Parker Pearson pers. comm.). Certainly by the late Neolithic, the 'core' landscapes of Wessex had become potent places with deep and politically complex histories.

Landscape

Could the very character of the Wessex landscape have afforded it qualities that were perceived as special and which set it apart from other regions of southern Britain? Especially when approached from their northern and western edges, the dramatic escarpments of the Wessex chalklands offer a striking and distinctive topography; while movement onto their tops gives the impression of entering a vast elevated plateau. The effect in places is somewhat like stepping onto an island surrounded by a sea of clay, gravel and greensand vales. That sense of height, and of a *different place* may have been regarded as highly significant. There is also something distinctive about the elemental constituents and qualities of the chalk: its weather (the chalk and its coombes capture moisture, resulting in distinctive mists and light); its springs and seasonal streams (the winterbournes: Cleal 2005); bands of flint and spreads of sarsen stone (Field 2005); and even the chalk itself. Form, texture, colour, and atmosphere all play their part.

The whiteness of chalk and its workability may have been important qualities, and these, along with presence of bands of flint contained within, perhaps made this rock a potent and generative substance rather than just inert geology (cf. papers in Boivin and Owoc 2004 for concepts of animate geology). It is surely not coincidental that chalk was preferentially chosen over other malleable substances such as clay as the medium for manufacturing a range of

FIGURE 5. THE AVEBURY HENGE DITCH UNDER EXCAVATION BY HAROLD ST. GEORGE GRAY DURING THE FIRST QUARTER OF THE 20TH CENTURY (PHOTO: ALEXANDER KEILLER MUSEUM, AVEBURY)

antler and human bone were sealed within the backfill of the shafts (Bradley 1975).

Shafts and pit-defined ditches are a feature of many of the Cranborne Chase and Dorchester henges. In addition to Maumbury Rings and Monkton-up-Wimborne, one can note their occurrence at the Wyke Down henges (Barrett et al. 1991; French et al. 2007), probably with the first phase at Site IV, Mount Pleasant (Wainwright 1979), at Flagstones, and forming the circuits of the small Conygar Hill monuments (Smith et al. 1997). There is a strong possibility that the deeper and more dramatic of these artificial pits were dug to emulate natural solution holes on the chalk of this region (Tilley 1999, 225-9). The natural collapse feature in Firtree Field on Cranborne Chase looks to have opened up during the late 5th millennium BC, and received a series of deposits in its upper fills (French et al. 2007, 76-8). Other possible solution/sink holes run alongside the Knowlton henge complex (French et al. 2007, 41), and it could be that their presence marked this location as one where enhanced intercession with the supernatural occurred. It is not difficult to image how these 'openings-up' into an underworld, into the heart of the chalk, were invested with enormous significance, being perceived as the actions of spirits, gods or other spiritual beings that dwelt in the rock and its underground streams.

objects likely linked to fertility concerns, notably phalli, balls and cups (Teather 2007). Direct links between this material and concepts of regeneration might be implied by the use of chalk capping on later round barrow mounds. That special quality afforded to chalk as a substance is also reflected in attempts to dig deep into the rock. At Avebury, Harold St George Gray's excavations during the early part of the 20th century dramatically illustrated the incredible depth (over 9m at the southern entrance) and narrowness of the henge ditch (Figure 5); in places its base reaching the interface between the chalk and water-table (Gray 1935). As Ashbee (2004) notes, the profile of the ditch ensured that its lower third silted rapidly, so depth here was not sought for lasting visual effect. The same desire for deep penetration of the chalk is seen with the shafts dug into the base of the henge ditch at Maumbury Rings (Bradley 1975), and with the shaft-within-pit feature of the late 4th millennium BC Monkton-up-Wimborne monument (French et al. 2007). At Maumbury Rings, in acts which suggest a complex reciprocal relationship with the chalk – literally an 'economy of substances' (Thomas 1999) – a remarkable series of deposits of carved chalk, stag's skulls,

Digging deep perhaps afforded communication and negotiation with those agencies. There can be little doubt that natural features were often ascribed great potency, and that their presence affected the way landscapes were understood and engaged with (Bradley 2000), often leading to significant acts of monumentalisation. Within the Stonehenge environs, the initial axis of the Greater Cursus was aligned on the distinctively-profiled Beacon Hill to the east (Thomas et al. 2009), one of the more remarkable landmarks in this otherwise 'unremarkable' landscape (Tilley et al. 2007). However, it is at Stonehenge itself where the most dramatic evidence of monumentalisation arising from the ascription of supernatural/mythic value to a natural feature can be found. Recent excavations by the Stonehenge Riverside Project have shown that the solstice-aligned section of the Avenue running from the north-east entrance of monument is essentially a geological feature, augmented around 2400BC by the cutting of shallow lengths of ditch (Parker Pearson 2012). Here, through a freak of geology, heaven and earth literally came together in a natural feature that emulated the form of a weathered and ancient earthwork possessed of a solstitial alignment. Perhaps recognised for millennia, given the presence close by of the remarkable 8th-millennium BC Stonehenge car park post-alignment (Cleal et al. 1995), its presence must surely provide the reason for the particular siting of the Stonehenge monument.

Around the headwaters of the Kennet near Avebury, and to a lesser extent in the Vale of Pewsey and on Salisbury Plain, another natural feature afforded these landscapes considerable significance – that was the presence in varying densities of spreads of resilient Tertiary sandstone known as sarsen. The greatest concentration occurred in the dry valleys bisecting the chalk around the headwaters of the River Kennet at Avebury, where its sheer presence must have given this landscape a distinctly 'foreign' feel; different from many other regions of chalk, and perhaps closely affiliated in the minds of Neolithic communities with the stoney uplands of the far west. (Again, the sense of the qualities of 'eastern' and 'western' worlds coming together in this region must be stressed.) Sarsen was widely used in the creation of burial chambers during the region's earlier Neolithic, and in circles, avenues and box-like 'cove' features during the late Neolithic (Gillings et al. 2008; Pollard and Reynolds 2002). The same stone was chosen for the outer circle and trilithon settings at Stonehenge (Cleal et al. 1995), and in the cove inside the Site IV henge at Mount Pleasant (Wainwright 1979). It would be a mistake, however, to think that this stone was simply regarded as a hindrance or inert building material (Gillings and Pollard 1999; Pollard and Gillings 2009). The way it was engaged with is telling of a recognition of an ontological status different to that of modern geological definitions; perhaps even, on occasions, stones being perceived as invested with a certain animism. During the 4th millennium BC even quite tiny blocks of sarsen could engender respectful treatment or actions of 'control', seen for example with the peculiar care taken with their incorporation within the non-funerary long mounds of South Street and Beckhampton Road (Ashbee et al. 1979).

During the 3rd millennium BC certain sarsens in the Stonehenge landscape – notably at Bulford and the Cuckoo Stone – were raised from their natural positions and set as standing stones; a process that surely altered their status, yet still respected their existing identity as important entities (Colin Richards pers. comm.). On a very different scale, those sarsens utilized for the outer circle and trilithons of the great monument at Stonehenge were both divorced from their locations of origin and modified in such a way that little of their given form remained evident. At Avebury, the stones used in the circles, avenues and other settings were left unworked (Smith 1965a). By virtue of their size, distinctive shape and prior histories (indicated by zones of axe polishing), at least some of these stones possessed an identity – as known and perhaps named things – that was not removed but transferred to the new locations where they were re-set. We could see that process as one in which the potency of stone was being harnessed (Gillings and Pollard 2004, 69).

Human history, geology and topography all collided to make the Wessex chalk a special place. Out of what we might call nature or geology, but which to Neolithic minds was a world of potent agencies and creative forces, some perhaps generated during a mythic time of beginning, came the conditions within which monumentalisation could occur.

A sense of place

We can therefore make a claim that the conditions for the creation of the major 3rd millennium BC ceremonial complexes around Avebury, Stonehenge, Knowlton and Dorchester arose, in part, from the particular location of Wessex, and the distinctiveness of its geology, topography and other elements. Occasionally, as with Stonehenge and its avenue, it might be the presence of remarkable natural features that provides the explanation for the location of major monuments – their building was a response to the qualities of place. Another dimension to this significance of place can be found in the relationship between the dynamic histories of settlement and monument creation. It is all too easy to think of these clusters of monuments as forming primarily 'ceremonial landscapes'. Admittedly, there are occasions when the evidence looks that way: when henge and other monuments have no obvious structural or spatial connection to contemporary settlement features. A case in point is provided by the Thornborough and Ferrybridge henge complexes in Yorkshire, where evidence suggests settlement at some distance (Harding 2000; Roberts 2005). That is not the case with any of the Wessex complexes, where monuments were built within landscapes with well-established histories of settlement, and where spatially the two sorts of activity might overlap. The ubiquity of contemporary lithic scatters and other traces of settlement show these landscapes to have been, periodically at least, quite densely occupied (Barrett et al. 1991; French et al. 2007; Holgate 1987; Richards 1990).

This leads on to the question of how the quotidian and the sacred intersect in the context of monument creation. Should we see the dynamics and imperatives of monument building as separate to the concerns of the everyday? On one level the dynamics of settlement and monument building have to be related, since the very process of mobilising resources and labour to create major structures involves people being drawn in to inhabit these landscapes while that work went on. The traces of this monument-driven settlement can be dramatic, as seen with the extensive, mid-3rd millennium BC seasonal settlement at Durrington Walls, linked to the building of the Southern Circle and likely main stone phase of Stonehenge (Parker Pearson 2007). In fact, the relationship between settlement and monument creation can be both more complicated and sometimes indirect, but nonetheless critical to understanding the imperative for making 'ceremonial' architecture, and it this issue which will be explored here.

At this point several strands of recent observation need to be drawn together. The first is Bradley's (2005) argument that ritualization often follows the logic of concerns of daily life, so we might expect that the format of particular

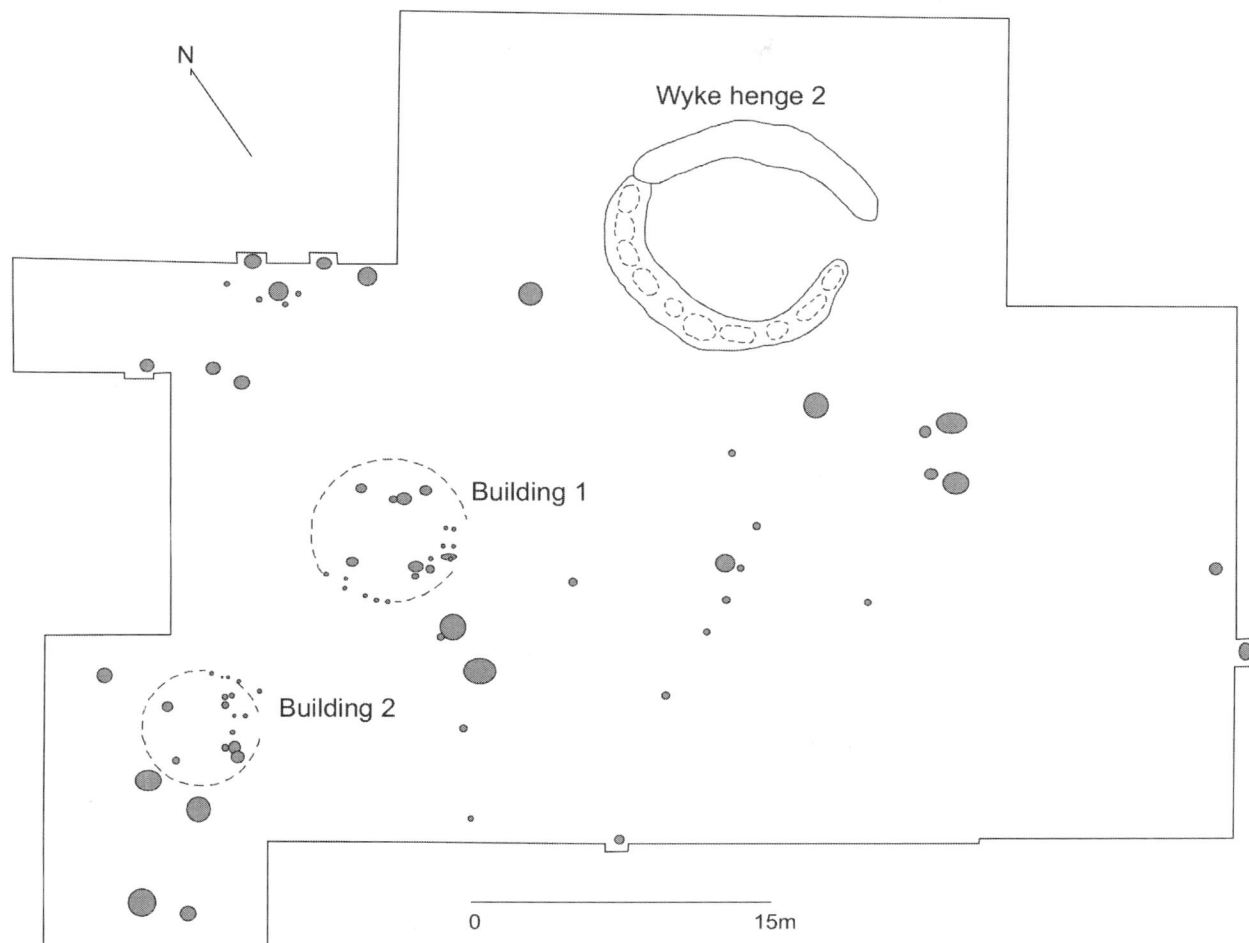

FIGURE 6. SETTLEMENT FEATURES AND STRUCTURES AND HENGE 2 AT WYKE DOWN (AFTER FRENCH ET AL. 2007)

monuments drew upon domestic architecture or that elements of routine practice might be elaborated to form the basis for ritual. The second relates directly to henge monuments and their function, and stresses their role as technologies of control. With reference to both henge-like enclosures of the Irish Iron Age and Neolithic and earlier Bronze Age earthworks of this kind, Warner (2000) and Gibson (2004) make the highly pertinent observation that their common 'inverted' earthwork format (with ditch inside bank) was designed to keep spiritual agencies or other kinds of sacred forces inside, thus protecting the outside world. The third is that there often exists a 'narrative' structure to individual henge sequences (Bradley 2011), and that where timber circles are present, they pre-date the henge earthworks themselves (Gibson 2004). It is certainly possible to see that sequence from radiocarbon chronologies at Durrington Walls and Woodhenge (Parker Pearson et al. in press). In this case, henges could be seen as a form of closure, marking the end point of sequences of activity (Gibson 2004, 79). Equally, and drawing upon the second of the observations highlighted here, the decision to enclose with a henge earthwork could reflect a change in the ontological status of the space and structural traces to be contained, signifying its newly enhanced potency or sacredness. With these observations in mind – and

with an awareness of how place, its history, associations and qualities mattered when it came to create sacred architecture – the relationship between sequences of settlement and the building of timber circles and henges can be explored.

Settlements and henges: the case of Wyke Down

The first case study relates to activity at Wyke Down/ Down Farm, on Cranborne Chase. This is an area with a record of dense middle and late Neolithic settlement that followed on from the construction of the Dorset Cursus (Barrett et al. 1991, French et al. 2007). In the case the Chalkpit Field site, middle Neolithic settlement was even located within the area between the ditches of the Cursus, and included a number of very distinctive artefact types (Barrett et al. 1991, 70-5).

At Wyke Down, Martin Green's excellent fieldwork revealed two small henge monuments set 40m apart, at least one of which (the northern-most) was located within or on the edge of an area of settlement-related features (Green, in French et al. 2007, 83-94) (Figure 6). Radiocarbon dates suggest that the settlement features and northern henge are broadly contemporary (Building 1: 2900-2830,

2820-2670 cal BC; Building 2: 2880-2570 cal BC; Henge 2: 2930-2860, 2810-2750 cal BC). Among the settlement features are pits, stake-holes, post lines and two post-built structures (Buildings 1 and 2), all associated with Grooved Ware. Such traces are typical of late Neolithic settlement activity, the exception being the two buildings to the west of the henge, both of which are circular with square central settings of posts. These are cautiously interpreted as elaborate houses or ceremonial structures; the difficulty in deciding their status reflecting the problem often encountered in deciding, quite erroneously, where the dividing line between the quotidian and the sacred should lie. That the walls of these structures were coated in daub (i.e. they were wall-enclosed rather than free-standing post rings), and that they should be associated with the same kinds of material as found within adjacent pits, could suggest they were lived in; but they were most probably not ordinary dwellings. Differences existed between the two structures. The clay-based daub from Building 2 – that furthest from the henge, and the smaller of the two structures – was coarse compared with that of Building 1. Exceptionally, decorated wall plaster was recovered from Building 1 (Green and Muros, in French et al. 2007, 333-4). Relative proximity to the henge might here be reflected in the scale and elaboration of the structures. In fact, the distinction between the structures and henge may be more a matter of degree than absolute kind. The buildings share the same south-east axis as the henge, they are set along a common east-west line, and the area enclosed by the henge earthwork is only slightly greater than that of Building 1. The relative status of the structures – and by that we might even mean degrees of sacredness, or connections to senior and junior lineages – increased from west to east: from Building 2, to Building 1, and then the henge.

All three constructions received deposits of pottery, lithics and animal bone. The Grooved Ware ceramics from the henge and the pits and structures share decorative features and fabrics in common (Cleal, in French et al. 2007, 322); and while there is a slightly higher percentage of retouched and utilised pieces from the settlement pits (7.4% as opposed to 4.4%), the lithic assemblages are similar. The only major distinction exists in the respective faunal assemblages, with cattle bone as opposed to pig being predominant in both henges (Rothwell and Maltby, in French et al. 2007, 320).

Here, there clearly exists a very close association between henge and settlement, both in terms of the level of spatial integration of different structures, and the generation and deposition of similar material assemblages. Given that their contents are not dissimilar to those placed within the settlement pits (perhaps as part of closing/commemorative rites: Thomas 2012), the deposits within the pit-defined ditches of both the Wyke Down 1 and 2 henges could even be seen as a translation and multiplication of practices routinely associated with settlement events – material performances at the henges condensed in some way the relations and practices that made up ordinary life.

However, while these connections and relations can be drawn out, the physical form of the henges – the use of enclosing earthworks – should not be neglected. Following the observations of Warner and Gibson, we should ask why the space enclosed within the henge earthworks needed to be *controlled*. Why would a timber circle, a simple fenced area or more elaborate version of the circular buildings not suffice? One possibility is that the henges contained spaces connected to funerary rites, and that the earthworks served to control the kinds of pollution or spiritual risk often associated with recent death (Bloch and Parry 1982; Hertz 1960). This gains some support from the subtle distinctions in the range of material from henge and settlement-feature contexts (Barrett et al. 1991, 92-106). Among those things deposited in the Wyke Down 1 henge were items of carved chalk and even human bone. Most telling of all though is the preponderance of cattle bone in the assemblages from both henges, contrasting with the pig-dominated assemblages from both the Wyke Down and Firtree Field pits, since the slaughter and consumption of cattle is routinely linked to mortuary feasting and other ritual occasions (Parker Pearson 2000). The ceramics, lithics and other material placed in the henge ditch pits could then be refuse connected to the households of the deceased, its incorporation linked to processes of control of death pollution. Whether this interpretation is accurate in its details is perhaps less important than the observation of the close relationship between kinds of signature (settlement versus monument) that we might normally regard as distinct or even antithetical.

The accruing significance and sacredness of place

While unusual, the two buildings at Wyke Down belong to a wider architectural tradition of 'square-in-circle' structures that take as their prototype small stake-built houses such as those excavated at Trelystan, Powys (Britnell 1982), and the eastern entrance at Durrington Walls (Parker Pearson 2007). It is possible to see a continuum from these small buildings, to those with internal settings of four posts, as at Wyke Down, to larger, more elaborated and clearly monumental versions such as the Northern Circle at Durrington Walls and that at Durrington 68 (Gibson 2005; Pollard 1995; Wainwright and Longworth 1971) (Figure 7). Through multiplication of enclosing post rings, at least one of these structures – that of the Southern Circle at Durrington Walls – was transformed into a highly elaborated timber circle that was the wooden equivalent of the stone settings at Stonehenge (Pollard 2009; Thomas 2007, 2010). Bradley has described this process of mimicry and elaboration as one of the 'consecration of the house' (Bradley 2005, 74). Using the house as a template for monumental constructions is by no means unusual, even in the Neolithic where we see the same process happening a millennium and a half earlier in the Paris Basin and Northern European Plain with the transformation of the long house into the long mound (Bradley 1998; Hodder 1994). The ethnographic record speaks of the power and complexity of the concept of the house, perhaps not surprising since it is the medium through which rights,

FIGURE 7. THE DURRINGTON 68 TIMBER SETTING UNDER EXCAVATION. THE CURVING DITCH BELONGS TO A LATER,
EARLY BRONZE AGE, ROUND BARROW (PHOTO: ADAM STANFORD © AERIAL-CAM)

responsibilities, structures of order, and the family as a social and biological unit are often reproduced (e.g. Parker Pearson and Richards 1994; Waterson 1990).

A variety of roles could be postulated for the square-in-circle structures at Wyke Down, Durrington 68 and elsewhere, ranging from the residences of high status individuals, to cult houses, origin houses and shrines. Their functions must have varied widely, and they should best be seen as an architectural resource to be drawn upon and developed according to context. What is pertinent to the discussion of henge monuments is the way in which these structures were treated at the end of their lives. As with the much smaller houses at Durrington Walls (Parker Pearson 2007), pairs of pits were cut in the former entrance areas of the Durrington 68 and 70 structures, into which were placed 'commemorative'/'decommissioning' deposits. In the case of the larger multiple circles of Woodhenge and the Southern Circle, a related practice saw pits cut into the tops of the larger post-holes after the timbers had rotted (Pollard and Robinson 2007; Thomas 2007). The status of these structures was such they could not simply be left – respectful and appropriate actions had to be performed, in much the same way as funerary feasts might be held for the dead.

In certain instances, notably with those structures at Wyke Down, Durrington 68 and 70, no further monumental

intervention was required, perhaps because they soon lost their significance. However, other comparable buildings in the western interior of Durrington Walls were enclosed within henge earthworks (Thomas 2007). It is not clear whether this happened after the structures went out of use, but elsewhere the sequence always runs from timber settings/structures to henge (Gibson 2004, 2005), implying a critical change in the ontological status of these places at the point when they were enclosed. Woodhenge provides a case in point (Cunnington 1929; Pollard and Robinson 2007). The henge earthwork was constructed in the third or fourth quarter of the 3rd millennium BC (2470-2030 BC and 2340-2010 BC), while the one radiocarbon date from the timber settings (a cremation from post-hole C14, dated to 2576-2468 cal BC) suggests a mid 3rd millennium BC date for their construction, perhaps contemporary with that of the nearby Southern Circle. The henge itself likely belongs with a megalithic phase to the monument. The sequence is in fact more complex, perhaps beginning with a phase of Grooved Ware associated settlement which may even have pre-dated the timber rings (Figure 8). Cunnington noted that 'wherever there were remains of the bank relics were found in the old surface layer beneath it, consisting mostly of broken animal bones and scattered fragments of pottery' (Cunnington 1929, 5). One area of buried soil on the western side included a layer of burnt flint, and on northern side a knapping scatter was found (Cunnington 1929, 6, 76). The large and fresh condition

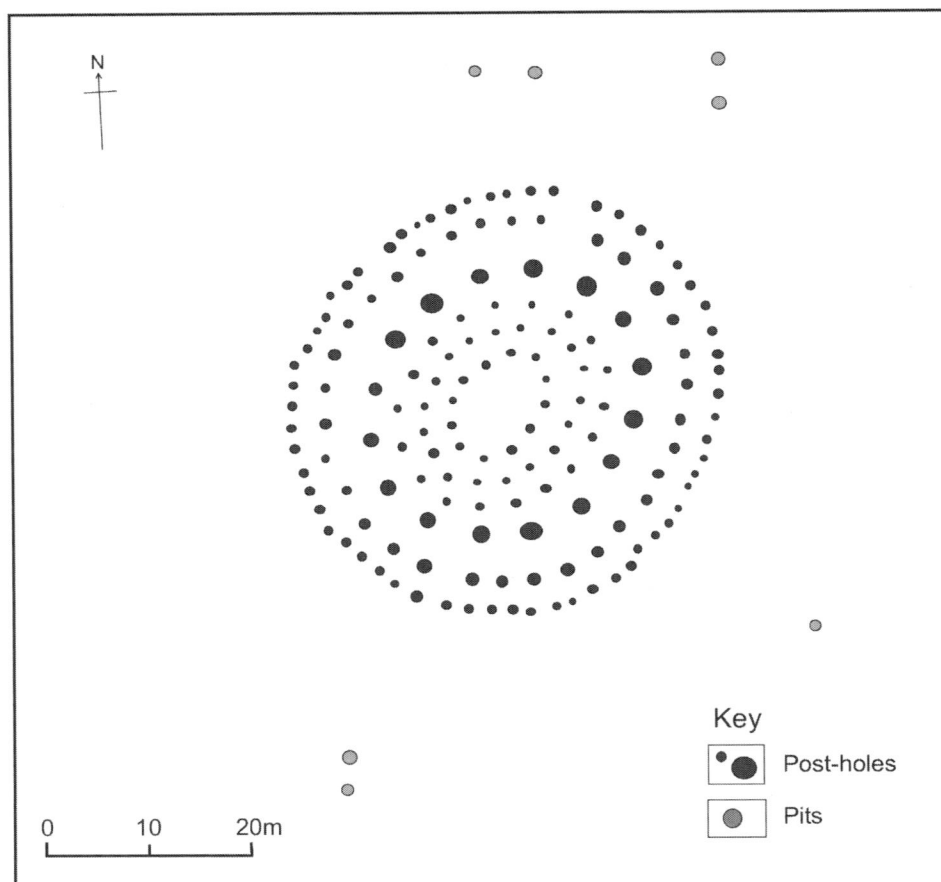

FIGURE 8. PRE-HENGE FEATURES AT WOODHENGE (AFTER CUNNINGTON 1931)

of Grooved Ware sherds from the buried soil hint at the presence of protective midden spreads. Three sets of paired pits under the bank and on the berm between the bank and ditch could mark the locations of houses, since they are similar in size and content to the 'decommissioning' pits associated with the Durrington houses. Here the sequence looks to run from settlement to henge.

Much the same sequence seems to characterise events at Coneybury, but at an earlier date, and without (so far as we are aware) a final megalithic phase (Richards 1990). Within the interior of the henge are a series of pits and post-holes that probably pre-date the earthwork (Figure 9). The larger of these, features 1608, 1619, 1603, 1601, 1177, look to have held uprights (Richards 1990, 13), describing either a six-post setting or square central setting with 'entrance' posts (1608 and 1619). 1608 is cut by a pit containing Grooved Ware, and there are two other pits (1844 and 1848) to the east that lie on the arc of a surrounding fence oval c.25m across. Their position recalls that of the 'commemorative'/'decommissioning' pits at Durrington 68 and 70. The whole is reminiscent of another square-in-circle structure, albeit on a fairly massive scale. Across the interior and outside the area of the ditch were numerous stake-holes, some of which must pre-date the earthwork since they occur in zones subsequently occupied by the bank. They may represent traces of stake-built houses of the kind found at Durrington.

At Coneybury the ploughsoil was subject to gridded excavation and the area around the monument fieldwalked. We can therefore link surface worked flint densities with sub-soil features. Both methods yielded large quantities of lithics that were generated through lengthy and/or intense periods of settlement. The results of extensive surface collection show the henge to lie within the centre of a large scatter at least 700 x 400m across (Richards 1990, fig. 10). In places, notably to the north-west, lithic densities reach 90+ pieces per 50m transect. While scatter sites often represent palimpsests of activity, that at Coneybury includes a good number of distinctive middle/ late Neolithic tool types, such as rods/fabricators, chisel and oblique arrowheads, the latter clustering close to the area of the henge (Richards 1990, fig. 158). Almost 12,000 pieces of worked flint came from the ploughsoil excavation across the henge interior and ditch, densities averaging 26.5 pieces of flint per square metre, but in places reaching over 50 per metre. Middle/late Neolithic chisel arrowheads are again well represented within this material (Richards 1990, 124-6). Of note is the fact that concentrations of tool types seem to ring the area of the fenced enclosure within which the timber structure sits (Richards 1990, fig. 96), suggesting it was surrounded by surface midden deposits.

The different strands of evidence point to Coneybury beginning as a large fenced structure sitting at the heart

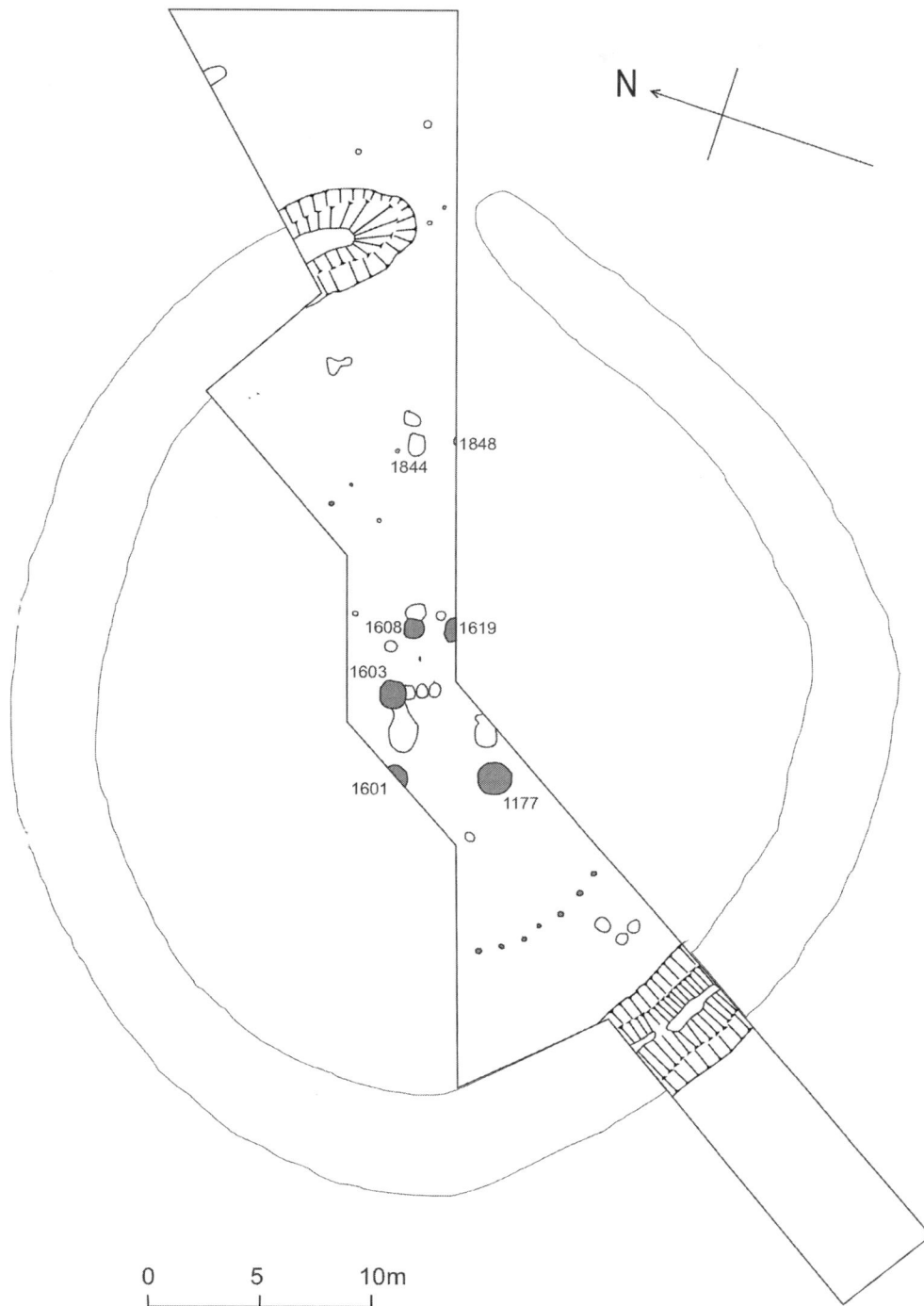

Figure 9. The henge and pre-henge internal features at Coneybury. Post-holes belonging to the timber structure shaded grey (after Richards 1990).

of an extensive settlement. At some point during the first half of the 3rd millennium BC the decision was made to enclose that structure within a henge earthwork; a very dramatic act that physically separated it from the rest of the settlement area and marked it out as something highly special or potent. We will probably never know the detail of events that led to this happening, but the sequence does highlight a process by which certain places or structures that formally operated within a routine context might eventually become so significant or sacred that they required being 'henged'. Those events could relate to the process of association then death of a prominent individual perceived to have real spiritual efficacy, an extreme ritual transgression, or simply a perception of accruing supernatural power within a place. The latter explanation might fit best those scenarios where the process leading from settlement to monument was more drawn out. This is probably the case at both Avebury and the Sanctuary, where there are lengthy histories of 4th and early 3rd millennium BC pre-monument activity that over time might have taken on strong ancestral connotations (Cunnington 1931; Pollard 2005). The agency or 'sense of weight' that those connections and connotations came to hold would have provide the pretext for the conversion of these locations into henge and timber circle respectively.

Discussion

This has been a rather oblique consideration of henges, but intentionally so, since the aim was to highlight the processes by which these monuments and larger monument complexes might have come into being within the Wessex landscape. In so doing, the focus has been on trying to understand both wider and more local historic conditions under which places became imbued with associations, qualities or a sense of sacredness that eventually had to be responded to through monumentalisation (see also Barrett 1994). What we are seeing are the outcomes of historical processes (here entwining religious and supernatural events), some perhaps quite contingent, but ones which can leave a material trace and so be detectable archaeologically. Hopefully, the case studies dealing with Woodhenge and Coneybury have stressed that sequences need not indicate a *continuity* of sacredness or ritual activity, but instead an *emergence* of these qualities and practices; sequences that eventually involved a process of ontological redefinition at the point when henge earthworks were constructed. In a place and time not too distant from late Neolithic Wessex, Bradley's (1998) account of the dynamics by which central European Neolithic long houses became long mounds provides a notable parallel.

There exists enormous potential for thinking about what monuments did and their intended affects. This could help us side-step the problems of categorization and attempts to ascribe strict functional attributes to these constructions. Particularly powerful is the idea that the process of henge enclosure served to control or contain perceived supernatural forces. Perhaps that could be extended to all forms of enclosure and mounding found in late Neolithic contexts; and perhaps the use of different materials reflected the temporality of that process, and/or the specific nature of the supernatural power that was being contained? In this case, wooden palisades served as mechanisms of temporary control, perhaps being linked to a sense of time-limited spiritual danger associated with certain activities. The destruction of their circuits through burning and post removal, seen at Mount Pleasant (Wainwright 1979), West Kennet (Whittle 1997) and much further afield (see papers in Gibson 2002), could then mark the end of a ritual cycle and a lifting of that sense of danger (cf. Whittle 1997, 158). Good arguments have already been made for close ontological connection between stone and ancestral states in the late Neolithic (Parker Pearson and Ramilisonina 1998). The use of stone in enclosures (specifically circles) or avenues/alignments might then be seen as a means by which ancestral presence and potency was brought in to protect spaces in a permanent fashion. Mounding might represent the ultimate strategy of control and containment, reserved for especially powerful agencies, places, or substances with which any further contact was not considered appropriate or desirable. In addition to the great Wessex mounds, one could note here the mounding over and ditch encircling of concentrations of occupation debris at Tye Field, Lawford, Essex (Shennan et al. 1985), Upper Ninepence, Powys (Gibson 1999), Ringlemere, Kent (Needham et al. 2006), and Avebury G55 (Smith 1965b); each a remarkable response to a particular settlement event.

Although a little unorthodox, I would like to end rather than begin with a little ethnographic analogy, simply because this may serve to ground some of the arguments presented above. In traditional Polynesian culture, much of life is regulated by the related concepts of *mana* and *tapu*. It is not easy to provide a solid definition of these (Shore 1989), but at the risk of generalisation *mana* can be seen as spiritual energy or efficacy that can reside in people, animals, places and things. It is often linked to authority and power (chiefs have *mana*), and may be inherited (i.e. deriving from an ancestral line), or come to people through achievement or contact with other powerful things or actions. It is intensely fluid, and can be lost and gained, and is made manifest through actions and events. *Tapu* is best defined as a state of extreme and potent sacredness – a state of contagious sacredness that might be a condition of *mana* – which must be carefully controlled because of its power. Again, it is not stable, and it can reside in people, places, things and events. Careful controls are put in place, including elaboration forms of segregation and wrapping, to avoid violation of *tapu*. There is no need to assume that direct equivalents of these concepts existed in the European Neolithic, but surely similar notions of spiritual power and efficacy, and the need for their harnessing and control were present, and they must have guided the way people conducted their lives. Critical though is awareness of how fluid such powers might be – how the ontological status of people, places and substances might shift – since this could help explain why seemingly ordinary places or traces of mundane events might suddenly become monumentalised.

Acknowledgements

Without wishing to implicate them in anything said here, a general acknowledgement is due to colleagues on the Stonehenge Riverside Project, especially Mike Parker Pearson, Colin Richards and Julian Thomas, for the thoughts and inspiration they have provided.

References

Ashbee, P. 2004. Early ditches: their forms and infills. In R. Cleal and J. Pollard (eds), *Monuments and Material Culture. Papers in honour of an Avebury archaeologist: Isobel Smith*, 1-14. Salisbury: Hobnob Press.

Ashbee, P., Smith, I. and Evans, J. 1979. Excavation of three long barrows near Avebury, Wiltshire. *Proceedings of the Prehistoric Society* 45, 207-300.

Barber, M. 2004. Mount Pleasant from the air: cropmarks old and new at the henge enclosure near Dorchester, Dorset. *Proceedings of the Dorset Natural History and Archaeological Society* 126, 7-14.

Barrett, J. C., Bradley, R. and Green, M. 1991. *Landscape, Monuments and Society: the prehistory of Cranborne Chase*. Cambridge: Cambridge University Press.

Barrett, J. 1994. *Fragments from Antiquity: an archaeology of social life in Britain, 2900-1200 BC*. Oxford: Blackwell.

Bloch, M. and Parry, J. (eds) 1982. *Death and the Regeneration of Life*. Cambridge: Cambridge University Press.

Boivin, N. and Owoc, M.A. (eds) 2004. *Soils, Stones and Symbols: cultural perceptions of the mineral world*. London: UCL Press.

Bradley, R. 1975. Maumbury Rings, Dorchester: the excavations of 1908-13. *Archaeologia* 105, 1-97.

Bradley, R. 1998. *The Significance of Monuments*. London: Routledge.

Bradley, R. 2000. *An Archaeology of Natural Places*. London: Routledge.

Bradley, R. 2005. *Ritual and Domestic Life in Prehistoric Europe*. London: Routledge.

Bradley, R. 2011. *Stages and Screens: An investigation of four henge monuments in northern and north-eastern Scotland*. Edinburgh: Society of Antiquaries of Scotland.

Britnell, W. 1982 The excavation of two round barrows at Trelystan, Powys. *Proceedings of the Prehistoric Society* 48, 133-201.

Cleal, R. M. J. 2005. 'The small compass of a grave': Early Bronze Age burial in and around Avebury and the Marlborough Downs. In G. Brown, D. Field, and D. McOmish (eds), *The Avebury Landscape: aspects of the field archaeology of the Marlborough Downs*, 115-32. Oxford: Oxbow Books.

Cleal, R. M. J. and Pollard, J. 2012. The Revenge of the Native: monuments, material culture, burial and other practices in the third quarter of the 3rd millennium BC in Wessex. In M.J. Allen, J. Gardiner and A. Sheridan (eds), *Is There a British Chalcolithic? people, place and polity in the later 3rd millennium BC*. Oxford: Prehistoric Society/Oxbow Books.

Cleal, R. M. J., Walker, K. E. and Montague, R. 1995. *Stonehenge in its Landscape: twentieth-century excavations*. London: English Heritage.

Cunnington, M. E. 1929. *Woodhenge*. Devizes: George Simpson.

Cunnington, M. E. 1931. The 'Sanctuary' on Overton Hill, near Avebury. *Wiltshire Archaeological and Natural History Magazine* 45, 300-35.

David, A., Cole, M., Horsley, T., Linford, N., Linford, P. and Martin, L. 2004. A rival to Stonehenge? Geophysical survey at Stanton Drew, England. *Antiquity* 78, 341-58.

Darvill, T., 2004. *Long Barrows of the Cotswolds and Surrounding Areas*. Stroud: Tempus.

Darvill, T. 2006. *Stonehenge: the biography of a landscape*. Stroud: Tempus.

Darvill, T. 2010. *Prehistoric Britain*. 2nd edition. London: Routledge.

Darvill, T. and Wainwright, G. 2009. Stonehenge Excavations 2008. *Antiquaries Journal* 89, 1-19.

Edmonds, M. 1999. *Ancestral Geographies of the Neolithic*. London: Routledge.

Field, D. 2005. Some observations on perception, consolidation and change in a land of stones. In G. Brown, D. Field, and D. McOmish (eds), *The Avebury Landscape: aspects of the field archaeology of the Marlborough Downs*, 87-94. Oxford: Oxbow Books.

French, C., Lewis, H., Allen, M. J., Green, M., Scaife, R. and Gardiner, J. 2007. *Prehistoric Landscape Development and Human Impact in the Upper Allen Valley, Cranborne Chase, Dorset*. Cambridge: MacDonald Institute.

Gibson, A. 1999. *The Walton Basin Project: excavation and survey in a prehistoric landscape 1993-7*. York: CBA Research Report 118.

Gibson, A. (ed.) 2002. *Behind Wooden Walls: the Neolithic palisaded enclosures of Europe*. Oxford: British Archaeological Reports International Series 1013.

Gibson, A. 2004. Round in circles. Timber circles, henges and stone circles: some possible relationships and transformations. In R. Cleal and J. Pollard (eds), *Monuments and Material Culture. Papers in honour of an Avebury archaeologist: Isobel Smith*, 70-82. Salisbury: Hobnob Press.

Gibson, A. 2005. *Stonehenge and Timber Circles*. 2nd edition. Stroud: Tempus.

Gillings, M. and Pollard, J. 1999. Non-portable stone artefacts and contexts of meaning: the tale of Grey Wether (www.museum.ncl.ac.uk/Avebury/stone4.htm). *World Archaeology* 31, 179-93.

Gillings, M. and Pollard, J. 2004. *Avebury*. London: Duckworth.

Gillings, M., Pollard, J., Wheatley, D. and Peterson, R. 2008. *Landscape of the Megaliths: Excavation and Fieldwork on the Avebury Monuments, 1997-2003*. Oxford: Oxbow Books.

Gray, H. St. G. 1935. The Avebury excavations, 1908-1922. *Archaeologia* 84, 99-162.

Harding, A. and Lee, G. 1987. *Henge Monuments and Related Sites of Great Britain: air photographic evidence and catalogue*. Oxford: British Archaeological Reports.

Harding, J. 2000. Later Neolithic ceremonial centres, ritual and pilgrimage: the monument complex of Thornborough, North Yorkshire. In A. Ritchie (ed.) *Neolithic Orkney in its European Context*, 31-46. Cambridge: McDonald Institute Monographs.

Harding, J. 2003. *Henge Monuments of the British Isles*. Stroud: Tempus.

Healy, F. 1997. 'Site 3, Flagstones' and 'Neolithic and Bronze Age'. In R. C. Smith, F. Healy, M. J. Allen, E.

L. Morris, I. Barnes and P. J. Woodward, *Excavations along the Route of the Dorchester By-pass, Dorset*, 27–48, 283-91. Salisbury: Wessex Archaeology.

Hertz, R. 1960. *Death and the Right Hand*. London: Cohen and West.

Hodder, I. 1994. Architecture and meaning: the example of Neolithic houses and tombs. In M. Parker Pearson and C. Richards (eds), *Architecture and Order: approaches to social space*, 73-86. London: Routledge.

Holgate, R. 1987. Neolithic settlement patterns at Avebury, Wiltshire. *Antiquity* 62, 349-53.

Kinnes, I. 1992. *Non-Megalithic Long Barrows and Allied Structures in the British Neolithic*. London: British Museum.

Lawson, A.J. 2007. *Chalkland: an archaeology of Stonehenge and its region*. East Knoyle: Hobnob Press.

Leary, J. and Field, D. 2010. *The Story of Silbury Hill*. London: English Heritage.

Leary, J., Field, D. and Russell, M. 2010. Marvels at Marden henge. *Past* 66, 14-16.

Mercer, R. and Healy, F. 2008. *Hambledon Hill, Dorset, England: excavation and survey of a Neolithic monument complex and its surrounding landscape*. London: English Heritage.

Needham, S., Parfitt, K. and Varndell, G. 2006. *The Ringlemere Cup: precious cups and the beginning of the Channel Bronze Age*. London: British Museum, Research Publication 163.

Oswald, A., Dyer, C. and Barber, M. 2001. *The Creation of Monuments: Neolithic Causewayed Enclosures in the British Isles*. London: English Heritage.

Parker Pearson, M. 2000. Eating Money: a study in the ethnoarchaeology of food. *Archaeological Dialogues* 7(2), 217-32.

Parker Pearson, M. 2007. The Stonehenge Riverside Project: excavations at the east entrance of Durrington Walls. In M. Larsson and M. Parker Pearson (eds), *From Stonehenge to the Baltic: living with cultural diversity in the third millennium BC*, 125-44. Oxford: British Archaeological Reports.

Parker Pearson, M. 2012. *Stonehenge Explained: exploring the greatest Stone Age mystery*. New York: Simon and Schuster.

Parker Pearson, M., Pollard, J., Richards, C., Thomas, J., Tilley, C., Welham, K. and Albarella, U. 2006. Materializing Stonehenge: the Stonehenge Riverside Project and new discoveries. *Journal of Material Culture* 11, 227-61.

Parker Pearson, M., Pollard, J., Thomas, J. and Welham, K. 2009. Newhenge. *British Archaeology* 110, 14-21.

Parker Pearson, M. and Ramilisonina, 1998. Stonehenge for the ancestors: the stones pass on the message. *Antiquity* 72, 308-26.

Parker Pearson, M. and Richards, C. (eds) 1994. *Architecture and Order: approaches to social space*. London: Routledge.

Pitts, M. 2001. *Hengeworld*. London: Arrow.

Pollard, J. 1995. The Durrington 68 Timber Circle: A Forgotten Late Neolithic Monument. *Wiltshire Archaeological and Natural History Magazine* 88, 122-5.

Pollard, J. 2005. Memory, Monuments and Middens in the Neolithic Landscape. In G. Brown, D. Field, and D. McOmish (eds), *The Avebury Landscape: aspects of the field archaeology of the Marlborough Downs*, 103-14. Oxford: Oxbow Books.

Pollard, J. 2009. The materialization of religious structures in the time of Stonehenge. *Material Religion* 5.3, 332-53.

Pollard, J. and Cleal. R. 2004. Dating Avebury. In R. Cleal and J. Pollard (eds), *Monuments and Material Culture. Papers in honour of an Avebury archaeologist: Isobel Smith*, 120-9. Salisbury: Hobnob Press.

Pollard, J. and Gillings, M. 2009. The world of the Grey Wethers. In B. O'Connor, G. Cooney and J. Chapman (eds), *Materialitas: working stone, carving identity*, 29-41. Oxford: Prehistoric Society/Oxbow Books.

Pollard, J. and Reynolds, A. 2002. *Avebury: the biography of a landscape*. Stroud: Tempus.

Pollard, J. and Robinson, D. 2007. A return to Woodhenge: the results and implications of the 2006 excavations. In M. Larsson and M. Parker Pearson (eds), *From Stonehenge to the Baltic: living with cultural diversity in the third millennium BC*, 159-68. Oxford: British Archaeological Reports.

Richards, J. 1990. *The Stonehenge Environs Project*. London: English Heritage.

Richards, C. (ed.) 2005. *Dwelling Among the Monuments: the Neolithic village of Barnhouse, Maeshowe passage grave and surrounding monuments at Stenness, Orkney*. Cambridge: McDonald Institute.

Roberts, I. (ed.) 2005. *Ferrybridge Henge: the ritual landscape*. Morley: Archaeological Services WYAS.

Shennan, S. J., Healy, F. and Smith, I. F. 1985. The excavation of a ring-ditch at Tye Field, Lawford, Essex. *Archaeological Journal* 142, 150-215.

Shore, B. 1989. *Mana* and *Tapu*. In A. Howard and R. Borofsky (eds), *Developments in Polynesian Ethnography*, 137-73. Honolulu: University of Hawaii Press.

Smith, I. F. 1965a. *Windmill Hill and Avebury: excavations by Alexander Keiller 1925-1939*. Oxford: Clarendon Press.

Smith, I. F. 1965b. Excavation of a Bell Barrow, Avebury G55. *Wiltshire Archaeological and Natural History Magazine* 60, 24-46.

Smith, R. C., Healy, F. Allen, M. J., Morris, E. L., Barnes, I. and Woodward, P. J. 1997. *Excavations along the Route of the Dorchester By-pass, Dorset*. Salisbury: Wessex Archaeology.

Teather, A. 2007. Neolithic phallacies: a discussion of some southern British artefacts. In M. Larsson and M. Parker Pearson (eds), *From Stonehenge to the Baltic: cultural diversity in the third millennium BC*, 205-11. Oxford: British Archaeological Reports.

Thomas, J. 1999. An economy of substances in earlier Neolithic Britain. In J. Robb (ed.), *Material Symbols:*

culture and economy in prehistory, 70-89. Carbondale: Southern Illinois University Press.

Thomas, J. 2004. The later Neolithic architectural repertoire: the case of the Dunragit complex. In R. Cleal and J. Pollard (eds), *Monuments and Material Culture. Papers in honour of an Avebury archaeologist: Isobel Smith*, 98-108. Salisbury: Hobnob Press.

Thomas, J. 2007. The internal features at Durrington Walls: investigations in the Southern Circle and Westrern Enclosures 2005-6. In M. Larsson and M. Parker Pearson (eds), *From Stonehenge to the Baltic: living with cultural diversity in the third millennium BC*, 145-57. Oxford: British Archaeological Reports.

Thomas, J. 2010. The return of the Rinyo-Clacton Folk? The cultural significance of the Grooved Ware complex in Later Neolithic Britain. *Cambridge Archaeological Journal* 20(1), 1-15.

Thomas, J. 2012. Introduction: beyond the mundane? In H. Anderson-Whymark and J. Thomas (eds), *Regional Perspectives on Neolithic Pit Deposition*, 1-12. Oxford: Oxbow Books.

Thomas, J., Marshall, P., Parker Pearson, Pollard, J., Richards, C., Tilley, C. and Welham, K. 2009. The date of the Greater Stonehenge Cursus. *Antiquity* 83, 40-53.

Tilley, C. 1999. *Metaphor and Material Culture*. Oxford: Blackwell.

Tilley, C., Richards, C., Bennett, W. and Field, D. 2007. Stonehenge – its landscape and its architecture: a reanalysis. In M. Larsson and M. Parker Pearson (eds), *From Stonehenge to the Baltic: cultural diversity in the third millennium BC*, 183-204. Oxford: British Archaeological Reports 1692.

Viner, S., Evans, J., Albarella, U. and Parker Pearson, M. 2010. Cattle mobility in prehistoric Britain: strontium isotope analysis of cattle teeth from Durrington Walls (Wiltshire, Britain). *Journal of Archaeological Science* 37, 2812-20.

Wainwright, G. J. 1971. The excavation of a Late Neolithic enclosure at Marden, Wiltshire. *Antiquaries Journal* 51, 177-239.

Wainwright, G. J. 1979. *Mount Pleasant, Dorset: excavations 1970-1971*. London: Society of Antiquaries of London.

Wainwright, G. J. and Longworth, I. H. 1971. *Durrington Walls: excavations 1966-1968*. London: Society of Antiquaries of London.

Warner, R. 2000. Keeping out the Otherworld: the internal ditch at Navan and other Iron Age 'hengiform' enclosures. *Emania* 18, 39-44.

Waterson, R. 1990. *The Living House: an anthropology of architecture in South-east Asia*. Oxford: Oxford University Press.

Whittle, A. 1990. A Model for the Mesolithic-Neolithic Transition in the Upper Kennet Valley, North Wiltshire. *Proceedings of the Prehistoric Society* 56, 101-10.

Whittle, A. 1997. *Sacred Mound, Holy Rings. Silbury Hill and the West Kennet palisade enclosures: a later Neolithic complex in north Wiltshire*. Oxford: Oxbow Books.

Whittle, A., Pollard, J. and Grigson, C. 1999. *The Harmony of Symbols: the Windmill Hill causewayed enclosure*. Oxford: Oxbow Books.

Mid Neolithic Enclosures in Southern Scandinavia

Lars Larsson

Abstract

There are two main types of enclosure during the Neolithic. The oldest type can be compared to causewayed enclosures with one or two ditch systems and with or without palisades. This is the most numerous type, constructed within the Funnel Beaker Culture from the later part of the Early Neolithic (EN II) until the early part of the early Middle Neolithic (MN AIB), *c.*3300-3100 BC.

During a later phase in the Middle Neolithic (*c.*2900-2600 BC) enclosures were constructed that consisted only of one or several palisades. They are contemporary with the latest part of the Funnel Beaker Culture and the early regional versions of the Corded Ware Culture. For both types of enclosure the inner area usually includes a small number of features or layers contemporaneous with the perimeter.

As regards the causewayed enclosures, they are often covered with intensive occupation layers accumulated a few generations after the enclosure was abandoned. Most of them were settled until the time when the 'second generation' of enclosures were built. The causewayed enclosures were erected during a period that also saw intensive megalith construction and consequently have been interpreted as being involved in mortuary practices, the bodies being deposited in the ditches together with a number of artefacts. The ditches were later re-opened and most of the skeletons removed. The re-opening of ditches continued throughout the settlement phase.

The palisade enclosures are only found in the southernmost part of Sweden and on Zealand, eastern Denmark. They are assumed to be assembly places, like the earlier enclosures. The building phase coincides with the transition from the late Funnel Beaker Culture to the early Battle Axe Culture, a stage that seems to include changes that placed a certain stress on the societies.

These two types of enclosures are well represented, however, other kinds of enclosure, both older and smaller, may also have existed.

Keywords: Southern Scandiavia, Denmark, Sweden, Neolithic, causewayed enclosure, palisade enclosure, megalithic tombs, Funnel Beaker Culture, Battle Axe Culture

Introduction

When studying enclosures in Europe, two characteristics are easily discernable: enclosures can show great variety in terms of structures and use, and they exist within a broad chronological framework. In southern Scandinavia they are quite a recent discovery, the first one having been identified in 1971 at Sarup, southern Funen, Denmark (Andersen 1974). With its ditch systems and palisade, parallel was drawn with the causewayed enclosures in Germany and Britain. About thirty enclosures of this kind have since been identified (Andersen 1997; Andersen 2002; Klatt 2009). They are described in Scandinavian archaeological research as Sarup enclosures, after the first site identified. Much more recently, another kind of enclosure, with palisades only, has also been recognized. The first was identified at Hyllie, southwestern Scania, Sweden. About ten sites of this kind have since been recorded. These two kinds of enclosures, or two generations of enclosures (Svensson 2002; Nielsen 2004), are sometimes dealt with as a group, but they differ in terms of structure, distribution and chronology.

In earlier presentations of the south Scandinavian causewayed enclosures the north German site at Büdelsdorf has been included. The reason is that this was the continental enclosure closest to the Scandinavian ones, but even more significantly, the identification of this causewayed enclosure in the 1960s gave hope that this kind of construction existed further north. Since then, a number of similar enclosures have been excavated in the same region. On one of these, Albersdorf-Dieksnöll, elements relating to an entrance suggest a link to similar structures further south, associated with the Michelsberg Culture (Dibbern and Hage 2010; Müller 2011).

When speaking about the Mid-Neolithic, we are dealing with an interval significantly, different in Scandinavia to other parts of Europe. The Mid-Neolithic or Middle Neolithic (MN) represents the phase 3300–2200 cal BC. The initial stage of enclosures begins even earlier, *c.*3400 BC, and the last enclosures are abandoned at about 2500 BC. This means that, in a broader continental perspective, the enclosures belong to the late Middle Neolithic and Late Neolithic.

Enclosures from the typological and chronological perspectives

At present, about thirty enclosures are known, most of them well proven, and a small number that are less certain. Detailed information about the individual structures can be found in Svensson 2002, Nielsen 2004 and Klatt 2009. Until the late 1990s the enclosures were regarded as comparatively uniform (Andersen 1997). With new discoveries a division became obvious between those with and without ditch systems (Svensson 2002). To classify the ditches according to shape, as in continental Europe (Meyer 2002), does not seem to be useful. In his presentation of the enclosures in the Baltic area, Klatt uses the following classification (2009, 67–70).

Type 1a:

During the period from the later part of the Early Neolithic to the early part of the Early Middle Neolithic, EN II-MN AI (3500–3100 BC) the enclosures belonging to Type 1 were constructed. In most of them the earliest pottery is dated to the Fuchsberg Phase, which means that they were probably built during a rather late part of EN II.

Most of the enclosures of Type 1a are constructed on spurs in the landscape. They are defined by ditches with or without a palisade. The size varies from 1.4 to 10ha. The construction is dependent on the topographical location, with an almost circular, elongated oval to triangular shape. The ditch system is either single or double. Intact vessels may be found at the bottom of ditches. The ditches of the causewayed enclosures commonly exhibit two or more episodes of re-opening. The posts of the internal palisades are set within a foundation ditch.

No traces of contemporary settlement have been found within the enclosed areas however, some are situated close to settlements. This type is commonly found all over the study area and most belong to this type. When the palisade is missing on some sites the most plausible explanation might be that the remains have totally eroded away either naturally or as a result of agricultural activity, or may not be detectable through survey. The variation in the depth of the postholes is considerable, from about 0.2 to 1.0m (Klatt 2009, Abb. 26) and the depth of the ditches also varies considerably from 0.8 to 2.5m. It is possible that some of the shallower ditches may not have been totally excavated.

Most of the enclosures are situated in proximity to megalithic graves. The extreme case is Sarup where four were known at the time of the site's discovery. However, due to intensive surveys and excavation over several years, the number of earthen long barrows, dolmens and passage graves now exceeds 120 (Andersen 2008, 2009)! This shows that the absence of graves, at least in some cases, is a result of low levels of research.

Type 1b:

This kind of causewayed enclosure is similar to the previous type, but located on or close to a hill. The ditch circuits are complete, they are smaller with an area of 1.6–3ha and they are more or less round or rectangular in shape. Palisades have not been recorded at these sites and megalithic tombs are normally situated some distance away from this type of enclosure. At a couple of enclosures craft activity, namely pottery making (Madsen and Fiedel 1987) and flint axe fabrication (Madsen 1988), seems to have taken place.

Type 1c:

This is a monumental type of enclosure of exceptional size, measuring up to 20ha. They are situated in a level locality or in connection to a ridge, and built with a double ditch system that totally encloses the area but palisades are again absent. Within this group just one (Liselund) is located in southern Scandinavia, while the others are in central northern Germany.

Type 2a:

The second generation of enclosures are dated to the period from the late Early Middle Neolithic to the early Late Middle Neolithic, MN AIV– MN BI (2900–2600 BC).

Type 2a only includes enclosures on the island of Bornholm, situated on level sites that are notable within the landscape. The palisade posts were placed in foundation ditches and contemporary occupation layers are encountered within the enclosures. Internal timber circles of free-standing posts have been identified, the largest with a diameter of 9m. At Rispebjerg a considerable number of timber circles have been found within the remains of the huge palisade structure (Nielsen 1998; 2000; Kaul et al. 2002) (Figure. 8). Although some have a central post, we do not know whether they were roofed. At some of the circles ritual depositions, such as pottery, were made.

At Vasagård the enclosure consists of two rows of palisades, while on Rispebjerg the number is 14 or even more. The palisades at Vasagård enclose an area of 3ha including a former causewayed enclosure, while the palisades at Rispebjerg cover an area of about 6ha. The Vasagård locality, at the eastern edge of a deep depression associated with a small river, include both a causewayed enclosure and an outer palisade enclosure. On the opposite side of the depression another causewayed enclosure has been identified. New geophysical measurements, together with a small excavation, have proved that this causewayed enclosure is also associated with an outer palisade enclosure (personal information by Dr. Finn Ole Nielsen).

Type 2 b:

This type of enclosure is located on level sites, but not exclusively so. The palisade(-s) completely enclose an area of 3–6ha. Usually, the palisade posts have been erected individually, in postholes rather than in a bedding trench, and comprise one to five rows of palisades. This type of enclosure is found in Scania, the southernmost part of Sweden, and on Zealand, eastern Denmark. A close connection with megalithic tombs has been established for the enclosures in Scania.

Causewayed enclosures

The causewayed enclosures are the most numerous kind of enclosure, with about 25 currently known (Figure 1). At most sites excavation has examined only a small area, so the extent of about half of the sites cannot be determined with any accuracy. The only site totally excavated is the first one discovered, at Sarup, southern Funen (Andersen 1999). During the end of the early Neolithic (TN II)

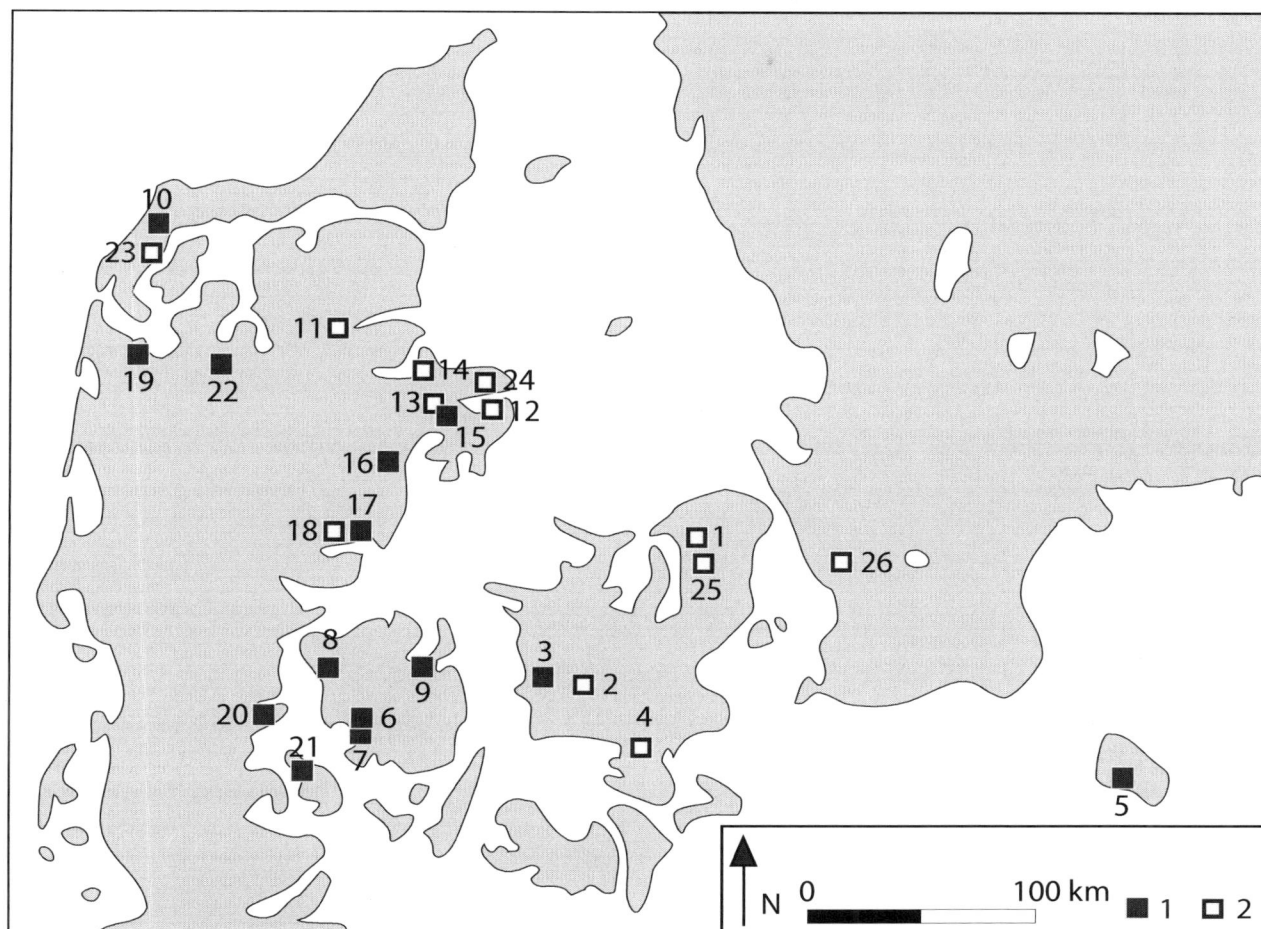

Figure 1. The causewayed enclosures in Southern Scandinavia. 1. Skævinge Boldbaner, 2. Sigersted I, 3. Trelleborg, 4. Markildegård, 5. Vasagård east and Vasagård west, 6. Sarup I and Sarup II, 7, Sarup Gamle Skole, 8. Hygind, 9. Åsum Enggård, 10. Liselund, 11. Lokes Hede, 12. Ginnerup, 13. Blakbjerg, 14. Store Brokhøj, 15. Ballegård, 16. Voldbæk, 17. Toftum, 18. Bjerggård, 19. Mølbjerg, 20. Lønt, 21. Bundsø, 22. Søby Møllegård, 23. Vilsund, 24. Kainsbakke, 25. Orebjerg Enge and 26. Stävie. Legend; 1: enclosures with two ditch systems, and 2: enclosures with one ditch system.

two parallel ditches were dug, covering an area at the confluence between a small river and its tributary (Sarup I) (Figure 2). The ditches run for 600m, covering an area of 8.5ha of the projecting area between the two streams. A palisade enclosed an inner area with just one very restricted entrance. Lines of posts were also erected between pits in which, about one metre deep, pottery vessels were deposited and fires were lit. Human bones were also found. The ditch system was intentionally refilled and then later reopened but this re-cutting was restricted to the inside the edge of the first ditch. Within the enclosed area was a small number of pits containing material similar to that which was found in the ditches.

About a century later (MN AIb) a second stage of the causeway enclosure was built, but now with a much shorter parallel system, 235m long, across the projecting section, only covering an area of 3.5ha (Sarup II). The ditch systems include shorter pits, most of them enclosed by rows of poles. Multiple lines of posts run along the

inner sides of the ditches. In the ditch of the palisades and in some of the postholes burnt human bones were recovered. The situation at Sarup is the only case where one causewayed enclosure has been replaced by another.

Some 100 years later the site was intensively settled with more or less continuous occupation until the end of MN A (Sarup III-V). The ditch system was frequently re-cut during the entire period, which proves that the memory of the initial stage of use was still in people's minds, even if the use of the site had changed rather radically.

Most causewayed enclosures are found at prominent locations in the landscape. However, at least a couple – Skævinge Boldbaner (Hedegaard Andersen 1987) and Liselund (Westphal 2000) – were located in flat areas. Enclosures with two or three rows of ditches predominate while the rest have just one row of ditches. These latter forms are dominant on Zealand, eastern Denmark.

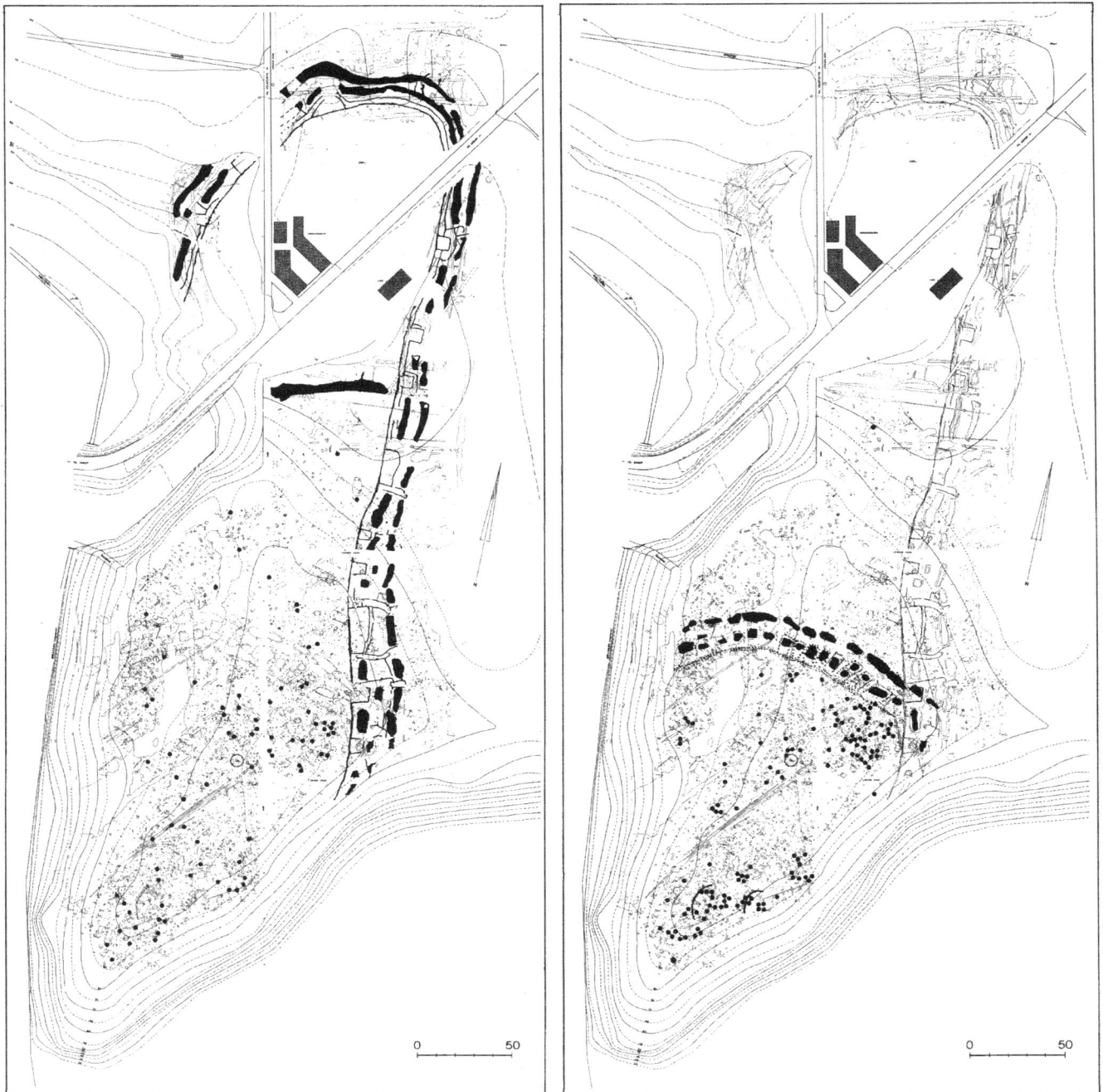

FIGURE 2. THE CAUSEWAYED ENCLOSURE AT SARUP, SOUTHERN FUNEN, DENMARK. SARUP I DATED TO THE FUCHBERG PHASE (EN II) (LEFT) AND SARUP II, DATED TO MN AIB (RIGHT). AFTER NIELSEN 1988.

The causewayed enclosures have been interpreted as meeting places of the inhabitants of small settlements who belonged to a supposedly segmented tribal society (Andersen 1999). Each settlement might have had access to their own ditch segment, perhaps as a place for temporary interments. The finds of human remains have been interpreted as the traces of original primary burials in the ditches that were later reopened to remove most of the bones and the re-cutting of the ditches might indicate that this practice continued for several centuries. Finds of burnt human bone in the postholes of the palisade of Sarup

II might also indicate some mortuary practice in the area between the ditches and the palisades and an interesting find related to mortuary practice is a miniature dolmen built inside a pit at the causewayed enclosure at Sarup Gamle Skole, close to Sarup (Andersen 2000a, 2000b). In the ditch system at Markildegård, where preservation conditions were exceptionally good, the bottom of the ditch was covered with a layer of wood and bark on which vessels and the bones of cattle and sheep were deposited (Sørensen 1995). In another causewayed enclosure, Store Brokhøj a structure interpreted as a pottery kiln was found

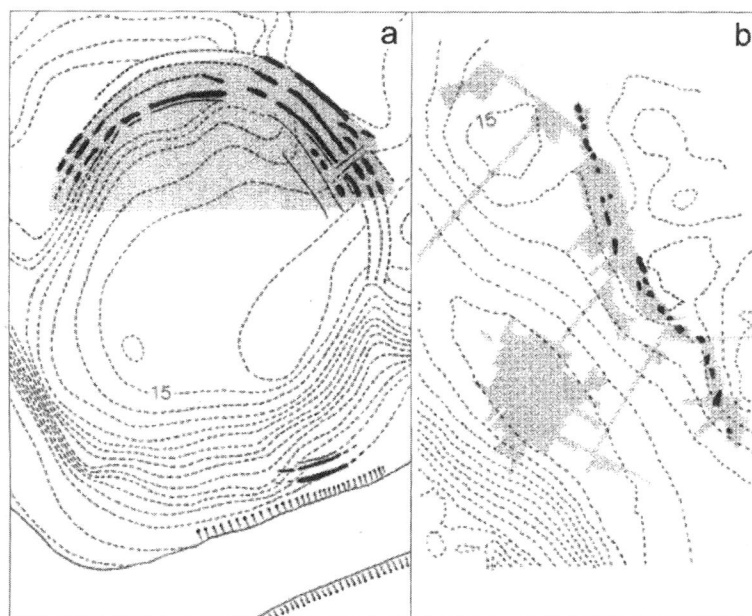

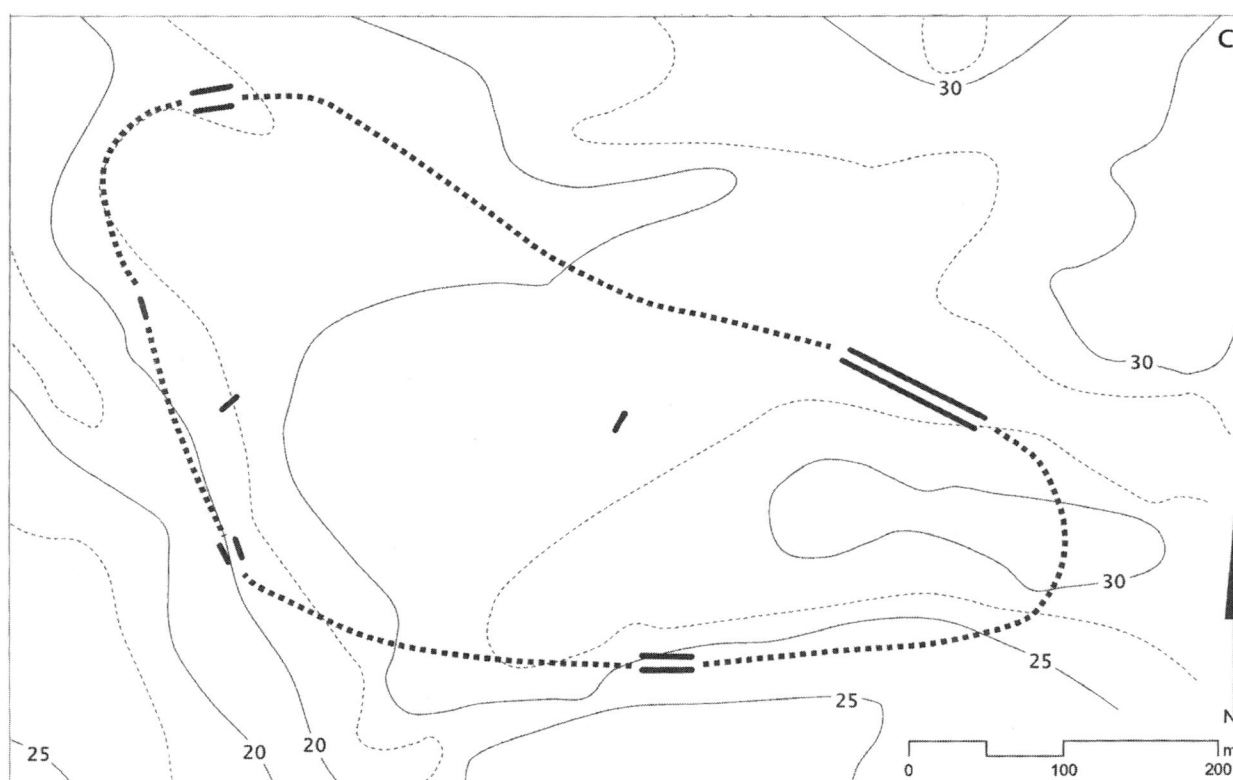

Figure 3. A number of causewayed enclosures: a. Büdelsdorf, b. Markildegård and c. Liselund. From Klatt 2009.

(Madsen and Fiedel 1988) and it has been suggested that ceramics were produced at these sites. The uniformity of the style of pottery encountered indicates that the causewayed enclosures were important in maintaining communication between groups (Nielsen 1999). At Stävie, western Scania, traces of the intensive firing of pottery were found within the material from re-opened ditches dated to MN AV, but these deposits were interpreted as representing the intentional destruction of vessels by fire,

much as was done to flint axes at a number of enclosures (Larsson 1989, 2000).

The relationship between the construction of causewayed enclosures and the use of the sites as settlements is still somewhat uncertain since in most cases there is a time interval between the two stages (Nielsen 2004). In Denmark some of the settlements at causewayed enclosures are large in comparison to sites from earlier periods of the Neolithic

113

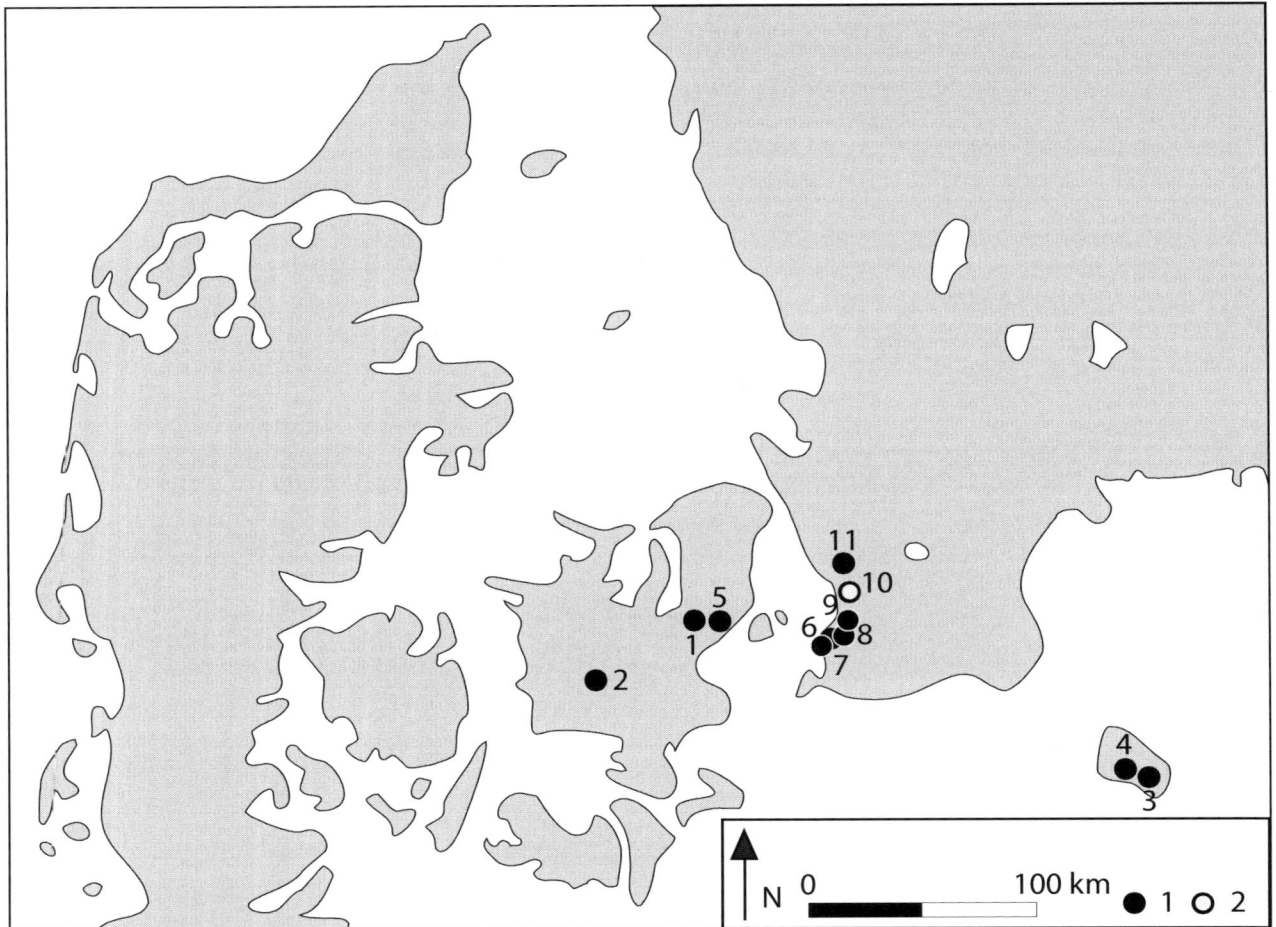

Figure 4. The palisade enclosures in Southern Scandinavia. 1. Helgeshøj, 2. Sigersted I, 3. Rispeberg, 4. Vasagård west and Vasagård east, 5. Bakkegård, 6.Bunkeflo, 7. Bunkeflostrand, 8. Hyllie, 9. Östra Torn, 10. Dösjöbro and 11. Stävie. Legend; 1: enclosures with two or more palisades and 2: enclosure with one palisade.

but even if the sites were used as 'ordinary' settlements, the ritual element involved in the re-cutting of the ditches still continued. It might be going too far to presume that causewayed enclosures formed the common initial stage of large settlements during the early part of MN A and there is at least one causewayed enclosure that was totally abandoned after its primary use (Westphal 2000). However, causewayed enclosures have been detected below some large settlements that were excavated decades ago, such as Budsø (Hoika 1987) and Trelleborg (Andersen 1982; Davidsen 1978) and others may yet remain to be found.

The palisade enclosures of the Middle Neolithic

Only about 11 palisade enclosures have been excavated (Figure 4) and the best excavated is that at Hyllie. It was excavated in two stages, with a gap of ten years between campaigns, in response to different kinds of exploitation affecting the hill on which it had been erected (Svensson 1991; Brinck 2002) (Figure 5). The first stage of excavation involved a cross-section of the feature that provided information about the size of the structure and

also revealed a well-shaped entrance. This meant that the second stage of excavation could be much better prepared in terms of survey, strategic excavation, sampling etc. Only the northernmost part of the enclosure as well as a small part to the east were not included in the threatened area and therefore were not excavated. The structure was situated on a fairly gentle south-facing slope with a height difference of about 3m. The structure was oval measuring 250m by 160m and enclosed an area of 4ha mostly comprising areas of clay with sandy patches. Judging from the traces of the posts, the palisades were built of round posts, each with a diameter of 0.2 – 0.4m and some were pointed and seem to have been driven into the soil. The depth of the postholes varied from 0.02 – 0.6m, with the deepest being found in the outer palisade whilst those of the inner circuit were shallower and therefore contained shorter posts. In the north-western part of the site there are indications to suggest that shallow ditches may have been made before the holes were dug. Based on the depth of the holes, the posts would have been 1.5 – 3.5m high and they were positioned close to each other but not contiguous, the distance between each post being more or less a post's

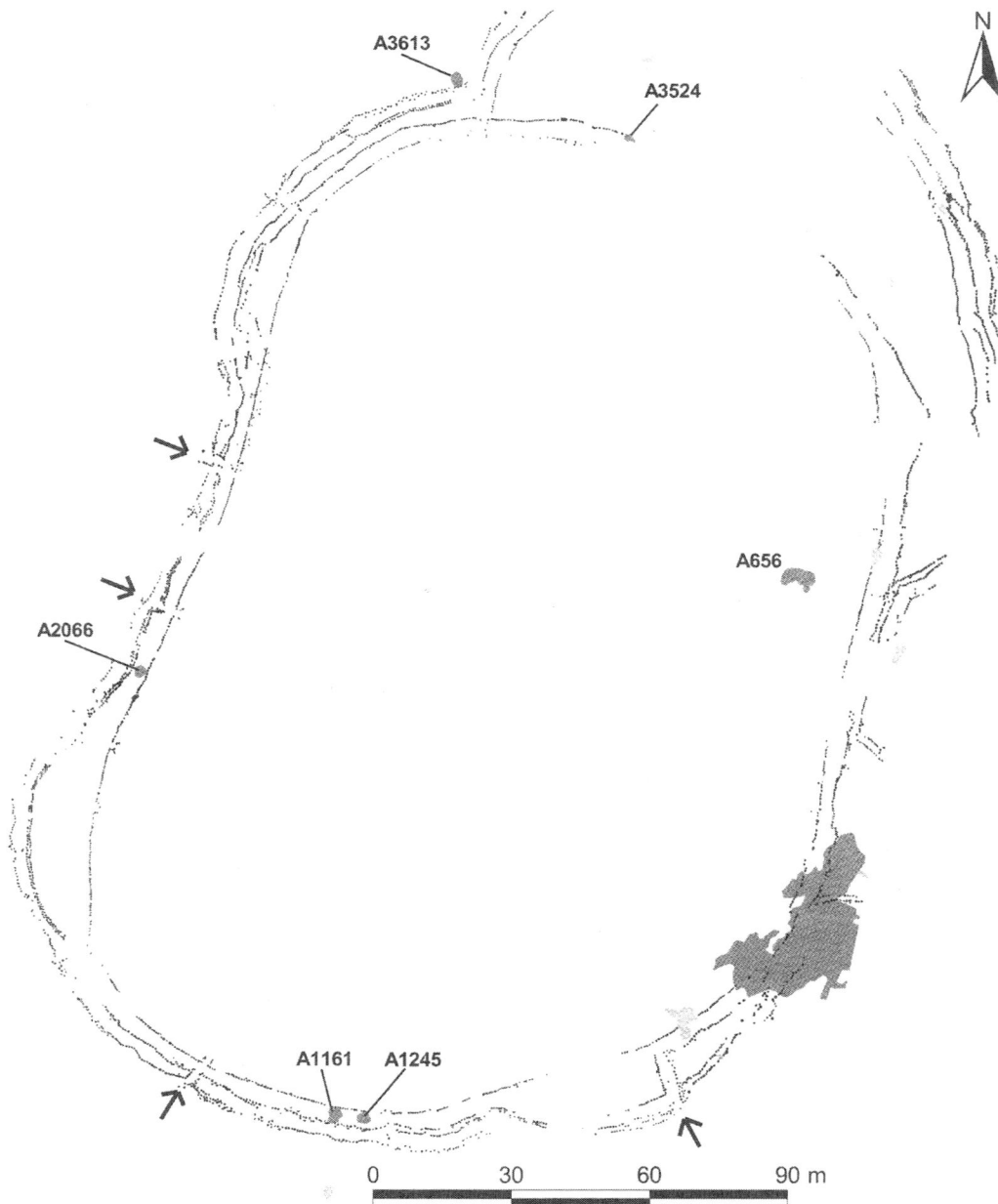

Figure 5. The palisade enclosures at Hyllie, southwestern Scania, Sweden. After Brink 2009.

width. Areas of interruption in the palisade are either the result of later disturbances or else they represent entrances. The number of rows of posts varies somewhat, from four to two. There were major extensions to the northeast and the southeast, but unfortunately they were only partly excavated due to the constraints of the excavation.

None of the posts or post rows overlap. The inner row is the most regular and is interpreted as the first, providing the starting point for the layout of the other rows. Four major entrances were identified: two on the western side and two on the southern side. Two entrances in the outer palisade do not correspond with gaps in the inner palisade, but rather the inner entrance is situated elsewhere. At least in one case, an outer row of poles changes to become the central

row. Entrances to the extensions are also well documented and this contradicts the interpretation of a palisade as having been a single-phased construction. Unfortunately, few datable finds come from either the postholes or the few pits situated inside the enclosure and believed to be contemporary. However, some postholes did contain numerous artefacts and at an entrance to the extension on the eastern side, some forty postholes contained various amounts of unburnt and burnt flint flakes mainly derived from the fabrication of axes, adzes or chisels. Samples of the topsoil were taken at regular intervals, and those with the highest number of burnt flints were also found at the same part of the site. Ground resistance measurements also indicate traces of burning within the same area (Brinck and Hydén 2006, Fig. 62).

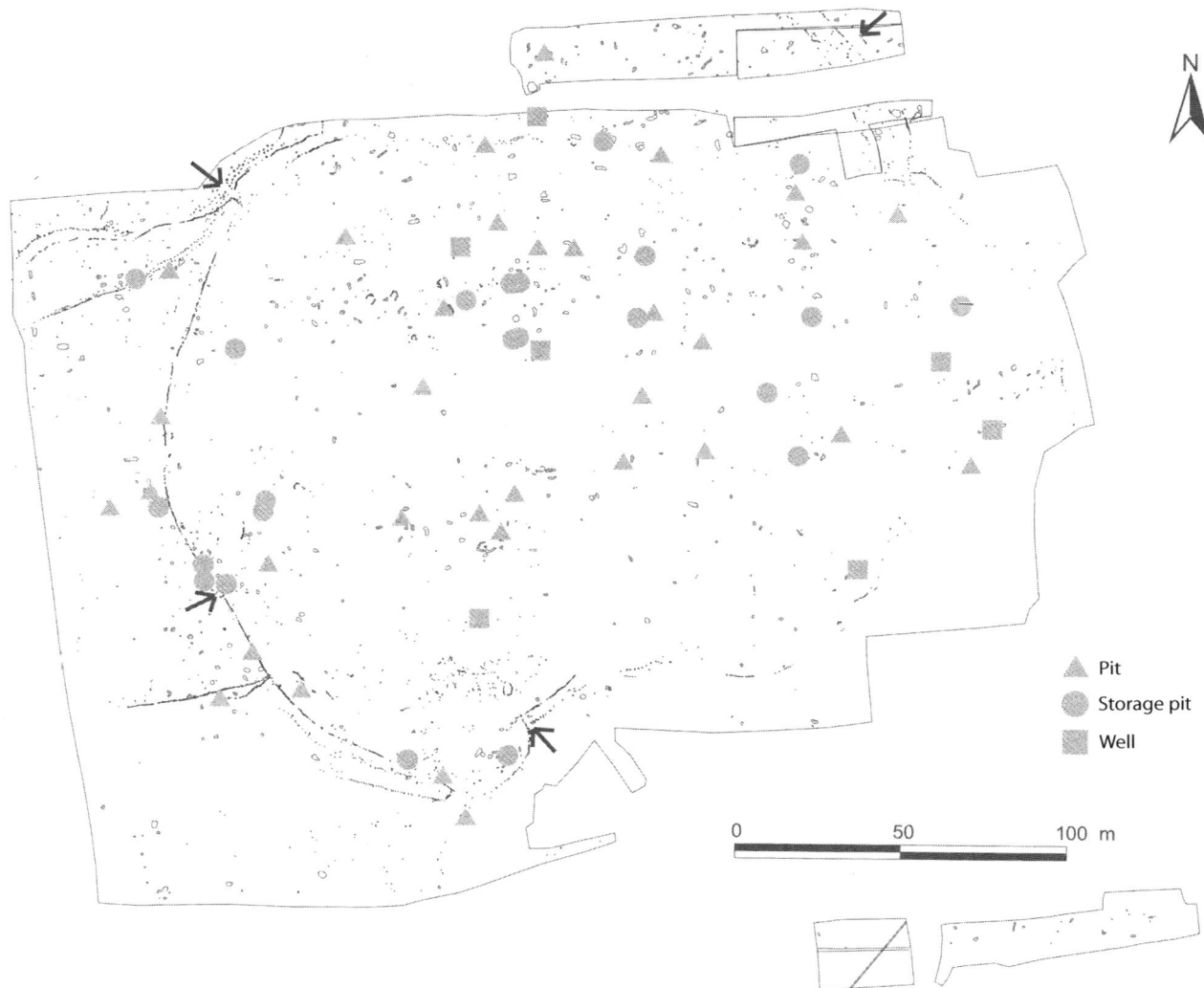

FIGURE 6. THE PALISADE ENCLOSURES AT BUNKEFLOSTRAND, SOUTHWESTERN SCANIA, SWEDEN. THE ENTRANCES AND FEATURES CONTEMPORANEOUS TO THE ENCLOSURE ARE MARKED. AFTER BRINK 2009.

Another enclosure, totally excavated except for a part in the north, is Bunkeflostrand, located in the same region, and situated in a low-lying landscape but on a slight rise sloping down to the former beach (Brink 2009; Brink et al. 2009) (Figure 6). It encloses an area of 300 x 240m totalling some 5.5ha and the height difference within the monument is just a couple of metres. As a result of agricultural activity, the palisade on the downslope is well preserved, while only parts of it can be identified on the higher part of the site and the average depth of the postholes (0.16m) reflects this agricultural degradation. Shallow sections of bedding trenches were also documented. Most parts of the enclosure were made up of three rows of palisades and the intervals between posts varied from just a few decimetres to 1.5m. Palisades leading towards the shoreline are also documented but these did not constitute part of an extension to the enclosure but instead ended after about fifty metres. The structure of the northern part of the enclosure is somewhat unclear though there may have been an extension with an inner row of posts, as at Hyllie

and at least four entrances have been documented. As at Hyllie, the rows of poles crossed, but in this case entrances could be followed through all the lines of palisade. This serves as an important indication that the structure was built either in a single phase or at least in sequences when earlier rows of posts were still in use.

The palisade enclosure at Dösjöbro was situated immediately on the southern bank of a small river (Svensson 2002, 2008) (Figure 7) and about two thirds of the 3 ha site has been excavated. It had almost the shape of a wide U but because the course of the river has been artificially changed, we do not know if there was a palisade running close to the riverbank, or if the river made up the northern side of the enclosure. The perimeter comprised a single palisade of posts spaced at 1m intervals. The existence of burnt clay in the postholes might indicate that the posts had been linked by some kind of wattle and daub screening. Charcoal and soot were documented in most of the postholes and in a part of the palisade the posts had been

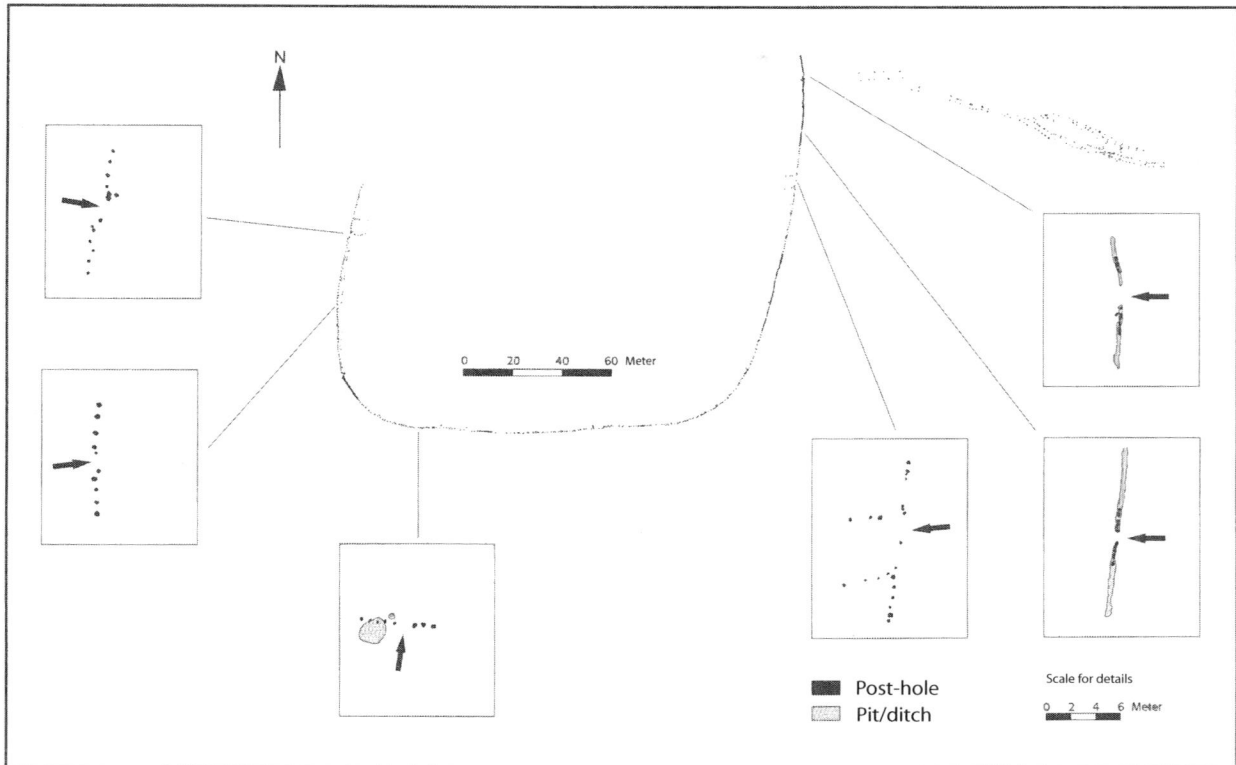

Figure 7. The palisade enclosures with entrances at Dösjöbro, southwestern Scania, Sweden. After Svensson 2008.

placed in a bedding trench. The posts varied between 0.15 and 0.3m in diameter and had been dug down to between 0.3 and 0.7m below the topsoil. As many as six entrances were recorded as either simple gaps in the perimeter or in some cases the entrances were marked with larger or with off-set posts. Some extra posts were interpreted as supports for the palisade. At a number of postholes, flakes from axe production were found. The amount and concentration of flint flakes in some postholes indicates that they had been put in a container and deposited at the same time as the post had been driven into the hole. The amount of burnt flint recovered from the postholes is higher than from other features in the excavated area.

The ploughsoil was stripped within a narrow area across the inner part of the enclosure but no definite features contemporary with the palisade were found. In the eastern part of the enclosure four irregular rows of posts were revealed, extending for about 100m, and in this area an occupation layer was discovered, mainly with finds from the latest part of the Funnel Beaker Culture, but also with a small number of sherds from the Battle Axe Culture. The few datable finds in the palisade and close to it indicate a date corresponding to the early Battle Axe Culture and just a couple of hundred metres to the north of the river, a cemetery with graves dated to the late Battle Axe Culture was excavated (Lagergren 2008). An area of extensive axe production dating to the same culture has been found just 100m further to the north (Runcis 2008).

There is a marked difference between the palisade enclosures at Hyllie and Bunkeflostrand, as the latter enclosed a large number of features. A small number of features were dated to the Early Neolithic, but the majority belong to MN B, according to the finds and radiocarbon dates. The features can be divided into pits, storage pits and wells. The storage pits are distinctive from ordinary pits and have flat or bowl-shaped bases. The topsoil covering the palisade enclosure was tested for flints, and specific concentrations are visible within the enclosure. This is especially obvious with regard to the distribution of waste flakes from axe production. In one pit there were flakes resulting from the same sequence of axe manufacturing. Despite the number of features, datable finds are rather few and this is most obvious with regard to the ceramics, though those sherds that are decorated all belong to the Battle Axe Culture. Observations at Bunkeflostrand, with a row of posts covering a pit and pottery with decoration spanning the entire MN B, indicate that all the activities from MN B at the site do not necessary have to be contemporaneous with the enclosure. They might be somewhat earlier but especially also later. Based on the pottery, most activities at this site date to the late Battle Axe Culture.

As to the shape of the palisade enclosures, the information is meagre. In most palisades the distance between the posts indicates that they were non-contiguous. If the purpose of the palisades was to restrict access then with the space between the posts being almost a metre in some cases,

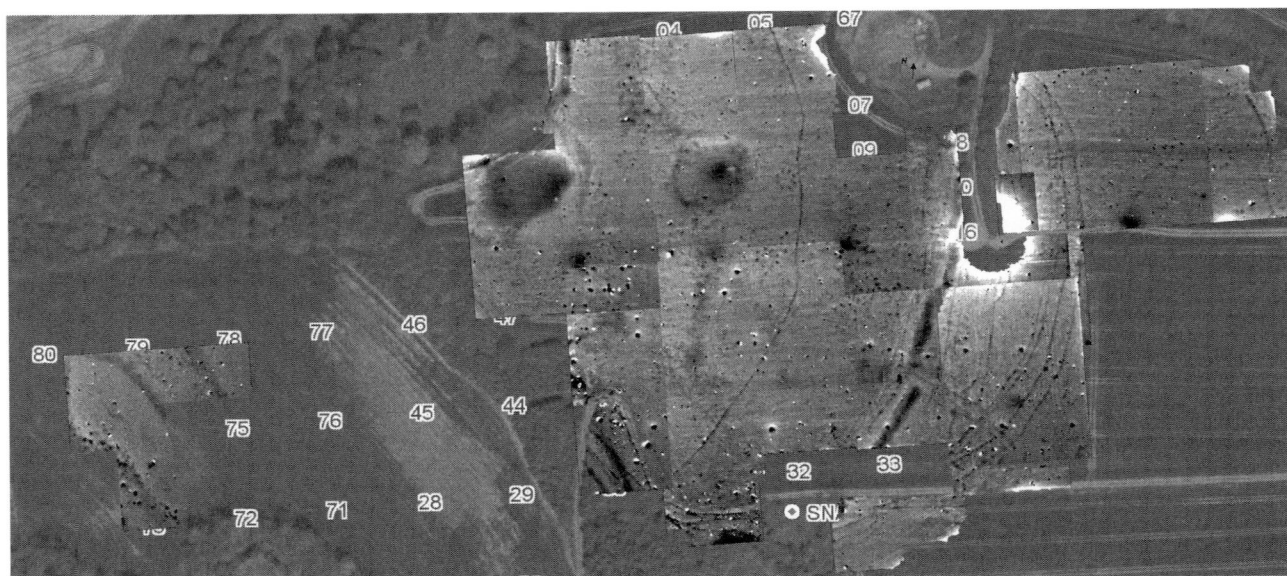

FIGURE 8. THE PALISADE ENCLOSURE AND CIRCLES OF POLES AT RISPEBJERG, BORNHOLM, DENMARK.

some kind of wattling, most probably combined with daub, must have existed, as has been suggested above at Dösjöbro. The examination of the charcoal from Hyllie indicates that most of the posts were made of oak.

The representativeness of the enclosures

According to present knowledge, in Scania, the southernmost part of Sweden, just one causewayed enclosure has been found, but at least five palisade enclosures but we now have a good dataset for both types of enclosure. The causewayed enclosure was found in 1978, but only identified for what it was a few years later (Larsson 1982), while the first palisade enclosure was found at Hyllie in 1989. Excavation teams from the museum at Malmö in the southwestern part of Scania have found four of the palisade enclosures that are known so far. An important factor in the discovery of the palisade enclosures in Scania is that they were found during large-scale rescue excavations involving extensive topsoil removal which facilitated the identification of rows of postholes. At the same time, these large areas of topsoil removal should also have facilitated the identification of causewayed enclosures but development seems to have been concentrated on parts of the landscape that were not suited for the construction of this type of enclosure.

The site of Stävie serves as a thought-provoking example regarding the representativeness of enclosures and elements within them. Previous to the excavation, the topsoil was removed by heavy machines that cut away more than 50cm of the topsoil prior to gravel extraction. The topsoil stripping was such that we do not know if remains of settlements existed on the site during the Funnel Beaker Culture or if the activities during MN AV were limited to the shallow pits that marked the ditch systems.

When archaeologists finally got access to the area no postholes contemporary with the ditch system were

identified and during the course of the excavation no connection was made to the then rather recent discovery of causewayed enclosures in Denmark. As a result the excavation of the ditches stopped after the removal of only the dark upper fill as the excavation team regarded the bottom of the dark fill as the bottom of the ditch (Nagmér 1979) and no testing of the sand below this was made. In addition, the material finds were of a kind not previously encountered (Larsson 1982). The time reserved for the excavation was very limited and the area also included a number of graves and settlement remains covering most of the prehistoric period. As has been observed in other causewayed enclosures, the deeper parts of the ditches are much less easily recognizable and most probably, the ditch system was much deeper than was documented, and probably dates to the first phase of the enclosures.

Some years later an area almost bordering the previous excavation was exposed for a pipeline. Here, the excavator worked in close contact with archaeologists, and a large number of postholes from different structures were identified (Nagmér 1985). A couple of rows of postholes were identified but these could not be stratigraphically linked to the houses. These might have been remains of later palisades from a new palisade enclosure. The way the topsoil was removed and the excavation team's knowledge of what it was confronted with were determining factors with regard to the identification of remains and how they were excavated.

In some areas, such as the southwestern part of Scania, the existence of palisades seems to exclude the presence of causewayed enclosures. The opposite situation seems to exist in the Sarup region, southern Funen where, despite an extremely thorough survey program, combined with a large number of excavations, palisade enclosures have not been identified (Andersen 2008, 2009).

Enclosures and social change

The two different types of enclosures are dated to two of what are perhaps the most interesting phases of cultural development during the Neolithic. The currency of causewayed enclosures is contemporary with the building of megalithic tombs, starting with dolmens at about 3500 BC and ending mainly with passage graves (Ebbesen 2011). The finds of Fuchsberg pottery at the bottom of the ditches indicate that the earliest enclosures date to a rather late phase of EN II, at about 3400 BC and the final period of use for most of the causewayed enclosures in MN AI at about 3200 BC. This final phase seems to have been an extremely intensive building phase, with as many as 650 tombs in Denmark built within a century. According to Ebbesen, this century is a period of extreme competition between societies based on chiefdoms which collapsed within a few generations. As most causewayed enclosures are found within areas of megalithic tombs, it is most plausible that these structures were built by societies experiencing extraordinary and stressful social conditions.

The palisade enclosures have a different distribution. So far, they have been found on the Baltic island of Bornholm, in Scania and in the eastern part of Zealand. They are in regions which have megalithic tombs, representing the old, traditionally settled areas, but they are not within landscapes with a high intensity of megaliths. Furthermore, most are located in topographically indistinctive locations.

The "second generation" (Svensson 2002) enclosures are associated with a much-discussed phase of the Neolithic. The palisade enclosures date to between the late Funnel Beaker Culture (MN AV) and the early part of the Battle Axe Culture (MN BI), 2800–2600 BC. This is a time when there is a marked change in the material culture combined with new social standards, exemplified among other things, by a new mortuary practice. Based on associated artefacts, some of the palisade enclosures are dated to the late Funnel Beaker Culture while others date to the early Battle Axe Culture but there seem to be no differences in terms of the structure of the enclosures.

The distribution of the palisade enclosures is rather complicated. No enclosures have been found on Jutland, where an early phase of the Single Grave Culture within the Corded Ware complex is well proven (Ebbesen 2006, Hübener 2005; Larsson 2007a). However, the Single Grave Culture is poorly represented on Zealand, eastern Denmark, where all the known palisades are located and where a prolonged sequence of the late Funnel Beaker Culture (MN AV) seems to have existed. In Scania, the southernmost part of Sweden, the late Funnel Beaker Culture has also been identified and seems to include at least a couple of stages (Larsson 1982, 1992). The large settlements, well known in Denmark (Davidsen 1978), are not found in Scania where the settlement sites seem to be of limited size.

In southern Sweden the Battle Axe Culture, another manifestation of the Corded Ware complex, was introduced. It has previously been understood that this first appeared in Scania (Malmer 1962) but there are indications to suggest that it was in fact introduced from present-day Finland (Larsson 2009). This hypothesis is much more in agreement with the few remains from the early part of the Battle Axe Culture, in contrast to the considerable number of finds from its later stage. The dates for the late Funnel Beaker Culture are few, but at c.2800 BC they are well in agreement with the dates for the early Corded Ware complex in Denmark (Larsson 1992). The date for the introduction of the Battle Axe Culture is somewhat uncertain, but it may have been broadly contemporary. There might also have been a co-existence of the late Funnel Beaker Culture and the Early Battle Axe Culture within the southernmost part of Sweden and this makes it particularly difficult to relate some of the palisade enclosures to a specific cultural complex as culturally distinctive finds are few. Most of the radiocarbon dates point to the period 2800–2600 BC (Brink 2009).

The ditch segments of the causewayed enclosures were reopened on two or more occasions and both the stratigraphy and the artefacts deposited make it easier to recognise the repeated processes. This is much more difficult for the palisade enclosures. The artefacts deposited in the postholes seem to have been placed there at the time when the posts were erected, but they are mainly waste from axe production or tools that are not closely datable. It is not possible to arrange the lines of palisades in stages. However, just as the ditches were filled and reopened within the limits of the initial segments, so might a palisade enclosure have been demolished and rebuilt without disturbing the remains of the earlier perimeter.

The use and re-use of enclosures

At a number of causewayed enclosures, occupation layers from MN A II onwards provide evidence for prolonged occupation of the site (Nielsen 2004, Table 2). If the original function involved actions relating to special aspects of the world-view, the site probably had to be de-ritualised before it could be accepted as an ordinary settlement and at most of the enclosures there seems to have been a short period of abandonment lasting for about a century prior to the settlement phase. Only a small number of causewayed enclosures seem to be totally abandoned after the end of their use as enclosures. As for the palisade enclosures, at least one (Vasagård east) on the island Bornholm seems to have been settled and, as mentioned above, the contemporaneity of the enclosure at Bunkflostrand and the features indicating a settlement has been questioned.

The mnemonic aspect seems to have been of importance when dealing with palisade enclosures. At Bunkeflostrand, a settlement site comprising houses and other features from the late MN B and Late Neolithic was found less than 100m south of the enclosure. At Dösjöbro a cemetery was excavated on the northern bank of the river, just opposite the enclosure. There may have been a time difference of a century or two between these external activities and the palisade enclosures and it seems very doubtful whether the posts were still standing, marking the location, when these other activities were taking place.

The fairly intensive deposition of late early Middle Neolithic (MN AV) material remains, has been recorded at Stävie and at other causewayed enclosures in Denmark (Nielsen 2004, Table 2). The difference in time between the enclosures and this deposition in these cases is at least half a millennium. Even if the ditches were reopened and later refilled, sometimes in several stages, it is reasonable to presume that the features were still visible as shallow depressions in the surface several generations after the site was abandoned and so the tradition of a special event might have been easier to maintain if the oral record could be linked to visible surface features. The actual relationship between the causewayed enclosures of the late Early Neolithic/early Early Middle Neolithic (TN II–MN AI) and the society of the late Early Middle Neolithic (MN AV) is easier to comprehend if we look to another phenomenon that seems to point in the same direction. The accumulated depositions of tools, especially axes, in wetlands cease at the MN AI but start again in MN AV and continue into MN B (Karsten 1994; Larsson 2007b). In the intermediate period the knowledge of where these depositions took place must have been kept alive, as the deposition would have been covered with water and organic litter within a generation. That palisade enclosures dated to MN AV are present in direct relationship to the earlier causewayed enclosures on the island of Bornholm is a strong indication of a link between the TN II/MN AI and MN AV and at the Danish site of Sigersted the causewayed enclosure and the palisade enclosure are documented just three hundred metres apart.

Whether the palisade enclosures were built and used with the same intentions and objectives as the causewayed enclosures is hard to say. Once again, the physical relationship of the two kinds of enclosures at Bornholm might provide a hint but even if the same location is selected, it does not mean that the functions of the enclosures were the same. The locations were in any case related to memories of exceptional significance and the palisades were erected at a respectable distance from the ditches. Artefacts suggest that the palisade enclosures at Bornholm can be dated to the latest part of the Funnel Beaker Culture (MN AV), while most of the palisade enclosures in Scania are somewhat later.

A number of activities of ritual significance were performed in the ditches of the causewayed enclosures: fires were lit and tools as well as vessels were deposited (Andersen 1997). Compared to the intensity of the activities taking place in the ditches, the number of contemporaneous features with similar remains within the enclosures is limited. This also seems to be true for most of the palisade enclosures.

What is an enclosure?

An important aspect of the discussion is what one means by 'enclosure'. The question is brought to a head when the pile dwelling at Alvastra in central southern Sweden is taken into account. Here, two square wooden platforms joined at an oblique angle were built during the Middle Neolithic (Malmer 2003). The platform measures 450m². These two square areas are in turn divided into several rectangular sections, each with a hearth and dendrochronological studies tell us that the structure was built in a single event as the piles for the frame of the platform were all driven into the mire at the same time. Some posts may have formed a wooden wall with a height of at least 2m. After just a year the platform was ravaged by fire, but parts were replaced shortly afterwards with new posts. Activities on the platform continued for a total of 42 years, but this included long periods when areas of the platform were abandoned. The composition of the finds assemblages distinguishes the site from more ordinary settlements as there is little waste or other remains of ordinary domestic activities. Instead, a large number of double-edged stone axes and scattered human bones from about 45 individuals were found. The animal bones and plant remains indicate that large feasts took place within the structure and it has been interpreted as an assembly place for two social groups, for example, two kin groups, with each family occupying its own rectangular cell (Browall 1986). Even though it is younger than the causewayed enclosures – with a mean value of several radiocarbon dates centring on 3060 cal. BC (Malmer 2003) – scholars have incorporated the structure within the same category (Andersen 1997) but in view of the dating of the construction, the age of the Alvastra pile dwelling fits better the time of the palisades than period of the causewayed enclosures.

In 2007 a new kind of palisade structure was recorded during excavations in an area of megalithic tombs at Håslöv in south-western Scania (Andersson and Wallebom 2011). About twenty destroyed megaliths, most of them dolmens, were identified, positioned more or less in two rows. Between these tombs a narrow area oriented north-south was visible, delimited on both sides by closely-spaced posts set in bedding trenches with packing stones to support the posts. The width of this area varies between 3-8m. Fragments of flint axes, waste from axe manufacturing, and burnt flints, a combination of artefacts well known at causewayed enclosures, were recovered from the bedding trenches. The delimited area is interpreted as a processional road and at intervals the rows of posts were flanked by rows of standing stones. The palisade 'road' could be detected for a distance of about 650m. At the southern end it turns to the east, leading down to a small river and this observation might support the idea that they represent the remains of a large enclosure. According to the radiocarbon dates, the palisade 'road' was constructed in the Early Neolithic, somewhat earlier than the first megalithic tombs.

Conclusion

Enclosures were built during two phases of the Neolithic. In both phases this is seemingly related to stress within the societies though probably for different reasons. The first phase, with the causewayed enclosures, includes a stage of intensive megalithic tomb construction, while the second phase, with palisade enclosures, occurred during a change in material culture and cosmology during the transition from Funnel Beaker Culture to the regional versions within the complex of the Corded Ware Culture. During both these phases the need for places for popular assemblies might have been related to the major importance of keeping control over the population. The building of the enclosures engaged a large number of people, providing work for them and perhaps preventing them from engaging in activities that could result in competition with the ruling elite. The ditch systems of the causewayed enclosures might have been important to most of the people – a focus for smaller groups as the place for ritual depositions and primary burials. Regarding the palisade enclosures, such activities are not so easily discernable, but features with ritual deposits have been identified. What happened within the area enclosed by the palisade might have been of importance for the ruling class and a means of marking the difference between the rulers and the rest of the population.

There is a time interval between the two generations of enclosures of about two to three hundred years. However, re-opening of the ditch systems during that interval proves that people were very conscious of the locales. That such elements as the ditch systems were excluded in the second generation might have to do with the change of views concerning how and what rituals were to be performed yet in some areas, such as western Denmark, enclosures of the second generation do not seem to have been built at all.

References

Andersen, N. H. 1974. En befæstet, yngre stenalderboplads i Sarup. Føreløbig meddelelse. *Fynske Minder* 1974, 49.

Andersen, N. H. 1982. A Neolithic Causewayed Camp at Trelleborg near Slagelse, West Zealand. *Journal of Danishish Archaeology* 1, 1982, 31–33.

Andersen, N. H. 1988. *Sarup. Befæstede kultpladser fra bondestenalderen.* Århus, Jysk Arkæologisk Selskab.

Andersen, N. H. 1997 *The Sarup Enclosures. The Funnel Beaker Culture of the Sarup site including two causewayed camps compared to the contemporary settlements in the area and other European enclosures.* Jutland Archaeological Society Publications XXXIII:1. Aarhus, Aarhus University Press.

Andersen, N. H. 1999. *Saruppladsen.* Sarup vol. 2. Jysk Archæologisk Selskabs Skrifter XXXIII:2. Aarhus, Aarhus Universitet Forlag.

Andersen, N. H. 2000a. Kult og ritualer i den ældre bondestenalder. *Kuml* 2000, 13–57.

Andersen, N. H. 2000b. Sarup Gamle Skole XII. *Arkæeologiske Udgravninger i Danmark* 1999, 2000, nr. 231.

Andersen, N. H. 2002. Neolithic Endosures of Scandinavia. In G. Varndell and P. Topping (eds.), *Enclosures in Neolithic Europe.* Essays on causewayed and noncausewayed sites, 1–10. Oxford, Oxbow books.

Andersen, N. H. 2008. Die Region um Saup in Südwesten der Insel Fünen (Dänemark) im 3. Jahrtausend v. Ch. In W. Döfler and J. Müller (eds.), *Umwelt – Wirtschaft – Siedlungen im dritten vorchristlichen Jahrtausend Mitteleuropas und Südskandinavien,* 35–47. Offa-Bücher Band 84. Neumünster, Wachholtz Verlag.

Andersen, N. H. 2009. Sarupområdet på Sydvestfyn i slutningen af det 4. årtusinde f. Kr. In A. Schülke (ed.), Plads og rum i tratbægerkulturen, 25–44. København, Det Konglige Nordiske Oldskriftselskab.

Andersson, M. and Wallebom, B. 2011. *Döserygg, Grav- och samlingsplats från början av yngre stenålder.* Skåne, Håslöv socken, Håslöv 10:1 och 13:1, RAÄ 47. Väg E6, Trelleborg–Vellinge. UV SYD Rapport 2010:30. Lund, Riksantikvarieämbetet.

Brink, K. 2004. The palisade enclosure at Hyllie, SW Scania. *Journal of Nordic Archaeological Science* 14, 35–44.

Brink, K. 2009. *I palissadernas tid. Om stolphål och skärvor och sociala relationer under yngre mellanneolitikum.* Malmöfynd 21. Malmö, Malmö Museer.

Brink, K. and Hydén, S. 2006. *Hyllie vattentorn – delområde 5 och Palissaden – delområde 5.* Rapport nr. 42. Malmö, Malmö kulturmiljö.

Brink, S., Kishonti, I. and Magnell, O. 2009. On the shore. Life inside a palisade enclosure and Cultural change during the Middle Neolithic B in Southern Sweden. *Current Swedish Archarology* 17, 79–107.

Browall, H. 1986 *Alvastra pålbyggnad: Social och ekonomisk bas.* Theses and Papers in North-European Archaeology 8. Stockholm: Institute of Archaeology.

Davidsen, K. 1978. *The Final TRB Culture in Denmark.* Arkæologiske Studier V. København, Akademisk Forlag.

Dibbern, H. and Hage, F. 2010. Erdwerk und Megalithgräber in der Region Albersdorf – Vorbericht zu den Grabungskampagneen am Dieksknöll und Brutkamp. *Archäologischen Nachrichten aus Schlewig-Holstein* 2010, 34–37.

Ebbesen, K. 2006. *The Battle Axe Period.* København, Attika.

Ebbesen, K. 2011. *Danmarks megalitgrave* 1, 1–2. København, Attika.

Hedegaard Andersen, A. 1987. Skævinge Boldbaner.nr. 16. *Arkæologiske udgravninge i Danmark* 1986.

Hingst, H. 1971. Eine befestigte jungsteinzeitliche Siedlung in Büdelsdorf, Krs. Rendsburg-Eckernrorde. *Offa* 28, 90–93.

Hoika, J. 1987. Das Mittelneolithikum zur ZeitDet Rrichterbecherkultur in Nordostholstein. Offa_bücher Band 61. Neumünster, Wachholtz Verlag.

Hübner, E. 2005. Jungneolithische Gräber auf der Jütischen Halbinsel. Typologische und chronologische Studien zur Einzelgrabkultur. Nordiske Fortidsminder Serie B, Band 24:1–3. Købehamn, Det Kongelige Nordiske Oldskriftselakab.

Karsten, P. 1994. *Att kasta ytan i sjön.* En studie over rituell tradition och förändring utifrån skånska neolitiska offerfynd. Acta Archaeologica Lundensia, Serries in 8°, N°. 23. Stockholm, Almquist & Wiksell International.

Kaul, F., Nielsen, P. O. and Nielsen, F. O. 2002. Vasagård og Rispebjerg. To indhegnede bopladser fra yngre stenalder på Bornholm. *Nationalmuseets Arbejdsmark* 2002, 119–138.

Klatt, S. 2009. Die neolithischen Einhegungen im westlischen Ostseeraum. Forschungsstand und Forschungsperspektiven. In T. Terberger (ed.), *Neue Forschungen zum Neolithikum im Ostseeraum, 7–134.* Archaeology and History of the Baltic 5. Rahden/Westf., Verlag Marie Leidorf GmbH.

Lagergren, A. 2008. Stridsyxegravfält och kommunikation och den rituella platsensom lank mellan kulturer. In P. Lagerås (ed.), *Dösjöbro, mötersplats för trattbägarkultur & stridsyxekultur,* 54–124. Skånska spår – arkeologi längs Västkustbanan. Lund, Riksantikvarieämbetet.

Larsson, L. 1982. A Causewayed Enclosure and a Site with Valby Pottery at Stävie, Western Scania. *Papers of the Archaeological Institute University of Lund* 1981–1982, 65–107.

Larsson, L, 1989. Brandopfer. Der frühneolithische Fundplatz Svartskylle im südlichen Schonen, Schweden. *Acta Archaeologica* 59, 143–53.

Larsson, L. 1992. Settlement and environment during the Middle Neolithic and Late Neolithic. In L. Larsson, J. Callmer and B. Stjernquist (eds.), *The Archaeology of the Cultural Landscape. Field work and research in a south Swedish Rural Region,* 91–159. Acta Archaeologica Lundensia Series I 4°, N°19. Lund, Almquist & Wiksell International.

Larsson, L. 2000. The passage of axes: fire transformation of flint objects in the Neolithic of southern Sweden. *Antiquity* 74, (No. 285), 602–610.

Larsson, L. 2007a. Regional development or external influences? The Battle Axe Period in south-western Scandinavia, In M. Larsson and M. Parker Pearson (eds.), *From Stonehenge to the Baltic.* Living with cultural diversity in the third millennium BC, 11–16. BAR International Series 1692. Oxford, Archaepress.

Larsson, L. 2007b. Wetland and Ritual Deposits during the Neolithic. A Local Study in a Micro-environment of a Macro-phenomenon. *Lund Archaeological Review* 2005–2006, 59–69.

Larsson, Å. M. 2009. *Breaking and Making Bodies and Ports.* Material and Ritual Practices in Sweden in the Third Millennium BC. Aun 40. Uppsala, Uppsala universitet.

Madsen, B. and Fiedel, E. R. 1987. Portery manufacture at a Neolithic Causewayed Enclosure near Hevringholm, East Jutland. *Journal of Danish Archaeology* 6, 78–86.

Madsen, T. 1988, Causewayed enclosures in South Scandinavia. In M. Maddison, C. Burgess P. Topping and C. Mordant (eds.), *Enclosures and defences in the Neolithic of western Europe.* Bd. 2, 301–336. BAR International Series 403(2). Oxford, Archaeopress.

Madsen, T. and Fiedel, R. 1988. Pottery manufacture at a Neolithic causewayed enclosure near Hevringholm, East Jutland. *Journal of Danish Archaeology,* 78–86.

Malmer, M.P. 1962. *Jungneolitische Studien.* Acta Archaeologica Lundensia Series in 8°. N° 2. Lund, Gleerups förlag.

Malmer, M.P. 2003. *The Neolithic of South Sweden. TRB, GRK, and STR.* Stockholm, Almquist & Wiksell International.

Müller, J. 2011. *Megaliths and funnel beakers; Societies in change 4100–2700 BC.* Drieendertigste Kroonvoordracht. Amsterdam, Amsterdam Archeologisch Centrum van de Universiteit Amsterdam.

Meyer, M. 2002. Palisaded Enclosures in the German Neolithic. In A. M. Gibson (ed.), *Behind wooden walls: Neolithic Palisaded Enclosures in Europe,* 59–92. BAR International Series 1013. Oxford, Archaeopress.

Nagmér, R. 1979. Gravfält från yngre järnålder–vikingatid samt boplats från gropkeramisk tid, bronsålder och älder järnålder, Sävie 4:1. Stävie sn., Skåne. Riksantikvarieämbetet och Statens Historiska Museer. *Rapporter Uppdragsverksamheten* 1979:47. Lund.

Nagmér, R. 1985. Stävie 4:1, Stävie socken, RAÄ 5. Arkeologisk slutundersökning. Sydgasprojektet, stamledning P30. In E. Rääf (ed.). Skåne på längden. Sydgasundersökningana 1983–1985, 102–105. Riksantikvarieämbetet Lund, Rapport UV Syd 1996:58. Lund, Riksantikvarieämbetet.

Nielsen, F. O. 1998. Nyt om Ringborgen paa Rispebjerg. *Bornholms Museum* 1996–1997, 77–96.

Nielsen, P. O. 2004. Causewayed camps, palisade enclosures and central settlements of the Middle Neolithic in Denmark. *Journal of Nordic Archaeological Science* 14, 19–33.

Nielsen, S. 1999. *The Domestic Mode of Production – and Beyond.* Nordiske Fortidsminder Serie B, Vol. 18. København, Det Kongelige Nordiske Oldtidselskap.

Runcis, J. 2008 Neolitisk yxtillverking. Produktion, organisation och kulturell kontext. In P Lagerås (ed) *Dösjebro. mötesplats för trattbägarkultur & stridsyxekultur,* 127–153. Skånska spår – arkeologi längs Västkustbanan. Lund, Riksantikvarieämbetet.

Svensson, M. 1991. A Palisade Enclosure in South-West Scania – a Site from the Battle-Axe Culture. In: K. Jennbert, L. Larsson, R. Petré and B. Wyszomirska-Werbart (eds.), *Regions and reflections.* In honour of Märta Strömberg, 97–109. Lund, Almquist & Wiksell International.

Svensson, M. 2002. Palisade enclosures – The Second Generation of Enclosed Sites in The Neolithic of Northern Europe. In A. Gibson (ed), *Behind Wooden Walls: Neolithic Palisaded Enclosures in Europe,* 28–58. BAR International Series 1013. Oxford: Archaeopress.

Svensson, M. 2008. Palissaden i Dösjöbro i ett nordeuropeiskt perspektiv. In P. Lagerås (ed.), *Dösjöbro, mötersplats för trattbägarkultur & stridsyxekultur*, 21–53. Skånska spår – arkeologi längs Västkustbanan. Lund, Riksantikvarieämbetet.

Sørensen, P. O. 1995. Markildegård. En tidligneolitisk samlingsplads. *Kulturhistoriske Studier, Sydsjællands Museum* 1995, 13–45.

Westphal, J. 2000. Liselund. In S. Hvass and Det Arkæologiske Nævn (eds.) *Vor skjulte kulturarv.* Arkæologien under overfladen, 50–51. Esbjerg, Det Konglige Nordiske Oldskriftselskab.

Mid- Late Neolithic Enclosures in the South of France

Fabien Convertini

Abstract

An overview of the Middle and Late Neolithic enclosures in the South of France will be presented primarily on the basis of recently excavated sites and those with updated publications. The proposed interpretations regarding function or status of these sites will be discussed for the two chronological horizons considered and for each of the geographic groups of enclosures.

The Middle Neolithic

In the South of France, no sites enclosed by ditches have been discovered for the Early Neolithic and enclosures dating to the Middle Neolithic remain fairly uncommon. Thirteen are located between the western Languedoc and Provence (Figure 1) and all have been attributed to the Chassean culture.

The earliest known enclosures were discovered in 1944, at Villeneuve-Tolosane/Cugnaux (Haute-Garonne), and have recently been published (Gandelin 2011). The enclosure system was investigated over a period of forty years in rescue excavations in advance of its destruction by urban expansion. Given the large number of such small-scale excavations, the remains were often not immediately interpreted as part of a single large site. It was only after 1978

that extensive excavations were carried out by J. Vaquer and these revealed the presence of one of the largest sites of the southern Middle Neolithic (around 30ha). Several palisades and many ditch sections seem to have coexisted with hundreds of pits containing heated cobbles, as well as dozens of other pits and individual burials (Vaquer 1990). Further rescue operations took place during the 1980s and 1990s up until 2000. This work complemented the overall plan of the site by mapping individual excavation zones distributed across the entire site. Despite this advance, the reconstruction of the complete site plan and the evaluation of the coherence of the recorded data proved difficult. Nevertheless, the combination of field data with the typological data and absolute chronology has enabled the identification of three architectural phases that correspond to three distinct and successive enclosure systems (Figure 2).

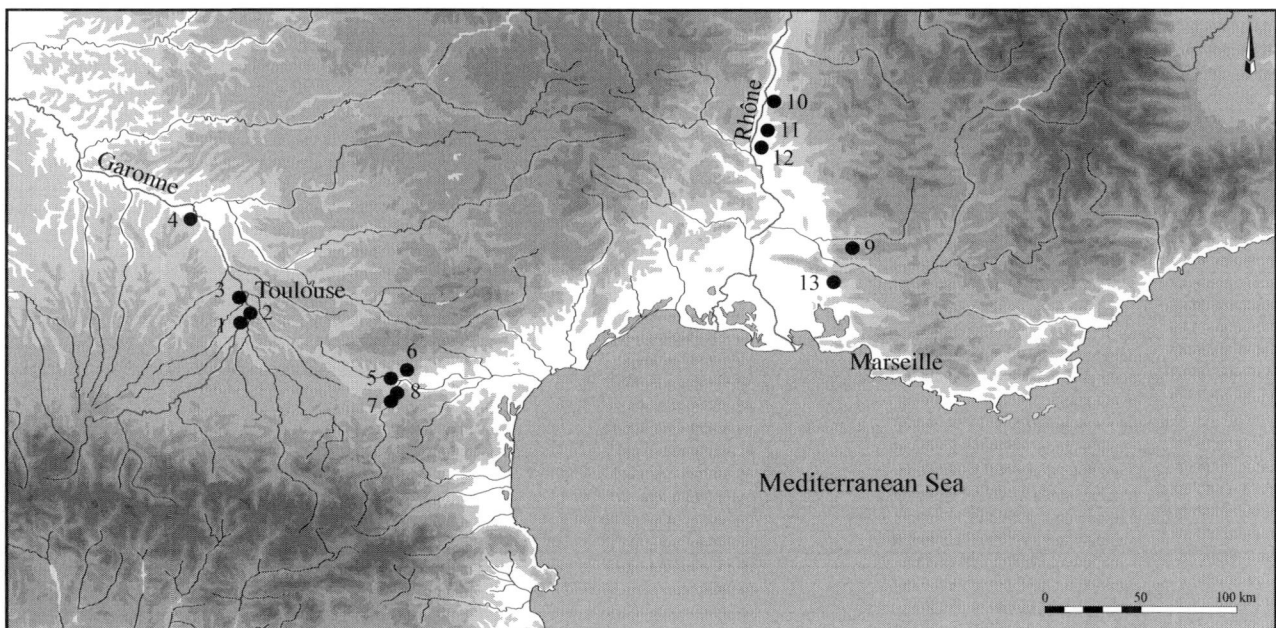

1 : Villeneuve-Tolosane / Cugnaux (Haute-Garonne), 2 : Saint-Michel-du-Touch (Toulouse, Haute-Garonne), 3 : Château-Percin (Seilh, Haute-Garonne), 4 : Saint-Genès (Castelferrus, Tarn-et-Garonne), 5 : La Poste Vieille (Pézens, Aude), 6 : Les Plos (Ventenac-Cabardès, Aude), 7 : La Farguette (Cavanac, Aude), 8 : Auriac (Carcassonne, Aude), 9 : Les Martins (Roussillon, Vaucluse), 10 : La Roberte (Châteauneuf-du-Rhône, Drôme), 11 : Clansayes 2 (Clansayes, Drôme), 12 : Les Moulins (Saint-Paul-Trois-Châteaux, Drôme), 13 : L'Héritière II (Vernègues, Bouches-du-Rhône)

FIGURE 1 : LOCATION OF THE MIDDLE NEOLITHIC ENCLOSURES IN THE SOUTH OF FRANCE

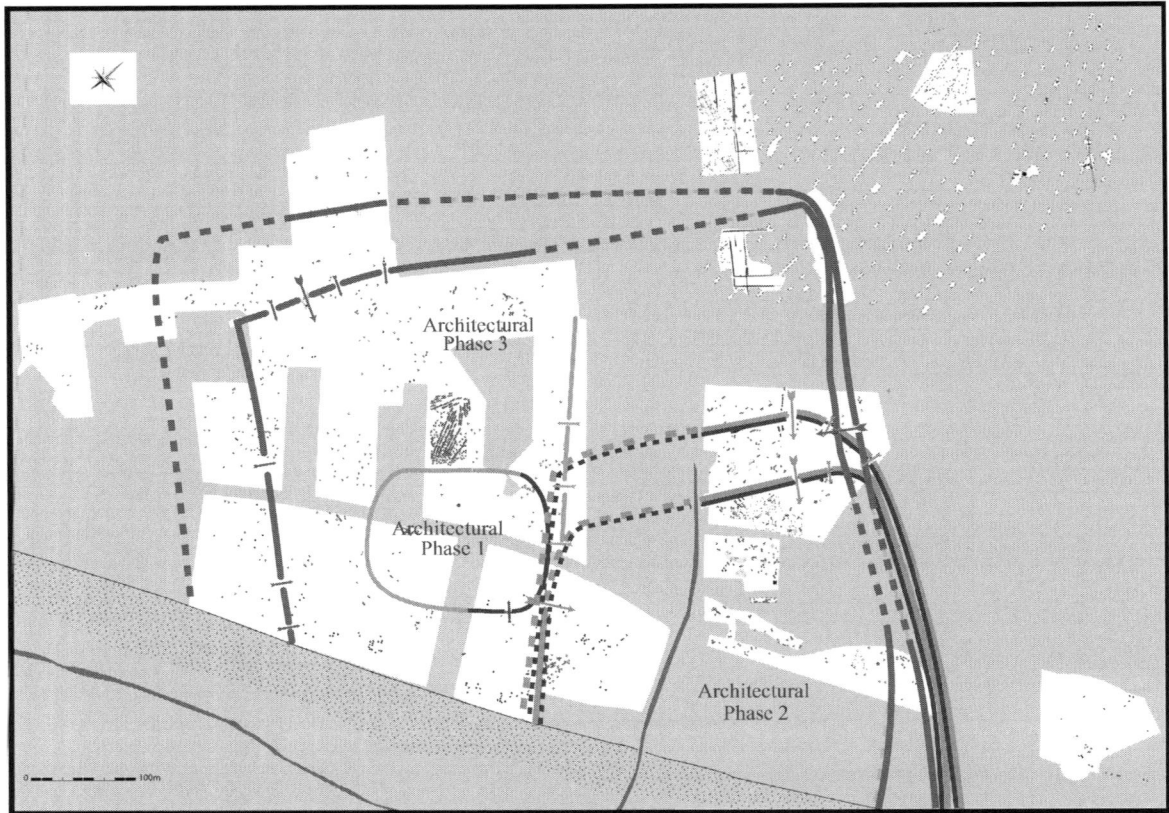

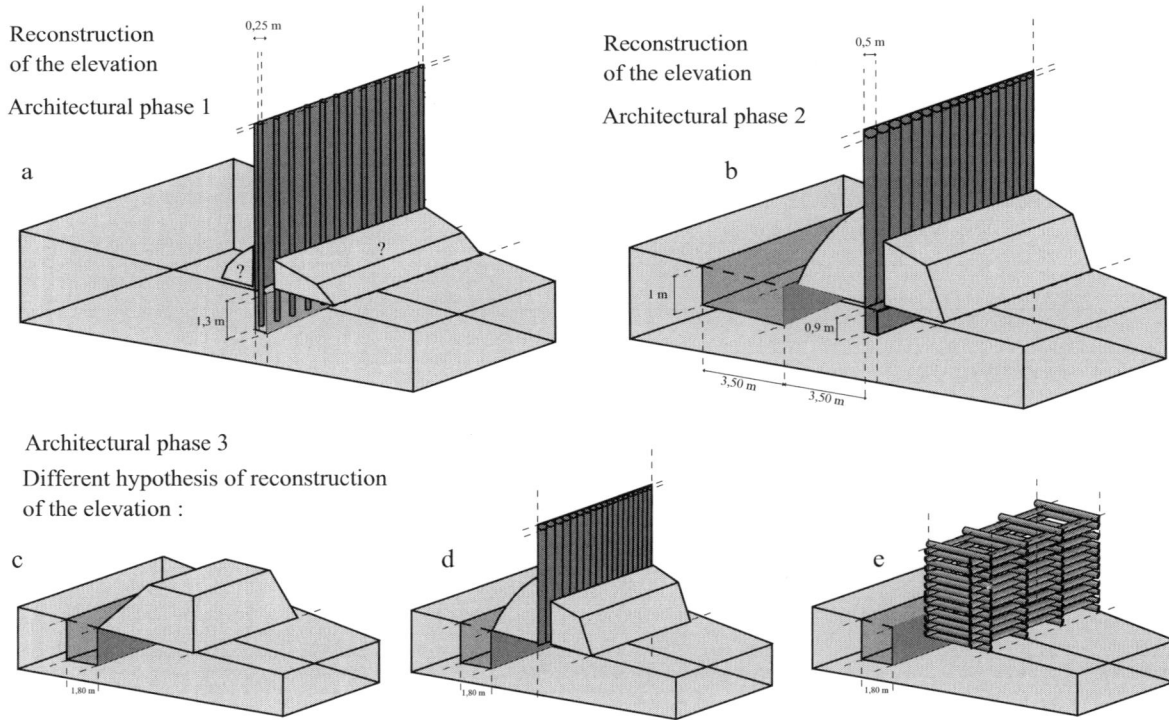

FIGURE 2 : SUCCESSIVE ARCHITECTURAL PHASES AT VILLENEUVE-TOLOSANE/CUGNAUX (HAUTE-GARONNE)
(ADAPTED FROM GANDELIN 2011, FIG. 12)

Phase 1 is characterized by the presence of a sub-circular palisade enclosure surrounding an area of 1-2ha (Figure 2). This has only been very partially excavated. This palisade comprised more than a thousand free-standing posts, deeply anchored in the ground, and possibly linked to one another by branches (hypothesis a). No gaps have so far been observed in the perimeter and this first occupation has not been directly dated.

Phase 2 comprises a double ditched enclosure associated with wooden palisades which enclosed a maximum area of 13ha (Figure 2). The first ditch was either continuous or sparsely segmented with a width of 3-4m and a palisade lay beyond the inner edge of this ditch. A second ditch, parallel to the first, was located to the northwest. It consisted of several ditch segments and was also associated with an inner palisade which resulted in the creation of an enclosed area between the two ditches. Analysis of the silting patterns within the ditch suggests that they were associated with banks. Both ditches were broken at the same point by an entrance causeway 5m wide suggesting that both ditches were either contemporary or constructed in quick succession. A possible second entrance was located to the east of the first. The posts of the palisade were firmly packed with soil and cobbles and the posts were possibly contiguous (hypothesis b). The enclosure seems to have been in use between 4200-3950 cal BC.

Phase 3 consists of a rectangular enclosure enclosing an area of 28ha and which seems to have been fortified on three sides (Figure 2). The interrupted ditch of this enclosure measured up to 2.8m wide and was preserved to a depth of 2m. It may have been associated with a second ditch along its entire length but the chronological relationship between the two wide-spaced ditches is as yet uncertain. No palisade has so far been discovered but the presence of an earthen bank is possible (hypothesis c) either revetted with soil (hypothesis d) or by timber (hypothesis e) though no trace of either has been found. Several entrances have been identified. The enclosure was constructed *c*. 3900 and abandoned *c*. 3800 cal BC.

The presence of other ditches suggests the possibility that there were other phases or stages within the life of the enclosure and as a result the reconstructions must remain hypothetical based on observations that can be difficult to interpret in some of the excavated areas.

No internal structures associated with Phase 1 have yet been identified with certainty thus its function and dating remain unknown. Given the scale of the perimeter, however, M. Gandelin (2011) considers it unlikely to have been a simple cattle enclosure. By contrast, several hundred structures and deposits are associated with Phases 2 and 3. These comprise pits, silos, structures with heat-cracked stones, postholes and a well and together they have produced considerable quantities of domestic artefacts. Space seems to have been carefully divided within the enclosures and at least 1 building has been associated with Phase 2 as well as 18 burials. In both Phases 2 and 3, the area to the northwest

delimited by the 2 ditches may have been a specialised zone such as a cattle enclosure separate to the occupation areas and a stream may have crossed the enclosure. It has been suggested that the occupation of Phase 2 lasted some 250 years whilst Phase 3 lasted a further century based around domestic occupation, animal husbandry, storage and the deposition of domestic waste. A large quantity of axes from the site also attests to woodland exploitation and perhaps even clearance. It has been suggested that the site was permanently occupied though changes in pottery style may suggest a hiatus between Phases 2 and 3. Periodic abandonment may have been deliberate to allow soil and forest regeneration.

Estimates as to population size have been based on several theoretical premises. It is assumed that the labour involved in digging the ditches and felling the thousands of trees for the construction of the palisade would have necessitated a population of 50 for Phase 2 and 400 for Phase 3.

Questions remain regarding the relationship between these enclosed sites and other contemporary unenclosed settlements. Were hierarchical relationships involved? These questions remain unanswered at the present stage of research however the presence of 2 other enclosures located at least 10km apart raises the question of the nature of inter-site relationships: were they involved in competition for land and resources or were they occupied at different times? The chronological relationships between the sites still need to be determined, but it is possible that all three sites were occupied by the same population at different times.

The first of these two enclosures is at Saint-Michel-du-Touch at Toulouse (Haute-Garonne) (Figure 1) and it is situated on a spur at the confluence of two waterways and only a few kilometres from Villeneuve-Tolosane/Cugnaux. Unfortunately the site has only been observed in foundation trenches however, despite this limited excavation, some 400 structures have been investigated (Vaquer 1990). Light and more robust 'defensive' palisades have been identified as well as sections of ditch some 3-4m wide belonging to several successive enclosures built across the spur (Figure 3). The ground plan is, unfortunately, far from clear but appears to have enclosed an area of *c*.35ha. Structures and archaeological features are abundant and represent the remains of several centuries of occupation suggesting the long term occupation of the site though whether this occupation was permanent or intermittent cannot yet be determined. Once again the abundance of axes suggests woodland exploitation as does the existence of the palisades. A rich secondary burial of 2 individuals represents the adoption of a new type of funerary practice.

The second enclosure at Château-Percin at Seilh (Haute-Garonne) (Figure 1) is also situated on a spur rising some 20m above the valley that it overlooks. Excavations in 2008 again revealed a palisaded enclosure with a continuous double ditch (Gandelin et al., 2011). Northwest of these enclosures, the site of Saint-Genès at Castelferrus

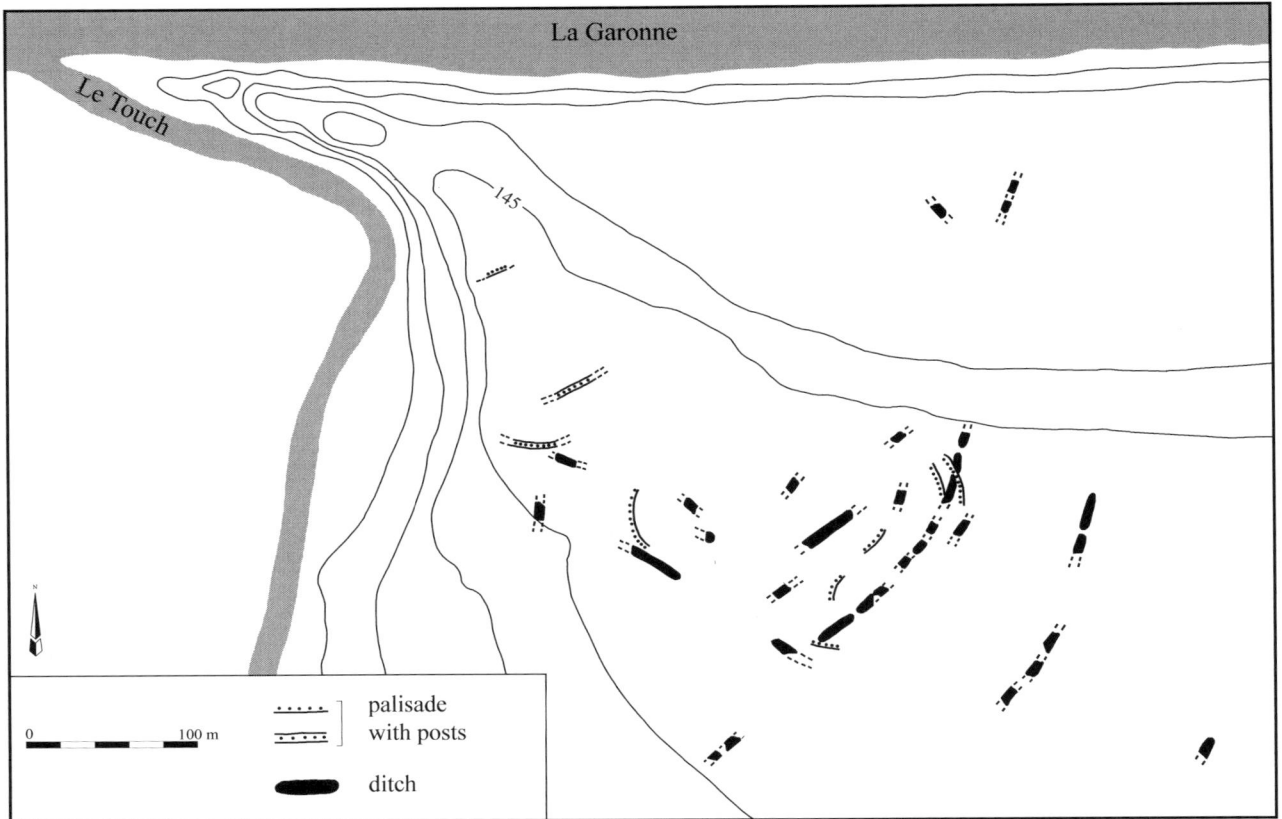

FIGURE 3 : CHASSEAN ENCLOSURE AT SAINT-MICHEL-DU-TOUCH (TOULOUSE, HAUTE-GARONNE)
(ADAPTED FROM VAQUER AND CLAUSTRE 1989, FIG. 1)

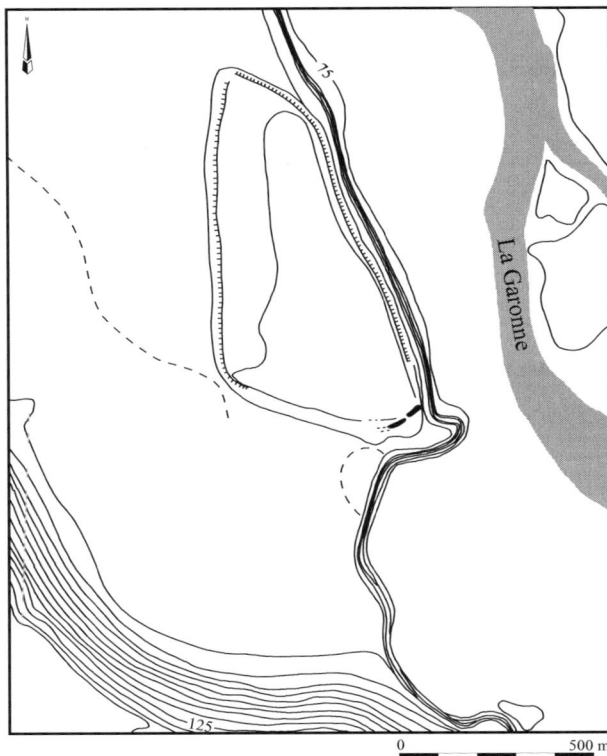

FIGURE 4 : CHASSEAN ENCLOSURE AT SAINT-GENÈS
(CASTELFERRUS, TARN-ET-GARONNE) (ADAPTED FROM
VAQUER AND CLAUSTRE 1989, FIG. 3)

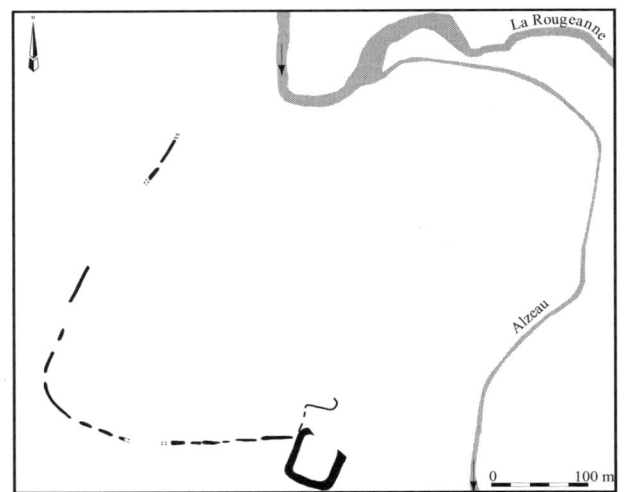

FIGURE 5 : CHASSEAN ENCLOSURE AT LA POSTE VIEILLE
(PÉZENS, AUDE) (ADAPTED FROM GUILAINE AND BARTHÈS
1997, FIG. 7)

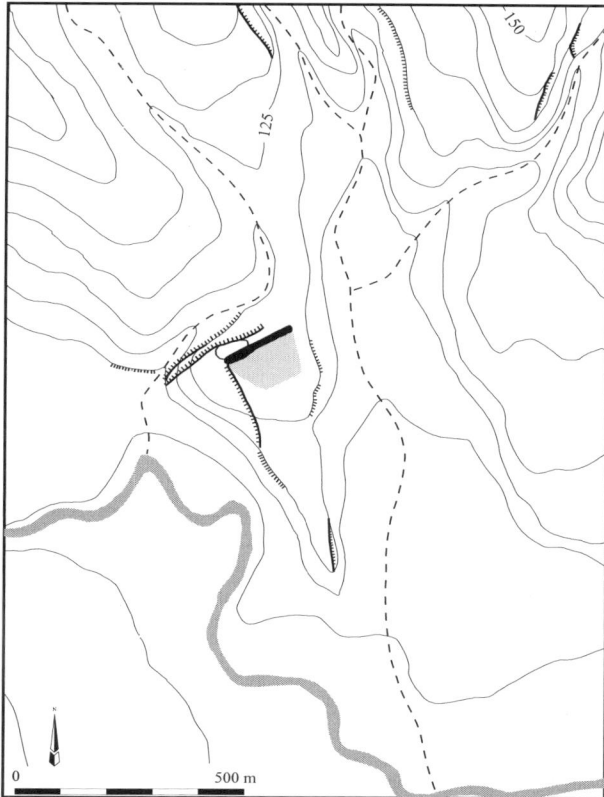

FIGURE 6 : CHASSEAN ENCLOSURE AT PLOS (VENTENAC-CABARDÈS, AUDE) (ADAPTED FROM VAQUER AND CLAUSTRE 1989, FIG. 4)

(Tarn-et-Garonne) (Figure 1) has produced aerial photographic evidence for ditches and palisades (Figure 4) and appears to have been a vast site enclosing some 30ha. Unfortunately only a small-scale test excavation has so far been undertaken (Beyneix and Humbert 1999).

A second geographical area to the east also seems to contain several enclosures. That at La Poste Vieille (Pezens, Aude) (Figure 1) is located in a dominant position on a terrace and is defined by a segmented ditch with earthen bank and with a palisade located 4m from the inner edge of the ditch (Figure 5). It encloses an area of around 12ha but excavation has only focused on a small part of the ditch and palisade (Guilaine and Barthès 1997). The ditch varies between 1.5 and 2.9m wide and two wider causeways of 7-8m have been noted in the segmented perimeter. The palisade posts had a diameter of 0.2m and were packed with soil. Excavations in the interior have produced evidence for hearths, pits, silos and postholes again suggesting that the enclosure was a settlement site. Another enclosure, Les Plos at Ventenac-Cabardès (Aude) is situated on a spur and is represented by a single ditch 5-6m wide enclosing an area of 2-3ha (Figure 6) (Vaquer and Claustre 1989).

The enclosure of La Farguette at Cavanac (Aude) (Figure 1) is also on a spur and delineated by multiple concentric ditches and palisades. It is only known from aerial photographs (Figure 7) but appears small only enclosing some 4ha (Vaquer 1990). Over 200 dark spots are visible on the aerial photographs suggesting dense archaeological

FIGURE 7 : AERIAL PHOTOGRAPH OF LA FARGUETTE (CAVANAC, AUDE) (PHOTO F. CLAUSTRE)

features some of which extend outside of the enclosure. Very close to La Farguette, Auriac (Carcassonne, Aude) (Figure 1) is a ditch interrupted by a single opening and which bars a spur delineating an area of 3ha. Part of the site has been excavated (Vaquer et al., 1996) demonstrating the ditch to be some 100m long and 4m wide with an earthen bank on the inside. Silos, hearths and structures associated with heat-cracked stones as well as some 20,000 artefacts have been found. La Poste Vieille, Les Plots, La Farguette and Auriac are the only 4 enclosures known out of 67 sites attributed to the Chassean in the middle Aude Valley.

To the east beyond the Rhône there is a notable lack of enclosures in an area where there is a lack of large scale excavations making the detection of such large sites difficult. Les Martins at Roussillon (Vaucluse) (Figure 1) has provided evidence for 2 narrow elongated structures that may be palisade trenches and may perhaps date to the Chassean (D'Anna 1993). Further north in the Rhône Valley, 3 occupation sites in the Drôme (La Roberte at Châteauneuf-du-Rhône, Clansayes 2 and Les Moulins at Saint-Paul-Trois-Châteaux) (Figure 1) have provided aerial photographic evidence for sections of ditch but have not been tested by excavation (Beeching 1989). The site of Clansayes 2 has segmented ditches as possibly does Les Moulins. In Provence, the site of L'Héritière II (Vernègues, Bouches-du-Rhône) has also produced evidence for a ditch that may be part of an enclosure (Chapon et al., 1997).

The Chassean enclosures of the south of France are therefore rare and of them only 4 have been the focus of sufficiently large scale excavations to allow meaningful discussion of their internal lay-out. The most complete and recently published results come from the site of Villeneuve-Tolosane/Cugnaux (Gandelin 2011). The enclosures at La Poste Vieille and Auriac have only been partially excavated and the excavation at Château-Percin is as yet unpublished.

These southern enclosures appeared later than their counterparts in northern France which were constructed from the end of the Early Neolithic (Villeneuve-Saint-Germain/Middle Neolithic I transition) and are based on LBK models present in Germany and Belgium from the end of the 6th millennium. BC. These were developed in the Cerny Culture and the Chambon Group in the Paris Basin and in the Rössen culture further to the east and their morphology and sizes vary. It is during the Middle Neolithic II that enclosures become widespread among the northern Chassean cultures, the Michelsberg culture and the Noyen group. These enclosures are adapted to their topography and most often defined by ditches with palisades and an earthen bank. Differences in morphology and size (1 – 20ha) may be significant amongst regional groupings of enclosures that are attributed to the same culture: palisades may or may not be present, ditches may vary between 2 and 7m wide, entrances may sometimes be monumental. Only a very few sites had stone-built ramparts (Camp de César at Catenoy and Cul Froid at Boury-en-Vexin in the Oise) (Blanchet et al., 1984; Lombardo et al., 1984).

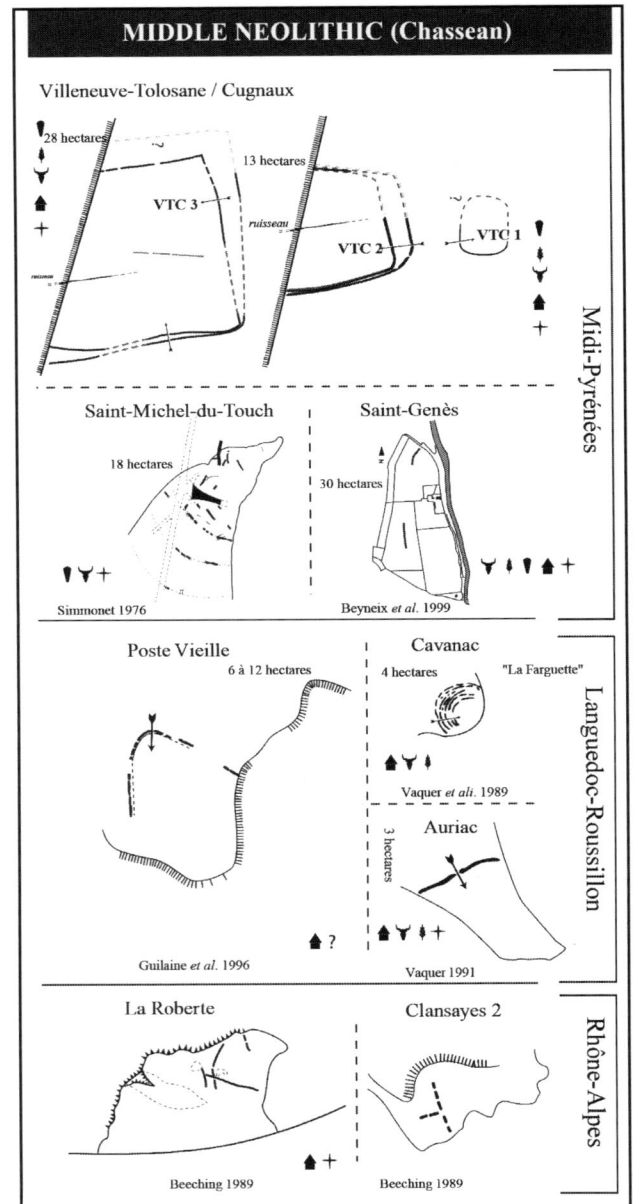

FIGURE 8 : PRINCIPAL CHASSEAN ENCLOSURES OF THE SOUTH OF FRANCE (ADAPTED FROM GANDELIN 2011, FIG. 56)

In the south of France, even with a smaller number of enclosures, variability also exists. Internal areas range from 3ha (Auriac) to 35ha (Saint-Michel-du-Touch) (Figure 8). Ditch width also varies as does the segmented or continuous nature of the ditches and the presence or absence of palisades. The enclosures are situated on spurs or dominant terrace edges and are usually close to streams or water courses. It is therefore difficult to construct a classification for these diverse sites hindered by their state of preservation and limited excavation.

Several hypotheses have been proposed to explain the appearance of these sites in southern France. These can be divided into two broad groups. The first concerns security and protection (defense of a settlement, conflict between groups, protection of livestock etc) whilst the second is more symbolic or ritualistic (cultural, funerary, display etc).

With regard to defense, a site surrounded by ditches alone would not have provided sufficiently strong lines of defense against a determined assailant or predator. Furthermore, the presence of causeways does not suggest a strong defensive boundary. However these ditches may have been reinforced with palisades or an earth bank that have since been destroyed and have left no trace and these palisades or banks need not have been interrupted or have had entrances coinciding with the causeways through the ditches as at La Poste Vieille. Openings through the palisade also tend to be much narrower than those through the ditches. Several researchers consider that the main function of the ditches was to produce material for a bank or rampart.

With regard to ritual the presence of faunal remains or human burials has been interpreted as symbolic actions but, as M. Gandelin (2011) points out, the presence of ritual deposits in a ditch does not necessarily imply a religious function for the entire enclosure or that they were necessarily directly linked to the enclosure. Whilst the presence of structures linked to domestic activities, or dwellings, within the enclosure clearly indicate a degree of occupation, their absence does not mean that they were never there for the interiors of the enclosure are rarely excavated and erosion may well have removed traces of flimsier structures. Equally, whilst the presence of waste in the ditches indicates the domestic nature of some of the activities taking place within the enclosure, the absence of such deposits does not infer a purely ritual role. In all cases, the excavated enclosures have yielded evidence for one or more periods of occupation contemporary with the enclosure ditches and palisades. Additionally, some of the lengths of palisade may have been used to delimit stockades for livestock as has been suggested at Villeneuve-Tolosane/Cugnaux.

It is most probable that the Chassean enclosures of southern France were occupation sites for people and their flocks. This does not exclude a secondary role of display and prestige as exemplified by their locations and monumental construction as demonstrated at Villeneuve-Tolosane/Cugnaux clearly visible from the valley below.

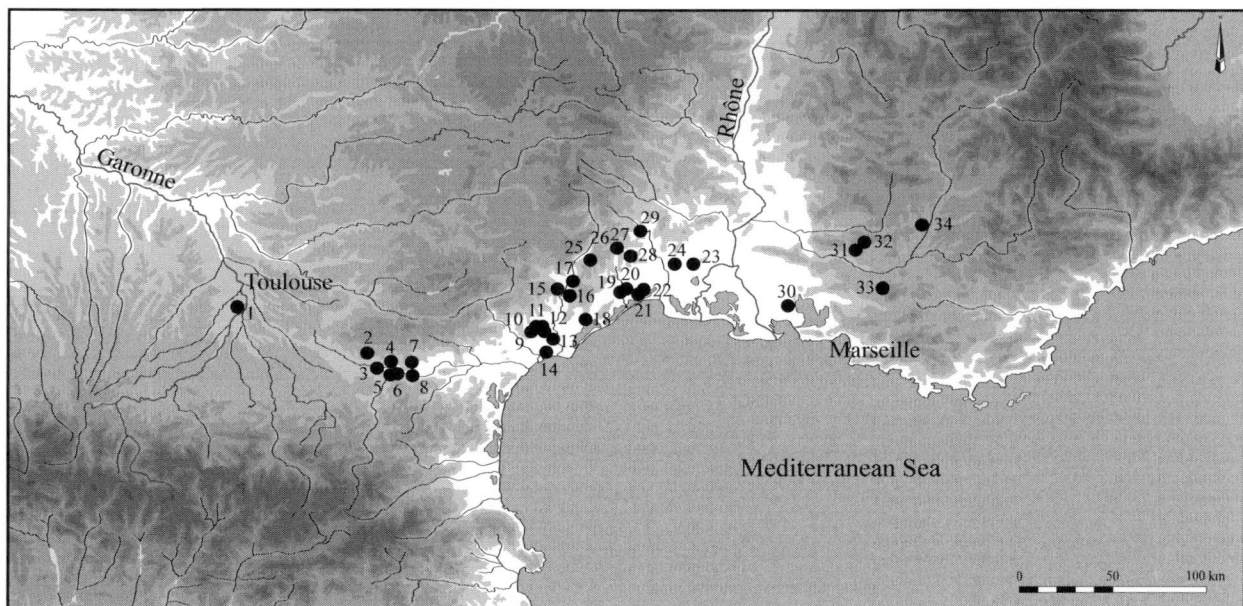

1 : Villeneuve-Tolosane (Haute-Garonne), 2 : Rocreuse (Raissac-sur-Lampy and Saint-Martin-le-Vieil, Aude), 3 : Saint-Antoine (Caux-et-Sauzens, Aude), 4 : Rivoire (Pennautier, Aude), 5 : Carsac-Mayrevieille (Carcassonne, Aude), 6 : Roc d'en Gabit (Carcassonne, Aude), 7 : La Serre (Laure-Minervois, Aude), 8 : Le Mourral (Trèbes, Aude), 9 : Le Grand Bosc (Lieuran-les-Béziers, Hérault), 10 : La Croix de Fer (Espondeilhan, Hérault), 11 : Machine de Laborde III (Abeilhan, Hérault), 12 : Le Pierras de l'Hermitage (Servian, Hérault), 13 : La Croix Vieille (Montblanc, Hérault), 14 : Les Mourguettes (Portiragnes, Hérault), 15 : Puech Haut (Paulhan, Hérault), 16 : Roquemengarde (Saint-Pons-de-Mauchiens, Hérault), 17 : Les Hermes (Bélarga, Hérault), 18 : Puech Badieu (Méze, Hérault), 19 : Richemont (Montpellier, Hérault), 20 : Stade Richter (Montpellier, Hérault), 21 : La Capoulière (Mauguio, Hérault), 22 : La Font de Mauguio (Mauguio, Hérault), 23 : Moulin Villard (Caissargues, Gard), 24 : Grange de Jaulmes (Congénies, Gard), 25 : Boussargues (Argelliers, Hérault), 26 : La Tailladette (Rouet, Hérault), 27 : Campmau (Rouet, Hérault), 28 : Le Lébous (Saint-Mathieu-de-Tréviers, Hérault), 29 : Le Rocher du Causse (Claret, Hérault), 30 : Miouvin 3 (Istres, Bouches-du-Rhône), 31 : Les Lauzières (Lourmarin, Vaucluse), 32 : La Brémonde (Buoux, Vaucluse), 33 : La Citadelle (Vauvenargues, Bouches-du-Rhône), 34 : La Fare (Forcalquier, Alpes-de-Haute-Provence)

FIGURE 9 : LOCATION OF THE FINAL NEOLITHIC ENCLOSURES OF THE SOUTH OF FRANCE

The Final Neolithic

Final Neolithic enclosures are more common (Figure 9) and are also more varied than those of the earlier period. As well as perimeters formed from ditches, palisades and earthen banks, there are also walled enclosures.

Western Languedoc

The westernmost enclosure is that at Villeneuve-Tolosane (Haute-Garonne) (Figure 9) but it is only known from small-scale test excavations (Vaquer 2001). The enclosure is of circular or near-circular shape, 114m in diameter, and was surrounded by a ditch over 4m wide. Inside the ditched perimeter, two palisades set 7 and 12m distant from the inner ditch edge, converge towards a causeway in the east. The space between the palisades may have been filled with earth. The entrance measured 20m wide at the ditches but narrowed to 2.6m at the palisades where it formed a corridor bordered by large posts.

The enclosure of Rivoire at Pennautier (Aude) (Figure 9) was discovered by aerial photography and is situated on an ancient terrace. The enclosure was defined by a single ditch 4-6m wide and enclosing an area around 100m in diameter. The ditch was broken by a single gap, 10m wide, in the east (Figure 10) (Vaquer 2001). At Carcassonne (Aude), the double-ditched circular enclosure of Carsac-Mayrevieille (Figures 9 and 11) describes two circuits measuring 100m and 60m in diameter. The inner ditch is 6-8m wide while the outer is somewhat narrower at 4-5m. Both ditches probably had an internal bank and a single entrance has been detected on aerial photographs. This site has been interpreted as a ritual enclosure (Vaquer

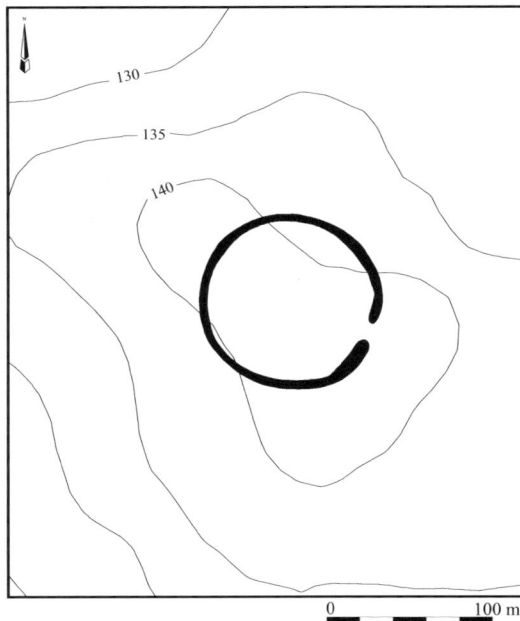

FIGURE 11 : FINAL NEOLITHIC ENCLOSURE AT CARSAC-MAYREVIEILLE (CARCASSONNE, AUDE) (ADAPTED FROM VAQUER 2001, FIG. 5)

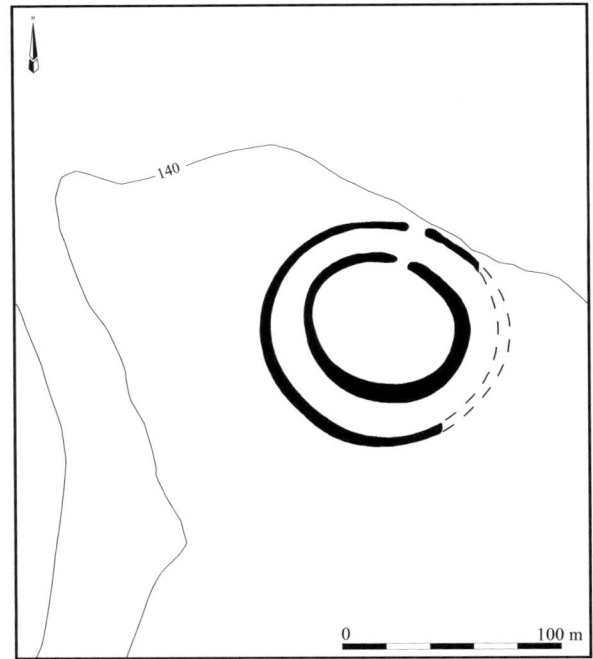

FIGURE 12 : FINAL NEOLITHIC ENCLOSURE AT ROC D'EN GABIT (CARCASSONNE, AUDE) (ADAPTED FROM VAQUER 2001, FIG. 7)

2001). The 100m diameter enclosure at Roc d'en Gabit (Carcassonne, Aude) (Figure 9) is surrounded by two arcs of ditches with wide interruptions 26m and 36m wide to the east and the west (Figure 12) and has been entirely excavated (Vaquer et al., 2004). The ditches were 8-10m wide and survived to a depth of 3.5m. Once again they were probably associated with internal banks. Finds from the ditches were rare and no structural evidence was located in the interior probably as a result of erosion. The paucity of material, the width of the causeways and the size of the ditches does not suggest an overtly domestic role and J. Vaquer (2001) considers the site to have been a sanctuary similar to British henges. The small enclosure at La Serre at Laure-Minervois (Aude) (Figure 9) was surrounded by a single ditch in 50m in diameter. The ditch was 2-4m wide and an entrance to the east measured 5m wide (Vaquer 2001).

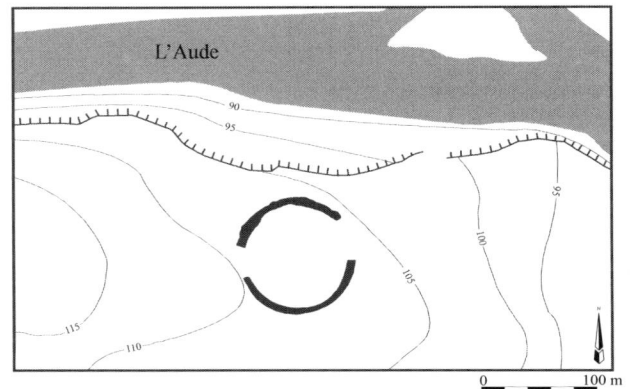

FIGURE 10 : FINAL NEOLITHIC ENCLOSURE AT RIVOIRE (PENNAUTIER, AUDE) (ADAPTED FROM VAQUER 2001, FIG. 3)

Figure 13 : Aerial photograph of Le Mourral (Trèbes, Aude) (photo J. Vaquer, CNRS)

The enclosure at Le Mourral at Trèbes (Aude) (Figure 9) was also completely excavated by J. Vaquer and was surrounded by a ditch 66m in diameter with a palisade set 4m inside the ditch (Vaquer et al., 2003). The palisade was eroded in the south (Figure 13). An entrance to the east measured 7m wide at the ditches and 2m at the palisade and a second opening to the west was later greatly reduced in width. The palisade was formed by contiguous logs each *c*.0.2m in diameter with larger uprights flanking the entrance. An earth bank probably occupied the area between the ditches and the palisade. Two aisled buildings were located in the interior (Figure 14) the larger measuring 29m x 4m. This type of architecture is rare in the South of France at the end of the 4th millennium BC. It has been suggested that these structures were high-status halls for an elite population (Vaquer 2001) and no other structures were located in close proximity to these halls. The ditches had filled up over several centuries. The basal layers produced abundant faunal remains dating to the end of the 4th millennium BC. The secondary silts have been dated to the early 3rd millennium BC. The site was then abandoned and the ruined site re-occupied by groups using Bell Beaker (Vaquer 1998). Vaquer has interpreted the site as a fortified settlement rather than a site of ritual significance based on the halls, contemporary domestic debris in the ditches and the evidence for processing artefacts and ecofacts but he contrasts the amount of labour needed to construct the site in comparison with the small estimated population (Vaquer 2001: Vaquer et al., 2003). Vaquer also considers the enclosure at Le Mourral to have been a defensive settlement occupied by a group that produced less than they consumed (Vaquer 2001).

The roles of the enclosures may have evolved over time, passing from the status of residence (Le Mourral) to sanctuary (Roc d'en Gabit, Carsac-Mayrevieille, Rivoire) and the presence of disarticulated human remains in the ditches supports this view. In Western Languedoc, the circular enclosures of the Final Neolithic (six in total) have yielded, in general, little evidence for domestic activities usually in the form of waste products or storage structures

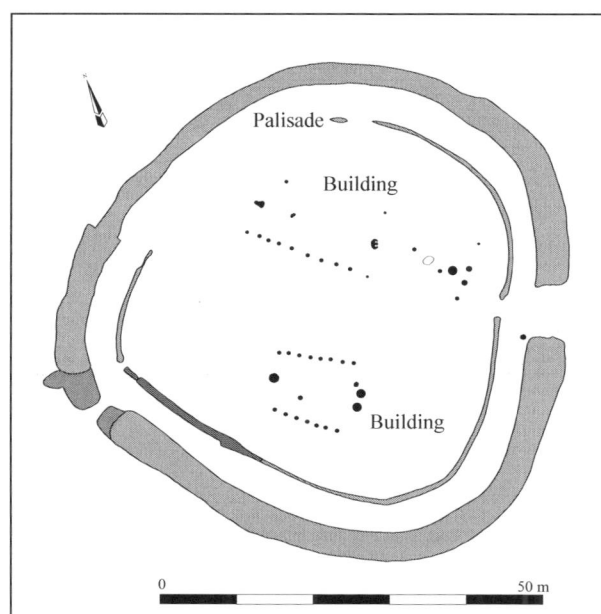

Figure 14 : Final Neolithic enclosure at Le Mourral (Trèbes, Aude) (adapted from Vaquer 2001, fig. 10)

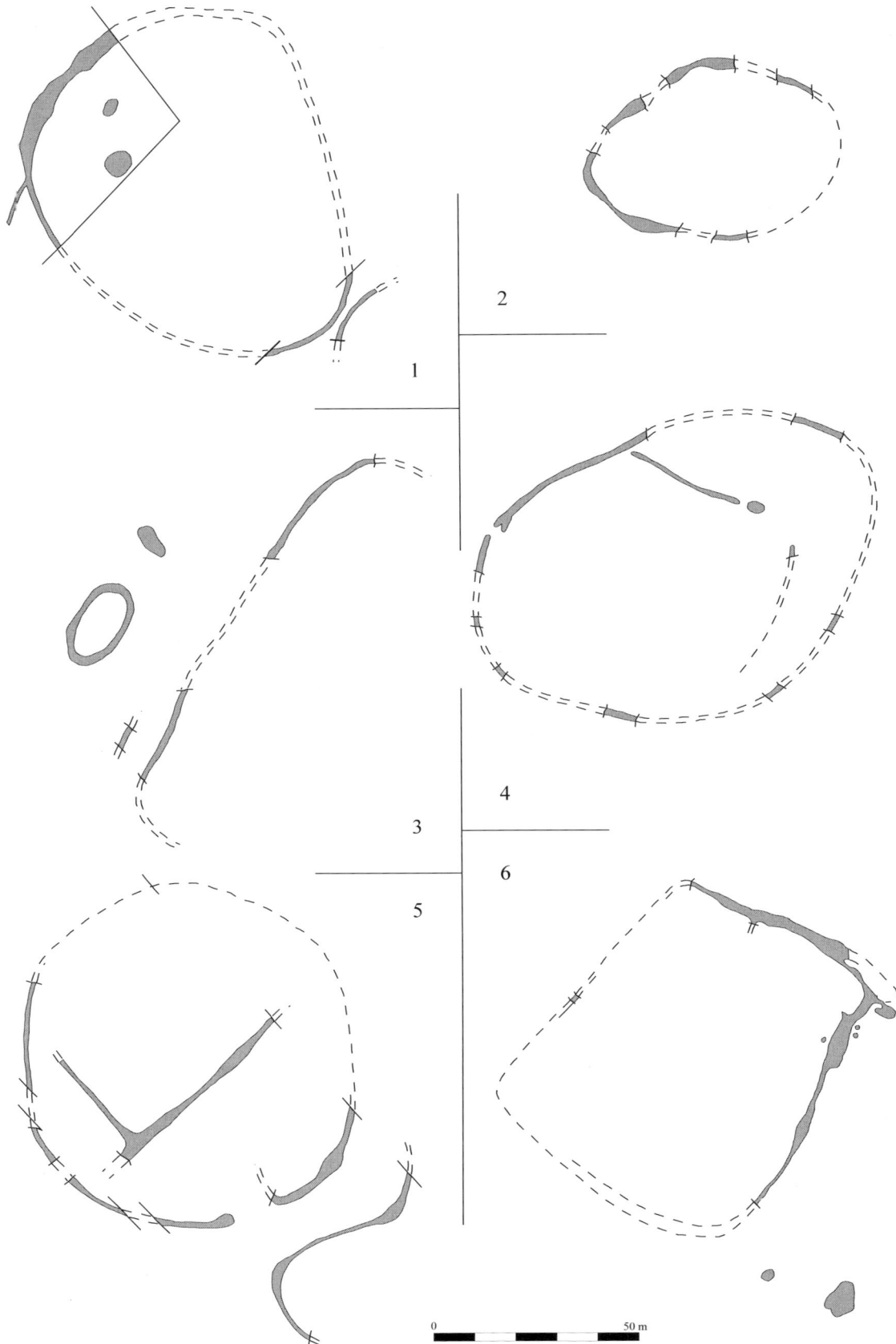

1 : Le Pierras de l'Hermitage (Servian, Hérault), 2 : Le Grand Bosc (Lieuran-les-Béziers, Hérault), 3 : Machine de Laborde III (Abeilhan, Hérault), 4 : Les Mourguettes (Portiragnes, Hérault), 5 : La Croix de Fer (Espondeilhan, Hérault), 6 : La Croix Vieille (Montblanc, Hérault)

FIGURE 15 : FINAL NEOLITHIC ENCLOSURES BETWEEN ORB AND HÉRAULT (ADAPTED FROM ESPÉROU 1999, FIG. 2) and this may be taken to reflect the increasingly important role of the symbolic domain during this period. M. Gandelin (2011) argues that at Le Mourral, the symbolic function was more important than the defensive function. In contrast, J. Guilaine argues that it could have been a farm (Guilaine 2001).

Quite often the circular shape of these enclosures is reminiscent of British henges. The phenomenon is accompanied by the increasing importance of worship and social hierarchy capable of mobilizing a large work force to undertake such monumental projects. All commentators place this in parallel with the appearance of large megalithic monuments at the end of the 4th and start of the 3rd millennium BC. J. Guilaine (2001) postulates that these enclosures played the same roles as those circles of wood and stone in Northwest Europe and perhaps they functioned as centres for the facilitation of group decision making, for resolving disputes and for the practice of ritual and ceremony.

Non-circular enclosures with double ditches are rarer, but are also found in the same geographic zones as the circular enclosures. Two have been subject to test excavations. The enclosure at Saint-Antoine at Caux-et-Sauzens (Aude) (Figure 9) is located on a spur and is sub-rectangular (166 by 125m) (Vaquer and Claustre 1989). The ditches are 3m wide and separated by 6 to 10m. The enclosure at Rocreuse at Raissac-sur-Lampy and Saint-Martin-le-Vieil (Aude) (Figure 9) was established on the edge of a limestone plateau and, though its form is difficult to determine since it is known only from on aerial photography, it may enclose a surface of 7ha (Vaquer and Claustre 1989).

In this intensively surveyed alluvial area around Carcassonne the enclosures seem to be spaced every 5km (Figure 9). Sites are frequently in dominant positions that control parts of the adjacent valley. The ditches were imposing and continuous, often with a single entrance and the enclosures are generally circular or sub-rectangular irrespective of the local topography (Vaquer 1995). They generally enclose areas of less than 1ha and all the archaeological remains from the excavations are attributable to the Véraza culture.

Central Languedoc

A second group of enclosures lies between the Orb and Hérault Rivers (Figure 9). They remain poorly known and have only been partially tested. However, three have been the focus of excavations. The first identified and to be tested was the enclosure of Le Pierras de l'Hermitage at Servian (Hérault) (Figure 9). It was probably circular (100m in diameter), but its outline remains incomplete (Figure 15-1). A second ditch tangential to the first may represent a second enclosure (Espérou 1989, 1999). The enclosure at La Croix de Fer (Espondeilhan, Hérault) (Figure 9) was oval (60 by 40m) and had segmented ditches (Figure 15-5) (Espérou 1989, 1999). The enclosure at Le Grand Bosc (Lieuran-les-Béziers, Hérault) (Figure 9),

also oval (65 by 45m) (Figure 15-2), had at least one wide entrance (Espérou 1989, 1999) while that at Machine de Laborde III at Abeilhan (Hérault) (Figure 9) was entirely enclosed (22 by 13m) (Figure 15-3) (Espérou 1989, 1999). The enclosure at La Croix Vieille (Montblanc, Hérault) (Figure 9) had a trapezoidal form (80 by 60m) (Figure 15-6) and the ditch fill yielded deposits of articulated cattle bones (Espérou and Roques 1994) as well as a stele. In contrast, the internal organization of the site remains poorly understood. Due to erosion, only two structures have been discovered. The enclosure Les Mourguettes at Portiragnes (Hérault) (Figure 9) was oval (100 by 70m) (Figure 15-4). It had a single 3m wide ditch and a single entrance in the form of a "crab claw" (Grimal 1992). The ditch was probably associated on the inside with an earthen bank supported by blocks of local stone. This enclosure has not produced evidence of inhabitation or internal pits, but artefacts, particularly Bell Beaker, were found in the ditch. On the left bank of the Hérault River, the dwelling site of Roquemengarde (Saint-Pons-de-Mauchiens, Hérault) (Figure 9) is located on a spur surrounded by cliffs and was delimited by a single ditch 75m long and a wall that blocked the only access (Figure 16). The ditch was 2-2.5m wide and was cut into the limestone bedrock (Guilaine et al., 1989). A wall, possibly of material derived from the ditch, followed the inside edge of the ditch. It is not impossible that a simple palisade existed prior to this arrangement, as is suggested at the eastern zone of the spur. Another palisade was built in part of the ditch.

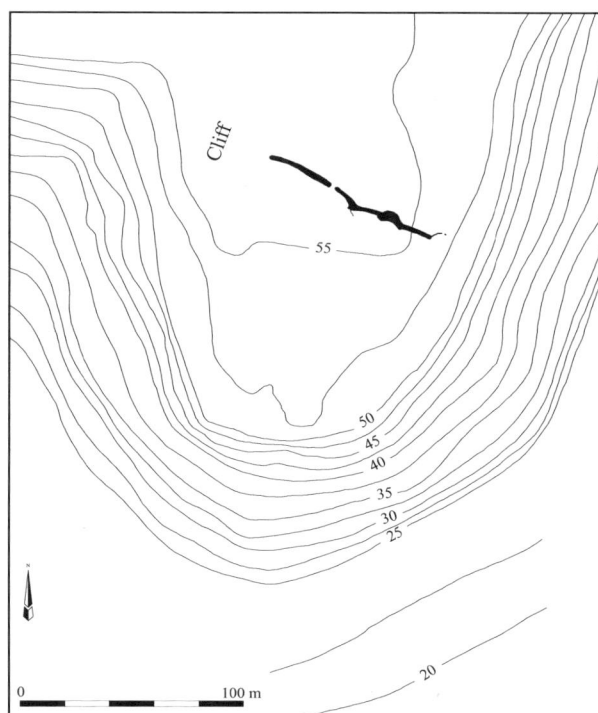

FIGURE 16 : FINAL NEOLITHIC ENCLOSURE AT ROQUEMENGARDE (SAINT-PONS-ET-MAUCHIENS, HÉRAULT) (ADAPTED FROM GUILAINE ET AL., 1989, FIG. 2)

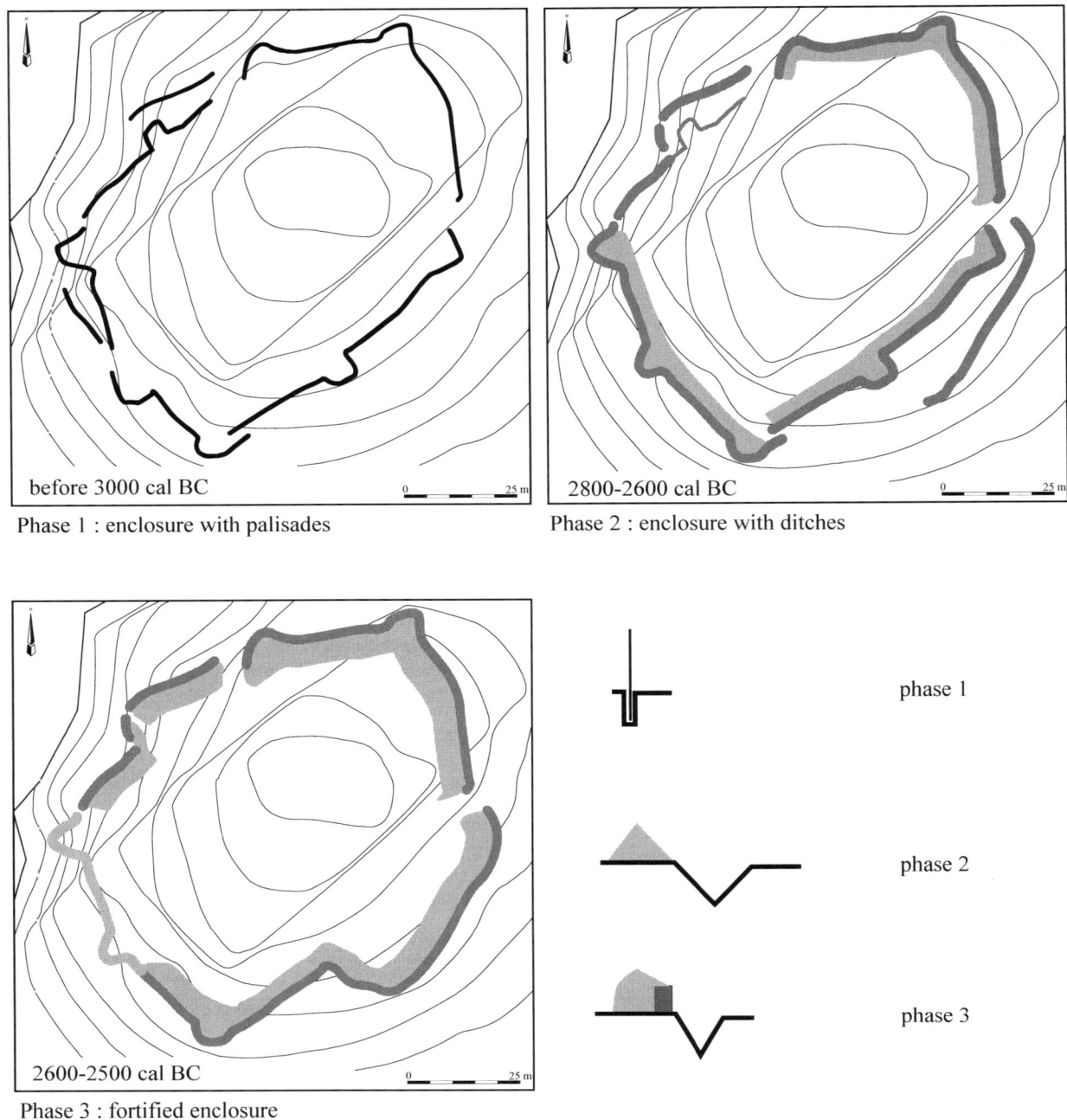

before 3000 cal BC

Phase 1 : enclosure with palisades

2800-2600 cal BC

Phase 2 : enclosure with ditches

2600-2500 cal BC

Phase 3 : fortified enclosure

phase 1

phase 2

phase 3

FIGURE 17 : SUCCESSIVE PHASES OF THE ENCLOSURE AT PUECH HAUT (PAULHAN, HÉRAULT)
(ADAPTED FROM CAROZZA ET AL., 2005)

In this region, the enclosure at Puech Haut at Paulhan (Hérault) (Figure 9) is the only one to have been entirely excavated as a result of rescue archaeology. The current plan suggests the succession of three enclosures built between the end of the 4th and the middle of the 3rd millennium BC (Figure 17). The enclosed area comprises 5000m² (Carozza et al., 2005). The primitive enclosure (phase 1) would correspond to a delimiting structure indicated by vertical posts (palisade) embedded in narrow trenches. After this initial phase, the plan of the enclosure was set and was subsequently barely altered. Five entrances existed in this enclosure. This construction phase occurred at the end of the 4th millennium BC. Between 2800 and 2600 cal BC, another ditch was superimposed on the earlier and largely

followed, the contour of the first. This second enclosure was formed by a discontinuous ditch with two large entrances and four smaller causeways. It also appears that an earthen bank lay inside the line of the ditch. The third phase (2600-2500 cal BC) saw more significant modifications with the construction of a wall behind the ditches in certain areas of the enclosure, such as the entrances, and on the southern slope. So, in some sectors of the enclosure, the site took on the aspect of a fortification composed of a wall and earthen bank whilst these features were less monumental or absent in other areas. L. Carozza sees this fortification as symbolic because the circuit is not complete and therefore a defensive function seems unlikely (Carozza et al., 2005). The walled section faces the river suggesting display and ostentation. All 3 phases of the enclosure were associated with structures and pits but after the collapse of the rampart there was only limited Bell Beaker occupation *c.*2400-2300 cal BC.

The site of Les Hermes at Bélarga (Hérault) (Figure 9) is situated on a terrace overlooking the Hérault River. It was a ditched enclosure perhaps associated with walls within the ditch circuits (Carozza et al., 2005). Finally, a spur bordered by cliffs was fortified at Puech Badieu at Mèze (Hérault) (Figure 9). A ditch more than 2.5m wide with a single entrance to the south, probably also with a rampart behind, surrounded occupation remains comprising apsidal buildings. The ditch fill included AOC Bell Beaker (Montjardin and Rouquette 2003).

Like western Languedoc, central Languedoc is rich in enclosures concentrated in a limited area. There was no single model for the enclosed sites at the end of the Neolithic in this region and modes of delimitation were varied. Spurs were enclosed by ditches with walls of stone and earth (Roquemengarde, Puech Badieu). On the plains or rolling landscapes, the alluvial terraces contain inhabitations enclosed by ditches, probably also associated with earthen banks. Oval forms are the most common, but more angular forms (La Croix Vieille), better adapted to the topography, are also present.

At the end of the 4th and start of the 3rd millennium BC, central Languedoc, like western Languedoc, sees the emergence of enclosed or fortified sites. This growth may be explained by the reorganization of territories and the development of a greater social hierarchy Carozza et al., 2005). The amount of labor involved in digging the ditches and building the wooden palisades required a significant collective investment. For the palisades, a series of activities was needed, from the felling of the trees to the placing of the posts in the trenches (Carozza et al., 2005). For L. Carozza, the study of the function of enclosed and fortified sites can only be done as part of an holistic analysis within which the weight of social and environmental dynamics must be taken into account and included in the modeling.

Two distinct types of enclosure were in existence in the middle of the 3rd millennium BC. The first comprised fortified sites, less common and with a privileged position within the organization of the territory. The second, more dominant type, consists of more modest enclosures that are circular or rectangular and less formalized in their delimitation of space. These sites continued to be domestic in character. Competition may have affected both the management of agricultural lands and the modes for the diffusion of products (Carozza et al., 2005). This geographic region, intermediate between western and eastern Languedoc, seems to have either come under the influence of one or the other of these zones, or to have developed independently.

Eastern Languedoc

This region has two clearly distinct geographic areas. To the south, the littoral plains are loamy and do not cover rocky geological formations while to the north, in the hinterland, the latter are omnipresent. This distribution of space led to two entirely different architectural traditions by a single cultural group during the 3rd millennium BC known as the Fontbouisse group.

One of the main contributions of rescue archaeology has been the discovery of several ditched enclosures on the littoral plains of the Gard and the Hérault. Unlike the more western sites, the ground plans are difficult to interpret since they are the result of successive phases of occupation over a long period. Palimpsests of enclosing ditches resulting from successive digging phases or the juxtaposition of elongated pits defined the areas of occupation: Richemont and Stade Richter at Montpellier (Hérault), Moulin Villard at Caissargues, Mas de Vignole at Nîmes (Gutherz and Jallot 1999; Convertini et al., 2004) (Figures 9 and 18). Other sites have more regular ditches (Font de Mauguio and La Capoulière at Mauguio, Hérault) (Figure 9) (Jallot 1994; Gutherz et al., 2011). Internal earthen banks are rare but palisades are sometimes associated with the ditches. The site of Richemont at Montpellier (Hérault) (Figure 18-4) consisted of an initial internal rectangular enclosure inserted within a later, more irregular but not fully defined enclosure (Thomas and Galant 1989). The internal ditches contained mainly anthropogenic fills while the external ditches probably supported a palisade. The presence of earthen banks is likely and causeways through the ditches were common. At the site of Moulin Villard at Caissargues (Gard) (Figure 18-1), the complex plan delineates a polygonal enclosure at least part of which was also defined by an earthen bank in one part and a palisade in another. Other stretches of palisade were discovered within curved trenches in other parts of the site. The enclosed area was divided into two parts: a living zone with evidence for domestic activity and an animal pen, particularly for bovids (De Freitas et al., 1992). However, no evidence for buildings was found, although subsequent agricultural activity may be responsible for this. Bell Beaker artefacts were found at the top of the fill of some ditches at Moulin Villard. No evidence for the fortification of these sites has been observed but they may have accommodated substantial communities over a period of several centuries. Such low lying ditch-defined settlements are only known in this region. They appear later than those in central and western Languedoc since they have been dated to the 3rd millennium BC. They represent occupation sites adapted to the plains environment where stone is absent (Gutherz and Jallot 1999). Interestingly, a single settlement (Grange de Jaulmes, Congénies, Gard) (Figure 9) situated at the junction between the lowlands and the limestone massifs of the hinterland (Boutié and Roger 1992), was enclosed by ditches dug into a soft substrate but surrounded buildings of dry-stone construction (Figure 18-3).

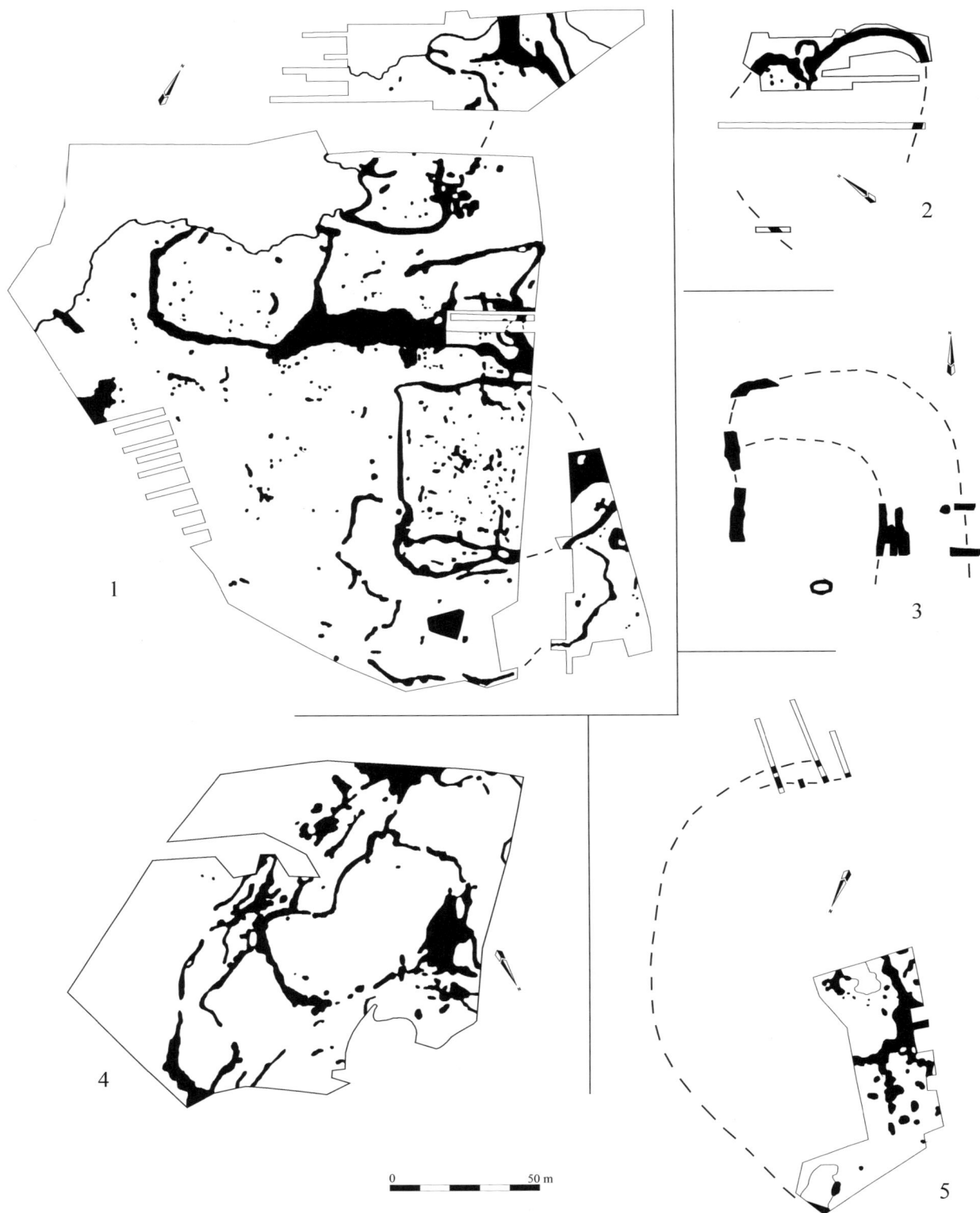

1 : Moulin Villard (Caissargues, Gard), 2 : Font de Mauguio (Mauguio, Hérault), 3 : Grange de Jaulmes (Congénies, Gard), 4 : Richemont (Montpellier, Hérault), 5 : Stade Richter (Montpellier, Hérault)

FIGURE 18 : FINAL NEOLITHIC LITTORAL ENCLOSURES OF EASTERN LANGUEDOC
(ADAPTED FROM GUTHERZ AND JALLOT 1999, FIG. 3)

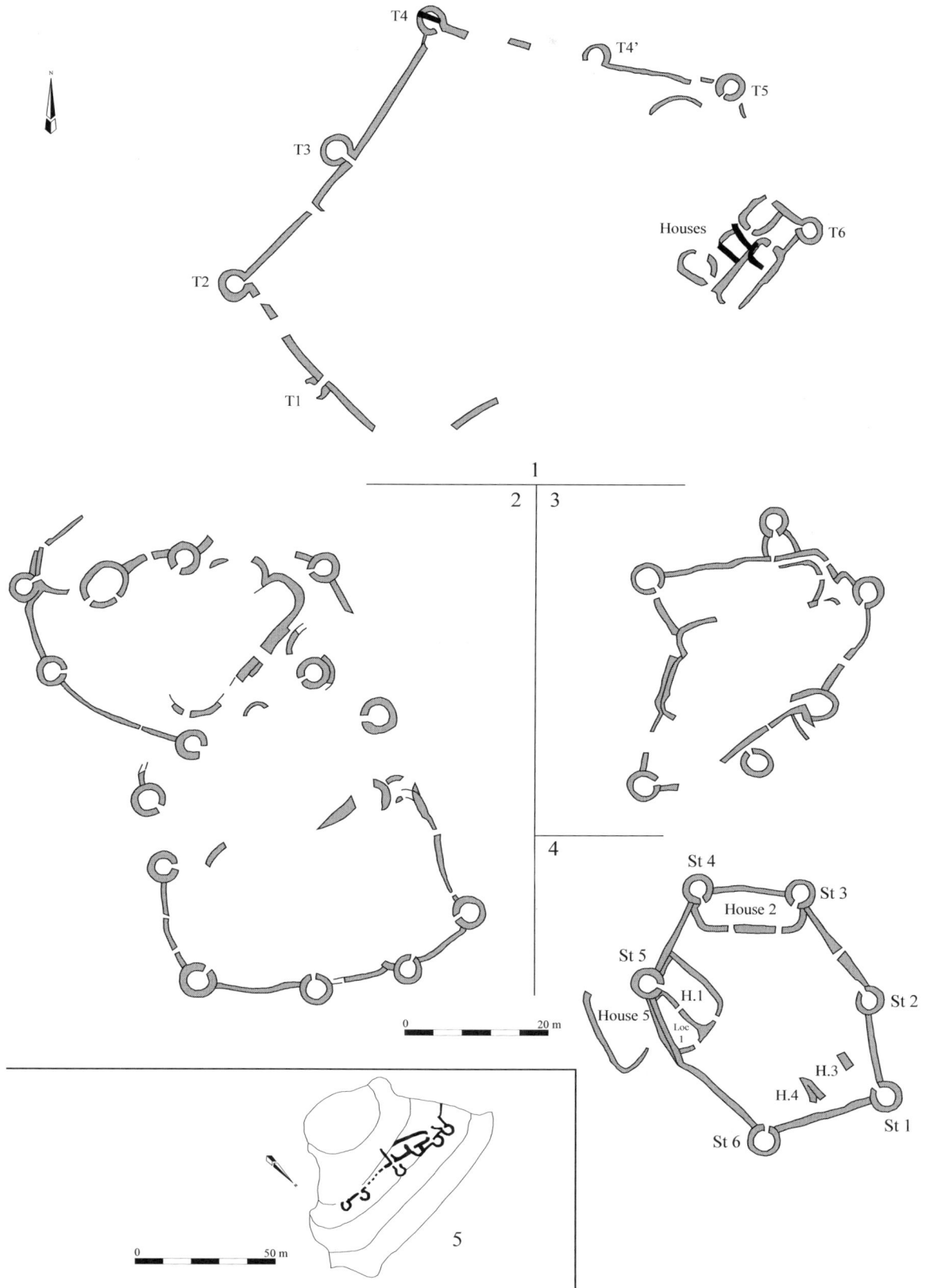

1 : Le Lébous (Saint-Mathieu-de-Tréviers, Hérault), 2 : La Tailladette (Rouet, Hérault), 3 : Campmau (Rouet, Hérault), 4 : Boussargues (Argelliers, Hérault), 5 : Le Rocher du Causse (Claret, Hérault)

Figure 19 : Final Neolithic dry stone enclosures of eastern Languedoc (adapted from Gutherz and Jallot 1989, fig. 2 and from Gutherz and Jallot 1999, fig. 3)

FIGURE 20 : AERIAL PHOTOGRAPH OF BOUSSARGUES (ARGELLIERS, HÉRAULT) (PHOTO J. COULAROU)

FIGURE 21 : AERIAL PHOTOGRAPH OF LES LAUZIÈRES (LOURMARIN, BOUCHES-DU-RHÔNE) (PHOTO A. D'ANNA, CNRS)

FIGURE 22 : AERIAL PHOTOGRAPH OF LA CITADELLE (VAUVENARGUES, BOUCHES-DU-RHÔNE) (PHOTO A. D'ANNA, CNRS)

This hinterland was occupied by agricultural communities who lived in villages of dry-stone apsidal houses. Around 150 of these settlements are known but only four have traces of walled perimeters. Only two of these have been excavated, one in its entirety. Le Lébous (Saint-Mathieu-de-Tréviers, Hérault) (Figure 9) had an area of 3500m² (Figure 19-1) and is the largest enclosed site known in this region. Unfortunately it is poorly preserved having suffered from medieval reconstruction. The enclosure was trapezoidal and constructed using large local limestone blocks arranged in the double cladding technique (Arnal 1973) and reaching 1m in thickness. The enclosure was lined with circular structures 2.5m in diameter, notably placed in the angles and the entrance opened toward the interior of the enclosure. Several dry-stone houses were found in the best preserved internal sector and are positioned against the enclosure wall. Boussargues (Argelliers, Hérault) (Figure 9) is the best known and best preserved of this type of site (Colomer et al., 1990; Coularou et al., 2008) and was excavated in the 1980s and 1990s. The site was hexagonal with an area of 860m² surrounded by a dry stone wall 1m thick (Figures 19-4 and 20). A circular structure was found in the six angles, each 2.5m in diameter and excavation demonstrated that they had been built first to a preconceived plan and that the walls were secondary. The stone houses were built after the enclosure wall had been completed. The site was accessed by a single entrance.

The final two enclosure villages are situated close together (200m apart) but have not been excavated (Gutherz and Jallot 1989). La Tailladette (Rouet, Hérault) (Figure 9) comprises two contiguous enclosures of 900 and 1300m², built on the same model as the preceding two (Figure 19-2). The enclosure further to the south contains nine circular structures 2.5m in diameter and has evidence for two entrances. The extent of the northern enclosure is only partially known but it was built after the first. At least four circular structures (2.5m in diameter) identical to the others have been identified and the remains of a large dry stone house are still visible within the enclosure. Finally, the enclosure at Campmau (Figure 9) surrounds an area of 800m². Three circular structures are visible within the corners of the enclosure while others were built outside (Figure 19-3). Several houses are also visible within the site.

These enclosures, which are very rare in comparison to the large number of unenclosed sites known in the same region, must have had a specific, even privileged, status (Gutherz and Jallot 1989). For example, in a radius of 5km around Boussargues, 30 unenclosed villages, 15 amorphous sites and 50 dolmens and tombs are known. The four enclosed sites in this area were constructed in varying locations but not at strategic points and their topographic positions are identical to those of the unenclosed villages. The chronology of the construction of the enclosure at Boussargues clearly demonstrates that it was built to a preconceived plan. In contrast, contemporaneous lowland sites, from the sequential construction of ditches and

episodes of recutting suggest the opposite. A final site in eastern Languedoc, Le Rocher du Causse (Claret, Hérault) (Figure 9), is situated on a spur and encloses an area of 1000m² defined by a row of dry stone houses, each independent and linked by a fence or wall (Figure 19-5). The row measured 53m long and ends at the cliff edges (Roux and Escallon 1992). A central entrance measured 1.1m wide. This kind of promontory settlement overlooking the plain is atypical of the settlements of the Fontbouisse culture and may rather be linked to the enclosures in Provence.

The archaeological data indicate that the ditched enclosures on the plains and dry stone villages on the limestone plateau are more recent than the ditched sites in western and central Languedoc.

Provence

The last geographical area to be considered here, relatively few enclosures are known in Provence. Two have been found in the Luberon, a limestone massif more than 1100m high and rich in Final Neolithic sites. Both have been excavated. Les Lauzières (Lourmarin, Vaucluse) (Figure 9 and 21) and La Brémonde (Buoux, Vaucluse) (Figure 9), 7km apart, each have a dry stone enclosure wall respectively 60m and 11m long (D'Anna et al., 1989). The wall was 1-1.4m wide at Lauzières where it surrounded an area of 2000m² and cuts across a plateau delimited elsewhere by cliffs, The site has domestic structures on both sides of the wall. The wall at La Brémonde is between 1.5 and 2m wide, but it is not entirely certain if this is an enclosure wall since much of it has been destroyed. The walls may not have functioned as ramparts *sensu stricto* but may have been protective rather than defensive. The enclosures in the Luberon are considered to be monuments symbolic territorial markers (D'Anna et al., 1989). The enclosed sites were located in marginal zones away from the prime agricultural lands.

The site of La Citadelle at Vauvenargues (Bouches-du-Rhône) (Figure 9) is located on the top of a hill more than 720m above sea level (Figure 22). An enclosure wall surrounded the site on three sides, the fourth being formed by 150m high cliffs (Figure 23). This 1-1.5m wide wall had been constructed with limestone blocks with a few meters of palisade in the south (D'Anna 1989). The length of the perimeter was 50m and enclosed an area of around 800m². No entrance was visible except for a causeway between the cliff and the end of the wall. Inside was at least one hut, hearths and pits. Like the two preceding sites, La Citadelle has been interpreted as a site away from the prime agricultural lands and the enclosure was not defensive, but simply indicated a local presence. The second occupation phase of the site at Miouvin 3 (Istres, Bouches-du-Rhône) (Figure 9), on a plateau overlooking a small lake and at the base of a hill, comprises a wall 1.45-1.7m wide traceable for a length of 4m (Camps-Fabrer and D'Anna 1989). The next phase saw the construction of another wall 1.5m wide, in part parallel to the first, 80m

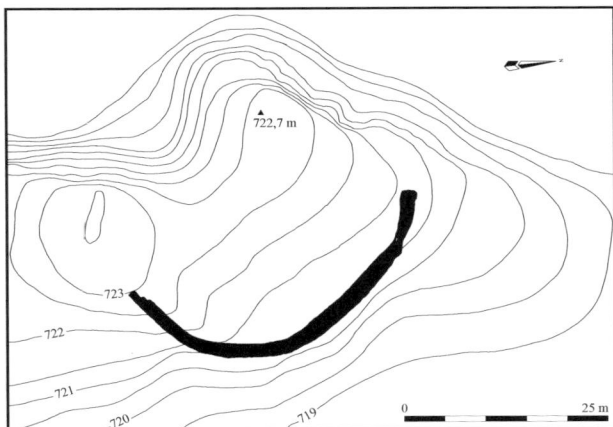

FIGURE 23 : FINAL NEOLITHIC ENCLOSURE AT LA CITADELLE (VAUVENARGUES, BOUCHES-DU-RHÔNE) (ADAPTED FROM D'ANNA 1989, FIG. 2)

long and built of large facing slabs placed vertically on each side of the wall, it was 80m long (Figure 24). Another wall perpendicular to the preceding one was built against the hill. The form of the enclosure was quadrangular and enclosed an area of 2000m², its position at the foot of the hill is unusual and it had a single entrance. After the final phase of construction of the perimeter, a rectangular hut of wood and earth was built parallel to the wall. Abundant archaeological artifacts resulting from domestic activities, reflecting long-term sedentary occupation were recovered from both inside and outside the enclosed area. The excavators suggested several hypotheses to explain the presence of the monumental enclosure at Miouvin 3: a

defensive site, a cattle pen or a prestigious edifice (Camps-Fabrer and D'Anna 1989). These enclosures in Provence have been dated to the first half of the 3rd millennium BC.

Finally, in the Durance Valley, the site of La Fare (Forcalquier, Alpes-de-Haute-Provence) (Figure 9) is a promontory on which two ditched enclosures, dated to the end of the 4th millennium BC, have been identified (Lemercier et al., 2004). The first has a 2m wide ditch with four causeways. A dry stone wall was located on the inner edge of the ditch. The enclosure could be traced for a length of 100m and appears to block the entire width of the plateau. Of the second partially destroyed enclosure, only a ditch with several sections remains. Palisades were set within the inside edge of the ditch of the second enclosure. The enclosure underwent significant later transformations. These enclosures differ from those described for Provence during the Final Neolithic and are comparable to the western enclosures with which they are contemporaneous (end of the 4th millennium BC). At present, their role in the organization of space and their status within the region has not been discussed in detail.

During the Final Neolithic, in each of the geographic zones considered, various enclosures adapted to the local environmental conditions and territorial management have been considered. In western Languedoc, the function of the enclosures seems to have changed over time from a defensive to a more symbolic role. In central Languedoc, this development toward symbolic status appears to be demonstrated only at Puech Haut. However, this particular enclosure may have had a special status since it is located not far from copper sources that were exploited from

FIGURE 24 : FINAL NEOLITHIC ENCLOSURE AT MIOUVIN 3 (ISTRES, BOUCHES-DU-RHÔNE) : WALL WITH LARGE VERTICAL FACING SLABS (PHOTO A. D'ANNA, CNRS)

the end of the 4th millennium BC. Moreover, the other sites are too poorly dated to be placed within a precise chronological sequence. In eastern Languedoc alone it is possible that the very rare dry stone walled enclosures represented high status sites while in Provence the enclosures were located in marginal areas far from prime agricultural lands. Finally, specialists in this field stress the fact that the emergence of these enclosures at the end of the 4th millennium BC was associated with the appearance of other communal monuments such as megaliths (Guilaine 2001; Vaquer 2001).

References

Arnal, J. 1973. Le Lébous à Saint-Mathieu-de-Tréviers. *Gallia Préhistoire*, 16 (1), 131-193.

Beeching, A. 1989. Un essai d'archéologie spatiale : les sites néolithiques à limitations naturelles ou aménagées dans le bassin du Rhône moyen. In *Enceintes, Habitats Ceinturés et Sites Perchés du Néolithique au Bronze Ancien*. Actes de la table ronde de Lattes et d'Aix (1987), Montpellier, Mémoire n° 2 de la Société Languedocienne de Préhistoire, 143-163.

Beyneix, A. and Humbert, M. 1999. La station chasséenne de Saint-Genès (Castelferrus, Tarn-et-Garonne). Les fouilles 1977-1978 du fossé sud. *Bulletin de la Société Préhistorique Française*, t. 96, n° 2, 209-219.

Blanchet, J.-C., Bouchain, P. and Decormeille, A. 1984. Le "Camp de César" à Catenoy (Oise). Bilan des anciennes recherches et des fouilles récentes de 1982 À 1983. In *Le Néolithique dans le Nord de la France et le Bassin Parisien*. Actes du neuvième colloque interregional sur le Néolithique, Compiègne, Revue Archéologique de Picardie n° 1-2, 173-204.

Camps-Fabrer, H. and D'Anna, A. 1989. Enceinte et structures d'habitat du Néolithique final. Miouvin 3 (Istres, Bouches-du-Rhône). In *Enceintes, Habitats Ceinturés et Sites Perchés du Néolithique au Bronze Ancien*. Actes de la table ronde de Lattes et d'Aix (1987), Montpellier, Mémoire n° 2 de la Société Languedocienne de Préhistoire, 195-208.

Carozza, L., Georjon, C. and Vignaud, A. 2005. *La Fin du Néolithique et les Débuts de la Métallurgie en Languedoc Central. Les Habitats de la Colline du Puech Haut à Paulhan, Hérault*. Recherches en Archéologie Préventives 3, Centre d'Anthropologie, Institut national de recherches archéologiques préventives, Toulouse, Ed. Archives d'Ecologie Préhistorique.

Chapon, P., Hasler, A. and Renault, S. 1997. Vernègues, L'Héritière II. *Bilan Scientifique Régional 1996, Provence-Alpes-Côtes d'Azur*, Ministère de la Culture, Aix-en-Provence, 104.

Colomer, A., Coularou, J. and Gutherz, X. 1990. *Boussargues (Argelliers, Hérault) : un Habitat Ceinturé Chalcolithique : les Fouilles du Secteur Ouest*. Paris, Maison des Sciences de l'Homme, Documents d'Archéologie Française.

Convertini, F., Furestier, R., Astruc, L., Forest, V. and Jallot, L. 2004. Le Mas de Vignole IV à Nîmes (Gard) : résultats préliminaires des fouilles d'un fossé à

occupation campaniforme. In H. Dartevelle (ed.), *Auvergne et Midi*. Actes des Cinquèmes Rencontres Méridionales de Préhistoire Récente, Clermont-Ferrand, Cressensac, Préhistoire du Sud-Ouest, suppl. n° 9, 493-507.

Coularou, J., Jallet, F., Colomer, A. and Balbure, J. 2008. *Boussargues. Une Enceinte Chalcolithique des Garrigues du Sud de la France*. Centre de Recherche sur la Préhistoire et la Protohistoire de la Méditerranée, EHESS, Musée du Pic Saint Loup, Toulouse, Ed. Archives d'Ecologie Préhistorique.

D'Anna, A. 1989. L'habitat perché néolithique final de La Citadelle (Vauvenargues, Bouches-du-Rhône). In *Enceintes, Habitats Ceinturés et Sites Perchés du Néolithique au Bronze Ancien*. Actes de la table ronde de Lattes et d'Aix (1987), Montpellier, Mémoire n° 2 de la Société Languedocienne de Préhistoire, 209-224.

D'Anna, A. 1993. L'habitat de plein air en Provence : recherches récentes. In J.-C. Blanchet (dir.), *Le Néolithique au Quotidien*. Actes du XVIème colloque interrégional sur le Néolithique, Parsi, 1989, Paris, Editions de la MSH, 1993, p. 72-84. (Documents d'Archéologie Française, 41).

D'Anna, A., Courtin, J., Coutel, R. and Müller, A. 1989. Habitats perchés et enceintes du Néolithique final et Chalcolithique dans le Lubéron central (Vaucluse). In *Enceintes, Habitats Ceinturés et Sites Perchés du Néolithique au Bronze Ancien*. Actes de la table ronde de Lattes et d'Aix (1987), Montpellier, Mémoire n° 2 de la Société Languedocienne de Préhistoire, 165-193.

De Freitas, L., Jallot, L., Pahin-Peytavy, A.-C. and Sénépart, I. 1992. Le site du Moulin Villard (Caissargues, Gard). Premiers éléments sur un site de plaine chalcolithique en Vistrenque. In *Le Chalcolithique en Languedoc: ses Relations Extra-Régionales*. Actes du colloque international Hommage au Dr J. Arnal, Saint-Mathieu-de-Tréviers, Archéologie en Languedoc, 1990/91, 95-108.

Espérou, J.-L. 1989. Les fossés néolithique final du Biterrois oriental. *Archéologie en Languedoc. Hommage à Henri Prades*, 4, 53-56.

Espérou, J.-L., 1999. Les enceintes chalcolithiques du Languedoc central. In A. Beeching and J. Vital (dir), *Préhistoire de l'Espace Habité en France du Sud*. Actes des Premières Rencontres Méridionales de Préhistoire Récente, Valence, CAP (Travaux du Centre archéologique de Valence, n° 1), 91-100.

Espérou, J.-L. and Roques, P. 1994. L'enceinte chalcolithique de la Croix Vieille à Montblanc (Hérault). Premiers résultats. *Bulletin de la Société Préhistorique Française*, t. 91, n° 6, 422-438.

Gandelin, M. 2011. *Les Enceintes Chasséennes de Villeneuve-Tolosane et de Cugnaux dans leur Contexte du Néolithique Moyen Européen*. Centre de Recherche sur la Préhistoire de la Méditerranée, Ecole des Hautes Etudes en Sciences Sociales, Toulouse, Ed. Archives d'Ecologie Préhistorique.

Gandelin, M., Pons, F. and De Chazelles, C.-A. 2011. L'enceinte chasséenne de Château-Percin. Un témoignage exceptionnel d'architecture monumentale néolithique en Haute-Garonne. *Archéopages*, t. 33, 12-15.

Grimal, J. 1992. Le gisement ceinturé des Mourguettes (Portiragnes, Hérault). Etude d'une coupe stratigraphique du fossé d'enceinte. In *Le Chalcolithique en Languedoc: ses Relations Extra-Régionales*. Actes du colloque international Hommage au Dr J. Arnal, St Mathieu de Tréviers, Archéologie en Languedoc, 1990/91, 109-113.

Guilaine, J. 2001. En Languedoc, grands fosses pour petits enclos. In J. Guilaine (dir.), *Communautés Villageoises du Proche-Orient à l'Atlantique (8000-2000 Avant Notre Ère)*. Séminaire du Collège de France, Ed. Errance, Collection des Hespérides, 221-222.

Guilaine, J., Coularou, J., Briois, F. and Rivenq, C. 1989. L'habitat néolithique de Roquemengarde (Saint-Pons-de-Mauchiens, Hérault). Premiers éléments sur le dispositif d'enceinte. In *Enceintes, Habitats Ceinturés et Sites Perchés du Néolithique au Bronze Ancien*. Actes de la Table Ronde de Lattes et d'Aix (1987), Montpellier, Mémoire n° 2 de la Société Languedocienne de Préhistoire, 21-29.

Guilaine, J. and Barthès, P. 1997. *La Poste-Vieille. De l'Enceinte Néolithique à la Bastide d'Alzau*. Toulouse, Centre d'Anthropologie, Carcassonne, Archéologie en Terre d'Aude.

Gutherz, X. and Jallot, L. with the collaboration of Coularou, J., Colomer, A. and Escalon, G. 1989. Les habitats chalcolithiques ceinturés de l'Hérault oriental. In *Enceintes, Habitats Ceinturés et Sites Perchés du Néolithique au Bronze Ancien*. Actes de la table ronde de Lattes et d'Aix (1987), Montpellier, Mémoire n° 2 de la Société Languedocienne de Préhistoire, 111-126.

Gutherz, X. and Jallot, L. 1999. Approche géoculturelle des pays fontbuxiens. In J. Vaquer (ed.), *Le Néolithique du Nord-Ouest Méditerranéen*. XXIVᵉ Congrès Préhistorique de France, Carcassonne, Société Préhistorique Française, 161-174.

Gutherz, X., Jallot, L., Wattez, J., Borgnon, C., Roux, J.-C., Thouvenot, Y. and Orgeval, M. with the collaboration of Blaise, E., Cros, J.-P., Diaz, A., Dubosq, S., Escallon, G., Fellot-Girard, J., Guerrero, Y., Kaenel, S., Raux, A., Recchia, J. and Rousselet, A. 2011. L'habitat néolithique final de la Capoulière IV (Mauguio, Hérault): présentation des principaux résultats 2004-2007. In I. Sénépart, T. Perrin, E. Thirault and S. Bonnardin (dir.), *Marges, Frontières et Transgressions. Actualité de la Recherche*. Actes des 8e Rencontres Méridionales de Préhistoire Récente, Marseille, Toulouse, Ed. Archives d'Écologie Préhistorique, 413-438.

Jallot, L. 1994. Les habitats chalcolithiques de la Font de Mauguio (Mauguio, Hérault) et de Las Planas (Mudaison, Hérault) et les sites fossoyés fontbuxiens en Languedoc oriental. *Archéologie en Languedoc*, n° 18, 49-68.

Lemercier, O., Furestier, R., Müller, A., Cauliez, J., Convertini, F., Lazard, N. and Provenzano, N. with the collaboration of Bouville, C., Gilabert, C., Jorda, C.,

Khedhaier, R., Loirat, D., Pellissier, M. and Verdin, P. 2004. Le site néolithique final de la Fare (Forcalquier, Alpes-de-Haute-Provence). Résultats 1995-1999 et révision chronoculturelle. In H. Dartevelle (ed.), *Auvergne et Midi*. Actes des Cinquèmes Rencontres Méridionales de Préhistoire Récente, Clermont-Ferrand, Cressensac, Préhistoire du Sud-Ouest, suppl. n° 9, 445-455.

Lombardo, J.-L., Martinez, R. and Verret, D. 1984. Le site chasséen du Culfroid, à Boury-en-Vexin dans son contexte historique et les apports de la stratigraphie de son fosse. In *Le Néolithique dans le Nord de la France et le Bassin Parisien*. Actes du neuvième colloque interrégional sur le Néolithique, Compiègne, Revue Archéologique de Picardie n° 1-2, 269-284.

Montjardin, R. and Rouquette, D. 2003. Le site chalcolithique fossoyé du Puech Badieu (Mèze, Hérault) et son évolution. In J. Gasco, X. Gutherz and P.-A. de Labriffe (dir.), *Temps et Espaces Culturels du 6° au 2° Millénaire en France du Sud*. Actes des Quatrièmes Rencontres Méridionales de Préhistoire Récente, Nîmes, 28 et 29 octobre 2000, Monographies d'Archéologie Méditerranéenne, 15, Lattes, ADAL, 299-310.

Roux, J.-C. and Escallon, G. 1992. L'éperon barré chalcolithique du Rocher du Causse. Bilan des recherches 1986-1989. In *Le Chalcolithique en Languedoc: ses Relations Extra-Régionales*. Actes du colloque international Hommage au Dr J. Arnal, St Mathieu de Tréviers, Archéologie en Languedoc, 1990/91, 141-146.

Thomas, J. and Galant, P. 1989. Le système de fossés du gisement chalcolithique de Montpellier-Richemont (Hérault). In *Enceintes, Habitats Ceinturés et Sites Perchés du Néolithique au Bronze Ancien*. Actes de la table ronde de Lattes et d'Aix (1987), Montpellier, Mémoire n° 2 de la Société Languedocienne de Préhistoire, 99-110.

Vaquer, J. 1990. *Le Néolithique en Languedoc Occidental*. Ed. C.N.R.S., Paris.

Vaquer, J. 1998. Le Mourral, Trèbes (Aude). A fortified languedocian late neolithic site reoccupied by Bell Beakers. In M. Benz and S. van Willigen (eds.), *Some Approaches to the Bell Beaker "Phenomenon". Lost paradise...?*. BAR International Series 690, Proceedings of the 2nd Meeting of the association "Archéologie et Gobelets", Feldberg, Germany, 18-20th April 1997, 15-22. Oxford: British Archaeological Reports.

Vaquer, J. 2001. Les enceintes annulaires du Néolithique final languedocien. Habitats ou sanctuaires ? In J. Guilaine (dir.), *Communautés Villageoises du Proche-Orient à l'Atlantique (8000-2000 Avant Notre Ère)*. Séminaire du Collège de France, Ed. Errance, Collection des Hespérides, 223-237.

Vaquer, J. and Claustre, F. 1989. Recherches sur les enceintes du Languedoc occidental. In *Enceintes, Habitats Ceinturés et Sites Perchés du Néolithique au Bronze Ancien*. Actes de la table ronde de Lattes et d'Aix (1987), Montpellier, Mémoire n° 2 de la Société Languedocienne de Préhistoire, 9-20.

Vaquer, J., Amiel, C., Briois, F., Consigny, A., Philibert, S. and Rigaud, L. 1996. Le site chasséen d'Auriac. In *La Vie Préhistorique*, Paris, Faton, 380-383.

Vaquer, J., Gandelin, M. and Marsac, R. 2003. L'enceinte du Néolithique final de Mourral, Trèbes (Aude). In J. Gasco, X. Gutherz and P.-A. de Labriffe (dir.), *Temps et Espaces Culturels du 6° au 2° Millénaire en France du Sud*. Actes des Quatrièmes Rencontres Méridionales de Préhistoire Récente, Nîmes, Monographies d'Archéologie Méditerranéenne, 15, Lattes, ADAL, 319-326.

Vaquer, J., Gandelin, M. and Marsac, R. 2004. Le site de Roc d'en Gabit, Carcassonne (Aude). In H. Dartevelle (ed.), *Auvergne et Midi*. Actes des Cinquèmes Rencontres Méridionales de Préhistoire Récente, Clermont-Ferrand, Cressensac, Préhistoire du Sud-Ouest, suppl. n° 9, 475-484.

Kreisgrabenanlagen – Middle Neolithic Ritual Enclosures in Austria 4800-4500 BC

Wolfgang Neubauer

Abstract

Kreisgrabenanlagen (KGAs) - the oldest known monumental sites in Central Europe dating from the Middle Neolithic (4800 – 4500 BC) - were mainly discovered by aerial archaeology and have been investigated by geophysical prospecting and archaeological excavation. They consist of up to four concentric circular v-shaped ditches with diameters typically ranging from 45 to 180 m, up to four internal wooden palisades, and at least two opposed entrances. They are an integral but separated part of the associated settlements indicating a central-place role with no obvious defensive function, but instead have deliberate astronomical orientations. These astronomical aspects indicate that the monuments had a calendrical function and were probably associated with ritual and festive events. They might have been used for the legitimation of cultural or social patterns through natural phenomena. Because these social patterns required such dramatic support, it may be supposed that they were novel. Their principal similarity and close contemporaneity across their distribution are unique in prehistory, perhaps representing the earliest found trans-cultural tradition of major public rituals, and are presumed to be part of the phenomenon of social control, marking the earliest conscious attempt at pan-European socio-economic and ideological integration. This process, attested by the appearance of the KGA phenomenon, emerges rapidly and then abruptly ceases throughout Central Europe in a defined time-span of not more than 200 - 300 years.

Keywords: Middle Neolithic monuments, enclosure, migration, Kreisgrabenanlage, KGA, Lengyel

Early monumental enclosures on the Continent - The Kreisgrabenanlagen phenomenon

On the continent, thousands of years prior to the henge monuments, prehistoric societies all over Central Europe created large timber circles enclosed by monumental circular ditch systems (Figure 1). Over 130 so called *Kreisgrabenanlagen or* KGAs (Melichar and Neubauer 2010; Trnka 1991; Petrasch 1990) were discovered mainly by aerial archaeology systematically applied since the 1970s in Austria (Doneus et al. 2005; Nikitsch 1985) and Bavaria (Schmotz 2007; Becker 1996a, 1996b, 1990;

FIGURE 1: VIRTUAL RECONSTRUCTION MODEL VISUALIZING THE DOUBLE KGA AT STEINABRUNN WITHIN ITS LANDSCAPE. THE MONUMENT SHOWS THREE RINGS OF PALISADES AND SINGLE TIMBER UPRIGHTS. THE ENTRANCE PATH APPROACHING THE EASTERN ENTRANCE IS ACCOMPANIED BY STEEP RADIAL DITCHES FORMING A VERY NARROW BRIDGE (IMAGINATION & VIAS-UNIVERSITY OF VIENNA).

Christlein and Braasch 1982). The rapid development and application of aerial archaeology after the fall of the iron curtain added to the known record many new sites from southwest Slovakia (Kuzma 2005), the Czech Republic (Kovarnik 2003; Hasek and Kovarnik 1999, Pavlu 1982), Saxony (Stäuble 2007; Bartels et al. 2003, Bertemes and Northe 2007, Bertemes et al. 2004), southern Poland and northern Hungary (Raczky et al. 2005; Gaal 1990). The highest density of these typical monuments can be found in Lower Austria, southern Moravia and western Slovakia. The radiocarbon dates so far date most of the monuments to the period 4850/4750 – 4650/4500 BC, conventionally the Middle Neolithic in Central Europe. In Austria, they have been investigated systematically by aerial photography and geophysical prospecting and by open area and targeted archaeological excavations (Melichar and Neubauer 2010). Thus, knowledge of the monuments in the central area of their distribution - in Lower Austria - is very detailed and forms the main background for the evidence and considerations presented here.

The KGAs consist of up to four concentric circular v-shaped ditches, originally 4 to 6m deep, with diameters typically ranging from 45 to 180ms. The ditches may enclose up to four concentric internal wooden palisades or rings of timber uprights. Access to the interior was only possible by narrow entrances formed by interruptions through the ditches and the palisade rings. The monuments have at least two radial opposed entrances, but might have up to six, more or less regularly arranged formal routes of admission into the central space. The monuments have many attributes in common like the approximately concentric arrangement of the ditches, the V-shaped section of the ditches, an interior delimited by concentric palisades and a delimited internal space accessible only by the narrow entrances and normally free of any remains of additional structures. Beside their similarity of form, which constitutes the basic argument for considering them as single units of a specific group of contemporary monuments, (Stäuble 2007, 170-172; Trnka 2005, 12-14; Trnka 1991, 11-12) many of the monuments are unique in their specific outline. Some monuments are nearly perfect circles whereas others are more irregular in outline. The narrow interruptions through the ditches and palisades are normally under 1.5m wide. Sometimes the ditches have radial annexes towards the interior or the exterior or join two of the concentric ditches, thus delineating a pathway into the central area of the monument. The wooden palisades were formed by posts 20 to 45cm in diameter that were set into foundation trenches normally 60cms wide and often over 1m deep. Most frequently KGAs have two rings of palisades enclosing a central area of up to 5000m^2 in area. Although many sites suffer from massive erosion the central areas are usually devoid of internal features. One of the open questions is whether the ditches were accompanied by external banks or whether the excavated soil mass was spread over a larger area (Trnka 1991, 308). None of the published 'evidence' from excavations has successfully addressed this problem so far.

The function of these exceptional monumental buildings, which were erected by early farming societies all over Europe involving considerable communal effort, is still under discussion. The interpretation models range from socio-cultural or socio-ritual centers (Neubauer 2007, 222-236; Podborský et al. 1999), fortifications (Nemejcová-Pavúková 1995), market places (Stäuble 2002, 307), places of refuge for people and their herds (Pertelwieser 2001) to functional explanations such as calendrical buildings, astronomical observatories or solar temples (Weber 1986; Becker 1996; Bertemes and Schlosser 2004; Zotti 2008; Schier 2008). Current opinion favours the multi-functional interpretation models (Neugebauer-Maresch 1995, 87; Stäuble 2007, 180; Neubauer 2007, 217-236; Petrasch 2001). As the monuments were not erected in strategic positions and because they have multiple regularly oriented entrances a defensive function seems unlikely (Trnka 1991, 317). We also do not think that they represent prestige settlement areas as there are no indications of dwellings, domestic evidence or other structures inside the monuments beside the timber palisades, single posts or pits. The ditches and palisades form an enclosed area, their perimeters separating the outside from the inside. The narrow entrances strictly control the access to the interior mainly invisible from the outside (Gibson 2005). This element of limited access seems not to be based on defense but rather may be based on ritual activities (Stäuble 2007; Neubauer 2007; Gibson 2005) to be seen in the social context of the early farming societies. Unlike many of the much younger British and Irish henge monuments, the continental KGAs are not preserved in the landscape but have, without exception, been ploughed flat.

The ditches, mainly dug into the Loess soil, were refilled quickly by washed in material or collapsing sides due to cyclical freezing and thawing. But the communities did keep them in order as various cleaning and re-cutting phases have been documented by excavation. Many of the excavation reports mention various phases of the ditches mainly derived from sectional evidence (Neugebauer-Maresch 1995, Trnka 1991; Petrasch 1990): evidence from earlier excavations might have been missed. Due to the fact that the interiors of the monuments are normally free of any sunken structures and the prehistoric surface layers have been eroded down to the parent soil horizon, it is up to the finds preserved in the ditch fills to add additional evidence for the function of the monuments and related activities. In the central area of their distribution the material remains belong to the Lengyel Culture, famous for the high quality and elaborate design of the characteristic polychromatic painted pottery.

The main types of pottery (Figure 2), painted in red and yellow, are curved bowls often with rather high hollow pedestals or conical bowls with pierced and un-pierced knobs. There are also various types of thin-walled painted pots, extremely thin-walled cups and beakers with complex painted motifs, large and mainly unpainted vessels with a low belly on a flat base and an elongated neck decorated only by knobs, and large slightly S-curved vessels (Stadler

FIGURE 2: SELECTED FINDS FROM A DEPOSITION INSIDE A DITCH IN FRONT OF THE SOUTHERN ENTRANCE OF THE DOUBLE KGA AT WILHELMSDORF 1 CONSISTING OF MOGIA POTTERY AND TWO FIGURINES. THE CENTRAL VESSEL IN THE TOP ROW IS AN SBK IV IMPORT. ANTLER ADZES AND A LARGE BUCRANIUM OF AN AUROCHS COMPLETING THE FIND ARE NOT DISPLAYED. (BUNDESDENKMALAMT, PHOTO A. SCHUHMACHER)

and Ruttkay 2007, 133, Tafel 1-3; Neugebauer-Maresch 1995, Abb. 24-27). There are also conical lids, sometimes with zoomorphic shaped lid-handles, within the ceramic assemblage as well as various sizes of spoons with spout handles, zoomorphic and anthropomorphic fragments and miniature ceramics sometimes interpreted as toys. The fragmentary remains of painted and unpainted ceramic idols in various sizes and types (Ruttkay 2005) might be interpreted as representations of the ancestors (Figure 3) and these are also frequently found inside the longhouses of the Lengyel Culture. Their frequency suggests that these specific objects are directly related to the activities that took place within the monuments. Many animal bones are found within the ditch fills especially from cattle, aurochs and bison, and particularly common are the crania of large animals with big horns. Less frequent than in settlement contexts are flints, stone adzes and, more rarely, axes. The ditch fills commonly contain human skeletal parts mainly from the extremities or from skulls. The human extremities are often found in close proximity and/or articulation proving that it was complete legs or arms that were deposited. At the site of Schletz a complete hand with cut marks made by a flint blade was detected within a deposit that had high magnetic susceptibility suggesting that it was deposited close to the former surface of the partly refilled ditch (Eder-Hinterleitner et al. 2005). These human remains might be interpreted as pieces of evidence for anthropophagic rituals, violent confrontations, judicial punishments or specific funeral rites.

The period of construction and use of the monuments is dated to approximately 4800-4500 BC. The ditches

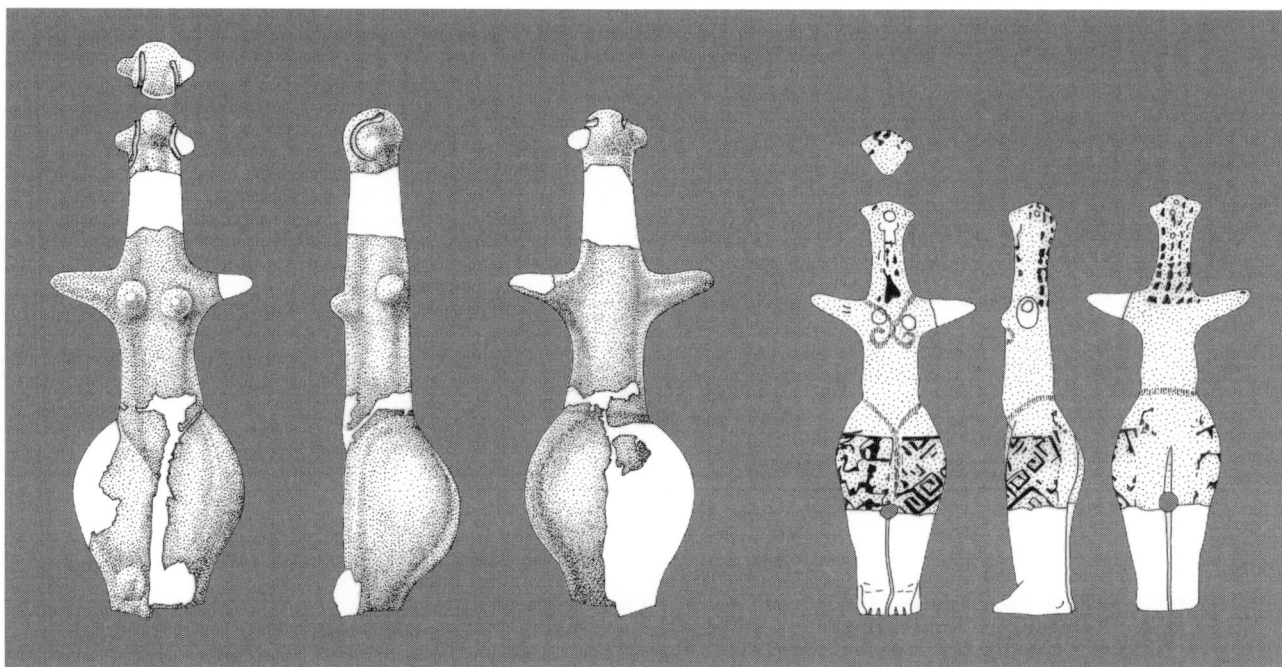

FIGURE 3: TYPICAL FEMALE FIGURINES OF THE MOG FOUND AT LANGENZERSDORF (LEFT) AND FALKENSTEIN-SCHANZBODEN (RIGHT). THE FEMALE FIGURINE FROM FALKENSTEIN IS PIERCED AND PAINTED IN RED AND BLACK REPRESENTING THE DRESS, JEWELLERY AND THE HAIRSTYLE. UNLIKE SIMILAR FINDS FROM THE SETTLEMENTS THE FIGURINES FOUND IN THE KGA DITCH FILLS ARE NORMALLY BROKEN. (GRAPHICS W. STRASIL)

were intentionally refilled at the end of this period. The surrounding settlements sometimes continue to be settled for another 100 or 200 years, whereas others were abandoned. The upper deposits in the ditch filling often contain remains from the Early Bronze Age, indicating that the ditch systems were still visible in the landscape and sometimes the interior was also reused for special Early Bronze Age funerary deposits (Neubauer and Neugebauer-Maresch 2005). The subsequent intensification of the agricultural use of the landscapes deleted these sites from living memory and the erosive processes dramatically increased as a result of modern mechanised agriculture causing massive loss of soil cover, in many cases down to the parent soil. Therefore none of the sites known so far has shown any preserved Neolithic deposits or surfaces in the interior except within rare sunken features. This severe truncation and lack of Neolithic land surfaces means that the evidence for the activities that took place within the monuments is severely limited.

The enclosures are an integral but separate part of the associated Middle Neolithic settlements, indicating a central communal role with no obvious defensive function, but instead deliberate orientation to the rising and setting points of the sun, moon and specific bright stars. These astronomical alignments or orientations indicate that the monuments had a kind of calendrical role and were probably associated with ritual and festive events. Their similarity within different archaeologically defined cultural groups is striking as is the widespread nature of the phenomenon which may be interpreted as the diffusion or spread of a 'Kreisgraben concept' through all the Middle Neolithic societies in the first half of the fifth millennium BC. This concept and its related ideas spread within fewer than three generations over the Early Lengyel (Phase I) in East Austria, southern Moravia, West Slovakia and West Hungary, the Stichbandkeramik (SBK IVa) in East Germany and Bohemia, the Early Rössen I in Nordrhein-Westfalen, the Grossgartach in Mittelfranken and the Oberlauterbach Group in Lower Bavaria (Neubauer and Melichar 2010, Abb. 2).

Systematic KGA research in Lower Austria

The KGAs as an impressive monumental phenomenon are well known in the archaeological prospection community. The striking aerial photographs and magnetograms from Germany, Slovakia, Hungary, the Czech Republic and especially from Austria have generated considerable public interest in these impressive monuments and the unsolved problems behind them. In 2003, the team from Archeo Prospections® in Vienna started a prospecting project, directed by the author, aiming to map and interpret all known monuments of this period in Austria (Figure 4).

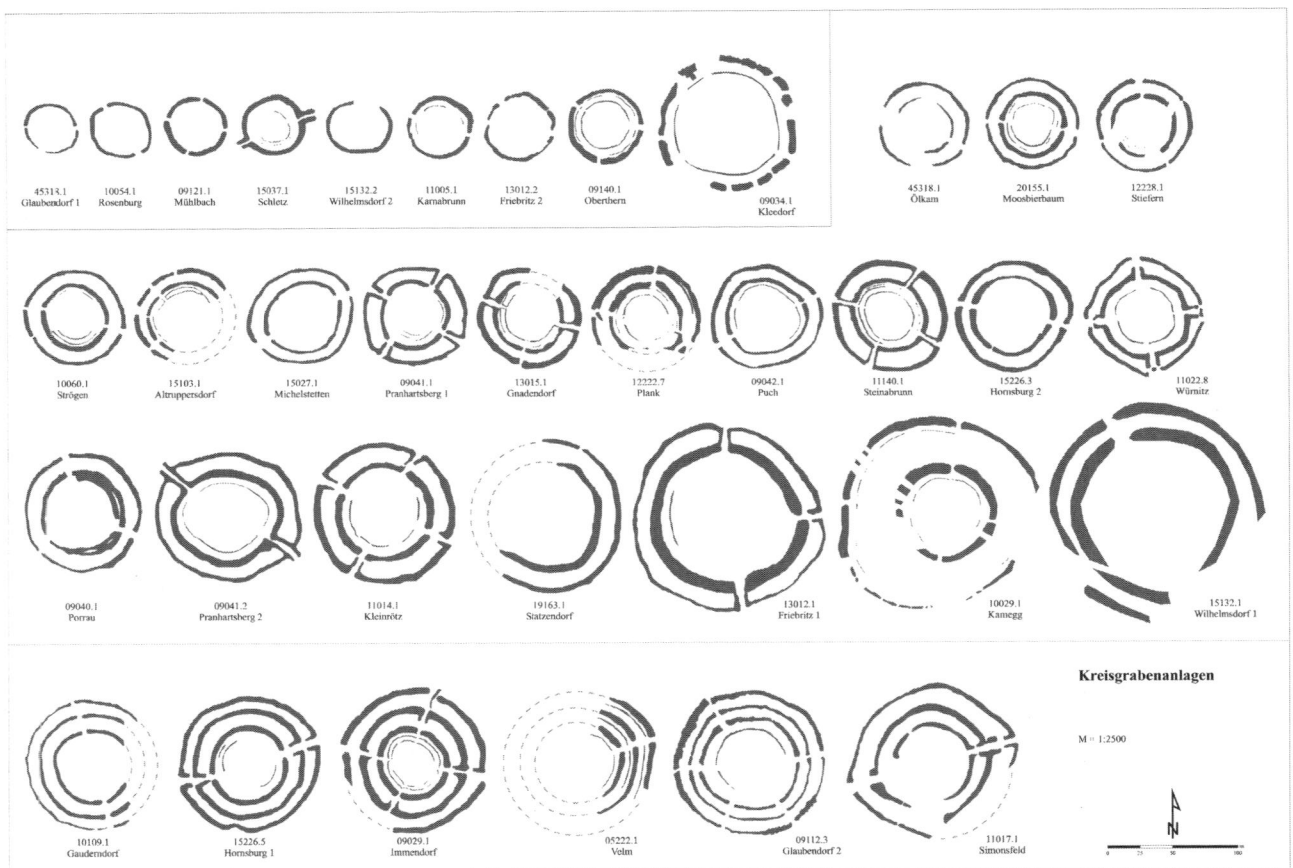

FIGURE 4: THE SINGLE, DOUBLE AND TRIPLE KGAs IN AUSTRIA INVESTIGATED BY MAGNETIC PROSPECTION SHOW A HIGH VARIETY IN SIZE AND SHAPE. (K. LÖCKER AND W. NEUBAUER)

The data collected systematically (aerial orthophotographs, digital terrain models, magnetograms, cadastral and hydrological data, pedological data) during three field campaigns formed the basis for various additional research projects focusing on the three-dimensional modeling of the magnetic data as well as archaeological interpretation (Melichar and Neubauer 2010). For the archaeological interpretation it became crucial to look for new ways of reasoning as well as to prove or disprove various hypotheses circulating in both academic and lay circles. Both the monuments and the prehistoric period were therefore presented in a county exhibition in 2005. This was an important impetus for developing strategies to go beyond the standard of interpreting geophysical or aerial evidence. The monuments had to be placed in their landscapes and their surroundings had to be taken into account. By extending the survey areas we found that, as expected, the monuments were situated within the settlements. The combination of all data in a GIS formed the primary inference machine. But since GIS still is a 2.5D tool and our needs extended to even 4D, full 3D visualisation and analysis of the data had to be employed and the construction of high quality 3D models of the sites situated in their landscapes was the next logical step. Combined with well-defined small-scale but targeted excavation campaigns it was possible to achieve impressive virtual reconstructions for exploration using immersive virtual reality devices. Whilst still far removed from a time machine, the virtual world was a helpful tool for the formation of new hypotheses regarding the function of these oldest monumental constructions from Middle Europe that unified various culture groups defined by material remains. The extended prospection work showed that there are many similarities as well as many differences within the monuments' layout, size and shape. However, there must have been an underlying idea or model that was responsible for the rapid spread of the phenomenon all over Central Europe. Time, the next dimension that became important, was investigated by the radiocarbon dating of nearly 100 samples and the results demonstrated that the adoption and use of these monuments occupied a very short period of time. They suddenly disappear some 150-250 years later. So what happened in and outside the monumental ditches; what was the function of these monuments?

Archaeoastronomical aspects of the KGAs

One of the most discussed theories is the astronomical aspect of this type of monument which imbues a ritual as well as calendrical importance. As soon as the first maps were available the KGAs became the subjects of archaeoastronomical investigation. The main focus was set on the orientation of the entrances (Weber 1986; Becker 1996; Karlovský 1999; Karlovský and Pavúk 2002). Ritual sky observations have been proposed most notably by Becker (1996), who based his analysis on magnetograms that indicated that the entrances of the Bavarian KGAs are oriented towards the rising or setting points of the sun at the solstices (Figure 5). In preparation

FIGURE 5: SUNSET IN THE ENTRANCE OF THE RECONSTRUCTED KGA AT SCHLETZ AT THE KREISGRABEN MUSEUM AT HELDENBERG, LOWER AUSTRIA. (PHOTO W. NEUBAUER)

for a large county exhibition on the Kreisgrabenanlagen in 2005, compiled and arranged by the author (Daim and Neubauer 2005), theoretical astronomical orientations were also investigated at the Lower Austrian KGAs (Zotti 2010, 2008, 2005; Kastowsky et al. 2005), based on the results of systematic archaeological prospection that combined field surveys, aerial archaeology and magnetic prospection (Neubauer 2007). Our approach was different to that previously employed as we based our studies on archaeological interpretation maps and reconstructions based on the magnetic modeling of the magnetic surveys (Eder-Hinterleitner and Neubauer 2001) combined with the digital terrain models derived from aerial archaeology (Neubauer 2001a; Doneus et al. 2005). Therefore it became possible to include the horizon and to derive virtual reality models for the monuments (Gervautz and Neubauer 2005). These models formed the input for astronomical simulation software, which made it possible to explore the potential astronomical orientations as well as the constraints in the reconstructed virtual Middle Neolithic environment (Zotti 2008). By animating the Middle Neolithic scenario of rising sun, moon and stars, the strict analysis of the virtual reconstructions formed the bases for strong arguments regarding the importance of the sky to the users of these monuments and also formed the bases for new research at the KGAs. An ongoing project (ASTROSIM, supported by the Austrian Science Fund, FWF P21208-G19) is currently studying the potential astronomical orientations in detail (Zotti and Neubauer 2011; Zotti 2010), combining geomagnetic results, field surveys, virtual reconstructions, and astronomical simulation.

The Late LBK and the formative phase of MOG (Lengyel)

The Early Neolithic Linearbandkeramik or LBK cultural groups (5700/5500 - 5000/4900 BC) originated from the same transdanubian region as the later core distribution of the Middle Neolithic KGAs and spread all over Central Europe. The latest phase of the LBK is characterized by a fragmentation into smaller cultural groups and large areas enclosed by ditches and/or palisades. Nevertheless these types of large Late LBK enclosures comprising rounded, irregular or rectangular perimeters, were situated on defended positions and enclosed areas of settlement: they are more likely to be interpreted as primarily defensive. We investigated the three rather large LBK enclosures, dating to after 5200 BC, situated in Lower Austria at Grossrussbach-Weinsteig (Doneus et al. 2001; Neubauer 2001, Figure 189), Wetzleinsdorf (Neubauer 2010, 410-415) and Asparn a.d. Zaya/Schletz (Neubauer 2001, Figure 160; Neubauer et. al. 1999) by means of large scale magnetic prospecting using high-resolution CS-magnetometers (Trnka 2005, Figure 1.8; Neubauer et. al 1999b) to map these extended monuments. They proved to have enclosed a settled area and to have had a steep U-shaped ditch cut into the loess soil. The monument at Grossrussbach-Weinsteig comprised a single ditch with only a few interruptions or entrances and enclosed a rectangular area of 24ha. The excavations indicated that agriculture had truncated the site by up to 1 to 2ms (Doneus et al. 2001) and consequently any potential remains of a bank or palisade have been destroyed. Nevertheless the ditch fills suggested the former presence of an internal bank. The site at Wetzleinsdorf situated only 3.5kms to the west had an interrupted (or causewayed) ditch enclosing a central area within an earlier extended LBK settlement. The site at Asparn a.d. Zaya/Schletz, situated 15kms north, was settled throughout the LBK. The settled area measures 18ha and was excavated during the 1990s (Windl 1999, 1996, 1994). In the final phase some 12ha of the hilltop were enclosed by an oval double ditch system and a trapezoid extension towards north capturing an area of artesian springs. Human remains in the ditches clearly prove the that the enclosure was defensive. A double palisade later occupied the interior. Wells exploiting the artesian springs were dug into the loess soil and formed important water sources inside the enclosed area despite the short distance to a small creek in the south and the river Zaya in the north. In the ditch fills the remains of more than 200 individuals were found, mainly male: the females and children were missing. Many of the skulls had been smashed with maces and these individuals are interpreted as the inhabitants killed in a warlike event dated by radiocarbon to 5070 – 4950 cal BC (personal communication Peter Stadler, 2004). The end of this large fortified LBK settlement which certainly played a central role around 5000 cal BC can be seen in conjunction with a general decline and diversification of the eastern LBK

groups. Whereas the western LBK groups developed further into various cultural groups defined by stroked ware pottery (e.g. Stichbandkeramik, Grossgartach or Rössen) indicating a continuous development from the incised ware to the stroked pottery, the eastern LBK in Northern Hungary, Austria and Slovakia ended abruptly overtly obvious in the ceramic record.

The MOG I (Lengyel)

From 4900 to 4850 cal BC onwards, polychromatic painted ware originating from the Lengyel cultural complex, dominates the material culture of the farming societies in Moravia and Eastern Austria. The pottery is richly ornamented in the early phase (MOG I) and is painted in red and yellow (Trnka 2005) and this decoration cannot be derived from LBK traditions. The formative phase is characterized by a find from Unterwölbling (Ruttkay 1978) and the grave finds within the interior of the KGA of Friebritz 1 (Neugebauer-Maresch et al. 2002). It is doubtful if this formative included early KGA monuments. The dating of the KGA monuments in Austria is based on a series of radiocarbon dates from finds from the ditch fills and ceramic typologies indicating the period of construction and use to within the MOG I, 4850/4750-4650/4550 cal BC in absolute terms (Stadler and Ruttkay 2007; Stadler et al. 2006). As far as we currently understand it all European KGA monuments date to this period. The existing radiocarbon dates do not yet permit a detailed analysis of the respective dates of construction and use for individual monuments largely due to the somewhat arbitrary excavation methods applied during the 1980s and 1990s. Recent excavations by VIAS-University of Vienna investigating the KGA sites at Schletz, Steinabrunn and Hornsburg 1 have produced well documented stratified contexts but are still unpublished. Despite the arbitrary but extensive excavations at Kamegg, a detailed seriation of the ceramic finds in combination with the radiocarbon dates has enabled a more detailed reconstruction of the site's history (Doneus and Trnka 2005; Doneus 2001). This almost completely excavated KGA has produced the most complete spectrum of ceramic types (Doneus 2001) found within the ditches and pits from the surrounding settlement. The material was divided into five sub-phases within MOG I and is dated to 4730/4635 – 4605/4515 cal BC (Stadler and Ruttkay 2007, Tab. 6) though does not appear to span the entire use of the monument. To date, the earliest KGAs are Friebritz 1 (Figure 6), Wilhelmsdorf 1 and Schletz though all are yet to be fully published.

Geographical and topographical location

The distribution the KGAs clearly indicates that they exploited the loess soils which were soft and easy to dig using wooden and antler tools (Melichar and Neubauer 2010, Abb. 52). The best time for digging into natural loess sediments is early spring to early summer when there is high water saturation and low precipitation. Loess is naturally very stable up to a slope of 60 – 70 % enabling the digging of the steep-sided ditches. Besides the soil the

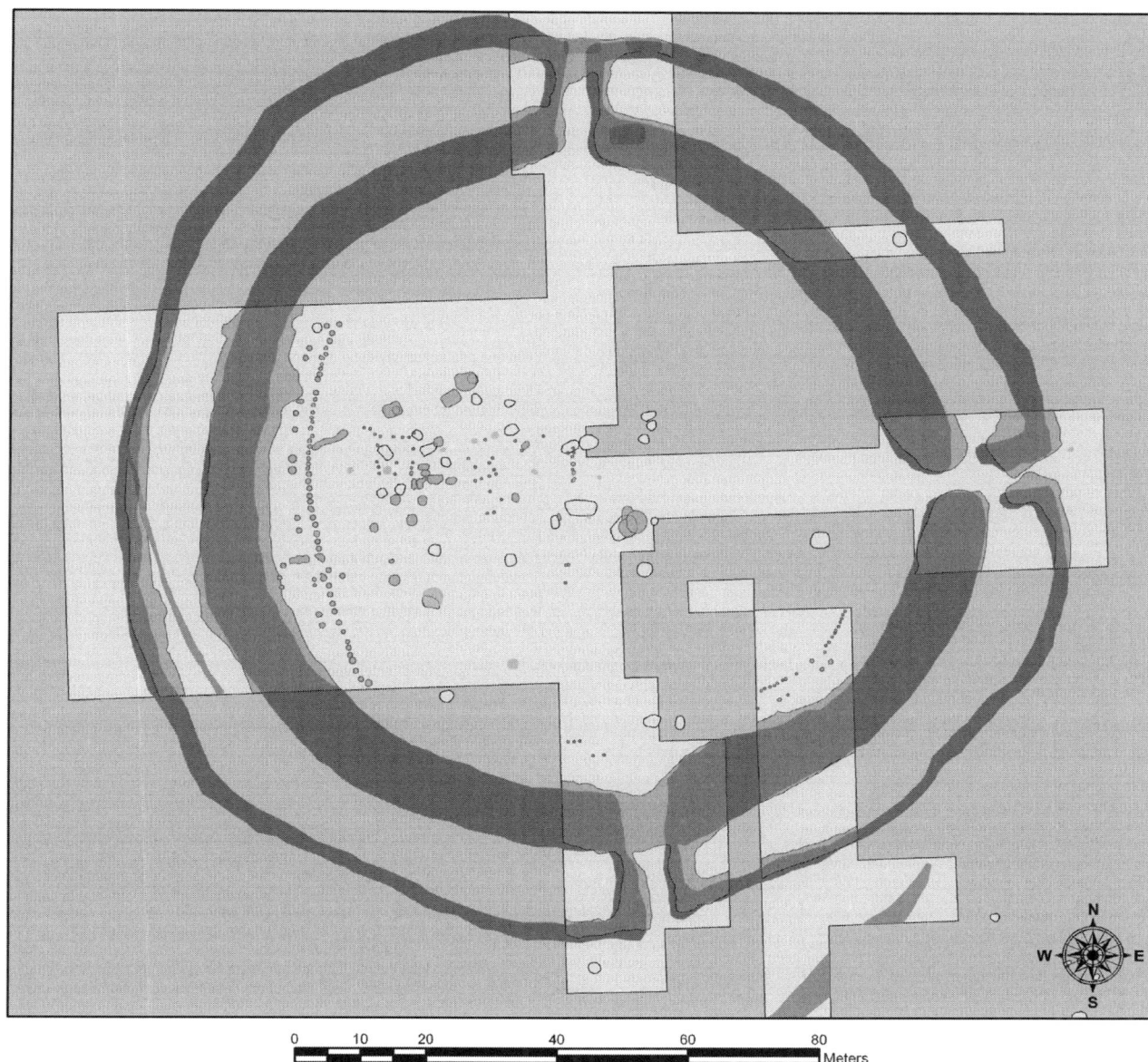

FIGURE 6: THE DOUBLE KGA AT FRIEBRITZ 1 COMBINING EXCAVATION RESULTS AND THE INTERPRETATION OF THE MAGNETIC DATA.
A GROUP OF BURIALS WAS DETECTED IN THE CENTRAL AREA ENCLOSED BY A PALISADE AND RING OF DOUBLE POSTS.
(NEUBAUER AND NEUGEBAUER-MARESCH 2005)

vegetation in the vicinity of the construction site might have been another important parameter and pollen analysis has shown that mixed oak forest mainly developed on acidic soils, while lime and elm also populated the loess. However whilst the composition of the forests is known we have no direct information on the density of vegetation. The formation of massive black earth soils is used by pedologists to argue for a steppe-like vegetation with isolated large trees (Loishandl-Weisz and Peticzka 2005) and the south-west facing slopes may have supported denser forests than the easterly sloping hillsides.

There is of course the fact that the area had been settled earlier, during the LBK, which would have had a major impact on the natural vegetation from 5300 cal BC. The transformation of the natural landscape due to clearance and the extraction of timber, the expansion of arable land

and forest grazing during the first 500 years of agricultural use must have been considerable mainly around the large settlements such as Asparn a.d. Zaya or Grossrussbach/ Weinsteig. Taking into account this detailed reconstruction of the environment, it is surprising that the more easily cultivated areas close to the LBK settlements (except Wetzleinsdorf and Eggendorf a. Walde) seem not to have been occupied. Indeed, most of the LBK sites are situated along small creeks and rivers (Lenneis 1995, Abb. 6) and the early Lengyel settlements are established close to sources and headwaters of the watersheds in Lower Austria. Some 84 % of the analyzed KGAs are directly associated with a spring or within an area of headwater and usually in areas remote from the LBK occupation. This concept of settling close to the sources of rivers is in clear contrast to the LBK farmers and can be explicitly demonstrated by the KGAs of Pranhartsberg 1 and 2 (Figure 7). They are not only

153

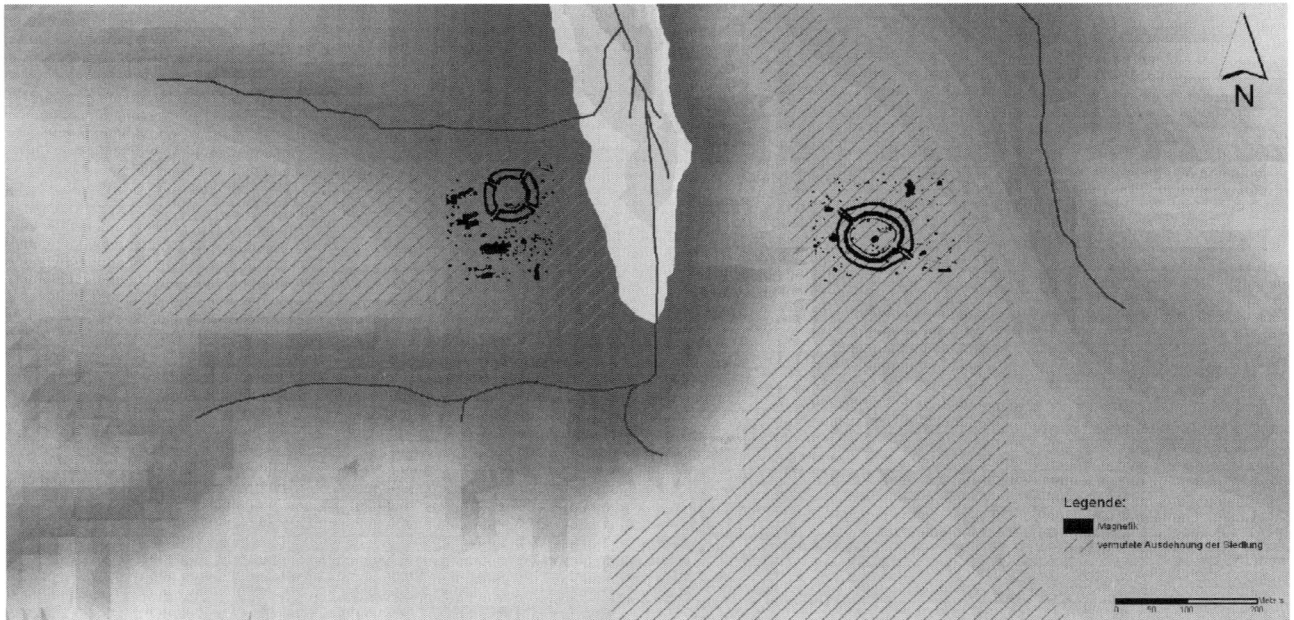

FIGURE 7: EXTENSION OF THE MOGI SETTLEMENT AROUND TWO DOUBLE KGAs AT PRANHARTSBERG 1 AND 2 SITUATED IN THE HEADWATERS. A HYPOTHETICAL SMALL LAKE WAS RECONSTRUCTED FROM THREE DIFFERENT WATERLINES IN THE PRESENT WETLANDS IN THE VALLEY BETWEEN THE TWO MONUMENTS. (GRAPHICS W. NEUBAUER)

situated in the headwaters but also on a plateau separating two regional watersheds as first identified by Trnka (1991). The MOG I people obviously followed the water courses up to the headwaters to set up their new settlements in remote places thus securing (or controlling) the fresh water supply. The depression in the valley between the two monuments today is marshy wetland and the topography indicates that it might have been a small lake during the Middle Neolithic adding pond mussels and turtles to the inhabitants' diet, elements that have also been noted at other comparably situated sites. Figure 7 shows a reconstruction of three equidistant levels of the reconstructed waterline probably resulting from a beaver dam – another animal well attested in the faunal finds record. The site at Friebritz with two KGAs, situated within an elongated settlement shows a comparable layout close to a pond or small lake within the headwaters and the magnetic prospection produced evidence for many other dried springs and watercourses in the area.

The mean slope direction or exposition of the monuments is 125 degrees or east-south-east. Slopes exposed to the west were not selected whereas those exposed to the north-west can be seen at Kleinrötz which is situated within a small basin close to a spring. The majority of the monuments are face between the north-east and south-east, which might be related to the fact that this is the lee of the hilly landscape where extensive deposits of loess were deposited at the end of the last glacial. Slope forms and slope directions do not show any observable regularity. The selection of place seems to be dependent on the local situation of the headwaters, which normally do not occupy flat valley bottoms. The selected slopes are frequently in the range of 2 – 9 % and only a few KGAs have been erected on plateaux (Oberthern, Immendorf, Hornsburg 2) suggesting

that it was not the intention to build the monuments on flat terrain. This is despite the obvious fact that the slopes caused major problems in the maintaining of the ditches due to heavy natural erosion. The reason for this selection has still has to be deduced.

Shape and size of the monuments

The magnetic imagery is perfectly suited for the analysis of the shape, size and general layout (Figure 4) with particular reference to the number of palisades and entrances of this group of Middle Neolithic monuments (Melichar and Neubauer 2010). The targeted excavations based on the magnetic evidence proved that these elements can be located with considerable accuracy from the magnetics combined with magnetic modeling. The size of the monuments in Austria is highly variable with one main similarity – the interior of the ditch systems is enclosed by one or more rings of timber palisades and is mainly empty (though truncation must be borne in mind). Another consistent similarity is the V-shaped deep ditches interrupted by small gaps that extend into the palisades.

Smaller systems comprising a single ditch range from 40 to 50m in average diameter. Most of the double systems have diameters between 60 and 90m – though the largest systems in Austria (Kamegg, Wilhelmsdorf I) are double ditched (up to 158m in diameter). For Kamegg, however, M. Doneus comprehensively demonstrated that the system developed from a smaller single ditch system into a larger single ditch system (Doneus 2001) and this is similar to the development at Svodín (Nemejcová-Pavúková 1995) (Figure 8). Triple ditch systems have average diameters between 100 and 120m and are more frequent in Lower

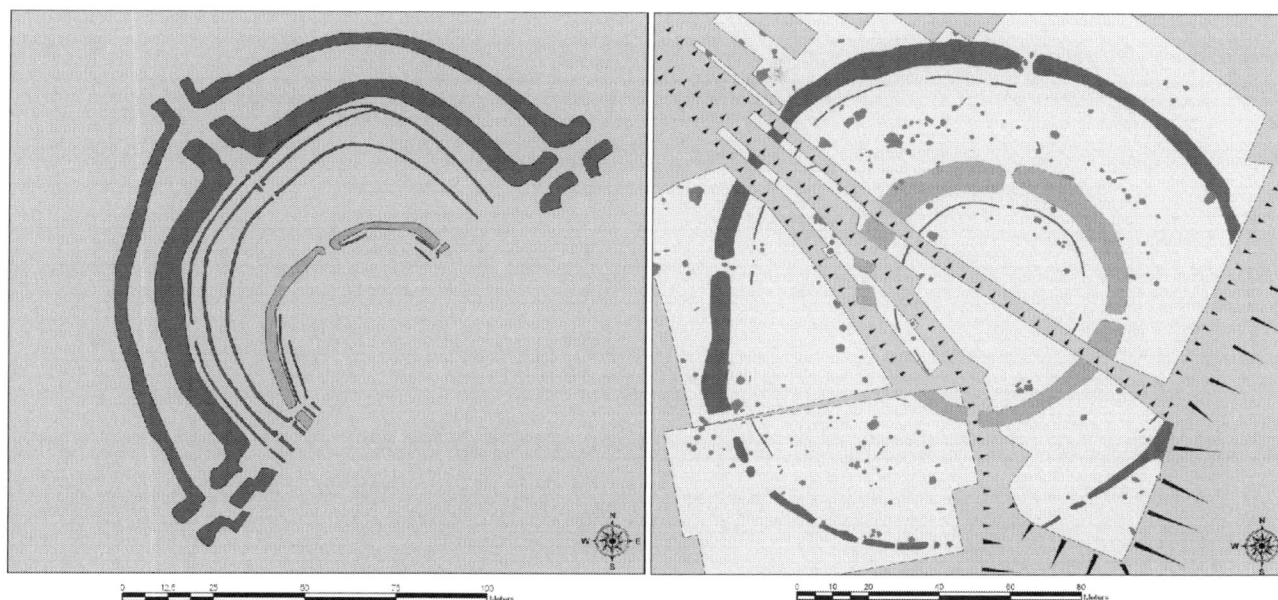

FIGURE 8: LAYOUT OF THE KGAS AT SVODIN(LEFT) AND KAMEGG (RIGHT) WHICH DEVELOPED FROM A PRIMARY MONUMENT INTO LARGER MONUMENTS CLEARLY EXTENDING THE CENTRAL ENCLOSED AREA. (GRAPHICS M. DONEUS AND W. NEUBAUER)

Austria. The number of palisades also varies from a single to five rings. The number of entrances ranges from two to five independent of the number of ditches. Quadruple ditch systems, known from Saxony (Kyhna 3, Nickern 4) or Slovakia (Cifer), have not yet been found in Austria (Stäuble 2007, Abb. 2; Kuzma and Tirpák 2001, 206). The ditch system at Polgár-Csőszhalom, situated at the river Tisza in Hungary, cannot yet be attributed to the KGA group. The monument partly shows five and, in one quarter, four ditches with four symmetrically opposed entrances (Raczky et al. 2007; Raczky et al. 2005). It is similar to the KGAs in form and with respect to the entrances but the interior is occupied by buildings. It is as yet unkown whether these buildings are normal dwellings such as have been excavated on a large scale in the surrounding settlement that extends over an area of at least 28ha. The excavators identified three main phases in the development of the monument from a single to a triple ditch system (Raczky et al. 2007, Figure 6). According to radiocarbon dates phases II and III of Polgár-Csőszhalom are contemporary with the monuments in the MOG I distribution area. The end of phase I is contemporary with the earliest MOG I sites (Raczky et al. 2007, Figure 10) which were networked via the obsidian trade originating at Polgár-Csőszhalom and the extraction mines in the Tokaj mountains. The evidence from Kamegg, Svodín, Wilhelmsdorf 1 and other sites indicate that at least the early monuments evolved from single into multiple ditch systems. This implies a continuous building activity and continued maintenance by recutting the ditches and the reorganization of the timber palisades observed within certain monuments (Steinabrunn, Friebritz 1).

The shape of the KGA monuments shows a high variation both in Austria (Figure 4) and elsewhere. Only a few

KGAs are of a nearly perfect circular shape with minor deviations from a true circle (Glaubendorf 2, Steinabrunn). Many are irregularly concentric, elliptical or have a ground plan close to a parallelogram (Pranhartsberg 2). Petrasch's initial analysis of the monuments' shape concluded that its builders intended the sites to be circular (Petrasch 1990, 442) and he argued that the deviations might be due to the topography and the construction process. Despite the fact that some of the nearly circular monuments have been erected on more or less flat areas, the deviations related to the topographical situations cannot be fully explained. No two KGA sites are directly parallel but rather they are all individually shaped yet are contemporary and share the aforementioned similarities placing them within a special group of monumental enclosures. The deviations from a circle were considered by earlier researchers as soon as the first complete plans became available but these deviations might not at all reflect the intention of the builders and might have been the result of the specific construction process. The magnetic map of the triple KGA at Glaubendorf 2 (Figure 9), revealing a distinct geometric shape made it possible to propose a construction process using a single divided rope to lay out the ditches and the positions of the entrances (Neubauer et. al. 1998). Most of the investigated sites are in such a topographic position as to make it impossible for a Neolithic spectator to appreciate the circularity of the monument. On the contrary many parts of the monuments are not visible from ground level as can clearly be demonstrated by virtual reality reconstructions and virtual walk throughs. The deep ditches only become visible when approaching the monument at a very close range and are more delimiting than monumental in character. The narrow entrances with the deep and steep ditches alongside and the narrow gaps in the palisades appear to restrict access suggesting the

155

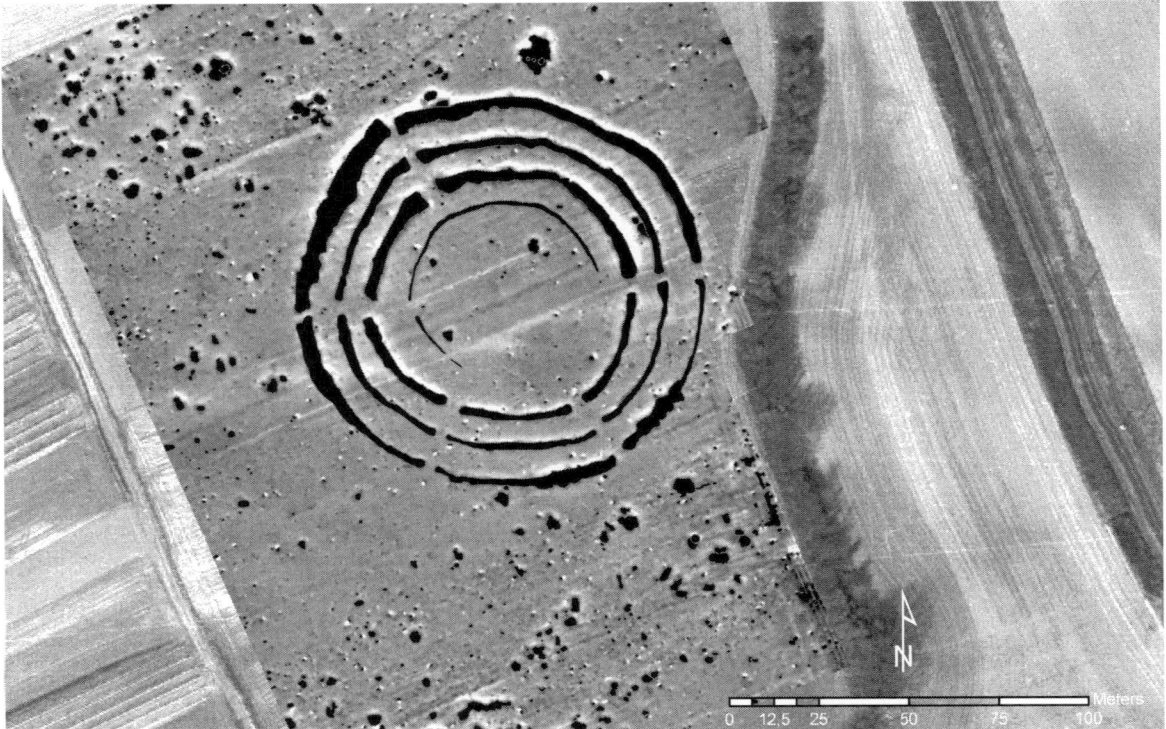

FIGURE 9: THE TRIPLE KGA AT GLAUBENDORF 2, SHOWING A NEARLY PERFECT CIRCULAR SHAPE AND SIX OPPOSED ENTRANCES. THE SIXTH ENTRANCE IN THE NORTH-EAST WAS DUG THROUGH IN A LATER PHASE OF THE MONUMENT. (GRAPHICS W. NEUBAUER)

FIGURE 10: THE FULL SCALE RECONSTRUCTION BASED ON THE SINGLE-DITCHED KGA MONUMENT AT SCHLETZ DURING ITS CONSTRUCTION AT THE KREISGRABEN MUSEUM HELDENBERG, LOWER AUSTRIA. THE KGA HAD A PALISADE AND SINGLE, RECTANGULAR SHAPED TIMBER UPRIGHTS, FORMING AN OUTER RING. THE FACES OF THE SHAPED TIMBERS WERE ALIGNED TO MEET IN A SINGLE POINT AT THE ENTRANCE. (PHOTO: W. LOBISSER)

exclusion of certain individuals. Circularity can only be appreciated when the palisades are viewed from the centre of the enclosure. The full scale reconstruction of Schletz (Lobisser and Neubauer 2005a, 2005b) proved that this palisade arrangement (Figure 10) also produces special acoustic phenomena, which might have been relevant during the activities performed in the interior. These observations are independent of the size or shape or the number of ditches and palisades at individual sites and may well be important design elements directly related to their function.

There is currently no means of relating the size of the monuments to their associated settlements. Enlargement of the monuments at Kamegg and Svodín clearly show that the internal areas of the larger monuments might increase over time and this may be evidence for a growing population. As the initial ditch systems were refilled the site did not develop into a more complex monument but a new and deliberately larger monument together with a larger enclosed interior. At Puch (Figure 11) a double system is closely related to the larger single ditch Kleedorf only some 250m distant. The overall size of Puch is equal to the area enclosed by the palisade of the single ditch system. Since the ditch of Kleedorf is built in single segments it might have been never finished (Trnka 1997) but it nevertheless provided a large enclosed area. It seems likely that access to the interior was restricted to certain individuals, privileged groups or parts of the community. The large interior spaces, however, and the obvious development and expansion of some sites may be used as evidence to suggest that during particular events, at least, larger groups had access to the monuments internal secrets.

We do not see any central role for the sites at Dresden-Nickern, Eythra und Khyna in Saxony-Anhalt (Stäuble 2007, 175). Therefore enlargement of these monuments cannot be explained by an expanding territory or community. At least for the site at Khyna, integration into a larger SBK settlement can be demonstrated. These SBK settlements further to the north might have been much larger with a more complex social organization than the newly founded MOG I settlements in the core distribution area.

The entrances, palisades and the interior of the ditched enclosures

The interior of the monuments can only be accessed through prescribed routes of admission in the form of specific entrances. Nearly half of the monuments have two opposite entrances, one third of the population has four entrances. Three entrances are less frequent and never appear with triple ditched KGAs. The number of entrances is not dependent on the size of the monument or the number of ditches. There is a tendency for monuments with three

FIGURE 11: MAGNETIC PROSPECTION RESULTS FROM THE MIDDLE NEOLITHIC SETTLEMENT AT PUCH/KLEEDORF WITH THE DOUBLE KGA AT PUCH AND THE SINGLE KGA AT KLEEDORF. THE TOTAL AREA ENCLOSED BY THE KGA AT PUCH IS EQUAL TO THE AREA ENCLOSED BY THE PALISADE OF THE KGA AT KLEEDORF. (GRAPHICS W. NEUBAUER)

entrances to have a larger interior. The KGA at Friebritz 1 (Figure 6) has an internal enclosed space exceeding three times the average and is also unique in the fact that there was a group of very peculiar burials found in the interior (Neugebauer-Maresch et al. 2001).

The entrances might be formed solely by interruptions of the ditches or accompanied by connecting radial ditches or the ditches may bend towards the inside or the outside of the monuments. However despite the variation of the entrance forms (Figure 10), which may or may not be of chronological relevance, they form long and narrowing passages that end in a small gap or gaps in the internal palisades. This implies an element of control first proposed by A. Gibson and presented as a major argument for the interpretation of the implications for social hierarchies.

As the inside is differentiated from the outside, so those within can permit, deny or restrict access to those without. The differentiation of space must reflect, even at a basic level, stratification within society. It represents a class possessing power, authority, and knowledge set aside from the rest of society. It does not imply conflict. Those with power may have held that power and authority with the full consent of the powerless by such means as lineage, wisdom or even election. They may have had the perceived ability to communicate on behalf of the community with the other world: the priesthood. We cannot but speculate when regarding these monuments as reflecting the society that they served and by which they were constructed (Gibson 2005).

We assume that passage from the outside into the monument and out again was integral to the functioning of the monument. The elongated narrow entrances clearly restrict access into the central space. The terminals of the ditches flanking the approaching individuals had extremely steep slopes and as the virtual walk throughs demonstrate, the ditches appeared bottomless. The narrow corridors obviously functioned restrictively and entry was only possible in single file or, at most, two abreast. This could be interpreted as defensive but it is more likely that it had ritual significance probably making people enter the KGA in procession, which might also have been an essential part of the ritual. Entry is not always possible in a straight line, the entrances through the palisades often being offset from the causeways through the ditches. The elongated passage-ways narrow the vision (Figure 10) and when approaching the monument, large areas of the interior are restricted from view, probably intentionally maintaining a degree of secrecy regarding the activities or installations within the central space.

The palisades might form single, double or even more complicated circular enclosures. There seems to be a formality when it comes to the relation of distances between the ditches and palisades but the detailed construction provided many degrees of freedom. The posts were embedded in narrow trenches up to 1.5ms deep and

FIGURE 12: OVERVIEW OF THE DIFFERENT TYPES OF DITCH TERMINALS OBSERVED AT THE AUSTRIAN KGA MONUMENTS FORMING THE ENTRANCE PATHS INTO THE ENCLOSED CENTRAL AREA. (GRAPHICS K. LÖCKER)

arranged to deny visual access into the central space. Some KGAs (Schletz, Friebritz 1, Steinabrunn) have additional concentric circles formed by spaced timber uprights. At Schletz (Figure 10) the excavated traces of the posts proved that these timbers had originally been squared off, probably indicating that they might have been shaped and carved like totems. At Friebritz and Steinabrunn (Figure 13) the posts were positioned uniformly in pairs indicating that they might have been supporting wooden lintels. The large number of very small and fine adzes found within the monuments (Trnka 1991, 54; Němejcová-Pavúková 1995, 86) might have been used for shaping these timbers. The KGA builders might even have painted the uprights with complicated motifs and patterns known from pottery and wall painting thus expressing their identity on a large screen and completely changing the appearance of the monument from a simplistic reconstruction to a more colourful and dynamic structure.

FIGURE 13: THE THREE RINGS OF PALISADES FOUND AT THE KGA AT STEINABRUNN. THE OUTER PALISADE WAS REPLACED IN A LATER PHASE BY A RING OF DOUBLE POSTS POSSIBLY SUPPORTING WOODEN LINTELS. (PHOTO O. RACHBAUER)

Flanking the formal entrances the magnetic images show slightly differing intensities in the magnetic anomalies produced by the ditch fills and some of them appear as small interruptions. Excavations at Kamegg (Figure 8, left), Strögen or Svodín (Figure 8, right) to name but three showed that the ditches were constructed in segments (Trnka 1997, Němejcová-Pavúková 1995) that had been joined together at a higher level in the ditch section before completion of the monument. This specific detail might be interpreted as the workload of distinct groups of people working individually on such a large monument. Since the segments were not completely joined at the bottom of the ditch; they may also have been intended to control the massive erosion within the sloping ditches.

Dynamics of the spread

The isolated sites related to the SBK in the Eastern part of Austria (Lenneis 1995, Abb. 18) indicate a decrease in the formerly dense LBK occupation. With the exception of one area around Horn related to the SBK in the Morava basin, none of the former LBK sites was continuously settled into the early phase of MOG I. There is a considerable body of evidence to suggest a colonisation from the south-east and this has recently and convincingly discussed by J. Pavúk in his analysis of the situation in Slovakia and the Morava basin (Pavúk 2007, 17). Based on the dense settlement pattern developing from the Early MOG I we would like to include the eastern part of Austria in this hypothesis. The Weinviertel, the north-eastern part of Lower Austria was sparsely occupied or even deserted around 4900 BC and was hypothetically occupied by MOG I people invading from the south-east – the core of the Lengyel culture. These people might have taken over the area completely in a phased but rapid colonization process combined with the formation of a new social identity, which appeared in the MOG I remains. There is no clear evidence for the coexistence or assimilation of a local and earlier population. Nevertheless the material remains indicate a fusion of various traditions from the south-east involving various different groups who were part of the formation of a new cultural identity.

From his analysis of the material remains, J. Pavúk envisages immigration from the Carpathian basin. The formative and early MOG I material has close relations with this area and its formation might be understood as a local result of this colonization process. The radiocarbon dates suggest a first phase of colonization around 4900 – 4850 cal BC (phase MOG Ia0) (Stadler and Ruttkay 2007). In the next phase the MOG expands and spreads into the Morava basin colonizing the area occupied by the SBK group. Whereas the evidence from Asparn a.d. Zaya indicates an early martial phase preceding the termination (cessation) of the LBK, the later expansion further north into the SBK territory might have been less violent. The site at Těšetice-Kyjovice, north of the river Thaya, was set up on a former SBK settlement by MOG people. The KGA monument and its related settlement was enclosed by an outer palisade, an element of fortification

not observed at the sites in the Weinviertel south of the river Thaya which may have formed the border of the first phase of colonisation. This second phase of expansion also included the Horn basin. There is certainly the need for more detailed research into this hypothesis, however such a colonisation or immigration process does shed a different light on the reasons for such a collective effort to build the KGA monuments.

Our research so far has shown that in Lower Austria many new settlements were founded during the initial phases of MOG I. The excavated sites at Kamegg and Svodín in Slovakia revealed features that predated the construction of the KGA but there had been no continuity from the LBK. Continuing occupation has been observed at a few sites after the intentional refilling of the ditches in the end of the KGA period. Parallel to that process of obliteration many new settlements were established in mainly strategic positions and enclosed by fortifications such as Falkenstein-Schanzboden (Neugebauer-Maresch 1978).

One main objective of the prospection project was to investigate not only the KGAs but also the settlement structures in the direct vicinity. Smaller houses with square dimensions of 8 to 20m and longhouses with bases of 8-10 to 40m were identified surrounding the monuments, demonstrating that the enclosures represent central delimited areas within distinct areas of settlement. The small distances between single KGA sites of 3 – 8km and the short period of use as documented by radiocarbon dates indicate an intensive and dense colonization of remote areas that were not settled with the same intensity during the Early Neolithic LBK. None of the KGAs and their related settlements had been situated in strategically prominent topographical positions, clearly available within the preferred headwaters. Settlements on hilltops, often combined with fortifications are known only from the later MOG Ib and MOG 2a and evolved after the KGA period (Neugebauer-Maresch 1995, 88-90, Trnka 1991).

The settlement pattern was dominated by the occupation of the headwaters within an undulating landscape and exploiting the easily cultivated and fertile loess-based soils. There is no continuity between the LBK and Early Lengyel. The MOG people did not reoccupy the earlier LBK settlements or take over the cultivated areas but occupied new and remote places. Most of the contemporary trees are deep rooting and would certainly have made the digging of ditches after clearance a laborious task, This raises the question as to why they did not occupy the cleared and cultivated areas that would certainly have been available in the vicinity. The availability of fresh water directly from springs in areas previously avoided or little used by the LBK groups seems to have been a major parameter for the selection of areas for settlement by the KGA builders. Another reason for the avoidance of cleared areas might have been the availability of sufficient amounts of timber for the building of houses and palisades. As we assume that the transportation of timber was not a main problem we favour the fresh water supply as the main explanation for occupying the headwaters, as also seems to be the case in the Bavarian examples (Petrasch 1990, Abb. 19).

It is possible that the MOG people avoided the river plains and therefore the threat of seasonal flooding. However, the river valleys and flood plains with their forested marshes and meanders were used for hunting aurochs, deer and beavers, for fishing and gathering mussels as is evident from the archaeozoological analysis. The narrow Kamp valley is the only river valley which was regularly settled but is morphologically clearly distinct from the wide river plains of the Danube, the Morava and Thaya.

Conclusions and further research objectives

The similarity of form and the contemporaneity of the KGAs across their distribution are unique in prehistory, perhaps representing the earliest visible transcultural tradition of major public ritual, and they are presumed to be part of a phenomenon of social control, marking the earliest conscious attempt at a pan-European socio-economic and ideological integration. This process, attested by the appearance of the KGA phenomenon, emerges rapidly and then abruptly ceases throughout Central Europe in a defined time-span of not more than 200 - 300 years. The facts so far indicate that the dense distribution of the monuments in Eastern Austria, the Czech Republic and Slovakia are related to migration from south-east Europe. It is reasonable to assume that the KGAs functioned in part in the legitimation of territorial ownership by new social groups and non-local traditions. The ritual or functional idea behind the KGAs or their expression of the power and strength of individuals or groups may have played a vital role in the formation of new cultural and/or political identities. The KGAs are communal constructions involving considerable numbers of people and effort thus unifying the groups involved in digging, cutting trees, transporting wood and erecting timber palisades (Gibson 2005).

The KGAs can be seen as the first reliable material imprint of the spread of new social practices in Central Europe. The main question to be investigated by future interdisciplinary archaeological research is to clarify the dynamic cultural processes in time and space that invoked the invention and spread of these monuments and the formation of the new cultural identities obvious in the independent archaeological records.

The most likely explanation is their use as some form of ritual place, a place for gatherings, or for certain ceremonies. Ritual activity represented by the deposition of artefacts like pottery, bucrania or broken idols (Figure 2, 3) and feasting remains like thin beakers or a variety of bones mainly from big cattle or aurochs formed most of the material record preserved in the ditch fillings and depositional pits.

The area of their distribution spans those of several archaeologically defined Neolithic cultural groups, so that they appear to represent an early transcultural idea (Trnka 2005a). It can be frequently shown that the azimuths of the entrances, as seen from the centre, are identical to certain important rising or setting solar azimuths in the course of the solar year such as at the solstices (Becker 1996, Bertemes and Schlosser 2004). About 40 KGAs are known in Austria, and almost all of them have been geomagnetically surveyed. An initial investigation supported the idea of solar orientation of several entrances, but also indicated that other azimuths can be explained by stellar orientation (Zotti 2008; Zotti and Neubauer 20110). These results suggest a calendrical use as one further aspect of the KGAs. The observation of heliacal risings or settings of certain stars may be linked to processes on Earth such as the start and end of the agricultural year and we can only vaguely guess the beliefs of the KGA builders. Clearly, a whole group of people had to work together under the command of a 'chief architect'.

The creation of astronomically orientated entrances required knowledge of and systematic observation of celestial phenomena as well as power over a sufficiently large population - a power that may have linked the celestial processes with an earthly authority. These astronomical orientations indicate that the monuments had a calendrical function and were probably associated with ritual and festive events at certain times of the year. They might have been used for the legitimation of cultural or social patterns through natural phenomena and because these social patterns required such dramatic support, it may be supposed that they were novel.

References

Bartels, R., Brestrich, W., de Vries, P., and Stäuble, H. 2003. Ein neolithisches Siedlungsareal mit Kreisgrabenanlagen bei Dresden-Nickern. Eine Übersicht, Arbeits- u. Forschungsber. *Sächs. Bodendenkmalpflege*. 45, 97-133.

Becker, H. 1990. Die Kreisgrabenanlage auf den Aschelbachäckern bei Meisternthal - ein Kalenderbau aus der mittleren Jungsteinzeit?, *Das archäologische Jahr in Bayern 1989*, 27ff.

Becker, H. 1996. Kultplätze, Sonnentempel und Kalenderbauten aus dem 5. Jahrtausend vor Chr. -- Die mittelneolithischen Kreisanlagen in Niederbayern. *Arbeitshefte des Bayrischen Landesamtes für Denkmalpflege*, Nr. 59.

Becker, H. 1996a Archäologische Prospektion und Luftbildarchäologie. *Arbeitshefte des Bayerischen Landesamtes für Denkmalpflege* 59, 15-18.

Bertemes, F. and Schlosser, W. 2004. Der Kreisgraben von Goseck und seine astronomischen Bezüge. in Meller, H. (ed.), *Der Geschmiedete Himmel -- Die Weite Welt im Herzen Europas vor 3600 Jahren*. 48-51. Theiss Verlag.

Bertemes, F., Biehl, P. F., Northe, A. and Schröder, O. 2004. Die neolithische Kreisgrabenanlage von Goseck, Ldkr. *Weißenfels, Archäologie in Sachsen-Anhalt* (NF) 2, 137-145.

Bertemes, F. and Northe, A. 2007. Der Kreisgraben von Goseck. Ein Beitrag zum Verständnis früher monumentaler Kultbauten Mittelauropas. *Vorträge des 25. Niederbayerischen Archäologentages,* 137-168.

Christlein, R. and Braasch, O. 1982. Das unterirdische Bayern, 7000 Jahre Geschichte und Archäologie im Luftbild,Stuttgart 1982.

Daim, F. and Neubauer, W. (eds), 2005. *Geheimnisvolle Kreisgräben - Niederösterreichische Landesausstellung,* Verlag Berger. (Exhibition Catalog). Horn, Wien.

Doneus, M. 2001. Die Keramik der mittelneolithischen Kreisgrabenanlage von Kamegg, Niederösterreich. Ein Beitrag zur Chronologie der Stufe MOGI der Lengyel-Kultur. *Mitteilungen der prähistorischen Kommission* 46.

Doneus, M. et al. 2001. The middle neolithic circular ditch systems of Puch and Kleedorf – A long term research project. In Doneus, M. et al., *Archaeological Prospection,* 4th int. conference, 36-46.

Doneus, M., Eder-Hinterleitner, A. and Neubauer, W. 2005. Entdeckungen aus der Luft. In Daim, F. and Neubauer, W. (Hg), 2005, 40-45.

Doneus, M. and Trnka, G. 2005. Jahrzehntelange Forschung – Die Kreisgrabenanlage von Kamegg im Kamptal. In Daim and Neubauer (Hg), 2005, 29-34.

Eder-Hinterleitner, A. 1994. Ein robustes Rekonstruktionsverfahren zur Bestimmung der Form von Gräben für die archäologische magnetische Prospektion. Tagungsband Musterkennung, *Informatik Xpress 5,* 532-539.

Eder-Hinterleitner, A., Einwögerer, C. and Neubauer, W. 2005. Grundlagen für eine Rekonstruktion – Die Kreisgrabenanlage Schletz. In: Daim, F. and Neubauer, W. (Hg), 2005, 85-92.

Gervautz, M. and Neubauer, W. 2005. Sonne, Mond und Sterne. in: Daim, F. and Neubauer, W. (Hg), 2005, 73-74.

Gibson, A. 2005. Monumente der Steinzeit. In Daim, F. and Neubauer, W (Hg)., 2005, 124-131.

Hašek, V. and Kovárník. J. 1999. Aerial and geophysical prospection in archaeological research of prehistoric circular ditches in Moravia, *Archaeological Prospection* 6/4, 187ff.

Karlovský , V. and Pavúk, J. 2002. Astronomická orientácia rondelov lengyelskej kultúry. In Cheben, I. and Kuzma, I. Otázky neolitu a eneolitu našich krajín – 2001, *Archaeologica Slovaca Monographiae – Communicationes* 4, 113-127.

Karlovský, V. 1999. Rondel v Bucanoch ako mozné slnecné a mesacné oberservatórium (Rondel in Bucany possibly served as a solar and lunar observatory). In Kuzma, I. (Hg.), Otázky neolitu a eneolitu našich krajín – 1998, *Materialia Archaeologica Slovaca – Communicationes* 2, 111ff.

Kastowski, K., Löcker, K., Neubauer, W. and Zotti, G. 2005. Drehscheibe des Sternenhimmels? Die Kreisgrabenanlage Immendorf. In Daim, F. and Neubauer, W. (Hg)., 2005, 80-82.

Kovárník, J. 2003. Jungneolithische und bronzezeitliche Kreisgrabenanlagen in Mähren. In Burdukiewicz , J. M. et al. (Hg.), Erkenntnisjäger – Kultur und Umwelt des frühen Menschen, *Festschrift für Dietrich Mania* (Veröffentlichungen des Landesamtes für Archäologie Sachsen-Anhalt – Landesmuseum für Vorgeschichte 57/1), 325-336.

Kuzma, I. 2005. Kruhové priekopové útvary na Slovensku - aktuálny stav (Kreisgrabenanlagen in der Slowakei - heutiger Forschungsstand). In Cheben, I. and Kuzma, I. (eds) Otázky neolitu a eneolitu našich krajín, *Archaeologica Slovaca Monographiae - Communicationes* 8, 185ff (185-223).

Kuzma, I. and Tirpák, J. 2001. Štvornásobný rondel v Cíferi, okr. Trnava, *Ve Službách Archeologie* 3, 205-210.

Lenneis, E. 1995. Altneolithikum: Die Bandkeramik. In Lenneis, E., Neugebauer-Maresch, C. Ruttkay, E.) Jungsteinzeit im Osten Österreichs, *Wissenschaftliche Schriftenreihe Niederösterreich* 102/103/104/105, 44-56.

Lobisser, W. and Neubauer, W. 2005a. Wiederaufbau einer Kreisgrabenanlage. In Daim, F. and Neubauer, W. (Hg) 2005, 95-101.

Lobisser, W. and Neubauer, W. 2005b. Im Kreisgrabenfieber: Experimentalarchäologische Studien zur Bautechnik der mittleren Jungsteinzeit. *Archäologie Österreichs* 16/1, 4-17.

Loishandl-Weisz, H. and Peticzka, R. 2005. Vom Winde verweht – Die Sedimente und Böden im Verbreitungsgebiet der niederösterreichischen Kreisgrabenanlagen. In Daim, F. and Neubauer, W. (Hg), 2005, 143-145.

Nemejcová-Pavúková, V. 1995. Svodín. Band 1 - Zwei Kreisgrabenanlagen der Lengyel-Kultur, *Studia Archaeologica et Mediaevalia* 2.

Melichar, P. and Neubauer, W. 2010. *Mitteilungen der prähistorischen Kommission der Österreichischen Akademie der Wissenschaften.*

Neubauer, W. 2001a. Geophysikalische Prospektion in der Archäologie. *Mitteilungen der anthropologischen Gesellschaft in Wien,* 120, 1-60.

Neubauer, W. 2001b. Images of the Invisible - Prospection methods for the documentation of threatened archaeological sites. *Naturwissenschaften* 88, 13-24.

Neubauer, W. 2007. Monumente der Steinzeit zwischen Himmel und Erde. Interdisziplinäre Kreisgrabenforschung in Österreich. *Vorträge des 25. Niederbayerischen Archäologentages,* 185-242.

Neubauer, W. 2010. Archäologische Auswertung der systematischen Prospektion. *Mitteilungen der Prähistorischen Kommission der österreichischen Akademie der Wissenschaften* 71, 2010, 56-135.

Neubauer, W. Eder-Hinterleitner, A. and Melichar, P., 1999. Large scale geomagnetic survey of an early neolithic settlement in Lower Austria (5250-4950 BC). In Faßbinder, J. and Irlinger W. Archaeological Prospection, *Arbeitshefte des Bayerischen Landesamtes für Denkmalpflege* 108, 58-59.

Neubauer, W. and Neugebauer-Maresch, C. 2005. Schwarze Kreise – Rote Erde. Kreisgrabenforschung in Niederösterreich. In Daim, F. and Neubauer, W. (Hg), 2005, 19- 28.

Neugebauer-Maresch, C. 1978. Befestigungsanlagen der Lengyel-Kultur von Falkenstein-„Schanzboden", Forschungsberichte zur Ur- und Frühgeschichte 10, 1978, 17ff.

Neugebauer-Maresch , C. 1995. Mittelneolithikum: Die Bemaltkeramik. In: (Lenneis E., Neugebauer-Maresch C., Ruttkay E. (eds), Jungsteinzeit im Osten Österreichs, Wissenschaftliche Schriftenreihe Niederösterreich 102/103/104/105, 1995, 57ff.

Neugebauer-Maresch, C., Neugebauer, J-W., Großschmidt, K., Randl, U. And Seemann, R. . 2002. Die Gräbergruppe vom Beginn der Bemaltkeramik im Zentrum der Kreisgrabenanlage Friebritz-Süd, Niederösterreich, Referat Tagung Poysdorf 1995, *Preistoria Alpina* 37, S. 187-253.

Nikitsch, R. 1985. *Kreisgrabenanlagen in Niederösterreich.* Unpublished Dissertation Wien.

Pavlů, I. 1982. Die neolithischen Kreisgrabenanlagen in Böhmen, *AR* 34, 176ff.

Pavúk, J. 2007. Zur Frage der Entstehung und Verbreitung der Lengyel-Kultur. In Kozlowski, J. K. and Raczky, P. (eds). The Lengyel, Polgár and related cultures in the Middle/Late Neolithic in Central Europe, *The Polish Academy of Arts and Sciences Kraków* - The Eötvös Loránd University, Institute of Archaeological Sciences Budapest,11-28.

Pertlwieser, M. 2001. Das kreisförmige Gehege. Ein Beitrag zur diskussion über die Funktion mittelneolithischer Kreisgrabenanlagen. in: Daim, F. and Kühtreiber T. (Hg.) Sein and Sinn/Burg und Mensch. *Katalog NÖ Landesausstellung*, 2001,182-184.

Petrasch, J. 1990. Mittelneolithische Kreisgrabenanlagen in Mitteleuropa. *Berichte der RGK Bd.* 71/1, 407-564.

Podborský, V. et al. 1999. *Praveká sociokultovní architektura na Moravě (Primeval socio-ritual architecture in Moravia*

Raczky, P., Domboroczki, L. And Hajdu, Z. 2005. Zwischen Himmel und Erde-Polgár-Czőszhalom, eine Siedlung in Ostungarn. In Daim, F. and Neubauer, W. (Hg), 2005, 203-209

Raczky , P. et al. 2007. The site of Polgár-Czőszhalom and its cultural and chronological connections with the Lengyel culture. in: Kozlowski, J. K. and Raczky, P. (eds). The Lengyel, Polgár and related cultures in the Middle/Late Neolithic in Central Europe, *The Polish Academy of Arts and Sciences Kraków* - The Eötvös Loránd University, Institute of Archaeological Sciences Budapest, 49-70.

Ruttkay, E. 2005. Innovation vom Balkan – Menschengestaltige Figuralplastik in Kreisgrabenanlagen. In Daim, F. and Neubauer, W. (Hg), 2005, 194-202.

Schier, W. 2008. Zur astronomischen Orientierung der mittelneolithischen Kreisgrabenanlage von Ippesheim, Mittelfranken, *Acta Praehistorica et Archaeologica* 40.

Schmotz, K. 2007. Die mittelneolithischen Kreisgrabenanlagen Niederbayerns. Anmerkungen zum Gang der Forschung. *Vorträge des 25. Niederbayerischen Archäologentages* 71-106.

Stadler, P. et al. 2006. Absolutchronologie der Mährisch-Ostösterreichischen Gruppe (MOG) der bemalten Keramik aufgrund von neuen 14C-Datierungen. *Archäologie Österreichs* 17/2, 41-69.

Stadler P. and Ruttkay, E. 2007. Absolute chronology of the Moravian-Eastern-Austrian Group (MOG) of the Painted Pottery (Lengyel-Culture) based on new radiocarbon dates from Austria. In J.K. Kozlowski, J. K. and Raczky, P. (eds), *The Lengyel, Polgár and related cultures in the Middle/Late Neolithic in Central Europe*, The Polish Academy of Arts and Sciences Kraków, The Eötvös Loránd University, Institute of Archaeological Sciences Budapest, 117-146.

Stäuble, H. 2002. From the air and on the ground: two aspects of the same archaeology? *Arch. Rozhledy* 54, 301-313.

Stäuble, H. 2007. Mittelneolithische Kreisgrabenanlagen im Wandel der Zeit. Die Sächsischen Beispiele. *Vorträge des 25. Niederbayerischen Archäologentages*, 169-184.

Trnka, G. 1981. Kamegg, *Fundberichte aus Österreich* 20, 300ff.

Trnka, G. 1981b. Straß im Straßertale, *Fundberichte aus Österreich* 20, 323f.

Trnka, G. 1983. Kamegg, *Fundberichte aus Österreich* 22, 227f.

Trnka, G. 1984. Kamegg, *Fundberichte aus Österreich* 23, 229f.

Trnka, G., 1986. Ergebnisse zu Untersuchungen der Kreisgrabenanlage von Kamegg, Niederösterreich, *Int. Symp. Lengyel* 289ff

Trnka, G. 1991. Studien zu mittelneolithischen Kreisgrabenanlagen, *Mitteilungen der Prähistorischen Kommission der Österreichischen Akademie der Wissenschaften* 26, 1-330.

Trnka, G. 1997. Zur Bauweise mittelneolithischer Kreisgrabenanlagen, *SPFFBU M* 2, 41ff.

Trnka, G. 2005 Kreise und Kulturen – Kreisgrabenanlagen in Mitteleuropa. In Daim , F. and Neubauer, W. (Hg), 2005, 10-18.

Trnka, G. 2005a. Kreise und Kulturen - *Kreisgrabenanlagen in Mitteleuropa.* 10-18

Trnka, G. 2005a. Katalog der mittelneolithischen Kreisgrabenanlagen. In Daim, F. and Neubauer, W. (Hg), 2005, 246-247.

Urban, O. H. 1980. Ein 5000 Jahre altes Langhaus aus Wetzleinsdorf, NÖ. *Antike Welt 11*, 3, 57ff.

Weber, Z. 1986. Astronomische Orientierung des Rondells von Těšetice-Kyjovice, Bez. Znojmo, *Internationales Symposium über die Lengyel-Kultur,* 313pp.

Windl, H. 1994. Zehn Jahre Grabung Schletz, VB Mistelbach, NÖ. *Archäologie Österreichs* 5/1, 11-23.

Windl, H. 1996. Rätsel um Gewalt und Tod und 7000 Jahren – Eine Spurensicherung. *Kat. des NÖ Landesmuseums, N.F.* 393, 1 ff.

Windl, H. 1999. Makaberes Ende einer Kultur. *Archäologie in Deutschland* 1 / 1999, 54-57.

Zalai-Gáal, I. 1990. A neolitikus körarokrendszerek kutatasa a Del-Dunantulon (Die Erforschung der neolithischen Kreisgrabensysteme in SO-Transdanubien), *Archaeologiai értesítö* 117, 3ff.

Zotti, G. 2005. Kalenderbauten? –Zur astronomischen Ausrichtung der Kreisgrabenanlagen in Niederösterreich. In Daim and Neubauer (eds) 2005, 75-79.

Zotti, G. 2008. Zur astronomischen Interpretation ausgezeichneter Richtungen der Kreisgrabenanlagen Niederösterreichs. In Wilfried Menghin (ed), *Acta Praehistorica et Archaeologica 40*. 61-67. Museum f. Vor- und Frühgeschichte, Berlin.

Zotti, G. 2010. Astronomische Aspekte der Kreisgrabenanlagen in Niederösterreich. In Melichar, P. and Neubauer, W. 2010, 136-167.

Zotti, G. and Neubauer, W. 2011. Astronomical Aspects of Kreisgrabenanlagen (Neolithic Circular Ditch Systems) - An Interdisciplinary Approach. In: Clive L. N. Ruggles (ed.): *Archaeoastronomy and Ethnoastronomy: Building Bridges between Cultures* (Proc. IAU Symp.278 (Oxford-IX Int. Symp. on Archaeoastronomy), Lima 2011), Cambridge University Press (in print).

Mind the Gap: Neolithic and Chalcolithic Enclosures of South Portugal

António Carlos Valera

Abstract

This paper examines the new data obtained during the last 15 years concerning ditched enclosures in Portugal, particularly the recent discoveries from the southern part of the country. Some of the problems raised by the recent proliferation of these sites in Western Iberia will be discussed. After describing their spatial distribution and chronological span, the dissimilarities with walled enclosures (and amongst ditched enclosures themselves) will be analysed. I shall dispute a homological reductionism and argue in favour of diversified social roles for these kinds of site. Particular attention will be given to size, landscape relationships (terrestrial and celestial), ditch filling processes and associated funerary practices. Finally it will be concluded that the diverse ditched enclosures of South Portugal must be read as an expression of Neolithic cosmogonies. The increasing size and complexity that can be observed in these monuments during the Chalcolithic is interpreted as a "singing of the swan" (the swan song) of those world views, and its abrupt decline, expressed by the apparently rapid disappearance of large ditched enclosures and ditched enclosure architecture as a result of that cosmogonic change.

Keywords: Neolithic, Chalcolithic, Ditched enclosures, Portugal, Cosmogonies

Filling the gap: the archaeological emergence of ditched enclosures

Being a European phenomenon, ditched enclosures were absent from the archaeological record of Portugal until the 1980s. In fact, by the end of that decade we knew of only one ditched enclosure, located in the hinterland of South Portugal: Santa Vitória in Campo Maior, Évora (Dias, 1996). By 1996 there were just five known in the region.

In the last decade and a half the archaeological record for ditched enclosures has changed dramatically. From 1997, with the discovery of the Perdigões set of ditched enclosures (Lago *et al*, 1998; Valera *et al*, 2000; Valera *et al*, 2007), to the present day, almost thirty new sites have been discovered as a result of infra-structure projects, but also in consequence of programmed research. They concentrate mainly in the South, in the middle Guadiana river basin, but some have also started to appear in the Lisbon Peninsula and in Central and North Portugal. The same has happened in Spain, bringing Iberia definitively into this phenomenon of European scale.

Today 34 ditched enclosures dating to the Neolithic and/or Chalcolithic are known in Portugal, spread all over the country, but with a particular concentration in the hinterland of Alentejo (Figure 1). Importantly, this "revolution" in the archaeological record has raised new questions and stimulated the development of new approaches to architecture, landscape and social practices of recent Prehistoric communities in Portuguese archaeology. Today, they are one of the most significant topics of research of Neolithic and Chalcolithic Western Iberia.

Time and space of ditched enclosures in Portugal

At the present time we have 23 radiocarbon dates from the ditch fills of only six sites, all from Alentejo's hinterland (South Portugal) but some sites have more than one ditch

and they are not always contemporary. As a result, these 23 dates are, in fact, related to specific enclosures, particularly at Perdigões (where three ditches of the eleven concentric enclosures have already been dated) and Porto Torrão (where two ditches were dated from a total number yet to

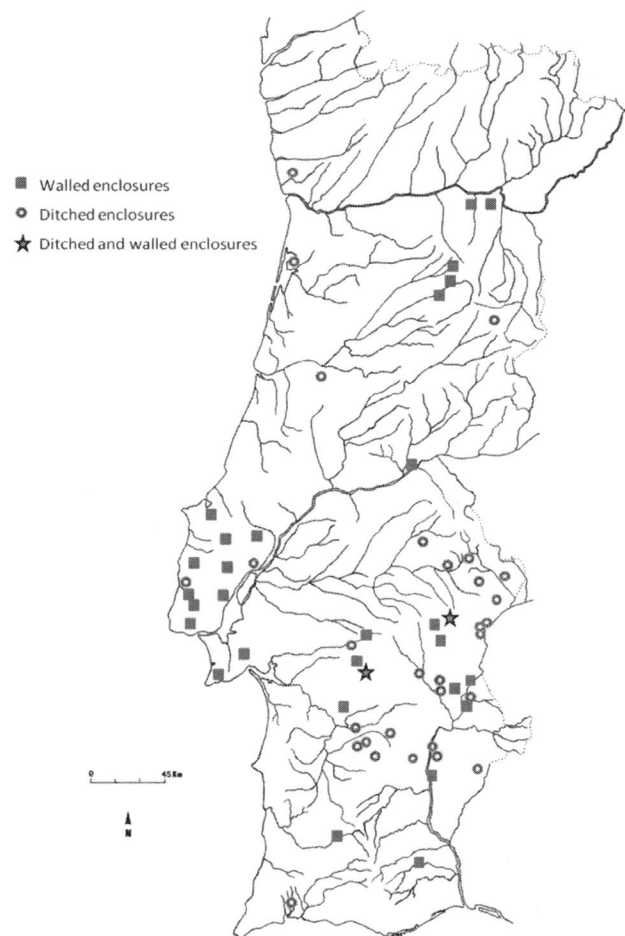

FIGURE 1: NEOLITHIC AND CHALCOLITHIC DITCHED AND WALLED ENCLOSURES IN PORTUGAL.

165

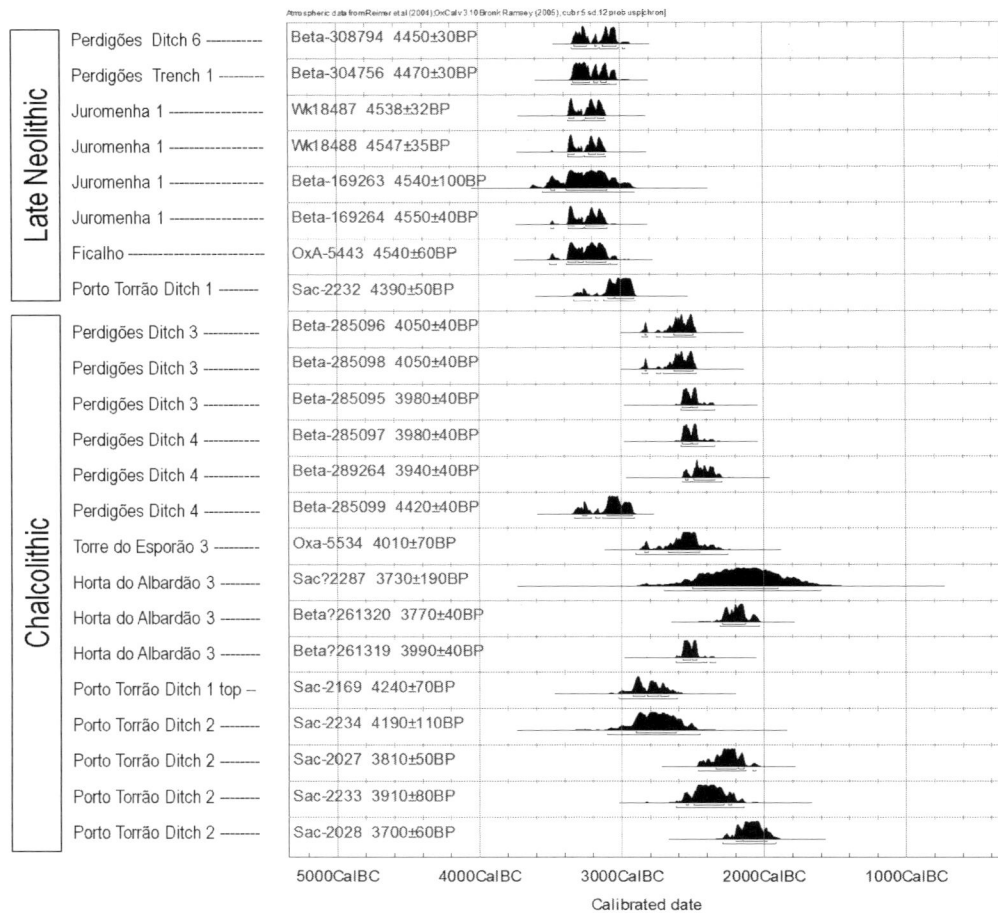

FIGURE 2: RADIOCABON DATES FOR THE NEOLITHIC AND CHALCOLITHIC DITCHED ENCLOSURES
IN PORTUGAL.

be determined). This raises the problem of the dynamics and growth of some enclosures through time while others present a much more restricted chronology. This will be considered later.

The material culture and the absolute chronologies available demonstrate that the oldest ditched enclosures known in South Portugal belong to the Late Neolithic and are dated from the second half of the 4th millennium BC, and especially from the last 400 years of that millennium (Figure 2). These early sites comprise the inner ditches (ditch 6 and trench 1) of Perdigões, Juromenha 1 (in Évora district), Ficalho and ditch 1 of Porto Torrão (in Beja district). Similarly early enclosures without an absolute chronology, but with identical material culture, are known at Torrão, Moreiros 2 (Portalegre district), Malhada das Mimosas, Águas Frias and Ponte da Azambuja (all in Évora district).

In the 3rd millennium BC, during the Chalcolithic, the number of ditched enclosures seems to increase in South Portugal, although currently only four sites have radiocarbon dates: Perdigões, Porto Torrão, Torre do Esporão and Horta do Albardão 3. Based on relative chronologies, however, several others can be included: Santa Vitória, Outeiro Alto 2, Xancra, Monte do Olival,

Luz 20, Monte da Ribeira, Salgada, Paraíso (all in Alentejo) and Alcalar (in Algarve). Most seem to be abandon during the millennium, after relatively short periods of use. In some cases (Perdigões and possibly Porto Torrão) the final occupation appears to extend to the first half of the 2nd millennium BC.

The great majority of these enclosures are concentrated in the middle Guadiana Basin or in the adjacent basins of Tagus (to the North) and Sado (to the West), in Alentejo's hinterland. In the South, only in Algarve do we find a ditched enclosure (Alcalar) near the coast.

The greatest concentration is in the inland South but in the last few years ditched enclosures have also started to appear in Central and North Portugal. Although few and scattered, they have a wider distribution not just in the hinterland (like that near Sabugal) but also in coastal areas and the Lisbon peninsula such as Gonçalvinhos (Sousa, 2010), Forca (Valera and Rebuge, 2008) and Angra do Castro in Aveiro (Almeida, in press). The most interesting example is still being excavated near Coimbra (Central Portugal). At Sra. da Alegria, located in the transitional area between the coastal plain and the high Central Mountains, there is a sequence of ditched and probably palisade enclosures dating from the Early/Middle to the Late Neolithic. The earliest ones cut earlier Early Neolithic occupation areas (with "cardial" decorated pottery) and are associated with sub rectangular houses. Although they have not been dated yet, the stratigraphy and associated materials suggest a chronology from the Early Neolithic/Middle Neolithic transition (late 5th/early 4th millennium BC). This is therefore the oldest ditched/palisade architecture presently known in western Iberia, following the examples of East and Northeast Spain, where ditched enclosures dating from the 6th and 5th millennium BC are known in the Valencia region (Bernabeu Auban *et al*, 2003; Köhler *et al*, 2008) and Navarra (Garcia Gazolaz and Sesma Sesma, 2007). According to the present data, therefore, we can anticipate a future increase in the number of ditched enclosures in Central/North Portugal (as is happening in Central Iberia) and perhaps earlier sites in the South.

Ditched enclosures are therefore a recent, but increasing, archaeological phenomenon adding to the well known walled enclosures. This raisesaan obvious question.

Are ditched and walled enclosures similar realities?

Ditched and walled enclosures share the same general space and if walled enclosures are clearly dominant in the Lisbon Peninsula, in Alentejo's hinterland the ditched enclosures prevail. In terms of chronologies, although both architectures were contemporaneous during the 3rd millennium BC, ditched and/or palisade enclosures appeared earlier, in the 4th millennium BC or even earlier (if we take into account the emerging data from Sra. da Alegria). Ditched enclosures therefore appear first and at the beginning of the 3rd millennium BC walled enclosures emerged, after which both types of architecture continued until the end of the millennium sharing the same general distribution.

They share the same areas but not the same sites. In fact, one interesting aspect is that walls and ditches appear side by side in only two cases (both in Alentejo – Salgadas and Monte da Ponte) but there is no evidence to suggest that they were contemporaneous. All the other Portuguese enclosures are delimited by ditches/palisades or by walls, but never by both (Figure 1). The same scenario seems to be the case in Spain and despite the large number of known enclosures, walls and ditches are both present in only two cases, Los Marroquiés Bajos and San Blás – the latter on the Spain/Portugal Guadiana border (Zafra *et al*, 2003; Hurtado, 2008).

The reality is that several dissimilarities between walled and ditched enclosures suggest that, in general, they might have served different purposes, although in some cases it is possible to argue for similar roles. In a recent paper (Valera, in press A) some of those differences were highlighted, such as the rarity of pits in walled enclosure and the association of ditched enclosures to tens, hundreds and sometimes thousands of them; the different sizes they can reach; the diversities in topographical location and landscape relations; the differences in design, architectonic

dynamics and associated practices; the unequal importance of cosmological bonds and funerary practices. Based on those dissimilarities it was argued that these two types of enclosures could, in general terms, have played different social roles. Here, I would like to return to some of those specifics in order to debate the interpretation of ditched enclosures.

Topography, planning and design: the architecture of ditched enclosures

One of the interesting aspects of South Iberian ditched enclosures is that despite a superficial similarity of appearance, they often have quite different topographical locations and some individualities in their design.

In terms of topography ditched enclosures can occupy flat hill tops (like the small enclosures of Santa Vitória, Outeiro Alto 2, Cortes 1 or Torrão) or crests (like Moreiros 2 or Alcalar). Others are located in the middle of smooth slopes, usually facing east, like Xancra or Monte do Olival, while some others were located in natural amphitheaters, also facing east such as Perdigões or Paraíso. Finally, they can also occur in open smooth valleys, crossed by streams, such as Porto Torrão. There is therefore no consistent topographical pattern, although facing East seems to be important.

These differences in topography (that do not exist in walled enclosures which are always located in hill tops or cliff edges) seem to have a relation with the ways the ditched enclosures are meant to relate to significant features in the local landscapes. This can be argued for several ditched enclosures, but is particularly evident in the case of Perdigões.

It was the analysis of the plan of Perdigões that, for the first time in Iberia, tried to understand the specific architectonic designs of the enclosures in their relation to topography, including landscape and skyscape (Valera, 2008 A; 2010 A). Based on the information provided by an aerial image published in 1998 (Lago et al, 1998), later reinforced by geophysical survey (Márquez Romero *et. al*, 2011; Valera *et. al.*, in press B), it was argued that the location of the site, its architecture and spatial organization could have considerable cosmogonic significance.

Perdigões is located in a natural amphitheatre opened to East. For one standing in the middle of the enclosures, the visibility is restricted to the limits of the amphitheatre (coincident with the outermost ditch circuit), except to the East, where the distant horizon is marked by the hill of Monsaraz and the valley of the Guadiana river. Between Perdigões and that horizon is the valley of Ribeira do Álamo, where more than a hundred megalithic monuments and some menhirs are known. In fact, Perdigões stands at the "back" (only few monuments are further West) of the famous megalithic group of Reguengos de Monsaraz and it was built in a locale and with such an orientation as to face this megalithic landscape (Figure 3).

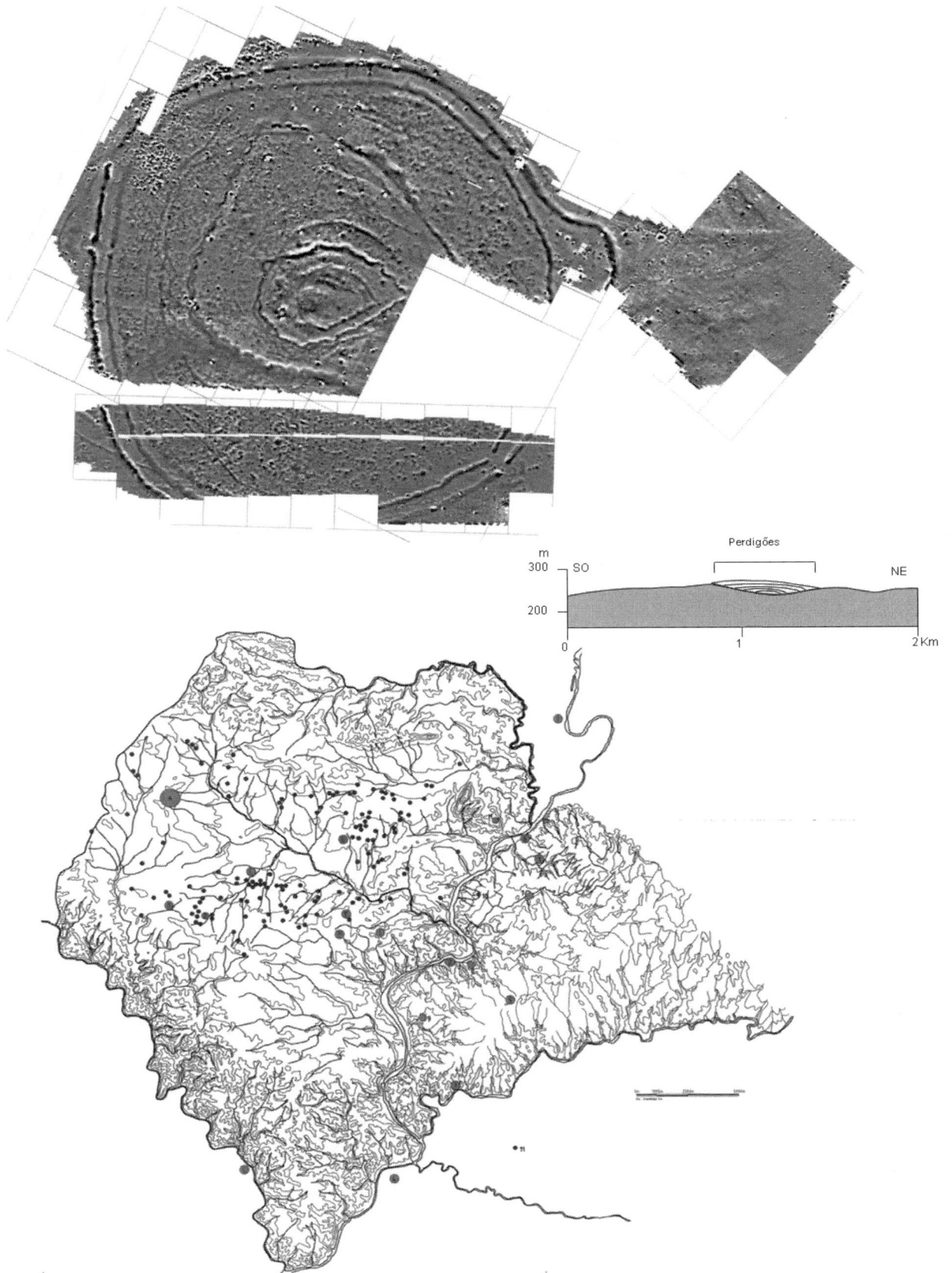

FIGURE 3: GEOPHYSICAL IMAGE (BY HELMUT BECKER) AND TOPOGRAPHICAL PROFILE OF PERDIGÕES (ABOVE); LOCATION OF PERDIGÕES IN THE RIBEIRA DO ÁLAMO SETTLEMENT AND MEGALITHIC NETWORK (BELOW).

According to the available data, in the Late Neolithic at least one ditched enclosure (with earlier or contemporary palisades) was constructed in the centre of the amphitheatre and a cromlech where it opens and meets the valley bottom. Later, in Chalcolithic times, the site grew larger and incorporated a necropolis in a semi circular area defined by the double ditches of the outside enclosure. This necropolis was again located in the Eastern side, where the topography opens to the valley and near the earlier cromlech.

This connection with the East and to the rising sun reinforced by the orientation of the eastern gates of the outside double ditches towards the sun's winter and summer solstices and the western gates to the corresponding sunsets. The inner enclosures that have gates detectable in the geophysical image are also orientated towards the m solstice sunrise. This suggests that the location chosen for the siting of the enclosure, cromlech, necropolis and the general architectural designs of the enclosures took into account both the local megalithic landscape and astronomically significant events, revealing the progressive construction of a meaningful cosmogonic landscape in that valley.

This line of inquiry developed into a research project entitled "Enclosure plans and Neolithic cosmogonies: a landscape, archaeoastronomic and geophysical approach" (Valera and Becker, 2010; Valera and Becker, in press;) that aimed to obtained integral plans of ditched enclosures through geophysical prospection and, together with other largely excavated sites, analyse them according to the criteria described above.

The results revealed an intentional tendency towards the observance of astronomic phenomena in the location and design of some ditched enclosures. This is clear in three enclosure that share a specific pattern of sinuous ditches (see below). The inner enclosure of Santa Vitória has its single entrance aligned towards the summer solstice. At Outeiro Alto 2 the entrance through the only ditch is facing the winter solstice; the three concentric ditches of Xancra have their gates perfectly aligned to the winter solstice or to the near moon standstill (Figure 4). Whilst Santa Vitória and Outeiro Alto 2 are located on the flat tops of small hills with a 360° visibility over the local landscape, Xancra has a topographical position similar to Perdigões and to some regional cromlechs (such as Almendres or Vale Maria do Meio). It is located in the middle of a smooth east-facing slope. The same topographical location occurs at the enclosure of Monte do Olival 1 or at Paraíso.

Although information is still limited due to the fact that these enclosures have only recently been briefly surveyed (with the exception of Santa Vitória and Perdigões), the observed recurrences suggest that, in several cases, their architecture and location in the landscape respond to symbolic needs and incorporate specific cosmogonies, which are central to understanding their social roles.

Architecture is a social practice that, through the organization and construction of space, built scenarios that express the way in which the world is perceived and we can hardly look to large architectural projects or building projects as meaningless, ideologically neutral and simply functional (functionalism is itself an ideology). Architecture expresses world views at several scales (landscapes, villages, houses) and all can act as metaphors for the cosmos or for certain aspects of the cosmogonies and "world order" that, through dwelling, are maintained and perpetuated.

This same line of inquiry can also be used to address the "strange" design that characterizes some ditches. In fact, a significant number of Portuguese ditched enclosures exhibit a specific kind of groundplan designated by a "sinuous ditch" (Figure 4). For some time this was only known in Santa Vitória (Dias, 1996), the first ditched enclosure to be discovered and excavated in Portugal, but in the recent years it has become increasingly recognised at other sites to the extent that they are present in almost 50% of the ditched enclosures of South Portugal, with a particular concentration in the Guadiana basin (although they are also present in the Algarve and in South Spain). On the contrary, the phenomenon is relatively rare in the rest of Europe, suggesting that this kind of design is particular to Iberia and, in some cases, a specific to South Portugal.

Traditional interpretations considered these sites as simple fortified settlements envisaging associated earth banks or palisades, even when no empirical evidence for these was present. It was considered that the design copied the bastions of walled enclosures (Dias, 1996). This was due to the similarity of the plans and because at the time the walled enclosures were considered to be the oldest. Subsequently, when it became clear that some 'wavy' enclosures were earlier, the design was naturally seen as an anticipation of walls with bastions (Mataloto and Costeira, 2008).

The form of the enclosures can generally be defined as a wavy in outline, for the whole or part of a ditch's perimeter and there are different types (Valera, in press b). There may be single ditch enclosures or examples with multiple ditches. These latter sites generally have the ditches arranged concentrically and may also appear alongside simple linear ditches. The available data indicates that they started to be built in the Neolithic during the second half of the 4th millennium BC (Juromenha 1, Malhada das Mimosas, Águas Frias) and continued into the Chalcolithic (Xancra, Santa Vitória, Outeiro Alto 2, Perdigões E, Alto do Outeiro), lasting until the second half of the 3rd millennium BC (Horta do Albardão).

Some plans comprise a regular pattern of semi circular lobes (such as Monte do Olival 1, Santa Vitória, Outeiro Alto 2 e Xancra, the last three with clear astronomically orientated gates – Figure 4), while others have a more wavy or irregular outline (such Perdigões C and E, Águas

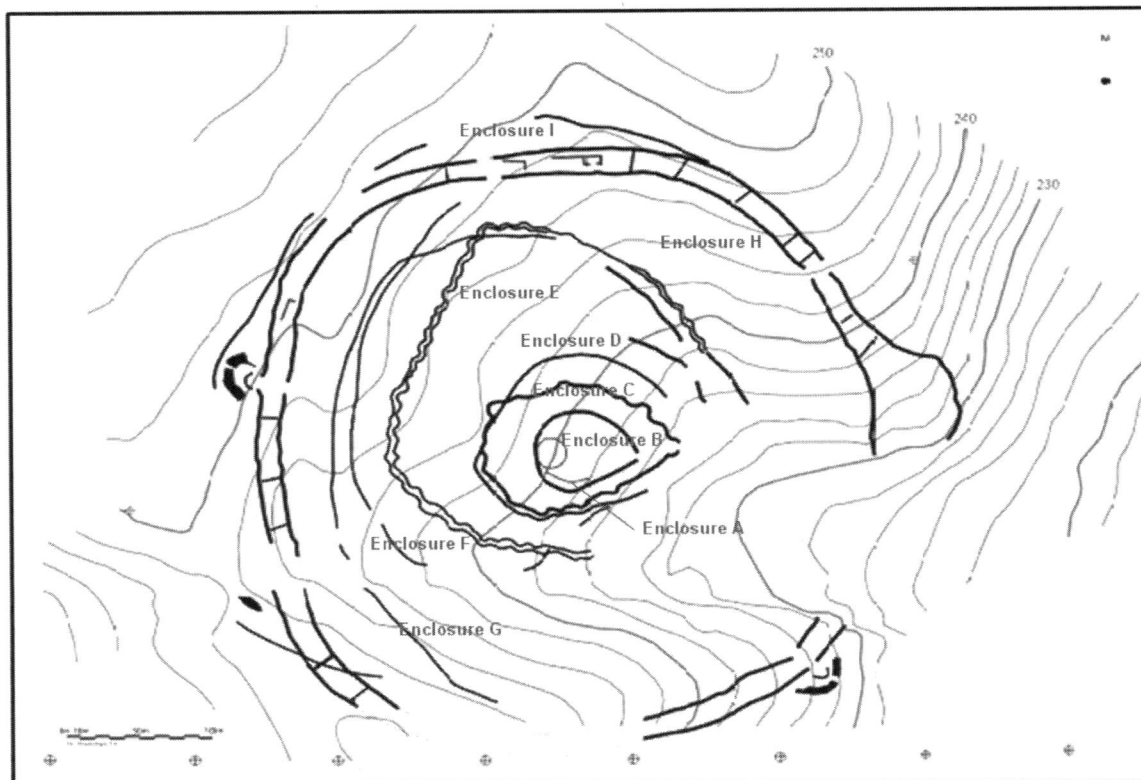

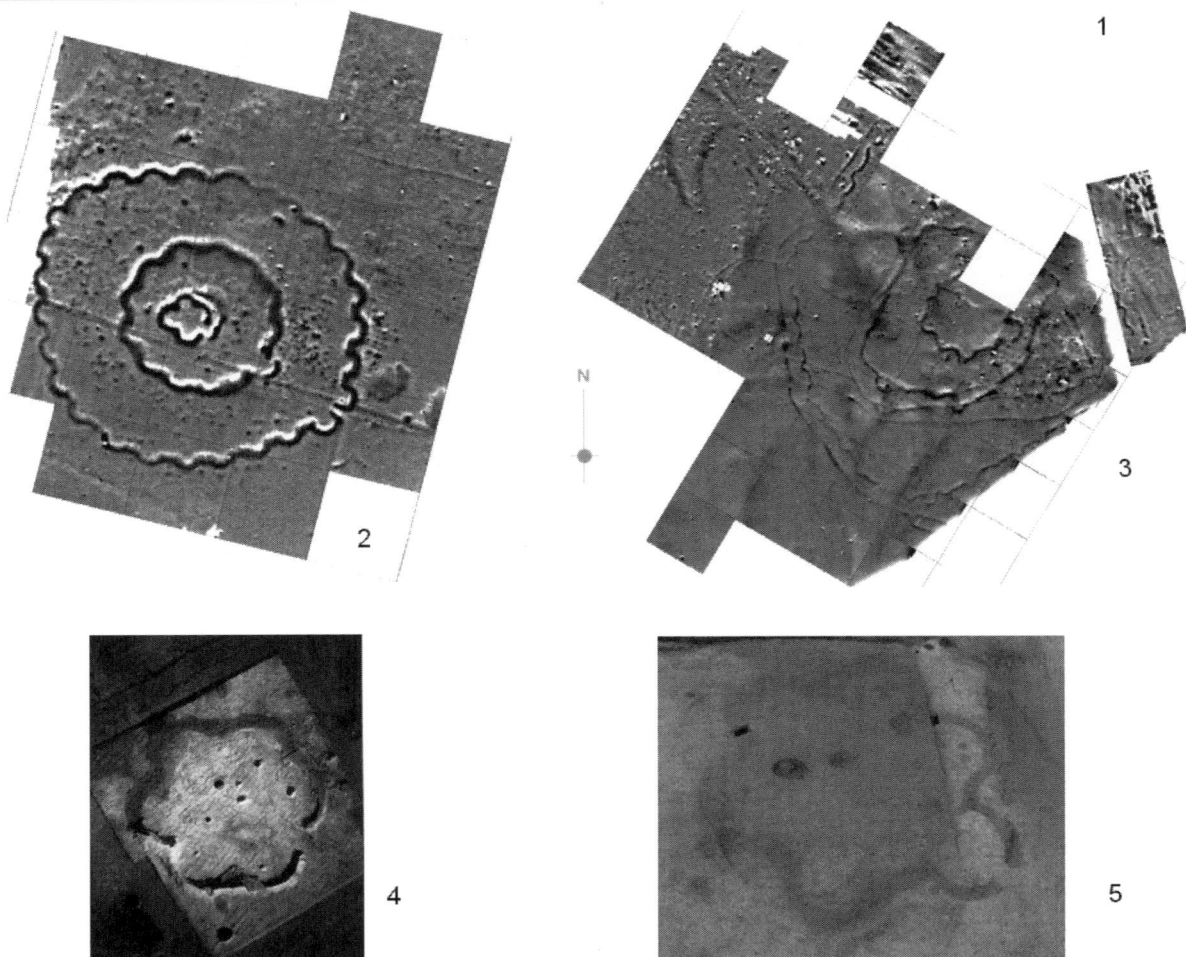

Figure 4: Sequence of enclosures at Perdigões (1). Geophysical image of Xancra by Helmut Becker (2). Geophysical image of Moreiros 2 by Helmut Becker (3). Aerial photograph of Santa Vitória (Miguel Lago) (4). Aerial photograph of Outeiro Alto 2 (Paulo Marques) (5).

Frias or Moreiros 2). The regularities of the first are far from random. Outeiro Alto 2 and Santa Vitória (inner ditch), share the same general plan and size, with six lobes and gates respectively aligned on the winter and summer solstice. Xancra has a numeric sequence of lobes (4, 12, 27) that is quite close to solar calendar numbers, or lunar calendar number if the entrances are taken into account (Valera and Becker, 2011 and in press).

No precise functional interpretation can be read into this design. There is no gain in defensive strategy and yet there is a considerable amount of work in the construction of these wavy ditches when compared to straight ones. Rather than protect and simply enclose, the reasons for these designs must lie elsewhere, in other dimensions of architecture. They seem to relate to earlier projects that respect the circle and principles of concentricity common to the ditched enclosure architecture of the period, but they appear to introduce a sort of movement suggested through wavy lines, reinforcing the bond between the building and living nature characterized by meandering paths. In other words, these architectural designs seem to be impregnated with ideology and to respond to certain cosmogonies:

It is not the right angle that attracts me neither the straight line, hard, inflexible, created by man. What attracts me is the free and sensual curved line, the curve that I found in the mountains of my country, in the sinuous path of its rivers, in the waves of the sea, in a woman's body. From curves is made the Universe – the infinite curved universe of Einstein (Oscar Niemeyer – my translation).

In fact, if the architectural design incorporates meanings, perspectives of the world and of its perceived organization, we should expect that many of the "world's shapes" and certain dimensions of the human way of experience may be represented in these enclosures. The sinuous ditches have been stressed as an important element in the construction and experience of the monumentalized Neolithic landscape (as suggested, for instance, for the connection between Durrington Walls and Stonehenge). In Portugal, the wavy line is also present in another dimension of the human symbolic behaviour, namely the rock and megalithic art or in pottery decoration. Are there bridges between these deferent dimensions of human representation that allow us to treat them in an integrated way?

Meaning is a difficult thing to deal with in Prehistory, but it becomes harder when, through our approach, we separate what is a transversal expression of a certain social environment and cosmogonical perception. Ideas, beliefs, perspectives of reality, meanings that conform and motivate action, can be expressed in quite diversified ways and in different dimensions of the social life and of the human achievements. The designs of the architectural elements of ditched enclosures are, in this respect, a written text in the landscape. But the encoded meaning is also expressed by the contextual specifics of those sites (what they enclose), their landscape relationships and by the historical dynamics that they reveal.

Dynamics of growth: a new scale for Portuguese (an Iberian) prehistoric sites

One of the main facets of ditched enclosures is that some of them grew to become large sites enclosing several hundred hectares and with almost two thousand years of occupation, while others stay quite small and existed for short periods of time.

The approach to size and growth dynamics of ditched enclosures, however, deals with two general problems. Firstly there are few sites where we have an image of the general plan and secondly for those that have such an image and have several ditches, we have little information about their chronological sequences.

At the moment, and for all 34 ditched enclosures recorded in Portugal, there are available plans that allow an estimation of the areas of Xancra, Monte do Olival 1, Perdigões, Moreiros 2, Luz 20 (through geophysical prospection – Figures 3 and 4) and Santa Vitória and Outeiro Alto 2 (through archaeological excavation – Figure 4). For the rest we only have a general idea of their sizes by the distribution surface materials or by partial and restricted archaeological surveys.

Figure 5 examines the known areas of those ditched enclosures with total or almost total plans (all from Alentejo), associated to the available absolute or relative chronologies. The majority of enclosures (59%) are small areas, corresponding to less than one ha. We can observe that Outeiro Alto 2 and the inner enclosures of Monte do Olival 1, Xancra and Santa Vitória are extraordinary small (and all present a similar plan), with areas that oscillate between 0,02 and 0,06ha. The only three enclosures in this corpus that can be assigned to the Late Neolithic (Perdigões B and Moreiros A and B) are included in this group of less than a hectare, but they are not the smallest. This seems to suggest that the Late Neolithic enclosures were relatively small, but also reveals that small enclosures were still present in the first half of the 3rd millennium. In fact, only the third enclosure of Xancra (which according to the homogeneity of the general plan of the site can be considered contemporaneous with the inner smaller ones) and the larger enclosures of Moreiros 2 and Perdigões have more than 1ha. There is a cluster between 1 and 2ha (Xancra C; Moreiros 2 C and Ca; Perdigões D), another between 2 and 5ha (Moreiros 2 D and E; Perdigões E and F) and a third over 13ha, corresponding to Perdigões H. Therefore, only at two sites do we have enclosures that have areas larger than 2ha, but the larger enclosure circuit at Perdigões reaches more than 16ha and through surface traces and rapid surveys we know that Alcalar and especially Porto Torrão must have been larger, the latter probably reaching areas in excess of 100ha, as is known for some of the South Spanish ditched enclosures.

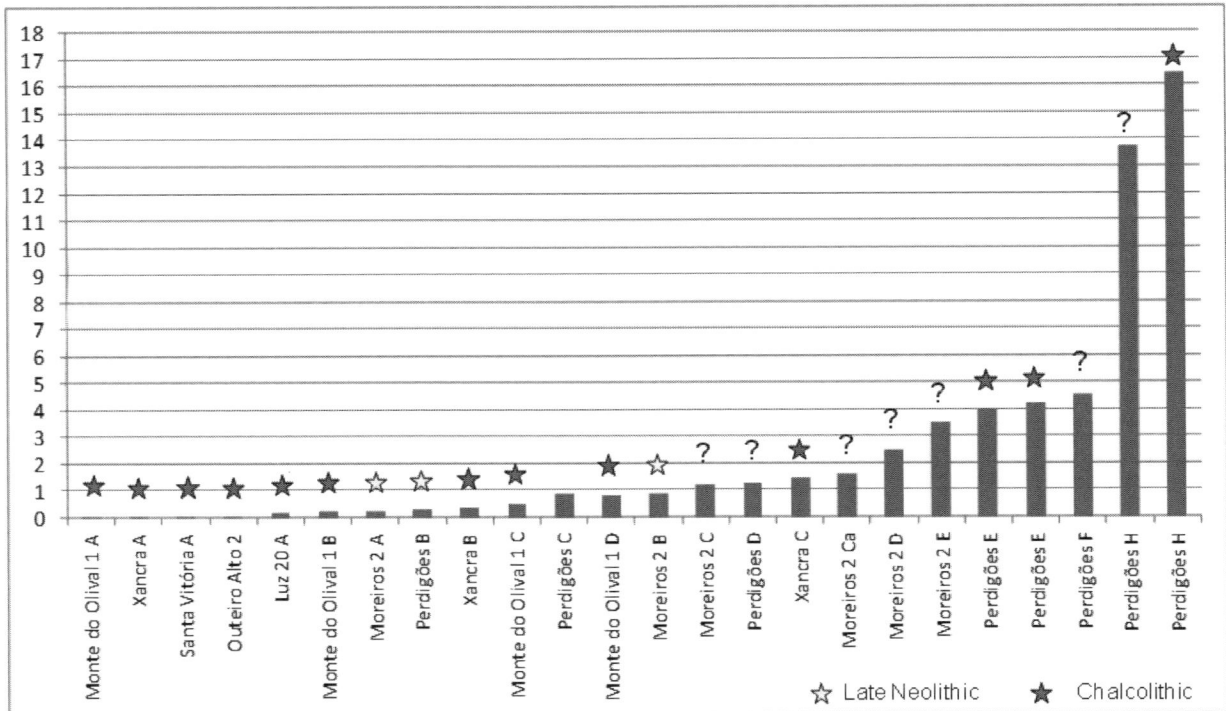

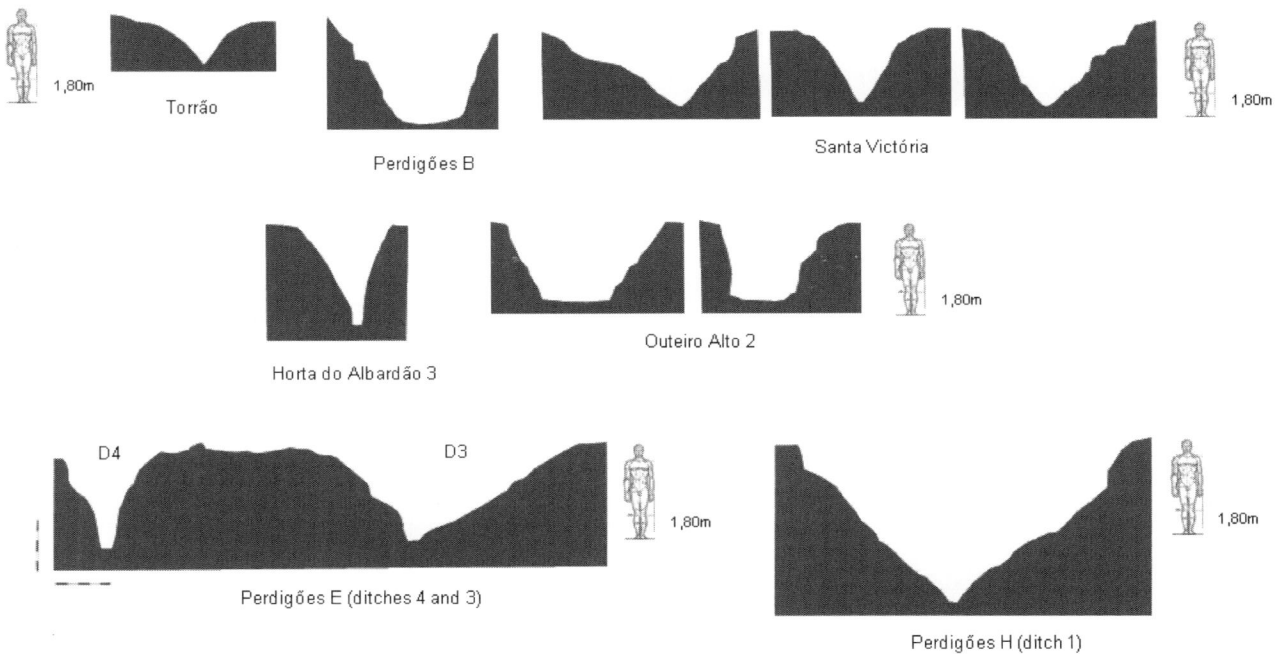

FIGURE 5: THE CALCULATED AREAS FOR SOME PORTUGUESE DITCHED ENCLOSURES (ABOVE);
DITCH SECTIONS OF SOME PORTUGUESE ENCLOSURES (BELOW).

From the available data it appears that during the 3rd millennium BC some ditched sites grew larger, with the construction of new ditches, usually concentric to the earlier ones which, although totally or partially filled, would still have been perceptible. The best evidence of this expansion comes, again, from Perdigões, where at least 11 roughly concentric ditches define 9 enclosures (Figure 4).

As we have already seen, the inner enclosures of Perdigões A and B are characterized by a possible palisade and ditch (ditch 6) that have been dated to the Late Neolithic from the second half of the 4th millennium BC (Figure 1). In the central area of the site, a double ditched enclosure (Perdigões E) is defined by ditches 3 and 4. Ditch 3 has dates from the first half of the 3rd millennium BC for the lower half of the fill and a date from middle 3rd millennium

BC for the upper half. Ditch 4, dug just two and half meters inside ditch 3, was dated from top to bottom to the middle 3rd millennium (an older date – Beta 285099 – from the top deposits is from old bone), which suggest that it was built when ditch 3 was already half full. This is consistent with a significant change in the filling process in the middle fills (Valera, 2008 B) and with the faunal taphonomic evidence (Costa, 2011). Finally, the larger double ditched enclosure (Perdigões H) is defined by ditches 1 and 2. Only ditch 1 was surveyed, but the results of the dating programs (one by radiocarbon made by Málaga University and another by optical stimulated luminescence made by the Portuguese Nuclear Technological Institute) are not yet published. Nevertheless, the filling materials of the bottom date to the Chalcolithic and the OSL preliminary dating suggests that the ditch was still partially open in the first half of the 2nd millennium BC, corresponding already to the Bronze Age. This is consistent with artefacts and other preliminary OSL results for a late stone structure in the centre of the enclosure.

What the actual chronology available for Perdigões suggests is that the site started with a small Late Neolithic enclosure in the centre of the natural amphitheatre formed by the slope (possibly contemporaneous with the cromlech situated to the East, where the slope meets the plane of the Ribeira do Álamo valley) and then grew progressively larger throughout the 3rd millennium and was still partially in use in the Bronze Age. Of course we still don't know the chronologies (absolute or relative) of all the other ditches present at Perdigões, and the fact that two pit graves from the Late Neolithic were detected near ditch 4, associated with the cromlech to the East, makes us exercise caution in estimating the size of the areas occupied during Neolithic times. The general plan, however, suggests expansion during the 3rd millennium BC.

Unfortunately, we do not have enough information about the largest enclosures of South Portugal to start to understand their spatial and architectural developments through time. Porto Torrão seems to have covered more than 100ha and to have had several ditches, with at least one dating from the Late Neolithic and others from the Chalcolithic (Figure 2), but no general plans are available. A similar situation is found at Alcalar (Algarve). But what is now clear is that some ditched enclosure in South Iberia (Perdigões, Porto Torrão and Alcalar in Portugal; Pijotilla, San Blás, Valencina de la Concépcion and Marroquiés Bajos in Spain) reach large dimensions during the 3rd millennium BC. They also enclose a density and complexity of occupation never seen before and that is unusual in the European enclosures of the Neolithic and Chalcolithic. Why did some of these enclosures continue to be occupied for such long periods of time and grow to such sizes and complexity whilst others didn't? Are all ditched enclosures to be interpreted in a similar way? What can internal arrangements tell us?

What is inside? Ritualized social practices of deposition?

Traditionally, these ditches are interpreted in terms of defensive structures (usually associated with banks and palisades) or as drainage structures, associated with domestic settlements (villages). But the evidence does not always support this claim.

There are significant differences noticeable in the size and especially the ditches of these enclosures. These differences are not just in the form of the perimeters (as described above) but also in their deepness and width (Figure 5). Ditches can vary from less than 1m deep and 1.5m wide as at Torrão, to ditches of 1m-2m deep and 2m to 4m wide (Santa Vitória, Outeiro Alto 2, Perdigões ditches 6, 3 and 4), and even to ditches that are more than 3m deep and 6 or 7m wideth (Perdigões ditch 1 and Porto Torrão ditches 1 and 2). Unpublished sites such as Porto Torrão may have even larger ditches. The differences can be remarkable and the available statistics for Perdigões serve to demonstrate this. When the length of the perimeter is combined with the estimated volume of rock removed from the surveyed ditches we have totals of 745m³ for the Late Neolithic ditch 6, 1838m³ and 2416m³ from ditches 4 and 3 and 14232m³ from ditch 1. All ditches date to the Chalcolithic. Enclosures such as Santa Vitória A and Outeiro Alto 2 produce values of 127m³ and 303m³, while Torrão would not have exceeded 100m³. This implies quite different social investments in the building of these structures and other inherent implications. It seems that throughout the 3rd millennium the ditches of some sites were getting larger and deeper, while in other contemporary sites they kept the dimensions smaller and similar to the earliest enclosures. Was there a different functionality expressed by ditch size? Small ditches, like the ones of Torrão, Ponte da Azambuja, Alto do Outeiro, Cortes 1 and others are not real barriers and there is no evidence for the existence of associated banks. On the other hand, ditches upwards of 9m wide and 3 to 6m deep (Perdigões or Porto Torrão) are far too big for the same general function (especially when we consider the effort needed in their construction). In fact, there are ditches too small to be considered defensive, while others are disproportionately large to fulfill this need. One interesting point, though, is that the largest ditches are related to the largest enclosures.

Another problem with the defensive or drainage theories is the fact that the ditches are filled, not with the original weathered bedrock that had used to build an accompanying bank, or by strata clearly related to water circulation and accumulation, but mostly with anthropogenic layers. At Perdigões, for example, the lower levels of the ditches reveled structured deposits of stones usually associated with large amounts of pottery and faunal remains. Only in some of the upper layers do we find evidence of fills resulting either from natural processes or unstructured human origin. In some cases, again, like Perdigões, or Santa Vitória or Porto Torrão there is evidence for pits, hearths or stone structures within the ditch fills (Figure

6). Other sites (e.g. Alcalar) have important deposits of articulated animal remains or human bone (such as at Porto Torrão and Perdigões E). Nothing inside the ditch fills suggests the existence of deposits derived from an associated bank: there is no evidence for the bedrock that was extracted during their initial construction. Some ditches seem to suggest rapid filling processes related to human activity, while others have phases of slow silting. At Perdigões ditch 3, the faunal remains reveal that the silting process was slow enough to enable soil formation (Costa, 2011). Basically, ditches of various sizes seem to have been constructed, the resulting excavated bedrock seems to have vanished and the ditches subsequently filled over time but mainly through human action.

The erosion theory, then, is far from satisfactory and it cannot explain the disappearance of tons of bedrock and, of course, for everything else that was inside these enclosures. Neither does topography since at sites like Perdigões, Porto Torrão, Paraíso, Xancra, Monte do Olival 1, sitting in natural hollows, the erosion would have been towards the inside, and the inside would have been protected.

The majority of excavated and published sites enclose only negative features. At Santa Vitória, Outeiro Alto 2, Alto do Outeiro, Ponte da Azambuja, Horta do Albardão 3 only pits or ditches survive. In the large enclosures, such as Perdigões or Alcalar, small walls, possibly of huts, made

1

3

2

4

Figure 6: Section of Ditch 6 at Perdigões (1). Stone structure in the bottom of Ditch 6 at Perdigões (2). Section of Ditch 3 at Perdigões (3). Structured deposit of stones, pottery and faunal remains in Ditch 3 at Perdigões (4).

of stone or clay were recorded, suggesting that during the Chalcolithic these large sites could have enclosed standing structures. Evidence such as this is scarce, however, and in Perdigões they were certainly affected by deep ploughing. They are exceptions to the general rule that a significant number of ditched enclosures (contrary to what can be observed in walled enclosures or in open sites) enclosed no standing structures.

The traditional argument used to explain this observation is, as said above, erosion but this has been challenged in recent years (Márquez Romero, 2003; Márquez Romero and Jiménez, 2008) in an Iberian context, where it has been argued that the structure of deposition inside the pits and ditches and the total absence of evidence for significant erosion either inside or outside the enclosures makes this theory unviable. Instead they claim that these sites should be integrated into the wider European tradition of placing structured deposits in negative contexts.

Indeed, inside the smaller South Portugal Late Neolithic and Chalcolithic ditched enclosures there are only negative features (pits and graves). But it is also important to notice that during the Chalcolithic (in the middle/3rd quarter of the 3rd millennium BC according to the dated contexts of the central sector at Perdigões) there is internal evidence for a positive stone structure suggesting that during the later phases of the sites that attain large proportions the conditions of use may have been different from those of the earlier moments. It is also in these larger enclosures, and especially during the 3rd millennium BC, that funerary practices seem to gain particular importance.

Enclosures and funerary practices

A specific connection between some ditched enclosures and funerary contexts has been recently been noted (Valera, in press; Valera and Godinho, 2009; 2010). The relationship can be seen in two ways: in the dialog that enclosures establish with megalithic landscapes and in the incorporation of funerary contexts and practices inside the enclosures. This is especially evident in the large enclosures of South Portugal, such as Perdigões, Alcalar and Porto Torrão, and in the large enclosures of South Spain (Pijotilla, San Bás, Valencina or Marroquiés).

Alcalar (Móran and Parrerira, 2009) is famous for its areas of clustered megalithic cemeteries, with orthostatic dolmens, hypogea and tholos monuments from the Late Neolithic and Chalcolithic. These cemeteries surround the Chalcolithic enclosures (Late Neolithic ditches have not yet been recorded at the site, but they are to be expected) and each have been considered as the necropolis of a "macro village". The excavated areas inside the enclosures and of their negative structures are, however, quite restricted and it would be dangerous to produce a definitive model based on such limited data. Nevertheless, a pit grave was recorded in the surveyed area, suggesting that funerary practices can have an important internal expression, just like in the other large South Iberian enclosures.

A similar connection with surrounding clusters of Chalcolithic hypogea and tholoi can be seen at Porto Torrão (Valera, 2010 B; Valera et al., in press c), where the known monuments do not reach the scale of Alcalar, but they are much more numerous and seem to concentrate in larger areas (Figure 7). But, even with a large number of surrounding graves, funerary contexts are also well represented inside the enclosures, with pit graves (Nuno Neto, personal information) and burial deposits within the ditches (Filipa Rodrigues, personal information) located in the albeit relatively restricted areas excavated in advance of development.

Again, it is in the Perdigões enclosure that these connections are more evident due to the fact that the surrounding megalithic monuments have been the focus of research since the mid 20thC and, since 1998, the site has been the focus of a permanent research program.

Perdigões, as we have seen, stands in an amphitheater open to the East, facing towards the valley of Ribeira do Álamo, where more than a hundred megalithic dolmens are known. Very few funerary monuments are located 'behind' the enclosure or outside of the corridor of visibityt established between the site and the valley. Considering the topography, location, the design of the enclosures, the astronomic orientation of the entrances, the presence of a cromlech and the specific viewshed, we can argue that Perdigões is clearly part of a "megalithic landscape", intended as a cosmological organization of space where funerary practices played an important role. The Perdigões enclosures simply cannot be understood outside that meaningful landscape.

At the enclosure itself, however, the funerary practices comprise a relevant and diversified activity throughout the lifetime of the site. From the Late Neolithic there are pit graves with primary deposits. During the Chalcolithic scattered human bones were deposited in the ditches, a necropolis of tholos monuments with secondary deposits was constructed and framed within a semi circular area formed by the outside ditches (further monuments have also been identified by geophysical survey, between this necropolis and the cromlech) and deposits of cremated remains were made in pits or in open areas (Valera et al., 2000 and 2007; Valera and Godinho, 2009; Valera and Silva, 2010). Archaeometric studies (Dias et al, 2008) suggest that the tholoi might have received secondary depositions of human remains provenance from the surrounding territory. In fact, the dimension and diversity of funerary practices at Perdigões, associated with the highlighted characteristics regarding location and architecture, suggest that the site was a space of social aggregation for ritualized practices during a significant period of time, and that sepulchro-ritual activities comprised some of the main activities taking place, participating in the construction of the meaning of the place and in the role of the place in the construction of the symbolic organization of the local landscape.

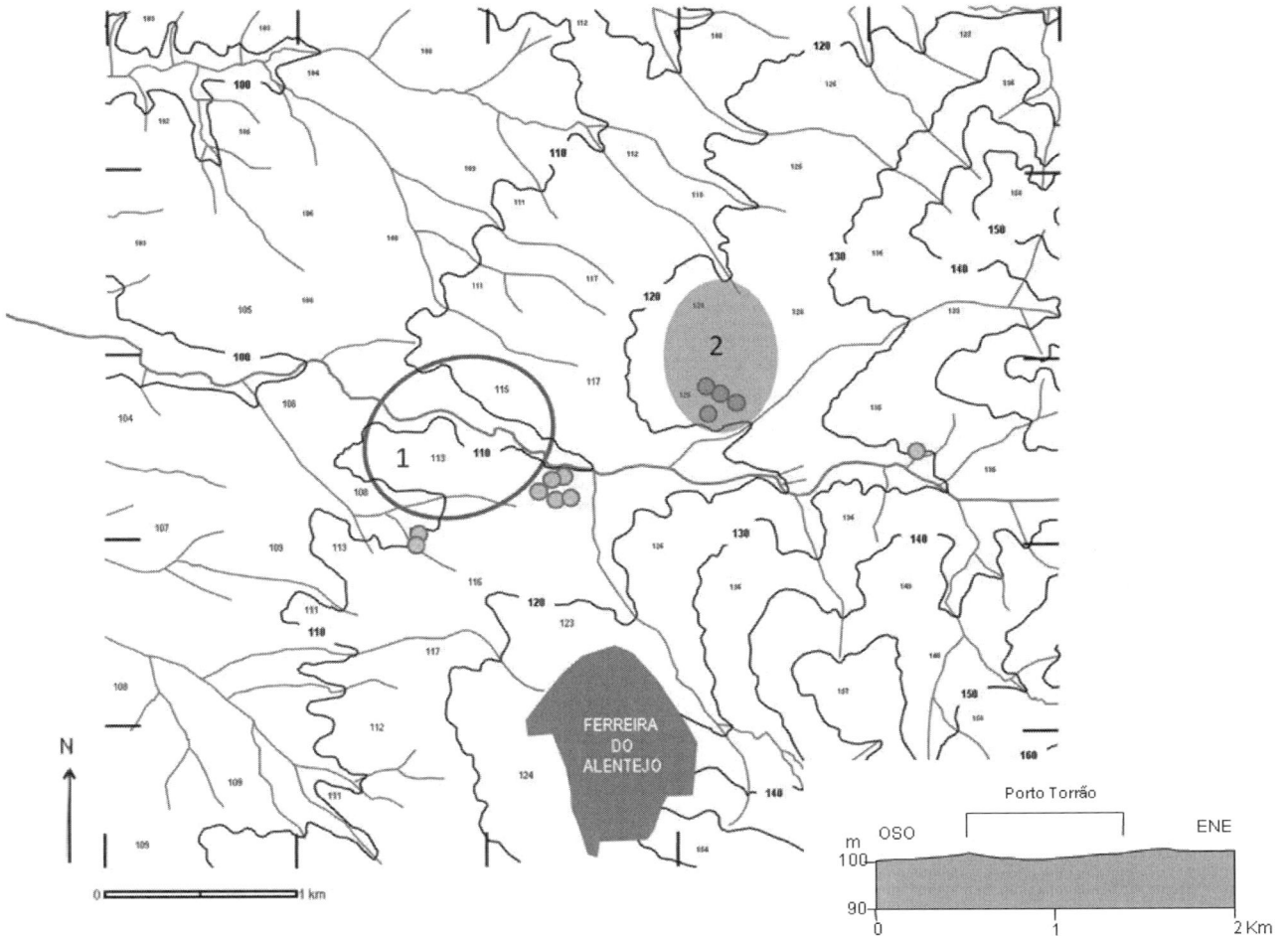

FIGURE 7: PORTO TORRÃO. ESTIMATED AREA OF THE ENCLOSURE (1) AND PERIPHERAL GRAVES (HYPOGEA AND THOLOI), WITH THE CONCENTRATED AREA AT CARRASCAL 2 (2). BOTTOM LEFT, A DITCH USED AS AN ACCESS CORRIDOR TO SEVERAL LATERAL HYPOGEA. BOTTOM RIGHT (LOWER) A DEPOSIT OF CREMATED HUMAN BONES AT CARRASCAL 2.

If this relationship between funerary practices, architecture and landscape is particularly evident in the large enclosures, especially during the 3rd millennium BC, it is not restricted to them. Very few small enclosures have been extensively surveyed, so there is currently insufficient empirical evidence on which to base any analysis of these kind of connections. Nevertheless, some older research interventions and some recent evidence from emergency archaeology are quite suggestive.

At Torrão (Lago and Albergaria, 2001), there is a small ditched enclosure located on the top of a small hill. Just at the SW limit of the ditch there was a cromlech also formed by small menhirs and, 100 meters way in the same direction, a proto-megalithic grave. The grave, the cromlech and the enclosure seem to be conected in the construction of a meaning for this local place.

Outeiro Alto 2 (Valera and Filipe, 2010) presents us with another interesting situation, since no direclyt related funerary contexts are known, but the site links through time two different funerary uses of the same place (Figure 9). It is a single sinuous-ditched enclosure with the entrance orientated to the winter solstice and has been dated to the Chalcolithic It is located on a flat hilltop. On the same hilltop we have two clustered necropolis areas, one dating from the Late Neolithic and other from the Bronze Age. The Late Neolithic area comprises three hypogea and a pit grave surrounding what seems to be a small timber circle (the first to have identified in Iberia). Close by, another group of hypogea and pit graves date from the Bronze Age. No chronological relation exists between these three nuclei (Neolithic graves, Chalcolithic enclosures and Bronze Age graves), but it is most significant that this symbolic use of a hill continued for a period of almost 2000 years. The necropolis and enclosure united to construct and express the continuity of use of a sacred and symbolic space through different cultural periods in which the earlier activity is a condition and attraction to the later, not just in a physical way, but also in a meaningful one. This has already been observed at several other megalithic areas in Portugal).

Just 5km northwest of Outeiro Alto, survey of the hilltop of Cortes (Valera et al. in press a) revealed a very small circular enclosure with a menhir in the centre. Nearby a large number of pits and a hypogeum dating from the Chalcolithic with fragments of a broken menhir were recorded. The emergency excavations were limited, but once more we have a spatial relationship between an enclosure, funerary contexts and evidence for a cromlech (just like at Perdigões and Torrão), suggesting that those different elements participated in the structuring of a specific symbolic and ritualized space.

Although information is wanting for most of the ditched enclosures in South Portugal, there is a picture emerging that suggests that there was a strong connection between these kinds of site, burials and related funerary practices and other ritual constructions (such as menhirs and cromlechs) in the creation of localized highly symbolic places in wider cosmogonic landscapes.

Filling the gap. Perspectives in dispute

Reaching this point it is now time to ask how the Iberian gap in the distribution of ditched enclosures has been filled. In other words, how is the emerging data being interpreted? The answer is that ditched enclosures are the centre of a conjectural dispute, based on different questions and different theoretical approaches.

In Portugal (as in general in Iberia) the traditional view of enclosure architecture (walled enclosures) can be summarised in two words: fortified settlements. Although some debates focussed on problems such as planning and sequences of construction, usually in the context of diffusion versus localism, little attention was paid to the nature of the designs of the enclosures and their relationships with landscape. When ditched enclosures started to appear in the archaeological record, they were naturally read within the same matrix. Historical Culturalism, Functionalism and Historical Materialism are the dominant theoretical frameworks in Iberia and diffusion, resource exploitation, product circulation and the emergence of social inequality are still the major research topics in Recent Prehistory. So, if the "truth" is to be provisionally established by the consensus of the majority of the scholars, in Iberia ditch enclosures would be (provisionally) unquestionably interpreted as domestic fortified settlements. The largest ones would provide evidence for a pristine form of state and of core – periphery dependencies or centres of territorial hierarchical settlement networks controlled by local elites. Perdigões, Porto Torrão and Alcalar would be seen as examples of "macro-villages" or political centres (the Portuguese equivalents of the Spanish Pijotilla, San Blás, Valencina or Marroquiés) and the smaller ditched enclosures (and walled) as sedentary fortified settlements integrated in (and protecting) these territorial units, ruled from one of those centres.

It has already been pointed out that in this theoretical framework those aggregation models are based on redistributive or classicist social relations (Valera, 2009). The motivation is usually the agrarian intensification and demographic growth, but a special role is reserved to control the labour force (based on coercion or persuasion), regarded as crucial to an increase in surplus in technologically primitive societies, and the control of circulation and distribution of critical resources and products considered central to reinforce dependency and increase inequality. The size of the settlements, their monumentality, their location, strategies relating to resource availability and differences in the amount of prestige goods (such as metals or products with a large circulation) are all indicators of the system. These indicators are regarded as revealing ranked or classicist social organization and the larger sites (the so called "macro-villages") are interpreted as political and economic centres that rule large territories protected by smaller fortified settlements and supported

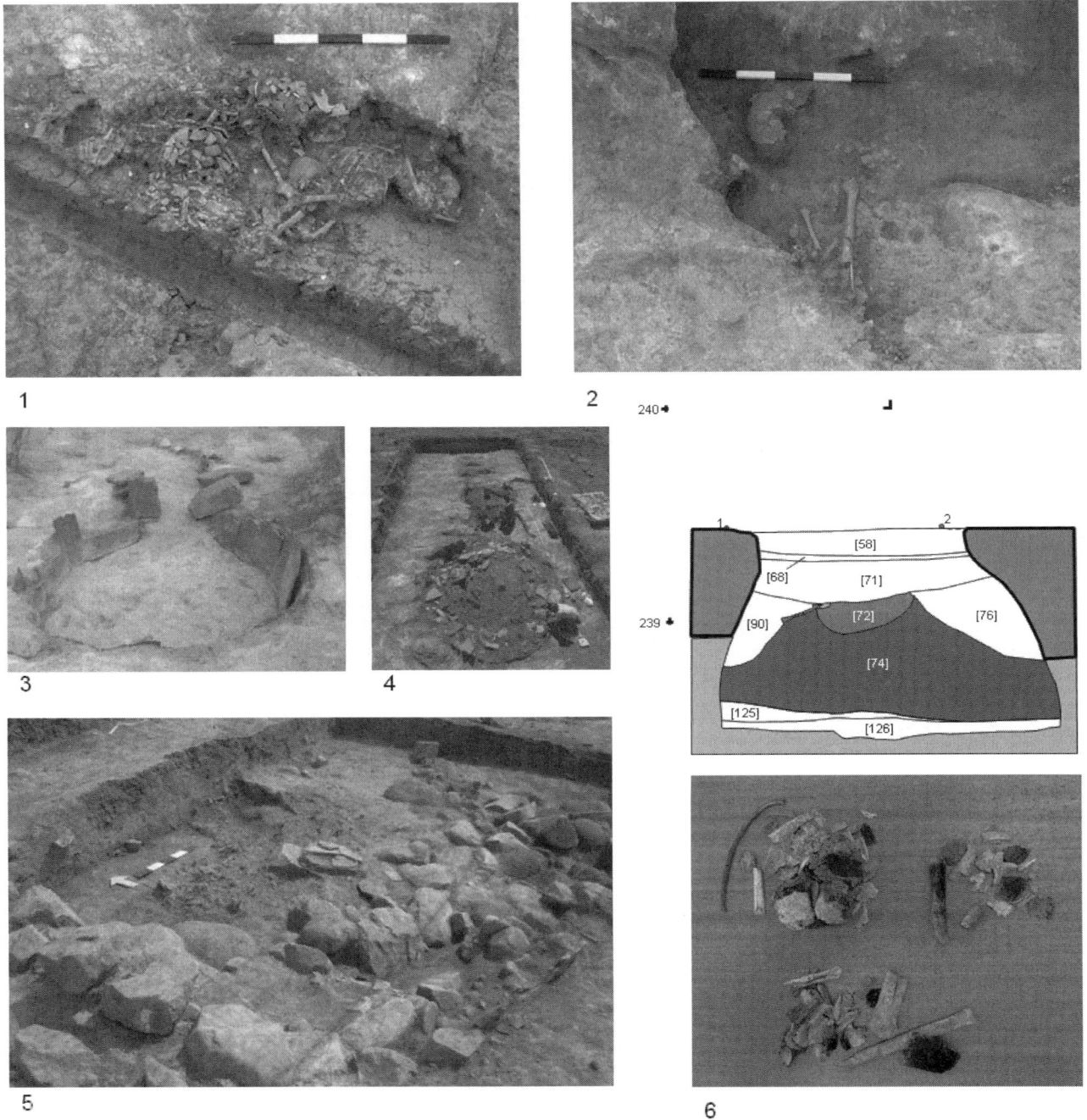

FIGURE 8: PERDIGÕES ENCLOSURE. LATE NEOLITHIC PIT GRAVES (1 AND 2). THOLOI TYPE TOMBS FROM THE EASTERN NECROPOLIS AREA (3 AND 4). STONE STRUCTURE WITH OPEN DEPOSITS OF CREMATED HUMAN REMAINS (5). PIT WITH A CONICAL DEPOSIT OF CREMATED HUMAN REMAINS (6).

by agrarian intensification, control of extraction areas or commercial routes. Monumental architecture, reflecting a large labour mobilization, is considered to express social asymmetry.

In Iberian terms, the standard interpretation outlined above has been criticised over the last decade by Málaga university (Márquez and Jiménez, 2010), suggesting that there are specific and contextual recurrences that might support other interpretations. They advocated a European scale approach focussing on the general phenomenon of structured deposition in pits and ditches. The rarity or absence of archaeological material and structures other than negative features is highlighted as an argument in favour of these practices. Nevertheless, this approach still did not pay sufficient attention to the nature of the architectural designs and topography. The theoretical discourse was concentrated on the function attributed to the negative features.

Considering both approaches, I assume the structural role of ideology (in its ontological and cosmological dimensions) as the main framework in which to understand the emergence and development of the ditched enclosures

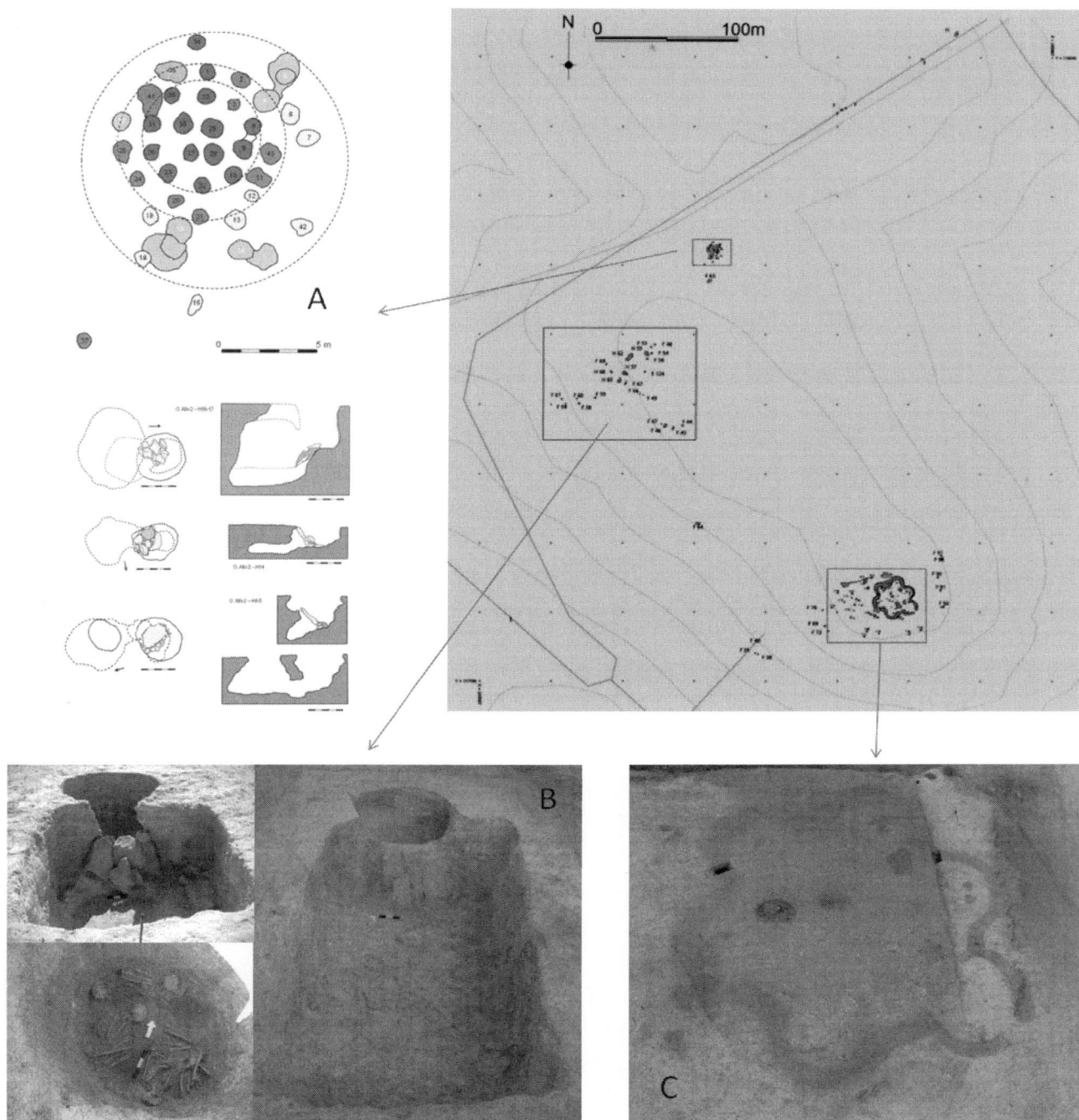

FIGURE 9: OUTEIRO ALTO 2. A SERIES OF LATE NEOLITHIC HYPOGEA SURROUNDING A POSSIBLE TIMBER CIRCLE (A). BRONZE AGE HYPOGEA AND PIT GRAVE (B). CHALCOLITHIC DITCHED ENCLOSURE (C).

of the 4th and 3rd millennia BC. To be clear in my statement, I am arguing that ditched enclosures emerged as an expression of Neolithic cosmogonies and that they also disappeared with them.

In South Portugal, ditched enclosures are very different monuments from walled enclosures. They differ in chronology, in location, in design, in architecture, in enclosed contexts and associated practices and also in the sizes that they can reach.

We must take into consideration several facts.

1. That ditched enclosures appear before walled sites.
2. That they tend to share a more patterned design.
3. That they emerge simultaneously with the floruit of megalithic passage graves (if not with the emergence of megalithism, as Sra. da Alegria seems to suggest).
4. That they seem to share the same general landscape semantics and be related to the same general celestial phenomena.
5. That they have strong spatial relationships with megalithic monuments (funerary or not).

6. That they integrate and diversify funerary practices connected with megalithic monuments and landscapes.

7. That they incorporate, as one of their most specific characteristics, the absence or rarity of lasting positive structures and the proliferation of negative structures associated with ritualized structured deposition.

With these facts in mind, we get a quite different picture from the one that we have for the 3rd millennium walled enclosures. The architectural designs of ditched enclosures are full of cosmogonic meaning. We have an extraordinary diversity of plans, all framed by the general tendency towards circularity and concentricity and by reverence to East. The topographical locations and relations established with landscapes reflect what we may call a megalithic landscape organization and cosmogony, structured on dichotomies associated with the sun's rising and setting in the East and West. In fact, the architecture, the location and the dialogue established with the landscape noted at several ditched enclosures where their plans are known, clearly relates them to the ideology expressed by megalithism in a way that is not visible in the walled enclosures.

The majority of ditched enclosures demonstrate the importance of cosmology to the way prehistoric communities spatially organized themselves and to the way they developed their architecture to emphasise their cosmogonies and to gain control of their world. The architecture and landscape organization seem to present themselves as forms of mapping the cosmos. Through them phenomena and associated stories are communicated, lived and remembered, encrypted in buildings, territories and natural elements. In a way, they highlight the inadequacy of sacred / profane dichotomies traditionally used in the approach to these communities.

In this context, the theory that ditched enclosures were essentially community meeting places for social aggregation, identity management, reproduction of the social status and preservation of cosmological order, where a diversified set of ritualized practices were performed in negative structures, seems more attractive.

The enclosure at Perdigões can serve as a paradigm for this thesis, as it clearly utilises the form of the local landscape in the design of the enclosures and in the way that they embrace funerary practices. The location of a necropolis between the entrances that were orientated towards the solstices and by that way is incorporated into the complex is an important statement. At Perdigões, as in other Iberian large enclosures (Costa Caramé et al., 2010), the notion of a necropolis as a well bounded and specific area of burial during the Chalcolithic is starting to be questioned, and is being replaced by a scene of generalized and diversified funerary practices. This is not coherent with the notion of a "macro-village" with its specific and separate graveyard area.

Funerary activity can hardly be approached in isolation from other social practices because its symbolic and social roles lie behind the simple ritualized disposal of the dead. It is part of a series of relationships with other performed ritualized practices that together participate in the construction of the site over time. As I suggested elsewhere, this is not a resurrection of the ritual/functional or meaningless argument. As Whittle suggested (Whittle, 1998 a and b), the discourse should move away from the need to strictly categorize a place or a practice as ritual or domestic, and aim to establish the degree of rituality and the meaning of the actions that give sense to a place. The ensemble of those actions and meanings would gradually construct the significance of each enclosure.

But this building of meaning over time also raises an important question. Why did some enclosures grow to became incredibly large and complex by the end of the 3rd millennium and others did not? Can we assume the same general "function" throughout the life time of those long-lived sites?

These questions are difficult to answer at the present moment, where we still have little information about the dynamics of the large ditched enclosures. But if we dare to answer, even hypothetically, once again we have to turn to Perdigões or to the "several" Perdigões that we can already detach from the conglomerated image.

What is evident is that the symbolic dimension expressed by location, by the orientation of the architectural design, by the relationship with the megalithic landscape, and by the presence of funerary contexts, was there at the very beginning in the Late Neolithic (second half of the 4th millennium BC). During the 3rd millennium the site grew, but seems to have maintained the same general logic, and the later enclosure is also perfectly adapted to the topography of the chosen location, developing a concentric relationship to the older enclosures and maintaining, through the orientation of the entrances and the framing of the necropolis, the existing visual dialog with the megalithic landscape of the valley and with the astronomically significant events related to the rising and setting of the sun. Funerary practices diversified and seem to have spread inside the enclosure, suggesting that the site became a large funerary chamber open to East as was usual in megaliths. What Perdigões seems to tell us is that the site grew, but kept the same general logic, and the small evidences that we have for some stone structures built outside negative structures during the Chalcolithic or the Bronze Age are not enough to question this general hypothesis. In fact, some of the stone structures are themselves clearly related to funerary contexts.

What apparently happens at Perdigões is that in the 3rd millennium BC, specifically in the second half the millennium, the ideological fundamentals behind the site were being emphasised, but mixed with some new elements (such as cremation rites or the manipulation of new transregional symbolic objects). How do we interpret this exuberance that seems to characterize Perdigões in the later centuries of its life?

Once again answering this question is dangerous. The end of these large enclosures throughout Iberia seems to have been abrupt at the end of the Chalcolithic / beginning of the Bronze Age and ditched enclosures cease to be constructed. The general character of the collapse means that it cannot be attributed to localized events yet there is no evidence for a large scale catastrophe. The reasons must lie in changes that were occurring in the deep structure of society: a change in cosmogonies that had been developing at least since the middle of the 3rd millennium BC and that can be seen as the death of the world views of the Neolithic and emergence of new Bronze Age cosmogonies, individuality expressed in death by such devices as orthogonal architecture, new icons and symbolisms, the affirmation of an hierarchic society, and the emergence of the warrior image.

It is suggested here that ditched enclosures were deeply linked to Neolithic cosmologies, that they built them at the same time that they were expressing their world views, and that the disappearance of this architecture is coincident with the fall of those ways of perceiving and experience the world. This change that marks the end of Neolithic ideology also marks, naturally, the end of ditched enclosures architectures. They simply lost their reason to be, and like the cathedrals of late medieval times, the exuberance presented by some enclosures in the late 3rd millennium BC can be read as the "singing of the swan".

References

Almeida, F., Moura, R., Constantino, F. and Tareco, H. (in press). Prospecção geofísica na Angra do Crasto, Aveiro), *Proceedings of the IX Congresso Ibérico de Arqueometria*, Lisboa.

Bernabeu Auban, J., Orozco Köhler, T., Díez Castillo, A., Gomez Punche, M. and Molina Hernández, F. J. 2003. Mas D'Is (Penàguila, Alicante): aldeãs y recintos monumentales del Neolítico Inicial en el valle del Serpis. *Trabajos de Prehistoria*, 60, n.2, 39–59.

Costa, C. 2011. Problemática do enchimento dos Fossos 3 e 4 (Sector I) dos Perdigões (Reguengos de Monsaraz) com base na análise estratigráfica dos restos faunísticos. *Estudos do Quaternário*, 6, Porto, APEQ, 113–124.

Bradley, R. 2003. A life less ordinary: the ritualization of the domestic sphere in Later Prehistoric Europe. *Cambridge Archaeological Journal*, 13:1, 5–23.

Bradley, R. 2005. *Ritual and domestic life in Prehistoric Europe*, London: Routledge.

Calado, M. and Rocha, L. 2007. As primeiras sociedades camponesas no Alentejo Central: a evolução do povoamento. In Cerrillo Cuenca, E. and Aladés Sierra, J-M (eds.), *Los primeros campesinos de La Raya: aportaciones recientes al conocimiento del Neolítico y Calcolítico en Extremadura y Alentejo*, 29–46. Cáceres: Museo.

Costa Camaré, M.E., Díaz–Zorzita, M., García Sanjúan, L. and Wheatley, D. W. 2010. The copper age settlement of Valencina de la Concepción (Seville, Spain): demography, metallurgy and spatial organization. *Trabajos de Prehistoria*, 67 (1), 85–117.

Dias, A. M. M. C. 1996. *Elementos para o estudo da sequência estratigráfica e artefactual do povoado calcolítico de Stª Vitória*, Dissertação de mestrado apresentada à FLUP, Policopiado.

Dias, M.I., Valera, A. C., Lago, M. and Prudêncio, M. I. 2008. Proveniência e tecnologia de produção de cerâmicas nos Perdigões. *Proceddeings of the III Encontro de Arqueologia do SW (Aljustrel, 2006)*, *Vipasca*, Nº 2, 2ª Série.

Edmonds, M. 1993. Interpreting causewayed enclosures in the past and the present. In Tilley, C. (Ed.), *Interpretative Archaeology*, 99–142. Oxford: Berg.

Fernández Gómez, F. and Oliva Alonso, D. 1986. Valencina de la Concepción (Sevilla): excavación de urgencia. *Revista de Arqueologia*, 58, 19–33.

Garcia Gazolaz, J. and Sesma Sesma, J. 2007. Enterramientos en el poblado neolítico de Los Cascajos (Los Arcos). *La tierra te sea leve. Arqueología de la muerte en Navarra*, 52–58.

Grilo, C. 2007. O povoado pré–histórico do Alto do Outeiro, Baleizão, Beja. *Vipasca*, Nº 2, II Série, 95–106.

Hurtado, V. 2008. Los recintos com fosos de la Cuenca Media del Guadiana. *ERA Arqueologia*, 8, 182–197.

Köhler T.O., Bernabeu Aubán, J., Molina Balanguer, L. and Diez Castillo, A. 2008. Los recintos Neolíticos como expresión de poder en el Mediterráneo Peninsular. *ERA Arqueologia,*8, 172–182.

Lago, M. and Albergaria, J. 2001. O Cabeço do Torrão (Elvas): contextos e interpretações prévias de um lugar do Neolítico alentejano. *Era Arqueologia,*4, 39–62.

Lago, M., Duarte, C., Valera, A., Albergaria, J., Almeida, F. and Carvalho, A. 1998. Povoado dos Perdigões (Reguengos de Monsaraz): dados preliminares dos trabalhos arqueológicos realizados em 1997. *Revista Portuguesa de Arqueologia*, 1:1, 45–152.

Márquez, J. E. 2003. Recintos Prehistóricos Atrincherados (RPA) en Andalucía (España): una propuesta interpretativa. In Jorge, S.O. (Ed.) *Recintos murados da Pré–história recente*, 269–284. Porto: Universidade do Porto.

Márquez, J. E. and Jiménez, V. 2008. Claves para el estudio de los Recintos de Fosos del sur de la Península Ibérica, *ERA–Arqueologia*, 8, 158–171.

Márquez, J.E and Jiménez, V. 2010. *Recintos de Fosos. Genealogía y significado de una tradición en la Prehistoria del suroeste de la Península Ibérica (IV–III milenios a.C.)*. Malaga: Servicios de publicaciones de la Universidad de Málaga.

Márquez, J.E., Valera, A.C., Becker, H., Jiménez, V. and Suárez, J. 2011. El Complexo Arqueológico dos Perdigões (Reguengos de Monsaraz, Portugal). Prospecciones Geofísicas – Campaña 2008–09. *Trabajos de Prehistoria*, Madrid.

Mataloto, R. and Boaventura, R. 2009. Entre vivos e mortos nos IV e III milénios a.n.e. do Sul de Portugal: um balanço relativo do povoamento com base em datações pelo radiocarbono. *Revista Portuguesa de Arqueologia*, 12:2, 31–77.

Morán, E. 2008. Organização espacial do Povoado Calcolítico de Alcalar (Algarve, Portugal). *ERA Arqueologia*, 8, 138–147.

Morán, E. and Parreira, R. 2009. La exhibición del poder en el megalitismo del suroeste: tres casos de studio en el extreme Sur de Portugal. *Cuadernos de Prehistoria y Arqueología de la Universidad de Granada*, 19, 139–162.

Nocete, F. 2001. *Tercer milenio antes de nuestra era. Relaciones y contradiciones centro/periferia en el Valle de! Guadalquivir*. Barcelona: Ediciones Bellaterra.

Santos, F., Soares, A., Rodrigues, Z., Queiroz Valério, P. and Araujo, M. F. 2009. Horta do Albardão 3: um sítio da Pré–História Recente, com fossos e fossas, na encosta do Albardão (S. Manços, Évora). *Revista Portguesa de Arqueologia*, 12:1, 53–71.

Soares, A. M. 1996. Datação absoluta da estrutura neolítica junto à Igreja Velha de S. Jorge (Vila Verde de Ficalho, Serpa). *Vipasca*, 5, 51–58.

Sousa, A. C. 2010. *O Penedo do Lexim e a sequência do Neolítico Final e Calcolítico da Península de Lisboa*. Dissertação de doutoramento, FLUL, policopiado.

Valera, A. C. 2008a. Mapeando o Cosmos. Uma abordagem cognitiva aos recintos da Pré–História Recente. *ERA Arqueologia*, 8, 112–127.

Valera, A. C. 2008b. Recinto Calcolítico dos Perdigões: fossos e fossas do Sector I, *Apontamentos de Arqueologia e Património 3*, 19–28. ERA Arqueologia.

Valera, A. C. 2009. Cosmological bonds and settlement aggregation processes during Late Neolithic and Copper Age in South Portugal. In Thurston, T. L. and Salisbury, R. B. (Eds), *Reimagining Regional Analyses: The Archaeology of Spatial and Social Dynamics*, 234–265. Newcastle: Cambridge Scholars Publishing.

Valera, A. C. 2010a. Mapping the Cosmos – A cognitive approach to Iberian prehistoric enclosures. In Valera, A. C. and Evangelista, L. S. (Eds.), 2010, 99 - 108

Valera, A. C. 2010b. Gestão da morte no 3° milénio AC no Porto Torrão (Ferreira do Alentejo): um primeiro contributo para a sua espacialidade. *Apontamentos de Arqueologia e Património*, 5, 57–62. Lisboa, NIA–ERA Arqueologia.

Valera, A. C. (in press a). Late Neolithic and Chalcolithic in South Portugal: aspects of the new agenda. In Kunst, M., Gauβ, R., and Bartelheim, M. (eds.), *Vom Erz zum Kupferartefakt. Metallurgie des 3. Jahrtausends in Zambujal und im Südwesten der Iberischen Halbinsel*, Madrid: Deutsches Archaeologisches Institut.

Valera, A. C. (in press b). Fossos sinuosos na Pré–História Recente do Sul de Portugal: ensaio de análise crítica. *Actas do V Encontro de Arqueologia do SW Peninsular*.

Valera, A. C. (in press C). Ditches, pits and hypogea: new data and new problems in South Portugal Late Neolithic and Chalcolithic funerary practices. Gibaja, J. F., Carvalho, A. F. and Chambom, P. (Eds.) *Funerary practices from the Mesolithic to the Chalcolithic of the Northwest Mediterranean*, British Archaeological Reports.

Valera, A. C. and Becker, H. 2011. Cosmologia e recintos de fossos da Pré–História Recente: resultados da prospecção geofísica em Xancra (Cuba, Beja). *Apontamentos de Arqueologia e Património*, 7, 23–32. Lisboa, NIA–ERA Arqueologia.

Valera, A. C. and Becker, H. (in press). Arqueoastronomia, geofísica e recintos de fossos e recintos de fossos da Pré–História Recente no Sul de Portugal, *Actas do 8° Encontro de Arqueologia do Algarve*, (2010), Silves.

Valera, A. C. and Evangelista, L. S. (Eds.) 2010. *Session WS29: The Idea of Enclosure in Recent Iberian Prehistory, Proceedings of the XV UISPP World Congress (Lisbon, 4–9 September 2006)*. BAR. International Series S2124. Oxford: Hadrian Books.

Valera, A. C. and Filipe, I. 2004. O povoado do Porto Torrão (Ferreira do Alentejo): novos dados e novas problemáticas no contexto da calcolitização do Sudoeste peninsular. *Era Arqueologia*, 6, 28–61.

Valera, A. C. and Filipe, V. 2010. Outeiro Alto 2 (Brinches, Serpa): nota preliminar sobre um espaço funerário e de socialização do Neolítico Final à Idade do Bronze. *Apontamentos de Arqueologia e Património*, 5, 49–56.

Valera, A. C. and Godinho, R. 2009. A gestão da morte nos Perdigões (Reguengos de Monsaraz): novos dados, novos problemas. *Estudos Arqueológicos de Oeiras*, 17, 371–387.

Valera, A. C. and Godinho, R. 2010. Ossos humanos provenientes dos fossos 3 e 4 e gestão da morte nos Perdigões. *Apontamentos de Arqueologia e Património*, 6, 29–40.

Valera, A. C., Lago, M., Duarte, C. and Evangelista, L. S. 2000. Ambientes funerários no complexo arqueológico dos Perdigões: uma análise preliminar no contexto das práticas funerárias calcolíticas no Alentejo. *ERA Aqueologia*, 2, 84–105.

Valera, A. C., Godinho, R., Calvo, E., Moro Berraquero, J., Filipe, V. and Santos, H. (in press a). Um mundo em negativo: fossos, fossas e hipogeus entre o Neolítico Final e a Idade do Bronze na margem esquerda do Guadiana (Brinches, Serpa). *Actas do 4° Colóquio de Arqueologia do Alqueva*, Beja (2010).

Valera, A. C, Márquez, J. E., Becker, H., Jiménez, V. and Suárez, J. (in press b). O Complexo Arqueológico dos Perdigões: nova imagem e novos problemas proporcionados pela prospecção geofísica" *Actas do 8° Encontro de Arqueologia do Algarve*, (2010), Silves.

Valera, A. C., Santos, H., Figueiredo, M. and Granja, R. (in press C). Contextos funerários na periferia do Porto Torrão: Cardim 6 e Carrascal 2. *Actas do 4° Colóquio de Arqueologia do Alqueva*, Beja (2010).

Valera, A. C. and Silva, A. M. 2011. Datações de radiocarbono para os Perdigões (1): contextos com restos humanos nos Sectores I e Q. *Apontamentos de Arqueologia e Património*, 7, 7–14.

Whittle, A. 1988a. Contexts, activities, events – aspects of neolithic and copper age enclosures in central and western Europe. In Burgess, C., Topping, P., Mordant, C. and Maddison, M. (Eds.), *Enclosures and defences in the Neolithic of Western Europe*, 1–19. BAR International Series S403(i). Oxford: British Archaeological Reports.

Whittle, A. 1988b. *Problems in Neolithic Archaeology*. New Studies in Archaeology. Cambridge: Cambridge University Press.

Zafra de la Torre, N., Castro López, M. and Hornos Mata, F. 2003. Sucesion y simultaneidad en un gran asentamiento: la cronologia de la macro–aldea de Marroquiés Bajos, Jaen. C.2500–2000 CAL ANE. *Trabajos de Prehistoria*, 60:2, 79–90.

The Neolithic Enclosures in Transition.
Tradition and Change in the Cosmology of Early Farmers in Central Europe

Jan Turek

Abstract

In this paper I am going to discuss the phenomenon of Neolithic enclosures as symbols of shared identity and their replacement by natural shrines and perhaps by new ideology and cult. The tradition of collective values gradually faded from the mid Fifth Millennium BC However, this dramatic change started at the beginning of the Third Millennium BC. The changes that I am going to discuss in this paper were not induced by any change in subsistence strategy or climatic influences. The Third Millennium changes comprise the development of social relations and transition of cosmology amongst the European Copper Age farming communities. What kind of changes were they? Mainly it was a sudden discontinuity in the long tradition of the construction of ditched and hill top enclosures that dominated the Neolithic Period in central Europe. This phenomenon has its pedigree in the early Neolithic round ditched shrines, so called roundels. Such monuments are traditionally interpreted as features of mainly sacral meaning (Podborský 2001 etc) but some other social functions are also being considered (Květina et al 2009).

Key words: Neolithic/Copper Age enclosures, Hilltop sites, Natural shrines, Beaker cosmology

Enclosures and Continuity

Despite many formal changes it is possible to trace the continuing tradition of ditched monuments during the Proto-Eneolithic period (4500–3800 cal. BC) in the form of so-called causewayed enclosures and in the early Eneolothic (3800–3350 cal. BC) as oval or square ditched enclosures of the TRB Culture (Pleslová-Štiková 1985). hilltops. I suppose that the hilltop ditched enclosures were also constructed at this time and were previously erroneously interpreted as hill-forts or fortified sites. Such an interpretation may be more related to the much later phenomenon of Iron Age and early Medieval forts and *oppidae*. The Eneolithic hilltop enclosures rather appear to continue the tradition of the lowland ditched enclosures. Together with emergence of the Corded Ware phenomenon at the beginning of the Late Eneolithic, roughly between 2900 and 2800 cal. BC, the habit of using hilltops disappeared in most regions of Central Europe. The same goes for the subsequent Bell Beaker period after 2500 cal. BC. Within the archaeological record of both periods funerary sites prevail. The symbolic structure of burial rites was fundamentally emphasized and the cult ceremonies probably transferred to natural shrines the existence of which is very hard to detect archaeologically.

The Purpose of Neolithic/Eneolithic enclosures

The re-examination of the purpose of prehistoric enclosures was carried out by Evžen Neustupný (1995 and 2007) and his argument can be summarised as follows:

Any fortification can serve its defensive purpose only if it is defended. But many prehistoric fortifications are so huge that small prehistoric communities of Central Europe, consisting of several families, could not guard and protect them.

In many instances prehistoric fortifications are situated far from the densely inhabited areas, frequently in places where there is sparse or no contemporaneous settlement around. This is typical for the case of La Tène period oppida.

In some locations "fortifications" are built on high mountains difficult to climb. The effort necessary to access them contrasts with the practical aspects of human life.There are many instances of so-called incomplete fortifications that leave considerable part of the defence line unprotected."

In some cases so-called fortifications are rather problematic because their defences are either too shallow (in the case of ditches) or too low (in the case of ramparts).

The ditches, especially those of the Neolithic and Eneolithic Age, have an unnecessary number of entrances (so-called causewayed camps) that weaken their defensive function.

If there was any military tactic in prehistoric times, in addition to ritual warfare, it was an unexpected attack on villages .... Large fortifications, which could not be defended by small prehistoric communities, provided dubious protection against such attacks.

Neustupný (2007) further states that: "While it is not excluded that so-called fortifications were used to defend people against human enemy from time to time, the arguments to the opposite clearly demonstrate that defence against human enemy could not be their prime purpose".

We have to bear in mind that the prehistoric ritual warfare was never mass slaughter and fighting mostly took place between individuals and/or small groups of people (Turek 2007).

In the following text I am going to interpret the Eneolithic enclosures in the overall context of prehistoric land use as the ritual and sacred human activities often spatially and functionally blended into the cultural landscape. Thus it is impossible to discuss the enclosures and not mention the settlement pattern and burial rites of the respective cultural groups.

The Neolithic ditch monuments

At the end of the Stroked Pottery and Lengyel Culture in Central Europe a new monumental phenomenon occurred, roundels. These circular ditched structures were traditionally interpreted as Neolithic shrines, eventually astronomic observatories with ritual functions. The archaeological evidence for such monuments usually consists of sunken ditches, palisade furrows or individual post holes. The dimensions of these monuments are varied, ranging from sites with rather small diameters of 40 to 60 m (for example Prague-Krč, Turek 2005) up to the gigantic outer ditch of a concentric system of roundels at Bylany (Pavlů - Rulf – Zápotocká 1995) some 250m in diameter (Figure 1). The ditches were usually interrupted on by four opposed entrances and some ditches extend to 2.5m deep. There are no traces of common dwellings or other settlement features within the roundels, just isolated pits and post holes. Vladimír Podborský (2001) has observed an increased number of clay female idol-figurines inside the enclosure at Těšetice-Kyjovice (District Znojmo). Such a specialised depositional context emphasizes the ritual nature of the site. A variety of cult and social rituals and ceremonies may well have been taking place in such sanctuaries. Scattered human remains were also found within the fills of the ditches at Těšetice. This may be evidence for human sacrifices and/or funerary ceremonies. Some roundel ditches were repeatedly cleaned, recut and reconstructed. These episodes may be related to changes of occupation phases within the associated settlement area shifting as a result of the technology of the Neolithic slash and burn agriculture, however this could be only one of many possible explanations.

What did the roundel sanctuary look like when in use? Looking at some earlier reconstructions (e.g. Podborský 1988, 175) we can see that most of Czech archaeologists do not visualize banks of soil along the ditches and it is likely that the removal of the soil quarried from the ditch would have represented an extra investment in labour yet it may have diminished the visual effect of monumentality. If the sites lacked banks, therefore, it would have to have been for an inevitable symbolical reason. The elevation between the bottom of the ditch and top of the bank would have been part of the desired monumentality and some of the roundels may therefore have been visible in the landscape for a long time after their abandonment. All ground features of the roundels were, however, completely wiped out by erosion and centuries of ploughing. The possible original appearance of Central European roundels may be compared to some of the later henge circles in the British Isles, where the elevated parts of the monuments create spectacular features still visible today (e.g. Avebury in Wiltshire). The excavations at roundels in Bohemia and Moravia, however, have produced no evidence for banks but it needs to be said that there is also no evidence against

them. There are visible traces of palisades creating timber enclosure interrupted in the areas of entrances bridging the main ditch enclosure. It may well be possible that these timber palisades perhaps acted as a revetment for the soil bank. The palisades, ditches and "walls" would have created an exceptional feeling for the visitor, perhaps a similar mysterious feeling to that of a labyrinth found at some Neolithic Balkan enclosures (Poljanitsa and Bailly 2000).

Early research on Neolithic roundels assumed that they represented a kind of centralised sanctuary used for ceremonial gatherings of a population drawn from a wider region and that each served more than one community who would also have shared the construction work. More recently, thanks to aerial survey (the aerial survey in Czech archaeology was very limited during the communist period) and thanks to large scale contract-funded excavations, the number of recorded roundels has grown dramatically. Over twenty roundels are currently known from Bohemia as well as many other palisade and ditched circles. This amount is obviously only the tip of the iceberg and while it is clearly possible that one roundel was shared by more than one community it is unlikely to have been shared by the population of a whole region: perhaps each large community area had its own ditched sanctuary.

Bylany (site 4) is currently the most systematically excavated roundel in Bohemia. It consists of three concentric ditches with diameters of 90, 110 and 240-250m. The inner ditches were 2.5 - 3.5m wide and 2.1 - 2.6m deep. They are interrupted on four sides by gates oriented towards NW, SE, NE and SW and the internal edge of the V-sectioned ditch is followed by a palisade. Three teams of researchers published the study on the Bylany roundel with three different interpretation models to explain the social meaning of this monument (Pavlů –Rulf – Zápotocká 1995). The authors agreed on the cult function of the monument, however they disagreed on the social context in which these monuments were created: namely whether they are signs of the stability and prosperity of the Neolithic society or just the opposite and that their creation heralds social decline. I am personally not convinced by any of these explanations. They seem to reflect the Marxist categories of economic basis and cultural/ritual superstructure without considering the coherence and indivisibility of sacred and profane activities. Also the discussion regarding the astronomical orientation of roundels is extensive (Podborský 1988, 268–276; Podborský 2001) but reaches only general conclusions. It is clear that the many of the gates were orientated to the position of Sun, Moon and perhaps some other planets at different times of year. More detailed archaeoastronomic reconstruction of the settings of the roundels is, however, disputable. The commitment of the European Neolithic cosmology towards a solar cult of some kind is presumed (Turek 2005) and the tradition of roundels may well be part of such a religion. The sacred function is usually blended with the profane and with social ceremonies and rituals, thus the spectrum of roles

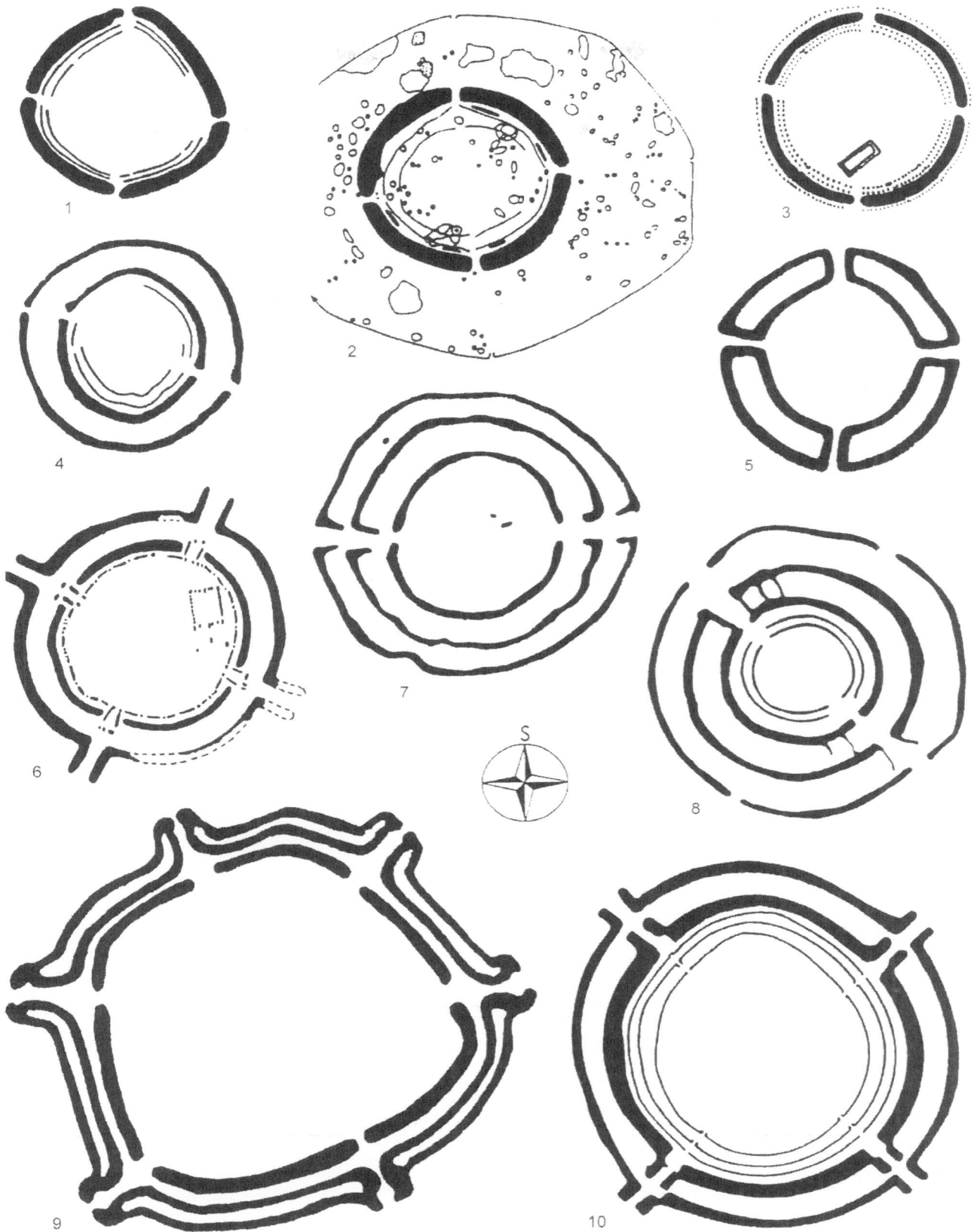

FIGURE 1: PLANS OF DIFFERENT TYPES OF NEOLITHIC ROUNDELS IN CENTRAL EUROPE: 1 - VEDROVICE, 2 -TĚŠETICE, 3 - NITRANSKÝ HRÁDOK, 4 – STRÖGEN, 5 – LOCHENICE, 6 – BUČANY, 7 - HORNSBURG, 8 – OSTERHOFEN, 9 – GOLIANOVO, 10 – SVODÍN (AFTER PODBORSKÝ, 2006, TAB. 18, DIFFERENT SCALES).

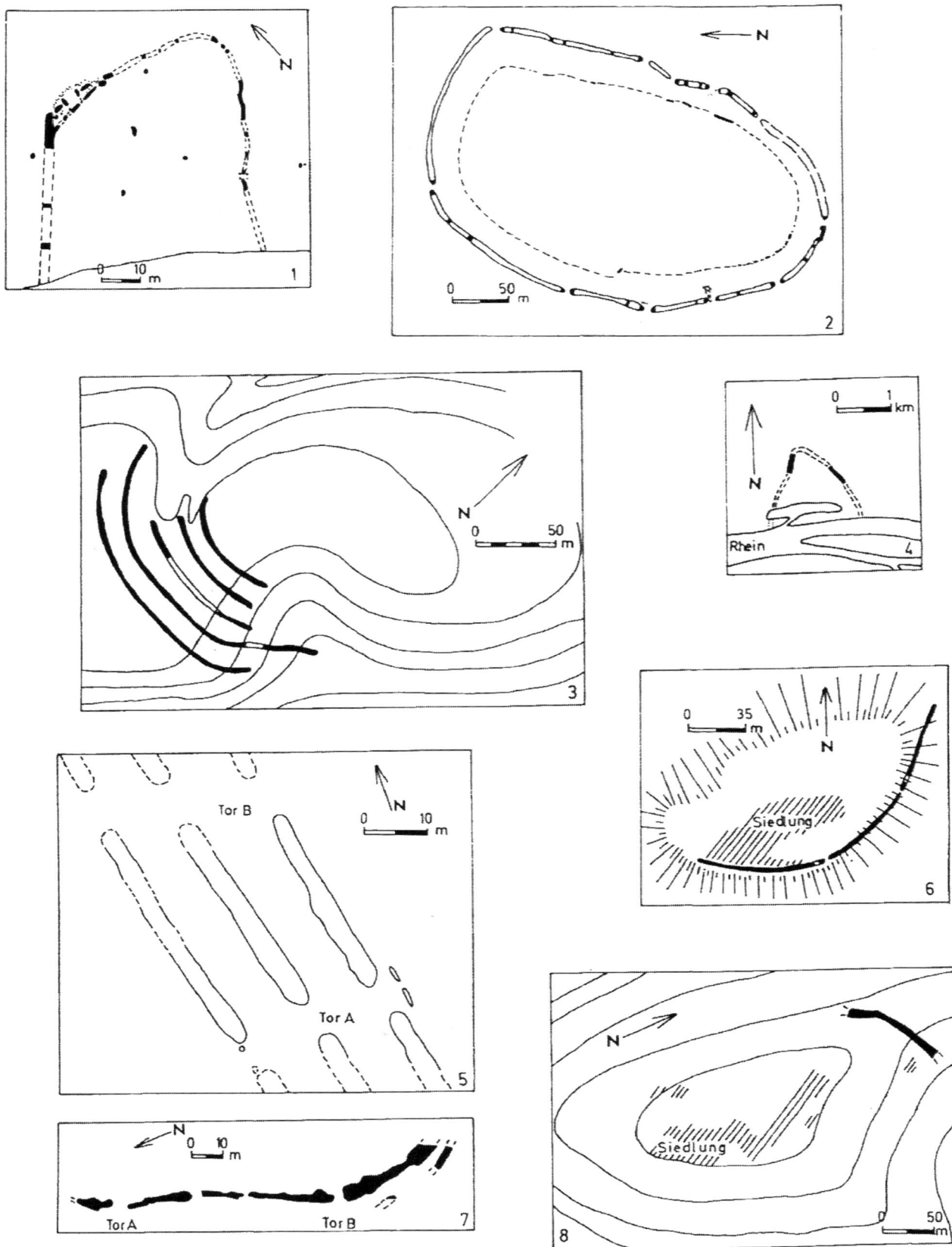

FIGURE 2: PLANS OF SOME MICHELBERG CAUSEWAYED ENCLOSURES IN GERMANY: 1 – MIEL, 2 – MAYEN, 3 – BOITSFORT, 4 – WIESBADEN-SCHIERSTEIN, 5 – HEILBRONN-HETZENBERG, 6 – MICHELSBERG-UNTERGROMBACH, 7 – HEILBRONN-ILSFELD, 8 - MÜNZINGEN (AFTER GOJDA 2004, FIG. 4.1).

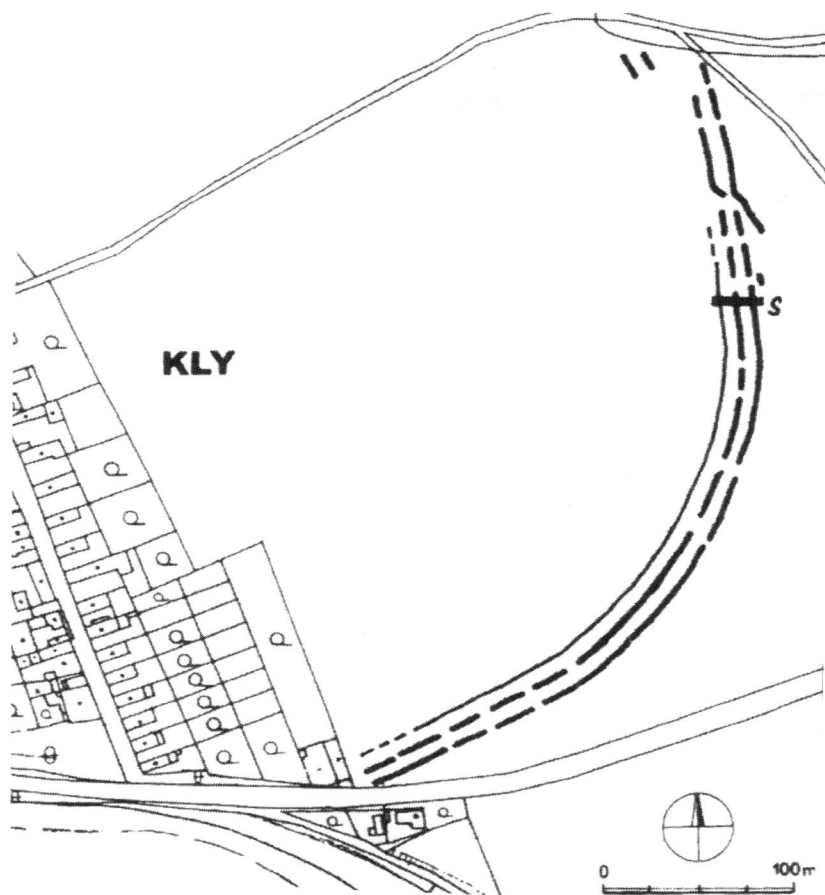

FIGURE 3: PLAN OF THE MICHELSBERG CAUSEWAYED ENCLOSURE IN CENTRAL BOHEMIA (AFTER GOJDA ET AL 2002)

total area, as well as in the number of recorded sunken features such as pits. This may be partly due to the change in the system of agriculture: large communities working on Neolithic fields were no longer needed. The system of ploughing offered people the possibility to create rather smaller communities dispersed throughout the landscape. Neustupný presumes that the typical Eneolithic community consisted of two to six families. One family was envisaged as comprising an average of four members (Neustupný 2001a, 121–122). The use and fortification of hilltops also starts during the early and middle Eneolithic. The hilltop finds of the early (TRB) and middle (Goldberg III – Cham – Řivnáč – Jevišovice B) Eneolithic are best known from hilltop enclosures as they are well visible and have been well known for a considerable time thus attracting archaeological attention. These hilltop sites could not have accommodated an entire community and therefore I believe that they played a predominantly symbolic role and that the majority of population lived on the lower ground.

Causewayed Enclosures and long barrows

A new type of ditched monument called "Causewayed enclosure" occurred in the Proto-Eneolithic period. These generally oval shaped enclosures usually covered vast areas of land. In Bohemia they can be identified with the Michelsberg Culture, such as the enclosures at Kly and Prague Krč (Gojda et al 2002; Turek 2005). Also the similar sites from Germany (Figure 2:2 - Mayen, 2:3 – Boitsfort, 2:5 – Heilbronn-Hetzenberg and 2:7 - Heilbronn–Ilsfeld; Keefer 1993, 152-153 - Heilbronn-Neckargartach and Klingenberg) have a similar cultural affinity. The site at Kly (District Mělník, central Bohemia) was first discovered by aerial survey and later surveyed by geophysics followed by a limited excavation. The enclosure consisted of a triple ditch line regularly interrupted by entrance gaps (Figure 3). The Kly monument is dated by the discovery of a tulip-like beaker found on the bottom of the ditch (Gojda et al 2002). A palisade ditch with four interruptions was uncovered at Prague-Krč (excavation by L. Smejtek in 2000) and this also produced Michelberg pottery. These monuments were certainly not of fortified and it is likely that the Proto-Eneolithic ditched enclosures are formally variable successors of the earlier Neolithic "ditch ideology". Another, much smaller monument of probably Proto-Eneolithic date was recently excavated at Tuchoměřice in central Bohemia (Sankot – Zápotocký 2011, 82-85) (Figure 4). It has a circular ground plan, 18m

that the roundels might have played in Neolithic society may be much wider than purely religious ceremonies and a variety of social functions should be also considered (cf. Květina et al 2009).

Enclosures in the context of changing settlement and social pattern

A wide range of technological, economic and social changes occurred during the Eneolithic Period. The introduction of copper metallurgy, ploughing together with the introduction of team traction initiated some distinctive changes in the social structure of these farming communities. The occurrence of specialised weapons and symbolic representations of warfare is symptomatic of the growing social importance of the male who accumulated power and wealth as a result of their control of the new agricultural technology and copper metallurgy. A more effective system of arable agriculture liberated the labour of many people and opened the opportunity for the beginning of craft specialisation (Neustupný 1995; Turek 2004), as well as the creation of monuments.

Compared to the Neolithic domestic sites the archaeological record of Eneolithic settlements seems to suggest that they were less extensive in terms of their

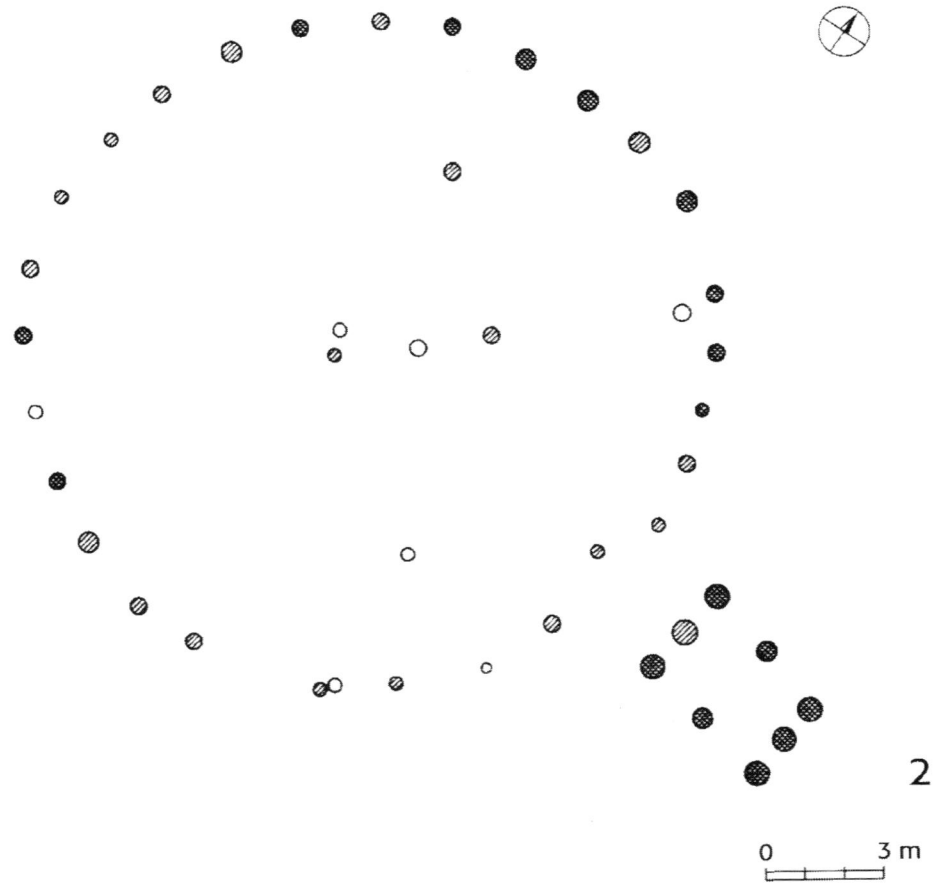

Figure 4: The Jordansmühl (?) round structure with an entrance extension from Tuchoměřice in Central Bohemia (after Sankot – Zápotocký 2010, obr. 14:2).

Figure 5: Reconstruction of the Michelsberg long barrow from Březno, Northwest Bohemia (after Pleinerová 1980).

in diameter, consisting of 29 post holes, with a rectangular entrance(?) structure attached to the eastern side of the ring (Figure 4). The Jordansmühl Culture circular structures perhaps represent a continuation of the early Lengyel structures, as is suggested by recuts and reconstructions of the Svodín roundel in Slovakia (Němejcová-Pavúková 1995, 216). Post-Lengyel roundels are also known from the Carpathian Basin, such as the one at Füzesabony (Kállay 1990), contemporary with the Jordansmühl Culture structure from Tuchoměřice.

It would be difficult to discuss the Proto-Eneolithic enclosures without mentioning the second distinctive type of monument, long barrows. There is lack of Jordansmühl and Michelsberg burials in Bohemia (Turek 2005). It may be due to the missing long mounds that perhaps contained the majority of burials at this time but have been eradicted due to centuries of ploughing. Březno in northwest Bohemia is important for understanding the burial rites and funerary constructions of the Michelsberg Culture. The foundations of two long barrows were uncovered and were the first known features of this kind in Bohemia (Pleinerová 1980). Both long barrows were oriented east - west. The shorter construction was over 24m long and of slightly trapezoid ground plan. The second longer oblong construction survived to 143.5m long and was originally even longer, but one end was impossible to excavate. (Figure 5). The longer structure was 4m wide and the shorter one about 3m. Three Michelsberg burials were found aligned with the main axis of the longer barrow. The radiocarbon date from one of the graves dates the structure to the late Michelsberg Culture.

The Michelsberg graves in Bohemia contain crouched inhumations lying on the right or left side with the head orientated to east or west. The burial assemblages were usually very poor and it is therefore sometimes difficult to classify some burials and link them conclusively to the Michelsberg Culture. Exceptions are graves with typical tulip-like beakers (Figure 6).

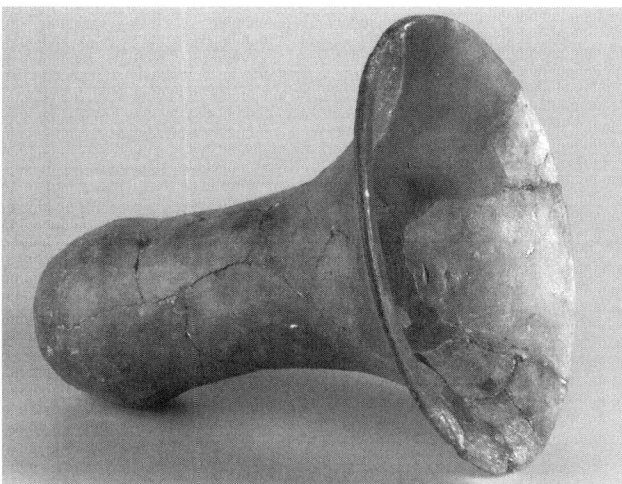

FIGURE 6: MICHELSBERG TULIP-LIKE BEAKER FROM PRAGUE-BUBENEČ (PHOTO: J. VRABEC)

There are some other sites with possible traces of Michelsberg long barrows in Bohemia. One such site is Klučov (District Kolín) or Velké Žernoseky (District Litoměřice, Krištuf 2003) for the subsequent TRB culture. The long barrows were typical of the burial monuments of the Proto-Eneolithic Period in central Europe, have their pedigree in the central European Neolithic Period (Turek 2005, 172–173; Turek 2010), and became the archetype for the later *megalithic circle* in Western Europe (Neustupný 2001b). The theory regarding the origins of long barrows based on their formal similarities with Neolithic long houses has generally been accepted for some time (Childe 1949; Bradley 1998; Turek 2005; 2010).

The TRB and Baden enclosures: the first hilltop enclosures

Two different groups of enclosures occurred during the TRB Period, those in flat open landscapes (Makotřasy) and the hilltop enclosures such as Rmíz, Baba or Cimburk. The use of hilltops had already been known since the late LBK Šárka Type, however, it was in the late Lengyel Period when the hilltop enclosures proliferated and this preference persisted during the Jordansmühl and Michelsberg period. The current state of knowledge suggests that only very basic methods were used to enclose hilltops such as simple palisades but no massive earthworks (Zápotocký 2000). During the subsequent TRB period the hilltop sites not only become more abundant, but also more elaborately enclosed (Zápotocký 2000). The TRB/Boleráz sites like Cimburk (Kutná Hora District, Zápotocký 2000), Baba (Prague 6, Havel 1986) and Rmíz (Laškov, District Prostějov, Šmíd 1995, see here Figure 7) produced evidence for ditches and also in some cases walls enclosing an area usually well-defined by the natural configuration of the terrain.

While these hilltop sites were traditionally considered to have been fortresses or fortified refuge places (Ehrich – Pleslová-Štiková 1968) sites such as the TRB square enclosure at Makotřasy were interpreted as shrines (Pleslová-Štiková 1985). Both types of enclosure might have combined the sacred function of a shrine with the profane functions of places for social gatherings. The re-examination of these sites requires a short summary of the evidence. First I shall describe the square enclosure at Makotřasy (Central Bohemia, Kladno District) as it was excavated by Emilie Plesová-Štiková (1995) in the 1960s and '70s. The square enclosure had an oval shaped predecessor (Figure 8), originally enclosing about 5ha. The later square enclosure covered area of 9ha, each side of the ditch being 300m long. This monument is interpreted as a ritual enclosure and evidence for such an interpretation can be seen in the occurrence of human remains within the ditch, unusual zoomorphic vessels and traces of copper metallurgy. The sacred and profane activities were probably mixed together but the supernatural meaning of copper should also be considered. The possible astronomical orientation of the Makotřasy enclosure was also considered (Pleslová-Štiková 1985).

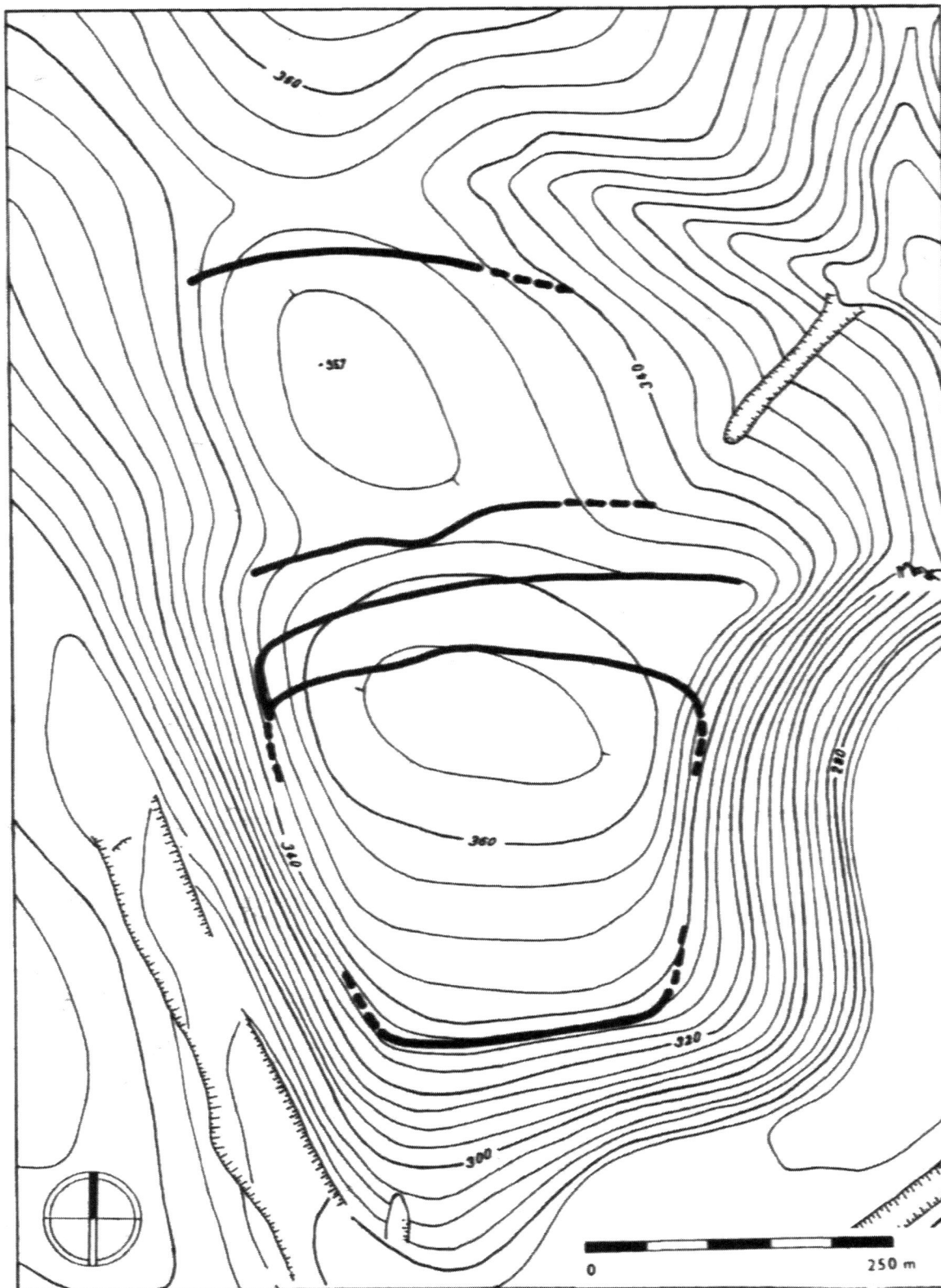

Figure 7: TRB hilltop enclosure at Rmízu near Laškov (after Šmíd 1995).

FIGURE 8: SQUARE (II) AND OVAL (I) DITCH ENCLOSURE ON THE TRB SITE AT MAKOTŘASY IN CENTRAL BOHEMIA
(AFTER PLESLOVÁ-ŠTIKOVÁ 1985).

Another type of the TRB enclosure is represented by the hilltop site at Prague Baba which was excavated prior to its redevelopment in 1974-78. The promontory above the Vltava River valley was enclosed by a 6m wide ditch. Five features were interpreted by J. Havel (1986) as semi sunken huts, three of which had traces of single or double hearths. The excavator calculated the overall interior area of these structures to vary between 5.5 - 16.1m². Artefacts such as quern stones, spindlewhorls and clay loom weights suggest that domestic activities were taking place within the enclosure. A large collection of green tuff axes also suggests the production and/or exchange of axes at the site. Havel also mentioned the presence of shallow ditches 0.60 – 0.70m wide evenly spread across the central flat area and aligned in a north-south direction. There were also some deep flat-bottomed cylindrical features interpreted as possible storage pits. The ceramic finds had decorative motives related to the early Baden Boleraz group.

Another similar site at Cimburk (District Kutná Hora) is represented by the earlier TRB (Baalberge) and later Boleraz pottery finds. The 1989 excavation by M. Zápotocký (2000) uncovered traces of an enclosure with two ditches each 4 - 5m wide and originally c.1.5 - 2m deep. Their fill suggested that the original banks had contained some fairly large stones. Another TRB Baalberge hilltop enclosure is known at Laškov - Rmíz (Prostějov District). The surface survey and limited excavations by M. Šmíd (1995) produced evidence for a complex promontory enclosure system (Figure 7). The enclosure consisted of several lines of walls and ditches and close by was a contemporary barrow cemetery.

A hilltop enclosure of the subsequent Baden Culture is known from Hlinsko (Přerov District). Excavations by J. Pavelčík (2001) uncovered a promontory enclosure with a total area about 2.5ha. The enclosure consisted of a wall, a palisade and a ditch and was associated with two occupation layers dating to the Baden Culture.

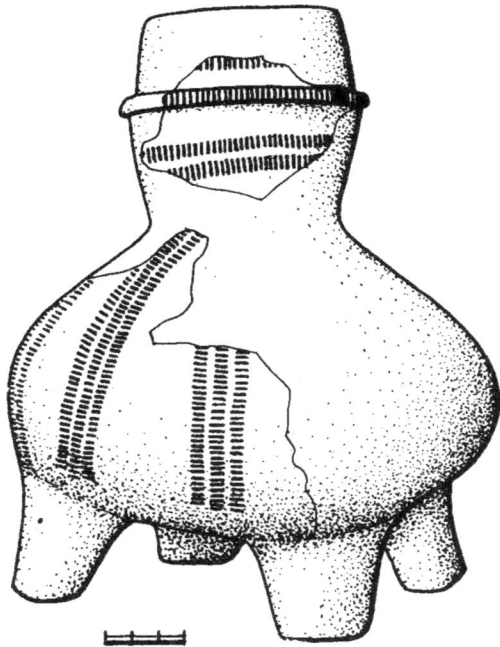

FIGURE 9: THE ZOOMORPHIC VESSEL FROM THE TRB ENCLOSURE AT MAKOTŘASY IN CENTRAL BOHEMIA (AFTER PLESLOVÁ-ŠTIKOVÁ 1985).

FIGURE 10: BOWL OF THE LAIBACHER MOOR TYPE FROM THE HILLTOP ENCLOSURE KLOBOUČEK AT PRAGUE-ZLÍCHOV (AFTER TUREK 1997).

Hilltop enclosures, *ansa cornuta,* Laibacher bowls and invisible funerary practices

After the period of the large multiregional cultural complexes of the TRB and Baden Cultures in the middle Eneolithic (3350 – 2900/2800 BC) came a period of cultural heterogeneity with many local cultures of similar character but of different formal appearance. In Bohemia and Moravia there occurred a range of regionally defined cultures such as the Jevišovice B, the Globular Amphora (GAC) and the Bošáca Culture in Moravia, the Řivnáč Culture and the GAC in central and northwest Bohemia and the Cham Culture in southwest Bohemia and eastern Bavaria. Despite this regional variability there are some common cultural features uniting most of central Europe. These include the hilltop enclosures (such as Homolka in Central Bohemia, Figure 11), archaeologically invisible burial rites, decorated bowls on stands and in some cultures also *ansa cornutae* the jug handles surmounted by representations of bulls' horns. This was a Baden motive that survived in some middle Eneolithic groups, especially in the Řivnáč Culture. Some Řivnáč hilltop sites were enclosed by walls, palisades and ditches. We also have to bear in mind that, especially for the Cham Culture, The majority of finds have been recovered from the hilltop sites. There is only one Cham site in western Bohemia that is not a hilltop enclosure (Město Touškov – Metlička 2000). It is more than obvious that the hilltop sites do not represent the everyday settlements of Eneolithic farmers especially due to their restricted area and sometimes extreme geomorphological location (John 2010). The

farmers therefore certainly would have lived in lower locations but their habitation activity has left few traces. The same pattern existed in the subsequent Corded Ware period in most of the central European regions (Turek 1995).

Artefacts indirectly supporting the ceremonial interpretation of these sites occurred amongst the finds from Řivnáč, Jevišovice B and Cham. Decorated bowls on stands were probably a product of local pottery production but their pattern and design (Figure 10) reaches far beyond Bohemia and Moravia, probably having its source in the Vučedol and Laibacher Moor area(Turek 1997). What function and symbolical role these bowls played remains a mystery but they were decorated with solar motives and it may be well possible that they represent ceremonial artefacts of some kind. Andrew Sherratt (1991, 54–55) presented similar bowls of the Ukrainian Michailovka Culture and Croatian Vučedol Culture to support his theory on the use of alcohol and/or narcotics in prehistoric social/religious ceremonies. In this respect it is worth emphasizing that the majority of these ceremonial bowls come from hilltop enclosures.

The hilltop enclosures are usually conspicuous from different viewpoints in the surrounding landscape. If the hilltops were kept deforested and the landscape below was covered with small settlements then the visibility of hilltop enclosures might underline their interpretation as central places. However, it was not just the visibility but also the mutual visibility between individual hilltop enclosures. This was perhaps an important phenomenon in structuring the landscape and connecting otherwise sparsely populated settlement areas. If we apply this model to the well-known landscape of Prague then we can be certain about visibility between Šárka and Bohnice Zámka and the view from Vyšehrad to Zlíchov-Klobouček and Prague Castle (Turek 2005).

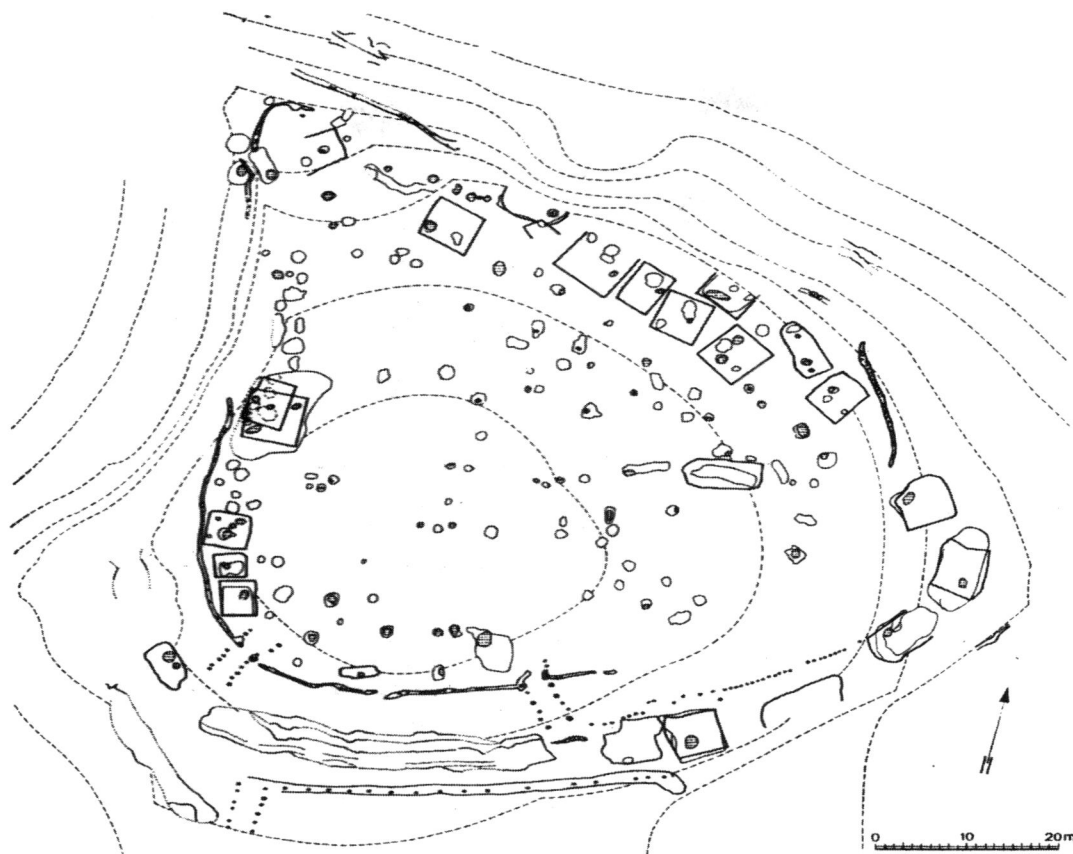

Figure 11: The Řivnáč hilltop enclosure Stehelčeves-Homolka (Central Bohemia) with large "ceremonial" gates in the southern part of the "fortification" (after Ehrich – Pleslová-Štiková 1968).

Evžen Neustupný reconsidered the Eneolithic hilltop sites in central Europe (1995, 199–201; 205–207). He questioned the interpretation of enclosures as strategic/defensive fortifications and introduced his own model of enclosures as symbols of human society and not as defensive artefacts (structures).

The fact that some Eneolithic hilltop enclosures occurred in locations that were later used for early Medieval hill-forts made some archaeologists draw a link between the function of the early historical fortifications and that of prehistoric enclosures however the overall structure and construction details of the Eneolithic enclosures differ from the early Medieval forts and castles (Turek 1997). The frequency and size of gates or gaps in the ditch circuits and palisades of the Eneolithic enclosures would seem to preclude these structures being forts (Figure 11). So what was their function? To answer this question we need to discuss their position in the overall middle Eneolithic settlement pattern. The archaeological record of this period consists mainly of the hilltop sites and funerary evidence is almost invisible. In the terms of the "pulsing" of archaeological cultures (Neustupný 2011) it is therefore no surprise that the subsequent Corded Ware and Bell Beaker Cultures are represented mainly by burials and their settlement activities are almost invisible in the archaeological record.

It is therefore very likely that these hilltop enclosures played a symbolical role similar to the Neolithic roundels, Michelsberg causewayed enclosures or TRB ditched enclosures. These sites might also have been the centres of ritualised production (stone axes etc.) and ceremonial exchange (Turek 2011, 385-398). Perhaps also the absence of funerary evidence may be explained by the use of the hilltop enclosures for archaeologically invisible burial methods such as excarnation or cremation and the surface scattering of ashes (Turek 1997). Generally speaking we can witness the transformation of earlier ditched shrine-enclosures onto hilltops and the use of distinctive natural landmarks as part of the contemporary cosmology and social interaction. Such processes perhaps continued in the natural shrines of the subsequent Corded Ware period.

The new phenomenon coming from east

At the beginning of the third millennium BC a new cultural phenomenon and perhaps a new ideology emerged in the north Black Sea area. A very influential concept of cultural uniformity with individual tombs emphasizing the social status of individuals symbolized by distinctive artefacts was established in the environment of the Yamnaya Culture (ямная культура, see Harrison - Heyd 2007, 193–203). It is likely that this provided the impulse that created the foundations for the early complex societies that dominated most of central, western and northern Europe during the third millennium BC and laid the foundations of the European Bronze Age.

This time sees the occurrence of the Corded Ware and Bell Beaker phenomena and represents a specific period that is in many respects different to the preceding cultural developments. The funerary activity is highly visible in the archaeological record. The individual burials represent age and gender as social categories in a very orthodox way. This is reflected by the symbolic positioning and orientation of the body in a grave as well as by gender specific burial assemblages. It is also the period with invisible settlement evidence. It is likely that the absence of visible traces of settlements was not caused by a different subsistence but more likely by strict and fundamental cultural norms that restricted vertical motion for profane purposes (Neustupný 1997: 2008).

Gender structure of the Copper Age burial customs

In the third millennium BC, some regions of Europe shared common elements of material culture, as well as similar burial rites. Vast areas of central, northern and eastern Europe shared a Corded Ware (CW) Culture (Single Grave) although later the Bell Beaker (BB) phenomenon spread through large parts of central, southern and western Europe. Both of these archaeological phenomena exhibit a degree of uniformity in their material culture as demonstrated by a specific range of symbolic, prestige goods found mainly in funerary contexts. The principles of the CW and BB burial rites arise from the same symbolic system probably reflecting a similar social and economic background for the Late Eneolithic communities. In the following paragraphs we shall review and compare the system of CW and BB burial rites.

Corded Ware cemeteries in Central Europe include primarily single flexed inhumations. Multiple burials are rare, represented mainly by dual "antipode" burials. The number of graves containing more than two persons is very small. CW female burials are usually placed on the left side with the head oriented to the east. For male burials the typical orientation is to the west, with the body placed on the right side. As a result of this practice burials of both sexes face south. This orientation may have been symbolically related to the location of some cemeteries on the landscape. A common location of CW cemeteries is on the edge of terraces or slopes, most of which are oriented to the south-east. BB cemeteries occurred in similar locations but with a preference for north-east slopes (Turek 1996; Turek and Peška 2001). Although the locations of these cemeteries may reflect some ritual commitment to the direction of the sunrise, the sheltered location of nearby habitation sites may also have been important. Possible evidence for a solar cult may be inferred from the shell disc amulets with motifs of double crosses or concentric circles, presumed to be symbols of the solar wheel. The same motif also appears on some of the V-perforated buttons of the subsequent Bell Beaker period. The BB

females were usually buried on their right side with head orientated to the south while males were on their left side, head orientated to the north. Therefore people buried in the Beaker period were facing east.

The position of the arms appears to have been highly symbolic within the Corded Ware burial rite (Turek, 1987; 1990), even though this placement was not specific to gender or age groups nor does it correlate to the amount of grave goods. The positioning of the arms was also important in the BB period, even though the amount of variation decreased (cf. Havel, 1978, Fig. 3). As such, the placement of the upper limbs may well relate to an alternative social category/identity but we have been unable, given our limited knowledge, to establish the meaning behind this.

Male and female burials appear to be accompanied by different "gendered" artefacts. Female burials include necklaces made of perforated animal teeth (wolf, dog, wild cat and fox in Corded Ware graves) as well as imitation teeth made from bone. Necklaces were also made from small perforated circular discs of fresh water shell. Another artefact appearing in female graves is the shell "solar" disc symbol. The pottery assemblage commonly found in female burials consists of ovoid pots and large amphora storage vessels although these also appear in male graves and in the subsequent BB period. Male burial assemblages include weapons symbolic of social power such as battle-axes, mace-heads or axes. In later BB burials, these weapons were replaced by copper daggers and archery equipment. The CW funerary pottery attributed to males is represented by beakers that have been decorated with cord impressions or herring-bone motif. In both periods the funerary ceramics were different from those found in domestic contexts.

Beakers are not exclusively male artefacts even though the majority of them were found in the graves of CW men. Beakers make up 19% of the pottery assemblages found within male graves and only 5% in female graves (Turek, 1987, 38). A similar observation was made by J. Havel (1978, Fig. 5) in the case of BB, where 20% of decorated beakers were associated with men and 11% with women. It is important to note that "gendered" artefacts need not only reflect the social status of the dead because some may also serve as symbolic representations of the relationships between the deceased and other members of the community. That is, some artefacts may represent the mourners and their relationships to the dead. A beaker or copper dagger in a BB female grave, for example, may be a symbolic gift from a father or husband, rather than an artefact used by the deceased in day to day practice. Brodie observed that: "Upon the occasion of burial it might have been the domestic duty of female relatives to provide the deceased with a serving of food and drink, together sometimes with their ceramic container [whereas] male relatives would be expected to provide weapons, ornaments or tools"(Brodie 1997, 300-301).

The CW and BB funerary practices seem to be a symbolic reflection of the division of labour within the family and a reflection of the different social status of men, women and children. The individuality expressed within the context of a single burial is indicative of an individual's association with a particular social category rather than a celebration of someone's special skills or the status achieved during their lifetime. The composition of the CW funeral assemblages seems to be quite uniform as is the number of items included in the grave. Thus, the average number of artefacts in the graves of adult males is 3.7 whereas, in the graves of adult females, it is 3.4 and in children's graves, 2.7 (Turek 1987).

The symbolic expression of male and female status in burial rites probably reflects different social roles for each sex within society. The evidence for the Corded Ware burial rite may also be considered as a reflection of social diversification among members of a society, including children.

Changing the ritual behaviour

Life of prehistoric farmers was structured by a wide range of symbols and rituals. People lived in constant contact with rituals that were not only devoted to cult. Virtually all human activities were more or less ritualized. The social norms created a framework of rules and restrictions that sometimes manifested themselves as some kind of taboo that defined some ritual, as well as, secular activities. After two thousand years of monotheism it is hard for us to find the correct view into prehistoric cults and it is probable that we are unable to interpret even some apparent structures in human behaviour.

New Eneolithic social-economic reality was naturally also reflected in the sphere of symbols and rituals. The early Neolithic female idols disappeared, the roundels were transformed into other forms of ditched enclosures and burial activities were organized in well-defined funerary areas. New farming technologies were also reflected in ritual behaviour. At the end of the TRB and in the Globular Amphora Culture ritual burials of oxen became common sometimes decorated with symbolic solar discs. They are probably ritual sacrifices of animals significant in the ploughing needs of arable agriculture. It does not only underline the ritual meaning of cattle but also its socio-economic importance. The ownership of a herd was perhaps an important part of growing social inequality and individual power. Since the beginning of the Copper Age stone battle axes acted as masculine attributes signifying male social superiority. Relation of this kind of artefact to the male phenomenon is not determined only by its interpretation as weapon but also by the phallic shape of some types of battle-axes (especially in the case of K-type of TRB battle-axe, see Zápotocký 1992, Abb. 2). There are also some clay amulets in shape of miniature battle-axes in the TRB as well as in the Corded Ware Period (Turek 2007, obr. 5).

FIGURE 12: Řivnáč Period jug with *ansa cornutae* from Prague-Bubeneč (photo: J. Vrabec).

Clay drums occurred During the TRB, Bernburg and Globular Amphora Period. They were usually found in male graves and especially in the case of the GAC burials in Bohemia we may presume that they were shamans. Another masculine motif is the bull's head, and especially the horns found in the Baden and mainly in the Řivnáč Culture. The *ansa cornutae* were applied only on jugs that were probably symbolically connected to male symbolism and perhaps drinking rituals (Figure 12). Such symbols occurred also on ceramic idols resembling a stylized quadratic human body with no head and horns (see the finds from Homolka in central Bohemia, Ehrich – Pleslová 1968). Besides the bulls' horns another archetypical motif representing the sun existed in Neolithic/Eneolithic Europe. This was the solar disc depicted as concentric circles or circles with a central cross. This motif is also known on Corded Ware discs and later on some V-perforated buttons of the Bell Beaker Period. In both cases they are mainly female artefacts. Similar signs were also incised on the bases of some jugs and Bell Beakers, but also later in the Bronze Age A1 on Únětice pins and some daggers. It is an important symbol of prehistoric cosmology distributed from England to Hungary. Also some aspects of burial rites (head orientation) and location of Corded Ware and Bell Beaker barrow cemeteries (Turek 1996) suggest that there might have been some ritual commitment towards solar symbolism.

An important part of orthodox Corded Ware social and ritual norms was that people did not appear to have dug pits for any reason other than funerary purposes. Only the dead might have been placed underground but no dwelling floor, storage or rubbish. The absence of any traces of domestic activity is perhaps due to a taboo connected with profane underground features.

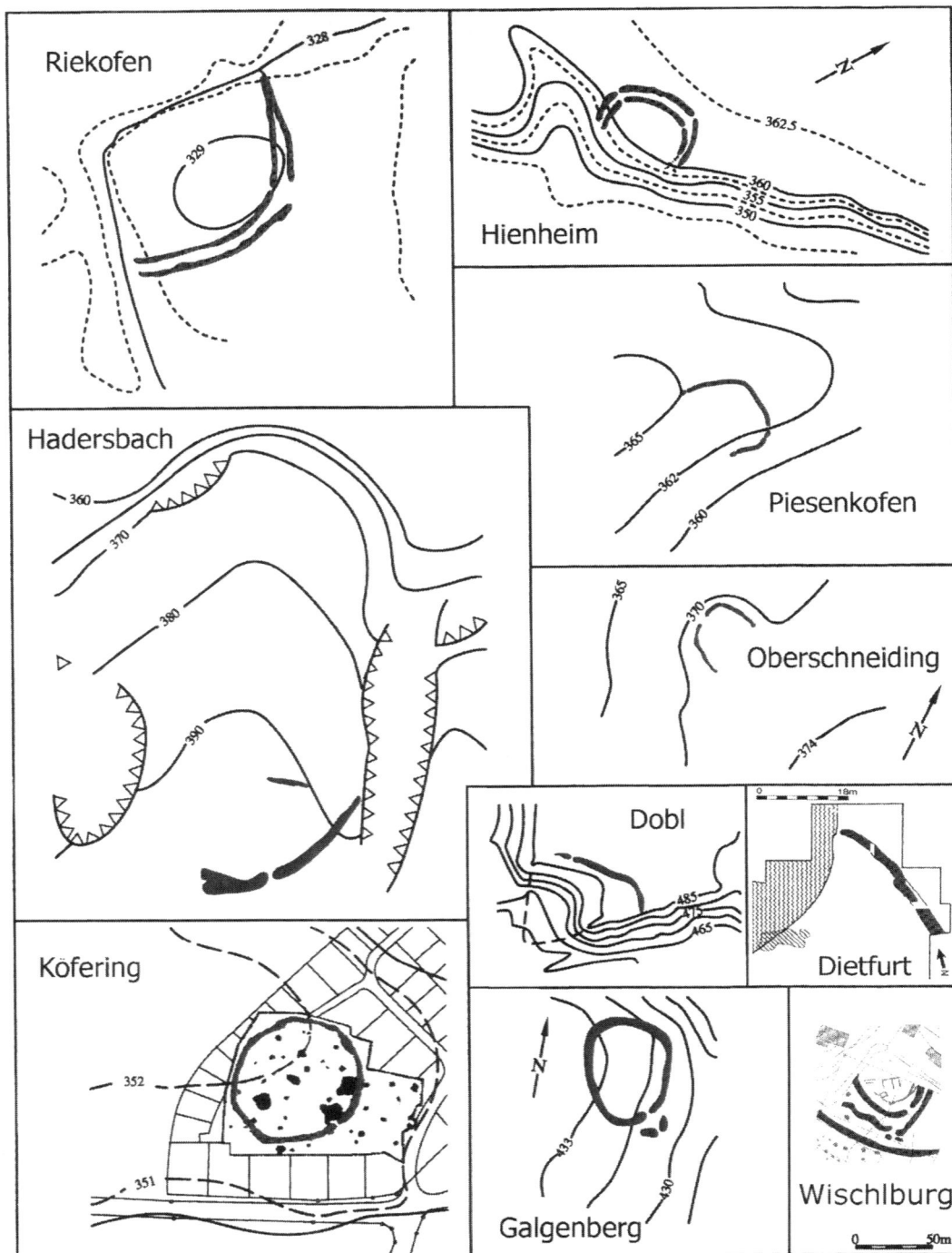

FIGURE 13: CHAM PERIOD HILLTOP SITES IN BAVARIA (AFTER JOHN 2010, FIG. 30).

Bull's horns, solar discs and the diversion from ditch enclosures

The main Copper Age cosmological motives in central Europe were the masculine bulls' horns and solar discs (possibly feminine). The symbolism of horns (*ansa cornuta*) and cattle burials (Pollex 1999, Szmyt 2006) suggests the growing importance of cattle in cult and religion. By contrast, the solar disc has a long pedigree in earlier Neolithic symbolism but it perhaps gained a higher significance during the Corded Ware and Bell Beaker

Period. These two symbolical traditions are not mutually exclusive as can be demonstrated by GAC cattle burials decorated with solar discs (Pollex 1999). However it could be generally observed that the symbolic presentation of bulls' horns and cattle herds is more connected with the TRB and middle Eneolithic Period (Řivnáč – Cham – Jevišovice B – Goldberg III) and that it was replaced by solar symbolism in the subsequent Corded Ware and Bell Beaker Period. It may well be possible that the diversion from the long tradition of ditched enclosures and the collapse of the earlier cult coincided with the introduction of a new or altered cosmological order and the worship of solar deity. The Corded Ware avoidance of pit-digging may possibly stem from a certain belief system that might have been connected to the concept of an underground world with spirits of ancestors worshiped at natural shrines: places of supposed entry to the underworld.

Collapse of monuments and the rise of natural shrines

In the third millennium BC a decisive change occurred in the conception of verticality (Neustupný 2008, 26). The people of the Michelsberg, TRB and Řivnáč/Cham (fig. 13) Periods preferred hilltop locations, mainly for their ceremonial activities. Conversely the Corded Ware and Bell Beaker populations abandoned the hilltops and their profane activities were limited to the lowlands, while the realization of their cult was directed vertically down, namely underground. It may be well possible that for the Corded Ware people the underworld started just below the ground surface and the living were not supposed to intervene in this realm other than for funeral or sacrificial causes. Evidence for such rituals is known from karst rock shrines in Central Europe, such as the one from the Bacín hill at Vinařice with its evidence of sacrificial tradition lasting over several millennia (Beroun District, see Matoušek and Turek 1998). Corded Ware domestic pottery was discovered inside one of the rock cracks (Figure 14). The votive offerings were usually deposited in rock cracks and cavities that might have been perceived as entrances to the underworld (Figure 15). The existence of natural shrines as an alternative to the man-made monuments is well documented throughout Prehistory and Antiquity (Bradley 2000). Such natural rock shrines are also known from Upper Franconia and at the site of Motzenstein, Wattendorf, the team of archaeologists from Bamberg University (Seregély 2008) discovered the remains of Corded Ware (and later) domestic and sacrificial activity.

FIGURE 14: DOMESTIC POT FROM THE SACRIFICIAL DEPOSIT IN THE ROCK SHRINE AT THE BACÍN HILL —DISTRICT OF BEROUN (PHOTO: H. TOUŠKOVÁ).

FIGURE 15: RECONSTRUCTION OF THE DEPOSITIONAL PROCESS OF THE VESSEL SACRIFICED IN THE LIMESTONE CRACK AT BACÍN (AFTER: MATOUŠEK – TUREK 1998, OBR. 8).

The finds were accumulated between two 10-15m high Jurassic limestone rocks that were, such as those at Bacín, characterised by cracks and cavities. Finds of miniature clay models of battle axes and wheels suggest some cultic activities. I believe that we should not be surprised by the presence of some domestic artefacts such as quern stones, as some seemingly profane activities might have blended with the sacred ones therefore also gaining some ritual meaning. Other karst rock shrines were probably identified at Stübig – Rothenstein and Voitmansdorf – Strohholz (cf. Seregély 2008).

Conclusion

It is possible that the changes that occurred during the third millennium BC in the society and cosmology of Copper Age farmers in Central Europe might have been a reflection of a much more general collapse of traditional Neolithic values that brought with it the new quality of Bronze Age society. The Copper Age innovations resulted in the deeper individualisation of some social principles and contributed towards greater social differentiation in the Early Bronze Age. Abandonment of the megalithic idea of collective burials and continuity in the use of funerary monuments together with a decline in ditched enclosures and the use of hilltop locations are not only evidence of changing social relations but also of far reaching changes in the cosmology of our ancestors. We can observe a reorientation from the Neolithic tradition of agricultural cults and a decline in the communal monuments (roundels, causewayed enclosures, hilltop enclosures) that were used to demonstrate and reinforce the collective identity and spiritual activities. The new cult was perhaps derived from the tradition of solar worship. Within the individualized funerary practices people emphasized their communication with the ancestors and the presentation of social status as well as the confirmation of social hierarchy and the reinforcement of a genealogical system of hereditary wealth of both individuals and families. It is also possible that the new Beaker ideology was rapidly spreading over Western and Central Europe to help enforce the new order of social relations. We can clearly see how some very distant regions of Europe with a variety of cultural traditions partook of this shared cultural uniformity, symbols, rituals and perhaps religion. In many other aspects, such as the tradition of the Central European Eneolithic-Bronze Age pottery complex (Neustupný 2008, 22) or the more intensive arable system of agriculture (Neustupný 2008, 18) we can, however, see a distinctive continuity throughout the whole Copper Age. The collapse of traditional values in the third millennium BC might be seen mainly in relation to changes in social structure, the rise of a new ideology and the transformation of cosmology. During the final stages of the Copper Age the foundations were laid for the forthcoming system of a greater stratified Bronze Age society and its new cosmological archetypes.

References

Bailey, D. W. 2000. *Balkan Prehistory*. London and New York: Routledge.

Bradley, R. 1998. *The Significance of Monuments. On the shaping of human experience in Neolithic and Bronze Age Europe*. London and New York: Routledge.

Bradley, R. 2000. *An Archaeology of Natural Places*. London and New York: Routledge.

Brodie, N. 1997. New perspectives on the Bell Beaker Culture. *Oxford Journal of Archaeology* ,16 (3), 297-314.

Childe, V. G. 1949: The origins of Neolithic culture in northern Europe. *Antiquity*, 32, 129-135.

Ehrich, R.W. and Pleslová-Štiková, E. 1968. *Homolka: An Eneolithic Site in Bohemia*. Praha: Academia.

Gojda, M., Dreslerová, D., Foster, P., Křivánek, R., Kuna, M., Vencl, S. and Zápotocký, M. 2002. Velké pravěké ohrazení v Klech (okr. Mělník). Využití nedestruktivních metod výzkumu k poznání nového typu areálu. *Archeologické Rozhledy*, 54, 371-430.

Gojda, M. (ed.) 2004. *Ancient Landscape, Settlement Dynamics and Non-Destructive Archaeology. Czech Research Project 1997-2002*. Praha: Academia.

Harrison, R. and Heyd, V. 2007. The Transformation of Europe in the third millennium BC: the example of 'Le Petit-Chasseur I + III' (Sion, Valais, Switzerland). *Prehistorisches Zeitschrift*, Band 82, S, 129–214.

Havel, J. 1986. Baba - výšinné sídliště kultury nálevkovitých pohárů v Praze 6 / Dejvicích. *Acta Musei Pragensis*, 82, Praha.

Havel, J. 1978. Pohřební ritus kultury zvoncovitých pohárů v Čechách a na Moravě. The Burial Rite of the Bell Beaker Culture in Bohemia and Moravia. *Praehistorica 7, Varia Archaeologica* 1, 91-117.

John, J. 2010. Výšinné lokality středního eneolitu v západních Čechách. *Opomíjená Archeologie* 1, Plzeň.

Kállay, A. 1990. Die kupferzeitliche Ringanlage von Füzesabony. *Jahresschrift für Mitteldeutsch Vorgeschichte*, 73, 125-130.

Keefer, E. 1993. *Steinzeit. Samlungen des Würtembergischen Landesmuseums Stuttgart, Bd. 1*. Stuttgart: Theiss.

Krištuf, P. 2003. Pohřebiště ve Velkých Žernosekách a problém mohyl KNP v Čechách, in: Lutovský, M. (ed.): *Otázky Neolitu a Eneolitu 2003*, ÚAPPSČ, Praha, 287-274.

Květina, P., Květina, P., Květinová, S. and Řídký, J. 2009. Význam her v archaických společnostech. Archeologické možnosti studia. The importance of games in archaic societies. Archaeological study options. *Archeologické Rozhledy*, 61, 3-30.

Matoušek, V. and Turek, J. 1998. Nález nádoby sídlištního typu šňůrové keramiky z vrchu Bacína (k.ú. Vinařice) The find of Corded Ware settlement pottery at Bacín (District Beroun). *Archeologické Rozhledy*, 50, 1998, 359-374.

Metlička, M. 2000. Rovinné sídliště chámské kultury u Města Touškova v okr. Plzeň-sever. In: P. Čech and M.

Dobeš (eds.), *Sborník Miroslavu Buchvaldkovi, Most,* 155-158.

Moucha, V. 1963. *Eneolitické pohřebiště ve Velkých Žernosekách Časopis NM,* 132, 125-136.

Němejcová-Pavúková, V. 1995. *Svodín. Zwei Kreisgrabenanlagen der Lengyel-Kultur.* Bratislava.

Neustupný, E. 1995. The significance of facts. *Journal of European Archaeology,* 3 (1), 189-212.

Neustupný, E. 1997. Šňůrová sídliště, kulturní normy a symboly - Settlement sites of the Corded Ware groups, cultural norms and symbols. *Archeologické Rozhledy,* 49, 304-322.

Neustupný, E. 2001a. The Origin of Megalithic Architecture in Bohemia and Moravia In: Biehl, P., Bertemes, F. and Meller, H (eds): *The Archaeology of Cult,* 203-207. Budapest: Archaeolingua.

Neustupný, E. 2001b. Grundzüge der Bevölkerungsgeschichte Böhmens im Äneolithikum. In A. Lippert, M. Schultz, S. Shennan and M. Teschler-Nicola (eds.), *Mensch und Umwelt während des Neolithikums und der Frühbronzezeit in Mitteleuropa,* 119-125. Rahden: Verlag Marie Leidorf GmbH.

Neustupný, E. 2008. *Čechy v Pravěku 4 – Eneolit.* Praha: Archeologický ústav v.v.i.

Neustupný, E. 2011. Pulzování archeologických kultur, in: Bárta, M. and Kovář, M., *Kolaps a regenerace: cesty civilizací a kultur: minulost, současnost a budoucnost komplexních společností,* 173-183. Praha: Academia.

Pavelčík, J. 2001. *Hlinsko. Hradisko lidu bádenské kultury.* Olomouc: Archeologické památky střední Moravy, sv. 2.

Pavlů, I., Rulf, J. and Zápotocká, M. 1995. Bylany Rondel. Model of the Neolithic site. *Praehistorica Archaeologica Bohemica, Památky Archeologické, Supplementum,* 3, 7-123.

Pleinerová 1980. Kultovní objekty z pozdní doby kamenné v Březně u Loun. *Památky Archeologické,* 71, 10 – 60.

Pleslová-Štiková, E. 1985. *Makotřasy: A TRB Site in Bohemia.* Praha: Fontes Archeologici Pragenses, 17.

Podborský, V. 1988. *Těšetice-Kyjovice IV. Rondel osady lidu s moravskou malovanou Keramikou.* Brno.

Podborský, V. 2001. *Pravěká sociokultovní architektura na Moravě.* Brno.

Podborský, V. 2006. *Náboženství pravěkých Evropanů.* Brno.

Pollex, A. 1999. Comments on the interpretation of the so-called Cattle burials of Neolithic Central Europe. *Antiquity,* 73, 542–550.

Segerély, T. 2008. Endneolitische Siedlungen in Oberfranken I. Wattendorf-Motzenstein: eine schnurkeramische Siedlung auf der Nördlichen Frankenalb I-II. *Studien zum Dritten Vorchristlichen Jahrtausend in Nordostbayern. Universitätsforschungen zur Archäologie, Band 154-155.* Bonn: Verlag R. Habelt.

Sherratt, A. G. 1991. Sacred and Profane Substances: the Ritual Use of Narcotics in Later Neolithic Europe. In Garwood, P., Jennings, D., Skeates, R. and Toms, J. (Eds.), *Sacred and Profane,* 50-64. Monograph No. 32. Oxford: Oxford University Committee for Archaeology.

Šmíd, M. 1995. Výsledky zjišťovacího výzkumu na eneolitickém hradisku Rmíz u Laškova. *Pravěk NŘ* 1993/3, 19-77.

Szmyt, M. 2006. Dead Animals and Living Society *http://www.jungsteinsite.uni-kiel.de/pdf/2006_szmyt_low.pdf* December 15th, 2006

Turek, J. 1987. *Sociální struktura kultury se šňůrovou keramikou v Čechách a na Moravě ve světle pohřebního ritu, SOČ.* Praha: Unpublished manuscript.

Turek, J. 1990. Pohřební ritus a otázky sociální struktury kultury se šňůrovou keramikou - The burial rite and a question on social structure of the Corded Ware culture. *Archaeologia Iuvenis* I-1990, 6-10.

Turek, J. 1996. Osídlení Pražské, kotliny v závěru eneolitu. Nástin problematiky období zvoncovitých pohárů. The Prague region in the Late Eneolithic period. *Archeologica Pragensia,* 12, 5-58.

Turek, J. 1997. Nález misky typu "Lublaňských blat" z Prahy Šárky. Úvahy o významu eneolitických opevněných výšinných sídlišt. The bowl of the "Laibacher Moor" type from Prague - Šárka. Thoughts on the social significance of Eneolithic fortifications. *Archaeologica Pragensia,* 13, 29-37.

Turek, J. 2004. Craft symbolism in the Bell Beaker burial customs. Resources, production and social structure at the end of Eneolithic period. In Besse, M. and Disideri, J. (eds), *Graves and Funerary Rituals during the Late Neolithic and the Early Bronze Age in Europe (2700-2000 BC,* 147-156. Proceedings of the International Conference held at the Cantonal Archaeological Museum, Sion (Switzerland) October 4th –7th 2001. BAR International Series 1284. Oxford: Archaeopress.

Turek, J. 2005. Praha kamenná. Neolit – mladší doba kamenná; Eneolit – pozdní doba kamenná. In Lutovský, M. and Smejtek, L. (eds.), *Pravěká Praha, Libri, Praha,* 157-348.

Turek, J. 2007. Počátky válečnictví v eneolitu. *Živá Archeologie,* 8/2007, 14-18.

Turek, J. 2010. Domy mrtvých ve světě prvních zemědělců. In: Hroby, pohřby a lidské ostatky na pravěkých a středověkých sídlištích. *Živá Archeologie, Supplementum* 3, 7-12.

Turek, J. 2011. Poháry místo monumentů. Tradice a změny ve společnosti a kosmologii evropských zemědělců ve 3. tisíciletí před Kristem. In Bárta, M. and Kovář, M. (eds), *Kolaps a regenerace: Cesty civilizací a kultur. Minulost, současnost a budoucnost komplexních společností,* 69-105. Praha: Academia.

Zápotocký, M. 1992. *Streitäxte des mitteleuropäischen Äneolithikums, Quellen und Forschungen zur prähistorischen und provinzialrömischen Archäologie.* Acta Humaniora, 16. Weinheim:VCH.

Zápotocký, M. 2000. Cimburk und die Höhensidelungen des frühen und älteren Äneolithikums in Böhmen. *Památky Archeologické, Supplementum* 12. Praha.

Journey to the Centre of the Earth

Richard Bradley

There is an obvious tension between two kinds of archaeology. Field survey is a method of classifying monuments by their surface appearance, but excavation can take those categories apart. It shows how different sequences may lead to the same result. Recent work, much of it reported here, suggests that the enclosures described as henges were built towards the end of a lengthy period of use. The implication is obvious. Like the Three Age System, 'henge' is a technical term which has outlived its usefulness.

This comment applies to prehistoric structures in Britain and Ireland, but a different approach extends to other parts of Europe. Rather than focussing on the *definition* of particular types of enclosure, it may be more helpful to ask what kind of phenomenon they represent. In the past, sites in Central Europe, Portugal and Southern France have been compared with henges in the British Isles. Now that more is known about them, it is obvious that this procedure was misguided. But why do they share features in common? In order to emphasise the distinctive nature of these places I have borrowed the title of a novel by Jules Verne, published in 1864: *A Journey to the Centre of the Earth.*

Centres

The word 'centre' has two connotations, one of them social and the other geographical. A place can be a centre if it plays a pivotal role in the activities of a particular community. It may be where assemblies come together, where gods are worshipped, the dead are celebrated and rites of passage take place. It need not be near a settlement, although that was the case in Central Europe. Such centres can also be in more distant areas, as they obviously were in Yorkshire. Their centrality depends on their *social* roles rather than their location on the ground.

In other instances they can be considered as central points in the terrain. That is particularly true of circular enclosures, whose earthwork perimeter may reflect the local topography. Thus major 'henges' are often in basins where their outer circuit mirrors the horizon. The royal centres of the Irish Iron Age illustrate the same principle, and it is not surprising that for a while their earthwork boundaries were dated to the Neolithic period. In this case they are on high ground where their perimeter commands a view in all directions. That is particularly true of Uisneach which was once considered as the *omphalos* of Ireland. In such cases a monument could be perceived as the centre of a wider world. The same relationship between a circular enclosure and the natural topography has been recognised

in Portugal. It is tempting to suggest that these earthworks were *microcosms* of a larger region.

One reason why certain monuments in Central and Southern Europe were compared with British henges was their circular ground plan (although this feature was not shared by every example). In many cases their shape was not suggested by the local topography, and another explanation is needed. One possibility is that the circular form was shared with domestic buildings. That is possible in Britain and Ireland and to a lesser extent in Iberia, but this idea would not apply to the sites in Central Europe where the contrast between Kreisgrabenanlagen and longhouses is especially striking. The same applies to occasional discoveries of post circles in Scandinavia: a region where the domestic dwellings of the same date are rectangular.

A feature which links some of the British henges to the Continental Kreisgrabenanlagen is the importance of celestial alignments. Again they are not found on every site. Even so, this feature is documented in an increasing number of cases. The circular plan may have been intended as a reference to the sky. That is especially obvious when the perimeter formed a conspicuous barrier, for it would have hidden the area beyond the monument, restricting long distance views to the axis of the entrance. Not only did this focus more attention on the sun and moon, it would also have emphasised the significance of particular orientations. They might have been towards the cardinal points or the turning points of the year.

It was once considered that such structures were used to establish a calendar, but there is a flaw in this argument, as the monuments could not have been laid out with so much precision unless that information was known in the first place. Perhaps the outline of these enclosures encapsulated beliefs about the cosmos. A useful comparison is with the Great Kivas in the South-western United States. They are circular buildings which were used in communal rituals. Again some examples were aligned on the solstices. Like the Kreisgrabenanlagen, they were associated with settlements of rectangular buildings.

In certain cases the siting of enclosures was not only connected with the sky, but also with an underworld. That may be one reason why their ditches were so deep and why some of them contained offerings. That is as true of the Kreisgrabenanlagen as it is of enclosures in the south of Portugal. It also applies to 'henge monuments' in Britain. The earthwork at Maumbury Rings illustrates this point. In its original form it was enclosed by a circle of over forty shafts excavated between ten and twelve metres into the bedrock. They had been refilled in an orderly sequence, with pieces of decorated pottery towards the bottom, red deer skulls and carved chalk objects above them, and human remains at the top. The alternative title of Verne's novel, *A Journey to the Interior of the Earth*, would be appropriate here.

Two of these features suggest links with other sites. Neolithic enclosures in Yorkshire and the Mendips are associated with natural sinkholes, where the ground surface opens to form deep shafts. This is a dramatic event and is difficult to comprehend without an understanding of geology. For that reason it is not surprising that features of this kind are often associated with deposits of artefacts and human bones. Springs are a similar phenomenon, as it would have been hard to work out why water was issuing from the ground. A number of British henges are associated with the sources of rivers, and it seems possible that some of their Irish counterparts even included ponds which celebrated the same connection. The ditches of other monuments were excavated to the water table.

The importance of water sources is not confined to insular prehistory, and it is clear that the Kreisgrabenanlagen illustrate a similar association. The same argument extends to South Scandinavia where Neolithic votive deposits were associated with bogs and pools. There was also a striking link between enclosures in North Yorkshire and the distribution of mires. Like the local sinkholes, their distinctive character might have attracted attention during the prehistoric period.

As well as springs, enclosures in Britain are frequently associated with rivers and particularly with confluences. The connection seems to be acknowledged by the alignment of their entrances. It is a moot point whether any of those rivers contained offerings, as they did in Scandinavia, but this may explain the concentration of Neolithic artefacts in the Middle Thames. Another link has been documented at Marden where the Avon forms one side of an unusually large enclosure. At Durrington Walls and Stonehenge, avenues communicate between the entrances of prehistoric earthworks and the bank of the same river.

In short, a number of enclosures in Britain and Continental Europe were organised in relation to both the sky and to an underworld. They were also located in places that might be considered as microcosms of the surrounding landscape. Their ditches might extend to the water table, and many 'henges' were associated with springs and rivers. Their circular outlines also mirrored the dome of the heavens. The placing of the entrances allowed the people inside them to observe celestial events. It may be that the communities who constructed these enclosures believed in a three-tier cosmology in which the plane on which they passed their daily lives was located between an upper world and an underworld. The forms of certain monuments suggest that the workforce that built the earthworks wished to communicate between these spheres in order to harness their powers.

To do so must have been dangerous, and it may be why such a sharp division was observed between the interior of the enclosure and the area outside it. That is true whether the barrier consisted of a bank and ditch, a fence or a series of palisades. There was a striking contrast between early enclosures with their segmented ditches and the forms adopted by later examples. Access to the interior became increasingly restricted. The ditches were deeper and the banks were higher than they had been before. There were fewer entrances, and some of them were narrower than their predecessors. Most important of all, the width of the outer barrier might be increased by the excavation of wider ditches or the creation of concentric earthworks and lines of posts.

In Britain and Ireland 'henges' are defined by an external bank and an internal ditch. There are two ways of interpreting this observation, but they can probably be combined. One possibility is that this was a kind of defence in reverse. Such places were associated with supernatural powers and it was important to prevent them from escaping. Just as the external ditch of a hillfort protected the inhabitants from attack, the internal ditch of a henge monument – almost its only defining feature – contained the dangerous forces associated with the site. The argument is plausible, but it may not provide a complete explanation, as there is evidence that these earthworks were among the latest structures to be built. If these places were imbued with danger, why had existing features, such as stone settings, been so permeable? Was it because the forces associated with these sites did not need to be contained until the monument went out of use? This interpretation does not explain why the earthworks had entrances. Nor can it account for those sites where activity continued after the bank and ditch had been built. On the other hand, the closing of these dangerous spaces may have gone one stage further where they were buried beneath a mound.

Another possibility is that the characteristic form of the perimeter was conceived as an explicit *reversal* of normal practice. Other Neolithic structures have their banks on the inside and their ditches on the exterior. Perhaps this distinctive configuration expressed the peculiar character of the rites of passage. They go through three distinct stages. The first are the *rites of separation* when people are removed from their normal lives to practice special rituals at a secluded location. There follows a *liminal phase* in which the conventions of everyday existence are inverted or overturned. Finally, there are *rites of incorporation* when the process is concluded and the participants return with their identities transformed. Such rituals include royal inaugurations, initiation ceremonies and funerals.

The enormous earthwork barriers of many British enclosures would have been well suited for this purpose, and the special character of the internal space is emphasised by the provision of a narrow entrance through the highest section of the bank. The earthworks separated the participants from people who remained outside and prevented any contact between them until the rituals were concluded. The same idea may apply to Kreisgrabenanlagen, and in each case the circular interior would have amplified the sounds created inside the enclosure. That could have added to the mystery associated with these places.

Again there is a difficulty with this approach. It might explain how public rituals became more exclusive or more rigidly controlled, but it is an argument that can only apply to those monuments that were eventually enclosed by an earthwork – in many cases that never happened. On the other hand, it may be that both processes were linked to one another. The rites of passage would have been a time of heightened awareness and it may have been important to contain the forces they unleashed. That could be achieved by making a clear distinction between the earthworks described as 'henges' and the forms of other monuments in the vicinity. In one sense the bank and ditch contained the ceremonies and hid them from view; in another, they emphasised the way in which the participants inverted the procedures associated with the wider world. One interpretation emphasises the reversal of normal practice, whilst the other stresses the dangers the use of these monuments involved.

Journeys

The locations of many enclosures meant that people had to travel there. This can be demonstrated by a number of methods. Field survey can show that they were situated in areas with few surface finds of artefacts, or that the objects deposited in the vicinity originated in distant areas. A good example is the use of flint from the Yorkshire Wolds in the Thornborough complex. Another method is to use laboratory analysis to establish the sources from which animals (or joints of meat) were introduced to the sites. It certainly suggests that Late Neolithic enclosures on the chalk of southern England were visited by people from distant areas. Similar considerations apply to the construction of the monuments themselves. In some cases it is hard to see how sufficient workers could be drawn from the settlements in the surrounding area, while there are sites where the very materials from which the structure was formed were introduced from different sources, some of them far away. That principle is well established at Newgrange and Stonehenge but may apply to other sites.

For a long time it has been accepted that concentrations of non-local artefacts are found in the vicinity of British monuments. There seems little reason to interpret them as chance losses. The presence of stone axes from distant quarries is a recurrent feature. There are similar finds from enclosures in Southern France, Scandinavia and Iberia. Such discoveries can be explained in anecdotal terms – English henges were among the pivotal points in an 'axe trade'; these artefacts were required to build timber structures – but such arguments are not entirely satisfactory. They would not explain why sites that were far apart were associated with very similar assemblages, nor can they account for the striking structural links between

the architecture of these monuments. Since it seems that some of the enclosures were on the margins of the settled landscape, it may be more appropriate to think of travel as a central element in the ceremonies that took place there. They may have been visited in the course of a pilgrimage.

It would certainly explain the siting of a number of the British monuments. Far from occupying the most productive land, they seem to have been built in locations that were accessible from a wider region. They were placed along important routes across the landscape, beside navigable rivers or, in a few cases, in upland passes or near harbours on the coast. The idea of seclusion is particularly relevant here, for by travelling to these special places the participants in ceremonies at these monuments would have removed themselves from their familiar surroundings.

There is no reason to suppose that such journeys were restricted to a single destination. Few of the monuments discussed in this book are found in total isolation. They can form part of larger complexes containing structures of other kinds. Particular forms of enclosure can occur more than once in the same place, and other examples were built at intervals along paths across the ancient landscape. It seems possible that the people who travelled there moved from one enclosure to another and that timber or earthwork monuments which have been assigned to the same class by archaeologists played a variety of different roles in the past. Some could accommodate larger audiences than others and it may be no accident that the most elaborate constructions were located in the borderland between different regions. That was the case in Wessex.

Journeys of any kind involve the transmission of knowledge as well as the movement of artefacts, and it is no accident that so many of the enclosures discussed by contributors to this volume date from periods when new networks were becoming established and fresh alliances were formed. That happened at various times during prehistory, but it may be no coincidence that in different regions the later histories of these monuments were associated with Bell Beaker ceramics. That was as true in Southern Europe as it was in the British Isles, yet many of the enclosures had been established during an earlier phase. It seems possible that the adoption of a new material culture was facilitated by existing contacts. In turn when visitors to the monuments were first exposed to new people, strange beliefs and unfamiliar technologies, it could have had a dramatic effect. It may be no coincidence that it was then that some of the largest monuments were built.

Epilogue in Oxford

I am not suggesting that the participants in the Oxford conference travelled there to communicate with higher powers, but the place where they stayed the night did have remarkable qualities - qualities that shed some light on the character of the structures they study.

Keble College opened in 1870 and was built opposite the University Museum where Thomas Huxley had debated the theory of evolution with the Bishop of Oxford ten years before. Their juxtaposition was no accident, for the college was founded in an attempt to reassert Catholic principles in the Church of England. For that reason its distinctive appearance evokes ecclesiastical architecture and one of the main buildings is a chapel. In other words its construction was inspired by a spiritual crisis and was an attempt to emphasise the power of traditional doctrine.

By a curious coincidence it was built in exactly the same place as a much older monument, although that was not recognised until 2008 when a neighbouring site was excavated in advance of development. This work exposed one segment of a curvilinear enclosure with an estimated diameter of 150 metres. Its ditch was eight metres wide and nearly three metres deep and was associated with animal bones, antler picks, sherds of Grooved Ware and Beaker, and radiocarbon dates in the later third millennium BC. It was strikingly similar to other 'henge monuments' in the region, but they had been discovered in farmland. This one would have enclosed virtually the entire area occupied Keble College.

Two striking monuments, both of them dating from periods when long-established beliefs came under pressure – the coincidence is remarkable. For the founders of the college it was a place where established values were celebrated and taught to a new generation. Similar notions may have been important in the Neolithic period. For the people who built the enclosure four thousand years before, that place could have been considered as the centre of the earth.